PRINCIPLES OF

MACRO-
ECONOMICS

Third Edition

PRINCIPLES OF
MACRO-
ECONOMICS
Third Edition

ROBERT H. FRANK
Cornell University

BEN S. BERNANKE
Princeton University (formerly)
Chairman of the President's Council of Economic Advisers

with the assistance of

ROGER T. KAUFMAN
Smith College

McGraw-Hill
Irwin

Boston   Burr Ridge, IL   Dubuque, IA   Madison, WI   New York   San Francisco   St. Louis
Bangkok   Bogotá   Caracas   Kuala Lumpur   Lisbon   London   Madrid   Mexico City
Milan   Montreal   New Delhi   Santiago   Seoul   Singapore   Sydney   Taipei   Toronto

McGraw-Hill
Irwin

PRINCIPLES OF MACROECONOMICS

Published by McGraw-Hill/Irwin, a business unit of The McGraw-Hill Companies, Inc., 1221 Avenue of the Americas, New York, NY, 10020. Copyright © 2007 by The McGraw-Hill Companies, Inc. All rights reserved. No part of this publication may be reproduced or distributed in any form or by any means, or stored in a database or retrieval system, without the prior written consent of The McGraw-Hill Companies, Inc., including, but not limited to, in any network or other electronic storage or transmission, or broadcast for distance learning.

Some ancillaries, including electronic and print components, may not be available to customers outside the United States.

This book is printed on acid-free paper.

1 2 3 4 5 6 7 8 9 0 QPD/QPD 0 9 8 7 6

ISBN-13: 978-0-07-319397-7
ISBN-10: 0-07-319397-6

Cover: Detail of the leaded glass entry ceiling light from the Frank Thomas house in Oak Park, Illinois.

Photo: © Chrysalis Books. Photographer—Simon Clay.

Design of book: The images in the design of this book are based on elements of the architecture of Frank Lloyd Wright, specifically from the leaded glass windows seen in many of his houses. Wright's design was rooted in nature and based on simplicity and harmony. His windows use elemental geometry to abstract natural forms, complementing and framing the natural world outside. This concept of seeing the world through an elegantly structured framework ties in nicely to the idea of framing one's view of the world through the window of economics.

The typeface used for some of the elements was taken from the Arts and Crafts movement. The typeface, as well as the color palette, bring in the feeling of that movement in a way that complements the geometric elements of Wright's windows. The Economic Naturalist icon is visually set apart from the more geometric elements but is a representation of the inspirational force behind all of Wright's work.

Publisher: *Gary Burke*
Executive sponsoring editor: *Paul Shensa*
Developmental editor: *Tom Thompson*
Editorial assistant: *Robin Pille*
Senior marketing manager: *Martin D. Quinn*
Media producer: *Jennifer Fisher*
Senior project manager: *Susanne Riedell*
Lead production supervisor: *Michael R. McCormick*
Lead designer: *Matthew Baldwin*
Photo research coordinator: *Lori Kramer*
Photo researcher: *PoYee Oster*
Lead media project manager: *Becky Szura*
Senior supplement producer: *Carol Loreth*
Typeface: *10/12 Sabon Roman*
Compositor: *TechBooks/GTS, York, PA*
Printer: *Quebecor World Dubuque Inc.*

Library of Congress Cataloging-in-Publication Data

Frank, Robert H.
    Principles of macroeconomics / Robert H. Frank, Ben S. Bernanke.—3rd ed.
      p. cm.
    Includes index.
    ISBN-13: 978-0-07-319397-7 (alk. paper)
    ISBN-10: 0-07-319397-6 (alk. paper)
    1. Macroeconomics. I. Bernanke, Ben. II. Title.
HB172.5.F69 2007
  339–dc22
                                                          2005054445

www.mhhe.com

DEDICATION

For Ellen

R. H. F.

For Anna

B. S. B.

ROBERT H. FRANK

Professor Frank is the Henrietta Johnson Louis Professor of Management and Professor of Economics at the Johnson Graduate School of Management at Cornell University, where he has taught since 1972. His "Economic Scene" column appears monthly in *The New York Times*. After receiving his B.S. from Georgia Tech in 1966, he taught math and science for two years as a Peace Corps Volunteer in rural Nepal. He received his M.A. in statistics in 1971 and his Ph.D. in economics in 1972 from The University of California at Berkeley. During leaves of absence from Cornell, he has served as chief economist for the Civil Aeronautics Board (1978–1980), a Fellow at the Center for Advanced Study in the Behavioral Sciences (1992–93), and Professor of American Civilization at l'École des Hautes Études en Sciences Sociales in Paris (2000–01).

Professor Frank is the author of a best-selling intermediate economics textbook—*Microeconomics and Behavior,* Sixth Edition (Irwin/McGraw-Hill, 2006). He has published on a variety of subjects, including price and wage discrimination, public utility pricing, the measurement of unemployment spell lengths, and the distributional consequences of direct foreign investment. His research has focused on rivalry and cooperation in economic and social behavior. His books on these themes, which include *Choosing the Right Pond* (Oxford, 1995), *Passions Within Reason* (W. W. Norton, 1988), and *What Price the Moral High Ground?* (Princeton, 2004), have been translated into 10 languages. *The Winner-Take-All Society* (The Free Press, 1995), co-authored with Philip Cook, received a Critic's Choice Award, was named a Notable Book of the Year by *The New York Times,* and was included in *Business Week*'s list of the 10 best books of 1995. *Luxury Fever* (The Free Press, 1999) was named to the *Knight-Ridder* Best Books list for 1999.

Professor Frank has been awarded an Andrew W. Mellon Professorship (1987–1990), a Kenan Enterprise Award (1993), and a Merrill Scholars Program Outstanding Educator Citation (1991). He is a co-recipient of the 2004 Leontief Prize for Advancing the Frontiers of Economic Thought. He was awarded the Johnson School's Stephen Russell Distinguished Teaching Award in 2004 and the School's Apple Distinguished Teaching Award in 2005. His introductory microeconomics course has graduated more than 6,000 enthusiastic economic naturalists over the years.

BEN S. BERNANKE

Professor Bernanke received his B.A. in economics from Harvard University in 1975 and his Ph.D. in economics from MIT in 1979. He taught at the Stanford Graduate School of Business from 1979 to 1985 and moved to Princeton University in 1985, where he was named the Howard Harrison and Gabrielle Snyder Beck Professor of Economics and Public Affairs, and where he served as Chairman of the Economics Department. He is a Fellow of the American Academy of Arts and Sciences and of the Econometrics Society. He was named a member of the Board of Governors of the Federal Reserve in 2002 and became the chairman of the President's Council of Economic Advisers in 2005.

Professor Bernanke's intermediate textbook, with Andrew Abel, *Macroeconomics,* Fifth Edition (Addison-Wesley, 2004) is a best seller in its field. He has authored more than 50 scholarly publications in macroeconomics, macroeconomic history, and finance. He has done significant research on the causes of the Great Depression, the role of financial markets and institutions in the business cycle, and measuring the effects of monetary policy on the economy. His two most recent books, both published by Princeton University Press, include *Inflation Targeting: Lessons from the International Experience* (with coauthors) and *Essays on the Great Depression.* He has served as the editor of the *American Economic Review* and was the founding editor of the *International Journal of Central Banking.* Professor Bernanke has taught principles of economics at both Stanford and Princeton.

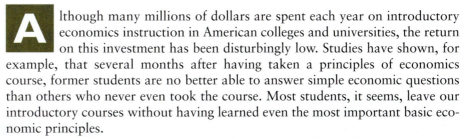

PREFACE

Although many millions of dollars are spent each year on introductory economics instruction in American colleges and universities, the return on this investment has been disturbingly low. Studies have shown, for example, that several months after having taken a principles of economics course, former students are no better able to answer simple economic questions than others who never even took the course. Most students, it seems, leave our introductory courses without having learned even the most important basic economic principles.

The problem, in our view, is that these courses almost always try to teach students far too much. In the process, really important ideas get little more coverage than minor ones, and everything ends up going by in a blur. Many instructors ask themselves, "How much can I cover today?" when instead they should be asking, "How much can my students absorb?"

Our textbook grew out of our conviction that students will learn far more if we attempt to cover much less. Our basic premise is that a small number of basic principles do most of the heavy lifting in economics, and that if we focus narrowly and repeatedly on those principles, students can actually master them in just a single semester.

The enthusiastic reactions of users of our first two editions affirm the validity of this premise. Although recent editions of a few other texts now pay lip service to the less-is-more approach, ours is by consensus the most carefully thought out and well-executed text in this mold. Avoiding excessive reliance on formal mathematical derivations, we present concepts intuitively through examples drawn from familiar contexts. We rely throughout on a well-articulated short list of core principles, which we reinforce repeatedly by illustrating and applying each principle in numerous contexts. We ask students periodically to apply these principles themselves to answer related questions, exercises, and problems.

Throughout this process, we encourage students to become "economic naturalists," people who employ basic economic principles to understand and explain what they observe in the world around them. An economic naturalist understands, for example, that infant safety seats are required in cars but not in airplanes because the marginal cost of space to accommodate these seats is typically zero in cars but often hundreds of dollars in airplanes. Scores of such examples are sprinkled throughout the book. Each one, we believe, poses a question that should make any normal, curious person eager to learn the answer. These examples stimulate interest while teaching students to see each feature of their economic landscape as the reflection of an implicit or explicit cost-benefit calculation. Students talk about these examples with their friends and families. Learning economics is like learning a language. In each case, there is no substitute for actually speaking. By inducing students to speak economics, the economic naturalist examples serve this purpose.

FEATURES

- **An emphasis on core principles:** As noted, a few core principles do most of the work in economics. By focusing almost exclusively on these principles, the text assures that students leave the course with a deep mastery of them. In contrast, traditional encyclopedic texts so overwhelm students with detail that they often leave the course with little useful working knowledge at all.

- **The Scarcity Principle:** Having more of one good thing usually means having less of another.

- **The Cost-Benefit Principle:** Take no action unless its marginal benefit is at least as great as its marginal cost.

- **The Incentive Principle:** Cost-benefit comparisons are relevant not only for identifying the decisions that rational people should make, but also for predicting the actual decisions they do make.

- **The Principle of Comparative Advantage:** Everyone does best when each concentrates on the activity for which he or she is relatively most productive.

- **The Principle of Increasing Opportunity Cost:** Use the resources with the lowest opportunity cost before turning to those with higher opportunity costs.

- **The Equilibrium Principle:** A market in equilibrium leaves no unexploited opportunities for individuals but may not exploit all gains achievable through collective action.

- **The Efficiency Principle:** Efficiency is an important social goal, because when the economic pie grows larger, everyone can have a larger slice.

- **Economic naturalism expanded in Macro:** Economic naturalist examples typically invoke a more aggregative perspective in macroeconomics, but still entail explicit or implicit cost-benefit calculations. In macro, for example, the economic naturalist might ask questions like these:

  - Why did the Federal Reserve lower interest rates in 2001–2003 and then raise them in 2004–2005?

  - China as Number One?

  - Why has U.S. labor productivity grown so rapidly since 1995?

- **Active learning stressed:** The only way to learn to hit an overhead smash in tennis is through repeated practice. The same is true for learning economics. Accordingly, we consistently introduce new ideas in the context of simple examples and then follow them with applications showing how they work in familiar settings. At frequent intervals, we pose exercises that both test and reinforce the understanding of these ideas. The end-of-chapter questions and problems are carefully crafted to help students internalize and extend core concepts. Experience with our first two editions confirms that this approach really does prepare students to apply basic economic principles to solve economic puzzles drawn from the real world.

- **Modern Macroeconomics:** Recent developments have renewed interest in cyclical fluctuations without challenging the importance of such long-run issues as growth, productivity, the evolution of real wages, and capital formation. Our treatment of these issues is organized as follows:

  - A five-chapter treatment of long-run issues prior to an analysis of short-run fluctuations, followed by a modern treatment of short-term fluctuations and stabilization policy, emphasizing the important distinction between short- and long-run behavior of the economy.

- Consistent with both media reporting and recent research on the central bank reaction function, we treat the interest rate rather than the money supply as the primary instrument of Fed policy.

- The analysis of aggregate demand and aggregate supply relates output to inflation, rather than to the price level, sidestepping the necessity of a separate derivation of the link between the output gap and inflation.

- This book places a heavy emphasis on globalization, starting with an analysis of its effects on real wage inequality and progressing to such issues as the benefits of trade, the causes and effects of protectionism, the role of capital flows in domestic capital formation, the link between exchange rates and monetary policy, and the sources of speculative attacks on currencies.

- **Web site:** Developed by Scott Simkins of North Carolina A & T State University, an expert in the growing field of economics education on the World Wide Web. The ambitious Web site contains a host of features that will enhance the principles classroom, including dynamic graphs, video lectures, e-mail updates, microeconomic experiments, current news articles, information about the text, an eLearning session, and more.

A NOTE ON THE WRITING OF THIS EDITION

For two-and-a-half years, Ben Bernanke served as a member of the Board of Governors of the Federal Reserve System, and he has recently been appointed as chairman of the President's Council of Economic Advisers. These positions have allowed him to play an active role in making U.S. economic policy, but the rules of government service have restricted his ability to participate in the preparation of the third edition.

Fortunately, we were able to enlist the aid of Roger Kaufman of Smith College to take the lead in revising the macro portions of the book. Roger, who is a long-time user of the book and a superb teacher, brings extensive classroom experience to the project. He has done an excellent job of updating the book to reflect the most important recent developments in the world economy. Pedagogically, he has made the book more student-friendly and the presentation more patient, while retaining the book's underlying approach and strengths. Ben Bernanke and Robert Frank express their deep gratitude to Roger for the energy and creativity he has brought to his work on the book. He has made the book a better tool for students and professors.

IMPROVEMENTS

- **Expanded discussion of macroeconomic policy:** The revised monetary policy reaction function we introduce in Chapter 14 is a more realistic description of the way in which the Fed actually conducts monetary policy and clarifies the Taylor rule. In Chapter 15 we use this policy reaction function to help students distinguish between a move along the aggregate demand curve and a shift in the aggregate demand curve resulting from a change in monetary policy. Then, in a new, optional Chapter 16, we provide a more complete analysis of the interaction between fiscal and monetary policy, illustrating the crucial role of the central bank in any long-run inflation. We also discuss how enhanced credibility can help to anchor inflationary expectations and explain the contributions of central bank independence, inflation targeting, and central bank reputation. In the last section of Chapter 16, we expand our discussion of the real-world difficulties in conducting macroeconomic policy.

- **More patient presentation of models:** In Chapter 13 we explain the effects of tax cuts on planned aggregate expenditure more carefully. In an optional box, we also solve a simple Keynesian model, leaving the full model in the appendix, as in the second edition. In the diagrams in Chapter 15, we include the transitional short-run aggregate supply lines to illustrate how the short-run aggregate supply line shifts when actual output deviates from potential output.

- **Expanded discussion of supply-side economics:** Most economists agree that changes in marginal tax rates can affect both aggregate demand and aggregate supply, but they disagree on the size of the effects. In Chapter 15 we describe this controversy in greater detail and present both the theoretical and empirical evidence of the effects of changes in marginal tax rates on aggregate supply.

- **Greater attention to asset prices:** In Chapter 8 we provide a clearer explanation of the inverse relationship between bond prices and interest rates. We also discuss the effects of changes in asset prices (especially stocks and houses) on aggregate demand.

- **Simpler presentation of exchange rates:** We use supply and demand curves to illustrate the determination of nominal exchange rates before we introduce the real exchange rate and purchasing power parity.

- **Additional material on China:** At its current rate of growth, the Chinese economy may become the largest economy in the world within the next generation. In this edition, we expand our discussion of China in the world economy. We discuss the determinants of its success and its management of its exchange rate.

- **New material on the acceleration of productivity growth:** The productivity slowdown of 1973–1995 has been followed by surprisingly strong productivity growth. We present and discuss the reasons for this acceleration.

- **Updated discussion of saving and investment:** In addition to emphasizing the importance of public and private saving and the relationship between the budget deficit, national saving, and capital flows, we discuss the recently divergent trends in business and household saving.

If free trade is so great, why do so many people oppose it?

THE CHALLENGE

The world is a more competitive place now than it was when we started teaching in the 1970s. In arena after arena, business as usual is no longer good enough. Baseball players used to drink beer and go fishing during the off season, but they now lift weights and ride exercise bicycles. Assistant professors used to work on their houses on weekends, but the current crop can now be found most weekends at the office. The competition for student attention has grown similarly more intense. There are many tempting courses in the typical college curriculum and even more tempting diversions outside the classroom. Students are freer than ever to pick and choose.

Yet many of us seem to operate under the illusion that most freshmen arrive with a burning desire to become economics majors. And many of us do not yet seem to have recognized that students' cognitive abilities and powers of concentration are scarce resources. To hold our ground, we must become not only more selective in what we teach, but also more effective as advocates for our discipline. We must persuade students that we offer something of value.

A well-conceived and well-executed introductory course in economics can teach our students more about society and human behavior in a single term than virtually any other course in the university. This course can and should be an intellectual adventure of the first order. Not all students who take the kind of course we envisioned when writing this book will go on to become economics majors, of course. But many will, and even those who do not will leave with a sense of admiration for the power of economic ideas.

A salesperson knows that he or she often gets only one chance to make a good first impression on a potential customer. Analogously, the principles course is often our only shot at persuading most students to appreciate the value of economics. By trying to teach them everything we know—rather than teaching them the most important things we know—we too often squander this opportunity.

SUPPLEMENTS FOR THE INSTRUCTOR

DiscoverEcon with Paul Solman Videos: DiscoverEcon, available at www.discoverecon.com/frankbernanke3, is an online economics discovery and course management system. DiscoverEcon is provided free to students via a code in every new copy of the third edition text. It precisely matches the book's topic sequence, terminology, and approach. The software acts like an interactive text; software chapters parallel text chapters and software pages include specific page references to the text. DiscoverEcon Plus adds a complete electronic version of the text, including the option to print. Hot links from the interactive software to the relevant text pages make it easier than ever for students to move between static explanations in the text and interactive explanations in the software.

For the instructor, DiscoverEcon provides easy-to-use course management options and pedagogically sound, self-grading exercises for homework assignments. The syllabus development tool allows an instructor to create an interactive syllabus by linking to the exercises, interactive explanations, and videos. DiscoverEcon includes preestablished syllabi to aid in course creation. It literally takes only a few moments to set up a course complete with homework.

All DiscoverEcon chapters contain a multiple-choice quiz, discussion questions with online links, and match-the-terms exercises. Interactive graphs, animated charts, and live tables let students manipulate variables and study the outcomes. The program provides links to videos created by Paul Solman of *The NewsHour with Jim Lehrer.* This video component consists of more than 30 short video segments. Each 5- to 10- minute video explains a key economic idea such as economic growth, elasticity, and production possibilities in a memorable, accessible way.

Students submit exercise results directly to their instructors with a click of a button. Multiple-choice and match-the-terms exercises are automatically graded and scores are added to the grade book.

Developed by Gerald C. Nelson of the University of Illinois at Urbana-Champaign, this fully updated and enhanced version of DiscoverEcon with Paul Solman Videos features new learning opportunities for students and easy integration into existing courses for the instructor.

Instructor's Manual: Prepared by Margaret Ray at the University of Mary Washington [micro] and Mary Lesser at Iona College [macro], this expanded manual will be extremely useful for all teachers, but especially for those new to the job. In addition to such general topics as Using the Web Site, Economic Education Resources, and Innovative Ideas, there will be for each chapter: An Overview, Core Principles, Important Concepts Covered, Teaching Objectives, Teaching Tips/Student Stumbling Blocks, More Economic Naturalists, In-Class and Web Activities, Annotated Chapter Outline, Answers to Textbook Problems, Sample Homework, and a Sample Reading Quiz.

Test Bank: Prepared by Nancy Jianakoplos at Colorado State University, this manual contains more than 3,000 multiple-choice questions categorized by Teaching Objective (from the Study Guide); Learning Level (knowledge, comprehension, application, analysis); Type (graph, calculation, word problem); and Source (textbook, Study Guide, Web, unique).

Computerized Test Bank: The print test bank is also available in the latest EZTest test-generating software, ensuring maximum flexibility in test preparation, including the reconfiguring of graphing exercises. EZTest is the gold standard of testing programs. It is available in both a Windows and Macintosh format.

PowerPoints: Prepared by Steve Smith and Jeff Caldwell at Rose State, these slides contain all of the illustrations in the textbook, along with a detailed, chapter-by-chapter review of the important ideas presented in the textbook. These teachers have done PowerPoints for many books at both the principles and intermediate level.

Overhead Transparencies: These more than 150, four-color acetates contain all the illustrations presented in the textbook. They are available on demand.

Instructor's CD-ROM: This remarkable Windows software program contains the complete Instructor's Manual, Computerized Test Banks, Power-Points, and a full set of lecture notes and accompanying PowerPoint files for principles of macroeconomics (see more detailed description above).

Online Learning Center (www.mhhe.com/economics/frankbernanke3): For teachers there are, among other things, an online newsletter called "Teaching Using the Web"; the Instructor's Manual; the PowerPoints; Economics on the Web, an annotated set of URLs/links to sites of interest to economists; a graphing library; along with a description of what's on the student site and some Optional Material from the book.

SUPPLEMENTS FOR THE STUDENT

Study Guide: Written by Jack Mogab at Southwest Texas State University and Louis Johnston at the College of St. Benedict/St. John's University, this book provides the following elements for each chapter: a Pretest; a Learning Objective Grid; a Key Point Review with Learning Tips; some Self-Tests (Key Term Matching, Multiple Choice, Problems) with answers; and an extension of the guide to the Web site, where students may practice with graphing.

Online Learning Center (www.mhhe.com/economics/frankbernanke3): For students there are such useful and exciting features for the book as a whole as Interpreting the News—articles and summaries of relevant articles with analysis and discussion questions; a Math Tutor—help for those whose math skills are rusty; e-mail Updates—periodic sending of information/study tips; the Glossary from the textbook; and Economics on the Web—annotated URLs useful for economics students. Additionally, for each chapter there is an Electronic Learning Session that opens with a brief recap of the chapter, is then followed by a test with answers and analysis; and is followed by a set of study sessions based on Economic Naturalist Exercises; Graphing Exercises; PowerPoints; and Key Terms; this is finally followed by a second quiz, with answers and analysis.

DiscoverEcon with Paul Solman Videos: DiscoverEcon, available at www.discoverecon.com/frankbernanke3, is provided free to students via a code within every new copy of the third edition textbook. The software acts like an interactive text; software chapters parallel text chapters and software pages include specific page references to the text. DiscoverEcon Plus adds a complete electronic version of the text, including the option to print text pages, for a substantially lower price. Hot links from the interactive software to the relevant text pages make it easier than ever for students to move between explanations in the text and interactive explanations in the software.

All DiscoverEcon chapters contain a multiple-choice quiz, discussion questions with online links, and match-the-terms exercises. Interactive graphs, animated charts, and live tables let students manipulate variables and study the outcomes. The program provides links to videos created by Paul Solman of *The NewsHour with Jim Lehrer.* This video component consists of more than 30 short video segments. Each 5- to 10- minute video explains a key economic idea such as economic growth, elasticity, and production possibilities in a memorable, accessible way.

Students submit exercise results directly to their instructors with the click of a button. Multiple-choice and match-the-terms exercises are automatically graded and scores are added to a gradebook.

Developed by Gerald C. Nelson of the University of Illinois at Urbana-Champaign, this fully updated and enhanced version of DiscoverEcon with Paul Solman Videos features new learning opportunities for students and easy integration into existing courses for the instructor.

Students who do not have a code or want the ebook version may purchase DiscoverEcon or DiscoverEconPlus at www.discoverecon.com/frankbernanke3.

BusinessWeek **Edition:** Your students can subscribe to 15 weeks of *Business-Week* for a special price in addition to the price of the text. Students will receive a pass code card shrink-wrapped with their new text. The card directs students to a Web site where they enter the code and then gain access to *BusinessWeek*'s registration page to enter address info and set up their print and online subscription as well.

Wall Street Journal **Edition:** Your students can subscribe to *The Wall Street Journal* for 15 weeks at a special price in addition to the price of the text. Students will receive a "How to Use the *WSJ*" handbook plus a pass code card shrink-wrapped with the text. The card directs students to a Web site where they enter the code and then gain access to the *WSJ* registration page to enter address info and set up their print and online subscription, and also set up their subscription to Dow Jones Interactive online for the span of the 15-week period.

ACKNOWLEDGMENTS

Our thanks first and foremost go to our publisher, Gary Burke, for his unwavering faith in our project since its inception. In an industry known for sticking with proven formulas, he has been willing from the outset to gamble that the market will embrace our somewhat unorthodox vision. Without his support and encouragement, we never could have produced this book. Tom Thompson, our development editor, was enormously helpful as he guided us with intelligence, patience, and tact through three major revisions of the original manuscript, and further extensive revisions for the second and third editions. We thank Paul Shensa, the sponsoring editor, whose considerable experience, insightful suggestions, and extensive knowledge of the marketplace were of great help. We also thank Marty Quinn, our creative marketing manager, for helping to get the message into the wider world. We are especially grateful to Betty Morgan, our superb manuscript editor. And we are also grateful to the production team, whose professionalism was outstanding: Susanne Riedell, Project Manager; Matthew Baldwin, Designer; Michael McCormick, Production Supervisor; Lori Kramer, Photo Research Coordinator; Carol Loreth, Supplement Producer; Becky Szura, Media Project Manager; and Jennifer Fisher, Media Producer. We would also like to thank Sarah Anders for her reliable assistance in updating the macroeconomic data.

Finally, our sincere thanks to the following teachers and colleagues, whose thorough reviews and thoughtful suggestions led to innumerable substantive improvements.

Reviewers for the third edition

Ugur Aker
Hiram College

Rashid Al-Hmoud
Texas Tech University

Sudeshna Bandyopadhay
West Virginia University

Michael Bar
University of Minnesota

Klaus Becker
Texas Tech University

Ariel Belason
Binghamton University

Calvin Blackwell
College of Charleston

Clair Brown
University of California–Berkeley

Andrew Buck
Temple University

James Butikofer
Washington University
in St. Louis

Randy Campbell
Mississippi State University

Lon Carlson
Illinois State University

Nevin Cavusoglu
University of New Hampshire

Xia Chen
Tulane University

Nan-Ting Chou
University of Louisville

Eleanor Craig
University of Delaware

Ward Curran
Trinity College

Donald Dale
Muhlenberg College

Fred Derrick
Loyola University [MD]

Linda Dynan
Northern Kentucky University

Michael Enz
Western New England College

Belton Fleisher
The Ohio State University

Robert Florence
St. Bonaventure University

Kent Ford
Onondaga Community College

Joseph Friedman
Temple University

Ynon Gablinger
City University of New
York–Hunter College

Rob Garnett
Texas Christian University

Gregory Green
Idaho State University

Sunil Gulati
Columbia University

Alan Gummerson
Florida International University

Paul Hamilton
DePauw University

Mehdi Haririan
Bloomsburg University of
Pennsylvania

Joe Haslag
University of Missouri–
Columbia

Jeff Hefel
Saint Mary's University

Barry Hirsch
Trinity University [TX]

Brett Katzman
Kennesaw State University

Brendan Kennelly
National University of Ireland

Frederick Kolb
University of Wisconsin–
Eau Claire

Stephan Kroll
California State University–
Sacramento

Christopher Laincz
Drexel University

Tom Lehman
Indiana Wesleyan

Patricia Lindsey
Butte College

Alina Luca
Drexel University

Jeffrey Macher
Georgetown University

Norman Miller
Miami University [OH]

Christopher Mushrush
Illinois State University

Wilhelm Neuefeind
Washington University in St. Louis

Norman Obst
Michigan State University

Frank O'Connor
Eastern Kentucky University

Thomas Odegaard
Baylor University

Ronald Olive
University of Massachusetts–Lowell

Terry Olson
Truman State University

Santiago Pinto
West Virginia University

Robert Rebelein
Vassar College

Michael Rolleigh
University of Minnesota

Dan Rubenson
Southern Oregon University

Sumati Srinivas
Radford University

Petia Stoytcheva
Louisiana State University

Marie Truesdell
Marian College [IN]

Nora Underwood
Central Florida University

Norman Van Cott
Ball State University

Kristin Van Gaasbeck
California State University–
Sacramento

William Welch
Saginaw Valley State University

Paula Worthington
University of Chicago

Micky Wu
Coe College

Zhenhui Xu
Georgia College and
State University

Reviewers for the first two editions

Ercument Aksoy
Los Angeles Valley College

Richard Anderson
Texas A&M University

Daniel Berkowitz
University of Pittsburgh

Guatam Bhattacharya
University of Kansas

Scott Bierman
Carleton College

Bruce Blonigen
University of Oregon

Beth Bogan
Princeton University

George Borts
Brown University

Nancy Brooks
University of Vermont

Douglas Brown
Georgetown University

Marie Bussings-Burk
Southern Indiana University

David Carr
University of Colorado

Jack Chambless
Valencia Community College

James Cover
University of Alabama

Carl Davidson
Michigan State University

Lynn Pierson Doti
Chapman College

Donald Dutkowsky
Syracuse University

Nancy Fox
Saint Joseph's College

Johah Gelbach
University of Maryland

Linda Ghent
East Carolina University

Kirk Gifford
Ricks College

Robert Gillette
University of Kentucky

Stephen Gohman
University of Louisville

Refet Gurkaynak
Princeton University

Mary Jean Horney
Furman University

Nancy Jianakoplos
Colorado State University

Robert Johnson
University of San Diego

Herbert Kiesling
Indiana University

Bruce Kingma
State University of New York–Albany

Leonard Lardaro
University of Rhode Island

Anthony Lima
California State University–Hayward

Tom Love
North Central University

Steven McCafferty
The Ohio State University

Edward McNertney
Texas Christian University

William Merrill
Iowa State University

Paul Nelson
Northeast Louisiana State University

Neil Niman
University of New Hampshire

Charles Okeke
Community College of
Southern Nevada

Duane Oyen
University of Wisconsin–Eau Claire

Theodore Palivos
Louisiana State University

Michael Potepan
San Francisco State University

Steve Robinson
University of North Carolina–
Wilmington

Christina Romer
University of California–Berkeley

David Romer
University of California–Berkeley

Greg Rose
Sacramento City College

Robert Rossana
Wayne State University

Richard Salvucci
Trinity University

Edward Scahill
University of Scranton

Pamela Schmitt
Indiana University

Esther-Mirjam Sent
University of Notre Dame

John Solow
University of Iowa

Dennis Starleaf
Iowa State University

Helen Tauchen
University of North Carolina–
Chapel Hill

Kay Unger
University of Montana

Stephan Weiler
Colorado State University

Jeffrey Weiss
City University of New York–
Baruch College

Richard Winkelman
Arizona State University

Mark Wohar
University of Nebraska–Omaha

Louise Wolitz
University of Texas–Austin

Darrel Young
University of Texas–Austin

Zenon Zygmont
Western Oregon University

BRIEF CONTENTS

CONTENTS

PART

I

INTRODUCTION

As you begin the study of economics, perhaps the most important thing to realize is that economics is not a collection of settled facts, to be copied down and memorized. Mark Twain said that nothing is older than yesterday's newspaper, and the same can be said of yesterday's economic statistics. Indeed, the only prediction about the economy that can be made with confidence is that there will continue to be large, and largely unpredictable, changes.

If economics is not a set of durable facts, then what is it? Fundamentally, it is a way of thinking about the world. Over many years economists have developed some simple but widely applicable principles that are useful for understanding almost any economic situation, from the relatively simple economic decisions that individuals make every day to the workings of highly complex markets, such as international financial markets. The principal objective of this book, and of this course, is to help you learn these principles and how to apply them to a variety of economic questions and issues.

The three chapters of Part 1 lay out the basic economic principles that will be used throughout the book. Chapter 1 introduces the notion of scarcity—the unavoidable fact that, although our needs and wants are boundless, the resources available to satisfy them are limited. The chapter goes on to show that deciding whether to take an action by comparing the cost and benefit of the action is a useful approach for dealing with the inevitable trade-offs that scarcity creates. Chapter 1 then discusses several important decision pitfalls and concludes by introducing the concept of *economic naturalism*. Chapter 2 goes beyond individual decision making to consider trade, among both individuals and countries. An important reason for trade is that it permits people (or countries) to specialize in the production of particular goods and services, which in turn enhances productivity and raises standards of living. Finally, Chapter 3 presents an overview of the concepts of supply and demand, perhaps the most basic and familiar tools used by economists.

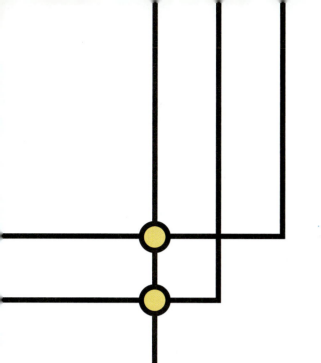

THINKING LIKE AN ECONOMIST

How many students are in your introductory economics class? Some classes have just 20 or so; others average 35, 100, or 200 students. At some schools, introductory economics classes may have as many as 2,000 students. What size is best?

If cost were no object, the best size for an introductory economics course—or any other course, for that matter—might be a single student. Think about it: the whole course, all term long, with just you and your professor! Everything could be custom-tailored to your own background and ability, allowing you to cover the material at just the right pace. The tutorial format would also promote close communication and personal trust between you and your professor. And your grade would depend more heavily on what you actually learned than on your luck when taking multiple-choice exams. We may even suppose, for the sake of discussion, that studies by educational psychologists prove definitively that students learn best in the tutorial format.

Why, then, do so many universities continue to schedule introductory classes with hundreds of students? The simple reason is that costs *do* matter. They matter not just to the university administrators who must build classrooms and pay faculty salaries, but also to *you*. The direct cost of providing you with your own personal introductory economics course—most notably, the professor's salary and the expense of providing a classroom in which to meet—might easily top $40,000. *Someone* has to pay these costs. In private universities, a large share of the cost would be recovered directly from higher tuition payments; in state universities, the burden would be split between higher tuition payments and higher tax payments. But in either case, the course would be unaffordable for many, if not most, students.

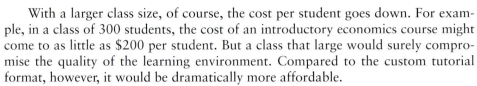

With a larger class size, of course, the cost per student goes down. For example, in a class of 300 students, the cost of an introductory economics course might come to as little as $200 per student. But a class that large would surely compromise the quality of the learning environment. Compared to the custom tutorial format, however, it would be dramatically more affordable.

In choosing what size introductory economics course to offer, then, university administrators confront a classic economic trade-off. In making the class larger, they lower the quality of instruction—a bad thing—but at the same time, they reduce costs, and hence the tuition students must pay—a good thing.

ECONOMICS: STUDYING CHOICE IN A WORLD OF SCARCITY

Even in rich societies like the United States, *scarcity* is a fundamental fact of life. There is never enough time, money, or energy to do everything we want to do or have everything we would like to have. **Economics** is the study of how people make choices under conditions of scarcity and of the results of those choices for society.

Are small classes "better" than large ones?

economics the study of how people make choices under conditions of scarcity and of the results of those choices for society

In the class-size example just discussed, a motivated economics student might definitely prefer to be in a class of 20 rather than a class of 100, everything else being equal. But other things, of course, are not equal. Students can enjoy the benefits of having smaller classes, but only at the price of having less money for other activities. The student's choice inevitably will come down to the relative importance of competing activities.

That such trade-offs are widespread and important is one of the core principles of economics. We call it the **scarcity principle**, because the simple fact of scarcity makes trade-offs necessary. Another name for the scarcity principle is the **no-free-lunch principle** (which comes from the observation that even lunches that are given to you are never really free—somebody, somehow, always has to pay for them).

The Scarcity Principle (also called the No-Free-Lunch Principle): Although we have boundless needs and wants, the resources available to us are limited. So having more of one good thing usually means having less of another.

Inherent in the idea of a trade-off is the fact that choice involves compromise between competing interests. Economists resolve such trade-offs by using *cost-benefit analysis*, which is based on the disarmingly simple principle that an action should be taken if, and only if, its benefits exceed its costs. We call this statement the **cost-benefit principle**, and it, too, is one of the core principles of economics:

The Cost-Benefit Principle: An individual (or a firm, or a society) should take an action if, and only if, the extra benefits from taking the action are at least as great as the extra costs.

With the cost-benefit principle in mind, let's think about our class-size question again. Imagine that classrooms come in only two sizes—100-seat lecture halls and 20-seat classrooms—and that your university currently offers introductory economics courses to classes of 100 students. Question: Should administrators reduce the class size to 20 students? Answer: Reduce if, and only if, the value of the improvement in instruction outweighs its additional cost.

This rule sounds simple, but to apply it we need some way to measure the relevant costs and benefits—a task that is often difficult in practice. If we make a few simplifying assumptions, however, we can see how the analysis might work. On the cost side, the primary expense of reducing class size from 100 to 20 is that we will now need five professors instead of just one. We'll also need five smaller classrooms rather than a single big one, and this too may add slightly to the expense of the move. For the sake of discussion, suppose that the cost with a class size of 20 turns out to be $1,000 per student more than the cost per student when the class size is 100. Should administrators switch to the smaller class size? If they apply the cost-benefit principle, they will realize that *the reduction in class size makes sense only if the value of attending the smaller class is at least $1,000 per student greater than the value of attending the larger class.*

Would you (or your family) be willing to pay an extra $1,000 for a smaller economics class? If not, and if other students feel the same way, then sticking with the larger class size makes sense. But if you and others would be willing to pay the extra tuition, then reducing the class size to 20 makes good economic sense.

Notice that the "best" class size, from an economic point of view, will generally not be the same as the "best" size from the point of view of an educational psychologist. The difference arises because the economic definition of "best" takes into account both the benefits *and* the costs of different class sizes. The psychologist ignores costs and looks only at the learning benefits of different class sizes.

In practice, of course, different people will feel differently about the value of smaller classes. People with high incomes, for example, tend to be willing to pay more for the advantage, which helps to explain why average class size is smaller, and tuition higher, at private schools whose students come predominantly from high-income families.

The cost-benefit framework for thinking about the class-size problem also suggests a possible reason for the gradual increase in average class size that has been taking place in American colleges and universities. During the last 15 years, professors' salaries have risen sharply, making smaller classes more costly. During the same period, median family income—and hence the willingness to pay for smaller classes—has remained roughly constant. When the cost of offering smaller classes goes up but willingness to pay for smaller classes does not, universities shift to larger class sizes.

Scarcity and the trade-offs that result also apply to resources other than money. Bill Gates is the richest man on Earth. His wealth was once estimated at over $100 billion—more than the combined wealth of the poorest 40 percent of Americans. Gates has enough money to buy more houses, cars, vacations, and other consumer goods than he could possibly use. Yet Gates, like the rest of us, has only 24 hours each day and a limited amount of energy. So even he confronts trade-offs, in that any activity he pursues—whether it be building his business empire or redecorating his mansion—uses up time and energy that he could otherwise spend on other things. Indeed, someone once calculated that the value of Gates's time is so great that pausing to pick up a $100 bill from the sidewalk simply wouldn't be worth his while.

If Bill Gates saw a $100 bill lying on the sidewalk, would it be worth his time to pick it up?

APPLYING THE COST-BENEFIT PRINCIPLE

In studying choice under scarcity, we'll usually begin with the premise that people are **rational,** which means they have well-defined goals and try to fulfill them as best they can. The cost-benefit principle illustrated in the class-size example is a fundamental tool for the study of how rational people make choices.

As in the class-size example, often the only real difficulty in applying the cost-benefit rule is to come up with reasonable measures of the relevant benefits and costs. Only in rare instances will exact dollar measures be conveniently available. But the cost-benefit framework can lend structure to your thinking even when no relevant market data are available.

To illustrate how we proceed in such cases, the following example asks you to decide whether to perform an action whose cost is described only in vague, qualitative terms.

rational person someone with well-defined goals who tries to fulfill those goals as best he or she can

EXAMPLE 1.1

Should you walk downtown to save $10 on a $25 computer game?

Imagine you are about to buy a $25 computer game at the nearby campus store when a friend tells you that the same game is on sale at a downtown store for only $15. If the downtown store is a 30-minute walk away, where should you buy the game?

The cost-benefit principle tells us that you should buy it downtown if the benefit of doing so exceeds the cost. The benefit of taking any action is the dollar value of everything you gain by taking it. Here, the benefit of buying downtown is exactly $10, since that is the amount you will save on the purchase price of the game. The cost of taking any action is the dollar value of everything you give up by taking it. Here, the cost of buying downtown is the dollar value you assign to the time and trouble it takes to make the trip. But how do we estimate that dollar value?

One way is to perform the following hypothetical auction. Imagine that a stranger has offered to pay you to do an errand that involves the same walk downtown (perhaps to drop off a letter for her at the post office). If she offered you a payment of, say, $1,000, would you accept? If so, we know that your cost of walking downtown and back must be less than $1,000. Now imagine her offer being reduced in small increments until you finally refuse the last offer. For example, if you would agree to walk downtown and back for $9.00 but not for $8.99, then your cost of making the trip is $9.00. In this case, you should buy the game downtown, because the $10 you'll save (your benefit) is greater than your $9.00 cost of making the trip.

But suppose, alternatively, that your cost of making the trip had been greater than $10. In that case, your best bet would have been to buy the game from the nearby campus store. Confronted with this choice, different people may choose differently, depending on how costly they think it is to make the trip downtown. But although there is no uniquely correct choice, most people who are asked what they would do in this situation say they would buy the game downtown.

ECONOMIC SURPLUS

economic surplus the economic surplus from taking any action is the benefit of taking that action minus its cost

Suppose again that in Example 1.1 your "cost" of making the trip downtown was $9. Compared to the alternative of buying the game at the campus store, buying it downtown resulted in an **economic surplus** of $1, the difference between the benefit of making the trip and its cost. In general, your goal as an economic decision maker is to choose those actions that generate the largest possible economic surplus. This means taking all actions that yield a positive total economic surplus, which is just another way of restating the cost-benefit principle.

Note that the fact that your best choice was to buy the game downtown doesn't imply that you *enjoy* making the trip, any more than choosing a large class means that you prefer large classes to small ones. It simply means that the trip is less unpleasant than the prospect of paying $10 extra for the game. Once again, you've faced a trade-off—in this case, the choice between a cheaper game and the free time gained by avoiding the trip.

OPPORTUNITY COST

opportunity cost the opportunity cost of an activity is the value of the next-best alternative that must be forgone in order to undertake the activity

Of course, your mental auction could have produced a different outcome. Suppose, for example, that the time required for the trip is the only time you have left to study for a difficult test the next day. Or suppose you are watching one of your favorite movies on cable, or that you are tired and would love a short nap. In such cases, we say that the **opportunity cost** of making the trip—that is, the value of what you must sacrifice to walk downtown and back—is high, and you are more likely to decide against making the trip.

In this example, if watching the last hour of the cable TV movie is the most valuable opportunity that conflicts with the trip downtown, the opportunity cost of making the trip is the dollar value you place on pursuing that opportunity—that is, the largest amount you'd be willing to pay to avoid missing the end of the movie. Note that the opportunity cost of making the trip is not the combined value of *all* possible activities you could have pursued, but only the value of your *best* alternative—the one you would have chosen had you not made the trip.

Throughout the text we will pose exercises like the one that follows. You'll find that pausing to answer them will help you to master key concepts in economics. Because doing these exercises isn't very costly (indeed, many students report that they are actually fun), the cost-benefit principle indicates that it's well worth your while to do them.

EXERCISE 1.1

You would again save $10 by buying the game downtown rather than at the campus store, but your cost of making the trip is now $12, not $9. How much economic surplus would you get from buying the game downtown? Where should you buy it?

THE ROLE OF ECONOMIC MODELS

Economists use the cost-benefit principle as an abstract model of how an idealized rational individual would choose among competing alternatives. (By "abstract model" we mean a simplified description that captures the essential elements of a situation and allows us to analyze them in a logical way.) A computer model of a complex phenomenon like climate change, which must ignore many details and includes only the major forces at work, is an example of an abstract model.

Noneconomists are sometimes harshly critical of the economist's cost-benefit model on the grounds that people in the real world never conduct hypothetical mental auctions before deciding whether to make trips downtown. But this criticism betrays a fundamental misunderstanding of how abstract models can help to explain and predict human behavior. Economists know perfectly well that people don't conduct hypothetical mental auctions when they make simple decisions. All the cost-benefit principle really says is that a rational decision is one that is explicitly or implicitly based on a weighing of costs and benefits.

Most of us make sensible decisions most of the time, without being consciously aware that we are weighing costs and benefits, just as most people ride a bike without being consciously aware of what keeps them from falling. Through trial and error, we gradually learn what kinds of choices tend to work best in different contexts, just as bicycle riders internalize the relevant laws of physics, usually without being conscious of them.

Even so, learning the explicit principles of cost-benefit analysis can help us make better decisions, just as knowing about physics can help in learning to ride a bicycle. For instance, when a young economist was teaching his oldest son to ride a bike, he followed the time-honored tradition of running alongside the bike and holding onto his son, then giving him a push and hoping for the best. After several hours and painfully skinned elbows and knees, his son finally got it. A year later, someone pointed out that the trick to riding a bike is to turn slightly in whichever direction the bike is leaning. Of course! The economist passed this information along to his second son, who learned to ride almost instantly. Just as knowing a little physics can help you learn to ride a bike, knowing a little economics can help you make better decisions.

RECAP	COST-BENEFIT ANALYSIS

Scarcity is a basic fact of economic life. Because of it, having more of one good thing almost always means having less of another (the scarcity principle). The cost-benefit principle holds that an individual (or a firm, or a society) should take an action if, and only if, the extra benefit from taking the action is at least as great as the extra cost. The benefit of taking any action minus the cost of taking the action is called the *economic surplus* from that action. Hence the cost-benefit principle suggests that we take only those actions that create additional economic surplus.

FOUR IMPORTANT DECISION PITFALLS*

Rational people will apply the cost-benefit principle most of the time, although probably in an intuitive and approximate way, rather than through explicit and precise calculation. Knowing that rational people tend to compare costs and benefits enables economists to predict their likely behavior. As noted earlier, for example, we can predict that students from wealthy families are more likely than others to attend colleges that offer small classes. (Again, while the cost of small classes is the same for all families, the benefit of small classes, as measured by what people are willing to pay for them, tends to be higher for wealthier families.)

PITFALL I: MEASURING COSTS AND BENEFITS AS PROPORTIONS RATHER THAN ABSOLUTE DOLLAR AMOUNTS

As the next example makes clear, the cost-benefit principle proves helpful in another way. The example demonstrates that people aren't born with an infallible instinct for weighing the relevant costs and benefits of many daily decisions. Indeed, one of the rewards of studying economics is that it can improve the quality of your decisions.

EXAMPLE 1.2

Should you walk downtown to save $10 on a $2,020 laptop computer?

You are about to buy a $2,020 laptop computer at the nearby campus store when a friend tells you that the same computer is on sale at a downtown store for only $2,010. If the downtown store is half an hour's walk away, where should you buy the computer?

Assuming that the laptop is light enough to carry without effort, the structure of this example is exactly the same as that of Example 1.1—the only difference being that the price of the laptop is dramatically higher than the price of the computer game. As before, the benefit of buying downtown is the dollar amount you'll save, namely, $10. And since it's exactly the same trip, its cost must also be the same as before. So if you are perfectly rational, you should make the same decision in both cases. Yet when real people are asked what they would do in these situations, the overwhelming majority say they would walk downtown to buy the game but would buy the laptop at the campus store. When asked to explain, most of them say something like "The trip was worth it for the game because you save 40 percent, but not worth it for the laptop because you save only $10 out of $2,020."

This is faulty reasoning. The benefit of the trip downtown is not the *proportion* you save on the original price. Rather, it is the *absolute dollar amount* you save.

*The examples in this section are inspired by the pioneering research of Daniel Kahneman and the late Amos Tversky. Kahneman was awarded the 2002 Nobel Prize in economics for his efforts to integrate insights from psychology into economics.

Since the benefit of walking downtown to buy the laptop is $10—exactly the same as for the computer game—and since the cost of the trip must also be the same in both cases, the economic surplus from making both trips must be exactly the same. And that means that a rational decision maker would make the same decision in both cases. Yet, as noted, most people choose differently.

EXERCISE 1.2

Which is more valuable: saving $100 on a $2,000 plane ticket to Tokyo or saving $90 on a $200 plane ticket to Chicago?

The pattern of faulty reasoning in the decision just discussed is one of several decision pitfalls to which people are often prone. In the discussion that follows, we will identify three additional decision pitfalls. In some cases, people ignore costs or benefits that they ought to take into account, while on other occasions they are influenced by costs or benefits that are irrelevant.

PITFALL 2: IGNORING OPPORTUNITY COSTS

Sherlock Holmes, Arthur Conan Doyle's legendary detective, was successful because he saw details that most others overlooked. In *Silver Blaze,* Holmes is called on to investigate the theft of an expensive racehorse from its stable. A Scotland Yard inspector assigned to the case asks Holmes whether some particular aspect of the crime requires further study. "Yes," Holmes replies, and describes "the curious incident of the dog in the nighttime." "The dog did nothing in the nighttime," responds the puzzled inspector. But as Holmes realized, that was precisely the problem. The watchdog's failure to bark when Silver Blaze was stolen meant that the watchdog knew the thief. This clue ultimately proved the key to unraveling the mystery.

Just as we often don't notice when a dog fails to bark, many of us tend to overlook the implicit value of activities that fail to happen. As discussed earlier, however, intelligent decisions require taking the value of forgone opportunities properly into account.

The opportunity cost of an activity, once again, is the value of the next-best alternative that must be forgone in order to engage in that activity. If buying a computer game downtown means not watching the last hour of a movie, then the value to you of watching the end of that movie is an opportunity cost of the trip. Many people make bad decisions because they tend to ignore the value of such forgone opportunities. To avoid overlooking opportunity costs, economists often translate questions like "Should I walk downtown?" into ones like "Should I walk downtown or watch the end of the movie?"

Opportunity costs are like dogs that fail to bark in the night.

Should you use your frequent-flyer coupon to fly to Fort Lauderdale for spring break?

With spring break only a week away, you are still undecided about whether to go to Fort Lauderdale with a group of classmates at the University of Iowa. The round-trip airfare from Cedar Rapids is $500, but you have a frequent-flyer coupon you could use to pay for the trip. All other relevant costs for the vacation week at the beach total exactly $1,000. The most you would be willing to pay for the Fort Lauderdale vacation is $1,350. That amount is your benefit of taking the vacation. Your only alternative use for your frequent-flyer coupon is for your plane trip to Boston the weekend after spring break to attend your brother's wedding. (Your coupon expires shortly thereafter.) If the Cedar Rapids–Boston round-trip airfare is $400, should you use your frequent-flyer coupon to fly to Fort Lauderdale for spring break?

The cost-benefit principle tells us that you should go to Fort Lauderdale if the benefits of the trip exceed its costs. If not for the complication of the frequent-flyer

EXAMPLE 1.3

Is your flight to Fort Lauderdale "free" if you travel on a frequent-flyer coupon?

coupon, solving this problem would be a straightforward matter of comparing your benefit from the week at the beach to the sum of all relevant costs. And since your airfare and other costs would add up to $1,500, or $150 more than your benefit from the trip, you would not go to Fort Lauderdale.

But what about the possibility of using your frequent-flyer coupon to make the trip? Using it for that purpose might make the flight to Fort Lauderdale seem free, suggesting you would reap an economic surplus of $350 by making the trip. But doing so would also mean you would have to fork over $400 for your airfare to Boston. So the opportunity cost of using your coupon to go to Fort Lauderdale is really $400. If you use it for that purpose, the trip still ends up being a loser, because the cost of the vacation, $1,400, exceeds the benefit by $50. In cases like these, you are much more likely to decide sensibly if you ask yourself, "Should I use my frequent-flyer coupon for this trip or save it for an upcoming trip?"

We cannot emphasize strongly enough that the key to using the concept of opportunity cost correctly lies in recognizing precisely what taking a given action prevents us from doing. The following exercise illustrates this point by modifying the details of Example 1.3 slightly.

EXERCISE 1.3

Same as Example 1.3, except that now your frequent-flyer coupon expires in a week, so your only chance to use it will be for the Fort Lauderdale trip. Should you use your coupon?

PITFALL 3: FAILURE TO IGNORE SUNK COSTS

The opportunity cost pitfall is one in which people ignore costs they ought to take into account. In another common pitfall, the reverse is true: People are influenced by costs they ought to ignore. *The only costs that should influence a decision about whether to take an action are those that we can avoid by not taking the action.* As a practical matter, however, many decision makers appear to be influenced by **sunk costs**—costs that are beyond recovery at the moment a decision is made. For example, money spent on a nontransferable, nonrefundable airline ticket is a sunk cost.

sunk cost a cost that is beyond recovery at the moment a decision must be made

Because sunk costs must be borne *whether or not an action is taken*, they are irrelevant to the decision of whether to take the action. The sunk-cost pitfall (the mistake of being influenced by sunk costs) is illustrated clearly in the following example.

EXAMPLE 1.4   **How much should you eat at an all-you-can-eat restaurant?**

Sangam, an Indian restaurant in Philadelphia, offers an all-you-can-eat lunch buffet for $5. Customers pay $5 at the door, and no matter how many times they refill their plates, there is no additional charge. One day, as a goodwill gesture, the owner of the restaurant tells 20 randomly selected guests that their lunch is on the house. The remaining guests pay the usual price. If all diners are rational, will there be any difference in the average quantity of food consumed by people in these two groups?

Having eaten their first helping, diners in each group confront the following question: "Should I go back for another helping?" For rational diners, if the benefit of doing so exceeds the cost, the answer is yes; otherwise it is no. Note that at the moment of decision about a second helping, the $5 charge for the lunch is a sunk cost. Those who paid it have no way to recover it. Thus, for both groups, the (extra) cost of another helping is exactly zero. And since the people who received the free lunch were chosen at random, there is no reason to suppose that their appetites or incomes are different from those of other diners. The benefit of another helping thus should be the same, on average, for people in both groups. And since their respective costs and benefits of an additional helping are the same, the two groups should eat the same number of helpings, on average.

Psychologists and economists have experimental evidence, however, that people in such groups do *not* eat similar amounts.[1] In particular, those for whom the luncheon charge is not waived tend to eat substantially more than those for whom the charge is waived. People in the former group seem somehow determined to "get their money's worth." Their implicit goal is apparently to minimize the average cost per bite of the food they eat. Yet minimizing average cost is not a particularly sensible objective. It brings to mind the man who drove his car on the highway at night, even though he had nowhere to go, because he wanted to boost his average fuel economy. The irony is that diners who are determined to get their money's worth usually end up eating too much, as evidenced later by their regrets about having gone back for their last helpings.

The fact that the cost-benefit criterion failed the test of prediction in this example does nothing to invalidate its advice about what people *should* do. If you are letting sunk costs influence your decisions, you can do better by changing your behavior.

PITFALL 4: FAILURE TO UNDERSTAND THE AVERAGE–MARGINAL DISTINCTION

Often we are confronted with the choice of whether or not to engage in an activity (for example, whether or not to shop downtown). But in many situations, the issue is not whether to pursue the activity at all, but rather the *extent* to which it should be pursued. We can apply the cost-benefit principle in such situations by repeatedly asking the question "Should I increase the level at which I am currently pursuing the activity?"

In attempting to answer this question, the focus should always be on the benefit and cost of an *additional* unit of activity. To emphasize this focus, economists refer to the cost of an additional unit of activity as the **marginal cost** of the activity. Similarly, the benefit of an additional unit of the activity is the **marginal benefit** of the activity.

When the problem is to discover the proper level at which to pursue an activity, the cost-benefit rule is to keep increasing the level as long as marginal benefit of the activity exceeds its marginal cost. As the following example illustrates, however, people often fail to apply this rule correctly.

marginal cost the increase in total cost that results from carrying out one additional unit of an activity

marginal benefit the increase in total benefit that results from carrying out one additional unit of an activity

Should NASA expand the space shuttle program from four launches per year to five?

EXAMPLE 1.5

Professor Kösten Banifoot, a prominent supporter of the National Aeronautics and Space Administration's (NASA) space shuttle program, estimated that the gains from the program are currently $24 billion per year (an average of $6 billion per launch) and that its costs are currently $20 billion per year (an average of $5 billion per launch). On the basis of these estimates, Professor Banifoot testified before Congress that NASA should definitely expand the space shuttle program. Should Congress follow his advice?

To discover whether expanding the program makes economic sense, we must compare the marginal cost of a launch to its marginal benefit. The professor's

[1]See, for example, Richard Thaler, "Toward a Positive Theory of Consumer Choice," *Journal of Economic Behavior and Organization* **1**, no. 1 (1980).

average cost the total cost of undertaking *n* units of an activity divided by *n*

average benefit the total benefit of undertaking *n* units of an activity divided by *n*

estimates, however, tell us only the **average cost** and **average benefit** of the program—which are, respectively, the total cost of the program divided by the number of launches and the total benefit divided by the number of launches. Knowing the average benefit and average cost per launch for all shuttles launched thus far is simply not useful for deciding whether to expand the program. Of course, the average cost of the launches undertaken so far *might* be the same as the cost of adding another launch. But it might also be either higher or lower than the marginal cost of a launch. The same statement holds true regarding average and marginal benefits.

Suppose, for the sake of discussion, that the benefit of an additional launch is in fact the same as the average benefit per launch thus far, $6 billion. Should NASA add another launch? Not if the cost of adding the fifth launch would be more than $6 billion. And the fact that the average cost per launch is only $5 billion simply does not tell us anything about the marginal cost of the fifth launch.

Suppose, for example, that the relationship between the number of shuttles launched and the total cost of the program is as described in Table 1.1. The average cost per launch (third column) when there are four launches would then be $20 billion/4 = $5 billion per launch, just as Professor Banifoot testified. But note in the second column of the table that adding a fifth launch would raise costs from $20 billion to $32 billion, making the marginal cost of the fifth launch $12 billion. So if the benefit of an additional launch is $6 billion, increasing the number of launches from four to five would make absolutely no economic sense.

TABLE 1.1
How Total Cost Varies with the Number of Launches

Number of launches	Total cost ($ billions)	Average cost ($ billion/launch)
0	0	0
1	3	3
2	7	3.5
3	12	4
4	20	5
5	32	6.4

The following example illustrates how to apply the cost-benefit principle correctly in this case.

EXAMPLE 1.6   **How many space shuttles should NASA launch?**

NASA must decide how many space shuttles to launch. The benefit of each launch is estimated to be $6 billion, and the total cost of the program again depends on the number of launches in the manner shown in Table 1.1. How many shuttles should NASA launch?

NASA should continue to launch shuttles as long as the marginal benefit of the program exceeds its marginal cost. In this example, the marginal benefit is constant at $6 billion per launch, regardless of the number of shuttles launched. NASA should thus keep launching shuttles as long as the marginal cost per launch is less than or equal to $6 billion.

TABLE 1.2
How Marginal Cost Varies with the Number of Launches

Number of launches	Total cost ($ billion)	Marginal cost ($ billion/launch)
0	0	
		3
1	3	
		4
2	7	
		5
3	12	
		8
4	20	
		12
5	32	

Applying the definition of marginal cost to the total cost entries in the second column of Table 1.1 yields the marginal cost values in the third column of Table 1.2. (Because marginal cost is the change in total cost that results when we change the number of launches by one, we place each marginal cost entry midway between the rows showing the corresponding total cost entries.) Thus, for example, the marginal cost of increasing the number of launches from one to two is $4 billion, the difference between the $7 billion total cost of two launches and the $3 billion total cost of one launch.

As we see from a comparison of the $6 billion marginal benefit per launch with the marginal cost entries in the third column of Table 1.2, the first three launches satisfy the cost-benefit test, but the fourth and fifth launches do not. NASA should thus launch three space shuttles.

EXERCISE 1.4

If the marginal benefit of each launch had been not $6 billion but $9 billion, how many shuttles should NASA have launched?

The cost-benefit framework emphasizes that the only relevant costs and benefits in deciding whether to pursue an activity further are *marginal* costs and benefits—measures that correspond to the *increment* of activity under consideration. In many contexts, however, people seem more inclined to compare the *average* cost and benefit of the activity. As Example 1.5 made clear, increasing the level of an activity may not be justified, even though its average benefit at the current level is significantly greater than its average cost.

Here's an exercise that further illustrates the importance of the average–marginal distinction.

EXERCISE 1.5

Should a basketball team's best player take all the team's shots?

A professional basketball team has a new assistant coach. The assistant notices that one player scores on a higher percentage of his shots than other players. Based on this information, the assistant suggests to the head coach that the star player should take *all* the shots. That way, the assistant reasons, the team will score more points and win more games.

On hearing this suggestion, the head coach fires his assistant for incompetence. What was wrong with the assistant's idea?

RECAP	FOUR IMPORTANT DECISION PITFALLS

1. **The pitfall of measuring costs or benefits proportionally.** Many decision makers treat a change in cost or benefit as insignificant if it constitutes only a small proportion of the original amount. Absolute dollar amounts, not proportions, should be employed to measure costs and benefits.

2. **The pitfall of ignoring opportunity costs.** When performing a cost-benefit analysis of an action, it is important to account for all relevant *opportunity costs,* defined as the values of the most highly valued alternatives that must be forgone in order to carry out the action. A resource (such as a frequent-flyer coupon) may have a high opportunity cost, even if you originally got it "for free," if its best alternative use has high value. The identical resource may have a low opportunity cost, however, if it has no good alternative uses.

3. **The pitfall of not ignoring sunk costs.** When deciding whether to perform an action, it is important to ignore sunk costs—those costs that cannot be avoided even if the action is not taken. Even though a ticket to a concert may have cost you $100, if you have already bought it and cannot sell it to anyone else, the $100 is a sunk cost and should not influence your decision about whether to go to the concert.

4. **The pitfall of using average instead of marginal costs and benefits.** Decision makers often have ready information about the total cost and benefit of an activity, and from these it is simple to compute the activity's average cost and benefit. A common mistake is to conclude that an activity should be increased if its average benefit exceeds its average cost. The cost-benefit principle tells us that the level of an activity should be increased if, and only if, its *marginal* benefit exceeds its *marginal* cost.

Some costs and benefits, especially marginal costs and benefits and opportunity costs, are important for decision making, while others, like sunk costs and average costs and benefits, are essentially irrelevant. This conclusion is implicit in our original statement of the cost-benefit principle (an action should be taken if, and only if, the extra benefits of taking it exceed the extra costs). When we encounter additional examples of decision pitfalls, we will flag them by inserting the icon for the cost-benefit principle in the margin.

NORMATIVE ECONOMICS VERSUS POSITIVE ECONOMICS

The examples discussed in the preceding section make the point that people *sometimes* choose irrationally. We must stress that our purpose in discussing these examples was not to suggest that people *generally* make irrational choices. On the contrary, most people appear to choose sensibly most of the time, especially when their decisions are important or familiar ones. The economist's focus on rational choice thus offers not only useful advice about making better decisions, but also a basis for predicting and explaining human behavior. We used the cost-benefit approach in this way when discussing how rising faculty salaries have led to larger class sizes. And as we will see, similar reasoning helps to explain human behavior in virtually every other domain.

normative economic principle
one that says how people
should behave

The cost-benefit principle is an example of a **normative economic principle,** one that provides guidance about how we *should* behave. For example, according to the cost-benefit principle, we should ignore sunk costs when making decisions about the future. As our discussion of the various decision pitfalls make clear, however, the cost-benefit principle is not always a **descriptive economic principle**, one that describes how we actually *will* behave. As we saw, the cost-benefit principle can be tricky to implement, and people sometimes fail to heed its prescriptions.

Positive economic principle one that predicts how people will behave

That said, we stress that knowing the relevant costs and benefits surely does enable us to predict how people will behave much of the time. If the benefit of an action goes up, it is generally reasonable to predict that people will be more likely to take that action. And conversely, if the cost of an action goes up, the safest prediction will be that people will be less likely to take that action. This point is so important that we designate it as the incentive principle.

The Incentive Principle: **A person (or a firm or a society) is more likely to take an action if its benefit rises, and less likely to take it if its cost rises. In short, incentives matter.**

The incentive principle is a positive economic principle. It stresses that the relevant costs and benefits usually help us predict behavior, but at the same time does not insist that people will behave rationally in each instance. For example, if the price of heating oil were to rise sharply, we would invoke the cost-benefit principle to say that people *should* turn their thermostats down, and invoke the incentive principle to predict that average thermostat settings *will* in fact go down in most cases.

ECONOMICS: MICRO AND MACRO

By convention, we use the term **microeconomics** to describe the study of individual choices and of group behavior in individual markets. **Macroeconomics,** by contrast, is the study of the performance of national economies and of the policies that governments use to try to improve that performance. Macroeconomics tries to understand the determinants of such things as the national unemployment rate, the overall price level, and the total value of national output.

microeconomics the study of individual choice under scarcity and its implications for the behavior of prices and quantities in individual markets

Our focus in this chapter is on issues that confront the individual decision maker, whether that individual confronts a personal decision, a family decision, a business decision, a government policy decision, or indeed any other type of decision. Further on, we'll consider economic models of groups of individuals, such as all buyers or all sellers in a specific market. Later still we will turn to broader economic issues and measures.

macroeconomics the study of the performance of national economies and the policies that governments use to try to improve that performance

No matter which of these levels is our focus, however, our thinking will be shaped by the fact that although economic needs and wants are effectively unlimited, the material and human resources that can be used to satisfy them are finite. Clear thinking about economic problems must therefore always take into account the idea of trade-offs—the idea that having more of one good thing usually means having less of another. Our economy and our society are shaped to a substantial degree by the choices people have made when faced with trade-offs.

THE APPROACH OF THIS TEXT

Choosing the number of students to register in each class is just one of many important decisions in planning an introductory economics course. Another decision, to which the scarcity principle applies just as strongly, concerns which of many different topics to include on the course syllabus. There is a virtually inexhaustible set of topics and issues that might be covered in an introductory course, but only limited time in which to cover them. There is no free lunch. Covering some topics inevitably means omitting others.

All textbook authors are necessarily forced to pick and choose. A textbook that covered *all* the issues ever written about in economics would take up more than a whole floor of your campus library. It is our firm view that most introductory textbooks try to cover far too much. One reason that each of us was drawn to the study of economics was that a relatively short list of the discipline's core ideas can explain a great deal of the behavior and events we see in the world around us. So rather than cover a large number of ideas at a superficial level, our strategy is to focus on this short list of core ideas, returning to each entry again and again, in many different contexts. This strategy will enable you to internalize these ideas remarkably well in the brief span of a single course. And the benefit of learning a small number of important ideas well will far outweigh the cost of having to ignore a host of other, less important ideas.

So far, we've already encountered three core ideas: the scarcity principle, the cost-benefit principle, and the incentive principle. As these core ideas reemerge in the course of our discussions, we'll call your attention to them. And shortly after a *new* core idea appears, we'll highlight it by formally restating it.

A second important element in the philosophy of this text is our belief in the importance of active learning. In the same way that you can learn Spanish only by speaking and writing it, or tennis only by playing the game, you can learn economics only by *doing* economics. And because we want you to learn how to do economics, rather than just to read or listen passively as the authors or your instructor does economics, we will make every effort to encourage you to stay actively involved.

For example, instead of just telling you about an idea, we will usually first motivate the idea by showing you how it works in the context of a specific example. Often, these examples will be followed by exercises for you to try, as well as applications that show the relevance of the idea to real life. Try working the exercises *before* looking up the answers (which are at the back of the corresponding chapter).

Think critically about the applications: Do you see how they illustrate the point being made? Do they give you new insight into the issue? Work the problems at the end of the chapters, and take extra care with those relating to points that you do not fully understand. Apply economic principles to the world around you. (We'll say more about this when we discuss economic naturalism below.) Finally, when you come across an idea or example that you find interesting, tell a friend about it. You'll be surprised to discover how much the mere act of explaining it helps you understand and remember the underlying principle. The more actively you can become engaged in the learning process, the more effective your learning will be.

ECONOMIC NATURALISM

With the rudiments of the cost-benefit framework under your belt, you are now in a position to become an "economic naturalist," someone who uses insights from economics to help make sense of observations from everyday life. People who have studied biology are able to observe and marvel at many details of nature that would otherwise have escaped their notice. For example, on a walk in the woods in early April the novice may see only trees whereas the biology student notices many different species of trees and understands why some are already into leaf while others still lie dormant. Likewise, the novice may notice that in some animal species males are much larger than females, but the biology student knows that pattern occurs only in species in which males take several mates. Natural selection favors larger males in those species because their greater size helps them prevail in the often bloody contests among males for access to females. By contrast, males tend to be roughly the same size as females in monogamous species, in which there is much less fighting for mates.

In similar fashion, learning a few simple economic principles enables us to see the mundane details of ordinary human existence in a new light. Whereas the uninitiated often fail even to notice these details, the economic naturalist not only sees them, but becomes actively engaged in the attempt to understand them. Let's consider a few examples of questions economic naturalists might pose for themselves.

Why do many hardware manufacturers include more than $1,000 worth of "free" software with a computer selling for only slightly more than that?

The software industry is different from many others in the sense that its customers care a great deal about product compatibility. When you and your classmates are working on a project together, for example, your task will be much simpler if you all use the same word-processing program. Likewise, an executive's life will be easier at tax time if her financial software is the same as her accountant's.

The implication is that the benefit of owning and using any given software program increases with the number of other people who use that same product. This unusual relationship gives the producers of the most popular programs an enormous advantage and often makes it hard for new programs to break into the market.

Recognizing this pattern, the Intuit Corporation offered computer makers free copies of *Quicken*, its personal financial-management software. Computer makers, for their part, were only too happy to include the program, since it made their new computers more attractive to buyers. *Quicken* soon became the standard for personal financial-management programs. By giving away free copies of the program, Intuit "primed the pump," creating an enormous demand for upgrades of *Quicken* and for more advanced versions of related software. Thus, *TurboTax* and *Macintax*, Intuit's personal income-tax software, have become the standards for tax-preparation programs.

Inspired by this success story, other software developers have jumped onto the bandwagon. Most hardware now comes bundled with a host of free software programs. Some software developers are even rumored to *pay* computer makers to include their programs!

ECONOMIC NATURALIST 1.1

DILBERT reprinted by permission of United Features Syndicates, Inc.

The free-software example illustrates a case in which the *benefit* of a product depends on the number of other people who own that product. As the next example demonstrates, the *cost* of a product may also depend on the number of others who own it.

Why don't auto manufacturers make cars without heaters?

Virtually every new car sold in the United States today has a heater. But not every car has a CD player. Why this difference?

One might be tempted to answer that although everyone *needs* a heater, people can get along without CD players. Yet heaters are of little use in places like Hawaii and southern California. What is more, cars produced as recently as the 1950s did *not* all have heaters. (The classified ad that led one young economic naturalist to his first car, a 1955 Pontiac, boasted that the vehicle had a radio, heater, and whitewall tires.)

ECONOMIC NATURALIST 1.2

Although heaters cost extra money to manufacture and are not useful in all parts of the country, they do not cost *much* money and are useful on at least a few days each year in most parts of the country. As time passed and people's incomes grew, manufacturers found that people were ordering fewer and fewer cars without heaters. At some point it actually became cheaper to put heaters in *all* cars, rather than bear the administrative expense of making some cars with heaters and others without. No doubt a few buyers would still order a car without a heater if they could save some money in the process. But catering to these customers is just no longer worth it.

Similar reasoning explains why certain cars today cannot be purchased without a CD player. Buyers of the 2006 BMW 745i, for example, got a CD player whether they wanted one or not. Most buyers of this car, which sells for approximately $75,000, have high incomes, so the overwhelming majority of them would have chosen to order a CD player had it been sold as an option. Because of the savings made possible when all cars are produced with the same equipment, it would have actually cost BMW more to supply cars for the few who would want them without CD players.

Buyers of the least-expensive makes of car have much lower incomes on average than BMW 745i buyers. Accordingly, most of them have more pressing alternative uses for their money than to buy CD players for their cars, and this explains why some inexpensive makes continue to offer CD players only as options. But as incomes continue to grow, new cars without CD players will eventually disappear.

The insights afforded by the preceding example suggest an answer to the following strange question:

Why do the keypad buttons on drive-up automatic teller machines have Braille dots?

ECONOMIC NATURALIST 1.3

Braille dots on elevator buttons and on the keypads of walk-up automatic teller machines enable blind people to participate more fully in the normal flow of daily activity. But even though blind people can do many remarkable things, they cannot drive automobiles on public roads. Why, then, do the manufacturers of automatic teller machines install Braille dots on the machines at drive-up locations?

The answer to this riddle is that once the keypad molds have been manufactured, the cost of producing buttons with Braille dots is no higher than the cost of producing smooth buttons. Making both would require separate sets of molds and two different types of inventory. If the patrons of drive-up machines found buttons with Braille dots harder to use, there might be a reason to incur these extra costs. But since the dots pose no difficulty for sighted users, the best and cheapest solution is to produce only keypads with dots.

Why do the keypad buttons on drive-up automatic teller machines have Braille dots?

The preceding example was suggested by Cornell student Bill Tjoa, in response to the following assignment:

EXERCISE 1.6

In 500 words or less, use cost-benefit analysis to explain some pattern of events or behavior you have observed in your own environment.

There is probably no more useful step you can take in your study of economics than to perform several versions of the assignment in Exercise 1.6. Students who do so almost invariably become lifelong economic naturalists. Their mastery of economic concepts not only does not decay with the passage of time; it actually grows stronger. We urge you, in the strongest possible terms, to make this investment!

■ SUMMARY ■

- Economics is the study of how people make choices under conditions of scarcity and of the results of those choices for society. Economic analysis of human behavior begins with the assumption that people are rational—that they have well-defined goals and try to achieve them as best they can. In trying to achieve their goals, people normally face trade-offs: Because material and human resources are limited, having more of one good thing means making do with less of some other good thing.

- Our focus in this chapter has been on how rational people make choices among alternative courses of action. Our basic tool for analyzing these decisions is cost-benefit analysis. The cost-benefit principle says that a person should take an action if, and only if, the benefit of that action is at least as great as its cost. The benefit of an action is defined as the largest dollar amount the person would be willing to pay in order to take the action. The cost of an action is defined as the dollar value of everything the person must give up in order to take the action.

- Often the question is not whether to pursue an activity but rather how many units of it to pursue. In these cases, the rational person pursues additional units as long as the marginal benefit of the activity (the benefit from pursuing an additional unit of it) exceeds its marginal cost (the cost of pursuing an additional unit of it).

- In using the cost-benefit framework, we need not presume that people choose rationally all the time. Indeed, we identified four common pitfalls that plague decision makers in all walks of life: a tendency to treat small proportional changes as insignificant, a tendency to ignore opportunity costs, a tendency not to ignore sunk costs, and a tendency to confuse average and marginal costs and benefits.

- Microeconomics is the study of individual choices and of group behavior in individual markets, while macroeconomics is the study of the performance of national economies and of the policies that governments use to try to improve economic performance.

■ CORE PRINCIPLES ■

The Scarcity Principle (also called the No-Free-Lunch Principle)
Although we have boundless needs and wants, the resources available to us are limited. So having more of one good thing usually means having less of another.

The Cost-Benefit Principle
An individual (or a firm, or a society) should take an action if, and only if, the extra benefits from taking the action are at least as great as the extra costs.

The Incentive Principle
A person (or a firm or a society) is more likely to take an action if its benefit rises, and less likely to take it if its cost rises.

■ KEY TERMS ■

average benefit (12)
average cost (12)
economic surplus (6)
economics (4)
macroeconomics (15)

marginal benefit (11)
marginal cost (11)
microeconomics (15)
normative economic principle (14)
opportunity cost (6)

positive economic principle (15)
rational person (5)
sunk cost (10)

■ REVIEW QUESTIONS ■

1. A friend of yours on the tennis team says, "Private tennis lessons are definitely better than group lessons." Explain what you think he means by this statement. Then use the cost-benefit principle to explain why private lessons are not necessarily the best choice for everyone.

2. True or false: Your willingness to drive downtown to save $30 on a new appliance should depend on what fraction of the total selling price $30 is. Explain.

3. Why might someone who is trying to decide whether to see a movie be more likely to focus on the $9 ticket

price than on the $20 she would fail to earn by not babysitting?

4. Many people think of their air travel as being free when they use frequent-flyer coupons. Explain why these people are likely to make wasteful travel decisions.

5. Is the nonrefundable tuition payment you made to your university this semester a sunk cost? How would your answer differ if your university were to offer a full tuition refund to any student who dropped out of school during the first two months of the semester?

▪ PROBLEMS ▪

1. The most you would be willing to pay for having a freshly washed car before going out on a date is $6. The smallest amount for which you would be willing to wash someone else's car is $3.50. You are going out this evening, and your car is dirty. How much economic surplus would you receive from washing it?

2. To earn extra money in the summer, you grow tomatoes and sell them at the farmers' market for 30 cents per pound. By adding compost to your garden, you can increase your yield as shown in the table below. If compost costs 50 cents per pound and your goal is to make as much money as possible, how many pounds of compost should you add?

Pounds of compost	Pounds of tomatoes
0	100
1	120
2	125
3	128
4	130
5	131
6	131.5

3. Residents of your city are charged a fixed weekly fee of $6 for garbage collection. They are allowed to put out as many cans as they wish. The average household disposes of three cans of garbage per week under this plan. Now suppose that your city changes to a "tag" system. Each can of refuse to be collected must have a tag affixed to it. The tags cost $2 each and are not reusable. What effect do you think the introduction of the tag system will have on the total quantity of garbage collected in your city? Explain briefly.

4. Once a week, Smith purchases a six-pack of cola and puts it in his refrigerator for his two children. He invariably discovers that all six cans are gone on the first day. Jones also purchases a six-pack of cola once a week for his two children, but unlike Smith, he tells them that each may drink no more than three cans. If the children use cost-benefit analysis each time they decide whether to drink a can of cola, explain why the cola lasts much longer at Jones's house than at Smith's.

5. Tom is a mushroom farmer. He invests all his spare cash in additional mushrooms, which grow on otherwise useless land behind his barn. The mushrooms double in weight during their first year, after which time they are harvested and sold at a constant price per pound. Tom's friend Dick asks Tom for a loan of $200, which he promises to repay after 1 year. How much interest will Dick have to pay Tom in order for Tom to recover his opportunity cost of making the loan? Explain briefly.

6. Suppose that in the last few seconds you devoted to question 1 on your physics exam you earned 4 extra points, while in the last few seconds you devoted to question 2 you earned 10 extra points. You earned a total of 48 and 12 points, respectively, on the two questions, and the total time you spent on each was the same. If you could take the exam again, how—if at all—should you reallocate your time between these questions?

7. Martha and Sarah have the same preferences and incomes. Just as Martha arrived at the theater to see a play, she discovered that she had lost the $10 ticket she had purchased

earlier. Sarah also just arrived at the theater planning to buy a ticket to see the same play when she discovered that she had lost a $10 bill from her wallet. If both Martha and Sarah are rational and both still have enough money to pay for a ticket, is one of them more likely than the other to go ahead and see the play anyway?

8.*You and your friend Joe have identical tastes. At 2 p.m., you go to the local Ticketmaster outlet and buy a $30 ticket to a basketball game to be played that night in Syracuse, 50 miles north of your home in Ithaca. Joe plans to attend the same game, but because he cannot get to the Ticketmaster outlet, he plans to buy his ticket at the game. Tickets sold at the game cost only $25, because they carry no Ticketmaster surcharge. (Many people nonetheless pay the higher price at Ticketmaster, to be sure of getting good seats.) At 4 p.m., an unexpected snowstorm begins, making the prospect of the drive to Syracuse much less attractive than before (but assuring the availability of good seats). If both you and Joe are rational, is one of you more likely to attend the game than the other?

9.*For each long-distance call anywhere in the continental United States, a new phone service will charge users 30 cents per minute for the first 2 minutes and 2 cents per minute for additional minutes in each call. Tom's current phone service charges 10 cents per minute for all calls, and his calls are never shorter than 7 minutes. If Tom's dorm switches to the new phone service, what will happen to the average length of his calls?

10.*The meal plan at university A lets students eat as much as they like for a fixed fee of $500 per semester. The average student there eats 250 pounds of food per semester. University B charges $500 for a book of meal tickets that entitles the student to eat 250 pounds of food per semester. If the student eats more than 250 pounds, he or she pays $2 for each additional pound; if the student eats less, he or she gets a $2 per pound refund. If students are rational, at which university will average food consumption be higher? Explain briefly.

■ ANSWERS TO IN-CHAPTER EXERCISES ■

1.1 The benefit of buying the game downtown is again $10 but the cost is now $12, so your economic surplus from buying it downtown would be $10 − $12 = −$2. Since your economic surplus from making the trip would be negative, you should buy at the campus store.

1.2 Saving $100 is $10 more valuable than saving $90, even though the percentage savings is much greater in the case of the Chicago ticket.

1.3 Since you now have no alternative use for your coupon, the opportunity cost of using it to pay for the Fort Lauderdale trip is zero. That means your economic surplus from the trip will be $1,350 − $1,000 = $350 > 0, so you should use your coupon and go to Fort Lauderdale.

1.4 The marginal benefit of the fourth launch is $9 billion, which exceeds its marginal cost of $8 billion, so the fourth launch should be added. But the fifth launch should not, since its marginal cost ($12 billion) exceeds its marginal benefit ($9 billion).

1.5 If the star player takes one more shot, some other player must take one less. The fact that the star player's *average* success rate is higher than the other players' does not mean that the probability of making his *next* shot (the marginal benefit of having him shoot once more) is higher than the probability of another player making his next shot. Indeed, if the best player took all his team's shots, the other team would focus its defensive effort entirely on him, in which case letting others shoot would definitely pay.

*Problems marked with an asterisk (*) are more difficult.

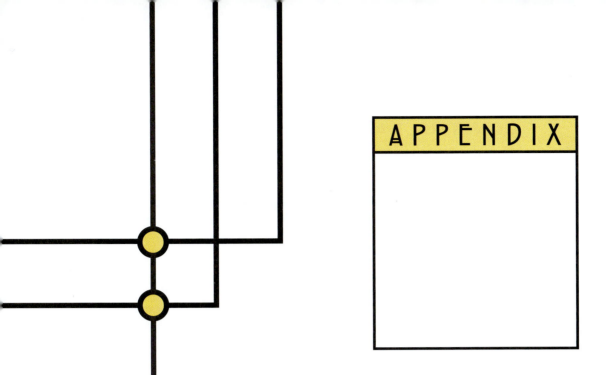

WORKING WITH EQUATIONS, GRAPHS, AND TABLES

Although many of the examples and most of the end-of-chapter problems in this book are quantitative, none requires mathematical skills beyond rudimentary high school algebra and geometry. In this brief appendix we review some of the skills you'll need for dealing with these examples and problems.

One important skill is to be able to read simple verbal descriptions and translate the information they provide into the relevant equations or graphs. You'll also need to be able to translate information given in tabular form into an equation or graph, and sometimes you'll need to translate graphical information into a table or equation. Finally, you'll need to be able to solve simple systems with two equations and two unknowns. The following examples illustrate all the tools you'll need.

USING A VERBAL DESCRIPTION TO CONSTRUCT AN EQUATION

We begin with an example that shows how to construct a long-distance telephone billing equation from a verbal description of the billing plan.

EXAMPLE 1A.1

Your long-distance telephone plan charges you $5 per month plus 10 cents per minute for long-distance calls. Write an equation that describes your monthly telephone bill.

equation a mathematical expression that describes the relationship between two or more variables

variable a quantity that is free to take a range of different values

dependent variable a variable in an equation whose value is determined by the value taken by another variable in the equation

independent variable a variable in an equation whose value determines the value taken by another variable in the equation

constant (or parameter) a quantity that is fixed in value

An **equation** is a simple mathematical expression that describes the relationship between two or more **variables,** or quantities that are free to assume different values in some range. The most common type of equation we'll work with contains two types of variable: **dependent variable** and **independent variable.** In this example, the dependent variable is the dollar amount of your monthly telephone bill, and the independent variable is the variable on which your bill depends, namely, the volume of long-distance calls you make during the month. Your bill also depends on the $5 monthly fee and the 10 cents per minute charge. But in this example, those amounts are **constants,** not variables. A constant, also called a **parameter,** is a quantity in an equation that is fixed in value, not free to vary. As the terms suggest, the dependent variable describes an outcome that depends on the value taken by the independent variable.

Once you've identified the dependent variable and the independent variable, choose simple symbols to represent them. In algebra courses, X is typically used to represent the independent variable and Y the dependent variable. Many people find it easier to remember what the variables stand for, however, if they choose symbols that are linked in some straightforward way to the quantities that the variables represent. Thus, in this example, we might use B to represent your monthly *bill* in dollars and T to represent the total *time* in minutes you spent during the month on long-distance calls.

Having identified the relevant variables and chosen symbols to represent them, you are now in a position to write the equation that links them:

$$B = 5 + 0.10T, \tag{1A.1}$$

where B is your monthly long-distance bill in dollars and T is your monthly total long-distance calling time in minutes. The fixed monthly fee (5) and the charge per minute (0.10) are parameters in this equation. Note the importance of being clear about the units of measure. Because B represents the monthly bill in dollars, we must also express the fixed monthly fee and the per-minute charge in dollars, which is why the latter number appears in Equation 1A.1 as 0.10 rather than 10. Equation 1A.1 follows the normal convention in which the dependent variable appears by itself on the left-hand side while the independent variable or variables and constants appear on the right-hand side.

Once we have the equation for the monthly bill, we can use it to calculate how much you'll owe as a function of your monthly volume of long-distance calls. For example, if you make 32 minutes of calls, you can calculate your monthly bill by simply substituting 32 minutes for T in Equation 1A.1:

$$B = 5 + 0.10(32) = 8.20. \tag{1A.2}$$

Your monthly bill when you make 32 minutes of calls is thus equal to $8.20.

EXERCISE 1A.1

Under the monthly billing plan described in Example 1A.1, how much would you owe for a month during which you made 45 minutes of long-distance calls?

GRAPHING THE EQUATION OF A STRAIGHT LINE

The next example shows how to portray the billing plan described in Example 1A.1 as a graph.

Construct a graph that portrays the monthly long-distance telephone billing plan described in Example 1A.1, putting your telephone charges, in dollars per month, on the vertical axis, and your total volume of calls, in minutes per month, on the horizontal axis.

EXAMPLE 1A.2

The first step in responding to this instruction is the one we just took, namely, to translate the verbal description of the billing plan into an equation. When graphing an equation, the normal convention is to use the vertical axis to represent the dependent variable and the horizontal axis to represent the independent variable. In Figure 1A.1, we therefore put B on the vertical axis and T on the horizontal axis. One way to construct the graph shown in the figure is to begin by plotting the monthly bill values that correspond to several different total amounts of long-distance calls. For example, someone who makes 10 minutes of calls during the month would have a bill of $B = 5 + 0.10(10) = \$6$. Thus, in Figure 1A.1 the value of 10 minutes per month on the horizontal axis corresponds to a bill of \$6 per month on the vertical axis (point A). Someone who makes 30 minutes of long-distance calls during the month will have a monthly bill of $B = 5 + 0.10(30) = \$8$, so the value of 30 minutes per month on the horizontal axis corresponds to \$8 per month on the vertical axis (point C). Similarly, someone who makes 70 minutes of long-distance calls during the month will have a monthly bill of $B = 5 + 0.10(70) = \$12$, so the value of 70 minutes on the horizontal axis corresponds to \$12 on the vertical axis (point D). The line joining these points is the graph of the monthly billing Equation 1A.1.

vertical intercept in a straight line, the value taken by the dependent variable when the independent variable equals zero

As shown in Figure 1A.1, the graph of the equation $B = 5 + 0.10T$ is a straight line. The parameter 5 is the **vertical intercept** of the line—the value of B when $T = 0$, or the point at which the line intersects the vertical axis. The parameter 0.10 is the **slope** of the line, which is the ratio of the **rise** of the line to the corresponding **run**. The ratio rise/run is simply the vertical distance between any two points on the line divided by the horizontal distance between those points. For example, if we choose points A and C in Figure 1A.1, the rise is $8 - 6 = 2$ and the corresponding run is $30 - 10 = 20$, so rise/run $= 2/20 = 0.10$. More generally, for the graph of any equation $Y = a + bX$, the parameter a is the vertical intercept and the parameter b is the slope.

slope in a straight line, the ratio of the vertical distance the straight line travels between any two points (**rise**) to the corresponding horizontal distance (**run**)

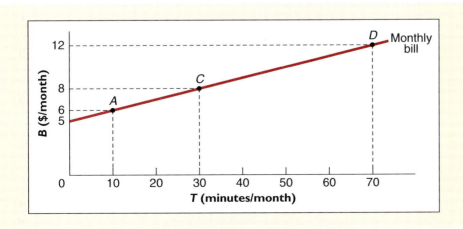

FIGURE 1A.1
The Monthly Telephone Bill in Example 1A.1.
The graph of the equation $B = 5 + 0.10T$ is the straight line shown. Its vertical intercept is 5, and its slope is 0.10.

DERIVING THE EQUATION OF A STRAIGHT LINE FROM ITS GRAPH

The next example shows how to derive the equation for a straight line from a graph of the line.

EXAMPLE IA.3

Figure IA.2 shows the graph of the monthly billing plan for a new long-distance plan. What is the equation for this graph? How much is the fixed monthly fee under this plan? How much is the charge per minute?

FIGURE IA.2

Another Monthly Long-Distance Plan.

The vertical distance between points A and C is 12 − 8 = 4 units, and the horizontal distance between points A and C is 40 − 20 = 20, so the slope of the line is 4/20 = 1/5 = 0.20. The vertical intercept (the value of B when T = 0) is 4. So the equation for the billing plan shown is B = 4 + 0.20T.

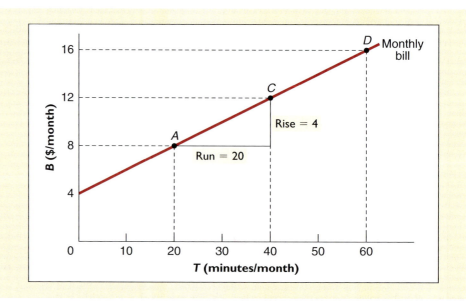

The slope of the line shown is the rise between any two points divided by the corresponding run. For points A and C, rise = 12 − 8 = 4, and run = 40 − 20 = 20, so the slope equals rise/run = 4/20 = 1/15 = 0.20. And since the horizontal intercept of the line is 4, its equation must be given by

$$B = 4 + 0.20T. \tag{1A.3}$$

Under this plan, the fixed monthly fee is the value of the bill when $T = 0$, which is $4. The charge per minute is the slope of the billing line, 0.20, or 20 cents per minute.

EXERCISE IA.2

Write the equation for the billing plan shown in the accompanying graph. How much is its fixed monthly fee? Its charge per minute?

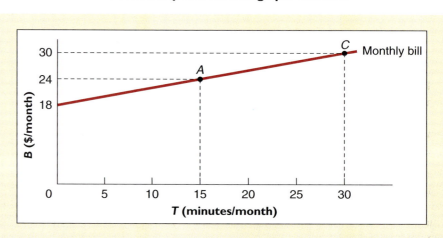

CHANGES IN THE VERTICAL INTERCEPT AND SLOPE

Examples 1A.4 and 1A.5 and Exercises 1A.3 and 1A.4 provide practice in seeing how a line shifts with a change in its vertical intercept or slope.

Show how the billing plan whose graph is in Figure 1A.2 would change if the monthly fixed fee were increased from $4 to $8.

An increase in the monthly fixed fee from $4 to $8 would increase the vertical intercept of the billing plan by $4 but would leave its slope unchanged. An increase in the fixed fee thus leads to a parallel upward shift in the billing plan by $4, as shown in Figure 1A.3. For any given number of minutes of long-distance calls, the monthly charge on the new bill will be $4 higher than on the old bill. Thus 20 min-

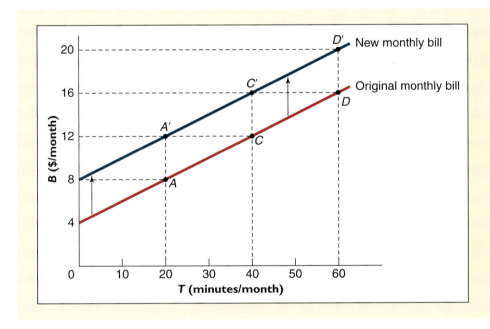

FIGURE 1A.3
The Effect of an Increase in the Vertical Intercept.
An increase in the vertical intercept of a straight line produces an upward parallel shift in the line.

utes of calls per month costs $8 under the original plan (point A) but $12 under the new plan (point A′). And 40 minutes costs $12 under the original plan (point C), $16 under the new plan (point C′); and 60 minutes costs $16 under the original plan (point D), $20 under the new plan (point D′).

EXERCISE 1A.3

Show how the billing plan whose graph is in Figure 1A.2 would change if the monthly fixed fee were reduced from $4 to $2.

Show how the billing plan whose graph is in Figure 1A.2 would change if the charge per minute were increased from 20 cents to 40 cents.

Because the monthly fixed fee is unchanged, the vertical intercept of the new billing plan continues to be 4. But the slope of the new plan, shown in Figure 1A.4, is 0.40, or twice the slope of the original plan. More generally, in the equation $Y = a + bX$, an increase in b makes the slope of the graph of the equation steeper.

FIGURE IA.4

The Effect of an Increase in the Charge per Minute.

Because the fixed monthly fee continues to be $4, the vertical intercept of the new plan is the same as that of the original plan. With the new charge per minute of 40 cents, the slope of the billing plan rises from 0.20 to 0.40.

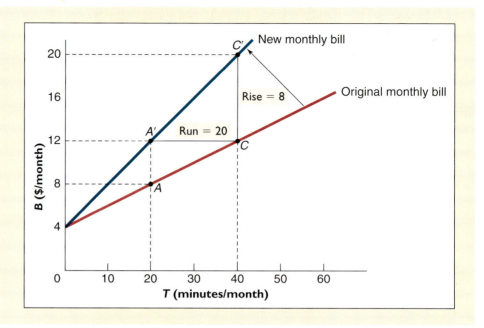

EXERCISE IA.4

Show how the billing plan whose graph is in Figure IA.2 would change if the charge per minute were reduced from 20 cents to 10 cents.

Exercise 1A.4 illustrates the general rule that in an equation $Y = a + bX$, a reduction in b makes the slope of the graph of the equation less steep.

CONSTRUCTING EQUATIONS AND GRAPHS FROM TABLES

Example 1A.6 and Exercise 1A.5 show how to transform tabular information into an equation or graph.

EXAMPLE IA.6

Table IA.I shows four points from a monthly long-distance telephone billing equation. If all points on this billing equation lie on a straight line, find the vertical intercept of the equation and graph it. What is the monthly fixed fee? What is the charge per minute? Calculate the total bill for a month with I hour of long-distance calls.

TABLE IA.I

Points on a Long-Distance Billing Plan

Long-distance bill ($/month)	Total long-distance calls (minutes/month)
10.50	10
11.00	20
11.50	30
12.00	40

One approach to this problem is simply to plot any two points from the table on a graph. Since we are told that the billing equation is a straight line, that line must be

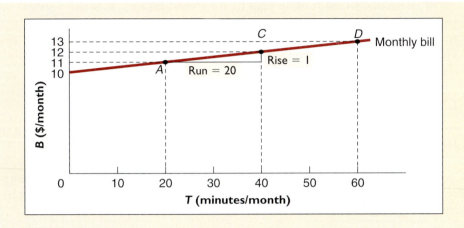

Plotting the Monthly Billing Equation from a Sample of Points.

Point *A* is taken from row 2, Table 1A.1, and point *C* from row 4. The monthly billing plan is the straight line that passes through these points.

the one that passes through any two of its points. Thus, in Figure 1A.5 we use *A* to denote the point from Table 1A.1 for which a monthly bill of $11 corresponds to 20 minutes per month of calls (second row) and *C* to denote the point for which a monthly bill of $12 corresponds to 40 minutes per month of calls (fourth row). The straight line passing through these points is the graph of the billing equation.

Unless you have a steady hand, however, or use extremely large graph paper, the method of extending a line between two points on the billing plan is unlikely to be very accurate. An alternative approach is to calculate the equation for the billing plan directly. Since the equation is a straight line, we know that it takes the general form $B = f + sT$, where f is the fixed monthly fee and s is the slope. Our goal is to calculate the vertical intercept f and the slope s. From the same two points we plotted earlier, *A* and *C*, we can calculate the slope of the billing plan as $s = \text{rise/run} = 1/20 = 0.05$.

So all that remains is to calculate f, the fixed monthly fee. At point *C* on the billing plan, the total monthly bill is $12 for 40 minutes, so we can substitute $B = 12$, $s = 0.05$, and $T = 40$ into the general equation $B = f + sT$ to obtain

$$12 = f + 0.05(40), \tag{1A.4}$$

or

$$12 = f + 2, \tag{1A.5}$$

which solves for $f = 10$. So the monthly billing equation must be

$$B = 10 + 0.05T. \tag{1A.6}$$

For this billing equation, the fixed fee is $10 per month, the calling charge is 5 cents per minute ($0.05/minute), and the total bill for a month with 1 hour of long-distance calls is $B = 10 + 0.05(60) = \$13$, just as shown in Figure 1A.5.

EXERCISE 1A.5

The following table shows four points from a monthly long-distance telephone billing plan.

Long-distance bill ($/month)	Total long-distance calls (minutes/month)
20.00	10
30.00	20
40.00	30
50.00	40

> If all points on this billing plan lie on a straight line, find the vertical intercept of the corresponding equation without graphing it. What is the monthly fixed fee? What is the charge per minute? How much would the charges be for 1 hour of long-distance calls per month?

SOLVING SIMULTANEOUS EQUATIONS

Example 1A.7 and Exercise 1A.6 demonstrate how to proceed when you need to solve two equations with two unknowns.

EXAMPLE 1A.7

Suppose you are trying to choose between two rate plans for your long-distance telephone service. If you choose Plan 1, your charges will be computed according to the equation

$$B = 10 + 0.04T, \tag{1A.7}$$

where B is again your monthly bill in dollars and T is your monthly volume of long-distance calls in minutes. If you choose Plan 2, your monthly bill will be computed according to the equation

$$B = 20 + 0.02T. \tag{1A.8}$$

How many minutes of long-distance calls would you have to make each month, on average, to make Plan 2 cheaper?

Plan 1 has the attractive feature of a relatively low monthly fixed fee, but also the unattractive feature of a relatively high rate per minute. In contrast, Plan 2 has a relatively high fixed fee but a relatively low rate per minute. Someone who made an extremely low volume of calls (for example, 10 minutes per month) would do better under Plan 1 (monthly bill = $10.40) than under Plan 2 (monthly bill = $20.20), because the low fixed fee of Plan 1 would more than compensate for its higher rate per minute. Conversely, someone who made an extremely high volume of calls (say, 10,000 minutes per month) would do better under Plan 2 (monthly bill = $220) than under Plan 1 (monthly bill = $410), because Plan 2's lower rate per minute would more than compensate for its higher fixed fee.

Our task here is to find the *break-even calling volume*, which is the monthly calling volume for which the monthly bill is the same under two plans. One way to answer this question is to graph the two billing plans and see where they cross. At that crossing point, the two equations are satisfied simultaneously, which means that the monthly call volumes will be the same under both plans, as will the monthly bills.

In Figure 1A.6, we see that the graphs of the two plans cross at A, where both yield a monthly bill of $30 for 500 minutes of calls per month. The break-even calling volume for these plans is thus 500 minutes per month. If your calling volume is higher than that, on average, you will save money by choosing Plan 2. For example, if you average 700 minutes, your monthly bill under Plan 2 ($34) will be $4 cheaper than under Plan 1 ($38). Conversely, if you average fewer than 500 minutes each month, your will do better under Plan 1. For example, if you average only 200 minutes, your monthly bill under Plan 1 ($18) will be $6 cheaper than under Plan 2 ($24). At 500 minutes per month, the two plans cost exactly the same ($30).

The question posed in Example 1A.7 also may be answered algebraically. As in the graphical approach just discussed, our goal is to find the point (T, B) that satisfies both billing equations simultaneously. As a first step, we rewrite the two billing equations, one on top of the other, as follows:

$$B = 10 + 0.04T \quad \text{(Plan 1)}$$

$$B = 20 + 0.02T \quad \text{(Plan 2)}.$$

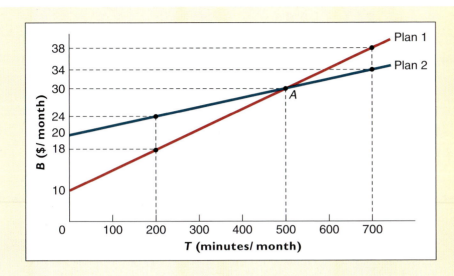

FIGURE 1A.6
The Break-Even Volume of Long-Distance Calls. When your volume of long-distance calls is 500 minutes per month, your monthly bill will be the same under both plans. For higher calling volumes, Plan 2 is cheaper; Plan 1 is cheaper for lower volumes.

As you'll recall from high school algebra, if we subtract the terms from each side of one equation from the corresponding terms of the other equation, the resulting differences must be equal. So if we subtract the terms on each side of the Plan 2 equation from the corresponding terms in the Plan 1 equation, we get

$$B = 10 + 0.04T \qquad \text{(Plan 1)}$$

$$-B = -20 - 0.02T \qquad \text{(}-\text{Plan 2)}$$

$$0 = -10 + 0.02T \qquad \text{(Plan 1} - \text{Plan 2).}$$

Finally, we solve the last equation (Plan 1 − Plan 2) to get $T = 500$.

Plugging $T = 500$ into either plan's equation, we then find $B = 30$. For example, Plan 1's equation yields $10 + 0.04(500) = 30$, as does Plan 2's: $20 + 0.2(500) = 30$.

Because, the point $(T, B) = (500, 30)$ lies on the equations for both plans simultaneously, the algebraic approach just described is often called *the method of simultaneous equations.*

EXERCISE 1A.6

Suppose you are trying to choose between two rate plans for your long-distance telephone service. If you choose Plan 1, your monthly bill will be computed according to the equation

$$B = 10 + 0.10T \qquad \textbf{(Plan 1),}$$

where B is again your monthly bill in dollars and T is your monthly volume of long-distance calls in minutes. If you choose Plan 2, your monthly bill will be computed according to the equation

$$B = 100 + 0.01T \qquad \textbf{(Plan 2).}$$

Use the algebraic approach described in Example 1A.7 to find the break-even level of monthly call volume for these plans.

■ KEY TERMS ■

constant (24)

dependent variable (24)

equation (24)

independent variable (24)

parameter (24)

rise (25)

run (25)

slope (25)

variable (24)

vertical intercept (25)

■ ANSWERS TO IN-APPENDIX EXERCISES ■

1A.1 To calculate your monthly bill for 45 minutes of calls, substitute 45 minutes for T in equation 1A.1 to get $B = 5 + 0.10(45) = \$9.50$.

1A.2 Calculating the slope using points A and C, we have rise $= 30 - 24 = 6$ and run $= 30 - 15 = 15$, so rise/run $= 6/15 = 2/5 = 0.40$. And since the horizontal intercept of the line is 18, its equation is $B = 18 + 0.40T$. Under this plan, the fixed monthly fee is \$18, and the charge per minute is the slope of the billing line, 0.40, or 40 cents per minute.

1A.3 A \$2 reduction in the monthly fixed fee would produce a downward parallel shift in the billing plan by \$2.

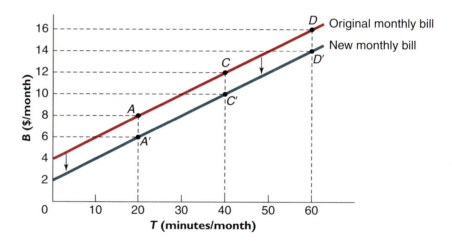

1A.4 With an unchanged monthly fixed fee, the vertical intercept of the new billing plan continues to be 4. The slope of the new plan is 0.10, half the slope of the original plan.

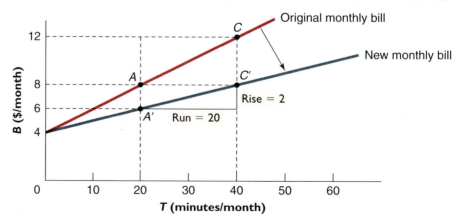

1A.5 Let the billing equation be $B = f + sT$, where f is the fixed monthly fee and s is the slope. From the first two points in the table, calculate the slope $s =$ rise/run $= 10/10 = 1.0$. To calculate f, we can use the information in row 1 of the table to write the billing equation as $20 = f + 1.0(10)$ and solve for $f = 10$. So the monthly billing equation must be $B = 10 + 1.0T$. For this billing equation, the fixed fee is \$10 per month, the calling charge is \$1 per minute, and the total bill for a month with 1 hour of long-distance calls is $B = 10 + 1.0(60) = \$70$.

1A.6 Subtracting the Plan 2 equation from the Plan 1 equation yields the equation

$$0 = -90 + 0.09T \qquad \text{(Plan 1 − Plan 2),}$$

which solves for $T = 1,000$. So if you average more than 1,000 minutes of long-distance calls each month, you'll do better on Plan 2.

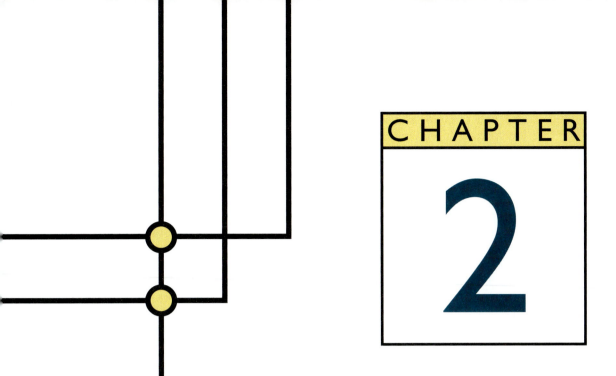

CHAPTER

2

COMPARATIVE ADVANTAGE: THE BASIS FOR EXCHANGE

During a stint as a Peace Corps volunteer in rural Nepal, a young economic naturalist employed a cook named Birkhaman, who came from a remote Himalayan village in neighboring Bhutan. Although Birkhaman had virtually no formal education, he was spectacularly resourceful. His primary duties, to prepare food and maintain the kitchen, he performed extremely well. But he also had other skills. He could thatch a roof, butcher a goat, and repair shoes. An able tinsmith and a good carpenter, he could sew and fix a broken alarm clock, as well as plaster walls. And he was a local authority on home remedies.

Birkhaman's range of skills was broad even in Nepal, where the least-skilled villager could perform a wide range of services that most Americans hire others to perform. Why this difference in skills and employment?

One might be tempted to answer that the Nepalese are simply too poor to hire others to perform these services. Nepal is indeed a poor country, whose income per person is less than one one-hundredth that of the United States. Few Nepalese have spare cash to spend on outside services. But as reasonable as this poverty explanation may seem, the reverse is actually the case. The Nepalese do not perform their own services because they are poor; rather, they are poor largely *because* they perform their own services.

The alternative to a system in which everyone is a jack of all trades is one in which people *specialize* in particular goods and services, then satisfy their needs

Did this man perform most of his own services because he was poor, or was he poor because he performed most of his own services?

by trading among themselves. Economic systems based on specialization and the exchange of goods and services are generally far more productive than those with less specialization. Our task in this chapter is to investigate why this is so. In doing so we will explore why people choose to exchange goods and services in the first place, rather than having each person produce his or her own food, cars, clothing, shelter, and the like.

As this chapter will show, the reason that specialization is so productive is the existence of what economists call *comparative advantage.* Roughly, a person has a comparative advantage at producing a particular good or service, say, haircuts, if that person is *relatively* more efficient at producing haircuts than at producing other goods or services. We will see that we can all have more of *every* good and service if each of us specializes in the activities at which we have a comparative advantage.

This chapter also will introduce the *production possibilities curve,* which is a graphical method of describing the combinations of goods and services that an economy can produce. The development of this tool will allow us to see much more precisely how specialization enhances the productive capacity of even the simplest economy.

EXCHANGE AND OPPORTUNITY COST

The scarcity principle (see Chapter 1) reminds us that the opportunity cost of spending more time on any one activity is having less time available to spend on others. As the following example makes clear, this principle helps explain why everyone can do better by concentrating on those activities at which he or she performs best relative to others.

EXAMPLE 2.1

Should a Joe Jamail prepare his own will?

Should Joe Jamail write his own will?

Joe Jamail, known in the legal profession as "The King of Torts," is the most renowned trial lawyer in American history. And at number 195 on the Forbes list of the 400 richest Americans, he is also one of the wealthiest, with net assets totaling more than $1 billion.

But although Mr. Jamail devotes virtually all of his working hours to high-profile litigation, he is also competent to perform a much broader range of legal services. Suppose, for example, that he could prepare his own will in two hours, only half as long as it would take any other attorney. Does that mean that Jamail should prepare his own will?

On the strength of his talent as a litigator, Jamail earns many millions of dollars a year, which means that the opportunity cost of any time he spends preparing his will would be several thousand dollars per hour. Attorneys who specialize in property law typically earn far less than that amount. Jamail would have little difficulty engaging a competent property lawyer who could prepare his will for him for less than $800. So even though Jamail's considerable skills would enable him to perform this task more quickly than another attorney, it would not be in his interest to prepare his own will.

absolute advantage one person has an absolute advantage over another if he or she takes fewer hours to perform a task than the other person

In the preceding example, economists would say that Jamail has an **absolute advantage** at preparing his will but a **comparative advantage** at trial work. He has an absolute advantage at preparing his will because he can perform that task in less time than a property lawyer could. Even so, the property lawyer has a comparative advantage at preparing wills because his opportunity cost of performing that task is lower than Jamail's.

The point of Example 2.1 is not that people whose time is valuable should never perform their own services. That example made the implicit assumption that Jamail would have been equally happy to spend an hour preparing his will or preparing for a trial. But suppose he was tired of trial preparation and felt it might be enjoyable to refresh his knowledge of property law. Preparing his own will might then have made perfect sense! But unless he expected to gain special satisfaction from performing that task, he would almost certainly do better to hire a property lawyer. The property lawyer would also benefit, or else she wouldn't have offered to prepare wills for the stated price.

THE PRINCIPLE OF COMPARATIVE ADVANTAGE

One of the most important insights of modern economics is that when two people (or two nations) have different opportunity costs of performing various tasks, they can always increase the total value of available goods and services by trading with one another. The following simple example captures the logic behind this insight.

Should Paula update her own Web page?

Consider a small community in which Paula is the only professional bicycle mechanic and Beth is the only professional HTML programmer. Paula also happens to be an even better HTML programmer than Beth. If the amount of time each of them takes to perform these tasks is as shown in Table 2.1, and if each regards the two tasks as equally pleasant (or unpleasant), does the fact that Paula can program faster than Beth imply that Paula should update her own Web page?

The entries in the table show that Paula has an absolute advantage over Beth in both activities. While Paula, the mechanic, needs only 20 minutes to update a Web page, Beth, the programmer, needs 30 minutes. Paula's advantage over Beth is even greater when the task is fixing bikes: She can complete a repair in only 10 minutes, compared to Beth's 30 minutes.

TABLE 2.1
Productivity Information for Paula and Beth

	Time to update a Web page	Time to complete a bicycle repair
Paula	20 minutes	10 minutes
Beth	30 minutes	30 minutes

But the fact that Paula is a better programmer than Beth does *not* imply that Paula should update her own Web page. As with the lawyer who litigates instead of preparing his own will, Beth has a comparative advantage over Paula at programming: She is *relatively* more productive at programming than Paula. Similarly, Paula has a comparative advantage in bicycle repair. (Remember that a person has a comparative advantage at a given task if his or her opportunity cost of performing that task is lower than another person's.)

What is Beth's opportunity cost of updating a Web page? Since she takes 30 minutes to update each page—the same amount of time she takes to fix a bicycle—her opportunity cost of updating a Web page is one bicycle repair. In other words, by taking the time to update a Web page, Beth is effectively giving up the opportunity to do one bicycle repair. Paula, in contrast, can complete two bicycle repairs in the time she takes to update a single Web page. For her, the opportunity cost of updating a Web page is two bicycle repairs. Paula's opportunity cost of programming, measured in terms of bicycle repairs forgone, is twice as high as Beth's. Thus Beth has a comparative advantage at programming.

comparative advantage one person has a comparative advantage over another if his or her opportunity cost of performing a task is lower than the other person's opportunity cost

EXAMPLE 2.2

TABLE 2.2
Opportunity Costs for Paula and Beth

	Opportunity cost of updating a Web page	Opportunity cost of a bicycle repair
Paula	2 bicycle repairs	0.5 Web page update
Beth	1 bicycle repair	1 Web page update

The interesting and important implication of the opportunity cost comparison summarized in Table 2.2 is that the total number of bicycle repairs and Web updates accomplished if Paula and Beth both spend part of their time at each activity will always be smaller than the number accomplished if each specializes in the activity in which she has a comparative advantage. Suppose, for example, that people in their community demand a total of 16 Web page updates per day. If Paula spent half her time updating Web pages and the other half repairing bicycles, an eight-hour workday would yield 12 Web page updates and 24 bicycle repairs. To complete the remaining 4 updates, Beth would have to spend two hours programming, which would leave her six hours to repair bicycles. And since she takes 30 minutes to do each repair, she would have time to complete 12 of them. So when the two women try to be jacks-of-all-trades, they end up completing a total of 16 Web page updates and 36 bicycle repairs.

Consider what would have happened had each woman specialized in her activity of comparative advantage. Beth could have updated 16 Web pages on her own, and Paula could have performed 48 bicycle repairs. Specialization would have created an additional 12 bicycle repairs out of thin air.

"We're a natural, Rachel. I handle intellectual property, and you're a content-provider."

When computing the opportunity cost of one good in terms of another, we must pay close attention to the form in which the productivity information is presented. In the preceding example, we were told how many minutes each person needed to perform each task. Alternatively, we might be told how many units of each task each person can perform in an hour. Work through the following exercise to see how to proceed when information is presented in this alternative format.

EXERCISE 2.1

Should Barb update her own Web page?

Consider a small community in which Barb is the only professional bicycle mechanic and Pat is the only professional HTML programmer. If their productivity rates at the two tasks are as shown in the table, and if each regards the two tasks as equally pleasant (or unpleasant), does the fact that Barb can program faster than Pat imply that Barb should update her own Web page?

	Productivity in programming	Productivity in bicycle repair
Pat	2 Web page updates per hour	1 repair per hour
Barb	3 Web page updates per hour	3 repairs per hour

The principle illustrated by the preceding examples is so important that we state it formally as one of the core principles of the course:

The Principle of Comparative Advantage: Everyone does best when each person (or each country) concentrates on the activities for which his or her opportunity cost is lowest.

Indeed, the gains made possible from specialization based on comparative advantage constitute the rationale for market exchange. They explain why each person does not devote 10 percent of his or her time to producing cars, 5 percent to growing food, 25 percent to building housing, 0.0001 percent to performing brain surgery, and so on. By concentrating on those tasks at which we are relatively most productive, together we can produce vastly more than if we all tried to be self-sufficient.

This insight brings us back to Birkhaman the cook. Though Birkhaman's versatility was marvelous, he was neither as good a doctor as someone who has been trained in medical school, nor as good a repairman as someone who spends each day fixing things. If a number of people with Birkhaman's native talents had joined together, each of them specializing in one or two tasks, together they would have enjoyed more and better goods and services than each could possibly have produced independently. Although there is much to admire in the resourcefulness of people who have learned through necessity to rely on their own skills, that path is no route to economic prosperity.

Specialization and its effects provide ample grist for the economic naturalist. Here's an example from the world of sports.

Where have all the .400 hitters gone?

In baseball, a .400 hitter is a player who averages at least four hits every 10 times he comes to bat. Though never common in professional baseball, .400 hitters used to appear relatively frequently. Early in the twentieth century, for example, a player known as Wee Willie Keeler batted .432, meaning that he got a hit in over 43 percent of his times at bat. But since Ted Williams of the Boston Red Sox batted .406 in 1941, there has not been a single .400 hitter in the major leagues. Why not?

Some baseball buffs argue that the disappearance of the .400 hitter means today's baseball players are not as good as yesterday's. But that claim does not

ECONOMIC NATURALIST 2.1

Why has no major league baseball player batted .400 since Ted Williams did it more than half a century ago?

withstand close examination. We can document, for example, that today's players are bigger, stronger, and faster than those of Willie Keeler's day. (Wee Willie himself was just a little over 5 feet, 4 inches, and he weighed only 140 pounds.)

Bill James, a leading analyst of baseball history, argues that the .400 hitter has disappeared because the quality of play in the major leagues has *improved,* not declined. In particular, pitching and fielding standards are higher, which makes batting .400 more difficult.

Why has the quality of play in baseball improved? Although there are many reasons, including better nutrition, training, and equipment, specialization also has played an important role.[1] At one time, pitchers were expected to pitch for the entire game. Now pitching staffs include pitchers who specialize in starting the game ("starters"), others who specialize in pitching two or three innings in the middle of the game ("middle relievers"), and still others who specialize in pitching only the last inning ("closers"). Each of these roles requires different skills and tactics. Pitchers also may specialize in facing left-handed or right-handed batters, in striking batters out, or in getting batters to hit balls on the ground. Similarly, few fielders today play multiple defensive positions; most specialize in only one. Some players specialize in defense (to the detriment of their hitting skills); these "defensive specialists" can be brought in late in the game to protect a lead. Even in managing and coaching, specialization has increased markedly. Relief pitchers now have their own coaches, and statistical specialists use computers to discover the weaknesses of opposing hitters. The net result of these increases in specialization is that even the weakest of today's teams play highly competent defensive baseball. With no "weaklings" to pick on, hitting .400 over an entire season has become a near-impossible task.

SOURCES OF COMPARATIVE ADVANTAGE

At the individual level, comparative advantage often appears to be the result of inborn talent. For instance, some people seem to be naturally gifted at programming computers while others seem to have a special knack for fixing bikes. But comparative advantage is more often the result of education, training, or experience. Thus, we usually leave the design of kitchens to people with architectural training, the drafting of contracts to people who have studied law, and the teaching of physics to people with advanced degrees in that field.

At the national level, comparative advantage may derive from differences in natural resources or from differences in society or culture. The United States, which has a disproportionate share of the world's leading research universities, has a comparative advantage in the design of electronic computing hardware and software. Canada, which has one of the world's highest per-capita endowments of farm and forest land, has a comparative advantage in the production of agricultural products. Topography and climate explain why Colorado specializes in the skiing industry while Hawaii specializes as an ocean resort.

Seemingly noneconomic factors also can give rise to comparative advantage. For instance, the emergence of English as the de facto world language gives English-speaking countries a comparative advantage over non–English-speaking nations in the production of books, movies, and popular music. Even a country's institutions may affect the likelihood that it will achieve comparative advantage in a particular pursuit. For example, cultures that encourage entrepreneurship will tend to have a comparative advantage in the introduction of new products, whereas those that promote high standards of care and craftsmanship will tend to have a comparative advantage in the production of high-quality variants of established products.

---

[1]For an interesting discussion of specialization and the decline of the .400 hitter from the perspective of an evolutionary biologist, see Stephen Jay Gould, *Full House* (New York: Three Rivers Press, 1996), Part 3.

Televisions and videocassette recorders were developed and first produced in the United States, but today the United States accounts for only a minuscule share of the total world production of these products. Why did the United States fail to retain its lead in these markets?

That televisions and VCRs were developed in the United States is explained in part by the country's comparative advantage in technological research, which in turn was supported by the country's outstanding system of higher education. Other contributing factors were high expenditures on the development of electronic components for the military and a culture that actively encourages entrepreneurship. As for the production of these products, America enjoyed an early advantage partly because the product designs were themselves evolving rapidly at first, which favored production facilities located in close proximity to the product designers. Early production techniques also relied intensively on skilled labor, which is abundant in the United States. In time, however, product designs stabilized and many of the more complex manufacturing operations were automated. Both of these changes gradually led to greater reliance on relatively less-skilled production workers. And at that point, factories located in high-wage countries like the United States could no longer compete with those located in low-wage areas overseas.

RECAP	EXCHANGE AND OPPORTUNITY COST

Gains from exchange are possible if trading partners have comparative advantages in producing different goods and services. You have a comparative advantage in producing, say, Web pages, if your opportunity cost of producing a Web page—measured in terms of other production opportunities forgone—is smaller than the corresponding opportunity costs of your trading partners. Maximum production is achieved if each person specializes in producing the good or service in which he or she has the lowest opportunity cost (the principle of comparative advantage). Comparative advantage makes specialization worthwhile even if one trading partner is more productive than others, in absolute terms, in every activity.

Why was the United States unable to remain competitive as a manufacturer of televisions and other electronic equipment?

COMPARATIVE ADVANTAGE AND PRODUCTION POSSIBILITIES

Comparative advantage and specialization allow an economy to produce more than if each person tries to produce a little of everything. In this section we gain further insight into the advantages of specialization by introducing a graph that can be used to describe the various combinations of goods and services that an economy can produce.

THE PRODUCTION POSSIBILITIES CURVE

We begin with a hypothetical economy in which only two goods are produced, coffee and pine nuts. It is a small island economy, and "production" consists either of picking coffee beans that grow on small bushes on the island's central valley floor or of gathering pine nuts that fall from trees on the steep hillsides overlooking the valley. The more time workers spend picking coffee, the less time they have available for picking nuts. So if people want to drink more coffee, they must make do with a smaller amount of nuts.

If we know how productive workers are at each activity, we can summarize the various combinations of coffee and nuts they can pick each day. This menu of possibilities is known as the **production possibilities curve**.

production possibilities curve a graph that describes the maximum amount of one good that can be produced for every possible level of production of the other good

To keep matters simple, we begin with an example in which the economy has only a single worker who can divide her time between the two activities.

EXAMPLE 2.3

What is the production possibilities curve for an economy in which Susan is the only worker?

Consider a society consisting only of Susan, who allocates her production time between coffee and nuts. She has nimble fingers, a quality that makes her more productive at picking coffee than at gathering nuts. She can gather 2 pounds of nuts or pick 4 pounds of coffee in an hour. If she works a total of 6 hours per day, describe her production possibilities curve—the graph that displays, for each level of nut production, the maximum amount of coffee that Susan can pick.

The vertical axis in Figure 2.1 shows Susan's daily production of coffee, and the horizontal axis shows her daily production of nuts. Let's begin by looking at two extreme allocations of her time. First, suppose she employs her entire workday (6 hours) picking coffee. In that case, since she can pick 4 pounds of coffee per hour, she would pick 24 pounds per day of coffee and gather zero pounds of nuts. That combination of coffee and nut production is represented by point A in Figure 2.1. It is the vertical intercept of Susan's production possibilities curve.

Now suppose, instead, that Susan devotes all her time to gathering nuts. Since she can gather 2 pounds of nuts per hour, her total daily production would be 12 pounds of nuts. That combination is represented by point D in Figure 2.1, the horizontal intercept of Susan's production possibilities curve. Because Susan's production of each good is exactly proportional to the amount of time she devotes to that good, the remaining points along her production possibilities curve will lie on the straight line that joins A and D.

For example, suppose that Susan devotes 4 hours each day to picking coffee and 2 hours to gathering nuts. She will then end up with (4 hours/day) × (4 pounds/hour) = 16 pounds of coffee per day and (2 hours/day) × (2 pounds/hour) = 4 pounds of nuts. This is the point labeled B in Figure 2.1. Alternatively, if she devotes 2 hours to coffee and 4 to nuts, she will get (2 hours/day) × (4 pounds/hour) = 8 pounds of coffee per day and (4 hours/day) × (2 pounds/hour) = 8 pounds of nuts. This alternative combination is represented by point C in Figure 2.1.

FIGURE 2.1

Susan's Production Possibilities.

For the production relationships given, the production possibilities curve is a straight line.

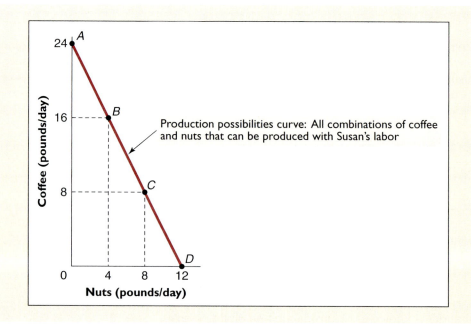

Since Susan's production possibilities curve (PPC) is a straight line, its slope is constant. The absolute value of the slope of Susan's PPC is the ratio of its vertical intercept to its horizontal intercept: (24 pounds of coffee/day)/(12 pounds of nuts/day) = (2 pounds of coffee)/(1 pound of nuts). (Be sure to keep track of the units of measure on each axis when computing this ratio.) *This ratio means that Susan's opportunity cost of an additional pound of nuts is 2 pounds of coffee.*

Note that Susan's opportunity cost (OC) of nuts can also be expressed as the following simple formula:

$$OC_{nuts} = \frac{\text{loss in coffee}}{\text{gain in nuts}}, \qquad (2.1)$$

where "loss in coffee" means the amount of coffee given up, and "gain in nuts" means the corresponding increase in nuts. Likewise, Susan's opportunity cost of coffee is expressed by this formula:

$$OC_{coffee} = \frac{\text{loss in nuts}}{\text{gain in coffee}}. \qquad (2.2)$$

To say that Susan's opportunity cost of an additional pound of nuts is 2 pounds of coffee is thus equivalent to saying that her opportunity cost of a pound of coffee is $\frac{1}{2}$ pound of nuts.

The downward slope of the production possibilities curve shown in Figure 2.1 illustrates the scarcity principle—the idea that because our resources are limited, having more of one good thing generally means having to settle for less of another (see Chapter 1). Susan can have an additional pound of coffee if she wishes, but only if she is willing to give up half a pound of nuts. If Susan is the only person in the economy, her opportunity cost of producing a good becomes, in effect, its price. Thus, the price she has to pay for an additional pound of coffee is half a pound of nuts; or the price she has to pay for an additional pound of nuts is 2 pounds of coffee.

Any point that lies either along the production possibilities curve or within it is said to be an **attainable point,** meaning that it can be produced with currently available resources. In Figure 2.2, for example, points *A, B, C, D,* and *E* are attainable

attainable point any combination of goods that can be produced using currently available resources

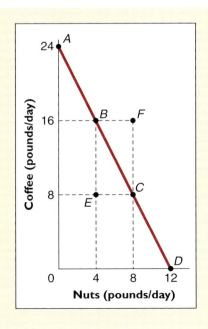

FIGURE 2.2

Attainable and Efficient Points on Susan's Production Possibilities Curve.

Points that lie either along the production possibilities curve (for example, *A, B, C,* and *D*) or within it (for example, *E*) are said to be attainable. Points that lie outside the production possibilities curve (for example, *F*) are unattainable. Points that lie along the curve are said to be efficient, while those that lie within the curve are said to be inefficient.

unattainable point any combination of goods that cannot be produced using currently available resources

inefficient point any combination of goods for which currently available resources enable an increase in the production of one good without a reduction in the production of the other

efficient point any combination of goods for which currently available resources do not allow an increase in the production of one good without a reduction in the production of the other

points. Points that lie outside the production possibilities curve are said to be **unattainable**, meaning that they cannot be produced using currently available resources. In Figure 2.2, *F* is an unattainable point because Susan cannot pick 16 pounds of coffee per day *and* gather 8 pounds of nuts. Points that lie within the curve are said to be **inefficient**, in the sense that existing resources would allow for production of more of at least one good without sacrificing the production of any other good. At *E*, for example, Susan is picking only 8 pounds of coffee per day and gathering 4 pounds of nuts, which means that she could increase her coffee harvest by 8 pounds per day without giving up any nuts (by moving from *E* to *B*). Alternatively, Susan could gather as many as 4 additional pounds of nuts each day without giving up any coffee (by moving from *E* to *C*). An **efficient** point is one that lies along the production possibilities curve. At any such point, more of one good can be produced only by producing less of the other.

EXERCISE 2.2

For the PPC shown in Figure 2.2, state whether the following points are attainable and/or efficient:

  a. **20 pounds per day of coffee, 4 pounds per day of nuts.**

  b. **12 pounds per day of coffee, 6 pounds per day of nuts.**

  c. **4 pounds per day of coffee, 8 pounds per day of nuts.**

HOW INDIVIDUAL PRODUCTIVITY AFFECTS THE SLOPE AND POSITION OF THE PPC

To see how the slope and position of the production possibilities curve depend on an individual's productivity, let's compare Susan's PPC to that of Tom, who is less productive at picking coffee but more productive at gathering nuts.

EXAMPLE 2.4

How do changes in productivity affect the opportunity cost of nuts?

Tom is short and has keen eyesight, qualities that make him especially well-suited for gathering nuts that fall beneath trees on the hillsides. He can gather 4 pounds of nuts or pick 2 pounds of coffee per hour. If Tom were the only person in the economy, describe the economy's production possibilities curve.

We can construct Tom's PPC the same way we did Susan's. Note first that if Tom devotes an entire workday (6 hours) to coffee picking, he ends up with (6 hours/day) $\times$ (2 pounds/hour) = 12 pounds of coffee per day and zero pounds of nuts. So the vertical intercept of Tom's PPC is *A* in Figure 2.3. If instead he devotes all his time to gathering nuts, he gets (6 hours/day) $\times$ (4 pounds/hour) = 24 pounds of nuts per day and no coffee. That means the horizontal intercept of his PPC is *D* in Figure 2.3. Because Tom's production of each good is proportional to the amount of time he devotes to it, the remaining points on his PPC will lie along the straight line that joins these two extreme points.

For example, if he devotes 4 hours each day to picking coffee and 2 hours to gathering nuts, he will end up with (4 hours/day) $\times$ (2 pounds/hour) = 8 pounds of coffee per day and (2 hours/day) $\times$ (4 pounds/hour) = 8 pounds of nuts per day. This is the point labeled *B* in Figure 2.3. Alternatively, if he devotes 2 hours to coffee and 4 to nuts, he will get (2 hours/day) $\times$ (2 pounds/hour) = 4 pounds of coffee per day and (4 hours/day) $\times$ (4 pounds/hour) = 16 pounds of nuts. This alternative combination is represented by point *C* in Figure 2.3.

How does Tom's PPC compare with Susan's? Note in Figure 2.4 that because Tom is absolutely less productive than Susan at picking coffee, the vertical intercept

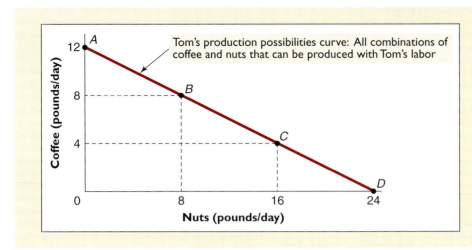

FIGURE 2.3
Tom's Production Possibilities Curve.
Tom's opportunity cost of producing one pound of nuts is only half a pound of coffee.

of his PPC lies closer to the origin than Susan's. By the same token, because Susan is absolutely less productive than Tom at gathering nuts, the horizontal intercept of her PPC lies closer to the origin than Tom's. For Tom, the opportunity cost of an additional pound of nuts is $\frac{1}{2}$ pound of coffee, which is one-fourth Susan's opportunity cost of nuts. This difference in opportunity costs shows up as a difference in the slopes of their PPCs: the absolute value of the slope of Tom's PPC is $\frac{1}{2}$, whereas Susan's is 2.

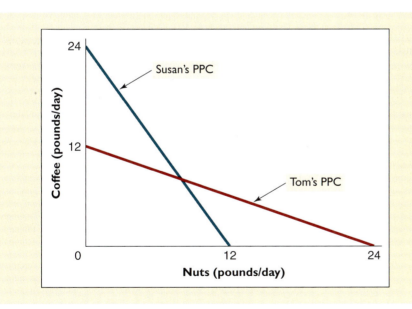

FIGURE 2.4
Individual Production Possibilities Curves Compared.
Tom is less productive in coffee than Susan, but more productive in nuts.

In this example, Tom has both an absolute advantage and a comparative advantage over Susan in gathering nuts. Susan, for her part, has both an absolute advantage and a comparative advantage over Tom in picking coffee.

We cannot emphasize strongly enough that the principle of comparative advantage is a relative concept—one that makes sense only when the productivities of two or more people (or countries) are being compared. To cement this idea, work through the following exercise.

EXERCISE 2.3

Suppose Susan can pick 2 pounds of coffee per hour or gather 4 pounds of nuts per hour; Tom can pick 1 pound of coffee per hour and gather 1 pound of nuts per hour. What is Susan's opportunity cost of gathering a pound of nuts? What is Tom's opportunity cost of gathering a pound of nuts? Where does Susan's comparative advantage now lie?

THE GAINS FROM SPECIALIZATION AND EXCHANGE

Earlier we saw that a comparative advantage arising from disparities in individual opportunity costs creates gains for everyone (see Examples 2.1 and 2.2). The following example shows how the same point can be illustrated using production possibility curves.

EXAMPLE 2.5

How costly is failure to specialize?

Suppose that in Example 2.4 Susan and Tom had divided their time so that each person's output consisted of half nuts and half coffee. How much of each good would Tom and Susan have been able to consume? How much could they have consumed if each had specialized in the activity for which he or she enjoyed a comparative advantage?

Since Tom can produce twice as many pounds of nuts in an hour as pounds of coffee, to produce equal quantities of each, he must spend 2 hours picking coffee for every hour he devotes to gathering nuts. And since he works a 6-hour day, that means spending 2 hours gathering nuts and 4 hours picking coffee. Dividing his time in this way, he will end up with 8 pounds of coffee per day and 8 pounds of nuts. Similarly, since Susan can produce twice as many pounds of coffee in an hour as pounds of nuts, to pick equal quantities of each, she must spend 2 hours gathering nuts for every hour she devotes to picking coffee. And since she too works a 6-hour day, that means spending 2 hours picking coffee and 4 hours gathering nuts. So, like Tom, she will end up with 8 pounds of coffee per day and 8 pounds of nuts. (See Figure 2.5.) Their combined daily production will thus be 16 pounds of each good. By contrast, had they each specialized in their respective activities of comparative advantage, their combined daily production would have been 24 pounds of each good.

FIGURE 2.5
Production without Specialization.
When Tom and Susan divide their time so that each produces the same number of pounds of coffee and nuts, they can consume a total of 16 pounds of coffee and 16 pounds of nuts each day.

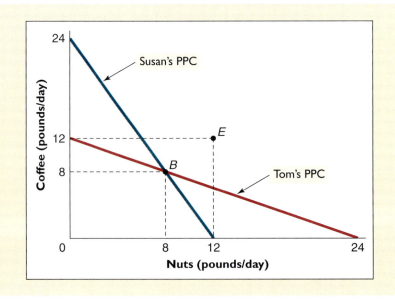

If they exchange coffee and nuts with one another, each can consume a combination of the two goods that would have been unattainable if exchange had not been possible. For example, Susan can give Tom 12 pounds of coffee in exchange for 12 pounds of nuts, enabling each to consume 4 pounds per day more of each good than when each produced and consumed alone. Note that point *E* in Figure 2.5, which has 12 pounds per day of each good, lies beyond each person's PPC, yet is easily attainable with specialization and exchange.

As the following exercise illustrates, the gains from specialization grow larger as the difference in opportunity costs increases.

EXERCISE 2.4

How do differences in opportunity cost affect the gains from specialization? Susan can pick 5 pounds of coffee or gather 1 pound of nuts in an hour. Tom can pick 1 pound of coffee or gather 5 pounds of nuts in an hour. Assuming they again work 6-hour days and want to consume coffee and nuts in equal quantities, by how much will specialization increase their consumption compared to the alternative in which each produced only for his or her own consumption?

Although the gains from specialization and exchange grow with increases in the differences in opportunity costs among trading partners, these differences alone still seem insufficient to account for the enormous differences in living standards between rich and poor countries. Average income in the 20 richest countries in the year 2000, for example, was over $27,000 per person, compared to only $211 per person in the 20 poorest countries.[2] Although we will say more later about specialization's role in explaining these differences, we first discuss how to construct the PPC for an entire economy and examine how factors other than specialization might cause it to shift outward over time.

A PRODUCTION POSSIBILITIES CURVE FOR A MANY-PERSON ECONOMY

Although most actual economies consist of millions of workers, the process of constructing a production possibilities curve for an economy of that size is really no different from the process for a one-person economy. Consider again an economy in which the only two goods are coffee and nuts, with coffee again on the vertical axis and nuts on the horizontal axis. The vertical intercept of the economy's PPC is the total amount of coffee that could be picked if all available workers worked full-time picking coffee. Thus, the maximum attainable amount of coffee production is shown for the hypothetical economy in Figure 2.6 as 100,000 pounds per day (an amount chosen arbitrarily, for illustrative purposes). The horizontal intercept of the PPC is the amount of nuts that could be gathered if all available workers worked full-time gathering nuts, shown for this same economy as 80,000 pounds per day (also an amount chosen arbitrarily). But note that the PPC shown in the diagram is not a straight line—as in the earlier examples involving only a single worker—but rather a curve that is bowed out from the origin.

[2]High-income countries: Australia, Austria, Belgium, Canada, China, Hong Kong, Denmark, Finland, France, Germany, Iceland, Ireland, Japan, Luxembourg, Netherlands, Norway, Singapore, Sweden, Switzerland, United Kingdom, and United States. Low-income countries: Burkina Faso, Burundi, Central African Republic, Chad, Ethiopia, Ghana, Guinea-Bisau, Kenya, Madagascar, Malawi, Mali, Mozambique, Myanmar, Nepal, Niger, Nigeria, Rwanda, Sierra Leone, Tanzania, and Uganda. (Source: Global Policy Forum, http://www.globalpolicy.org/).

FIGURE 2.6

Production Possibilities Curve for a Large Economy.

For an economy with millions of workers, the PPC typically has a gentle outward bow shape.

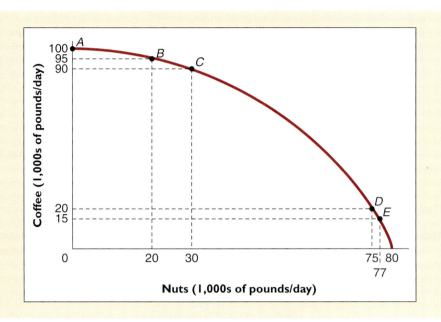

Nuts (1,000s of pounds/day)

We'll say more in a moment about the reasons for this shape. But first note that a bow-shaped PPC means that the opportunity cost of producing nuts increases as the economy produces more of them. Notice, for example, that when the economy moves from *A*, where it is producing only coffee, to *B*, it gets 20,000 pounds of nuts per day by giving up only 5,000 pounds per day of coffee. When nut production is increased still further, however—for example, by moving from *B* to *C*—the economy again gives up 5,000 pounds per day of coffee, yet this time gets only 10,000 additional pounds of nuts. This pattern of increasing opportunity cost persists over the entire length of the PPC. For example, note that in moving from *D* to *E,* the economy again gives up 5,000 pounds per day of coffee but now gains only 2,000 pounds a day of nuts. Note, finally, that the same pattern of increasing opportunity cost applies to coffee. Thus, as more coffee is produced, the opportunity cost of producing additional coffee—as measured by the amount of nuts that must be sacrificed—also rises.

Why is the PPC for the multiperson economy bow-shaped? The answer lies in the fact that some resources are relatively well-suited for gathering nuts while others are relatively well-suited for picking coffee. If the economy is initially producing only coffee and wants to begin producing some nuts, which workers will it reassign? Recall Susan and Tom, the two workers discussed in Example 2.5, in which Tom's comparative advantage was gathering nuts and Susan's comparative advantage was picking coffee. If both workers were currently picking coffee and you wanted to reassign one of them to gather nuts instead, whom would you send? Tom would be the clear choice, because his departure would cost the economy only half as much coffee as Susan's and would augment nut production by twice as much.

The principle is the same in any large multiperson economy, except that the range of opportunity cost differences across workers is even greater than in the earlier two-worker example (Example 2.5). As we keep reassigning workers from coffee production to nut production, sooner or later we must withdraw even coffee specialists like Susan from coffee production. Indeed, we must eventually reassign others whose opportunity cost of producing nuts is far higher than hers.

The shape of the production possibilities curve shown in Figure 2.6 illustrates the general principle that when resources have different opportunity costs, we should always exploit the resource with the lowest opportunity cost first. We call this the *low-hanging-fruit principle*, in honor of the fruit picker's rule of picking the most accessible fruit first:

The Principle of Increasing Opportunity Cost (also called "The Low-Hanging-Fruit Principle"): In expanding the production of any good, first employ those resources with the lowest opportunity cost, and only afterward turn to resources with higher opportunity costs.

A Note on the Logic of the Fruit Picker's Rule

Why should a fruit picker harvest the low-hanging fruit first? This rule makes sense for several reasons. For one, the low-hanging fruit is easier (and hence cheaper) to pick, and if he planned on picking only a limited amount of fruit to begin with, he would clearly come out ahead by avoiding the less-accessible fruit on the higher branches. But even if he planned on picking all the fruit on the tree, he would do better to start with the lower branches first, because this would enable him to enjoy the revenue from the sale of the fruit sooner.

The fruit picker's job can be likened to the task confronting a new CEO who has been hired to reform an inefficient, ailing company. The CEO has limited time and attention, so it makes sense to focus first on problems that are relatively easy to correct and whose elimination will provide the biggest improvements in performance—the low-hanging fruit. Later on, the CEO can worry about the many smaller improvements needed to raise the company from very good to excellent.

Again, the important message of the low-hanging-fruit principle is to be sure to take advantage of your most favorable opportunities first.

RECAP	COMPARATIVE ADVANTAGE AND PRODUCTION POSSIBILITIES

For an economy that produces two goods, the production possibilities curve describes the maximum amount of one good that can be produced for every possible level of production of the other good. Attainable points are those that lie on or within the curve, and efficient points are those that lie along the curve. The slope of the production possibilities curve tells us the opportunity cost of producing an additional unit of the good measured along the horizontal axis. The principle of increasing opportunity cost, or the low-hanging-fruit principle, tells us that the slope of the production possibilities curve becomes steeper as we move downward to the right. The greater the differences among individual opportunity costs, the more bow-shaped the production possibilities curve will be, and the more bow-shaped the production possibilities curve, the greater will be the potential gains from specialization.

FACTORS THAT SHIFT THE ECONOMY'S PRODUCTION POSSIBILITIES CURVE

As its name implies, the production possibilities curve provides a summary of the production options open to any society. At any given moment, the PPC confronts society with a trade-off. The only way people can produce and consume more nuts is to produce and consume less coffee. In the long run, however, it is often possible to increase production of all goods. This is what is meant when people speak of economic growth. As shown in Figure 2.7, economic growth is an outward shift in the economy's production possibilities curve. It can result from increases in the amount of productive resources available or from improvements in knowledge or technology that render existing resources more productive.

FIGURE 2.7

Economic Growth: An Outward Shift in the Economy's PPC.
Increases in productive resources (such as labor and capital equipment) or improvements in knowledge and technology cause the PPC to shift outward. They are the main factors that drive economic growth.

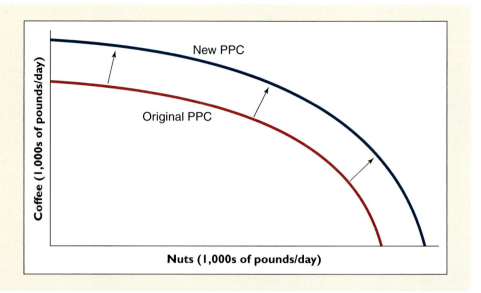

What causes the quantity of productive resources to grow in an economy? One factor is investment in new factories and equipment. When workers have more and better equipment to work with, their productivity increases, often dramatically. This is surely an important factor behind the differences in living standards between rich and poor countries. According to one study, for example, the value of capital investment per worker in the United States is about $30,000, while in Nepal the corresponding figure is less than $1,000.[3]

Such large differences in capital per worker don't occur all at once. They are a consequence of decades, even centuries, of differences in rates of savings and investment. Over time, even small differences in rates of investment can translate into extremely large differences in the amount of capital equipment available to each worker. Differences of this sort are often self-reinforcing: Not only do higher rates of saving and investment cause incomes to grow, but the resulting higher income levels also make it easier to devote additional resources to savings and investment. Over time, then, even small initial productivity advantages from specialization can translate into very large income gaps.

Population growth also causes an economy's PPC curve to shift outward and thus is often listed as one of the sources of economic growth. But because population growth also generates more mouths to feed, it cannot by itself raise a country's standard of living. Indeed it may even cause a decline in the standard of living if existing population densities have already begun to put pressure on available land, water, and other scarce resources.

Perhaps the most important source of economic growth is improvements in knowledge and technology. As economists have long recognized, such improvements often lead to higher output through increased specialization. Improvements in technology often occur spontaneously, but more frequently they are directly or indirectly the result of increases in education.

Earlier we discussed a two-person example in which individual differences in opportunity cost led to a threefold gain from specialization (Exercise 2.4). Real-world gains from specialization often are far more spectacular than those in the example. One reason is that specialization not only capitalizes on preexisting differences in individual skills but also deepens those skills through practice and experience. Moreover, it eliminates many of the switching and start-up costs people incur when they move back and forth among numerous tasks. These gains apply

[3]Alan Heston and Robert Summers, "The Penn World Table (Mark 5): An Expanded Set of International Comparisons, 1950–1988," *Quarterly Journal of Economics*, May 1991, pp. 327–68.

not only to people but also to the tools and equipment they use. Breaking a task down into simple steps, each of which can be performed by a different machine, greatly multiplies the productivity of individual workers.

Even in simple settings, these factors can combine to increase productivity hundreds- or even thousands-fold. Adam Smith, the Scottish philosopher who is remembered today as the founder of modern economics, was the first to recognize the enormity of the gains made possible by the division and specialization of labor. Consider, for instance, his description of work in an eighteenth-century Scottish pin factory:

> One man draws out the wire, another straightens it, a third cuts it, a fourth points it, a fifth grinds it at the top for receiving the head; to make the head requires two or three distinct operations . . . I have seen a small manufactory of this kind where only ten men were employed . . . [who] could, when they exerted themselves, make among them about twelve pounds of pins in a day. There are in a pound upwards of four thousand pins of middling size. Those ten persons, therefore, could make among them upwards of forty-eight thousand pins in a day. Each person, therefore, making a tenth part of forty-eight thousand pins, might be considered as making four thousand eight hundred pins in a day. But if they had all wrought separately and independently, and without any of them having been educated to this peculiar business, they certainly could not each of them have made twenty, perhaps not one pin in a day.[4]

The gains in productivity that result from specialization are indeed often prodigious. They constitute the single most important explanation for why societies that don't rely heavily on specialization and exchange are rapidly becoming relics.

WHY HAVE SOME COUNTRIES BEEN SLOW TO SPECIALIZE?

You may be asking yourself, "If specialization is such a great thing, why don't people in poor countries like Nepal just specialize?" If so, you are in good company. Adam Smith spent many years attempting to answer precisely the same question. In the end, his explanation was that population density is an important precondition for specialization. Smith, ever the economic naturalist, observed that work tended to be far more specialized in the large cities of England in the eighteenth century than in the rural highlands of Scotland:

> In the lone houses and very small villages which are scattered about in so desert a country as the Highlands of Scotland, every farmer must be butcher, baker and brewer for his own family. . . . A country carpenter . . . is not only a carpenter, but a joiner, a cabinet maker, and even a carver in wood, as well as a wheelwright, a ploughwright, a cart and waggon maker.[5]

In contrast, each of these same tasks was performed by a different specialist in the large English and Scottish cities of Smith's day. Scottish highlanders also would have specialized had they been able to, but the markets in which they participated were simply too small and fragmented. Of course, high population density by itself provides no guarantee that specialization will result in rapid economic growth. But especially before the arrival of modern shipping and electronic communications technology, low population density was a definite obstacle to gains from specialization.

Nepal remains one of the most remote and isolated countries on the planet. As recently as the mid-1960s, its average population density was less than 30 people per square mile (as compared, for example, to more than 1,000 people per square

[4]Adam Smith, *The Wealth of Nations* (New York: Everyman's Library, 1910 (1776)), book 1.
[5]*Id.*, chapter 3.

Can specialization proceed too far?

Drawing by Gini Kennedy

mile in New Jersey). Specialization was further limited by Nepal's rugged terrain. Exchanging goods and services with residents of other villages was difficult, because the nearest village in most cases could be reached only after trekking several hours, or even days, over treacherous Himalayan trails. More than any other factor, this extreme isolation accounts for Nepal's longstanding failure to benefit from widespread specialization.

Population density is by no means the only important factor that influences the degree of specialization. Specialization may be severely impeded, for example, by laws and customs that limit people's freedom to transact freely with one another. The communist governments of North Korea and the former East Germany restricted exchange severely, which helps explain why those countries achieved far less specialization than South Korea and the former West Germany, whose governments were far more supportive of exchange.

CAN WE HAVE TOO MUCH SPECIALIZATION?

Of course, the mere fact that specialization boosts productivity does not mean that more specialization is always better than less, for specialization also entails costs. For example, most people appear to enjoy variety in the work they do, yet variety tends to be one of the first casualties as workplace tasks become ever more narrowly specialized.

Indeed, one of Karl Marx's central themes was that the fragmentation of workplace tasks often exacts a heavy psychological toll on workers. Thus, he wrote,

> All means for the development of production . . . mutilate the laborer into a fragment of a man, degrade him to the level of an appendage of a machine, destroy every remnant of charm in his work and turn it into hated toil.[6]

Charlie Chaplin's 1936 film, *Modern Times,* paints a vivid portrait of the psychological costs of repetitive factory work. As an assembly worker, Chaplin's only task, all day every day, is to tighten the nuts on two bolts as they pass before him on the assembly line. Finally, he snaps and staggers from the factory, wrenches in hand, tightening every nutlike protuberance he encounters.

[6]Karl Marx, *Das Kapital* (New York: Modern Library), pp. 708, 709.

Do the extra goods made possible by specialization simply come at too high a price? We must certainly acknowledge at least the *potential* for specialization to proceed too far. Yet specialization need not entail rigidly segmented, mind-numbingly repetitive work. And it is important to recognize that *failure* to specialize entails costs as well. Those who don't specialize must accept low wages or work extremely long hours.

When all is said and done, we can expect to meet life's financial obligations in the shortest time—thereby freeing up more time to do whatever else we wish—if we concentrate at least a significant proportion of our efforts on those tasks for which we have a comparative advantage.

COMPARATIVE ADVANTAGE AND INTERNATIONAL TRADE

The same logic that leads the individuals in an economy to specialize and exchange goods with one another also leads nations to specialize and trade among themselves. As with individuals, each nation can benefit from exchange, even though one may be generally more productive than the other in absolute terms.

If trade between nations is so beneficial, why are free-trade agreements so controversial?

One of the most heated issues in the 1996 presidential campaign was President Clinton's support for the North American Free Trade Agreement (NAFTA), a treaty to sharply reduce trade barriers between the United States and its immediate neighbors north and south. The treaty attracted fierce opposition from third-party candidate Ross Perot, who insisted that it would mean unemployment for millions of American workers. If exchange is so beneficial, why does anyone oppose it?

The answer is that while reducing barriers to international trade increases the total value of all goods and services produced in each nation, it does not guarantee that each individual citizen will do better. One specific concern regarding NAFTA was that it would help Mexico to exploit a comparative advantage in the production of goods made by unskilled labor. Although U.S. consumers would benefit from reduced prices for such goods, many Americans feared that unskilled workers in the United States would lose their jobs to workers in Mexico.

In the end, NAFTA was enacted over the vociferous opposition of American labor unions. So far, however, studies have failed to detect significant job losses among unskilled workers in the United States.

We will look at international trade in much more detail in Chapter 9.

ECONOMIC NATURALIST 2.3

If free trade is so great, why do so many people oppose it?

RECAP	COMPARATIVE ADVANTAGE AND INTERNATIONAL TRADE

Nations, like individuals, can benefit from exchange, even though one trading partner may be more productive than the other in absolute terms. The greater the difference between domestic opportunity costs and world opportunity costs, the more a nation benefits from exchange with other nations. But expansions of exchange do not guarantee that each individual citizen will do better. In particular, unskilled workers in high-wage countries may be hurt in the short run by the reduction of barriers to trade with low-wage nations.

▪ SUMMARY ▪

- One person has an *absolute* advantage over another in the production of a good if she can produce more of that good than the other person. One person has a *comparative* advantage over another in the production of a good if she is relatively more efficient than the other person at producing that good, meaning that her opportunity cost of producing it is lower than her counterpart's. Specialization based on comparative advantage is the basis for economic exchange. When each person specializes in the task at which he or she is relatively most efficient, the economic pie is maximized, making possible the largest slice for everyone.

- At the individual level, comparative advantage may spring from differences in talent or ability or from differences in education, training, and experience. At the national level, sources of comparative advantage include these innate and learned differences, as well as differences in language, culture, institutions, climate, natural resources, and a host of other factors.

- The production possibilities curve is a simple device for summarizing the possible combinations of output that a society can produce if it employs its resources efficiently. In a simple economy that produces only coffee and nuts, the PPC shows the maximum quantity of coffee production (vertical axis) possible at each level of nut production (horizontal axis). The slope of the PPC at any point represents the opportunity cost of nuts at that point, expressed in pounds of coffee.

- All production possibilities curves slope downward because of the scarcity principle, which states that the only way a consumer can get more of one good is to settle for less of another. In economies whose workers have different opportunity costs of producing each good, the slope of the PPC becomes steeper as consumers move downward along the curve. This change in slope illustrates the principle of increasing opportunity cost (or the low-hanging-fruit principle), which states that in expanding the production of any good, a society should first employ those resources that are relatively efficient at producing that good, only afterward turning to those that are less efficient.

- Factors that cause a country's PPC to shift outward over time include investment in new factories and equipment, population growth, and improvements in knowledge and technology.

- The same logic that prompts individuals to specialize in their production and exchange goods with one another also leads nations to specialize and trade with one another. On both levels, each trading partner can benefit from an exchange, even though one may be more productive than the other, in absolute terms, for each good. For both individuals and nations, the benefits of exchange tend to be larger the larger are the differences between the trading partners' opportunity costs.

▪ CORE PRINCIPLES ▪

The Principle of Comparative Advantage
Everyone does best when each person (or each country) concentrates on the activities for which his or her opportunity cost is lowest.

The Principle of Increasing Opportunity Cost (also called "The Low-Hanging-Fruit Principle")
In expanding the production of any good, first employ those resources with the lowest opportunity cost, and only afterward turn to resources with higher opportunity costs.

▪ KEY TERMS ▪

absolute advantage (36) efficient point (44) production possibilities curve (41)
attainable point (43) inefficient point (44) unattainable point (44)
comparative advantage (36)

▪ REVIEW QUESTIONS ▪

1. Explain what "having a comparative advantage" at producing a particular good or service means. What does "having an absolute advantage" at producing a good or service mean?

2. How will a reduction in the number of hours worked each day affect an economy's production possibilities curve?

3. How will technological innovations that boost labor productivity affect an economy's production possibilities curve?

4. Why does saying that people are poor because they do not specialize make more sense than saying that people perform their own services because they are poor?

5. What factors have helped the United States to become the world's leading exporter of movies, books, and popular music?

▪ PROBLEMS ▪

1. Ted can wax 4 cars per day or wash 12 cars. Tom can wax 3 cars per day or wash 6. What is each man's opportunity cost of washing a car? Who has a comparative advantage in washing cars?

2. Ted can wax a car in 20 minutes or wash a car in 60 minutes. Tom can wax a car in 15 minutes or wash a car in 30 minutes. What is each man's opportunity cost of washing a car? Who has a comparative advantage in washing cars?

3. Toby can produce 5 gallons of apple cider or 2.5 ounces of feta cheese per hour. Kyle can produce 3 gallons of apple cider or 1.5 ounces of feta cheese per hour. Can Toby and Kyle benefit from specialization and trade? Explain.

4. Nancy and Bill are auto mechanics. Nancy takes 4 hours to replace a clutch and 2 hours to replace a set of brakes. Bill takes 6 hours to replace a clutch and 2 hours to replace a set of brakes. State whether anyone has an absolute advantage at either task and, for each task, identify who has a comparative advantage.

5. Consider a society consisting only of Helen, who allocates her time between sewing dresses and baking bread. Each hour she devotes to sewing dresses yields 4 dresses, and each hour she devotes to baking bread yields 8 loaves of bread. If Helen works a total of 8 hours per day, graph her production possibilities curve.

6. Refer to the preceding question. Which of the points listed below is efficient? Which is attainable?
   a. 28 dresses per day, 16 loaves per day.
   b. 16 dresses per day, 32 loaves per day.
   c. 18 dresses per day, 24 loaves per day.

7. Suppose that in Problem 5 a sewing machine is introduced that enables Helen to sew 8 dresses per hour rather than only 4. Show how this development shifts her production possibilities curve.

8. Refer to the preceding question to explain what is meant by the following statement: "An increase in productivity with respect to any one good increases our options for producing and consuming all other goods."

9. Susan can pick 4 pounds of coffee in an hour or gather 2 pounds of nuts. Tom can pick 2 pounds of coffee in an hour or gather 4 pounds of nuts. Each works 6 hours per day.
   a. What is the maximum number of pounds of coffee the two can pick in a day?
   b. What is the maximum number of pounds of nuts the two can gather in a day?
   c. If Susan and Tom were picking the maximum number of pounds of coffee when they decided that they would like to begin gathering 4 pounds of nuts per day, who would gather the nuts, and how many pounds of coffee would they still be able to pick?
   d. Now suppose Susan and Tom were gathering the maximum number of pounds of nuts when they decided that they would like to begin picking 8 pounds of coffee per day. Who would pick the coffee, and how many pounds of nuts would they still be able to gather?
   e. Would it be possible for Susan and Tom in total to gather 26 pounds of nuts and pick 20 pounds of coffee each day? If so, how much of each good should each person pick?

10.* Refer to the two-person economy described in the preceding problem.
   a. Is the point (30 pounds of coffee per day, 12 pounds of nuts per day) an attainable point? Is it an efficient point? What about the point (24 pounds of coffee per day, 24 pounds of nuts per day)?
   b. On a graph with pounds of coffee per day on the vertical axis and pounds of nuts per day on the horizontal axis, show all the points you identified in Problem 9, parts a–e, and Problem 10a. Connect these points with straight lines. Is the result the PPC for the economy consisting of Susan and Tom?
   c. Suppose that Susan and Tom could buy or sell coffee and nuts in the world market at a price of $2 per pound for coffee and $2 per pound for nuts. If each person specialized completely in the good for which he or she had a comparative advantage, how much could they earn by selling all their produce?
   d. At the prices just described, what is the maximum amount of coffee Susan and Tom could buy in the world market? The maximum amount of nuts? Would it be possible for them to consume 40 pounds of nuts and 8 pounds of coffee each day?
   e. In light of their ability to buy and sell in world markets at the stated prices, show on the same graph all combinations of the two goods it would be possible for them to consume.

■ ANSWERS TO IN-CHAPTER EXERCISES ■

2.1

	Productivity in programming	**Productivity in bicycle repair**
Pat	2 Web page updates per hour	1 repair per hour
Barb	3 Web page updates per hour	3 repairs per hour

The entries in the table tell us that Barb has an absolute advantage over Pat in both activities. While Barb, the mechanic, can update 3 Web pages per hour, Pat, the programmer, can update only 2. Barb's absolute advantage over Pat is even greater in the task of fixing bikes—3 repairs per hour versus Pat's 1.

But as in Example 2.2, the fact that Barb is a better programmer than Pat does not imply that Barb should update her own Web page. Barb's opportunity cost of updating a Web page is 1 bicycle repair, whereas Pat must give up only half a repair to update a Web page. Pat has a comparative advantage over Barb at programming, and Barb has a comparative advantage over Pat at bicycle repair.

2.2 In the accompanying graph, A (20 pounds per day of coffee, 4 pounds per day of nuts) is unattainable; B (12 pounds per day of coffee, 6 pounds per day of nuts) is both attainable and efficient; and C (4 pounds per day of coffee, 8 pounds per day of nuts) is both attainable and inefficient.

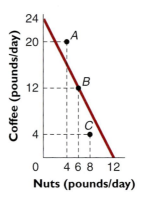

*Problems marked with an asterisk (*) are more difficult.

2.3 Susan's opportunity cost of gathering a pound of nuts is now $\frac{1}{2}$ pound of coffee, and Tom's opportunity cost of gathering a pound of nuts is now only 1 pound of coffee. So Tom has a comparative advantage at picking coffee, and Susan has a comparative advantage at gathering nuts.

2.4 Since Tom can produce five times as many pounds of nuts in an hour as pounds of coffee, to produce equal quantities of each, he must spend 5 hours picking coffee for every hour he devotes to gathering nuts. And since he works a 6-hour day, that means spending 5 hours picking coffee and 1 hour gathering nuts. Dividing his time in this way, he will end up with 5 pounds of each good. Similarly, if she is to produce equal quantities of each good, Susan must spend 5 hours gathering nuts and 1 hour picking coffee. So she too produces 5 pounds of each good if she divides her 6-hour day in this way. Their combined daily production will thus be 10 pounds of each good. By working together and specializing, however, they can produce and consume a total of 30 pounds per day of each good.

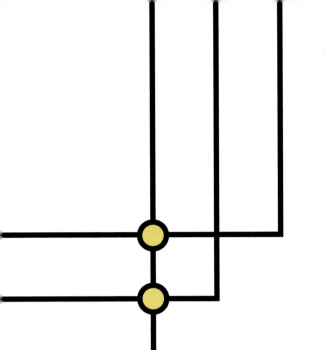

SUPPLY AND DEMAND:
AN INTRODUCTION

The stock of foodstuffs on hand at any moment in New York City's grocery stores, restaurants, and private kitchens is sufficient to feed the area's 10 million residents for at most a week or so. Since most of these residents have nutritionally adequate and highly varied diets, and since almost no food is produced within the city proper, provisioning New York requires that millions of pounds of food and drink be delivered to locations throughout the city each day.

No doubt many New Yorkers, buying groceries at their favorite local markets or eating at their favorite Italian restaurants, give little or no thought to the nearly miraculous coordination of people and resources that is required to feed city residents on a daily basis. But near-miraculous it is, nevertheless. Even if the supplying of New York City consisted only of transporting a fixed collection of foods to a given list of destinations each day, it would be quite an impressive operation, requiring at least a small (and well-managed) army to carry out.

Yet the entire process is astonishingly more complex than that. For example, the system must somehow ensure that not only *enough* food is delivered to satisfy New Yorkers' discriminating palates, but also the *right kinds* of food. There mustn't be too much pheasant and not enough smoked eel; or too much bacon and not enough eggs; or too much caviar and not enough canned tuna; and so on. Similar judgments must be made *within* each category of food and drink: There must be the right amount of Swiss cheese, and the right amounts of provolone, gorgonzola, and feta.

But even this doesn't begin to describe the complexity of the decisions and actions required to provide our nation's largest city with its daily bread. Someone has to decide where each particular type of food gets produced, and how, and by whom. Someone must decide how much of each type of food gets delivered to *each* of the tens of thousands of restaurants and grocery stores in the city. Someone must determine whether the deliveries should be made in big trucks or small ones, arrange that the trucks be in the right place at the right time, and ensure that gasoline and qualified drivers be available.

Thousands of individuals must decide what role, if any, they will play in this collective effort. Some people—just the right number—must choose to drive food-delivery trucks rather than trucks that deliver lumber. Others must become the mechanics who fix these trucks rather than carpenters who build houses. Others must become farmers rather than architects or bricklayers. Still others must become chefs in upscale restaurants, or flip burgers at McDonald's, instead of becoming plumbers or electricians.

Yet despite the almost incomprehensible number and complexity of the tasks involved, somehow the supplying of New York City manages to get done remarkably smoothly. Oh, a grocery store will occasionally run out of flank steak, or a diner will sometimes be told that someone else has just ordered the last serving of roast duck. But if episodes like these stick in memory, it is only because they are rare. For the most part, New York's food delivery system—like that of every other city in the country—functions so seamlessly that it attracts virtually no notice.

The situation is strikingly different in New York City's rental housing market. According to one recent estimate, the city needs between 20,000 and 40,000 new housing units each year merely to keep up with population growth and to replace existing housing that is deteriorated beyond repair. The actual rate of new construction in the city, however, is only 6,000 units per year. As a result, America's most densely populated city has been experiencing a protracted housing shortage. Yet, paradoxically, in the midst of this shortage, apartment houses are being demolished; and in the vacant lots left behind, people from the neighborhoods are planting flower gardens!

New York City is experiencing not only a growing shortage of rental housing, but also chronically strained relations between landlords and tenants. In one all-too-typical case, for example, a photographer living in a loft on the Lower East Side waged an eight-year court battle with his landlord that generated literally thousands of pages of legal documents. "Once we put up a doorbell for ourselves," the photographer recalled, "and [the landlord] pulled it out, so we pulled out the wires to his doorbell."[1] The landlord, for his part, accused the photographer of obstructing his efforts to renovate the apartment. According to the landlord, the tenant preferred for the apartment to remain in substandard condition, since that gave him an excuse to withhold rent payments.

Same city, two strikingly different patterns: In the food industry, goods and services are available in wide variety, and people (at least those with adequate income) are generally satisfied with what they receive and the choices available to them. In contrast, in the rental housing industry, chronic shortages and chronic dissatisfaction are rife among both buyers and sellers. Why this difference?

The brief answer is that New York City relies on a complex system of administrative rent regulations to allocate housing units but leaves the allocation of food essentially in the hands of market forces—the forces of supply and demand. Although intuition might suggest otherwise, both theory and experience suggest that the seemingly chaotic and unplanned outcomes of market forces, in most cases, can do a better job of allocating economic resources than can (for example) a government agency, even if the agency has the best of intentions.

Why does New York City's food distribution system work so much better than its housing market?

---

[1]Quoted by John Tierney, "The Rentocracy: At the Intersection of Supply and Demand," *New York Times Magazine,* May 4, 1997, p. 39.

In this chapter we'll explore how markets allocate food, housing, and other goods and services, usually with remarkable efficiency despite the complexity of the tasks. To be sure, markets are by no means perfect, and our stress on their virtues is to some extent an attempt to counteract what most economists view as an under-appreciation by the general public of their remarkable strengths. But in the course of our discussion we'll see why markets function so smoothly most of the time, and why bureaucratic rules and regulations rarely work as well in solving complex economic problems.

To convey an understanding of how markets work is a major goal of this course, and in this chapter we provide only a brief introduction and overview. As the course proceeds, we will discuss the economic role of markets in considerably more detail, paying attention to some of the problems of markets as well as their strengths.

WHAT, HOW, AND FOR WHOM? CENTRAL PLANNING VERSUS THE MARKET

No city, state, or society—regardless of how it is organized—can escape the need to answer certain basic economic questions. For example, how much of our limited time and other resources should we devote to building housing, how much to the production of food, and how much to providing other goods and services? What techniques should we use to produce each good? Who should be assigned to each specific task? And how should the resulting goods and services be distributed among people?

In the thousands of different societies for which records are available, issues like these have been decided in essentially one of two ways. One approach is for all economic decisions to be made centrally, by an individual or small number of individuals on behalf of a larger group. For example, in many agrarian societies throughout history, families or other small groups consumed only those goods and services that they produced for themselves, and a single clan or family leader made most important production and distribution decisions. On an immensely larger scale, the economic organization of the former Soviet Union (and other communist countries) was also largely centralized. In so-called centrally planned communist nations, a central bureaucratic committee established production targets for the country's farms and factories, developed a master plan for how to achieve the targets (including detailed instructions concerning who was to produce what), and set up guidelines for the distribution and use of the goods and services produced.

Neither form of centralized economic organization is much in evidence today. When implemented on a small scale, as in a self-sufficient family enterprise, centralized decision making is certainly feasible. For the reasons discussed in the preceding chapter, however, the jack-of-all-trades approach was doomed once it became clear how dramatically people could improve their living standards by specialization—that is, by having each individual focus his or her efforts on a relatively narrow range of tasks. And with the fall of the Soviet Union and its satellite nations in the late 1980s, there are now only three communist economies left in the world: Cuba, North Korea, and China. The first two of these appear to be on their last legs, economically speaking, and China has by now largely abandoned any attempt to control production and distribution decisions from the center. The major remaining examples of centralized allocation and control now reside in the bureaucratic agencies that administer programs like New York City's rent controls—programs that are themselves becoming increasingly rare.

At the beginning of the twenty-first century we are therefore left, for the most part, with the second major form of economic system, one in which production and distribution decisions are left to individuals interacting in private markets. In the so-called capitalist, or free-market, economies, people decide for themselves which careers to pursue and which products to produce or buy. In fact, there are no *pure* free-market economies today. Modern industrial countries are more properly described as "mixed economies," meaning that goods and services are allocated by a combination of free markets, regulation, and other forms of collective control. Still, it makes sense to refer to such systems as free-market economies, because people are for the most part free to start businesses, to shut them down, or to sell them. And within broad limits, the distribution of goods and services is determined by individual preferences backed by individual purchasing power, which in most cases comes from the income people earn in the labor market.

In country after country, markets have replaced centralized control for the simple reason that they tend to assign production tasks and consumption benefits much more effectively. The popular press, and the conventional wisdom, often asserts that economists disagree about important issues. (As someone once quipped, "If you lay all the economists in the world end to end, they still wouldn't reach a conclusion.") The fact is, however, that there is overwhelming agreement among economists about a broad range of issues, with the great majority accepting the efficacy of markets as means for allocating society's scarce resources. For example, a recent survey found that more than 90 percent of American professional economists believe that rent regulations like the ones implemented by New York City do more harm than good. That the stated aim of these regulations—to make rental housing more affordable for middle- and low-income families—is clearly benign was not enough to prevent them from wreaking havoc on New York City's housing market. To see why, we must explore how goods and services are allocated in private markets, and why nonmarket means of allocating goods and services often do not produce the expected results.

market the market for any good consists of all buyers or sellers of that good

Why do Pablo Picasso's paintings sell for so much more than Jackson Pollock's?

BUYERS AND SELLERS IN MARKETS

Beginning with some simple concepts and definitions, we will explore how the interactions among buyers and sellers in markets determine the prices and quantities of the various goods and services traded in those markets. We begin by defining a market: The **market** for any good consists of all the buyers and sellers of that good. So, for example, the market for pizza on a given day in a given place is just the set of people (or other economic actors, such as firms) potentially able to buy or sell pizza at that time and location.

In the market for pizza, sellers comprise the individuals and companies that either do sell—or might, under the right circumstances, sell—pizza. Similarly, buyers in this market include all individuals who buy—or might buy—pizza.

In most parts of the country, a decent pizza—or some other life-sustaining meal—can still be had for less than $10. Where does the market price of pizza come from? Looking beyond pizza to the vast array of other goods that are bought and sold every day, we may ask, "Why are some goods cheap and others expensive?" Aristotle had no idea. Nor did Plato, or Copernicus, or Newton. On reflection, it is astonishing that, for almost the entire span of human history, not even the most intelligent and creative minds on Earth had any real inkling of how to answer that seemingly simple question. Even Adam Smith, the Scottish moral philosopher whose *Wealth of Nations* launched the discipline of economics in 1776, suffered confusion on this issue.

Smith and other early economists (including Karl Marx) thought that the market price of a good was determined by its cost of production. But although costs surely do affect prices, they cannot explain why one of Pablo Picasso's paintings sells for so much more than one of Jackson Pollock's.

Stanley Jevons and other nineteenth-century economists tried to explain price by focusing on the value people derived from consuming different goods and services. It certainly seems plausible that people will pay a lot for a good they value highly. Yet willingness to pay cannot be the whole story, either. Deprive a person in the desert of water, for example, and he will be dead in a matter of hours, and yet water sells for less than a penny a gallon. By contrast, human beings can get along perfectly well without gold, and yet gold sells for more than $400 an ounce.

Cost of production? Value to the user? Which is it? The answer, which seems obvious to today's economists, is that both matter. Writing in the late nineteenth century, the British economist Alfred Marshall was among the first to show clearly how costs and value interact to determine both the prevailing market price for a good and the amount of it that is bought and sold. Our task in the pages ahead will be to explore Marshall's insights and gain some practice in applying them. As a first step, we introduce the two main components of Marshall's pathbreaking analysis: the demand curve and the supply curve.

THE DEMAND CURVE

In the market for pizza, the **demand curve** for pizza is a simple schedule or graph that tells us how many slices people would be willing to buy at different prices. By convention, economists usually put price on the vertical axis of the demand curve and quantity on the horizontal axis.

A fundamental property of the demand curve is that it is downward-sloping with respect to price. For example, the demand curve for pizza tells us that as the price of pizza falls, buyers will buy more slices. Thus, the daily demand curve for pizza in Chicago on a given day might look like the curve seen in Figure 3.1. (Although economists usually refer to demand and supply "curves," we often draw them as straight lines in examples.)

The demand curve in Figure 3.1 tells us that when the price of pizza is low—say $2 per slice—buyers will want to buy 16,000 slices per day, whereas they will want to buy only 12,000 slices at a price of $3, and only 8,000 at a price of $4. The demand curve for pizza—as for any other good—slopes downward for multiple reasons. Some of these reasons have to do with the individual consumer's reactions to price changes. Thus, as pizza becomes more expensive, a consumer may switch to chicken sandwiches, hamburgers, or other foods that substitute for pizza. This is called the **substitution effect** of a price change. In addition, a price increase reduces the quantity demanded because it reduces purchasing power: A consumer simply can't afford to buy as many slices of pizza at higher prices as at lower prices. This is called the **income effect** of a price change.

Another reason that the demand curve slopes downward is that consumers differ in terms of how much they are willing to pay for the good. The cost-benefit principle tells us that a given person will buy the good if the benefit he expects to

demand curve a schedule or graph showing the quantity of a good that buyers wish to buy at each price

substitution effect the change in the quantity demanded of a good that results because buyers switch to or from substitutes when the price of the good changes

income effect the change in the quantity demanded of a good that results because a change in the price of a good changes the buyer's purchasing power

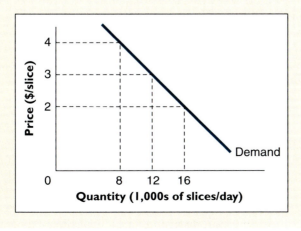

FIGURE 3.1
The Daily Demand Curve for Pizza in Chicago.
The demand curve for any good is a downward-sloping function of its price.

buyer's reservation price the largest dollar amount the buyer would be willing to pay for a good

receive from it exceeds its cost. The benefit is the **buyer's reservation price,** the highest dollar amount he would be willing to pay for the good. The cost of the good is the actual amount that the buyer actually must pay for it, which is the market price of the good. In most markets, different buyers have different reservation prices. Thus, when the good sells for a high price, it will satisfy the cost-benefit test for fewer buyers than when it sells for a lower price.

To put this same point another way, the fact that the demand curve for a good is downward-sloping reflects the fact that the reservation price of the marginal buyer declines as the quantity of the good bought increases. Here the marginal buyer is the person who purchases the last unit of the good that is sold. If buyers are currently purchasing 12,000 slices of pizza a day in Figure 3.1, for example, the reservation price for the buyer of the 12,000th slice must be $3. (If someone had been willing to pay more than that, the quantity demanded at a price of $3 would have been more than 12,000 to begin with.) By similar reasoning, when the quantity sold is 16,000 slices per day, the marginal buyer's reservation price must be only $2.

We defined the demand curve for any good as a schedule telling how much of it consumers wish to purchase at various prices. This is called the *horizontal interpretation* of the demand curve. Using the horizontal interpretation, we start with price on the vertical axis and read the corresponding quantity demanded on the horizontal axis. Thus, at a price of $4 per slice, the demand curve in Figure 3.1 tells us that the quantity of pizza demanded will be 8,000 slices per day.

The demand curve also can be interpreted in a second way, which is to start with quantity on the horizontal axis and then read the marginal buyer's reservation price on the vertical axis. Thus, when the quantity of pizza sold is 8,000 slices per day, the demand curve in Figure 3.1 tells us that the marginal buyer's reservation price is $4 per slice. This second way of reading the demand curve is called the *vertical interpretation*.

EXERCISE 3.1

In Figure 3.1, what is the marginal buyer's reservation price when the quantity of pizza sold is 10,000 slices per day? For the same demand curve, what will be the quantity of pizza demanded at a price of $2.50 per slice?

THE SUPPLY CURVE

supply curve a graph or schedule showing the quantity of a good that sellers wish to sell at each price

In the market for pizza, the **supply curve** is a simple schedule or graph that tells us, for each possible price, the total number of slices that all pizza vendors would be willing to sell at that price. What does the supply curve of pizza look like? The answer to this question is based on the logical assumption that suppliers should be willing to sell additional slices as long as the price they receive is sufficient to cover their opportunity costs of supplying them. Thus, if what someone could earn by selling a slice of pizza is insufficient to compensate her for what she could have earned if she had spent her time and invested her money in some other way, she will not sell that slice. Otherwise, she will.

Just as buyers differ with respect to the amounts they are willing to pay for pizza, sellers also differ with respect to their opportunity costs of supplying pizza. For those with limited education and work experience, the opportunity cost of selling pizza is relatively low (because such individuals typically do not have a lot of high-paying alternatives). For others, the opportunity cost of selling pizza is of moderate value, and for still others—like rock stars and professional athletes—it is prohibitively high. In part because of these differences in opportunity cost among people, the daily supply curve of pizza will be *upward-sloping* with respect to price. As an illustration, see Figure 3.2, which shows a hypothetical supply curve for pizza in the Chicago market on a given day.

The fact that the supply curve slopes upward may be seen as a consequence of the low-hanging-fruit principle, discussed in the preceding chapter. This principle

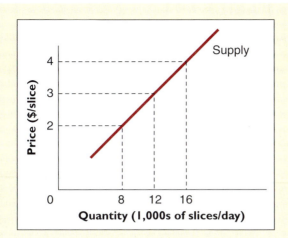

FIGURE 3.2
**The Daily Supply Curve
of Pizza in Chicago.**
At higher prices, sellers
generally offer more units
for sale.

tells us that as we expand the production of pizza, we turn first to those whose opportunity costs of producing pizza are lowest, and only then to others with higher opportunity costs.

Like the demand curve, the supply curve can be interpreted either horizontally or vertically. Under the horizontal interpretation, we begin with a price, then go over to the supply curve to read the quantity that sellers wish to sell at that price on the horizontal axis. For instance, at a price of $2 per slice, sellers in Figure 3.2 wish to sell 8,000 slices per day.

Under the vertical interpretation, we begin with a quantity, then go up to the supply curve to read the corresponding marginal cost on the vertical axis. Thus, if sellers in Figure 3.2 are currently supplying 12,000 slices per day, the opportunity cost of the marginal seller is $3 per slice. In other words, the supply curve tells us that the marginal cost of producing the 12,000th slice of pizza is $3. (If someone could produce a 12,001st slice for less than $3, she would have an incentive to supply it, so the quantity of pizza supplied at $3 per slice would not have been 12,000 slices per day to begin with.) By similar reasoning, when the quantity of pizza supplied is 16,000 slices per day, the marginal cost of producing another slice must be $4. The **seller's reservation price** for selling an additional unit of a good is her marginal cost of producing that good. It is the smallest dollar amount for which she would not be worse off if she sold an additional unit.

seller's reservation price the smallest dollar amount for which a seller would be willing to sell an additional unit, generally equal to marginal cost

EXERCISE 3.2

In Figure 3.2, what is the marginal cost of a slice of pizza when the quantity of pizza sold is 10,000 slices per day? For the same supply curve, what will be the quantity of pizza supplied at a price of $3.50 per slice?

RECAP	DEMAND AND SUPPLY CURVES

The *market* for a good consists of the actual and potential buyers and sellers of that good. For any given price, the *demand curve* shows the quantity that demanders would be willing to buy, and the *supply curve* shows the quantity that suppliers of the good would be willing to sell. Suppliers are willing to sell more at higher prices (supply curves slope upward) and demanders are willing to buy less at higher prices (demand curves slope downward).

MARKET EQUILIBRIUM

equilibrium a system is in equilibrium when there is no tendency for it to change

The concept of **equilibrium** is employed in both the physical and social sciences, and it is of central importance in economic analysis. In general, a system is in equilibrium when all forces at work within the system are canceled by others, resulting in a balanced or unchanging situation. In physics, for example, a ball hanging from a spring is said to be in equilibrium when the spring has stretched sufficiently that the upward force it exerts on the ball is exactly counterbalanced by the downward force of gravity. In economics, a market is said to be in equilibrium when no participant in the market has any reason to alter his or her behavior, so that there is no tendency for production or prices in that market to change.

equilibrium price and **equilibrium quantity** the values of price and quantity for which quantity supplied and quantity demanded are equal

If we want to determine the final position of a ball hanging from a spring, we need to find the point at which the forces of gravity and spring tension are balanced and the system is in equilibrium. Similarly, if we want to find the price at which a good will sell (which we will call the **equilibrium price**) and the quantity of it that will be sold (the **equilibrium quantity**), we need to find the equilibrium in the market for that good. The basic tools for finding the equilibrium in a market for a good are the supply and demand curves for that good. For reasons that we will explain, the equilibrium price and equilibrium quantity of a good are the price and quantity at which the supply and demand curves for the good intersect. For the hypothetical supply and demand curves shown earlier for the pizza market in Chicago, the equilibrium price will therefore be $3 per slice, and the equilibrium quantity of pizza sold will be 12,000 slices per day, as shown in Figure 3.3.

In Figure 3.3, note that at the equilibrium price of $3 per slice, both sellers and buyers are "satisfied" in the following sense: Buyers are buying exactly the quantity of pizza they wish to buy at that price (12,000 slices per day) and sellers are selling exactly the quantity of pizza they wish to sell (also 12,000 slices per day). And since they are satisfied in this sense, neither buyers nor sellers face any incentives to change their behavior.

market equilibrium occurs in a market when all buyers and sellers are satisfied with their respective quantities at the market price

Note the limited sense of the term "satisfied" in the definition of **market equilibrium**. It doesn't mean that sellers would not be pleased to receive a price higher than the equilibrium price. Rather, it means only that they're able to sell all they wish to sell at that price. Similarly, to say that buyers are satisfied at the equilibrium price doesn't mean that they would not be happy to pay less than the equilibrium price. Rather, it means only that they're able to buy exactly as many units of the good as they wish to at the equilibrium price.

Note also that if the price of pizza in our Chicago market were anything other than $3 per slice, either buyers or sellers would be frustrated. Suppose, for example, that the price of pizza were $4 per slice, as shown in Figure 3.4. At that price, buyers wish to buy only 8,000 slices per day, but sellers wish to sell 16,000. And since no one can force someone to buy a slice of pizza against her wishes, this means that

FIGURE 3.3
The Equilibrium Price and Quantity of Pizza in Chicago.
The equilibrium quantity and price of a product are the values that correspond to the intersection of the supply and demand curves for that product.

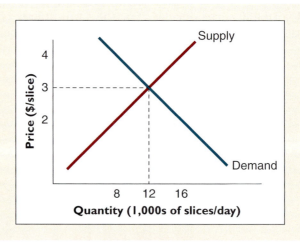

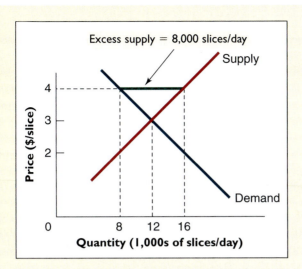

FIGURE 3.4

Excess Supply.
When price exceeds the
equilibrium price, there is
excess supply, or surplus,
the difference between
quantity supplied and
quantity demanded.

buyers will buy only the 8,000 slices they wish to buy. So when the price exceeds
the equilibrium price, it is sellers who end up being frustrated. At a price of $4 in
this example, they are left with an **excess supply** of 8,000 slices per day.

Conversely, suppose that the price of pizza in our Chicago market were less
than the equilibrium price—say, $2 per slice. As shown in Figure 3.5, buyers want
to buy 16,000 slices per day at that price, whereas sellers want to sell only 8,000.
And since sellers cannot be forced to sell pizza against their wishes, this time it is the
buyers who end up being frustrated. At a price of $2 per slice in this example, they
experience an **excess demand** of 8,000 slices per day.

An extraordinary feature of private markets for goods and services is their automatic tendency to gravitate toward their respective equilibrium prices and quantities.
This tendency is a simple consequence of the incentive principle. The mechanisms by
which the adjustment happens are implicit in our definitions of excess supply and excess demand. Suppose, for example, that the price of pizza in our hypothetical market
was $4 per slice, leading to excess supply as shown in Figure 3.4. Because sellers are
frustrated in the sense of wanting to sell more pizza than buyers wish to buy, sellers
have an incentive to take whatever steps they can to increase their sales. The simplest
strategy available to them is to cut their price slightly. Thus, if one seller reduced his
price from $4 to, say, $3.95 per slice, he would attract many of the buyers who had
been paying $4 per slice for pizza supplied by other sellers. Those sellers, in order to
recover their lost business, would then have an incentive to match the price cut. But

excess supply the amount by
which quantity supplied exceeds
quantity demanded when the
price of a good exceeds the
equilibrium price

excess demand the amount by
which quantity demanded
exceeds quantity supplied when
the price of a good lies below
the equilibrium price

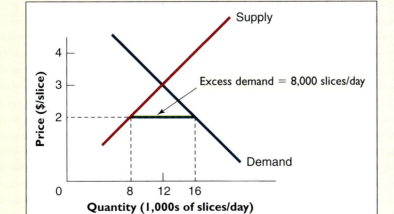

FIGURE 3.5

Excess Demand.
When price lies below the
equilibrium price, there is
excess demand, the difference
between quantity demanded
and quantity supplied.

notice that if all sellers lowered their prices to $3.95 per slice, there would still be considerable excess supply. So sellers would face continuing incentives to cut their prices. This pressure to cut prices will not go away until price falls all the way to $3 per slice.

Conversely, suppose that price starts out less than the equilibrium price—say, $2 per slice. This time it is buyers who are frustrated. A person who can't get all the pizza he wants at a price of $2 per slice has an incentive to offer a higher price, hoping to obtain pizza that would otherwise have been sold to other buyers. And sellers, for their part, will be only too happy to post higher prices as long as queues of frustrated buyers remain.

The upshot is that price has a tendency to gravitate to its equilibrium level under conditions of either excess supply or excess demand. And when price reaches its equilibrium level, both buyers and sellers are satisfied in the technical sense of being able to buy or sell precisely the amounts of their choosing.

EXAMPLE 3.1

Samples of points on the demand and supply curves of a pizza market are provided in Table 3.1. Graph the demand and supply curves for this market, and find its equilibrium price and quantity.

TABLE 3.1
Points along the Demand and Supply Curves of a Pizza Market

Demand for Pizza		Supply of Pizza	
Price ($/slice)	Quantity demanded (1,000s of slices/day)	Price ($/slice)	Quantity supplied (1,000s of slices/day)
1	8	1	2
2	6	2	4
3	4	3	6
4	2	4	8

The points in the table are plotted in Figure 3.6. and then joined to indicate the supply and demand curves for this market. These curves intersect to yield an equilibrium price of $2.50 per slice and an equilibrium quantity of 5,000 slices per day.

FIGURE 3.6
Graphing Supply and Demand and Finding the Equilibrium Price and Quantity.
To graph the demand and supply curves, plot the relevant points given in the table and then join them with a line. The equilibrium price and quantity occur at the intersection of these curves.

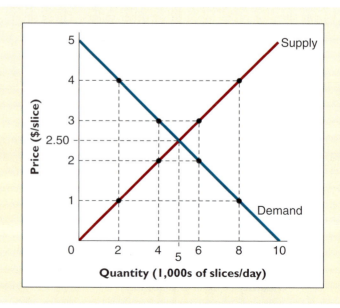

We emphasize that market equilibrium does not necessarily produce an ideal outcome for all market participants. Thus, in the example just considered, market participants are satisfied with the amount of pizza they buy and sell at a price of $2.50 per slice, but for a poor buyer this may signify little more than that he *can't* buy additional pizza without sacrificing other more highly valued purchases.

Indeed, buyers with extremely low incomes often have difficulty purchasing even basic goods and services, which has prompted governments in almost every society to attempt to ease the burdens of the poor. Yet the laws of supply and demand cannot simply be repealed by an act of the legislature. In the next section we will see that when legislators attempt to prevent markets from reaching their equilibrium prices and quantities, they often do more harm than good.

RENT CONTROLS RECONSIDERED

Consider again the market for rental housing units in New York City, and suppose that the demand and supply curves for one-bedroom apartments are as shown in Figure 3.7. This market, left alone, would reach an equilibrium monthly rent of $1,600, at which 2 million one-bedroom apartments would be rented. Both landlords and tenants would be satisfied, in the sense that they would not wish to rent either more or fewer units at that price.

This would not necessarily mean, of course, that all is well and good. Many potential tenants, for example, might simply be unable to afford a rent of $1,600 per month and thus be forced to remain homeless (or to move out of the city to a cheaper location). Suppose that, acting purely out of benign motives, legislators made it unlawful for landlords to charge more than $800 per month for one-bedroom apartments. Their stated aim in enacting this law was that no person should have to remain homeless because decent housing was unaffordable.

But note in Figure 3.8 that when rents for one-bedroom apartments are prevented from rising above $800 per month, landlords are willing to supply only 1 million apartments per month, 1 million fewer than at the equilibrium monthly rent of $1,600. Note also that at the controlled rent of $800 per month, tenants want to rent 3 million one-bedroom apartments per month. (For example, many people who would have decided to live in New Jersey rather than pay $1,600 a month in New York will now choose to live in the city.) So when rents are prevented from rising above $800 per month, we see an excess demand for one-bedroom apartments of 2 million units each month. Put another way, the rent controls result in a housing shortage of 2 million units each month. What is more, the number of apartments actually available *declines* by 1 million units per month.

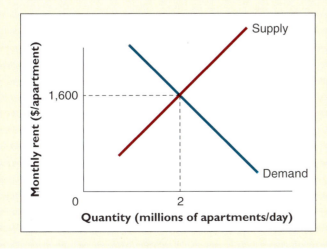

FIGURE 3.7
An Unregulated Housing Market.
For the supply and demand curves shown, the equilibrium monthly rent is $1,600, and 2 million apartments will be rented at that price.

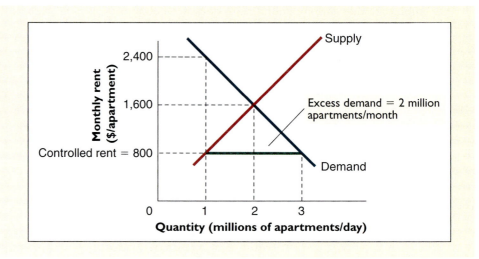

FIGURE 3.8
Rent Controls.
When rents are prohibited
from rising to the equilibrium
level, the result is excess
demand in the housing
market.

If the housing market were completely unregulated, the immediate response to such a high level of excess demand would be for rents to rise sharply. But here the law prevents them from rising above $800. Many other ways exist, however, in which the pressures of excess demand can make themselves felt. For instance, owners will quickly learn that they are free to spend less on maintaining the quality of their rental units. After all, if there are scores of renters knocking at the door of each vacant apartment, a landlord has considerable room to maneuver. Leaking pipes, peeling paint, broken furnaces, and other problems are less likely to receive prompt attention—or, indeed, any attention at all—when rents are set well below market-clearing levels.

Nor are reduced availability of apartments and poorer maintenance of existing apartments the only difficulties. With an offering of only 1 million apartments per month, we see in Figure 3.8 that there are renters who would be willing to pay as much as $2,400 per month for an apartment. As the incentive principle suggests, this pressure will almost always find ways, legal or illegal, of expressing itself. In New York City, for example, it is not uncommon to see "finder's fees" or "key deposits" as high as several thousand dollars. Owners who cannot charge a market-clearing rent for their apartments also have the option of converting them to condominiums or co-ops, which enables them to sell their assets for prices much closer to their true economic value.

Even when rent-controlled apartment owners do not hike their prices in these various ways, serious misallocations result. For instance, ill-suited roommates often remain together despite their constant bickering, because each is reluctant to reenter the housing market. Or a widow might steadfastly remain in her seven-room apartment even after her children have left home, because it is much cheaper than alternative dwellings not covered by rent control. It would be much better for all concerned if she relinquished that space to a larger family that valued it more highly. But under rent controls, she has no economic incentive to do so.

There is also another more insidious cost of rent controls. In markets without rent controls, landlords cannot discriminate against potential tenants on the basis of race, religion, sexual orientation, physical disability, or national origin without suffering an economic penalty. Refusal to rent to members of specific groups would reduce the demand for their apartments, which would mean having to accept lower rents. When rents are artificially pegged below their equilibrium level, however, the resulting excess demand for apartments enables landlords to engage in discrimination with no further economic penalty.

Rent controls are not the only instance in which governments have attempted to repeal the law of supply and demand in the interest of helping the poor. During

*"If you leave me, you know, you'll
never see this kind of rent again"*

the late 1970s, for example, the federal government tried to hold the price of gasoline below its equilibrium level out of concern that high gasoline prices imposed unacceptable hardships on low-income drivers. As with controls in the rental housing market, unintended consequences of price controls in the gasoline market made the policy an extremely costly way of trying to aid the poor. For example, gasoline shortages resulted in long lines at the pumps, a waste not only of valuable time, but also of gasoline as cars sat idling for extended periods.

In their opposition to rent controls and similar measures, are economists revealing a total lack of concern for the poor? Although this claim is sometimes made by those who don't understand the issues, or who stand to benefit in some way from government regulations, there is little justification for it. *Economists simply realize that there are much more effective ways to help poor people than to try to give them apartments and other goods at artificially low prices.*

One straightforward approach would be to give the poor additional income and let them decide for themselves how to spend it. True, there are also practical difficulties involved in transferring additional purchasing power into the hands of the poor—most importantly, the difficulty of targeting cash to the genuinely needy without weakening others' incentives to fend for themselves. But there are practical ways to overcome this difficulty. For example, for far less than the waste caused by price controls, the government could afford generous subsidies to the wages of the working poor and could sponsor public-service employment for those who are unable to find jobs in the private sector.

Regulations that peg prices below equilibrium levels have far-reaching effects on market outcomes. The following exercise asks you to consider what happens when a price control is established at a level above the equilibrium price.

EXERCISE 3.3

In the rental housing market whose demand and supply curves are shown below, what will be the effect of a law that prevents rents from rising above $1,200 per month?

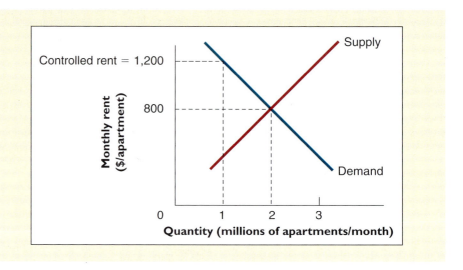

PIZZA PRICE CONTROLS?

The sources of the contrast between the rent-controlled housing market and the largely unregulated food markets in New York City can be seen more vividly by trying to imagine what would happen if concern for the poor led the city's leaders to implement price controls on pizza. Suppose, for example, that the supply and demand curves for pizza are as shown in Figure 3.9, and that the city imposes a **price ceiling** of $2 per slice, making it unlawful to charge more than that amount. At $2 per slice, buyers want to buy 16,000 slices per day, but sellers want to sell only 8,000.

At a price of $2 per slice, every pizza restaurant in the city will have long queues of buyers trying unsuccessfully to purchase pizza. Frustrated buyers will behave rudely to clerks, who will respond in kind. Friends of restaurant managers will begin to get preferential treatment. Devious pricing strategies will begin to

price ceiling a maximum allowable price, specified by law

FIGURE 3.9
Price Controls in the Pizza Market.
A price ceiling below the equilibrium price of pizza would result in excess demand for pizza.

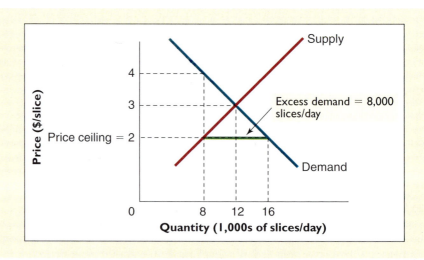

emerge (such as the $2 slice of pizza sold in combination with a $5 cup of Coke). Pizza will be made from poorer-quality ingredients. Rumors will begin to circulate about sources of black-market pizza. And so on.

The very idea of not being able to buy a pizza seems absurd, yet precisely such things happen routinely in markets in which prices are held below the equilibrium levels. For example, prior to the collapse of communist governments, it was considered normal in those countries for people to stand in line for hours to buy basic goods, while the politically connected had first choice of those goods that were available.

RECAP	MARKET EQUILIBRIUM

Market equilibrium, the situation in which all buyers and sellers are satisfied with their respective quantities at the market price, occurs at the intersection of the supply and demand curves. The corresponding price and quantity are called the *equilibrium price* and the *equilibrium quantity.*

Unless prevented by regulation, prices and quantities are driven toward their equilibrium values by the actions of buyers and sellers. If the price is initially too high, so that there is excess supply, frustrated sellers will cut their price in order to sell more. If the price is initially too low, so that there is excess demand, competition among buyers drives the price upward. This process continues until equilibrium is reached.

PREDICTING AND EXPLAINING CHANGES IN PRICES AND QUANTITIES

If we know how the factors that govern supply and demand curves are changing, we can make informed predictions about how prices and the corresponding quantities will change. But when describing changing circumstances in the marketplace, we must take care to recognize some important terminological distinctions. For example, we must distinguish between the meanings of the seemingly similar expressions **change in the quantity demanded** and **change in demand**. When we speak of a "change in the quantity demanded," this means the change in the quantity that people wish to buy that occurs in response to a change in price. For instance, Figure 3.10(a) depicts an increase in the quantity demanded that occurs in response to

change in the quantity demanded a movement along the demand curve that occurs in response to a change in price

change in demand a shift of the entire demand curve

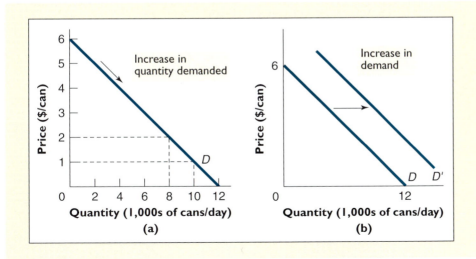

FIGURE 3.10

An Increase in the Quantity Demanded versus an Increase in Demand.
(a) An increase in quantity demanded describes a downward movement along the demand curve as price falls. (b) An increase in demand describes an outward shift of the demand curve.

a reduction in the price of tuna. When the price falls from $2 to $1 per can, the quantity demanded rises from 8,000 to 10,000 cans per day. By contrast, when we speak of a "change in demand," this means a *shift in the entire demand curve*. For example, Figure 3.10(b) depicts an increase in demand, meaning that at every price the quantity demanded is higher than before. In summary, a "change in the quantity demanded" refers to a movement *along* the demand curve, and a "change in demand" means a *shift* of the entire curve.

A similar terminological distinction applies on the supply side of the market. A **change in supply** means a shift in the entire supply curve, whereas a **change in the quantity supplied** refers to a movement along the supply curve.

Alfred Marshall's supply and demand model is one of the most useful tools of the economic naturalist. Once we understand the forces that govern the placements of supply and demand curves, we are suddenly in a position to make sense of a host of interesting observations in the world around us.

> *change in supply* a shift of the entire supply curve
>
> *change in the quantity supplied* a movement along the supply curve that occurs in response to a change in price

SHIFTS IN DEMAND

To get a better feel for how the supply and demand model enables us to predict and explain price and quantity movements, it is helpful to begin with a few simple examples. The first one illustrates a shift in demand that results from events outside the particular market itself.

EXAMPLE 3.2

What will happen to the equilibrium price and quantity of tennis balls if court rental fees decline?

> *complements* two goods are complements in consumption if an increase in the price of one causes a leftward shift in the demand curve for the other (or if a decrease causes a rightward shift)

Let the initial supply and demand curves for tennis balls be as shown by the curves *S* and *D* in Figure 3.11, where the resulting equilibrium price and quantity are $1 per ball and 40 million balls per month, respectively. Tennis courts and tennis balls are what economists call **complements**, goods that are more valuable when used in combination than when used alone. Tennis balls, for example, would be of little value if there were no tennis courts on which to play. (Tennis balls would still have *some* value even without courts—for example, to the parents who pitch them to their children for batting practice.) As tennis courts become cheaper to use, people will respond by playing more tennis, and this will increase their demand for tennis balls. A decline in court-rental fees will thus shift the demand curve for tennis balls rightward to *D'*. (A "rightward shift" of a demand curve also can be described as an "upward shift." These distinctions correspond, respectively, to the horizontal and vertical interpretations of the demand curve.)

FIGURE 3.11
The Effect on the Market for Tennis Balls of a Decline in Court-Rental Fees.
When the price of a complement falls, demand shifts right, causing equilibrium price and quantity to rise.

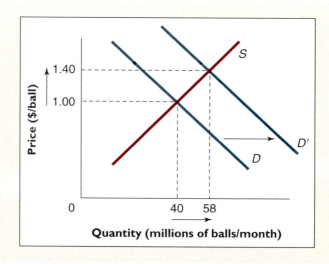

Note in Figure 3.11 that for the illustrative demand shift shown, the new equilibrium price of tennis balls, $1.40, is higher than the original price, and the new equilibrium quantity, 58 million balls per month, is higher than the original quantity.

What will happen to the equilibrium price and quantity of overnight letter delivery service as the price of Internet access falls?

Suppose the initial supply and demand curves for overnight letter deliveries are as shown by the curves S and D in Figure 3.12, and that the resulting equilibrium price and quantity are denoted P and Q. E-mail messages and overnight letters are examples of what economists call **substitutes**, meaning that, in many applications at least, the two serve similar functions for people. (Many noneconomists would call them substitutes, too. Economists don't *always* choose obscure terms for important concepts!) When two goods or services are substitutes, a decrease in the price of one will cause a leftward shift in the demand curve for the other. (A "leftward shift" in

EXAMPLE 3.3

substitutes two goods are substitutes in consumption if an increase in the price of one causes a rightward shift in the demand curve for the other (or if a decrease causes a leftward shift).

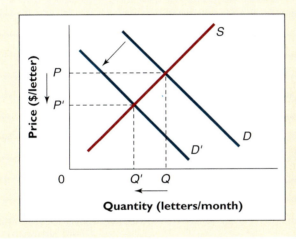

FIGURE 3.12
The Effect on the Market for Overnight Letter Delivery of a Decline in the Price of Internet Access.
When the price of a substitute falls, demand shifts left, causing equilibrium price and quantity to fall.

a demand curve can also be described as a "downward shift.") Diagrammatically, the demand curve for overnight delivery service shifts from D to D' in Figure 3.12.

As the figure shows, both the new equilibrium price, P', and the new equilibrium quantity, Q', are lower than the initial values, P and Q. Cheaper Internet access probably won't put Federal Express and UPS out of business, but it will definitely cost them many customers.

To summarize, economists define goods as substitutes if an increase in the price of one causes a rightward shift in the demand curve for the other. By contrast, goods are complements if an increase in the price of one causes a leftward shift in the demand curve for the other.

The concepts of substitutes and complements enable you to answer questions like the one posed in the following exercise.

EXERCISE 3.4

How will a decline in airfares affect intercity bus fares and the price of hotel rooms in resort communities?

Demand curves are shifted not just by changes in the prices of substitutes and complements but also by other factors that change the amounts that people are willing to pay for a given good or service. One of the most important such factors is income.

ECONOMIC NATURALIST 3.1

Who gets to live in the most conveniently located apartments?

When the federal government implements a large pay increase for its employees, why do rents for apartments located near Washington Metro stations go up relative to rents for apartments located far away from Metro stations?

For the citizens of Washington, D.C., a substantial proportion of whom are government employees, it is more convenient to live in an apartment located one block from the nearest subway station than to live in one that is 20 blocks away. Conveniently located apartments thus command relatively high rents. Suppose the initial demand and supply curves for such apartments are as shown in Figure 3.13. Following a federal pay raise, some government employees who live in less convenient apartments will be willing and able to use part of their extra income to bid for more conveniently located apartments, and those who already live in such apartments will be willing and able to pay more to keep them. The effect of the pay raise is thus to shift the demand curve for conveniently located apartments to the right, as indicated by the demand curve labeled D' in Figure 3.13. As a result, both the equilibrium price and quantity of such apartments, P' and Q', will be higher than before.

FIGURE 3.13
The Effect of a Federal Pay Raise on the Rent for Conveniently Located Apartments in Washington, D.C.
An increase in income shifts demand for a normal good to the right, causing equilibrium price and quantity to rise.

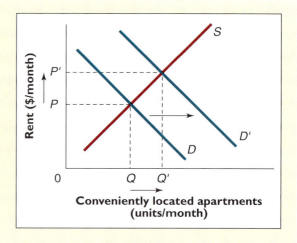

It might seem natural to ask how there could be an increase in the number of conveniently located apartments, which might appear to be fixed by the constraints of geography. But the incentive principle reminds us never to underestimate the ingenuity of sellers when they confront an opportunity to make money by supplying more of something that people want. For example, if rents rose sufficiently, some landlords might respond by converting warehouse space to residential use. Or perhaps people with cars who do not place high value on living near a subway station might sell their apartments to landlords, thereby freeing them for people eager to rent them. (Note that these responses constitute movements along the supply curve of conveniently located apartments, as opposed to shifts in that supply curve.)

When incomes increase, the demand curves for most goods will behave like the demand curve for conveniently located apartments, and in recognition of that fact, economists have chosen to call such goods **normal goods.**

Not all goods are normal goods, however. In fact, the demand curves for some goods actually shift leftward when income goes up; such goods are called **inferior goods.**

When would having more money tend to make you want to buy less of something? In general, this will happen in the case of goods for which there exist attractive substitutes that sell for only slightly higher prices. Apartments in an unsafe, inconveniently located neighborhood are an example. Most residents would

normal good one whose demand curve shifts rightward when the incomes of buyers increase and leftward when the incomes of buyers decrease

inferior good one whose demand curve shifts leftward when the incomes of buyers increase and rightward when the incomes of buyers decrease

choose to move out of such neighborhoods as soon as they could afford to, which means that an increase in income would cause the demand for such apartments to shift leftward.

EXERCISE 3.5

How will a large pay increase for federal employees affect the rents for apartments located far away from Washington Metro stations?

Ground beef with high fat content is another example of an inferior good. For health reasons, most people prefer grades of meat with low fat content, and when they do buy high-fat meats it is usually a sign of budgetary pressure. When people in this situation receive higher incomes, they usually switch quickly to leaner grades of meat.

Preferences, or tastes, are another important factor that determines whether a given good will meet the cost-benefit test. Steven Spielberg's film *Jurassic Park* appeared to kindle a powerful, if previously latent, preference among children for toy dinosaurs. When this film was first released, the demand for such toys shifted sharply to the right. And the same children who couldn't find enough dinosaur toys suddenly seemed to lose interest in toy designs involving horses and other present-day animals, whose respective demand curves shifted sharply to the left.

Expectations about the future are another factor that may cause demand curves to shift. If Apple Macintosh users hear a credible rumor, for example, that a cheaper or significantly upgraded model will be introduced next month, the demand curve for the current model is likely to shift leftward.

SHIFTS IN THE SUPPLY CURVE

The preceding examples involved changes that gave rise to shifts in demand curves. Next, we'll look at what happens when supply curves shift. Because the supply curve is based on costs of production, anything that changes production costs will shift the supply curve, and hence will result in a new equilibrium quantity and price.

What will happen to the equilibrium price and quantity of skateboards if the price of fiberglass, a substance used for making skateboards, rises?

EXAMPLE 3.4

Suppose the initial supply and demand curves for skateboards are as shown by the curves *S* and *D* in Figure 3.14, resulting in an equilibrium price and quantity of

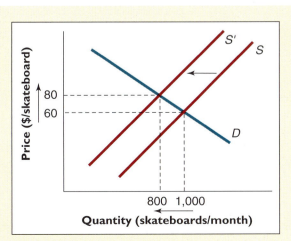

FIGURE 3.14

The Effect on the Skateboard Market of an Increase in the Price of Fiberglass.

When input prices rise, supply shifts left, causing equilibrium price to rise and equilibrium quantity to fall.

$60 per skateboard and 1,000 skateboards per month, respectively. Since fiberglass is one of the ingredients used to produce skateboards, the effect of an increase in the price of fiberglass is to raise the marginal cost of producing skateboards. How will this affect the supply curve of skateboards? Recall that the supply curve is upward-sloping because when the price of skateboards is low, only those potential sellers whose marginal cost of making skateboards is low can sell boards profitably, whereas at higher prices, those with higher marginal costs also can enter the market profitably (again, the low-hanging-fruit principle). So if the cost of one of the ingredients used to produce skateboards rises, the number of potential sellers who can profitably sell skateboards at any given price will fall. And this, in turn, implies a leftward shift in the supply curve for skateboards. Note that a "leftward shift" in a supply curve also can be viewed as an "upward shift" in the same curve. The first corresponds to the horizontal interpretation of the supply curve, while the second corresponds to the vertical interpretation. We will use these expressions to mean exactly the same thing. The new supply curve (after the price of fiberglass rises) is the curve labeled S' in Figure 3.14.

Does an increase in the cost of fiberglass have any effect on the demand curve for skateboards? The demand curve tells us how many skateboards buyers wish to purchase at each price. Any given buyer is willing to purchase a skateboard if his reservation price for it exceeds its market price. And since each buyer's reservation price, which is based on the benefits of owning a skateboard, does not depend on the price of fiberglass, there should be no shift in the demand curve for skateboards.

In Figure 3.14, we can now see what happens when the supply curve shifts leftward and the demand curve remains unchanged. For the illustrative supply curve shown, the new equilibrium price of skateboards, $80, is higher than the original price, and the new equilibrium quantity, 800 per month, is lower than the original quantity. (These new equilibrium values are merely illustrative. There is insufficient information provided in the example to determine their exact values.) People who don't place a value of at least $80 on owning a skateboard will choose to spend their money on something else.

The effects on equilibrium price and quantity run in the opposite direction whenever marginal costs of production decline, as illustrated in the next example.

EXAMPLE 3.5

What will happen to the equilibrium price and quantity of new houses if the wage rate of carpenters falls?

Suppose the initial supply and demand curves for new houses are as shown by the curves S and D in Figure 3.15, resulting in an equilibrium price of $120,000 per

FIGURE 3.15
The Effect on the Market for New Houses of a Decline in Carpenters' Wage Rates.
When input prices fall, supply shifts right, causing equilibrium price to fall and equilibrium quantity to rise.

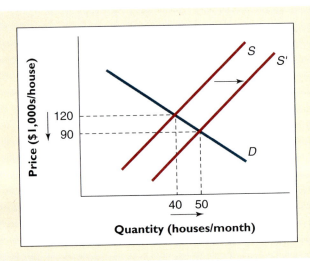

house and an equilibrium quantity of 40 houses per month. A decline in the wage rate of carpenters reduces the marginal cost of making new houses, and this means that, for any given price of houses, more builders can profitably serve the market than before. Diagrammatically, this means a rightward shift in the supply curve of houses, from S to S'. (A "rightward shift" in the supply curve also can be described as a "downward shift.")

Does a decrease in the wage rate of carpenters have any effect on the demand curve for houses? The demand curve tells us how many houses buyers wish to purchase at each price. Because carpenters are now earning less than before, the maximum amount that they are willing to pay for houses may fall, which would imply a leftward shift in the demand curve for houses. But because carpenters make up only a tiny fraction of all potential home buyers, we may assume that this shift is negligible. Thus, a reduction in carpenters' wages produces a significant rightward shift in the supply curve of houses, but no appreciable shift in the demand curve.

We see from Figure 3.15 that the new equilibrium price, $90,000 per house, is lower than the original price, and the new equilibrium quantity, 50 houses per month, is higher than the original quantity.

Both of the preceding examples involved changes in the cost of an ingredient, or input, in the production of the good in question—fiberglass in the production of skateboards and carpenters' labor in the production of houses. As the following example illustrates, supply curves also shift when technology changes.

Why do major term papers go through so many more revisions today than in the 1970s?

Students in the dark days before word processors were in widespread use could not make even minor revisions in their term papers without having to retype their entire manuscripts from scratch. The availability of word-processing technology has, of course, radically changed the picture. Instead of having to retype the entire draft, now only the changes need be entered.

In Figure 3.16, the curves labeled S and D depict the supply and demand curves for revisions in the days before word processing, and the curve S' depicts the supply curve for revisions today. As the diagram shows, the result is not only a sharp decline in the price per revision, but also a corresponding increase in the equilibrium number of revisions.

ECONOMIC NATURALIST 3.2

Why does written work go through so many more revisions now than in the 1970s?

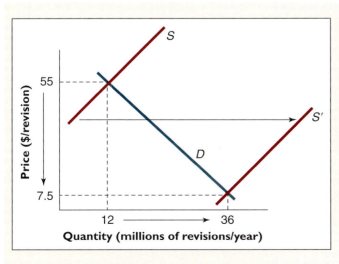

FIGURE 3.16
The Effect of Technical Change on the Market for Term-Paper Revisions.
When a new technology reduces the cost of production, supply shifts right, causing equilibrium price to fall and equilibrium quantity to rise.

Note that in the preceding discussion we implicitly assumed that students purchased typing services in a market. In fact, however, many students type their own term papers. Does that make a difference? Even if no money actually changes hands, students pay a price when they revise their term papers—namely, the opportunity cost of the time it takes to perform that task. Because technology has radically reduced that cost, we would expect to see a large increase in the number of term-paper revisions even if most students type their own work.

Changes in input prices and technology are two of the most important factors that give rise to shifts in supply curves. In the case of agricultural commodities, weather may be another important factor, with favorable conditions shifting the supply curves of such products to the right, and unfavorable conditions shifting them to the left. (Weather also may affect the supply curves of nonagricultural products through its effects on the national transportation system.) Expectations of future price changes also may shift current supply curves, as when the expectation of poor crops from a current drought causes suppliers to withhold supplies from existing stocks in the hope of selling at higher prices in the future. Changes in the number of sellers in the market also can cause supply curves to shift.

FOUR SIMPLE RULES

For supply and demand curves that have the conventional slopes (upward-sloping for supply curves, downward-sloping for demand curves), the preceding examples illustrate the four basic rules that govern how shifts in supply and demand affect equilibrium prices and quantities. These rules are summarized in Figure 3.17.

FIGURE 3.17
Four Rules Governing the Effects of Supply and Demand Shifts.

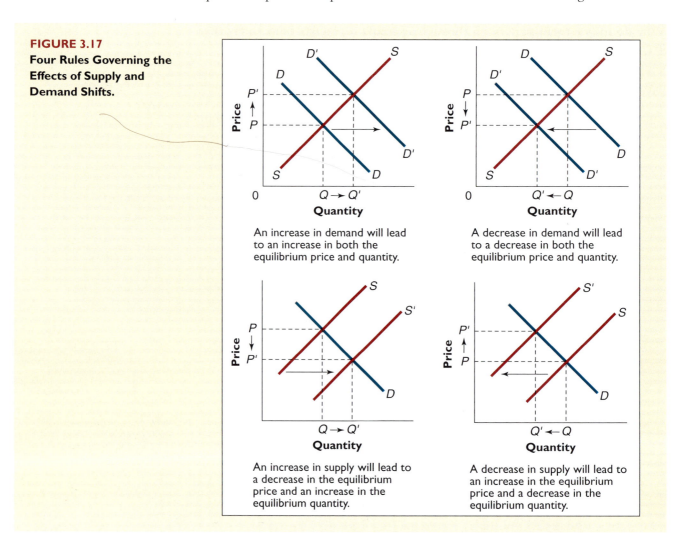

An increase in demand will lead to an increase in both the equilibrium price and quantity.

A decrease in demand will lead to a decrease in both the equilibrium price and quantity.

An increase in supply will lead to a decrease in the equilibrium price and an increase in the equilibrium quantity.

A decrease in supply will lead to an increase in the equilibrium price and a decrease in the equilibrium quantity.

RECAP	FACTORS THAT SHIFT SUPPLY AND DEMAND

Factors that cause an increase (rightward or upward shift) in demand:

1. A decrease in the price of complements to the good or service.

2. An increase in the price of substitutes for the good or service.

3. An increase in income (for a normal good).

4. An increased preference by demanders for the good or service.

5. An increase in the population of potential buyers.

6. An expectation of higher prices in the future.

When these factors move in the opposite direction, demand will shift left.

Factors that cause an increase (rightward or downward shift) in supply:

1. A decrease in the cost of materials, labor, or other inputs used in the production of the good or service.

2. An improvement in technology that reduces the cost of producing the good or service.

3. An improvement in the weather (especially for agricultural products).

4. An increase in the number of suppliers.

5. An expectation of lower prices in the future.

When these factors move in the opposite direction, supply will shift left.

The qualitative rules summarized in Figure 3.17 hold for supply or demand shifts of any magnitude, provided the curves have their conventional slopes. But as the next example demonstrates, when both supply and demand curves shift at the same time, the direction in which equilibrium price or quantity changes will depend on the relative magnitudes of the shifts.

How do shifts in *both* demand and supply affect equilibrium quantities and prices?

EXAMPLE 3.6

What will happen to the equilibrium price and quantity in the corn tortilla chip market if both of the following events occur: (1) researchers prove that the oils in which tortilla chips are fried are harmful to human health and (2) the price of corn harvesting equipment falls?

The conclusion regarding the health effects of the oils will shift the demand for tortilla chips to the left, because many people who once bought chips in the belief that they were healthful will now switch to other foods. The decline in the price of harvesting equipment will shift the supply of chips to the right, because additional farmers will now find it profitable to enter the corn market. In Figures 3.18(a) and 3.18(b), the original supply and demand curves are denoted by S and D, while the new curves are denoted by S' and D'. Note that in both panels, the shifts lead to a decline in the equilibrium price of chips.

But note also that the effect of the shifts on equilibrium quantity cannot be determined without knowing their relative magnitudes. Taken separately, the demand shift causes a decline in equilibrium quantity, whereas the supply shift causes an increase in equilibrium quantity. The net effect of the two shifts thus depends on which of the individual effects is larger. In Figure 3.18(a), the demand shift dominates, so equilibrium quantity declines. In Figure 3.18(b), the supply shift dominates, so equilibrium quantity goes up.

FIGURE 3.18
The Effects of Simultaneous Shifts in Supply and Demand.
When demand shifts left and supply shifts right, equilibrium price falls, but equilibrium quantity may either rise (b) or fall (a).

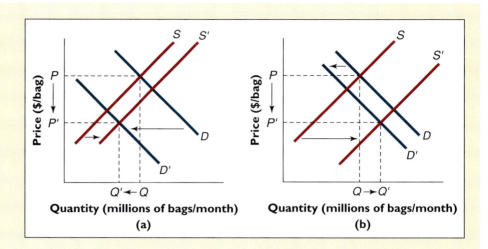

Quantity (millions of bags/month)
(a)

Quantity (millions of bags/month)
(b)

The following exercise asks you to consider a simple variation on the problem posed in Example 3.6.

EXERCISE 3.6

What will happen to the equilibrium price and quantity in the corn tortilla chip market if both of the following events occur: (1) researchers discover that a vitamin found in corn helps protect against cancer and heart disease and (2) a swarm of locusts destroys part of the corn crop?

Why do the prices of some goods, like airline tickets to Europe, go up during the months of heaviest consumption, while others, like sweet corn, go down?

Seasonal price movements for airline tickets are primarily the result of seasonal variations in demand. Thus, ticket prices to Europe are highest during the summer months because the demand for tickets is highest during those months, as shown in Figure 3.19(a), where the *w* and *s* subscripts denote winter and summer values, respectively.

ECONOMIC NATURALIST 3.3

Why are some goods cheapest during the months of heaviest consumption, while others are most expensive during those months?

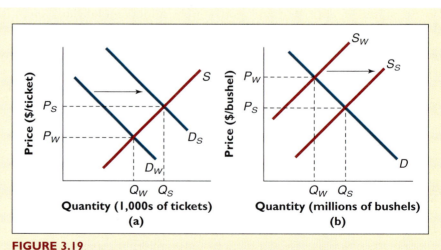

Quantity (1,000s of tickets)
(a)

Quantity (millions of bushels)
(b)

FIGURE 3.19
Seasonal Variation in the Air Travel and Corn Markets.
(a) Prices are highest during the period of heaviest consumption when heavy consumption is the result of high demand. (b) Prices are lowest during the period of heaviest consumption when heavy consumption is the result of high supply.

By contrast, seasonal price movements for sweet corn are primarily the result of seasonal variations in supply. The price of sweet corn is lowest in the summer months because its supply is highest during those months, as seen in Figure 3.19(b).

MARKETS AND SOCIAL WELFARE

Markets represent a highly effective system of allocating resources. When a market for a good is in equilibrium, the equilibrium price conveys important information to potential suppliers about the value that potential demanders place on that good. At the same time, the equilibrium price informs potential demanders about the opportunity cost of supplying the good. This rapid, two-way transmission of information is the reason that markets can coordinate an activity as complex as supplying New York City with food and drink, even though no one person or organization oversees the process.

But are the prices and quantities determined in market equilibrium socially optimal, in the sense of maximizing total economic surplus? That is, does equilibrium in unregulated markets always maximize the difference between the total benefits and total costs experienced by market participants? As we will see, the answer is "it depends": A market that is out of equilibrium, such as the rent-controlled New York housing market, always creates opportunities for individuals to arrange transactions that will increase their individual economic surplus. As we will see, however, a market for a good that is in equilibrium makes the largest possible contribution to total economic surplus only when its supply and demand curves fully reflect the costs and benefits associated with the production and consumption of that good.

CASH ON THE TABLE

In economics we assume that all exchange is purely voluntary. This means that a transaction cannot take place unless the buyer's reservation price for the good exceeds the seller's reservation price. When that condition is met and a transaction takes place, both parties receive an economic surplus. The **buyer's surplus** from the transaction is the difference between his reservation price and the price he actually pays. The **seller's surplus** is the difference between the price she receives and her reservation price. The **total surplus** from the transaction is the sum of the buyer's surplus and the seller's surplus. It is also equal to the difference between the buyer's reservation price and the seller's reservation price.

Suppose there is a potential buyer whose reservation price for an additional slice of pizza is $4 and a potential seller whose reservation price is only $2. If this buyer purchases a slice of pizza from this seller for $3, the total surplus generated by this exchange is $4 − $2 = $2, of which $4 − $3 = $1 is the buyer's surplus and $3 − $2 = $1 is the seller's surplus.

A regulation that prevents the price of a good from reaching its equilibrium level unnecessarily prevents exchanges of this sort from taking place, and in the process reduces total economic surplus. Consider again the effect of price controls imposed in the market for pizza. The demand curve in Figure 3.20 tells us that if a price ceiling of $2 per slice were imposed, only 8,000 slices of pizza per day would be sold. At that quantity, the vertical interpretations of the supply and demand curves tell us that a buyer would be willing to pay as much as $4 for an additional slice and that a seller would be willing to sell one for as little $2. The difference—$2 per slice—is the additional economic surplus that would result if an additional slice were produced and sold. As noted earlier, an extra slice sold at a price of $3 would result in an additional $1 of economic surplus for both buyer and seller.

When a market is out of equilibrium, it is always possible to identify mutually beneficial exchanges of this sort. When people have failed to take advantage of all mutually beneficial exchanges, we often say that there is **"cash on the table"**—the economist's metaphor for unexploited opportunities. When the price in a market is below the equilibrium price, there is cash on the table, because the reservation price of

buyer's surplus the difference between the buyer's reservation price and the price he or she actually pays

seller's surplus the difference between the price received by the seller and his or her reservation price

total surplus the difference between the buyer's reservation price and the seller's reservation price

cash on the table economic metaphor for unexploited gains from exchange

FIGURE 3.20
Price Controls in the Pizza Market.
A price ceiling below the equilibrium price of pizza would result in excess demand for pizza.

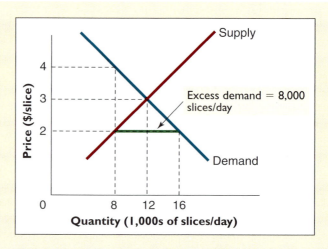

sellers (marginal cost) will always be lower than the reservation price of buyers. In the absence of a law preventing buyers paying more than $2 per slice, restaurant owners would quickly raise their prices and expand their production until the equilibrium price of $3 per slice was reached. At that price, buyers would be able to get precisely the 12,000 slices of pizza they want to buy each day. All mutually beneficial opportunities for exchange would have been exploited, leaving no more cash on the table.

With the incentive principle in mind, it should be no surprise that buyers and sellers in the marketplace have an uncanny ability to detect the presence of cash on the table. It is almost as if unexploited opportunities gave off some exotic scent triggering neurochemical explosions in the olfactory centers of their brains. The desire to scrape cash off the table and into their pockets is what drives sellers in each of New York City's thousands of individual food markets to work diligently to meet their customers' demands. That they succeed to a far higher degree than participants in the city's rent-controlled housing market is plainly evident. Whatever flaws it might have, the market system moves with considerably greater speed and agility than any centralized allocation mechanisms yet devised. But as we emphasize in the following section, this does not mean that markets *always* lead to the greatest good for all.

SMART FOR ONE, DUMB FOR ALL

socially optimal quantity the quantity of a good that results in the maximum possible economic surplus from producing and consuming the good

The **socially optimal quantity** of any good is the quantity that maximizes the total economic surplus that results from producing and consuming the good. From the cost-benefit principle, we know that we should keep expanding production of the good as long as its marginal benefit is at least as great as its marginal cost. This means that the socially optimal quantity is that level for which the marginal cost and marginal benefit of the good are the same.

When the quantity of a good is less than the socially optimal quantity, boosting its production will increase total economic surplus. By the same token, when the quantity of a good exceeds the socially optimal quantity, reducing its production will increase total economic surplus. **Economic efficiency,** or **efficiency,** occurs when all goods and services in the economy are produced and consumed at their respective socially optimal levels.

efficiency (also called **economic efficiency**) occurs when all goods and services are produced and consumed at their respective socially optimal levels

Efficiency is an important social goal. Failure to achieve efficiency means that total economic surplus is smaller than it could have been. Movements toward efficiency make the total economic pie larger, making it possible for everyone to have a larger slice. The importance of efficiency will be a recurring theme as we move forward, and we state it here as one of the core principles:

The Efficiency Principle: Efficiency is an important social goal, because when the economic pie grows larger, everyone can have a larger slice.

Is the market equilibrium quantity of a good efficient? That is, does it maximize the total economic surplus received by participants in the market for that good? When the private market for a given good is in equilibrium, we can say that the cost *to the seller* of producing an additional unit of the good is the same as the benefit *to the buyer* of having an additional unit. If all costs of producing the good are borne directly by sellers, and if all benefits from the good accrue directly to buyers, it follows that the market equilibrium quantity of the good will equate the marginal cost and marginal benefit of the good. And this means that the equilibrium quantity also maximizes total economic surplus. (We'll discuss this issue in greater detail in Chapter 7.)

But sometimes the production of a good entails costs that fall on people other than those who sell the good. This will be true, for instance, for goods whose production generates significant levels of environmental pollution (a topic we will explore in much greater detail in Chapter 12). As extra units of these goods are produced, the extra pollution harms other people besides sellers. In the market equilibrium for such goods, the benefit *to buyers* of the last good produced is, as before, equal to the cost incurred by sellers to produce that good. But since producing that good also imposed pollution costs on others, we know that the *full* marginal cost of the last unit produced—the seller's private marginal cost plus the marginal pollution cost borne by others—must be higher than the benefit of the last unit produced. So in this case the market equilibrium quantity of the good will be larger than the socially optimal quantity. Total economic surplus would be higher if output of the good were lower. Yet neither sellers nor buyers have any incentive to alter their behavior.

Another possibility is that people other than those who buy a good may receive significant benefits from it. For instance, when someone purchases a vaccination against measles from her doctor, she not only protects herself against measles, but she also makes it less likely that others will catch this disease. From the perspective of society as a whole, we should keep increasing the number of vaccinations until their marginal cost equals their marginal benefit. The marginal benefit of a vaccination is the value of the protection it provides the person vaccinated *plus* the value of the protection it provides all others. Private consumers, however, will choose to be vaccinated only if the marginal benefit *to them* exceeds the price of the vaccination. In this case, then, the market equilibrium quantity of vaccinations will be smaller than the quantity that maximizes total economic surplus. Again, however, individuals would have no incentive to alter their behavior.

Situations like the ones just discussed provide examples of behaviors that we may call "smart for one but dumb for all." In each case, the individual actors are behaving rationally. They are pursuing their goals as best they can, and yet there remain unexploited opportunities for gain from the point of view of the whole society. The difficulty is that these opportunities cannot be exploited by individuals acting alone. In subsequent chapters, we will see how people can often organize collectively to exploit such opportunities. For now, we simply summarize this discussion in the form of the following core principle:

The Equilibrium Principle (also called the "No-Cash-on-the-Table" Principle): A market in equilibrium leaves no unexploited opportunities for individuals but may not exploit all gains achievable through collective action.

RECAP	MARKETS AND SOCIAL WELFARE

When the supply and demand curves for a good reflect all significant costs and benefits associated with the production and consumption of that good, the market equilibrium will result in the largest possible economic surplus. But if people other than buyers benefit from the good, or if people other than sellers bear costs because of it, market equilibrium need not result in the largest possible economic surplus.

▪ SUMMARY ▪

- Eighteenth-century economists tried to explain differences in the prices of goods by focusing on differences in their cost of production. But this approach cannot explain why a conveniently located house sells for more than one that is less conveniently located. Early nineteenth-century economists tried to explain price differences by focusing on differences in what buyers were willing to pay. But this approach cannot explain why the price of a lifesaving appendectomy is less than that of a surgical facelift.

- Alfred Marshall's model of supply and demand explains why neither cost of production nor value to the purchaser (as measured by willingness to pay) is, by itself, sufficient to explain why some goods are cheap and others are expensive. To explain variations in price, we must examine the interaction of cost and willingness to pay. As we've seen in this chapter, goods differ in price because of differences in their respective supply and demand curves.

- The demand curve is a downward-sloping line that tells what quantity buyers will demand at any given price. The supply curve is an upward-sloping line that tells what quantity sellers will offer at any given price. Market equilibrium occurs when the quantity buyers demand at the market price is exactly the same as the quantity that sellers offer. The equilibrium price-quantity pair is the one at which the demand and supply curves intersect. In equilibrium, market price measures both the value of the last unit sold to buyers and the cost of the resources required to produce it.

- When the price of a good lies above its equilibrium value, there is an excess supply of that good. Excess supply motivates sellers to cut their prices, and price continues to fall until the equilibrium price is reached. When price lies below its equilibrium value, there is excess demand. With excess demand, frustrated buyers are motivated to offer higher prices, and the upward pressure on prices persists until equilibrium is reached. A remarkable feature of the market system is that, relying only on the tendency of people to respond in self-interested ways to market price signals, it somehow manages to coordinate the actions of literally billions of buyers and sellers worldwide. When excess demand or excess supply occurs, it tends to be small and brief, except in markets where regulations prevent full adjustment of prices.

- The efficiency of markets in allocating resources does not eliminate social concerns about how goods and services are distributed among different people. For example, we often lament the fact many buyers enter the market with too little income to buy even the most basic goods and services. Concern for the well-being of the poor has motivated many governments to intervene in a variety of ways to alter the outcomes of market forces. Sometimes these interventions take the form of laws that peg prices below their equilibrium levels. Such laws almost invariably generate harmful, if unintended, consequences. Programs like rent-control laws, for example, lead to severe housing shortages, black marketeering, and a rapid deterioration of the relationship between landlords and tenants.

- If the difficulty is that the poor have too little money, the best solution is to discover ways of boosting their incomes directly. The law of supply and demand cannot be repealed by the legislature. But legislatures do have the capacity to alter the underlying forces that govern the shape and position of supply and demand schedules.

- The basic supply and demand model is a primary tool of the economic naturalist. Changes in the equilibrium price of a good, and in the amount of it traded in the marketplace, can be predicted on the basis of shifts in its supply or demand curves. The following four rules hold for any good with a downward-sloping demand curve and an upward-sloping supply curve:
  - An increase in demand will lead to an increase in equilibrium price and quantity.
  - A reduction in demand will lead to a reduction in equilibrium price and quantity.
  - An increase in supply will lead to a reduction in equilibrium price and an increase in equilibrium quantity.
  - A decrease in supply will lead to an increase in equilibrium price and a reduction in equilibrium quantity.

- Incomes, tastes, population, expectations, and the prices of substitutes and complements are among the factors that shift demand schedules. Supply schedules, in turn, are primarily governed by such factors as technology, input prices, expectations, the number of sellers, and, especially for agricultural products, the weather.

- When the supply and demand curves for a good reflect all significant costs and benefits associated with the production and consumption of that good, the market equilibrium price will guide people to produce and consume the quantity of the good that results in the largest possible economic surplus. This conclusion, however, does not apply if others, besides buyers, benefit from the good (as when someone benefits from his neighbor's purchase of a vaccination against measles), or if others besides sellers bear costs because of the good (as when its production generates pollution). In such cases, market equilibrium does not result in the greatest gain for all.

▪ CORE PRINCIPLES ▪

The Efficiency Principle
Efficiency is an important social goal, because when the economic pie grows larger, everyone can have a larger slice.

The Equilibrium Principle (also called the "No-Cash-on-the-Table" Principle)
A market in equilibrium leaves no unexploited opportunities for individuals but may not exploit all gains achievable through collective action.

■ KEY TERMS ■

buyer's reservation price (64)
buyer's surplus (83)
cash on the table (83)
change in demand (73)
change in quantity demanded (73)
change in quantity supplied (74)
change in supply (74)
complements (74)
demand curve (63)
economic efficiency (84)

efficiency (84)
equilibrium (66)
equilibrium price (66)
equilibrium quantity (66)
excess demand (67)
excess supply (67)
income effect (63)
inferior good (76)
market (62)
market equilibrium (66)

normal good (76)
price ceiling (72)
seller's reservation price (65)
seller's surplus (83)
socially optimal quantity (84)
substitutes (75)
substitution effect (63)
supply curve (64)
total surplus (83)

■ REVIEW QUESTIONS ■

1. Why isn't knowing the cost of producing a good sufficient to predict its market price?

2. Distinguish between the meaning of the expressions "change in demand" and "change in the quantity demanded."

3. Last year a government official proposed that gasoline price controls be imposed to protect the poor from rising gasoline prices. What evidence could you consult to discover whether this proposal was enacted?

4. Explain the distinction between the horizontal and vertical interpretations of the demand curve.

5. Give an example of behavior you have observed that could be described as "smart for one but dumb for all."

■ PROBLEMS ■

1. State whether the following pairs of goods are complements or substitutes. (If you think a pair is ambiguous in this respect, explain why.)
   a. Tennis courts and squash courts.
   b. Squash racquets and squash balls.
   c. Ice cream and chocolate.
   d. Cloth diapers and paper diapers.

2. How would each of the following affect the U.S. market supply curve for corn?
   a. A new and improved crop rotation technique is discovered.
   b. The price of fertilizer falls.
   c. The government offers new tax breaks to farmers.
   d. A tornado sweeps through Iowa.

3. Indicate how you think each of the following would shift demand in the indicated market:
   a. Incomes of buyers in the market for Adirondack vacations increase.
   b. Buyers in the market for pizza read a study linking hamburger consumption to heart disease.
   c. Buyers in the market for CDs learn of an increase in the price of audiocassettes (a substitute for CDs).
   d. Buyers in the market for CDs learn of an increase in the price of CDs.

4. An Arizona student claims to have spotted a UFO over the desert outside of Tucson. How will his claim affect the *supply* (not the quantity supplied) of binoculars in Tucson stores?

5. What will happen to the equilibrium price and quantity of oranges if the wage paid to orange pickers rises?

6. How will an increase in the birth rate affect the equilibrium price of land?

7. What will happen to the equilibrium price and quantity of fish if fish oils are found to help prevent heart disease?

8. What will happen to the equilibrium price and quantity of beef if the price of chicken-feed increases?

9. Use supply and demand analysis to explain why hotel room rental rates near your campus during parents' weekend and graduation weekend might differ from the rates charged during the rest of the year.

10. How will a new law mandating an increase in required levels of automobile insurance affect the equilibrium price and quantity in the market for new automobiles?

11. Suppose the current issue of the *New York Times* reports an outbreak of mad cow disease in Nebraska, as well as the discovery of a new breed of chicken that gains more weight than existing breeds that consume the same amount of food. How will these developments affect the equilibrium price and quantity of chickens sold in the United States?

12. What will happen to the equilibrium quantity and price of potatoes if population increases and a new, higher-yielding variety of potato plant is developed?

13. What will happen to the equilibrium price and quantity of apples if apples are discovered to help prevent colds and a fungus kills 10 percent of existing apple trees?

14. What will happen to the equilibrium quantity and price of corn if the price of butter (a complement) increases and the price of fertilizer decreases?

15. Twenty-five years ago, tofu was available only from small businesses operating in predominantly Asian sections of large cities. Today tofu has become popular as a high-protein health food and is widely available in supermarkets throughout the United States. At the same time, tofu production has evolved to become factory-based using modern food-processing technologies. Draw a diagram with demand and supply curves depicting the market for tofu 25 years ago and the market for tofu today. Given the information above, what does the demand-supply model predict about changes in the volume of tofu sold in the United States between then and now? What does it predict about changes in the price of tofu?

■ ANSWERS TO IN-CHAPTER EXERCISES ■

3.1 At a quantity of 10,000 slices per day, the marginal buyer's reservation price is $3.50 per slice. At a price of $2.50 per slice, the quantity demanded will be 14,000 slices per day.

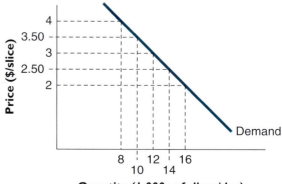

3.2 At a quantity of 10,000 slices per day, the marginal cost of pizza is $2.50 per slice. At a price of $3.50 per slice, the quantity supplied will be 14,000 slices per day.

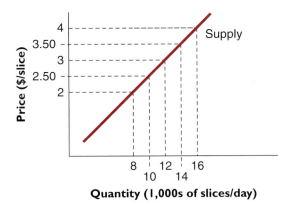

Quantity (1,000s of slices/day)

3.3 Since landlords are permitted to charge less than the maximum rent established by rent-control laws, a law that sets the maximum rent at $1,200 will have no effect on the rents actually charged in this market, which will settle at the equilibrium value of $800 per month.

3.4 Travel by air and travel by intercity bus are substitutes, so a decline in airfares will shift the demand for bus travel to the left, resulting in lower bus fares and fewer bus trips taken. Travel by air and the use of resort hotels are complements, so a decline in airfares will shift the demand for resort hotel rooms to the right, resulting in higher hotel rates and an increase in the number of rooms rented.

3.5 Apartments located far from Washington Metro stations are an inferior good. A pay increase for federal workers will thus shift the demand curve for such apartments downward, which will lead to a reduction in their equilibrium rent.

3.6 The vitamin discovery shifts the demand for chips to the right, and the crop losses shift the supply of chips to the left. Both shifts result in an increase in the equilibrium price of chips. But depending on the relative magnitude of the shifts, the equilibrium quantity of chips may either rise (left panel) or fall (right panel).

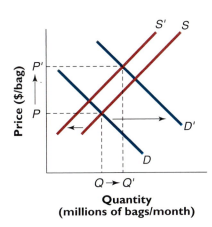

**Quantity
(millions of bags/month)**

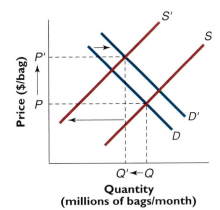

**Quantity
(millions of bags/month)**

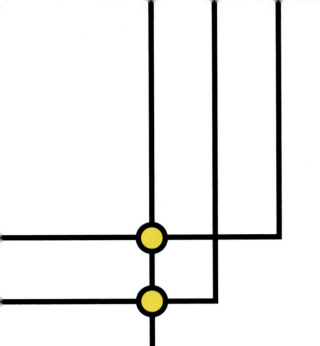

THE ALGEBRA OF SUPPLY AND DEMAND

In the text of this chapter, we developed supply and demand analysis in a geometric framework. The advantage of this framework is that many find it an easier one within which to visualize how shifts in either curve affect equilibrium price and quantity.

It is a straightforward extension to translate supply and demand analysis into algebraic terms. In this brief appendix, we show how this is done. The advantage of the algebraic framework is that it greatly simplifies computing the numerical values of equilibrium prices and quantities.

Consider, for example, the supply and demand curves in Figure 3A.1, where P denotes the price of the good and Q denotes its quantity. What are the equations of these curves?

Recall from the appendix to Chapter 1 that the equation of a straight-line demand curve must take the general form $P = a + b Q^d$, where P is the price of the product (as measured on the vertical axis), Q^d is the quantity demanded at that price (as measured on the horizontal axis), a is the vertical intercept of the demand curve, and b is its slope. For the demand curve shown in Figure 3A.1, the vertical intercept is 16 and the slope is -2. So the equation for this demand curve is

$$P = 16 - 2Q^d. \tag{3A.1}$$

Similarly, the equation of a straight-line supply curve must take the general form $P = c + dQ^s$, where P is again the price of the product, Q^s is the quantity supplied at that price, c is the vertical intercept of the supply curve, and d is its

FIGURE 3A.1
Supply and Demand Curves

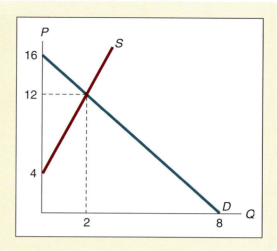

slope. For the supply curve shown in Figure 3A.1, the vertical intercept is 4 and the slope is also 4. So the equation for this supply curve is

$$P = 4 + 4Q^s. \tag{3A.2}$$

If we know the equations for the supply and demand curves in any market, it is a simple matter to solve them for the equilibrium price and quantity using the method of simultaneous equations described in the appendix to Chapter 1. The following example illustrates how to apply this method.

EXAMPLE 3A.1

If the supply and demand curves for a market are given by $P = 4 + 4Q^s$ and $P = 16 - 2Q^d$, respectively, find the equilibrium price and quantity for this market.

In equilibrium, we know that $Q^s = Q^d$. Denoting this common value as Q^*, we may then equate the right-hand sides of Equations 3A.1 and 3A.2 and solve:

$$4 + 4Q^* = 16 - 2Q^*, \tag{3A.3}$$

which yields $Q^* = 2$. Substituting $Q^* = 2$ back into either the supply or demand equation gives the equilibrium price $P^* = 12$.

Of course, having already begun with the graphs of Equations 3A.1 and 3A.2 in hand, we could have identified the equilibrium price and quantity by a simple glance at Figure 3A.1. (That is why it seems natural to say that the graphical approach helps us visualize the equilibrium outcome.) As the following exercise illustrates, the advantage of the algebraic approach to finding the equilibrium price and quantity is that it is much less painstaking than having to produce accurate drawings of the supply and demand schedules.

EXERCISE 3A.1

Find the equilibrium price and quantity in a market whose supply and demand curves are given by $P = 2Q^s$ and $P = 8 - 2Q^d$, respectively.

ANSWER TO IN-APPENDIX EXERCISE ■

3A.1 Let Q^* denote the equilibrium quantity. Since the equilibrium price and quantity lie on both the supply and demand curves, we equate the right-hand sides of the supply and demand equations to obtain

$$2Q^* = 8 - 2Q^*,$$

which solves for $Q^* = 2$. Substituting $Q^* = 2$ back into either the supply or demand equation gives the equilibrium price $P^* = 4$.

PART

2

MACROECONOMICS: ISSUES AND DATA

■

Physical scientists study the world at many different scales, ranging from the inner workings of the atom to the vast dimensions of the cosmos. Although the laws of physics are thought to apply at all scales, scientists find that some phenomena are best understood "in the small" and some "in the large." Although the range of scales they must deal with is much more modest than in physics, economists also find it useful to analyze economic behavior at both the small-scale, or "micro" level, and the large-scale, or "macro-" level. This section introduces you to *macroeconomics,* the study of the performance of national economies. Unlike *microeconomics,* which focuses on the behavior of individual households, firms, and markets, macroeconomics takes a bird's-eye view of the economy. So, while a microeconomist might study the determinants of consumer spending on personal computers, macroeconomists analyze the factors that determine aggregate, or total, consumer spending. Experience has shown that, for many issues, the macroeconomic perspective is the more useful.

Chapter 4 begins our discussion of macroeconomics by introducing you to some of the key macroeconomic issues and questions. These include the search for the factors that cause economies to grow, productivity to improve, and living standards to rise over long periods of time. Macroeconomists also study shorter-term fluctuations in the economy (called recessions and expansions), unemployment, inflation, and the economic interdependence among nations, among other topics. Macroeconomic policies—government actions to improve the performance of the economy—are of particular concern to macroeconomists, as the quality of macroeconomic policymaking is a major determinant of a nation's economic health.

To study phenomena like economic growth scientifically, economists must have accurate measurements. Chapters 5 and 6 continue the introduction to macroeconomics by discussing how some key macroeconomic concepts are measured and interpreted. Chapter 5 discusses two important measures of the level of economic activity: the gross domestic product and the unemployment rate. Besides describing how these variables are constructed in practice, this chapter also discusses the issue of how these measures are related to the economic well-being of the typical person. Chapter 6 concerns the measurement of the price level and inflation and includes a discussion of the costs that inflation imposes on the economy. When you have completed Part 2, you will be familiar not only with the major questions that macroeconomists ask but also with some of the most important tools that they use to try to find the answers.

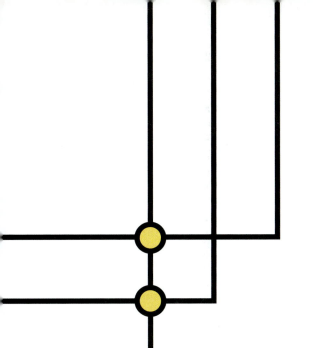

CHAPTER

4

MACROECONOMICS: THE BIRD'S-EYE VIEW OF THE ECONOMY

In 1929 the economy of the United States slowed dramatically. Between August of 1929 and the end of 1930, the nation's factories and mines, facing sharp declines in sales, cut their production rates by a remarkable 31 percent. These cutbacks led in turn to mass layoffs: Between 1929 and 1930, the number of people without jobs almost tripled, from about 3 percent of the workforce to nearly 9 percent.[1] Financial markets were equally shaky. The stock market crashed in October 1929, and stocks lost nearly a third of their value in just three weeks.

At first, policymakers and the general public (except for those people who had put their life savings into the stock market) were concerned but not panic-stricken. Americans remembered that the nation had experienced a similar slowdown only eight years earlier, in 1921–1922. That episode had ended quickly, apparently on its own, and the decade that followed (popularly known as the roaring twenties) had been one of unparalleled prosperity. But the fall in production and the rise in unemployment that began in 1929 continued into 1931. In the spring of 1931, the economy seemed to stabilize briefly, and President Herbert Hoover optimistically proclaimed that "prosperity is just around the corner." But in mid-1931 the economy went into an even steeper dive. What historians now call the Great Depression had begun in earnest.

[1]The source for these and most other pre-1960 statistics cited in this chapter is the U.S. Bureau of the Census, *Historical Statistics of the United States: Colonial Times to 1970*, Washington, 1975.

Labor statistics tell the story of the Great Depression from the worker's point of view. Unemployment was extremely high throughout the 1930s, despite government attempts to reduce it through large-scale public employment programs. At the worst point of the Depression, in 1933, one out of every four American workers was unemployed. Joblessness declined gradually to 17 percent of the workforce by 1936 but remained stuck at that level through 1939. Of those lucky enough to have jobs, many were able to work only part-time, while others worked for near-starvation wages.

In some other countries, conditions were even worse. In Germany, which had never fully recovered from its defeat in World War I, nearly a third of all workers were without jobs, and many families lost their savings as major banks collapsed. Indeed, the desperate economic situation was a major reason for Adolf Hitler's election as chancellor of Germany in 1933. Introducing extensive government control over the economy, Hitler rearmed the country and ultimately launched what became the most destructive war in history, World War II.

How could such an economic catastrophe have happened? One often-heard hypothesis is that the Great Depression was caused by wild speculation on Wall Street, which provoked the stock market crash. But though stock prices may have been unrealistically high in 1929, there is little evidence to suggest that the fall in stock prices was a major cause of the Depression. A similar crash in October 1987, when stock prices fell a record 23 percent in one day—an event comparable in severity to the crash of October 1929—did not slow the economy significantly. Another reason to doubt that the 1929 stock market crash caused the Great Depression is that, far from being confined to the United States, the Depression was a worldwide event, affecting countries that did not have well-developed stock markets at the time. The more reasonable conclusion is that the onset of the Depression probably caused the stock market crash, rather than the other way round.

Another explanation for the Depression, suggested by some economists in the 1930s, was that free-market economies like those of the United States and Germany are "naturally" unstable, prone to long periods of low production and high unemployment. But this idea too has fallen out of favor, since the period after World War II has generally been one of prosperity and economic growth throughout the industrialized world.

What *did* cause the Great Depression, then? Today most economists who have studied the period blame *poor economic policymaking* both in the United States and in other major industrialized countries. Of course, policymakers did not set out to create an economic catastrophe. Rather, they fell prey to misconceptions of the time about how the economy worked. In other words, the Great Depression, far from being inevitable, *might have been avoided*—if only the state of economic knowledge had been better. From today's perspective, the Great Depression was to economic policymaking what the voyage of the *Titanic* was to ocean navigation.

Could better economic policies have prevented the Great Depression?

One of the few benefits of the Great Depression was that it forced economists and policymakers of the 1930s to recognize that there were major gaps in their understanding of how the economy works. This recognition led to the development of a new subfield within economics, called macroeconomics. Recall from Chapter 1 that *macroeconomics* is the study of the performance of national economies and the policies governments use to try to improve that performance.

This chapter will introduce the subject matter and some of the tools of macroeconomics. Although understanding episodes like the Great Depression remains an important concern of macroeconomists, the field has expanded to include the analysis of many other aspects of national economies. Among the issues macroeconomists study are the sources of long-run economic growth and development, the causes of high unemployment, and the factors that determine the rate of inflation. Appropriately enough in a world in which economic "globalization" preoccupies businesspeople and policymakers, macroeconomists also study how national economies interact. Since the performance of the national economy has an important bearing on the availability of jobs, the wages workers earn, the prices they pay, and the rates of return they receive on their saving, it's clear that macroeconomics addresses bread-and-butter issues that affect virtually everyone.

In light of the nation's experience during the Great Depression, macroeconomists are particularly concerned with understanding how *macroeconomic policies* work and how they should be applied. **Macroeconomic policies** are government actions designed to affect the performance of the economy as a whole (as opposed to policies intended to affect the performance of the market for a particular good or service, such as sugar or haircuts). The hope is that by understanding more fully how government policies affect the economy, economists can help policymakers do a better job—and avoid serious mistakes, such as those that were made during the Great Depression. On an individual level, educating people about macroeconomic policies and their effects will make for a better-informed citizenry, capable of making well-reasoned decisions in the voting booth.

macroeconomic policies
government actions designed to affect the performance of the economy as a whole

THE MAJOR MACROECONOMIC ISSUES

We defined macroeconomics as the study of the performance of the national economy as well as the policies used to improve that performance. Let's now take a closer look at some of the major economic issues that macroeconomists study.

ECONOMIC GROWTH AND LIVING STANDARDS

Although the wealthy industrialized countries (such as the United States, Canada, Japan, and the countries of western Europe) are certainly not free from poverty, hunger, and homelessness, the typical person in those countries enjoys a standard of living better than at any previous time or place in history. By *standard of living* we mean the degree to which people have access to goods and services that make their lives easier, healthier, safer, and more enjoyable. People with a high living standard enjoy more and better consumer goods: sports utility vehicles, camcorders, cellular phones, and the like. But they also benefit from a longer life expectancy and better general health (the result of high-quality medical care, good nutrition, and good sanitation), from higher literacy rates (the result of greater access to education), from more time and opportunity for cultural enrichment and recreation, from more interesting and fulfilling career options, and from better working conditions. Of course, the *scarcity principle* will always apply—even for the citizen of a rich country, having more of one good thing means having less of another. But higher incomes make these choices much less painful than they would be otherwise. Choosing between a larger apartment and a nicer car is much easier than choosing between feeding your children adequately and sending them to school, the kind of hard choice people in the poorest nations face.

Americans sometimes take their standard of living for granted, or even as a "right." As a Paul Simon lyric proclaims, "God bless our standard of living—let's keep it that way!" But we should realize that the way we live today is radically different from the way people have lived throughout most of history. The current standard of living in the United States is the result of several centuries of sustained *economic growth*, a process of steady increase in the quantity and quality of the goods and services the economy can produce. The basic equation is simple: The more we can produce, the more we can consume. Though not everyone in a society shares equally in the fruits of economic growth, in most cases growth brings an improvement in the average person's standard of living.

To get a sense of the extent of economic growth over time, examine Figure 4.1, which shows how the output of the U.S. economy has increased since 1900. (We discuss the measure of output used here, real gross domestic product, in the next chapter.) Although output fluctuates at times, the overall trend has been unmistakably upward. Indeed, in 2004 the output of the U.S. economy was more than 33 times what it was in 1900 and more than 6 times its level in 1950. What caused this remarkable economic growth? Can it continue? Should it? These are some of the questions macroeconomists try to answer.

FIGURE 4.1

Output of the U.S. Economy, 1900–2004.

The output of the U.S. economy has increased by more than 33 times since 1900 and by more than 6 times since 1950.

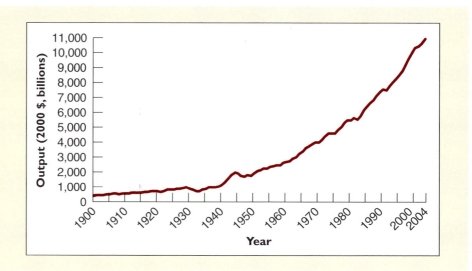

One reason for the growth in U.S. output over the last century has been the rapid growth of the U.S. population, and hence the number of workers available. Because of population growth, increases in *total* output cannot be equated with improvements in the general standard of living. Although increased output means that more goods and services are available, increased population implies that more people are sharing those goods and services. Because the population changes over time, output *per person* is a better indicator of the average living standard than total output.

Figure 4.2 shows output per person in the United States since 1900 (the blue line). Note that the long-term increase in output per person is smaller than the increase in total output shown in Figure 4.1 because of population growth. Nevertheless, the gains made over this long period are still impressive: In 2004 a typical U.S. resident consumed over eight times the quantity of goods and services available to a typical resident at the beginning of the century. As Table 4.1 illustrates, the United States has one of the highest standards of living, and there are substantial differences in consumption patterns around the world. Americans have more television sets, personal computers, and motor vehicles per person than any other country listed in Table 4.1. According to recent estimates, there are 1.9 automobiles per U.S. household, and only roughly 8 percent of U.S. households (many of them located in cities, with good access to public transportation) do not have a car. On the other hand, Hungarians are more likely to be cell telephone subscribers than any of the

Nearly 60 million American households own two or more automobiles.

FIGURE 4.2

Output per Person and per Worker in the U.S. Economy, 1900–2004.

The red line shows the output per worker in the U.S. economy since 1900, and the blue line shows output per person. Both have risen substantially. Relative to 1900, output per person today is eight times greater, and output per worker is more than six times greater.

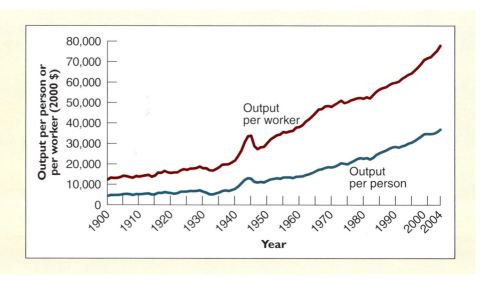

TABLE 4.1
Consumption Patterns around the World

Country	Television sets (per 1,000 people)	Cellular subscribers (per 1,000 people)	Internet users (per 1,000 people)	Personal computers (per 1,000 people)	Motor vehicles (per 1,000 people)	Energy use (kg of oil equivalent per capita)	Electricity consumption per capita (kilowatt-hours)
High income							
Canada	691	377	512.8	487.0	581.1	7,972.6	18,212
Germany	675	727	411.9	431.3	585.9	4,197.8	7,207
Japan	785	637	448.9	382.2	598.9	4,057.5	8,203
United States	938	488	551.4	658.9	811.7	7,942.6	13,241
Middle income							
Argentina	326	178	112.0	82.0	186.7	1,543.2	2,453
China	350	161	46.0	27.6	16.0	959.5	1,139
Hungary	119	676	157.6	108.4	306.0	2,505.1	3,886
Mexico	282	255	98.5	82.0	165.4	1,560.3	2,228
Low income							
India	83	12	15.9	7.2	16.5	513.3	561
Indonesia	153	55	37.7	11.9	28.8	736.9	469
Pakistan	150	8	10.3	4.2	11.7	454.1	479

Data in Columns 2–6 are for the year 2002, data in Column 1 are for 2003, and data in Column 7 are for 2001.
SOURCE: Column 1: http://www.worldbank.org/data/wdi2005/pdfs/Table5_11.pdf; Columns 2, 3, 7: Human Development Report 2004, http://hdr.undp.org/reports/global/2004/; Columns 4, 6: http://www.worldbank.org/data/dataquery.html; Column 5: http://www.imf.org/external/pubs/ft/weo/2005/01/chp4data/fig4_7.csv.

other 10 nationalities listed in Table 4.1.[2] And while many of China's consumption patterns are comparable to what the World Bank calls "low income" countries, the Chinese have more televisions per person than most developing countries.

The rise in U.S. output during the past century has been accompanied by greater access to education. For example, as late as 1960, only 41 percent of U.S. adults over age 25 had completed high school, and less than 8 percent had completed four years of college. Today, over 85 percent of the adult population have at least a high school diploma, and about 27 percent have a college degree. Over half the students currently leaving high school will go on to college. Higher incomes, which allow young people to continue their schooling rather than work to support themselves and their families, are a major reason for these increases in educational levels.

PRODUCTIVITY

While growth in output per person is closely linked to changes in what the typical person can *consume*, macroeconomists are also interested in changes in what the average worker can *produce*. Figure 4.2 shows how output per employed worker (that is, total output divided by the number of people working) has changed since 1900 (red line). The figure shows that in 2004 a U.S. worker could produce more than six times the quantity of goods and services produced by a worker at the beginning of the twentieth century, despite the fact that the workweek is now much shorter than it was 100 years ago.

Economists refer to output per employed worker as **average labor productivity**. As Figure 4.2 shows, average labor productivity and output per person are closely related. This relationship makes sense—as we noted earlier, the more we can produce, the more we can consume. Because of this close link to the average living standard, average labor productivity and the factors that cause it to increase over time are of major concern to macroeconomists.

average labor productivity
output per employed worker

[2]Cellphones are popular in many middle-income countries because of weaknesses in their traditional landline infrastructures.

Although the long-term improvement in output per worker is impressive, the *rate* of improvement slowed during the 1970s and 1980s. Between 1950 and 1973 in the United States, output per employed worker increased by 2.3 percent per year. But from 1973 to 1995 the average rate of increase in output per worker was only 1.1 percent per year. Since 1995 the pace of productivity growth seems to have picked up again, however, to 2.1 percent per year. Slowing productivity growth leads to less rapid improvement in living standards, since the supply of goods and services cannot grow as quickly as it does during periods of rapid growth in productivity. Identifying the causes of productivity slowdowns and speedups is thus an important challenge for macroeconomists.

The current standard of living in the United States is not only much higher than in the past but also much higher than in many other nations today. Why have many of the world's countries, including both the developing nations of Asia, Africa, and Latin America and some formerly communist countries of eastern Europe, not enjoyed the same rates of economic growth as the industrialized countries? How can the rate of economic growth be improved in these countries? Once again, these are questions of keen interest to macroeconomists.

EXAMPLE 4.1

Productivity and living standards in China and the United States

In 2004, the value of the output of the U.S. economy was about $11,734 billion. In the same year, the estimated value of the output of the People's Republic of China was $7,291 billion. The populations of the United States and China in 2004 were about 294 million and 1,300 million, respectively, while the number of employed workers in the two countries were approximately 139 million and 752 million.[3]

Find output per person and average labor productivity for the United States and China in 2004. What do the results suggest about comparative living standards in the two countries?

Output per person is simply total output divided by the number of people in an economy, and average labor productivity is output divided by the number of employed workers. Doing the math, we get the following results for 2004:

	United States	China
Output per person	$39,912	$5,608
Average labor productivity	$84,417	$9,695

Note that, although the total output of the Chinese economy is roughly 62 percent that of the U.S. output, output per person and average labor productivity in China are each only about 14 and 11 percent, respectively, of what they are in the United States. Thus, though the Chinese economy may someday rival the U.S. economy in total output, for the time being there remains a large gap in productivity. This gap translates into striking differences in the living standard between the two countries—in access to consumer goods, health care, transportation, education, and other benefits of affluence.

RECESSIONS AND EXPANSIONS

Economies do not always grow steadily; sometimes they go through periods of unusual strength or weakness. A look back at Figure 4.1 shows that although output

[3]Chinese output is converted to U.S. dollars using an exchange rate that adjusts for differences in the cost of various goods and services in China and the United States. The sources for the data are for PPP GDP: the *CIA factbook,* http://www.cia.gov/cia/publications/factbook/, adjusted by the author; population (China): http://www.economist.com/countries/China/profile.cfm?folder=Profile-FactSheet; employment (China): http://english.people.com.cn/200504/01/eng20050401_179049.html; U.S. population: *Economic Report of the President,* 2005; U.S. employment: http://www.bls.gov.

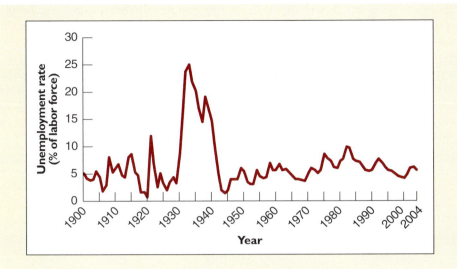

FIGURE 4.3
The U.S. Unemployment Rate, 1900–2004.
The unemployment rate is the percentage of the labor force that is out of work. Unemployment spikes upward during recessions and depressions, but the unemployment rate is always above zero, even in good times.

generally grows over time, it does not always grow smoothly. Particularly striking is the decline in output during the Great Depression of the 1930s, followed by the sharp increase in output during World War II (1941–1945). But the figure shows many more moderate fluctuations in output as well.

Slowdowns in economic growth are called *recessions;* particularly severe economic slowdowns, like the one that began in 1929, are called *depressions.* In the United States, major recessions occurred in 1973–1975 and 1981–1982 (find those recessions in Figure 4.1). More modest downturns occurred in 1990–1991 and 2001. During recessions economic opportunities decline: Jobs are harder to find, people with jobs are less likely to get wage increases, profits are lower, and more companies go out of business. Recessions are particularly hard on economically disadvantaged people, who are most likely to be thrown out of work and have the hardest time finding new jobs.

Sometimes the economy grows unusually quickly. These periods of rapid economic growth are called *expansions,* and particularly strong expansions are called *booms.* During an expansion, jobs are easier to find, more people get raises and promotions, and most businesses thrive.

The alternating cycle of recessions and expansions raises some questions that are central to macroeconomics. What causes these short-term fluctuations in the rate of economic growth? Can government policymakers do anything about them? Should they try?

UNEMPLOYMENT

The *unemployment rate,* the fraction of people who would like to be employed but can't find work, is a key indicator of the state of the labor market. When the unemployment rate is high, work is hard to find, and people who do have jobs typically find it harder to get promotions or wage increases.

Figure 4.3 shows the unemployment rate in the United States since 1900. Unemployment rises during recessions—note the dramatic spike in unemployment during the Great Depression, as well as the increases in unemployment during the 1973–1975 and 1981–1982 recessions. But even in the so-called good times, such as the 1960s and the 1990s, some people are unemployed. Why does unemployment rise so sharply during periods of recession? And why are there always unemployed people, even when the economy is booming?

Increases in unemployment during recessions

EXAMPLE 4.2

Using monthly data on the national civilian unemployment rate, find the increase in the unemployment rate between the onset of recession in November 1973, January

1980, July 1990, and March 2001 and the peak unemployment rate in the following three years. Compare these increases in unemployment to the increase during the Great Depression.

Unemployment data are collected by the U.S. Bureau of Labor Statistics (BLS) and can be obtained from the BLS home page (http://stats.bls.gov/datahome.htm). Hard-copy sources include the *Survey of Current Business*, the *Federal Reserve Bulletin*, and *Economic Indicators*. Monthly data from the BLS home page yield the following comparisons:

Unemployment rate at beginning of recession (%)	Peak unemployment rate (%)	Increase in unemployment rate (%)
4.8 (Nov. 1973)	9.0 (May 1975)	+4.2
6.3 (Jan. 1980)	10.8 (Nov./Dec. 1982)	+4.5
5.5 (July 1990)	7.8 (June 1992)	+2.3
4.3 (March 2001)	6.3 (June 2003)	+2.0

Unemployment increased significantly following the onset of each recession, although the impact of the 1990 and 2001 recessions on the labor market was clearly less serious than that of the 1973 and the 1980 recessions. (Actually, the 1980 recession was a "double dip"—a short recession in 1980, followed by a longer one in 1981–82.) In comparison, during the Great Depression the unemployment rate rose from about 3 percent in 1929 to about 25 percent in 1933, as we mentioned in the introduction to this chapter. Clearly, the 22 percentage point change in the unemployment rate that Americans experienced in the Great Depression dwarfs the effects of these four postwar recessions.

One question of great interest to macroeconomists is why unemployment rates sometimes differ markedly from country to country. For the past two decades, unemployment rates in western Europe have more often than not been measured in the "double digits." On average, about 10 percent of the European workforce has been out of a job during this period, a rate roughly double that in the United States. The high unemployment is particularly puzzling, because during the 1950s and 1960s, European unemployment rates were generally much lower than those in the United States. What explains these differences in the unemployment rate in different countries at different times?

EXERCISE 4.1

Find the most recent unemployment rates for France, Germany, and the United Kingdom, and compare them to the most recent unemployment rate for the United States. A useful source is the home page of the Organization for Economic Cooperation and Development (OECD), an organization of industrialized countries (http://www.oecd.org/). See also the OECD's publication *Main Economic Indicators*. Is unemployment still lower in the United States than in western Europe?

INFLATION

Another important economic statistic is the rate of *inflation*, which is the rate at which prices in general are increasing over time. As we discuss in the chapter "Measuring the Price Level and Inflation," inflation imposes a variety of costs on the economy. And when the inflation rate is high, people on fixed incomes, such as pensioners who receive a fixed dollar payment each month, can't keep up with the rising cost of living.

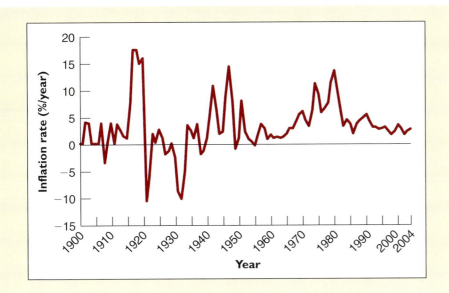

FIGURE 4.4
The U.S. Inflation Rate,
1900–2004.
The U.S. inflation rate has
fluctuated over time.
Inflation was high in the
1970s but has been quite
low recently.

In recent years, inflation has been relatively low in the United States, but that has not always been the case (see Figure 4.4 for data on U.S. inflation since 1900). During the 1970s, inflation was a major problem; in fact, many people told poll takers that inflation was "public enemy number one." Why was inflation high in the 1970s, and why is it relatively low today? What difference does it make to the average person?

As with unemployment rates, the rate of inflation can differ markedly from country to country. For example, in 2004 the inflation rate was about 3 percent in the United States, but the nation of Ukraine averaged over 400 percent annual inflation for the whole decade of the 1990s. What accounts for such large differences in inflation rates between countries?

Inflation and unemployment are often linked in policy discussions. One reason for this linkage is the oft-heard argument that unemployment can be reduced only at the cost of higher inflation and that inflation can be reduced only at the cost of higher unemployment. Must the government accept a higher rate of inflation to bring down unemployment, and vice versa?

ECONOMIC INTERDEPENDENCE AMONG NATIONS

National economies do not exist in isolation but are increasingly interdependent. The United States, because of its size and the wide variety of goods and services it produces, is one of the most self-sufficient economies on the planet. Even so, in 2004, the United States exported about 10.0 percent of all the goods and services it produced and imported from abroad 14.4 percent of the goods and services that Americans used.

Sometimes international flows of goods and services become a matter of political and economic concern. For example, congressional representatives of states producing steel or textiles repeatedly complain that low-priced imports of these goods threaten the jobs of their constituents. Ross Perot, the Texas businessman and presidential candidate, predicted such problems when he opposed the adoption of the North American Free Trade Agreement (NAFTA) and similar agreements designed to promote international trade in goods and services. (Perot made famous the phrase "giant sucking sound" to describe what he thought free trade would do to American jobs.) Are free trade agreements, in which countries agree not to tax or otherwise block the international flow of goods and services, a good or bad thing?

A related issue is the phenomenon of *trade imbalances*, which occur when the quantity of goods and services that a country sells abroad (its *exports*) differs significantly from the quantity of goods and services its citizens buy from abroad (its *imports*). Figure 4.5 shows U.S. exports and imports (of goods only to allow

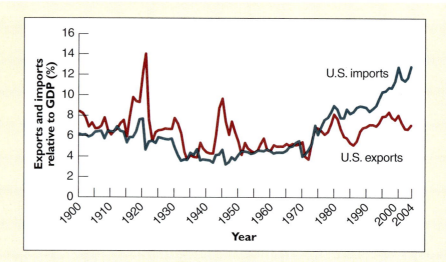

for a longer data series) since 1900, measured as a percentage of the economy's total output. Prior to the 1970s, the United States generally exported more than it imported. (Notice the major export booms that occurred after both world wars, when the United States was helping to reconstruct Europe.) Since the 1970s, however, imports to the United States have outstripped exports, creating a situation called a *trade deficit*. Other countries—Japan, for example—export much more than they import. A country such as Japan is said to have a *trade surplus*. What causes trade deficits and surpluses? Are they harmful or helpful?

RECAP	THE MAJOR MACROECONOMIC ISSUES

- *Economic growth and living standards.* Over the last century, the industrialized nations have experienced remarkable economic growth and improvements in living standards. Macroeconomists study the reasons for this extraordinary growth and try to understand why growth rates vary markedly among nations.

- *Productivity.* Average labor productivity, or output per employed worker, is a crucial determinant of living standards. Macroeconomists ask, What causes slowdowns and speedups in the rate of productivity growth?

- *Recessions and expansions.* Economies experience periods of slower growth (recessions) and more rapid growth (expansions). Macroeconomists examine the sources of these fluctuations and the government policies that attempt to moderate them.

- *Unemployment.* The unemployment rate is the fraction of people who would like to be employed but can't find work. Unemployment rises during recessions, but there are always unemployed people even during good times. Macroeconomists study the causes of unemployment, including the reasons why it sometimes differs markedly across countries.

- *Inflation.* The inflation rate is the rate at which prices in general are increasing over time. Questions macroeconomists ask about inflation include, Why does inflation vary over time and across countries? Must a reduction in inflation be accompanied by an increase in unemployment, or vice versa?

- *Economic interdependence among nations.* Modern economies are highly interdependent. Related issues studied by macroeconomists include the desirability of free trade agreements and the causes and effects of trade imbalances.

MACROECONOMIC POLICY

We have seen that macroeconomists are interested in why different countries' economies perform differently and why a particular economy may perform well in some periods and poorly in others. Although many factors contribute to economic performance, government policy is surely among the most important. Understanding the effects of various policies and helping government officials develop better policies are important objectives of macroeconomists.

TYPES OF MACROECONOMIC POLICY

We defined macroeconomic policies as government policies that affect the performance of the economy as a whole, as opposed to the market for a particular good or service. There are three major types of macroeconomic policy: *monetary policy*, *fiscal policy*, and *structural policy*.

The term **monetary policy** refers to the determination of the nation's money supply. (Cash and coin are the basic forms of money, although, as we will see, modern economies have other forms of money as well.) For reasons that we will discuss in later chapters, most economists agree that changes in the money supply affect important macroeconomic variables, including national output, employment, interest rates, inflation, stock prices, and the international value of the dollar. In virtually all countries, monetary policy is controlled by a government institution called the *central bank*. The Federal Reserve System, often called the Fed for short, is the central bank of the United States.

monetary policy determination of the nation's money supply

Fiscal policy refers to decisions that determine the government's budget, including the amount and composition of government expenditures and government revenues. The balance between government spending and taxes is a particularly important aspect of fiscal policy. When government officials spend more than they collect in taxes, the government runs a *deficit*, and when they spend less, the government's budget is in *surplus*. As with monetary policy, economists generally agree that fiscal policy can have important effects on the overall performance of the economy. For example, many economists believe that the large deficits run by the federal government during the 1980s were harmful to the nation's economy. Likewise, many would say that the balancing of the federal budget that occurred during the 1990s contributed to the nation's strong economic performance during that decade. Most recently, the federal budget has moved once again into deficit.

fiscal policy decisions that determine the government's budget, including the amount and composition of government expenditures and government revenues

Fiscal policies sometimes involve very long time horizons. For example, the Social Security and Medicare programs, which provide income support and medical care to retirees, face the need to meet their commitments to currently young workers, who will not retire for decades. Current proposals to reform these programs often consider projected revenues and payouts over a horizon of 75 years or more.

EXERCISE 4.2

The Congressional Budget Office (CBO) is the government agency that is charged with projecting the federal government's surpluses or deficits. From the CBO's home page (http://www.cbo.gov/), find the most recent value of the federal government's surplus or deficit and the CBO's projected values for the next five years. How do you think these projections are likely to affect congressional deliberations on taxation and government spending?

Finally, the term **structural policy** includes government policies aimed at changing the underlying structure, or institutions, of the nation's economy. Structural policies come in many forms, from minor tinkering to ambitious overhauls of the entire economic system. One example is the participation of the United States and many other countries in international trade agreements, starting with the Kennedy Round, that have greatly opened up the global economy to the free flow of goods

structural policy government policies aimed at changing the underlying structure, or institutions, of the nation's economy

and services across borders. A second example is the move away from government control of the economy and toward a more market-oriented approach in many formerly communist countries, such as Poland, the Czech Republic, and Hungary. Many developing countries have tried similar structural reforms. Supporters of structural policy hope that, by changing the basic characteristics of the economy or by remaking its institutions, they can stimulate economic growth and improve living standards.

POSITIVE VERSUS NORMATIVE ANALYSES OF MACROECONOMIC POLICY

Macroeconomists are frequently called upon to analyze the effects of a proposed policy. For example, if Congress is debating a tax cut, economists in the Congressional Budget Office or the Treasury may be asked to prepare an analysis of the likely effects of the tax cut on the overall economy, as well as on specific industries, regions, or income groups. An objective analysis aimed at determining only the economic consequences of a particular policy—not whether those consequences are desirable—is called a **positive analysis.** In contrast, a **normative analysis** includes recommendations on whether a particular policy *should* be implemented. While a positive analysis is supposed to be objective and scientific, a normative analysis involves the *values* of the person or organization doing the analysis—conservative, liberal, or middle-of-the-road.

positive analysis addresses the economic consequences of a particular event or policy, not whether those consequences are desirable

normative analysis addresses the question of whether a policy *should* be used; normative analysis inevitably involves the values of the person doing the analysis

While pundits often joke that economists cannot agree among themselves, the tendency for economists to disagree is exaggerated. When economists do disagree, the controversy often centers on normative judgments (which relate to economists' personal values) rather than on positive analysis (which reflects objective knowledge of the economy). For example, liberal and conservative economists might agree that a particular tax cut would increase the incomes of the relatively wealthy (positive analysis). But they might vehemently disagree on whether the policy *should* be enacted, reflecting their personal views about whether wealthy people deserve a tax break (normative analysis).

The next time you hear or read about a debate over economic issues, try to determine whether the differences between the two positions are primarily *positive* or *normative.* If the debate focuses on the actual effects of the event or policy under discussion, then the disagreement is over positive issues. But if the main question has to do with conflicting personal opinions about the *desirability* of those effects, the debate is normative. The distinction between positive and normative analyses is important, because objective economic research can help to resolve differences over positive issues. When people differ for normative reasons, however, economic analysis is of less use.

EXERCISE 4.3

Which of the following statements are positive and which are normative? How can you tell?

a. **A tax increase is likely to lead to lower interest rates.**

b. **Congress should increase taxes to reduce the inappropriately high level of interest rates.**

c. **A tax increase would be acceptable if most of the burden fell on those with incomes over $100,000.**

d. **Higher tariffs (taxes on imports) are needed to protect American jobs.**

e. **An increase in the tariff on imported steel would increase employment of American steelworkers.**

RECAP	MACROECONOMIC POLICY

Macroeconomic policies affect the performance of the economy as a whole. The three types of macroeconomic policy are monetary policy, fiscal policy, and structural policy. *Monetary policy,* which in the United States is under the control of the Federal Reserve System, refers to the determination of the nation's money supply. *Fiscal policy* involves decisions about the government budget, including its expenditures and tax collections. *Structural policy* refers to government actions to change the underlying structure or institutions of the economy. Structural policy can range from minor tinkering to a major overhaul of the economic system, as with the formerly communist countries that are attempting to convert to market-oriented systems.

The analysis of a proposed policy can be positive or normative. A *positive analysis* addresses the policy's likely economic consequences, but not whether those consequences are desirable. A *normative analysis* addresses the question of whether a proposed policy *should* be used. Debates about normative conclusions inevitably involve personal values and thus generally cannot be resolved by objective economic analysis alone.

AGGREGATION

In Chapter 1 we discussed the difference between macroeconomics, the study of national economies, and microeconomics, the study of individual economic entities, such as households and firms, and the markets for specific goods and services. The main difference between the fields is one of perspective: Macroeconomists take a "bird's-eye view" of the economy, ignoring the fine details to understand how the system works as a whole. Microeconomists work instead at "ground level," studying the economic behavior of individual households, firms, and markets. Both perspectives are useful—indeed essential—to understand what makes an economy work.

Although macroeconomics and microeconomics take different perspectives on the economy, the basic tools of analysis are much the same. In the chapters to come, you will see that macroeconomists apply the same core principles as microeconomists in their efforts to understand and predict economic behavior. Even though a national economy is a much bigger entity than a household or even a large firm, the choices and actions of individual decision makers ultimately determine the performance of the economy as a whole. So, for example, to understand saving behavior at the national level, the macroeconomist must first consider what motivates an individual family or household to save. The core principles introduced in Part 1 prove very useful for attacking such questions.

EXERCISE 4.4

Which of the following questions would be studied primarily by macroeconomists? By microeconomists? Explain.

a. **Does increased government spending lower the unemployment rate?**

b. **Does Microsoft Corporation's dominance of the software industry harm consumers?**

c. **Would a school voucher program improve the quality of education in the United States? (Under a voucher program, parents are given a fixed amount of government aid, which they may use to send their children to any school, public or private.)**

d. **Should government policymakers aim to reduce inflation still further?**

> **e. Why is the average rate of household saving low in the United States?**
>
> **f. Does the increase in the number of consumer products being sold over the Internet threaten the profits of conventional retailers?**

aggregation the adding up of individual economic variables to obtain economywide totals

While macroeconomists use the core principles of economics to understand and predict individual economic decisions, they need a way to relate millions of individual decisions to the behavior of the economy as a whole. One important tool they use to link individual behavior to national economic performance is **aggregation,** the adding up of individual economic variables to obtain economywide totals.

For example, macroeconomists don't care whether consumers drink Pepsi or Coke, go to the movie theater or rent videos, drive a convertible or a sports utility vehicle. These individual economic decisions are the province of microeconomics. Instead, macroeconomists add up consumer expenditures on all goods and services during a given period to obtain *aggregate*, or total, consumer expenditure. Similarly, a macroeconomist would not focus on plumbers' wages versus electricians' but would concentrate instead on the average wage of all workers. By focusing on aggregate variables, like total consumer expenditures or the average wage, macroeconomists suppress the mind-boggling details of a complex modern economy to see broad economic trends.

EXAMPLE 4.3

Aggregation (1): A national crime index

To illustrate not only why aggregation is needed but also some of the problems associated with it, consider an issue that is only partly economic: crime. Suppose policymakers want to know whether *in general* the problem of crime in the United States is getting better or worse. How could an analyst obtain a statistical answer to that question?

Police keep detailed records of the crimes reported in their jurisdictions, so in principle a researcher could determine precisely how many purse snatchings occurred last year on New York City subways. But data on the number of crimes of each type in each jurisdiction would produce stacks of computer output. Is there a way to add up, or aggregate, all the crime data to get some sense of the national trend?

Law enforcement agencies such as the FBI use aggregation to obtain national *crime rates*, which are typically expressed as the number of "serious" crimes committed per 100,000 population. For example, the FBI reported that in 2003 some 11.8 million serious crimes (both violent crimes and property crimes) occurred in the United States (http://www.fbi.gov). Dividing the number of crimes by the U.S. population in 2003, which was about 290 million, and multiplying by 100,000 yields the crime rate for 2003, equal to about 4,000 crimes per 100,000 people. This rate represented a substantial drop from the crime rate in 1992, which was nearly 5,700 crimes per 100,000 people. So aggregation (the adding up of many different crimes into a national index) indicates that, in general, serious crime decreased in the United States between 1992 and 2003.

Although aggregation of crime statistics reveals the "big picture," it may obscure important details. The FBI crime index lumps together relatively minor crimes such as petty theft with very serious crimes such as murder and rape. Most people would agree that murder and rape do far more damage than a typical theft, so adding together these two very different types of crimes might give a false picture of crime in the United States. For example, although the U.S. crime rate fell 29 percent between 1992 and 2003 the murder rate fell by 39 percent. Since murder is the most serious of crimes, the reduction in crime between 1992 and 2003 was probably more significant than the change in the overall crime rate indicates. The aggregate crime rate glosses over other important details, such as the fact that the most dramatic reductions in crime occurred in urban areas. This loss of detail is a cost of aggregation, the price analysts pay for the ability to look at broad economic or social trends.

Aggregation (2): U.S. exports

EXAMPLE 4.4

The United States exports a wide variety of products and services to many different countries. Kansas farmers sell grain to Russia, Silicon Valley programmers sell software to France, and Hollywood movie studios sell entertainment the world over. Suppose macroeconomists want to compare the total quantities of American-made goods sold to various regions of the world. How could such a comparison be made?

Economists can't add bushels of grain, lines of code, and movie tickets—the units aren't comparable. But they can add the *dollar values* of each—the revenue farmers earned from foreign grain sales, the royalties programmers received for their exported software, and the revenues studios reaped from films shown abroad. By comparing the dollar values of U.S. exports to Europe, Asia, Africa, and other regions in a particular year, economists are able to determine which regions are the biggest customers for American-made goods.

RECAP	AGGREGATION

Macroeconomics, the study of national economies, differs from microeconomics, the study of individual economic entities (such as households and firms) and the markets for specific goods and services. Macroeconomists take a "bird's-eye view" of the economy. To study the economy as a whole, macroeconomists make frequent use of aggregation, the adding up of individual economic variables to obtain economywide totals. For example, a macroeconomist is more interested in the determinants of total U.S. exports, as measured by total dollar value, than in the factors that determine the exports of specific goods. A cost of aggregation is that the fine details of the economic situation are often obscured.

STUDYING MACROECONOMICS: A PREVIEW

This chapter introduced many of the key issues of macroeconomics. In the chapters to come we will look at each of these issues in more detail. The next two chapters (Chapters 5 and 6) cover the *measurement* of economic performance, including key variables like the level of economic activity, the extent of unemployment, and the rate of inflation. Obtaining quantitative measurements of the economy, against which theories can be tested, is the crucial first step in answering basic macroeconomic questions like those raised in this chapter.

In Part 3 we will study economic behavior over relatively long periods of time. Chapter 7 examines economic growth and productivity improvement, the fundamental determinants of the average standard of living in the long run. Chapter 8 discusses the long-run determination of employment, unemployment, and wages. In Chapter 9 we study saving and its link to the creation of new capital goods, such as factories and machines. The role played in the economy by money, and its relation to the rate of inflation, is covered in Chapter 10, which also introduces

the Federal Reserve, the central bank of the United States, and discusses some of its policy tools. Chapter 11 looks at both domestic and international financial markets and their role in allocating saving to productive uses, in particular their role in promoting international capital flows.

John Maynard Keynes, a celebrated British economist, once wrote that "In the long run, we are all dead." Keynes's statement was intended as an ironic comment on the tendency of economists to downplay short-run economic problems on the grounds that "in the long run," the operation of the free market will always restore economic stability. Keynes, who was particularly active and influential during the Great Depression, correctly viewed the problem of massive unemployment, whether "short run" or not, as the most pressing economic issue of the time.

So why start our study of macroeconomics with the long run? Keynes's comment notwithstanding, long-run economic performance is extremely important, accounting for most of the substantial differences in living standards and economic well-being the world over. Furthermore, studying long-run economic behavior provides important background for understanding short-term fluctuations in the economy.

We turn to those short-term fluctuations in Part 4. Chapter 12 provides background on what happens during recessions and expansions, as well as some historical perspective. Chapter 13 discusses one important source of short-term economic fluctuations: variations in aggregate spending. The chapter also shows how, by influencing aggregate spending, fiscal policy may be able to moderate economic fluctuations. The second major policy tool for stabilizing the economy, monetary policy, is the subject of Chapter 14. Chapter 15 brings inflation into the analysis and discusses the circumstances under which macroeconomic policymakers may face a short-term trade-off between inflation and unemployment. Chapter 16 extends the analysis and discusses the practices and pitfalls of macroeconomic policymaking in more detail.

The international dimension of macroeconomics is the focus of Part 5. (Chapter 17 focused on the issue of international trade and the costs and benefits of unrestricted trade.) Chapter 18 introduces exchange rates between national currencies. We will discuss how exchange rates are determined and how they affect the workings of the economy and macroeconomic policy.

■ SUMMARY ■

- Macroeconomics is the study of the performance of national economies and of the policies governments use to try to improve that performance. Some of the broad issues macroeconomists study are

  Sources of economic growth and improved living standards.

  Trends in *average labor productivity,* or output per employed worker.

  Short-term fluctuations in the pace of economic growth (recessions and expansions).

  Causes and cures of unemployment and inflation.

  Economic interdependence among nations.

- To help explain differences in economic performance among countries, or in economic performance in the same country at different times, macroeconomists study the implementation and effects of macroeconomic policies. *Macroeconomic policies* are government actions designed to affect the performance of the economy as a whole. Macroeconomic policies

include *monetary policy* (the determination of the nation's money supply), *fiscal policy* (relating to decisions about the government's budget), and *structural policy* (aimed at affecting the basic structure and institutions of the economy).

- In studying economic policies, economists apply both *positive analysis* (an objective attempt to determine the consequences of a proposed policy) and *normative analysis* (which addresses whether a particular policy *should* be adopted). Normative analysis involves the values of the person doing the analysis.

- Macroeconomics is distinct from microeconomics, which focuses on the behavior of individual economic entities and specific markets. Macroeconomists make heavy use of *aggregation,* which is the adding up of individual economic variables into economywide totals. Aggregation allows macroeconomists to study the "big picture" of the economy, while ignoring fine details about individual households, firms, and markets.

▪ KEY TERMS ▪

aggregation (110)
average labor productivity (101)
fiscal policy (107)

macroeconomic policies (99)
monetary policy (107)
normative analysis (108)

positive analysis (108)
structural policy (107)

▪ REVIEW QUESTIONS ▪

1. How did the experience of the Great Depression motivate the development of the field of macroeconomics?

2. Generally, how does the standard of living in the United States today compare to the standard of living in other countries? To the standard of living in the United States a century ago?

3. Why is average labor productivity a particularly important economic variable?

4. True or false: Economic growth within a particular country generally proceeds at a constant rate. Explain.

5. True or false: Differences of opinion about economic policy recommendations can always be resolved by objective analysis of the issues. Explain.

6. Baseball statistics, such as batting averages, are calculated and reported for each individual player, for each team, and for the league as a whole. What purposes are served by doing this? Relate to the idea of aggregation in macroeconomics.

7. What type of macroeconomic policy (monetary, fiscal, structural) might include each of the following actions?
   a. A broad government initiative to reduce the country's reliance on agriculture and promote high-technology industries.
   b. A reduction in income tax rates.
   c. Provision of additional cash to the banking system.
   d. An attempt to reduce the government budget deficit by reducing spending.
   e. A decision by a developing country to reduce government control of the economy and to become more market-oriented.

▪ PROBLEMS ▪

1. Over the next 50 years the Japanese population is expected to decline, while the fraction of the population that is retired is expected to increase sharply. What are the implications of these population changes for total output and average living standards in Japan, assuming that average labor productivity continues to grow? What if average labor productivity stagnates?

2. Is it possible for average living standards to rise during a period in which average labor productivity is falling? Discuss, using a numerical example for illustration.

3. The Bureau of Economic Analysis, or BEA, is a government agency that collects a wide variety of statistics about the U.S. economy. From the BEA's home page (http://www.bea.doc.gov) find data for the most recent year available on U.S. exports and imports of goods and services. Is the United States running a trade surplus or deficit? Calculate the ratio of the surplus or deficit to U.S. exports.

4. Which of the following statements are positive and which are normative?
   a. If the Federal Reserve raises interest rates, demand for housing is likely to fall.
   b. The Federal Reserve should raise interest rates to keep inflation at an acceptably low level.
   c. Stock prices are likely to fall over the next year as the economy slows.
   d. A reduction in the capital gains tax (the tax on profits made in the stock market) would lead to a 10 to 20 percent increase in stock prices.
   e. Congress should not reduce capital gains taxes without also providing tax breaks for lower-income people.

5. Which of the following would be studied by a macroeconomist? By a microeconomist?
   a. The worldwide operations of General Motors.
   b. The effect of government subsidies on sugar prices.
   c. Factors affecting average wages in the U.S. economy.
   d. Inflation in developing countries.
   e. The effects of tax cuts on consumer spending.

■ ANSWERS TO IN-CHAPTER EXERCISES ■

4.1 Your answer will depend upon the current unemployment rate available at the OECD Web site.

4.2 Your answer will depend upon the current CBO budget data.

4.3 a. Positive. This is a prediction of the effect of a policy, not a value judgment on whether the policy should be used.
 b. Normative. Words like *should* and *inappropriately* express value judgments about the policy.
 c. Normative. The statement is about the desirability of certain types of policies, not their likely effects.
 d. Normative. The statement is about desirability of a policy.
 e. Positive. The statement is a prediction of the likely effects of a policy, not a recommendation on whether the policy should be used.

4.4 a. Macroeconomists. Government spending and the unemployment rate are aggregate concepts pertaining to the national economy.
 b. Microeconomists. Microsoft, though large, is an individual firm.
 c. Microeconomists. The issue relates to the supply and demand for a specific service, education.
 d. Macroeconomists. Inflation is an aggregate, economywide concept.
 e. Macroeconomists. Average saving is an aggregate concept.
 f. Microeconomists. The focus is on a relatively narrow set of markets and products rather than on the economy as a whole.

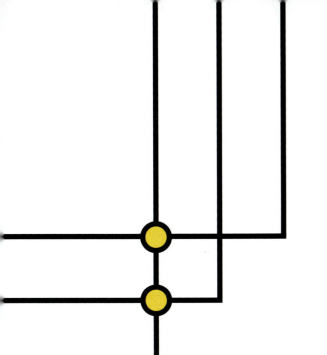

CHAPTER 5

MEASURING ECONOMIC ACTIVITY: GDP AND UNEMPLOYMENT

"**N**onfarm payrolls grew at a 2 percent rate in the third quarter . . ."

"The Dow Jones stock market index closed up 93 points yesterday in moderate trading . . ."

"Inflation appears subdued as the consumer price index registered an increase of only 0.2 percent last month . . ."

"The unemployment rate last month rose to 5.8 percent, its highest level since . . ."

News reports like these fill the airwaves—some TV and radio stations carry nothing else. In fact, all kinds of people are interested in economic data. The average person hopes to learn something that will be useful in a business decision, a financial investment, or a career move. The professional economist depends on economic data in much the same way that a doctor depends on a patient's vital signs—pulse, blood pressure, and temperature—to make an accurate diagnosis. To understand economic developments and to be able to give useful advice to policymakers, businesspeople, and financial investors, an economist simply must have up-to-date, accurate data. Political leaders and policymakers also need economic data to help them in their decisions and planning.

Interest in measuring the economy, and attempts to do so, date back as far as the mid-seventeenth century, when Sir William Petty (1623–1687) conducted a detailed survey of the land and wealth of Ireland. Not until the twentieth century, though, did economic measurement come into its own. World War II was an important catalyst for the development of accurate economic statistics, since its very outcome was thought to depend on the mobilization of economic resources. Two economists—Simon Kuznets in the United States and Richard Stone in the United Kingdom—developed comprehensive systems for measuring a nation's output of goods and services, which were of great help to Allied leaders in their wartime planning. Kuznets and Stone each received a Nobel Prize in economics for their work, which became the basis for the economic accounts used today by almost all the world's countries. The governments of the United States and many other countries now collect and publish a wealth of statistics covering all aspects of their economies.

In this chapter and the next, we will discuss how economists measure three basic macroeconomic variables that arise frequently in analyses of the state of the economy: the *gross domestic product,* or *GDP;* the *rate of unemployment;* and the *rate of inflation.* The focus of this chapter is on the first two of these statistics, GDP and the unemployment rate, which both measure the overall level of economic activity in a country.

Measuring economic activity might sound like a straightforward and uncontroversial task, but that is not the case. Indeed, the basic measure of a nation's output of goods and services, the gross domestic product, or GDP, has been criticized on many grounds. Some critics have complained that GDP does not adequately reflect factors such as the effect of economic growth on the environment or the rate of resource depletion. Because of problems like these, they charge, policies based on GDP statistics are likely to be flawed. Unemployment statistics also have been the subject of some controversy. By the end of this chapter, you will understand how official measures of output and unemployment are constructed and used and will have gained some insight into these debates over their accuracy. Understanding the strengths and limitations of economic data is the first critical step toward becoming an intelligent user of economic statistics, as well as a necessary background for the economic analysis in the chapters to come.

GROSS DOMESTIC PRODUCT: MEASURING THE NATION'S OUTPUT

The previous chapter emphasized the link between an economy's output of goods and services and its living standard. We noted that high levels of output per person, and per worker, are typically associated with a high standard of living. But what, exactly, does "output" mean? To study economic growth and productivity scientifically, we need to be more precise about how economists define and measure an economy's output.

The most frequently used measure of an economy's output is called the *gross domestic product,* or *GDP.* GDP is intended to measure how much an economy produces in a given period, such as a quarter (three months) or a year. More precisely, **gross domestic product (GDP)** is the market value of the final goods and services produced in a country during a given period. To understand this definition, let's take it apart and examine each of its parts separately. The first key phrase in the definition is "market value."

gross domestic product (GDP) the market value of the final goods and services produced in a country during a given period

MARKET VALUE

A modern economy produces many different goods and services, from dental floss (a good) to acupuncture (a service). Macroeconomists are not interested in this kind of detail, however; rather, their goal is to understand the behavior of the economy as a whole. For example, a macroeconomist might ask, Has the overall capacity of the economy to produce goods and services increased over time? If so, by how much?

To be able to talk about concepts like the "total output" or "total production"— as opposed to the production of specific items like dental floss—economists need to *aggregate* the quantities of the many different goods and services into a single number.

They do so by adding up the *market values* of the different goods and services the economy produces. A simple example will illustrate the process. In the imaginary economy of Orchardia, total production is 4 apples and 6 bananas. To find the total output of Orchardia, we could add the number of apples to the number of bananas and conclude that total output is 10 pieces of fruit. But what if this economy also produced 3 pairs of shoes? There really is no sensible way to add apples and bananas to shoes.

Suppose, though, that we know that apples sell for $0.25 each, bananas for $0.50 each, and shoes for $20.00 a pair. Then the market value of this economy's production, or its GDP, is equal to

$$(4 \text{ apples} \times \$0.25/\text{apple}) + (6 \text{ bananas} \times \$0.50/\text{banana}) \\ + (3 \text{ pairs of shoes} \times \$20.00/\text{pair}) = \$64.00.$$

Notice that when we calculate total output this way, the more expensive items (the shoes) receive a higher weighting than the cheaper items (the apples and bananas). In general, the amount people are willing to pay for an item is an indication of the economic benefit they expect to receive from it (see Chapter 3). For this reason, higher-priced items should count for more in a measure of aggregate output.

Orchardia's GDP

EXAMPLE 5.1

Suppose Orchardia were to produce 3 apples, 3 bananas, and 4 pairs of shoes at the same prices as in the preceding text. What is its GDP now?

Now the Orchardian GDP is equal to

$$(3 \text{ apples} \times \$0.25/\text{apple}) + (3 \text{ bananas} \times \$0.50/\text{banana}) \\ + (4 \text{ pairs of shoes} \times \$20.00/\text{pair}) = \$82.25.$$

Notice that Orchardian GDP is higher in Example 5.1 even though two of the three goods (apples and bananas) are being produced in smaller quantities than before. The reason is that the good whose production has increased (shoes) is much more valuable than the goods whose production has decreased (apples and bananas).

EXERCISE 5.1

Suppose Orchardia produces the original quantities of the three goods at the same prices (see text preceding Example 5.1). In addition, it produces 5 oranges at $0.30 each. What is the GDP of Orchardia now?

EXERCISE 5.2

Following are data for April 2005 on U.S. production of passenger cars and other light vehicles (a category that includes minivans, light trucks, and sports utility vehicles). The data are broken down into two categories: U.S. auto producers (GM, Ford, and Chrysler, now DaimlerChrysler) and foreign-owned plants (such as Honda, Toyota, and BMW). Suppose the average selling price is $25,000 for passenger cars and $30,000 for other light vehicles.

	Passenger cars	Other light vehicles
U.S. producers	223,480	507,640
Foreign-owned plants	156,757	124,487

Compare the output of U.S. producers to that of foreign-owned plants in terms of both the total number of vehicles produced and their market values (contribution to GDP). Explain why the two measures give different impressions of the relative importance of production by U.S.-owned and foreign-owned plants.

Market values provide a convenient way to add together, or aggregate, the many different goods and services produced in a modern economy. A drawback of using market values, however, is that not all economically valuable goods and services are bought and sold in markets. For example, the unpaid work of a homemaker, although it is of economic value, is not sold in markets and so isn't counted in GDP. But paid housekeeping and child care services, which are sold in markets, do count. This distinction can create some pitfalls, as Example 5.2 shows.

EXAMPLE 5.2

Women's labor force participation and GDP measurement

The percentage of adult American women working outside the home has increased dramatically in the past four decades, from less than 40 percent in 1960 to about 60 percent today (see Figure 5.1). This trend has led to a substantial increase in the demand for paid day care and housekeeping services, as working wives and mothers require more help at home. How have these changes affected measured GDP?

FIGURE 5.1

Percentages of American Men and Women over Age 16 Working Outside the Home, 1960–2004.
The fraction of American women working outside the home has risen by about 20 percentage points since 1960, while the fraction of men working outside the home has declined slightly.

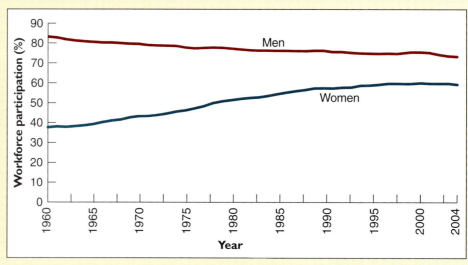

SOURCE: *Economic Report of the President*, February 2005 (http://www.gpoaccess.gov/eop/.

The entry of many women into the labor market has raised measured GDP in two ways. First, the goods and services that women produce in their new jobs have contributed directly to increasing GDP. Second, the fact that paid workers took over previously unpaid housework and child care duties has increased measured GDP by the amount paid to those workers. The first of these two changes represents a genuine increase in economic activity, but the second reflects a transfer of existing economic activities from the unpaid sector to the market sector. Overall, then, the increase in measured GDP associated with increased participation in the labor force by women probably overstates the actual increase in economic activity.

Why has female participation in the labor market increased by so much? What explains the trends illustrated in Figure 5.1?

In a world governed only by economic principles—without social conventions, customs, or traditions—homemaking tasks like cleaning, cooking, and child rearing would be jobs like any other. As such, they would be subject to the principle of comparative advantage: Those people (either men or women) whose comparative advantage lay in performing homemaking tasks would specialize in them, freeing people whose comparative advantage lies elsewhere to work outside the home. In

ECONOMIC NATURALIST
5.1

other words, homemaking tasks would be done by those with the lowest opportunity cost in those tasks. In such a world, to see a woman with a medical degree doing housework would be very unusual—her opportunity cost of doing housework would be too high.

But of course we don't live in a world driven only by economic considerations. Traditionally, social custom has severely limited the economic opportunities of women (and in some societies still does). However, social restrictions on women have weakened considerably over the past century, particularly in the industrialized countries, as a result of the increased educational attainment of women, the rise of the feminist movement, and other factors. As traditional social restraints on women have loosened, domestic arrangements have moved in the direction dictated by comparative advantage—to an increasing degree, homemaking tasks are now performed by paid specialists, while the majority of women (and men) work outside the home.

Although homemaking activities are excluded from measured GDP, in a few cases goods and services that are not sold in markets are included in GDP. By far the most important are the goods and services provided by federal, state, and local governments. The protection provided by the army and navy, the transportation convenience of the interstate highway system, and the education provided by the public school system are examples of publicly provided goods and services that are not sold in markets. As market prices for publicly provided goods and services do not exist, economic statisticians add to the GDP the *costs* of providing those goods and services as rough measures of their economic value. For example, to include public education in the GDP, the statisticians add to GDP the salaries of teachers and administrators, the costs of textbooks and supplies, and the like. Similarly, the economic value of the national defense establishment is approximated, for the purposes of measuring GDP, by the *costs* of defense: the pay earned by soldiers and sailors, the costs of acquiring and maintaining weapons, and so on.

With a few exceptions, like publicly provided goods and services, GDP is calculated by adding up market values. However, not all goods and services that have a market value are counted in GDP. As we will see next, GDP includes only those goods and services that are the end products of the production process, called *final goods and services*. Goods and services that are used up in the production process are not counted in GDP.

FINAL GOODS AND SERVICES

Many goods are used in the production process. Before a baker can produce a loaf of bread, grain must be grown and harvested, then the grain must be ground into flour, and, together with other ingredients, baked into bread. Of the three major goods that are produced during this process—the grain, the flour, and the bread—only the bread is used by consumers. Because producing the bread is the ultimate purpose of the process, the bread is called a *final good*. In general, a **final good or service** is the end product of a process, the product or service that consumers actually use. The goods or services produced on the way toward making the final product—here, the grain and the flour—are called **intermediate goods or services.**

Since we are interested in measuring only those items that are of direct economic value, *only final goods and services are included in GDP.* Intermediate goods and services are *not* included. To illustrate, suppose that the grain from the previous example has a market value of $0.50 (the price the milling company paid for the grain). The grain is then ground into flour, which has a market value of $1.20 (the price the baker paid for the flour). Finally, the flour is made into a loaf of fine French bread, worth $2.00 at the local store. In calculating the

Why is the female labor force participation rate now more than 50 percent greater than in the 1960s?

final goods or services goods or services consumed by the ultimate user; because they are the end products of the production process, they are counted as part of GDP

intermediate goods or services goods or services used up in the production of final goods and services and therefore not counted as part of GDP

contribution of these activities to GDP, would we want to add together the values of the grain, the flour, and the bread? No. This would incorrectly measure GDP as $.50 + $1.20 + $2.00 = $3.70. The value of the grain would then be counted three times: once as grain, then as part of the value of the flour, and finally as part of the value of the bread. The grain and flour are valuable only because they are intermediate goods that can be used to make bread. Since their value is included in the $2.00 value of the final product, the loaf of bread, the total contribution to GDP is $2.00.

Example 5.3 illustrates the same distinction but this time with a focus on services.

EXAMPLE 5.3   **The barber and his assistant**

Your barber charges $10 for a haircut. In turn, the barber pays his assistant $2 per haircut in return for sharpening the scissors, sweeping the floor, and other chores. For each haircut given, what is the total contribution of the barber and his assistant, taken together, to GDP?

The answer to this problem is $10, the price, or market value, of the haircut. The haircut is counted in GDP because it is the final service, the one that actually has value to the final user. The services provided by the assistant have value only because they contribute to the production of the haircut. Their $2 value is included in the $10 price of the haircut.

Example 5.4 illustrates that the same good can be either intermediate or final, depending on how it is used.

EXAMPLE 5.4   **A good that can be either intermediate or final**

Farmer Brown produces $100 worth of milk. He sells $40 worth of milk to his neighbors and uses the rest to feed his pigs, which he sells to his neighbors for $120. What is Farmer Brown's contribution to the GDP?

The final goods in this example are the $40 worth of milk and the $120 worth of pigs sold to the neighbors. Adding $40 and $120, we get $160, which is Farmer Brown's contribution to the GDP. Note that part of the milk Farmer Brown produced serves as an intermediate good and part as a final good. The $60 worth of milk that is fed to the pigs is an intermediate good, and so it is not counted in GDP. The $40 worth of milk sold to the neighbors is a final good, and so it is counted.

capital good a long-lived good that is used in the production of other goods and services

A special type of good that is difficult to classify as intermediate or final is a capital good. A **capital good** is a long-lived good that is used in the production of other goods or services. Factories and machines are examples of capital goods. Houses and apartment buildings, which produce dwelling services, are also a form of capital good. Capital goods do not fit the definition of final goods, since their purpose is to produce other goods. On the other hand, they are not used up during the production process, except over a very long period, so they are not exactly intermediate goods either. For purposes of measuring GDP, economists have agreed to classify newly produced capital goods as final goods even though they are not consumed by the ultimate user. Otherwise, a country that invested in its future by building modern factories and buying new machines would be counted as having a lower GDP than a country that devoted all its resources to producing consumer goods.

We have established the rule that only final goods and services (including newly produced capital goods) are counted in GDP. Intermediate goods and services, which are used up in the production of final goods and services, are not counted. In practice, however, this rule is not easy to apply, because the production process often stretches over several periods. To illustrate, recall the earlier example of the grain that was milled into flour, which in turn was baked into a loaf of French bread. The contribution of the whole process to GDP is $2, the value of the bread (the final product). Suppose, though, that the grain and the flour were produced near the end of the year 2005 and the bread was baked early the next year in 2006. In this case, should we attribute the $2 value of the bread to the GDP for the year 2005 or to the GDP for the year 2006?

Neither choice seems quite right, since part of the bread's production process occurred in each year. Part of the value of the bread should probably be counted in the year 2005 GDP and part in the year 2006 GDP. But how should we make the split? To deal with this problem, economists determine the market value of final goods and services indirectly, by adding up the *value added* by each firm in the production process. The **value added** by any firm equals the market value of its product or service minus the cost of inputs purchased from other firms. As we'll see, summing the value added by all firms (including producers of both intermediate and final goods and services) gives the same answer as simply adding together the value of final goods and services. But the value-added method eliminates the problem of dividing the value of a final good or service between two periods.

value added for any firm, the market value of its product or service minus the cost of inputs purchased from other firms

To illustrate this method, let's revisit the example of the French bread, which is the result of multiple stages of production. We have already determined that the total contribution of this production process to GDP is $2, the value of the bread. Let's show now that we can get the same answer by summing value added. Suppose that the bread is the ultimate product of three corporations: ABC Grain Company, Inc., produces grain; General Flour produces flour; and Hot'n'Fresh Baking produces the bread. If we make the same assumptions as before about the market value of the grain, the flour, and the bread, what is the value added by each of these three companies?

ABC Grain Company produces $0.50 worth of grain, with no inputs from other companies, so ABC's value added is $0.50. General Flour uses $0.50 worth of grain from ABC to produce $1.20 worth of flour. The value added by General Flour is thus the value of its product ($1.20) less the cost of purchased inputs ($0.50), or $0.70. Finally, Hot'n'Fresh Baking buys $1.20 worth of flour from General Flour and uses it to produce $2.00 worth of bread. So the value added by Hot'n'Fresh is $0.80. These calculations are summarized in Table 5.1.

You can see that summing the value added by each company gives the same contribution to GDP, $2.00, as the method based on counting final goods and services only. Basically, the value added by each firm represents the portion of the value of the final good or service that the firm creates in its stage of production. Summing the value added by all firms in the economy yields the total value of final goods and services, or GDP.

TABLE 5.1
Value Added in Bread Production

Company	Revenues	− Cost of purchased inputs	= Value added
ABC Grain	$0.50	$0.00	$0.50
General Flour	$1.20	$0.50	$0.70
Hot'n'Fresh	$2.00	$1.20	$0.80
Total			$2.00

You also can see now how the value-added method solves the problem of production processes that bridge two or more periods. Suppose that the grain and flour are produced during the year 2005, but the bread is not baked until 2006. Using the value-added method, the contribution of this production process to the year 2005 GDP is the value added by the grain company plus the value added by the flour company, or $1.20. The contribution of the production process to the year 2006 GDP is the value added by the baker, which is $0.80. Thus, part of the value of the final product, the bread, is counted in the GDP for each year, reflecting the fact that part of the production of the bread took place in each year.

EXERCISE 5.3

Amy's card shop receives a shipment of Valentine's Day cards in December 2005. Amy pays the wholesale distributor of the cards a total of $500. In February 2006 she sells the cards for a total of $700. What are the contributions of these transactions to GDP in the years 2005 and 2006?

We have now established that GDP is equal to the market value of final goods and services. Let's look at the last part of the definition, "produced within a country during a given period."

PRODUCED WITHIN A COUNTRY DURING A GIVEN PERIOD

The word *domestic* in the term *gross domestic product* tells us that GDP is a measure of economic activity within a given country. Thus, only production that takes place within the country's borders is counted. For example, the GDP of the United States includes the market value of *all* cars produced within U.S. borders, even if they are made in foreign-owned plants (recall Exercise 5.2). However, cars produced in Mexico by a U.S.-based company like General Motors are *not* counted.

We have seen that GDP is intended to measure the amount of production that occurs during a given period, such as the calendar year. For this reason, only goods and services that are actually produced during a particular year are included in the GDP for that year. Example 5.5 and Exercise 5.4 illustrate.

EXAMPLE 5.5   **The sale of a house and GDP**

A 20-year-old house is sold to a young family for $200,000. The family pays the real estate agent a 6 percent commission, or $12,000. What is the contribution of this transaction to GDP?

Because the house was not produced during the current year, its value is *not* counted in this year's GDP. (The value of the house was included in the GDP 20 years earlier, the year the house was built.) In general, purchases and sales of existing assets, such as old houses or used cars, do not contribute to the current year's GDP. However, the $12,000 fee paid to the real estate agent represents the market value of the agent's services in helping the family find the house and make the purchase. Since those services were provided during the current year, the agent's fee *is* counted in current-year GDP.

EXERCISE 5.4

Lotta Doe sells 100 shares of stock in Benson Buggywhip for $50 per share. She pays her broker a 2 percent commission for executing the sale. How does Lotta's transaction affect the current-year GDP?

RECAP	MEASURING GDP

Gross domestic product (GDP) equals

the market value
GDP is an aggregate of the market values of the many goods and services produced in the economy.

Goods and services that are not sold in markets, such as unpaid housework, are not counted in GDP. An important exception is goods and services provided by the government, which are included in GDP at the government's cost of providing them.

of final goods and services
Final goods and services—goods and services consumed by the ultimate user—are counted in GDP. By convention, newly produced capital goods, such as factories and machines, also are treated as final goods and are counted in GDP. Intermediate goods and services, which are used up in the production of final goods and services, are not counted.

In practice, the value of final goods and services is determined by the value-added method. The value added by any firm equals the firm's revenue from selling its product minus the cost of inputs purchased from other firms. Summing the value added by all firms in the production process yields the value of the final good or service.

produced in a country during a given period.
Only goods and services produced within a nation's borders are included in GDP.

Only goods and services produced during the current year (or the portion of the value produced during the current year) are counted as part of the current-year GDP.

THE EXPENDITURE METHOD FOR MEASURING GDP

GDP is a measure of the quantity of goods and services *produced* by an economy. But any good or service that is produced also will be *purchased* and used by some economic agent—a consumer buying Christmas gifts or a firm investing in new machinery, for example. For many purposes, knowing not only how much is produced, but who uses it and how, is important.

Economic statisticians divide the users of the final goods and services that make up the GDP for any given year into four categories: *households, firms, governments,* and the *foreign sector* (that is, foreign purchasers of domestic products). They assume that all the final goods and services that are produced in a country in a given year will be purchased and used by members of one or more of these four groups. Furthermore, the amounts that purchasers spend on various goods and services should be equal to the market values of those goods and services. As a result, GDP can be measured with equal accuracy by either of two methods: (1) adding up the market values of all the final goods and services that are produced domestically or (2) adding up the total amount spent by each of the four groups on final goods and services and subtracting spending on imported goods and services. The values obtained by the two methods will be the same.

Corresponding to the four groups of final users are four components of expenditure: consumption, investment, government purchases, and net exports. That is,

TABLE 5.2
Expenditure Components of U.S. GDP, 2004 (billions of dollars)

Consumption		8,214.3
Durable goods	987.8	
Nondurable goods	2,368.3	
Services	4,858.2	
Investment		1,928.1
Business fixed investment	1,198.8	
Residential investment	673.8	
Inventory investment	55.4	
Government purchases		2,215.9
Net exports		−624.0
Exports	1,173.8	
Imports	1,797.8	
Total: Gross domestic product		11,734.3

Source: http://www.bea.gov.

households consume, firms invest, governments make government purchases, and the foreign sector buys the nation's exports. Table 5.2 gives the dollar values for each of these components for the U.S. economy in 2004. As the table shows, GDP for the United States in 2004 was about $11.7 trillion, roughly $40,000 per person. Detailed definitions of the components of expenditure, and their principal subcomponents, follow. As you read through them, refer to Table 5.2 to get a sense of the relative importance of each type of spending.

consumption expenditure, or consumption spending by households on goods and services such as food, clothing, and entertainment

Consumption expenditure, or simply **consumption,** is spending by households on goods and services such as food, clothing, and entertainment. Consumption expenditure is subdivided into three subcategories:

■ *Consumer durables* are long-lived consumer goods such as cars and furniture. Note that new houses are not treated as consumer durables but as part of investment.

■ *Consumer nondurables* are shorter-lived goods like food and clothing.

■ *Services,* a large component of consumer spending, include everything from haircuts and taxi rides to legal, financial, and educational services.

investment spending by firms on final goods and services, primarily capital goods

Investment is spending by firms on final goods and services, primarily capital goods. Investment is divided into three subcategories:

■ *Business fixed investment* is the purchase by firms of new capital goods such as machinery, factories, and office buildings. (Remember that for the purposes of calculating GDP, long-lived capital goods are treated as final goods rather than as intermediate goods.) Firms buy capital goods to increase their capacity to produce.

■ *Residential investment* is construction of new homes and apartment buildings. Recall that homes and apartment buildings, sometimes called residential capital, are also capital goods. For GDP accounting purposes, residential investment is treated as an investment by the business sector, which then sells the homes to households.

■ *Inventory investment* is the addition of unsold goods to company inventories. In other words, the goods that a firm produces but doesn't sell during the current period are treated, for accounting purposes, as if the firm had bought those goods from itself. (This convention guarantees that production equals expenditure.) Inventory investment can be positive or negative, depending on whether the value of inventories rises or falls over the course of the year.

People often refer to purchases of financial assets, such as stocks or bonds, as "investments." That use of the term is different from the definition we give here. A person who buys a share of a company's stock acquires partial ownership of the *existing* physical and financial assets controlled by the company. A stock purchase does not usually correspond to the creation of *new* physical capital, however, and so is not investment in the sense we are using the term in this chapter. We will generally refer to purchases of financial assets, such as stocks and bonds, as "financial investments," to distinguish them from a firm's investment in new capital goods, such as factories and machines.

Government purchases are purchases by federal, state, and local governments of final goods, such as fighter planes, and services, such as teaching in public schools. Government purchases do *not* include *transfer payments,* which are payments made by the government in return for which no current goods or services are received. Examples of transfer payments (which, again, are *not* included in government purchases) are Social Security benefits, unemployment benefits, pensions paid to government workers, and welfare payments. Interest paid on the government debt is also excluded from government purchases.

Net exports equal exports minus imports.

- *Exports* are domestically produced final goods and services that are sold abroad.

- *Imports* are purchases by domestic buyers of goods and services that were produced abroad. Since imports are included in consumption, investment, and government purchases but do not represent spending on domestic production, they must be subtracted. A shorthand way of adding exports and subtracting imports is to add net exports, which equal exports minus imports.

government purchases purchases by federal, state, and local governments of final goods and services; government purchases do *not* include *transfer payments,* which are payments made by the government in return for which no current goods or services are received, nor do they include interest paid on the government debt

net exports exports minus imports

A country's net exports reflect the net demand by the rest of the world for its goods and services. Net exports can be negative, since imports can exceed exports in any given year. As Table 5.2 shows, the United States had significantly greater imports than exports in 2004.

The relationship between GDP and expenditures on goods and services can be summarized by an equation. Let

$$Y = \text{gross domestic product, or output}$$
$$C = \text{consumption expenditure}$$
$$I = \text{investment}$$
$$G = \text{government purchases}$$
$$NX = \text{net exports.}$$

Using these symbols, we can write that GDP equals the sum of the four types of expenditure algebraically as

$$Y = C + I + G + NX.$$

EXAMPLE 5.6

Measuring GDP by production and by expenditure

An economy produces 1,000,000 automobiles valued at $15,000 each. Of these, 700,000 are sold to consumers, 200,000 are sold to businesses, 50,000 are sold to the government, and 25,000 are sold abroad. No automobiles are imported. The automobiles left unsold at the end of the year are held in inventory by the auto producers. Find GDP in terms of (a) the market value of production and (b) the components of expenditure. You should get the same answer both ways.

The market value of the production of final goods and services in this economy is 1,000,000 autos times $15,000 per auto, or $15 billion.

To measure GDP in terms of expenditure, we must add spending on consumption, investment, government purchases, and net exports. Consumption is 700,000 autos times $15,000, or $10.5 billion. Government purchases are 50,000 autos times $15,000, or $0.75 billion. Net exports are equal to exports (25,000 autos at $15,000, or $0.375 billion) minus imports (zero), so net exports are $0.375 billion.

But what about investment? Here we must be careful. The 200,000 autos that are sold to businesses, worth $3 billion, count as investment. But notice too that the auto companies produced 1,000,000 automobiles but sold only 975,000 (700,000 + 200,000 + 50,000 + 25,000). Hence 25,000 autos were unsold at the end of the year and were added to the automobile producers' inventories. This addition to producer inventories (25,000 autos at $15,000, or $0.375 billion) counts as inventory investment, which is part of total investment. Thus, total investment spending equals the $3 billion worth of autos sold to businesses plus the $0.375 billion in inventory investment, or $3.375 billion.

Recapitulating, in this economy consumption is $10.5 billion, investment (including inventory investment) is $3.375 billion, government purchases equal $0.75 billion, and net exports are $0.375 billion. Summing these four components of expenditure yields $15 billion—the same value for GDP that we got by calculating the market value of production.

EXERCISE 5.5

Extending Example 5.6, suppose that 25,000 of the automobiles purchased by households are imported rather than domestically produced. Domestic production remains at 1,000,000 autos valued at $15,000 each. Once again, find GDP in terms of (a) the market value of production and (b) the components of expenditure.

RECAP	EXPENDITURE COMPONENTS OF GDP

GDP can be expressed as the sum of expenditures on domestically produced final goods and services. The four types of expenditure that are counted in the GDP, and the economic groups that make each type of expenditure, are as follows:

Who makes the expenditure?	Type of expenditure	Examples
Households	Consumption	Food, clothes, haircuts, new cars
Business firms	Investment	New factories and equipment, new houses, increases in inventory stocks
Governments	Government purchases	New school buildings, new military hardware, salaries of soldiers and government officials
Foreign sector	Net exports, or exports minus imports	Exported manufactured goods, legal or financial services provided by domestic residents to foreigners

GDP AND THE INCOMES OF CAPITAL AND LABOR

The GDP can be thought of equally well as a measure of total production or as a measure of total expenditure—either method of calculating the GDP gives the same final answer. There is yet a third way to think of the GDP, which is as the *incomes of capital and labor.*

Whenever a good or service is produced or sold, the revenue from the sale is distributed to the workers and the owners of the capital involved in the production of the good or service. Thus, except for some technical adjustments that we will ignore, GDP also equals labor income plus capital income. *Labor income* (equal to about two-thirds of GDP) comprises wages, salaries, and the incomes of the self-employed. *Capital income* (about one-third of GDP) is made up of payments to owners of physical capital (such as factories, machines, and office buildings) and intangible capital (such as copyrights and patents). The components of capital income include items such as profits earned by businessowners, the rents paid to owners of land or buildings, interest received by bondholders, and the royalties received by the holders of copyrights or patents. Both labor income and capital income are to be understood as measured prior to payment of taxes; ultimately, of course, a portion of both types of income is captured by the government in the form of tax collections.

Figure 5.2 may help you visualize the three equivalent ways of thinking about GDP: the market value of production, the total value of expenditure, and the sum of labor income and capital income. The figure also roughly captures the relative importance of the expenditure and income components. About 70 percent of expenditure is consumption spending, about 20 percent is government purchases, and the rest is investment spending and net exports. (Actually, as Table 5.2 or Figure 4.5 shows, net exports have been negative in recent years, reflecting the U.S. trade deficit.) As we mentioned, labor income is about two-thirds of total income, with capital income making up the rest.

FIGURE 5.2

The Three Faces of GDP.

The GDP can be expressed equally well as (1) the market value of production, (2) total expenditure (consumption, investment, government purchases, net exports), or (3) total income (labor income and capital income).

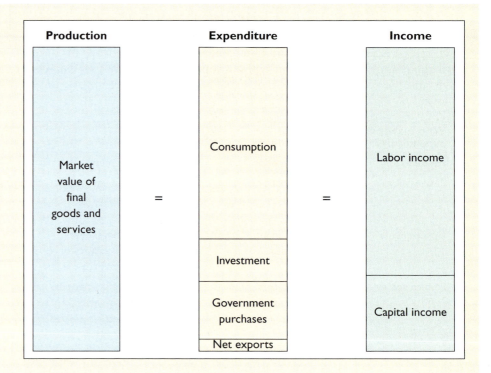

NOMINAL GDP VERSUS REAL GDP

As a measure of the total production of an economy over a given period, such as a particular year, GDP is useful in comparisons of economic activity in different places. For example, GDP data for the year 2004, broken down state by state, could be used to compare aggregate production in New York and California during that year. However, economists are interested in comparing levels of economic activity not only in different *locations* but *over time* as well. For example, a president who is running for reelection on the basis of successful economic policies might want to know by how much output in the U.S. economy had increased during his term.

Using GDP to compare economic activity at two different points in time may give misleading answers, however, as the following example shows. Suppose, for the sake of illustration, that the economy produces only pizzas and calzones. The prices and quantities of the two goods in the years 2004 and 2008, the beginning and end of the president's term, are shown in Table 5.3. If we calculate GDP in each year as the market value of production, we find that the GDP for 2004 is (10 pizzas × \$10/pizza) + (15 calzones × \$5/calzone) = \$175. The GDP for 2008 is (20 pizzas × \$12/pizza) + (30 calzones × \$6/calzone) = \$420. Comparing the GDP for the year 2008 to the GDP for the year 2004, we might conclude that it is 2.4 times greater (\$420/\$175).

TABLE 5.3

Prices and Quantities in 2004 and 2008

	Quantity of pizzas	Price of pizzas	Quantity of calzones	Price of calzones
2004	10	\$10	15	\$5
2008	20	\$12	30	\$6

But look more closely at the data given in Table 5.3. Can you see what is wrong with this conclusion? The quantities of both pizzas and calzones produced in the year 2008 are exactly twice the quantities produced in the year 2004. If economic activity, as measured by actual production of both goods, exactly doubled over the four years, why do the calculated values of GDP show a greater increase?

The answer, as you also can see from the table, is that prices as well as quantities rose between 2004 and 2008. Because of the increase in prices, the *market value* of production grew more over those four years than the *physical volume* of production. So in this case, GDP is a misleading gauge of economic growth during the president's term, since the physical quantities of the goods and services produced in any given year, not the dollar values, are what determine people's economic well-being. Indeed, if the prices of pizzas and calzones had risen 2.4 times between 2004 and 2008, GDP would have risen 2.4 times as well, with no increase in physical production! In that case, the claim that the economy's (physical) output had more than doubled during the president's term would obviously be wrong.

As this example shows, if we want to use GDP to compare economic activity at different points in time, we need some method of excluding the effects of price changes. In other words, we need to adjust for inflation. To do so, economists use a common set of prices to value quantities produced in different years. The standard approach is to pick a particular year, called the *base year,* and use the prices from that year to calculate the market value of output. There is no particular rule about which year to choose as the base year, but it is usually some recent year. When GDP is calculated using the prices from a base year, rather than the current year's prices, it is called **real GDP,** to indicate that it is a measure of real physical production. Real GDP is GDP adjusted for inflation. To distinguish real GDP, in which quantities produced are valued at base-year prices, from GDP valued at current-year prices, economists refer to the latter measure as **nominal GDP.**

real GDP a measure of GDP in which the quantities produced are valued at the prices in a base year rather than at current prices; real GDP measures the actual *physical volume* of production

nominal GDP a measure of GDP in which the quantities produced are valued at current-year prices; nominal GDP measures the *current dollar value* of production

Calculating the change in real GDP over the president's term

EXAMPLE 5.7

Using data from Table 5.3 and assuming that 2004 is the base year, find real GDP for the years 2008 and 2004. By how much did real output grow between 2004 and 2008?

To find real GDP for the year 2008, we must value the quantities produced that year using the prices in the base year, 2004. Using the data in Table 5.3:

Year 2008 real GDP = (year 2008 quantity of pizzas $\times$ year 2004 price of pizzas) + (year 2008 quantity of calzones $\times$ year 2004 price of calzones)

= $(20 \times \$10) + (30 \times \$5)$

= \$350.

The real GDP of this economy in the year 2008 is \$350. What is the real GDP for 2004?

By definition, the real GDP for 2004 equals 2004 quantities valued at base-year prices. The base year in this example happens to be 2004, so real GDP for 2004 equals 2004 quantities valued at 2004 prices, which is the same as nominal GDP for 2004. In general, in the base year, real GDP and nominal GDP are the same. We already found nominal GDP for 2004, \$175, so that is also the real GDP for 2004.

We can now determine how much real production has actually grown over the four-year period. Since real GDP was \$175 in 2004 and \$350 in 2008, the physical volume of production doubled between 2004 and 2008. This conclusion makes good sense, since Table 5.3 shows that the production of both pizzas and calzones exactly doubled over the period. By using real GDP, we have eliminated the effects of price changes and obtained a reasonable measure of the actual change in physical production over the four-year span.

Of course, the production of all goods will not necessarily grow in equal proportion, as in Example 5.7. Exercise 5.6 asks you to find real GDP when pizza and calzone production grow at different rates.

EXERCISE 5.6

Suppose production and prices of pizza and calzone in 2004 and 2008 are as follows:

	Quantity of pizzas	Price of pizzas	Quantity of calzones	Price of calzones
2004	10	$10	15	$5
2008	30	$12	30	$6

These data are the same as those in Table 5.3, except that pizza production has tripled rather than doubled between 2004 and 2008. Find real GDP in 2008 and 2004, and calculate the growth in real output over the four-year period. (Continue to assume that 2004 is the base year.)

If you complete Exercise 5.6, you will find that the growth in real GDP between 2004 and 2008 reflects a sort of average of the growth in physical production of pizzas and calzones. Real GDP therefore remains a useful measure of overall physical production, even when the production of different goods and services grows at different rates.

The method of calculating real GDP just described was followed for many decades by the Bureau of Economic Analysis (BEA), the U.S. government agency responsible for GDP statistics. However, in recent years the BEA has adopted a more complicated procedure of determining real GDP, called *chain weighting*. The new procedure makes the official real GDP data less sensitive to the particular base year chosen. However, the chain-weighting and traditional approaches share the basic idea of valuing output in terms of base-year prices, and the results obtained by the two methods are generally similar.

ECONOMIC NATURALIST 5.2

Can nominal and real GDP ever move in different directions?

In most countries, both nominal and real GDP increase in almost every year. It is quite possible, however, for them to move in opposite directions. The last time this happened in the United States was 1990–1991. In that period real GDP using the year 2000 as a base year *fell* by 0.2 percent, from $7,113 billion to $7,101 billion. This reflected an overall reduction in the physical quantities of goods and services produced. Nominal GDP, however, rose by 3.3 percent, from $5,803 billion to $5,996 billion, during the same period because prices rose by more than quantities fell.

The preceding example also illustrates the fact that nominal GDP will be *less* than real GDP if prices during the current year are less than prices during the base year. This will generally be the case when the current year is earlier than the base year.

Could real GDP ever rise during a year in which nominal GDP fell? Once again, the answer is yes. This may occur in some (but not all) instances in which a country is experiencing economic growth and deflation (falling prices) at the same time. If the rate at which prices are falling (indicating deflation) is greater than the rate at which the production of physical quantities is rising, real GDP will rise and nominal GDP will decrease. This actually happened in Japan during several years in the 1990s.

BOX 5.1: CHAIN WEIGHTING

Students who are comfortable with square roots may find it interesting to see how *chain weighting* actually works. As the name implies, annual data are "linked" with data from adjacent years using what is called a geometric average. The ratio of real GDP in 2005 relative to real GDP in 2004 is calculated using prices from both 2004 and 2005 as follows:

Ratio of real GDP in 2005 relative to real GDP in 2004

$$= \sqrt{\text{(Ratio of real GDPs using 2004 prices)}}\ \sqrt{\text{(Ratio of real GDPs using 2005 prices)}}.$$

The first term, the ratio of real GDPs using 2004 prices, is equal to

$$\frac{\text{Year 2005 real GDP using 2004 prices}}{\text{Year 2004 real GDP using 2004 prices}}.$$

Recall that this calculation would first use 2004 prices to value the quantities produced in 2005. It would then divide this sum by the value of the quantities produced in 2004 using 2004 prices once again. (This, of course, also will equal nominal GDP in year 2004.) Suppose this ratio were 1.06.

The ratio of real GDPs using 2005 prices, on the other hand, is equal to

$$\frac{\text{Year 2005 real GDP using 2005 prices}}{\text{Year 2004 real GDP using 2005 prices}}.$$

This second calculation would first use 2005 prices to value the quantities produced in 2005. (This would also equal nominal GDP in 2005.) It would then divide this sum by the value of the quantities produced in 2004 using 2005 prices. Suppose this ratio were 1.03.

The chain-weighted ratio of real GDP between 2005 and 2004 would then equal the geometric average of these two ratios. In our example, this would equal

$$\sqrt{1.06}\sqrt{1.03} = 1.0449.$$

This would imply that real GDP grew by 4.49 percent between 2004 and 2005. (Note that this is very close to the simple arithmetic average of 4.5 percent.)

Recall that real GDP in the base year is equal to nominal GDP in that same year. Consequently, we can use the chain-weighted growth rates of real GDP in each successive year to compute the level of real GDP in each year.

RECAP	NOMINAL GDP VERSUS REAL GDP

Real GDP is calculated using the prices of goods and services that prevailed in a base year rather than in the current year. Nominal GDP is calculated using current-year prices. Real GDP is GDP adjusted for inflation; it may be thought of as measuring the physical volume of production. Comparisons of economic activity at different times should always be done using real GDP, not nominal GDP.

REAL GDP IS NOT THE SAME AS ECONOMIC WELL-BEING

Government policymakers pay close attention to real GDP, often behaving as if the greater the GDP, the better. However, real GDP is *not* the same as economic well-being. At best, it is an imperfect measure of economic well-being because, for the most part, it captures only those goods and services that are priced and sold in markets. Many factors that contribute to people's economic well-being are not priced and sold in markets and thus are largely or even entirely omitted from GDP. Maximizing real GDP is not, therefore, always the right goal for government policymakers. Whether or not policies that increase GDP will also make people better off has to be determined on a case-by-case basis.

To understand why an increase in real GDP does not always promote economic well-being, let's look at some factors that are not included in GDP but do affect whether people are better off.

LEISURE TIME

Most Americans (and most people in other industrialized countries as well) work many fewer hours than their great-grandparents did 100 years ago. Early in the twentieth century some industrial workers—steelworkers, for example—worked as many as 12 hours a day, 7 days a week. Today, the 40-hour workweek is typical. Today, Americans also tend to start working later in life (after college or graduate school), and, in many cases, they are able to retire earlier. The increased leisure time available to workers in the United States and other industrialized countries—which allows them to pursue many worthwhile activities, including being with family and friends, participating in sports and hobbies, and pursuing cultural and educational activities—is a major benefit of living in a wealthy society. These extra hours of leisure are not priced in markets, however, and therefore are not reflected in GDP.

ECONOMIC
NATURALIST
5.3

Why do people work fewer hours today than their great-grandparents did?

Americans start work later in life, retire earlier, and in many cases work fewer hours per week than people of 50 or 100 years ago.

The *opportunity cost* of working less—retiring earlier, for example, or working fewer hours per week—is the earnings you forgo by not working. If you can make $400 per week at a summer job in a department store, for example, then leaving the job two weeks early to take a trip with some friends has an opportunity cost of $800. The fact that people are working fewer hours today suggests that their opportunity cost of forgone earnings is lower than their grandparents' and great-grandparents' opportunity cost. Why this difference?

Over the past century, rapid economic growth in the United States and other industrialized countries has greatly increased the purchasing power of the average worker's wages (see the chapter "Workers, Wages, and Unemployment in the Modern Economy"). In other words, the typical worker today can buy more goods and services with his or her hourly earnings than ever before. This fact would seem to suggest that the opportunity cost of forgone earnings (measured in terms of what those earnings can buy) is greater, not smaller, today than in earlier times. But because the buying power of wages is so much higher today than in the past, Americans can achieve a reasonable standard of living by working fewer hours than they did in the past. Thus, while your grandparents may have had to work long hours to pay the rent or put food on the table, today the extra income from working long hours is more likely to buy relative luxuries, like nicer clothes or a fancier car. Because such discretionary purchases are easier to give up than basic food and shelter, the true opportunity cost of forgone earnings is lower today than it was 50 years ago. As the opportunity cost of leisure has fallen, Americans have chosen to enjoy more of it.

NONMARKET ECONOMIC ACTIVITIES

Not all economically important activities are bought and sold in markets; with a few exceptions, such as government services, nonmarket economic activities are omitted from GDP. We mentioned earlier the example of unpaid housekeeping services. Another example is volunteer services, such as the volunteer fire and rescue squads that serve many small towns. The fact that these unpaid services are left out of GDP does *not* mean that they are unimportant. The problem is that, because there are no market prices and quantities for unpaid services, estimating their market values is very difficult.

How far do economists go wrong by leaving nonmarket economic activities out of GDP? The answer depends on the type of economy being studied. Although nonmarket economic activities exist in all economies, they are particularly important in poor economies. For example, in rural villages of developing countries, people commonly trade services with each other or cooperate on various tasks without exchanging any money. Families in these communities also tend to be relatively self-sufficient, growing their own food and providing many of their own basic services (recall the many skills of the Nepalese cook Birkhaman, described in Chapter 2). Because such nonmarket economic activities are not counted in official statistics, GDP data may substantially understate the true amount of economic activity in the poorest countries. In 2003, according to the World Bank,[1] the official GDP per person in Nepal was about $240, an amount that seems impossibly low. Part of the explanation for this figure is that because the Nepalese seldom use formal markets, many economic activities that would ordinarily be included in GDP are excluded from it in Nepal.

Closely related to nonmarket activities is what is called the *underground economy*, which includes transactions that are never reported to government officials and data collectors. The underground economy encompasses both legal and illegal activities, from informal babysitting jobs to organized crime. For instance, some people pay temporary or part-time workers like housecleaners and painters in cash, which allows these workers to avoid paying taxes on their income. Economists who have tried to estimate the value of such services by studying how much cash the public holds have concluded that these sorts of transactions make up an important share of overall economic activity, even in advanced industrial economies.

ENVIRONMENTAL QUALITY AND RESOURCE DEPLETION

China has recently experienced tremendous growth in real GDP. But in expanding its manufacturing base, it also has suffered a severe decline in air and water quality. Increased pollution certainly detracts from the quality of life, but because air and water quality are not bought and sold in markets, the Chinese GDP does not reflect this downside of their economic growth.

The exploitation of finite natural resources also tends to be overlooked in GDP. When an oil company pumps and sells a barrel of oil, GDP increases by the value of the oil. But the fact that there is one less barrel of oil in the ground, waiting to be pumped sometime in the future, is not reflected in GDP.

A number of efforts have been made to incorporate factors like air quality and resource depletion into a comprehensive measure of GDP. Doing so is difficult, since it often involves placing a dollar value on intangibles, like having a clean river to swim in instead of a dirty one. But the fact that the benefits of environmental quality and resource conservation are hard to measure in dollars and cents does not mean that they are unimportant.

---

[1]http://www.worldbank.org/cgi-bin/sendoff.cgi?page=/data/countrydata/aag/np/_aag.pdf.

QUALITY OF LIFE

What makes a particular town or city an attractive place in which to live? Some desirable features you might think of are reflected in GDP: spacious, well-constructed homes, good restaurants and stores, a variety of entertainment, and high-quality medical services. However, other indicators of the good life are not sold in markets and so may be omitted from GDP. Examples include a low crime rate, minimal traffic congestion, active civic organizations, and open space. Thus, while some citizens of a community may oppose the construction of a new Wal-Mart because they believe it may have a negative effect on the quality of life, others may support it because Wal-Mart sells goods at lower prices and may increase local GDP.

POVERTY AND ECONOMIC INEQUALITY

GDP measures the *total* quantity of goods and services produced and sold in an economy, but it conveys no information about who gets to enjoy those goods and services. Two countries may have identical GDPs but differ radically in the distribution of economic welfare across the population. Suppose, for example, that in one country—call it Equalia—most people have a comfortable middle-class existence; both extreme poverty and extreme wealth are rare. But in another country, Inequalia—which has the same real GDP as Equalia—a few wealthy families control the economy, and the majority of the population lives in poverty. While most people would say that Equalia has a better economic situation overall, that judgment would not be reflected in the GDPs of the two countries, which are the same.

In the United States absolute poverty has been declining. Today, many families whose income is below today's official "poverty line" (in 2005, $19,350 for a family of four) own a television, a car, and in some cases their own home. Some economists have argued that people who are considered poor today live as well as many middle-class people did in the 1950s.

But, though absolute poverty seems to be decreasing in the United States, inequality of income has generally been rising. The chief executive officer of a large U.S. corporation may earn hundreds of times what the typical worker in the same firm receives. Psychologists tell us that people's economic satisfaction depends not only on their absolute economic position—the quantity and quality of food, clothing, and shelter they have—but on what they have compared to what others have. If you own an old, beat-up car but are the only person in your neighborhood to have a car, you may feel privileged. But if everyone else in the neighborhood owns a luxury car, you are likely to be less satisfied. To the extent that such comparisons affect people's well-being, inequality matters as well as absolute poverty. Again, because GDP focuses on total production rather than on the distribution of output, it does not capture the effects of inequality.

BUT GDP IS RELATED TO ECONOMIC WELL-BEING

You might conclude from the list of important factors omitted from the official figures that GDP is useless as a measure of economic welfare. Indeed, numerous critics have made that claim. Clearly, in evaluating the effects of a proposed economic policy, considering only the likely effects on GDP is not sufficient. Planners must also ask whether the policy will affect aspects of economic well-being that are not captured in GDP. Environmental regulations may reduce production of steel, for example, which reduces the GDP. But that fact is not a sufficient basis on which to decide whether such regulations are good or bad. The right way to decide such questions is to apply the *cost-benefit principle* (see Chapter 1). Are the benefits of cleaner air worth more to people than the costs the regulations impose in terms of lost output and lost jobs? If so, then the regulations should be adopted; otherwise, they should not.

Although looking at the effects of a proposed policy on real GDP is not a good enough basis on which to evaluate a policy, real GDP per person *does* tend to be positively associated with many things people value, including a high material standard of living, better health and life expectancies, and better education. We discuss next some of the ways in which a higher real GDP implies greater economic well-being.

AVAILABILITY OF GOODS AND SERVICES

Obviously, citizens of a country with a high GDP are likely to possess more and better goods and services (after all, that is what GDP measures). On average, people in high-GDP countries enjoy larger, better-constructed, and more comfortable homes; higher-quality food and clothing; a greater variety of entertainment and cultural opportunities; better access to transportation and travel; better communications and sanitation; and other advantages. While social commentators may question the value of material consumption—and we agree that riches do not necessarily bring happiness or peace of mind—the majority of people in the world place great importance on achieving material prosperity. Throughout history people have made tremendous sacrifices and taken great risks to secure a higher standard of living for themselves and their families. In fact, to a great extent the United States was built by people who were willing to leave their native lands, often at great personal hardship, in hopes of bettering their economic condition.

HEALTH AND EDUCATION

Beyond an abundance of consumer goods, a high GDP brings other more basic advantages. Table 5.4 shows the differences between rich and poor countries with

TABLE 5.4
GDP and Basic Indicators of Well-Being

Indicator	All developing countries	Least developed countries	Industrialized countries
GDP per person (U.S. dollars)	4,054	1,307	29,000
Life expectancy at birth (years)	64.6	50.6	78.3
Infant mortality rate (per 1,000 live births)	61	99	5
Under-5 mortality rate (per 1,000 live births)	89	157	7
Births attended by skilled health personnel (%)	55	33	99
Prevalence of HIV/AIDS (% in 15–49 age group)	1.2	3.4	0.3
Undernourished people (%)	17	37	Negligible
Combined gross enrollment rate for primary, secondary, and tertiary schools (%)	60	43	93
Adult literacy rate (%)	76.7	52.5	99
Total population in group of countries (millions)	4,936.9	700.9	911.6

Source: United Nations, *Human Development Report,* 2004, available at http://hdr.undp.org/. All data are for 2002, except births attended by skilled health personnel (1995–2002), prevalence of HIV/AIDS (2003), and undernourished people (1999–2001). GDP data are adjusted to account for local differences in prices of basic commodities and services (adjusted for purchasing power parity).

regard to some important indicators of well-being, including life expectancy, infant and child mortality rates, number of doctors, measures of nutrition, and educational opportunity. Three groups of countries are compared: (1) developing countries as a group (total population, 4.9 billion); (2) the least developed countries (49 countries with a total population of about 700 million); and (3) the industrialized countries (24 countries, including the United States, Canada, the western European countries, and Japan, with a total population of about 900 million). As the first row of Table 5.4 shows, these three groups of countries have radically different levels of GDP per person. Most notably, GDP per person in the industrialized countries is more than 20 times that of the least developed countries.[2]

How do these large differences in GDP relate to other measures of well-being? Table 5.4 shows that on some of the most basic measures of human welfare, the developing countries fare much worse than the industrial countries. A child born in one of the least developed countries has a 10 percent (99/1,000) chance of dying before its first birthday and about a 16 percent (157/1,000) chance of dying before its fifth birthday. The corresponding figures for the industrialized countries are 0.5 percent (5/1,000) and 0.7 percent (7/1,000), respectively. A child born in an industrialized country has a life expectancy of about 78 years, compared to about 51 years for a child born in one of the least developed countries. Superior nutrition, sanitation, and medical services in the richer countries account for these large discrepancies in basic welfare. Skilled health personnel assist in the delivery of 99 percent of births in industrialized countries but only 33 percent of births in the least developed countries. The poor also experience much higher rates of illness. For example, the incidence of HIV/AIDS in the least developed countries is 3.4 percent of the population aged 15–49, about 11 times the rate in industrialized countries.

On another important dimension of human well-being, literacy and education rates, high-GDP countries also have the advantage. As Table 5.4 shows, in the industrialized countries, the percentage of adults who can read and write is virtually 100 percent, almost twice the percentage (53 percent) in the poorest developing countries. The percentage of children enrolled in primary, secondary, and tertiary schools is 93 percent in industrialized countries, compared to 43 percent in the least developed countries. Furthermore, enrollment rates do not capture important differences in the quality of education available in rich and poor countries, as measured by indicators such as the educational backgrounds of teachers and student–teacher ratios. Once again, the average person in an industrialized country seems to be better off than the average person in a poor developing country.

A child born in one of the least developed countries has a 16 percent chance of dying before its fifth birthday.

© Bettmann/CORBIS

ECONOMIC
NATURALIST
5.4

Why do far fewer children complete high school in poor countries than in rich countries?

One possible explanation is that people in poor countries place a lower priority on getting an education than people in rich countries. But immigrants from poor countries often put a heavy emphasis on education—though it may be that people who emigrate from poor countries are unrepresentative of the population as a whole.

An economic naturalist's explanation for the lower schooling rates in poor countries would rely not on cultural differences but on differences in *opportunity cost*. In poor societies, most of which are heavily agricultural, children are an important source of labor. Beyond a certain age, sending children to school imposes a high opportunity cost on the family. Children who are in school are not available to help with planting, harvesting, and other tasks that must be done if the family is to survive. In addition, the cost of books and school supplies imposes a major hardship on poor families. In rich, nonagricultural countries, school-age children have few work opportunities, and their potential earnings are small relative to other sources

[2]The GDP data in Table 5.4 use U.S. prices to value goods and services in developing nations. Since basic goods and services tend to be cheaper in poor countries, this adjustment significantly increases measured GDP in those countries.

of family income. The low opportunity cost of sending children to school in rich countries is an important reason for the higher enrollment rates in those countries.

In the chapter "Economic Growth, Productivity, and Living Standards," we will discuss the costs and benefits of economic growth—which in practice means growth in real GDP per person—in greater depth. In that context we will return to the question of whether a growing real GDP is necessarily equated with greater economic well-being.

How do economists identify the determinants of happiness?

Several economists have used survey data to study the extent to which a variety of socioeconomic factors affect happiness. In these surveys, respondents are asked to describe or rank their level of happiness. They are then asked questions about their incomes, marital and family circumstances, employment situations, and so on. Economists use statistical techniques to determine the extent to which each socioeconomic variable affects people's reported levels of happiness.

In most studies, economists have found that adults are happier if they are married, employed, and earn more money, as one might expect. In one recent study,[3] 32 percent of Americans classify themselves as "very happy," 56 percent say they are "pretty happy," and 12 percent are "not too happy." In addition to the usual factors, this study also found that adults are happier if they have sex more frequently. (The typical American has sex two to three times per month.) People who had sex with more than one partner during the preceding year reported lower levels of happiness than those who had only one sex partner. The authors note, however, that the results should be treated "cautiously," because it was impossible to verify the validity of the survey responses. This is often a problem with studies that use survey response data.

ECONOMIC NATURALIST 5.5

RECAP	**REAL GDP AND ECONOMIC WELL-BEING**

Real GDP is at best an imperfect measure of economic well-being. Among the factors affecting well-being omitted from real GDP are the availability of leisure time, nonmarket services such as unpaid homemaking and volunteer services, environmental quality and resource conservation, and quality-of-life indicators such as a low crime rate. The GDP also does not reflect the degree of economic inequality in a country. Because real GDP is not the same as economic well-being, proposed policies should not be evaluated strictly in terms of whether or not they increase the GDP.

Although GDP is not the same as economic well-being, it is positively associated with many things that people value, including a higher material standard of living, better health, longer life expectancies, and higher rates of literacy and educational attainment. This relationship between real GDP and economic well-being has led many people to emigrate from poor nations in search of a better life and has motivated policymakers in developing countries to try to increase their nations' rates of economic growth.

THE UNEMPLOYMENT RATE

In assessing the level of economic activity in a country, economists look at a variety of statistics. Besides real GDP, one statistic that receives a great deal of attention, both from economists and from the general public, is the rate of unemployment. The unemployment rate is a sensitive indicator of conditions in the

[3]David G. Blanchflower and Andrew J. Oswald, "Money, Sex, and Happiness: An Empirical Study," National Bureau of Economic Research Working Paper 10499, May 2004.

labor market. When the unemployment rate is low, jobs are secure and relatively easier to find. Low unemployment is often associated with improving wages and working conditions as well, as employers compete to attract and retain workers.

We will discuss labor markets and unemployment in detail in the chapter "Workers, Wages, and Unemployment in the Modern Economy." This chapter will explain how the unemployment rate and some related statistics are defined and measured. It will close with a discussion of the costs of unemployment, both to the unemployed and to the economy as a whole.

MEASURING UNEMPLOYMENT

In the United States, defining and measuring unemployment is the responsibility of the Bureau of Labor Statistics, or BLS. Each month the BLS surveys about 60,000 randomly selected households. Each person in those households who is 16 years or older is placed in one of three categories:

1. *Employed.* A person is employed if he or she worked full-time or part-time (even for a few hours) during the past week or is on vacation or sick leave from a regular job.

2. *Unemployed.* A person is unemployed if he or she did not work during the preceding week but made some effort to find work (for example, by going to a job interview) in the past four weeks.

3. *Out of the labor force.* A person is considered to be out of the labor force if he or she did not work in the past week and did not look for work in the past four weeks. In other words, people who are neither employed nor unemployed (in the sense of looking for work but not being able to find it) are "out of the labor force." Full-time students, unpaid homemakers, retirees, and people unable to work because of disabilities are examples of people who are out of the labor force.

Based on the results of the survey, the BLS estimates how many people in the whole country fit into each of the three categories.

labor force the total number of employed and unemployed people in the economy

To find the unemployment rate, the BLS must first calculate the size of the *labor force.* The **labor force** is defined as the total number of employed and unemployed people in the economy (the first two categories of respondents to the BLS survey). The **unemployment rate** is then defined as the number of unemployed people divided by the labor force. Notice that people who are out of the labor force (because they are in school, have retired, or are disabled, for example) are not counted as unemployed and thus do not affect the unemployment rate. In general, a high rate of unemployment indicates that the economy is performing poorly.

unemployment rate the number of unemployed people divided by the labor force

participation rate the percentage of the working-age population in the labor force (that is, the percentage that is either employed or looking for work)

Another useful statistic is the **participation rate,** or the percentage of the working-age population in the labor force (that is, the percentage that is either employed or looking for work). Figure 5.1 showed participation rates for American women and men since 1960. The participation rate is calculated by dividing the labor force by the working-age (16+) population.

Table 5.5 illustrates the calculation of key labor market statistics, using data based on the BLS survey for April 2005. In that month unemployment was 5.2 percent of the labor force. The participation rate was 66 percent; that is, about two out of every three adults had a job or were looking for work. Figure 5.3 shows the U.S. unemployment rate since 1960. Unemployment rates were exceptionally low—just above 4 percent—in the late 1960s and the late 1990s. By this measure, the latter part of the 1990s was an exceptionally good time for American workers. However, unemployment rose in 2001–2003 following a recession in 2001.

TABLE 5.5
U.S. Employment Data, April 2005 (in millions)

Employed	141.10
Plus:	
Unemployed	7.66
Equals: Labor force	148.76
Plus:	
Not in labor force	76.68
Equals:	
Working-age (over 16) population	225.44
Unemployment rate = unemployed/labor force = 7.66/148.76 = 5.2%	
Participation rate = labor force/working-age population = 148.76/225.44 = 66.0%	

SOURCE: Bureau of Labor Statistics (http://stats.bls.gov).

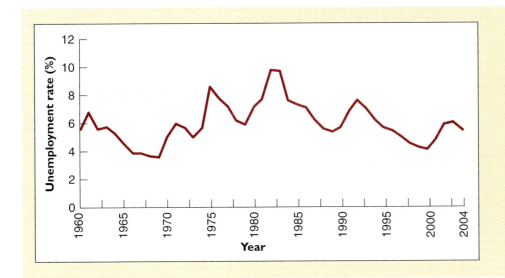

FIGURE 5.3
The U.S. Unemployment Rate since 1960.
The unemployment rate—the fraction of the U.S. labor force that is unemployed—was just above 4 percent in the late 1990s, the lowest recorded rate since the latter part of the 1960s. Unemployment rose above 6 percent in 2003, following a recession.

EXERCISE 5.7

Following are April 2005 BLS U.S. employment data for African Americans.

Employed	15.184 million
Unemployed	1.756 million
Not in the labor force	9.473 million

Find the labor force, the working-age population, the unemployment rate, and the participation rate for African Americans and compare your results to those in Table 5.5.

THE COSTS OF UNEMPLOYMENT

Unemployment imposes *economic, psychological,* and *social* costs on a nation. From an economic perspective, the main cost of unemployment is the output that is lost because the workforce is not fully utilized. Much of the burden of the reduced output is borne by the unemployed themselves, whose incomes fall when they are not working and whose skills may deteriorate from lack of use. However, society at large also bears part of the economic cost of unemployment. For example, workers who become unemployed are liable to stop paying taxes and start receiving government support payments, such as unemployment benefits. This net drain on the government's budget is a cost to all taxpayers.

The *psychological* costs of unemployment are felt primarily by unemployed workers and their families. Studies show that lengthy periods of unemployment can lead to a loss of self-esteem, feelings of loss of control over one's life, depression, and even suicidal behavior.[4] The unemployed worker's family is likely to feel increased psychological stress, compounded by the economic difficulties created by the loss of income.

The *social* costs of unemployment are a result of the economic and psychological effects. People who have been unemployed for a while tend not only to face severe financial difficulties but also to feel anger, frustration, and despair. Not surprisingly, increases in unemployment tend to be associated with increases in crime, domestic violence, alcoholism, drug abuse, and other social problems. The costs created by these problems are borne not only by the unemployed but by society in general, as more public resources must be spent to counteract these problems—for example, by hiring more police to control crime or increasing spending on social services.

THE DURATION OF UNEMPLOYMENT

In assessing the impact of unemployment on jobless people, economists must know how long individual workers have been without work. Generally, the longer a person has been out of work, the more severe are the economic and psychological costs that person will face. People who are unemployed for only a few weeks, for example, are not likely to suffer a serious reduction in their standard of living, since for a short period they can draw upon their savings and perhaps on government benefits. Nor would we expect someone who is unemployed for only a short time to experience psychological problems such as depression or loss of self-esteem, at least not to the same extent as someone who has been out of work for months or years.

unemployment spell a period during which an individual is continuously unemployed

duration the length of an unemployment spell

In its surveys, therefore, the BLS asks respondents how long they have been unemployed. A period during which an individual is continuously unemployed is called an **unemployment spell**; it begins when the worker becomes unemployed and ends when the worker either finds a job or leaves the labor force. (Remember, people outside the labor force are not counted as unemployed.) The length of an unemployment spell is called its **duration**. The duration of unemployment rises during recessions, reflecting the greater difficulty of finding work during those periods.

At any given time, a substantial fraction of unemployed workers have been unemployed for six months or more; we will refer to this group as the *long-term unemployed*. Long-term unemployment creates the highest economic, psychological, and social costs, both for the unemployed themselves and for society as a whole.

Although long-term unemployment is a serious problem, many unemployment spells are quite short. For example, April 2005, 35 percent of the unemployed had been out of work for just 5 weeks or less, another 30 percent had been unemployed for 5 to 14 weeks, and about 35 percent of the unemployed had been without a job for more than 14 weeks (about three months). These statistics are a bit deceptive, however, because short unemployment spells can arise from two very different patterns of labor-market experience. Some people have short unemployment spells that

[4]For a survey of the literature on the psychological effects of unemployment, see William Darity Jr. and Arthur H. Goldsmith, "Social Psychology, Unemployment and Macroeconomics," *Journal of Economic Perspectives*, **10**:121–140, Winter 1996.

end in their finding a stable long-term job. For the most part, these workers, whom we will refer to as the *short-term unemployed*, do not bear a high cost of unemployment. But other workers have short unemployment spells that typically end either in their withdrawal from the labor force or in a short-term or temporary job that soon leaves the worker unemployed again. Workers whose unemployment spells are broken up by brief periods of employment or withdrawal from the labor force are referred to as the *chronically unemployed*. In terms of the costs of unemployment, the experience of these workers is similar to that of the long-term unemployed.

THE UNEMPLOYMENT RATE VERSUS "TRUE" UNEMPLOYMENT

Like GDP measurement, unemployment measurement has its critics. Most of them argue that the official unemployment rate understates the true extent of unemployment. They point in particular to two groups of people who are not counted among the unemployed: so-called *discouraged workers* and *involuntary part-time workers*.

Discouraged workers are people who say they would like to have a job but have not made an effort to find one in the past four weeks. Often, discouraged workers tell the survey takers that they have not searched for work because they have tried without success in the past, or because they are convinced that labor-market conditions are such that they will not be able to find a job. Because they have not sought work in the past four weeks, discouraged workers are counted as being out of the labor force rather than unemployed. Some observers have suggested that treating discouraged workers as unemployed would provide a more accurate picture of the labor market.

Involuntary part-time workers are people who say they would like to work full-time but are able to find only part-time work. Because they do have jobs, involuntary part-time workers are counted as employed rather than unemployed. Some economists have suggested that these workers should be counted as partially unemployed.

In response to these criticisms, in recent years the BLS has released special unemployment rates that include estimates of the number of discouraged workers and involuntary part-time workers. In April 2005, when the official unemployment rate was 5.2 percent (see Table 5.5), the BLS calculated that if both discouraged workers and involuntary part-time workers were counted as unemployed, the unemployment rate would have been 9.0 percent. So the problem of discouraged and underemployed workers appears to be fairly significant.

Whether in an official or adjusted version, the unemployment rate is a good overall indicator of labor-market conditions. A high unemployment rate tends to be bad news even for those people who are employed, since raises and promotions are hard to come by in a "slack" labor market. We will discuss the causes and cures of unemployment at some length in the chapter "Workers, Wages, and Unemployment in the Modern Economy" and subsequent chapters.

discouraged workers people who say they would like to have a job but have not made an effort to find one in the past four weeks

■ SUMMARY ■

- The basic measure of an economy's output is *gross domestic product (GDP)*, the market value of the final goods and services produced in a country during a given period. Expressing output in terms of market values allows economists to aggregate the millions of goods and services produced in a modern economy.

- Only *final goods and services* (which include *capital goods*) are counted in GDP, since they are the only goods and services that directly benefit final users. *Intermediate goods and services*, which are used up in the production of final goods and services, are not counted in GDP, nor are sales of existing assets, such as a 20-year-old house. Summing the value added by each firm in the production process is a useful method of determining the value of final goods and services.

- GDP also can be expressed as the sum of four types of expenditure: *consumption, investment, government purchases,* and *net exports*. These four types of expenditure correspond to the spending of households, firms, the government, and the foreign sector, respectively.

- To compare levels of GDP over time, economists must eliminate the effects of inflation. They do so by measuring the market value of goods and services in terms of the prices in a base year. GDP measured in this way is called *real GDP*, while GDP measured in terms of current-year prices is called *nominal GDP*. Real GDP should always be used in making comparisons of economic activity over time.

- Real GDP per person is an imperfect measure of economic well-being. With a few exceptions, notably government purchases of goods and services (which are included in GDP at their cost of production), GDP includes only those goods and services sold in markets. It excludes important factors that affect people's well-being, such as the amount of leisure time available to them, the value of unpaid or volunteer services, the quality of the environment, the quality of life indicators such as the crime rate, and the degree of economic inequality.

- Real GDP is still a useful indicator of economic well-being, however. Countries with a high real GDP per person not only enjoy high average standards of living; they also tend to have higher life expectancies, low rates of infant and child mortality, and high rates of school enrollment and literacy.

- The unemployment rate, perhaps the best-known indicator of the state of the labor market, is based on surveys conducted by the Bureau of Labor Statistics. The surveys classify all respondents over age 16 as employed, unemployed, or not in the labor force. The *labor force* is the sum of employed and unemployed workers—that is, people who have a job or are looking for one. The *unemployment rate* is calculated as the number of unemployed workers divided by the labor force. The *participation rate* is the percentage of the working-age population that is in the labor force.

- The costs of unemployment include the economic cost of lost output, the psychological costs borne by unemployed workers and their families, and the social costs associated with problems like increased crime and violence. The greatest costs are imposed by long *unemployment spells* (periods of unemployment). Critics of the official unemployment rate argue that it understates "true" unemployment by excluding *discouraged workers* and involuntary part-time workers.

■ KEY TERMS ■

capital good (120)
consumption expenditure (124)
discouraged workers (141)
duration (of an unemployment
 spell) (140)
final goods or services (119)

government purchases (125)
gross domestic product (GDP) (116)
intermediate goods or services (119)
investment (124)
labor force (138)
net exports (125)

nominal GDP (129)
participation rate (138)
real GDP (129)
unemployment rate (138)
unemployment spell (140)
value added (121)

■ REVIEW QUESTIONS ■

1. Why do economists use market values when calculating GDP? What is the economic rationale for giving high-value items more weight in GDP than low-value items?

2. A large part of the agricultural sector in developing countries is subsistence farming, in which much of the food that is produced is consumed by the farmer and the farmer's family. Discuss the implications of this fact for the measurement of GDP in poor countries.

3. Give examples of each of the four types of aggregate expenditure. Which of the four represents the largest share of GDP in the United States? Can an expenditure component be negative? Explain.

4. Al's Shoeshine Stand shined 1,000 pairs of shoes last year and 1,200 pairs this year. He charged $4 for a shine last year and $5 this year. If last year is taken as the base year, find Al's contribution to both nominal GDP and real GDP in both years. Which measure would be better to use if you were trying to measure the change in Al's productivity over the past year? Why?

5. Would you say that real GDP per person is a useful measure of economic well-being? Defend your answer.

6. True or false: A high participation rate in an economy implies a low unemployment rate. Explain.

7. What are the costs of a high unemployment rate? Do you think providing more generous government benefits to the unemployed would increase these costs, reduce these costs, or leave them unchanged? Discuss.

■ PROBLEMS ■

1. George and John, stranded on an island, use clamshells for money. Last year George caught 300 fish and 5 wild boars. John grew 200 bunches of bananas. In the two-person economy that George and John set up, fish sell for 1 clamshell each, boars sell for

10 clamshells each, and bananas go for 5 clamshells a bunch. George paid John a total of 30 clamshells for helping him to dig bait for fishing, and he also purchased five of John's mature banana trees for 30 clamshells each. What is the GDP of George's and John's island in terms of clamshells?

2. How would each of the following transactions affect the GDP of the United States?
   a. The U.S. government pays $1 billion in salaries for government workers.
   b. The U.S. government pays $1 billion to Social Security recipients.
   c. The U.S. government pays a U.S. firm $1 billion for newly produced airplane parts.
   d. The U.S. government pays $1 billion in interest to holders of U.S. government bonds.
   e. The U.S. government pays $1 billion to Saudi Arabia for crude oil to add to U.S. official oil reserves.

3. Intelligence Incorporated produces 100 computer chips and sells them for $200 each to Bell Computers. Using the chips and other labor and materials, Bell produces 100 personal computers. Bell sells the computers, bundled with software that Bell licenses from Macrosoft at $50 per computer, to PC Charlie's for $800 each. PC Charlie's sells the computers to the public for $1,000 each. Calculate the total contribution to GDP using the value-added method. Do you get the same answer by summing up the market values of final goods and services?

4. For each of the following transactions, state the effect both on U.S. GDP and on the four components of aggregate expenditure.
   a. Your mother-in-law buys a new car from a U.S. producer.
   b. Your mother-in-law buys a new car imported from Sweden.
   c. Your mother-in-law's car rental business buys a new car from a U.S. producer.
   d. Your mother-in-law's car rental business buys a new car imported from Sweden.
   e. The U.S. government buys a new, domestically produced car for the use of your mother-in-law, who has been appointed the ambassador to Sweden.

5. Here are some data for an economy. Find its GDP. Explain your calculation.

Consumption expenditures	$600
Exports	75
Government purchases of goods and services	200
Construction of new homes and apartments	100
Sales of existing homes and apartments	200
Imports	50
Beginning-of-year inventory stocks	100
End-of-year inventory stocks	125
Business fixed investment	100
Government payments to retirees	100
Household purchases of durable goods	150

6. The nation of Potchatoonie produces hockey pucks, cases of root beer, and back rubs. Here are data on prices and quantities of the three goods in the years 2000 and 2007.

	Pucks		Root beer		Back rubs	
Year	Quantity	Price	Quantity	Price	Quantity	Price
2000	100	$5	300	$20	100	$20
2007	125	$7	250	$20	110	$25

Assume that 2000 is the base year. Find nominal GDP and real GDP for both years.

7. The government is considering a policy to reduce air pollution by restricting the use of "dirty" fuels by factories. In deciding whether to implement the policy, how, if

at all, should the likely effects of the policy on real GDP be taken into account? Discuss.

8. Here is a report from a not-very-efficient BLS survey taker: "There were 65 people in the houses I visited, 10 of them children under 16 and 10 retired; 25 people had full-time jobs, and 5 had part-time jobs. There were 5 full-time homemakers, 5 full-time students over age 16, and 2 people who were disabled and cannot work. The remaining people did not have jobs but all said they would like one. One of these people had not looked actively for work for 3 months, however."

   Find the labor force, the unemployment rate, and the participation rate implied by the survey taker's report.

9. Ellen is downloading labor market data for the most recent month, but her connection is slow and so far this is all she has been able to get:

Unemployment rate	5.0%
Participation rate	62.5%
Not in the labor force	60 million

   Find the labor force, the working-age population, the number of employed workers, and the number of unemployed workers.

10. The towns of Sawyer and Thatcher each has a labor force of 1,200 people. In Sawyer, 100 people were unemployed for the entire year, while the rest of the labor force was employed continuously. In Thatcher, every member of the labor force was unemployed for 1 month and employed for 11 months.
   a. What is the average unemployment rate over the year in each of the two towns?
   b. What is the average duration of unemployment spells in each of the two towns?
   c. In which town do you think the costs of unemployment are higher? Explain.

■ ANSWERS TO IN-CHAPTER EXERCISES ■

5.1 In the text, GDP was calculated to be $64.00. If in addition Orchardia produces 5 oranges at $0.30 each, GDP is increased by $1.50 to $65.50.

5.2 Plants owned by U.S. companies produced a total of 731,120 vehicles, or 2.60 times the 281,244 vehicles produced by foreign-owned plants. In market value terms, with passenger cars valued at $25,000 and other light vehicles at $30,000 plants owned by U.S. companies produced (223,480 × $25,000) + (507,640 × $30,000) = $20.82 billion worth of vehicles. Foreign-owned plants produced (156,757 × $25,000) + (124,487 × $30,000) = $7.65 billion worth of vehicles. In market value terms, U.S.-owned plants outproduced the foreign-owned plants by a ratio of 2.72 to 1. The U.S. producers have a greater advantage when output is compared in market value terms instead of in terms of number of vehicles because the U.S. companies produce relatively more of the higher-value types of vehicles than the foreign companies do.

5.3 The value added of the wholesale distributor together with the ultimate producers of the cards is $500. Amy's value added—her revenue less her payments to other firms—is $200. Since the cards were produced and purchased by Amy during the year 2005 (we assume), the $500 counts toward year 2005 GDP. The $200 in value added originating in Amy's card shop counts in year 2006 GDP, since Amy actually sold the cards in that year.

5.4 The sale of stock represents a transfer of ownership of part of the assets of Benson Buggywhip, not the production of new goods or services. Hence, the stock sale itself does not contribute to GDP. However, the broker's commission of $100 (2 percent of the stock sale proceeds) represents payment for a current service and is counted in GDP.

5.5 As in Example 5.6, the market value of domestic production is 1,000,000 autos times $15,000 per auto, or $15 billion.

Also as in Example 5.6, consumption is \$10.5 billion and government purchases are \$0.75 billion. However, because 25,000 of the autos that are purchased are imported rather than domestic, the domestic producers have unsold inventories at the end of the year of 50,000 (rather than 25,000 as in Example 5.6). Thus, inventory investment is 50,000 autos times \$15,000, or \$0.75 billion, and total investment (autos purchased by businesses plus inventory investment) is \$3.75 billion. Since exports and imports are equal (both are 25,000 autos), net exports (equal to exports minus imports) are zero. Notice that since we subtract imports to get net exports, it is unnecessary also to subtract imports from consumption. Consumption is defined as total purchases by households, not just purchases of domestically produced goods.

Total expenditure is $C + I + G + NX$ = \$10.5 billion + \$3.75 billion + \$0.75 billion + 0 = \$15 billion, the same as the market value of production.

5.6   Real GDP in the year 2008 equals the quantities of pizzas and calzones produced in the year 2008, valued at the market prices that prevailed in the base year 2004. So real GDP in 2008 = (30 pizzas $\times$ \$10/pizza) + (30 calzones $\times$ \$5/calzone) = \$450.

Real GDP in 2004 equals the quantities of pizzas and calzones produced in 2004, valued at 2004 prices, which is \$175. Notice that since 2004 is the base year, real GDP and nominal GDP are the same for that year.

The real GDP in the year 2008 is \$450/\$175, or about 2.6 times what it was in 2004. Hence the expansion of real GDP lies between the threefold increase in pizza production and the doubling in calzone production that occurred between 2004 and 2008.

5.7

$$\text{Labor force} = \text{Employed} + \text{Unemployed}$$
$$= 15.184 \text{ million} + 1.756 \text{ million} = 16.940 \text{ million}$$

$$\text{Working-age population} = \text{Labor force} + \text{Not in labor force}$$
$$= 16.940 \text{ million} + 9.473 \text{ million} = 26.413 \text{ million}$$

$$\text{Unemployment rate} = \frac{\text{Unemployed}}{\text{Labor force}}$$
$$= \frac{1.756 \text{ million}}{16.940 \text{ million}} = 10.4\%$$

$$\text{Participation rate} = \frac{\text{Labor force}}{\text{Working-age population}}$$
$$= \frac{16.940 \text{ million}}{26.413 \text{ million}} = 64.1\%$$

In April 2005, African Americans represented 11.4 percent of the U.S. labor force and 11.8 percent of the working-age population. Note that while the participation rate for African Americans is similar to that of the overall population, the unemployment rate for African Americans is substantially higher.

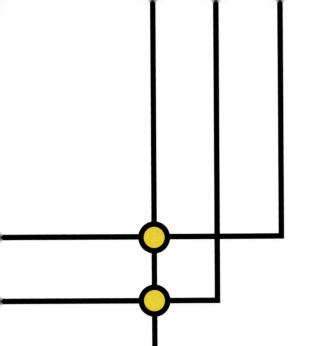

MEASURING THE PRICE LEVEL AND INFLATION

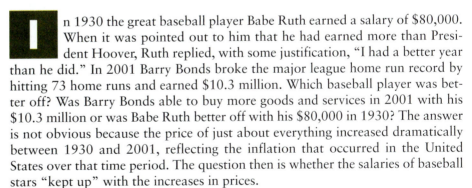

In 1930 the great baseball player Babe Ruth earned a salary of $80,000. When it was pointed out to him that he had earned more than President Hoover, Ruth replied, with some justification, "I had a better year than he did." In 2001 Barry Bonds broke the major league home run record by hitting 73 home runs and earned $10.3 million. Which baseball player was better off? Was Barry Bonds able to buy more goods and services in 2001 with his $10.3 million or was Babe Ruth better off with his $80,000 in 1930? The answer is not obvious because the price of just about everything increased dramatically between 1930 and 2001, reflecting the inflation that occurred in the United States over that time period. The question then is whether the salaries of baseball stars "kept up" with the increases in prices.

Inflation can make a comparison of economic conditions at different points in time quite difficult. Your grandparents remember being able to buy both a comic book and a chocolate sundae for a quarter. Today the same two items might cost $4 or $5. You might conclude from this fact that kids were much better off in "the good old days," but were they really? Without more information, we can't tell, for though the prices of comic books and sundaes have gone up, so have allowances. The real question is whether young people's spending money has increased as much as or more than the prices of the things they want to buy. If so, then they are no worse off today than their grandparents were when they were young and candy bars cost a nickel.

Inflation also creates uncertainty when we try to look into the future, to ask questions such as, "How much should I plan to save for retirement?" The answer to this question depends on how much inflation is likely to occur before one retires (and thus how much heating oil, food, and clothing will cost). Inflation can pose similar problems for policymakers. For example, to plan long-term government spending programs they must estimate how much the government's purchases will cost several years in the future.

An important benefit of studying macroeconomics is learning how to avoid the confusion inflation interjects into comparisons of economic conditions over time or projections for the future. In this chapter, a continuation of our study of the construction and interpretation of economic data, we will see how both prices and inflation are measured and how dollar amounts, such as the price of a comic book, can be "adjusted" to eliminate the effects of inflation. Quantities that are measured in dollars (or other currency units) and then adjusted for inflation are called *real* quantities (recall, for example, the concept of real GDP in the last chapter). By working with real quantities, economists can compare the real incomes of Babe Ruth and Barry Bonds.

More important than the complications inflation creates for economic measurement are the costs that it imposes on the economy. In this chapter we will see why high inflation can significantly impair an economy's performance, to the extent that economic policymakers claim a low and stable rate of inflation as one of their chief objectives. We will conclude the chapter by showing how inflation is linked to another key economic variable, the rate of interest on financial assets.

THE CONSUMER PRICE INDEX: MEASURING THE PRICE LEVEL

consumer price index (CPI)
for any period, measures the cost in that period of a standard basket of goods and services relative to the cost of the same basket of goods and services in a fixed year, called the *base year*

The basic tool economists use to measure the price level and inflation in the U.S. economy is the *consumer price index,* or CPI for short. The CPI is a measure of the "cost of living" during a particular period. Specifically, the **consumer price index (CPI)** for any period measures the cost in that period of a standard set, or basket, of goods and services *relative* to the cost of the same basket of goods and services in a fixed year, called the *base year*.

To illustrate how the CPI is constructed, suppose the government has designated 2000 as the base year. Assume for the sake of simplicity that in 2000 a typical American family's monthly household budget consisted of spending on just three items: rent on a two-bedroom apartment, hamburgers, and movie tickets. In reality, of course, families purchase hundreds of different items each month, but the basic principles of constructing the CPI are the same no matter how many items are included. Suppose too that the family's average monthly expenditures in 2000, the base year, were as shown in Table 6.1.

Now let's fast-forward to the year 2005. Over that period, the prices of various goods and services are likely to have changed; some will have risen and some fallen. Let's suppose that by the year 2005 the rent that our family pays for their two-bedroom apartment has risen to $630. Hamburgers now cost $2.50 each, and the price of movie tickets has risen to $7.00 each. So, in general, prices have been rising.

TABLE 6.1
Monthly Household Budget of the Typical Family in 2000 (Base Year)

Item	Cost (in 2000)
Rent, two-bedroom apartment	$500
Hamburgers (60 at $2.00 each)	120
Movie tickets (10 at $6.00 each)	60
Total expenditure	$680

By how much did the family's cost of living increase between 2000 and 2005? Table 6.2 shows that if the typical family wanted to consume the *same basket of goods and services* in the year 2005 as they did in the year 2000, they would have to spend $850 per month, or $170 more than the $680 per month they spent in 2000. In other words, to live the same way in the year 2005 as they did in the year 2000, the family would have to spend 25 percent more ($170/$680) each month. So, in this example, the cost of living for the typical family rose 25 percent between 2000 and 2005.

TABLE 6.2
Cost of Reproducing the 2000 (Base-Year) Basket of Goods and Services in Year 2005

Item	Cost (in 2005)	Cost (in 2000)
Rent, two-bedroom apartment	$630	$500
Hamburgers (60 at $2.50 each)	150	120
Movie tickets (10 at $7.00 each)	70	60
Total expenditure	$850	$680

The government—actually, the Bureau of Labor Statistics (BLS), the same agency that is responsible for determining the unemployment rate—calculates the official consumer price index (CPI) using essentially the same method. The first step in deriving the CPI is to pick a base year and determine the basket of goods and services that were consumed by the typical family during that year. In practice, the government learns how consumers allocate their spending through a detailed survey, called the Consumer Expenditure Survey, in which randomly selected families record every purchase they make and the price they paid over a given month. (Quite a task!) Let's call the basket of goods and services that results the *base-year basket*. Then, each month BLS employees visit thousands of stores and conduct numerous interviews to determine the current prices of the goods and services in the base-year basket. The CPI in any given year is computed using this formula:

$$\text{CPI} = \frac{\text{Cost of base-year basket of goods and services in current year}}{\text{Cost of base-year basket of goods and services in base year}}.$$

Returning to the example of the typical family that consumes three goods, we can calculate the CPI in the year 2005 as

$$\text{CPI in year 2005} = \frac{\$850}{\$680} = 1.25.$$

In other words, in this example, the cost of living in the year 2005 is 25 percent higher than it was in 2000, the base year. Notice that the base-year CPI is always equal to 1.00, since in that year the numerator and the denominator of the CPI formula are the same. The CPI for a given period (such as a month or year) measures the cost of living in that period *relative* to what it was in the base year.

Often news reporters multiply the CPI by 100 to get rid of the decimal point. If we were to do that here, the year 2005 CPI would be expressed as 125 rather than 1.25, and the base-year CPI would be expressed as 100 rather than 1.00. However, some calculations we will do later in the chapter are simplified if the CPI is stated in decimal form, so we will not adopt the convention of multiplying it by 100.

EXAMPLE 6.1

Measuring the typical family's cost of living

Suppose that in addition to the three goods and services the typical family consumed in 2000 they also bought four sweaters at $30 each. In the year 2005 the same sweaters cost $50 each. The prices of the other goods and services in 2000 and 2005 were the same as in Table 6.2. Find the change in the family's cost of living between 2000 and 2005.

In the example in the text, the cost of the base-year (2000) basket was $680. Adding four sweaters at $30 each raises the cost of the base-year basket to $800. What does this same basket (including the four sweaters) cost in 2005? The cost of the apartment, the hamburgers, and the movie tickets is $850, as before. Adding the cost of the four sweaters at $50 each raises the total cost of the basket to $1,050. The CPI equals the cost of the basket in 2005 divided by the cost of the basket in 2000 (the base year), or $1,050/$800 = 1.31. We conclude that the family's cost of living rose 31 percent between 2000 and 2005.

EXERCISE 6.1

Returning to the three-good example in Tables 6.1 and 6.2, find the year 2005 CPI if the rent on the apartment falls from $500 in 2000 to $400 in 2005. The prices for hamburgers and movie tickets in the two years remain the same as in the two tables.

The CPI is not itself the price of a specific good or service. Indeed, it has no units of measurement at all since the dollars in the numerator of the fraction cancel with the dollars in the denominator. Rather, the CPI is an *index*. The *value* of an index in a particular year has meaning only in comparison with the value of that index in another year. Thus, a **price index** measures the average price of a class of goods or services relative to the price of those same goods or services in a base year. The CPI is an especially well-known price index, one of many economists use to assess economic trends. For example, because manufacturers tend to pass on increases in the prices of raw materials to their customers, economists use indexes of raw materials' prices to try to forecast changes in the prices of manufactured goods. Other indexes are used to study the rate of price change in energy, food, health care, and other major sectors.

price index a measure of the average price of a given class of goods or services relative to the price of the same goods and services in a base year

EXERCISE 6.2

The consumer price index captures the cost of living for the "typical" or average family. Suppose you were to construct a personal price index to measure changes in your own cost of living over time. In general, how would you go about constructing such an index? Why might changes in your personal price index differ from changes in the CPI?

INFLATION

The CPI provides a measure of the average *level* of prices relative to prices in the base year. *Inflation*, in contrast, is a measure of how fast the average price level is *changing* over time. The **rate of inflation** is defined as the annual percentage rate of change in the price level, as measured, for example, by the CPI. Suppose, for example, that the CPI has a value of 1.25 in the year 2005 and a value of 1.30 in the year 2006. The rate of inflation between 2005 and 2006 is the percentage increase in the price level, or the increase in the price level (0.05) divided by the initial price level (1.25), which is equal to 4 percent.

rate of inflation the annual percentage rate of change in the price level, as measured, for example, by the CPI

Calculating inflation rates: 2000–2004

EXAMPLE 6.2

CPI values for the years 2000 through 2004 are shown below. Find the rates of inflation between 2000 and 2001, 2001 and 2002, 2002 and 2003, and 2003 and 2004.

Year	CPI
2000	1.722
2001	1.771
2002	1.799
2003	1.840
2004	1.889

The inflation rate between 2000 and 2001 is the percentage increase in the price level between those years, or $(1.771 - 1.722)/1.722 = 0.049/1.722 = 0.028 = 2.8$ percent. Do the calculations on your own to confirm that inflation during each of the next three years was 1.6, 2.3, and 2.7 percent. The last time inflation exceeded 3.5 percent in the United States was between 1990 and 1991, when it was 4.2 percent. Between 1979 and 1980, however, inflation reached 13.5 percent.

EXERCISE 6.3

Below are CPI values for the years 1929 through 1933. Find the rates of inflation between 1929 and 1930, 1930 and 1931, 1931 and 1932, and 1932 and 1933.

Year	CPI
1929	0.171
1930	0.167
1931	0.152
1932	0.137
1933	0.130

How did inflation rates in the 1930s differ from those since 2000.

The results of the calculations for Exercise 6.3 include some examples of *negative* inflation rates. A situation in which the prices of most goods and services are falling over time so that inflation is negative is called **deflation.** The early 1930s was the last time the United States experienced significant deflation. Japan has experienced relatively mild deflation during the past decade.

deflation a situation in which the prices of most goods and services are falling over time so that inflation is negative

ADJUSTING FOR INFLATION

The CPI is an extremely useful tool. Not only does it allow us to measure changes in the cost of living; it also can be used to adjust economic data to eliminate the effects of inflation. In this section we will see how the CPI can be used to convert quantities measured at current dollar values into real terms, a process called *deflating.* We also will see that the CPI can be used to convert real quantities into current-dollar terms, a procedure called *indexing.* Both procedures are useful not only to economists but to anyone who needs to adjust payments, accounting measures, or other economic quantities for the effects of inflation.

DEFLATING A NOMINAL QUANTITY

nominal quantity a quantity that is measured in terms of its current dollar value

An important use of the CPI is to adjust **nominal quantities**—quantities measured at their current dollar values—for the effects of inflation. To illustrate, suppose we know that the typical family in a certain metropolitan area had a total income of $20,000 in 2000 and $22,000 in the year 2005. Was this family economically better off in the year 2005 than in 2000?

Without any more information than this, we might be tempted to say yes. After all, their income rose by 10 percent over the five-year period. But prices also might have been rising, as fast or faster than the family's income. Suppose the prices of the goods and services the family consumes rose 25 percent over the same period. Since the family's income rose only 10 percent, we would have to conclude that the family is worse off, in terms of the goods and services they can afford to buy, despite the increase in their *nominal*, or current-dollar, income.

real quantity a quantity that is measured in physical terms—for example, in terms of quantities of goods and services

We can make a more precise comparison of the family's purchasing power in 2000 and 2005 by calculating their incomes in those years in *real* terms. In general, a **real quantity** is one that is measured in physical terms—for example, in terms of quantities of goods and services. To convert a nominal quantity into a real quantity, we must divide the nominal quantity by a price index for the period, as shown in Table 6.3. The calculations in the table show that in *real* or purchasing power terms, the family's income actually *decreased* by $2,400, or 12 percent of their initial real income of $20,000, between 2000 and 2005.

TABLE 6.3
Comparing the Real Values of a Family's Income in 2000 and 2005

Year	Nominal family income	CPI	Real family income = Nominal family income/CPI
2000	$20,000	1.00	$20,000/1.00 = $20,000
2005	$22,000	1.25	$22,000/1.25 = $17,600

deflating (a nominal quantity) the process of dividing a nominal quantity by a price index (such as the CPI) to express the quantity in real terms

The problem for this family is that though their income has been rising in nominal (dollar) terms, it has not kept up with inflation. Dividing a nominal quantity by a price index to express the quantity in real terms is called **deflating** the nominal quantity. (Be careful not to confuse the idea of deflating a nominal quantity with deflation, or negative inflation. The two concepts are different.)

Dividing a nominal quantity by the current value of a price index to measure it in real or purchasing power terms is a very useful tool. It can be used to eliminate the effects of inflation from comparisons of any nominal quantity—workers' wages, health care expenditures, the components of the federal budget—over time. Why does this method work? In general, if you know both how many dollars you have spent on a given item and the item's price, you can figure out how many of the item you bought (by dividing your expenditures by the price). For example, if you spent $100 on hamburgers last month and hamburgers cost $2.50 each, you can determine that you purchased 40 hamburgers. Similarly, if you divide a family's dollar income or expenditures by a price index, which is a measure of the average price of the goods and services they buy, you will obtain a measure of the real quantity of goods and services they purchased. Such real quantities are sometimes referred to as *inflation-adjusted* quantities.

Home run hitters drive Cadillacs

EXAMPLE 6.3

Let's return to the question posed at the beginning of this chapter. When Barry Bonds earned $10.3 million in 2001, was he better or worse off than Babe Ruth was in 1930 earning $80,000?

To answer this question, we need to convert both men's earnings into real terms. The CPI (using the average of 1982–1984 as the base year since an extensive survey of consumer purchases was made in this period) was 0.167 in 1930 and 1.78 in 2001. Dividing Babe Ruth's salary by 0.167, we obtain approximately $479,000, which is Ruth's salary "in 1982–1984 dollars." In other words someone would need $479,000 in the 1982–1984 period to buy the same amount of goods and services as Babe Ruth could in 1930 with his $80,000 salary. Dividing Barry Bonds' 2001 salary by the 2001 CPI, 1.78, yields a salary of $5.79 million in 1982–1984 dollars. Thus, someone would need $5.79 million in the 1982–1984 period to buy the same amount of goods and services as Barry Bonds could in 2001 with his $10.3 million salary. We can now compare the real earnings of the two power hitters in 1982–1984 dollars: $479,000 and $5.79 million. Although adjusting for inflation brings the two figures closer together (since part of Bonds' higher salary compensates for the increase in prices between 1930 and 2001), in real terms Bonds still earned more than 12 times Ruth's salary. Incidentally, Bonds also earned about 25 times what President Bush earned in 2001.

Clearly, in comparing wages or earnings at two different points in time, we must adjust for changes in the price level. Doing so yields the **real wage**—the wage measured in terms of real purchasing power. The real wage for any given period is calculated by dividing the nominal (dollar) wage by the CPI for that period.

real wage the wage paid to workers measured in terms of purchasing power; the real wage for any given period is calculated by dividing the nominal (dollar) wage by the CPI for that period

EXERCISE 6.4

In 2004 Alex Rodriguez of the New York Yankees earned $18 million. In that year the CPI was 1.89. How did Rodriguez's 2004 real earnings compare to Bond's 2001 real earnings?

Real wages of U.S. production workers

EXAMPLE 6.4

Production workers are nonsupervisory workers, such as those who work on factory assembly lines. The average U.S. production worker earned $3.40 per hour in 1970 and $15.68 per hour in 2004.[1] Compare the real wages for this group of workers in these years.

To find the real wage in 1970 and 2004, we need to know that the CPI was 0.388 in 1970 and 1.889 in 2004 (again using the 1982–1984 average as the base period). Dividing $3.40 by 0.388, we find that the real wage in 1970 was $8.76. Dividing $15.68 by 1.889, we find that the real wage in 2004 was only $8.30. In real or purchasing power terms, production workers' wages actually fell between 1970 and 2004, despite the fact that the nominal or dollar wage almost quintupled.

Figure 6.1 shows nominal wages and real wages for U.S. production workers for the period 1960–2004. Notice the dramatic difference between the two trends. Looking only at nominal wages, one might conclude that production-line workers were much better paid in 2004 than in 1960. But once wages are adjusted for inflation, we see that, in terms of buying power, production-line workers' wages have stagnated since the early 1970s. This example illustrates the crucial importance of adjusting for inflation when comparing dollar values over time.

---

[1] http://www.gpoaccess.gov/eop.

FIGURE 6.1

Nominal and Real Wages for Production Workers, 1960–2004.

Though nominal wages of production workers have risen dramatically since 1960, real wages have stagnated.

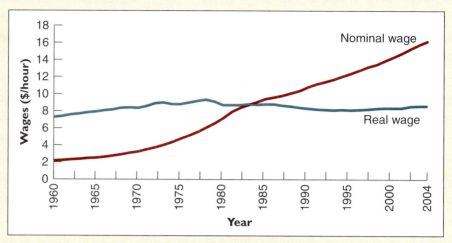

SOURCE: *Economic Report of the President* (http://www.gpoaccess.gov/eop/).

EXERCISE 6.5

In 1950 the minimum wage prescribed by federal law was $0.75 per hour. In April 2005 it was $5.15 per hour. How does the real minimum wage in April 2005 compare to that of 1950? The CPI was 0.241 in 1950 and 1.946 in April 2005.

INDEXING TO MAINTAIN BUYING POWER

The consumer price index also can be used to convert real quantities to nominal quantities. Suppose, for example, that in the year 2000 the government paid certain Social Security recipients $1,000 per month in benefits. Let's assume that Congress would like the buying power of these benefits to remain constant over time so that the recipients' standard of living is unaffected by inflation. To achieve that goal, at what level should Congress set the monthly Social Security benefit in the year 2005?

The nominal, or dollar, benefit Congress should pay in the year 2005 to maintain the purchasing power of retired people depends on how much inflation has taken place between 2000 and 2005. Suppose that the CPI has risen 20 percent between 2000 and 2005. That is, on average the prices of the goods and services consumers buy have risen 20 percent over that period. For Social Security recipients to "keep up" with inflation, their benefit in the year 2005 must be $1,000 + .20($1,000) = $1,200 per month, or 20 percent more than it was in 2000. In general, to keep purchasing power constant, the dollar benefit must be increased each year by the percentage increase in the CPI.

The practice of increasing a nominal quantity according to changes in a price index to prevent inflation from eroding purchasing power is called **indexing**. In the case of Social Security, federal law provides for the automatic indexing of benefits. Each year, without any action by Congress, benefits increase by an amount equal to the percentage increase in the CPI. Some labor contracts are indexed as well so that wages are adjusted fully or partially for changes in inflation (see Example 6.5).

indexing the practice of increasing a nominal quantity each period by an amount equal to the percentage increase in a specified price index. Indexing prevents the purchasing power of the nominal quantity from being eroded by inflation

EXAMPLE 6.5

An indexed labor contract

A labor contract provides for a first-year wage of $12.00 per hour and specifies that the real wage will rise by 2 percent in the second year of the contract and by another 2 percent in the third year. The CPI is 1.00 in the first year, 1.05 in the second year, and 1.10 in the third year. Find the dollar wage that must be paid in the second and third years.

Because the CPI is 1.00 in the first year, both the nominal wage and the real wage are $12.00. Let W_2 stand for the nominal wage in the second year. Deflating by the CPI in the second year, we can express the real wage in the second year as $W_2/1.05$. The contract says that the second-year real wage must be 2 percent higher than the real wage in the first year, so $W_2/1.05 = \$12.00 \times 1.02 = \$12.24$. Multiplying through by 1.05 to solve for W_2, we get $W_2 = \$12.85$, the nominal wage required by the contract in the second year. In the third year the nominal wage W_3 must satisfy the equation $W_3/1.10 = \$12.24 \times 1.02 = \$12.48$. (Why?) Solving this equation for W_3 yields $\$13.73$ as the nominal wage that must be paid in the third year.

EXERCISE 6.6

The minimum wage is not indexed to inflation, but suppose it had been starting in 1950. What would the nominal minimum wage have been in April 2005? See Exercise 6.5 for the data necessary to answer this question.

Every few years there is a well-publicized battle in Congress over whether the minimum wage should be raised. Why do these heated legislative debates recur so regularly?

ECONOMIC NATURALIST 6.1

Because the minimum wage is not indexed to inflation, its purchasing power falls as prices rise. Congress must therefore raise the nominal minimum wage periodically to keep the real value of the minimum wage from eroding. Ironically, despite the public's impression that Congress has raised the nominal minimum wage steeply over the years, the real minimum wage has fallen about one-third since 1970.

Why doesn't Congress index the minimum wage to the CPI and eliminate the need to reconsider it so often? Evidently, some members of Congress prefer to hold a highly publicized debate on the issue every few years—perhaps because it mobilizes both advocates and opponents of the minimum wage to make campaign donations to those members who represent their views.

RECAP	METHODS TO ADJUST FOR INFLATION

Deflating. To correct a nominal quantity, such as a family's dollar income, for changes in the price level, divide it by a price index such as the CPI. This process, called *deflating* the nominal quantity, expresses the nominal quantity in terms of real purchasing power. If nominal quantities from two different years are deflated by a price index with the same base year, the purchasing power of the two deflated quantities can be compared.

Indexing. To ensure that a nominal payment, such as a Social Security benefit, represents a constant level of real purchasing power, increase the nominal quantity each year by a percentage equal to the rate of inflation for that year (a procedure known as *indexing*).

DOES THE CPI MEASURE "TRUE" INFLATION?

You may have concluded that measuring inflation is straightforward, but as with GDP and the unemployment rate, the issue is not free from controversy. Indeed the question of whether U.S. inflation is properly measured has been the subject of serious debates in recent years. Because the CPI is one of the most important U.S. economic statistics, the issue is far from academic. Policymakers pay close attention to the latest inflation numbers when deciding what actions to take. Furthermore, because of the widespread use of indexing, changes in the CPI directly impact the government's budget. For example, if the CPI rises by 3 percent during a given year, by law Social Security benefits—which are a significant part of federal government spending—increase automatically by 3 percent. Many other government payments and private contracts, such as union labor contracts, are indexed to the CPI as well.

When a 1996 report concluded that changes in the CPI are a poor measure of "true" inflation, therefore, a major controversy ensued. The report, prepared by a commission headed by Michael Boskin, formerly the chief economic adviser to President George H. W. Bush, concluded that the official CPI inflation rate *overstates* the true inflation rate by as much as one to two percentage points a year. In other words, if the official CPI inflation rate is reported to be 3 percent, the "true" inflation rate might be 2 percent, or even 1 percent.

If this assessment is in fact correct, the indexing of Social Security and other government benefits to the CPI could be costing the federal government billions of dollars more than necessary every year. In addition, an overstated rate of inflation would lead to an underestimation of the true improvement in living standards over time. If the typical family's nominal income increases by 3 percent per year, and inflation is reported to be 3 percent per year, economists would conclude that American families are experiencing no increase in their real income. But if the "true" inflation rate is really 2 percent per year, then the family's real income is actually rising by 1 percent per year (the 3 percent increase in nominal income minus 2 percent inflation).

The Boskin Commission gave a number of reasons why the official inflation rate, based on the CPI, may overestimate the true rate of inflation. Two are particularly important. First, in practice, government statisticians cannot always adjust adequately for changes in the *quality* of goods and services. Suppose a new personal computer has 20 percent more memory, computational speed, and data storage capacity than last year's model. Suppose too for the sake of illustration that its price is 20 percent higher. Has there been inflation in computer prices? Economists would say no; although consumers are paying 20 percent more for a computer, they are getting a 20 percent better machine. The situation is really no different from paying 20 percent more for a pizza that is 20 percent bigger. However, because quality change is difficult to measure precisely and because they have many thousands of goods and services to consider, government statisticians often miss or understate changes in quality. In general, whenever statisticians fail to adjust adequately for improvements in the quality of goods or services, they will tend to overstate inflation. This type of overstatement is called *quality adjustment bias*.[2]

An extreme example of quality adjustment bias can occur whenever a totally new good becomes available. For example, the introduction of the first effective AIDS drugs significantly increased the quality of medical care received by AIDS patients. In practice, however, quality improvements that arise from totally new products are likely to be poorly captured by the CPI, if at all. The problem is that since the new good was not produced in the base year, there is no base-year price with which to compare the current price of the good. Government statisticians use various approaches to correct for this problem, such as comparing the cost of the new drug to the cost of the next-best therapies. But such methods are necessarily imprecise and open to criticism.

The second problem emphasized by the Boskin Commission arises from the fact that the CPI is calculated for a fixed basket of goods and services. This procedure does not allow for the possibility that consumers can switch from products whose prices are rising to those whose prices are stable or falling. Ignoring the fact that consumers can switch from more expensive to less expensive goods leads statisticians to overestimate the true increase in the cost of living.

---

[2]There are many hard-working employees at the Bureau of Labor Statistics trying to measure quality changes. Some improvements, such as increases in computer speeds and memory, are relatively easy to measure. But many others are much harder to quantify.

Suppose, for instance, that people like coffee and tea equally well and in the base year consumed equal amounts of each. But then a frost hits a major coffee-producing nation, causing the price of coffee to double. The increase in coffee prices encourages consumers to forgo coffee and drink tea instead—a switch that doesn't make them worse off, since they like coffee and tea equally well. However, the CPI, which measures the cost of buying the base-year basket of goods and services, will rise significantly when the price of coffee doubles. This rise in the CPI, which ignores the fact that people can substitute tea for coffee without being made worse off, exaggerates the true increase in the cost of living. This type of overstatement of inflation is called *substitution bias*.

Substitution bias

EXAMPLE 6.6

Suppose the CPI basket for 2000, the base year, is as follows:

Item	Expenditure
Coffee (50 cups at $1/cup)	$ 50.00
Tea (50 cups at $1/cup)	50.00
Scones (100 at $1 each)	100.00
Total	$200.00

Assume that consumers are equally happy to drink coffee or tea with their scones. In 2000, coffee and tea cost the same, and the average person drinks equal amounts of coffee and tea.

In the year 2005, coffee has doubled in price to $2 per cup. Tea remains at $1 per cup, and scones are $1.50 each. What has happened to the cost of living as measured by the CPI? How does this result compare to the true cost of living?

To calculate the value of the CPI for the year 2005, we must first find the cost of consuming the 2000 basket of goods in that year. At year 2005 prices, 50 cups each of coffee and tea and 100 scones cost $(50 \times \$2) + (50 \times \$1) + (100 \times \$1.50) = \$300$. Since consuming the same basket of goods cost $200 in 2000, the base year, the CPI in 2005 is $300/$200, or 1.50. This calculation leads us to conclude that the cost of living has increased 50 percent between 2000 and 2005.

However, we have overlooked the possibility that consumers can substitute a cheaper good (tea) for the more expensive one (coffee). Indeed, since consumers like coffee and tea equally well, when the price of coffee doubles they will shift entirely to tea. Their new consumption basket—100 cups of tea and 100 scones—is just as enjoyable to them as their original basket. If we allow for the substitution of less expensive goods, how much has the cost of living really increased? The cost of 100 cups of tea and 100 scones in the year 2005 is only $250, not $300. From the consumer's point of view, the true cost of living has risen by only $50, or 25 percent. The 50 percent increase in the CPI therefore overstates the increase in the cost of living as the result of substitution bias.

The Boskin Commission's findings have been controversial. While quality adjustment bias and substitution bias undoubtedly distort the measurement of inflation, estimating precisely how much of an overstatement they create is difficult. (If economists knew exactly how big these biases were, they could simply correct the data.) But the Bureau of Labor Statistics (the agency responsible for calculating the CPI) has recently made significant efforts to improve the quality of its data as a result of the Commission's report.

ECONOMIC NATURALIST 6.2

Why is inflation in the health care sector apparently high?

Government statisticians report inflation rates for different categories of goods and services, as well as for the overall consumer basket. According to the official measures, over recent decades the prices of medical services have tended to rise much more rapidly than the prices of other goods and services. Why is inflation in the health care sector apparently high?

Although inflation rates in the health care sector are high, some economists have argued that reported rates greatly overstate the true rate of inflation in that sector. The reason, claim critics, is the quality adjustment bias. Health care is a dynamic sector of the economy, in which ongoing technological change has significantly improved the quality of care. To the extent that official data fail to account for improvements in the quality of medical care, inflation in the health care sector will be overstated.

Economists Matthew Shapiro and James Wilcox[3] illustrated the problem with the example of changes in the treatment of cataracts, a cloudiness in the lens of the eye that impairs vision. The lens must still be removed surgically, but there have been important improvements in the procedure over the past 30 years. First, surgeons can now replace the defective lens with an artificial one, which improves the patient's vision considerably without contact lenses or thick glasses. Second, the techniques for making and closing the surgical incision have been substantially improved. Besides reducing complications and therefore follow-up visits, the new techniques can be performed in the physician's office, with no hospital stay (older techniques frequently required three nights in the hospital). Thus, the new technologies have both improved patient outcomes and reduced the number of hours doctors and nurses spend on the procedure.

Shapiro and Wilcox point out that official measures of health care inflation are based primarily on data such as the doctor's hourly rate or the cost of a night in the hospital. They do not take into account either the reduction in a doctor's time or the shorter hospital stay now needed for procedures such as cataract surgery. Furthermore, Shapiro and Wilcox argue, official measures do not take adequate account of improvements in patient outcomes, such as the improved vision cataract patients now enjoy. Because of the failure to adjust for improvements in the quality of procedures, including increased productivity of medical personnel, official measures may significantly overstate inflation in the health care sector.

THE COSTS OF INFLATION: NOT WHAT YOU THINK

In the late 1970s, when inflation was considerably higher than it is now, the public told poll takers that they viewed it as "public enemy number one"—that is, as the nation's most serious problem. Although U.S. inflation rates have not been very high in recent years, today many Americans remain concerned about inflation or the threat of inflation. Why do people worry so much about inflation? Detailed opinion surveys often find that many people are confused about the meaning of inflation and its economic effects. When people complain about inflation, they are often concerned primarily about relative price changes. Before describing the true economic costs of inflation, which are real and serious, let's examine this confusion people experience about inflation and its costs.

We need first to distinguish between the *price level* and the *relative price* of a good or service. The **price level** is a measure of the overall level of prices at a particular point in time as measured by a price index such as the CPI. Recall that the

price level a measure of the overall level of prices at a particular point in time as measured by a price index such as the CPI

[3]"Mismeasurement in the Consumer Price Index: An Evaluation," in Ben Bernanke and Julio Rotemberg (eds.), NBER *Macroeconomics Annual*, 1996.

inflation rate is the percentage change in the price level from year to year. In contrast, a **relative price** is the price of a specific good or service *in comparison to* the prices of other goods and services. For example, if the price of oil were to rise by 10 percent while the prices of other goods and services were rising on average by 3 percent, the relative price of oil would increase. But if oil prices rise by 3 percent while other prices rise by 10 percent, the relative price of oil would decrease. That is, oil would become cheaper relative to other goods and services, even though it has not become cheaper in absolute terms.

relative price the price of a specific good or service *in comparison to* the prices of other goods and services

Public opinion surveys suggest that many people are confused about the distinction between inflation, or an increase in the overall *price level*, and an increase in a specific *relative price*. Suppose that supply disruptions in the Middle East were to double the price of gas at the pump, leaving other prices unaffected. Appalled by the increase in gasoline prices, people might demand that the government do something about "this inflation." But while the increase in gas prices hurts consumers, is it an example of inflation? Gasoline is only one item in a consumer's budget, one of the thousands of goods and services that people buy every day. Thus, the increase in the price of gasoline might affect the overall price level, and hence the inflation rate, only slightly. In this example, inflation is not the real problem. What upsets consumers is the change in the *relative price* of oil, particularly compared to the price of labor (wages). By increasing the cost of using a car, the increase in the relative price of oil reduces the income people have left over to spend on other things.

Again, changes in relative prices do *not* necessarily imply a significant amount of inflation. For example, increases in the prices of some goods could well be counterbalanced by decreases in the prices of other goods, in which case the price level and the inflation rate would be largely unaffected. Conversely, inflation can be high without affecting relative prices. Imagine, for example, that all prices in the economy, including wages and salaries, go up exactly 10 percent each year. The inflation rate is 10 percent, but relative prices are not changing. Indeed, because wages (the price of labor) are increasing by 10 percent per year, people's ability to buy goods and services is unaffected by the inflation.

These examples show that changes in the average price level (inflation) and changes in the relative prices of specific goods are two quite different issues. The public's tendency to confuse the two is important, because the remedies for the two problems are different. To counteract changes in relative prices, the government would need to implement policies that affect the supply and demand for specific goods. In the case of an increase in oil prices, for example, the government could try to encourage the development of alternative sources of energy. To counteract inflation, however, the government must resort (as we will see) to changes in macroeconomic policies, such as monetary or fiscal policies. If, in confusion, the public forces the government to adopt anti-inflationary policies when the real problem is a relative price change, the economy could actually be hurt by the effort. Here is an example of why economic literacy is important, both to policymakers and the general public.

The price level, relative prices, and inflation

EXAMPLE 6.7

Suppose the value of the CPI is 1.20 in the year 2000, 1.32 in 2001, and 1.40 in 2002. Assume also that the price of oil increases 8 percent between 2000 and 2001 and another 8 percent between 2001 and 2002. What is happening to the price level, the inflation rate, and the relative price of oil?

The price level can be measured by the CPI. Since the CPI is higher in 2001 than in 2000 and higher still in 2002 than in 2001, the price level is rising throughout the period. The inflation rate is the *percentage increase* in the CPI. Since the CPI increases by 10 percent between 2000 and 2001, the inflation rate between those years is 10 percent. However, the CPI increases only about 6 percent between 2001 and 2002 ($1.40/1.32 \approx 1.06$), so the inflation rate decreases to about 6 percent between those years. The decline in the inflation rate implies that although the price level is still rising, it is doing so at a slower pace than the year before.

The price of oil rises 8 percent between 2000 and 2001. But because the general inflation over that period is 10 percent, the relative price of oil—that is, its price *relative to all other goods and services*—falls by about 2 percent ($8\% - 10\% = -2\%$). Between 2001 and 2002 the price of oil rises by another 8 percent, while the general inflation rate is about 6 percent. Hence the relative price of oil rises between 2001 and 2002 by about 2 percent ($8\% - 6\%$).

EXERCISE 6.7

In April 1980, unleaded, regular gasoline cost $1.26 per gallon and the CPI was 0.810. In April 2005, unleaded, regular gas cost $2.24 per gallon and the CPI was 1.946. Did the price of gasoline relative to the other items in the CPI rise or fall between these two years?

EXERCISE 6.8

In 1980, when the CPI was 0.824, the cost of attending a leading private university was $8,761, including tuition, room, board, and fees. In 2004, when the CPI was 1.889, the cost was $38,297. By how much had the cost risen relative to other items in the CPI?

THE TRUE COSTS OF INFLATION

Having dispelled the common confusion between inflation and relative price changes, we are now free to address the true economic costs of inflation. There are a variety of such costs, each of which tends to reduce the efficiency of the economy. Five of the most important are discussed here.

"NOISE" IN THE PRICE SYSTEM

In Chapter 3 we described the remarkable economic coordination that is necessary to provide the right amount and the right kinds of food to New Yorkers every day. This feat is not orchestrated by some Food Distribution Ministry staffed by bureaucrats. It is done much better than a Ministry ever could by the workings of free markets, operating without central guidance.

How do free markets transmit the enormous amounts of information necessary to accomplish complex tasks like the provisioning of New York City? The answer, as we saw in Chapter 3, is through the price system. When the owners of French restaurants in Manhattan cannot find sufficient quantities of chanterelles, a particularly rare and desirable mushroom, they bid up its market price. Specialty food suppliers notice the higher price for chanterelles and realize that they can make a profit by supplying more chanterelles to the market. At the same time, price-conscious diners will shift to cheaper, more available mushrooms. The market for chanterelles will reach equilibrium only when there are no more unexploited opportunities for profit, and both suppliers and demanders are satisfied at the market price (the *equilibrium principle*). Multiply this example a million times, and you will gain a sense of how the price system achieves a truly remarkable degree of economic coordination.

When inflation is high, however, the subtle signals that are transmitted through the price system become more difficult to interpret, much in the way that static, or "noise," makes a radio message harder to interpret. In an economy with little or no inflation, the supplier of specialty foodstuffs will immediately recognize the increase in chanterelle prices as a signal to bring more to market. If inflation is high, however, the supplier must ask whether a price increase represents a true increase in the demand for chanterelles or is just a result of the general inflation, which causes all food prices to rise. If the price rise reflects only inflation, the price of chanterelles *relative to other goods and services* has not really changed. The supplier therefore should not change the quantity of mushrooms he brings to market.

In an inflationary environment, to discern whether the increase in chanterelle prices is a true signal of increased demand, the supplier needs to know not only the price of chanterelles but also what is happening to the prices of other goods and services. Since this information takes time and effort to collect, the supplier's response to the change in chanterelle prices is likely to be slower and more tentative.

In summary, price changes are the market's way of communicating information to suppliers and demanders. An increase in the price of a good or service, for example, tells demanders to economize on their use of the good or service and suppliers to bring more of it to market. But in the presence of inflation, prices are affected not only by changes in the supply and demand for a product but by changes in the general price level. Inflation creates static, or "noise," in the price system, obscuring the information transmitted by prices and reducing the efficiency of the market system. This reduction in efficiency imposes real economic costs.

DISTORTIONS OF THE TAX SYSTEM

Just as some government expenditures, such as Social Security benefits, are indexed to inflation, many taxes are also indexed. In the United States, people with higher incomes pay a higher *percentage* of their income in taxes. Without indexing, an inflation that raises people's nominal incomes would force them to pay an increasing percentage of their income in taxes, even though their *real* incomes may not have increased. To avoid this phenomenon, which is known as *bracket creep*, Congress has indexed income tax brackets to the CPI. The effect of this indexation is that a family whose nominal income is rising at the same rate as inflation does not have to pay a higher percentage of income in taxes.

Inflation adds static to the information conveyed by changes in prices.

Although indexing has solved the problem of bracket creep, many provisions of the tax code have not been indexed, either because of lack of political support or because of the complexity of the task. As a result, inflation can produce unintended changes in the taxes people pay, which in turn may cause them to change their behavior in economically undesirable ways.

To illustrate, an important provision in the business tax code for which inflation poses problems is the *capital depreciation allowance*, which works as follows. Suppose a firm buys a machine for $1,000, expecting it to last for 10 years. Under U.S. tax law, the firm can take one-tenth of the purchase price, or $100, as a deduction from its taxable profits in each of the 10 years. By deducting a fraction of the purchase price from its taxable profits, the firm reduces its taxes. The exact amount of the yearly tax reduction is the tax rate on corporate profits times $100.

The idea behind this provision of the tax code is that the wearing out of the machine is a cost of doing business that should be deducted from the firm's profit. Also, in giving firms a tax break for investing in new machinery, Congress intended to encourage firms to modernize their plants. Yet capital depreciation allowances are not indexed to inflation. Suppose that, at a time when the inflation rate is high, a firm is considering purchasing a $1,000 machine. The managers know that the purchase will allow them to deduct $100 per year from taxable profits for the next 10 years. But that $100 is a fixed amount that is not indexed to inflation. Looking forward, managers will recognize that 5, 6, or 10 years into the future, the real value of the $100 tax deduction will be much lower than at present because of inflation. They will have less incentive to buy the machine and may decide not to make the investment at all. Indeed, many studies have found that a high rate of inflation can significantly reduce the rate at which firms invest in new factories and equipment.

Because the complex U.S. tax code contains hundreds of provisions and tax rates that are not indexed, inflation can seriously distort the incentives provided by the tax system for people to work, save, and invest. The resulting adverse effects on economic efficiency and economic growth represent a real cost of inflation.

"SHOE-LEATHER" COSTS

As all shoppers know, cash is convenient. Unlike checks, which are not accepted everywhere, and credit cards, for which a minimum purchase is often required, cash can be used in almost any routine transaction. Businesses, too, find cash convenient to hold. Having plenty of cash on hand facilitates transactions with customers and reduces the need for frequent deposits and withdrawals from the bank.

Inflation raises the cost of holding cash to consumers and businesses. Consider a miser with $10,000 in $20 bills under his mattress. What happens to the buying power of his hoard over time? If inflation is zero so that on average the prices of goods and services are not changing, the buying power of the $10,000 does not change over time. At the end of a year, the miser's purchasing power is the same as it was at the beginning of the year. But suppose the inflation rate is 10 percent. In that case, the purchasing power of the miser's hoard will fall by 10 percent each year. After a year, he will have only $9,000 in purchasing power. In general, the higher the rate of inflation, the less people will want to hold cash because of the loss of purchasing power that they will suffer.

Technically, currency is a debt owed by the government to the currency holder. So when currency loses value, the losses to holders of cash are offset by gains to the government, which now owes less in real terms to currency holders. Thus, from the point of view of society as a whole, the loss of purchasing power is not in itself a cost of inflation, because it does not involve wasted resources. (Indeed, no real goods or services were used up when the miser's currency hoard lost part of its value.) However, when faced with inflation, people are not likely to accept a loss in purchasing power but instead will take actions to try to "economize" on their cash holdings. For example, instead of drawing out enough cash for a month the next time they visit the bank, they will draw out only enough to last a week. The inconvenience of visiting the bank more often to minimize one's cash holdings is a real cost of inflation. Similarly, businesses will reduce their cash holdings by sending employees to the bank more frequently, or by installing computerized systems to monitor cash usage. To deal with the increase in bank transactions required by consumers and businesses trying to use less cash, banks will need to hire more employees and expand their operations.

The costs of more frequent trips to the bank, new cash management systems, and expanded employment in banks are real costs. They use up resources, including time and effort, that could be used for other purposes. Traditionally, the costs of economizing on cash have been called *shoe-leather costs*—the idea being that shoe leather is worn out during extra trips to the bank. Shoe-leather costs probably are not a significant problem in the United States today, where inflation is only 2 to 3 percent per year. But in economies with high rates of inflation, they can become quite significant.

EXAMPLE 6.8   **Shoe-leather costs at Woodrow's Hardware**

Woodrow's Hardware needs $5,000 cash per day for customer transactions. Woodrow has a choice between going to the bank first thing on Monday morning to withdraw $25,000—enough cash for the whole week—or going to the bank first thing every morning for $5,000 each time. Woodrow puts the cost of going to the bank, in terms of inconvenience and lost time, at $4 per trip. Assume that funds left in the bank earn precisely enough interest to keep their purchasing power unaffected by inflation.

If inflation is zero, how often will Woodrow go to the bank? If it is 10 percent? In this example, what are the shoe-leather costs of a 10 percent inflation rate?

If inflation is zero, there is no cost to holding cash. Woodrow will go to the bank only once a week, incurring a shoe-leather cost of $4 per week. But if inflation is 10 percent, Woodrow may need to change his banking habits. If he continues to go to the bank only on Monday mornings, withdrawing $25,000 for the week, what will be Woodrow's average cash holding over the week? At the beginning of each day, his cash holding will be as follows:

Monday	$25,000
Tuesday	20,000
Wednesday	15,000
Thursday	10,000
Friday	5,000

Averaging the holdings on those five days, we can calculate that Woodrow's average cash holding at the beginning of each day is $75,000/5 = $15,000. If inflation is 10 percent a year, over the course of a year the cost to Woodrow of holding an average of $15,000 in cash equals 10 percent of $15,000, or $1,500.

On the other hand, if Woodrow goes to the bank every day, his average cash holding at the beginning of the day will be only $5,000. In that case, his losses from inflation will be $500 (10 percent of $5,000) a year. Will Woodrow start going to the bank every day when inflation reaches 10 percent? The *benefit* of changing his banking behavior is a loss of only $500 per year to inflation, rather than $1,500, or $1,000 saved. The *cost* of going to the bank every day is $4 per trip. Assuming Woodrow's store is open 50 weeks a year, going to the bank 5 days a week instead of 1 day a week adds 200 trips per year, at a total cost of $800. Since the $800 cost is less than the $1,000 benefit, Woodrow will begin going to the bank more often.

To repeat, the shoe-leather costs of a high inflation rate are the extra costs incurred to avoid holding cash. In this example, they are the additional $800 per year associated with Woodrow's daily trips to the bank.

UNEXPECTED REDISTRIBUTION OF WEALTH

When inflation is unexpected, it may arbitrarily redistribute wealth from one group to another. Consider a group of union workers who signed a contract setting their wages for the next three years. If those wages are not indexed to inflation, then the workers will be vulnerable to upsurges in the price level. Suppose, for example, that inflation is much higher than expected over the three years of the contract. In that case, the buying power of the workers' wages—their real wages—will be less than anticipated when they signed the contract.

From society's point of view, is the buying power that workers lose to inflation really "lost"? The answer is no; the loss in their buying power is exactly matched by an unanticipated gain in the employer's buying power, because the real cost of paying the workers is less than anticipated. In other words, the effect of the inflation is not to *destroy* purchasing power but to *redistribute* it, in this case from the workers to the employer. If inflation had been *lower* than expected, the workers would have enjoyed greater purchasing power than they anticipated and the employer would have been the loser.

Another example of the redistribution caused by inflation takes place between borrowers (debtors) and lenders (creditors). Suppose one of the authors of this book wants to buy a house on a lake and borrows $150,000 from the bank to pay for it. Shortly after signing the mortgage agreement, he learns that inflation is likely to be much higher than expected. How should he react to the news? Perhaps as a public-spirited macroeconomist the author should be saddened to hear that inflation is rising, but as a consumer he should be pleased. In real terms, the dollars with which he will repay his loan in the future will be worth much less than expected. The loan officer should be distraught, because the dollars the bank will receive from the author will be worth less, in purchasing power terms, than expected at contract signing. Once again, no real wealth is "lost" to the inflation; rather, the borrower's gain is just offset by the lender's loss. *In general, unexpectedly high inflation rates help borrowers at the expense of lenders,* because borrowers are able to repay their loans in less valuable dollars. Unexpectedly low inflation rates, in contrast, help lenders and hurt borrowers by forcing borrowers to repay in dollars that are worth more than expected when the loan was made.

Although redistributions caused by inflation do not directly destroy wealth, but only transfer it from one group to another, they are still bad for the economy. Our economic system is based on incentives. For it to work well, people must know that if they work hard, save some of their income, and make wise financial investments, they will be rewarded in the long run with greater real wealth and a better standard of living. Some observers have compared a high-inflation economy to a casino, in which wealth is distributed largely by luck—that is, by random fluctuations in the inflation rate. In the long run, a "casino economy" is likely to perform poorly, as its unpredictability discourages people from working and saving. (Why bother if inflation can take away your savings overnight?) Rather, a high-inflation economy encourages people to use up resources in trying to anticipate inflation and protect themselves against it.

INTERFERENCE WITH LONG-RUN PLANNING

The fifth and final cost of inflation we will examine is its tendency to interfere with the long-run planning of households and firms. Many economic decisions take place within a long time horizon. Planning for retirement, for example, may begin when workers are in their twenties or thirties. And firms develop long-run investment and business strategies that look decades into the future.

Clearly, high and erratic inflation can make long-term planning difficult. Suppose, for example, that you want to enjoy a certain standard of living when you retire. How much of your income do you need to save to make your dreams a reality? That depends on what the goods and services you plan to buy will cost 30 or 40 years from now. With high and erratic inflation, even guessing what your chosen lifestyle will cost by the time you retire is extremely difficult. You may end up saving too little and having to compromise on your retirement plans; or you may save too much, sacrificing more than you need to during your working years. Either way, inflation will have proved costly.

In summary, inflation damages the economy in a variety of ways. Some of its effects are difficult to quantify and are therefore controversial. But most economists agree that a low and stable inflation rate is instrumental in maintaining a healthy economy.

RECAP	THE TRUE COSTS OF INFLATION

The public sometimes confuses changes in relative prices (such as the price of oil) with inflation, which is a change in the overall level of prices. This confusion can cause problems, because the remedies for undesired changes in relative prices and for inflation are different.

There are a number of true costs of inflation, which together tend to reduce economic growth and efficiency. These include

- "Noise" in the price system, which occurs when general inflation makes it difficult for market participants to interpret the information conveyed by prices.

- Distortions of the tax system, for example, when provisions of the tax code are not indexed.

- Shoe-leather costs, or the costs of economizing on cash (for example, by making more frequent trips to the bank or installing a computerized cash management system).

- Unexpected redistributions of wealth, as when higher-than-expected inflation hurts wage earners to the benefit of employers or hurts creditors to the benefit of debtors.

- Interference with long-term planning, arising because people find it difficult to forecast prices over long periods.

HYPERINFLATION

Although there is some disagreement about whether an inflation rate of, say, 5 percent per year imposes important costs on an economy, few economists would question the fact that an inflation rate of 500 percent or 1,000 percent per year disrupts economic performance. A situation in which the inflation rate is extremely high is called **hyperinflation**. Although there is no official threshold above which inflation becomes hyperinflation, inflation rates in the range of 500 to 1,000 percent per year would surely qualify. In the past few decades, episodes of hyperinflation have occurred in Israel (400 percent inflation in 1985), several South American countries (including Bolivia, Argentina, and Brazil), Nicaragua (33,000 percent inflation in 1988), and several countries attempting to make the transition from communism to capitalism, including Russia. Perhaps the most well-known episode occurred in Germany in 1923 when inflation was 102,000,000 percent. In the German hyperinflation, prices rose so rapidly that for a time workers were paid twice each day so their families could buy food before the afternoon price increases, and many people's life savings became worthless. But the most extreme hyperinflation ever recorded was in Hungary in 1945, at the end of the Second World War, when inflation peaked at 3.8×10^{27} percent. The United States has never experienced hyperinflation, although the short-lived Confederate States of America suffered severe inflation during the Civil War. Between 1861 and 1865, prices in the Confederacy rose to 92 times their prewar levels.

Hyperinflation greatly magnifies the costs of inflation. For example, shoe-leather costs—a relatively minor consideration in times of low inflation—become quite important during hyperinflation, when people may visit the bank two or three times per day to hold money for as short a time as possible. With prices changing daily or even hourly, markets work quite poorly, slowing economic growth. Massive redistributions of wealth take place, impoverishing many. Not surprisingly, episodes of hyperinflation rarely last more than a few years; they are so disruptive that they quickly lead to public outcry for relief.

hyperinflation a situation in which the inflation rate is extremely high

ECONOMIC
NATURALIST
6.3

How costly is high inflation?

Economic theory suggests that high inflation rates, especially those associated with hyperinflation, reduce economic efficiency and growth. Most economists believe that the economic costs associated with high inflation outweigh the perceived benefits, yet we continue to see episodes of high inflation throughout the world. In reality, how costly are high inflation rates?

Economists Stanley Fischer, Ratna Sahay, and Carlos A. Végh[4] examined the economic performance of 133 market economies over the period 1960–96 and uncovered 45 episodes of high inflation (12-month inflation rates greater than 100 percent) among 25 different countries. They found that, while uncommon, episodes of high inflation impose significant economic costs on the countries experiencing them. During periods of high inflation, these countries saw real GDP per person fall by an average of 1.6 percent per year, real consumption per person fall by an average of 1.3 percent per year, and real investment per person fall by an average of 3.3 percent per year. During low inflation years these same countries experienced positive growth in each of these variables. In addition, during periods of high inflation, these countries' trade and government budget deficits were larger than during low inflation years.

Falling output and consumption levels caused by high inflation reduce the economic well-being of households and firms, and have a disproportionate effect on poor workers, who are least likely to have their wages indexed to the inflation rate and thus avoid a real loss in purchasing power. As pointed out in the last section, high inflation rates also distort relative prices in the marketplace, leading to a misallocation of resources that can have long-term economic consequences. Falling investment in new capital caused by high inflation, for example, leads not only to a slowdown in current economic activity but also to reduced growth rates of future output. Because of these adverse economic effects, policymakers have an incentive to keep inflation rates low.

INFLATION AND INTEREST RATES

So far we have focused on the measurement and economic costs of inflation. Another important aspect of inflation is its close relationship to other key macroeconomic variables. For example, economists have long realized that during periods of high inflation, interest rates tend to be high as well. We will close this chapter with a look at the relationship between inflation and interest rates, which will provide a useful background in the chapters to come.

INFLATION AND THE REAL INTEREST RATE

Earlier in our discussion of the ways in which inflation redistributes wealth, we saw that inflation tends to hurt creditors and help debtors by reducing the value of the dollars with which debts are repaid. The effect of inflation on debtors and creditors can be explained more precisely using an economic concept called the *real interest rate*. An example will illustrate.

Suppose that there are two neighboring countries, Alpha and Beta. In Alpha, whose currency is called the alphan, the inflation rate is zero and is expected to remain at zero. In Beta, where the currency is the betan, the inflation rate is 10 percent and is expected to remain at that level. Bank deposits pay 2 percent annual interest in Alpha and 10 percent annual interest in Beta. In which countries are bank depositors getting a better deal?

[4]"Modern Hyper- and High Inflations," *Journal of Economic Literature*, Vol. 11 (September 2002), pp. 837–880.

You may answer "Beta," since interest rates on deposits are higher in that country. But if you think about the effects of inflation, you will recognize that Alpha, not Beta, offers the better deal to depositors. To see why, think about the change over a year in the real purchasing power of deposits in the two countries. In Alpha, someone who deposits 100 alphans in the bank on January 1 will have 102 alphans on December 31. Because there is no inflation in Alpha, on average prices are the same at the end of the year as they were at the beginning. Thus, the 102 alphans the depositor can withdraw represent a 2 percent increase in buying power.

In Beta, the depositor who deposits 100 betans on January 1 will have 110 betans by the end of the year—10 percent more than she started with. But the prices of goods and services in Beta, we have assumed, also will rise by 10 percent. Thus, the Beta depositor can afford to buy precisely the same amount of goods and services at the end of the year as she could at the beginning; she gets no increase in buying power. So the Alpha depositor has the better deal, after all.

Economists refer to the annual percentage increase in the *real* purchasing power of a financial asset as the **real interest rate,** or the *real rate of return,* on that asset. In our example, the real purchasing power of deposits rises by 2 percent per year in Alpha and by 0 percent per year in Beta. So the real interest rate on deposits is 2 percent in Alpha and 0 percent in Beta. The real interest rate should be distinguished from the more familiar market interest rate, also called the *nominal interest rate.* The **nominal interest rate** is the annual percentage increase in the nominal, or dollar, value of an asset.

As the example of Alpha and Beta illustrates, we can calculate the real interest rate for any financial asset, from a checking account to a government bond, by subtracting the rate of inflation from the market or nominal interest rate on that asset. So in Alpha, the real interest rate on deposits equals the nominal interest rate (2 percent) minus the inflation rate (0 percent), or 2 percent. Likewise in Beta, the real interest rate equals the nominal interest rate (10 percent) minus the inflation rate (10 percent), or 0 percent.

We can write this definition of the real interest rate in mathematical terms:

$$r = i - \pi,^5$$

where

r = the real interest rate,

i = the nominal, or market, interest rate,

π = the inflation rate.

real interest rate the annual percentage increase in the purchasing power of a financial asset; the real interest rate on any asset equals the nominal interest rate on that asset minus the inflation rate

nominal interest rate (or market interest rate) the annual percentage increase in the nominal value of a financial asset

Real interest rates in the 1970s, 1980s, and 1990s

EXAMPLE 6.9

Following are interest rates on government bonds for selected years since 1970. In which of these years did the financial investors who bought government bonds get the best deal? The worst deal?

Year	Interest rate (%)	Inflation rate (%)
1970	6.5	5.7
1975	5.8	9.1
1980	11.5	13.5
1985	7.5	3.6
1990	7.5	5.4
1995	5.5	2.8
2000	5.9	3.4
2004	1.4	2.7

[5]Note that the real interest rate is *not* equal to the nominal interest rate divided by the price level. The reason is that the nominal interest rate is a rate of return, measured in percent, not a nominal quantity measured in dollars.

Financial investors and lenders do best when the real (not the nominal) interest rate is high, since the real interest rate measures the increase in their purchasing power. We can calculate the real interest rate for each year by subtracting the inflation rate from the nominal interest rate. The results are 0.8 percent for 1970, −3.3 percent for 1975, −2.0 percent for 1980, 3.9 percent for 1985, 2.1 percent for 1990, 2.7 percent for 1995, 2.5 percent for 2000, and −1.3 percent for 2004. For purchasers of government bonds, the best of these years was 1985, when they enjoyed a real return of 3.9 percent. The worst year was 1975, when their real return was actually negative. In other words, despite receiving 5.8 percent nominal interest, financial investors ended up losing buying power in 1975, as the inflation rate exceeded the interest rate earned by their investments.

Figure 6.2 shows the real interest rate in the United States since 1960 as measured by the nominal interest rate paid on the federal government's debt minus the inflation rate. Note that the real interest rate was negative in the 1970s and in 2003–2004 but reached historically high levels in the mid-1980s.

FIGURE 6.2

The Real Interest Rate in the United States, 1960–2004.

The real interest rate is the nominal interest rate—here the interest rate on funds borrowed by the federal government for a term of three months—minus the rate of inflation. In the United States, the real interest rate was negative in the 1970s and in 2003–2004 but reached historically high levels in the mid-1980s.

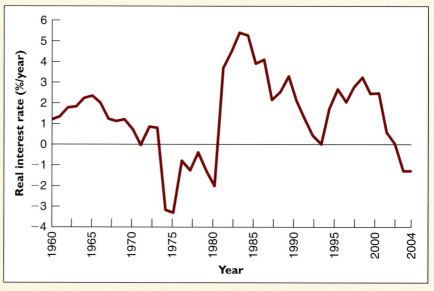

SOURCE: *Economic Report of the President* (http://www.gpoaccess.gov/eop/) and authors' calculations.

EXERCISE 6.9

You have some funds to invest but are unimpressed with the low interest rates your bank offers. You consult a broker, who suggests a bond issued by the government of a small island nation. The broker points out that these bonds pay 25 percent interest—much more than your bank—and that the island's government has never failed to repay its debts. What should be your next question?

The concept of the real interest rate helps to explain more precisely why an unexpected surge in inflation is bad for lenders and good for borrowers. For any given nominal interest rate that the lender charges the borrower, the higher the inflation rate, the lower the real interest rate the lender actually receives. So unexpectedly high inflation leaves the lender worse off. Borrowers, on the other hand, are better off when inflation is unexpectedly high, because their real interest rate is lower than anticipated.

Although unexpectedly high inflation hurts lenders and helps borrowers, a high rate of inflation that is *expected* may not redistribute wealth at all, because expected inflation can be built into the nominal interest rate. Suppose, for example, that the lender requires a real interest rate of 2 percent on new loans. If the inflation rate is confidently expected to be zero, the lender can get a 2 percent real interest rate by charging a nominal interest rate of 2 percent. But if the inflation rate is expected to be 10 percent, the lender can still ensure a real interest rate of 2 percent by charging a nominal interest rate of 12 percent. Thus, high inflation, if it is *expected*, need not hurt lenders—as long as the lenders can adjust the nominal interest they charge to reflect the expected inflation rate.

In response to people's concerns about unexpected inflation, in 1997 the United States Treasury introduced **inflation-protected bonds**, which pay a fixed real interest rate. People who buy these bonds receive a nominal interest rate each year equal to a fixed real rate plus the actual rate of inflation during that year. Owners of inflation-protected bonds suffer no loss in real wealth even if inflation is unexpectedly high.

inflation-protected bonds
bonds that pay a nominal interest rate each year equal to a fixed real rate plus the actual rate of inflation during that year

EXERCISE 6.10

In early 2005, the annual real rate of return on a 10-year inflation-protected bond was 1.8 percent. The annual nominal rate of return on a 10-year bond without inflation protection was about 4.4 percent. Who made the better financial investment if inflation averages 2 percent over the next 10 years? What if inflation averages 3 percent per year? What inflation rate will make holders of inflation-protected bonds and holders of bonds without inflation protection equally well off?

EXERCISE 6.11

What is the real rate of return to holding cash? (*Hint:* Does cash pay interest?) Does this real rate of return depend on whether the rate of inflation is correctly anticipated? How does your answer relate to the idea of shoe-leather costs?

THE FISHER EFFECT

Earlier we mentioned the observation that interest rates tend to be high when inflation is high and low when inflation is low. This relationship can be seen in Figure 6.3, which shows both the U.S. inflation rate and a nominal interest rate (the rate at which the government borrows for short periods) from 1960 to the present. Notice that nominal interest rates have tended to be high in periods of high inflation, such as the late 1970s, and relatively low in periods of low inflation, such as the early 1960s and the late 1990s.

Why do interest rates tend to be high when inflation is high? Our discussion of real interest rates provides the answer. Suppose inflation has recently been high, so borrowers and lenders anticipate that it will be high in the near future. We would expect lenders to raise their nominal interest rate so that their real rate of return will be unaffected. For their part, borrowers are willing to pay higher nominal interest rates when inflation is high, because they understand that the higher nominal interest rate only serves to compensate the lender for the fact that the loan will be repaid in dollars of reduced real value—in real terms, their cost of borrowing is unaffected by an equal increase in the nominal interest rate and the inflation rate.

FIGURE 6.3

Inflation and Interest Rates in the United States, 1960–2004.

Nominal interest rates tend to be high when inflation is high and low when inflation is low, a phenomenon called the Fisher effect.

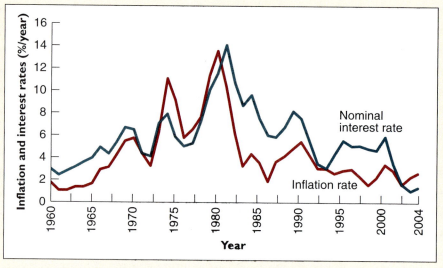

SOURCE: *Economic Report of the President* (http://www.gpoaccess.gov/eop/).

Conversely, when inflation is low, lenders do not need to charge so high a nominal interest rate to ensure a given real return. Thus, nominal interest rates will be high when inflation is high and low when inflation is low. This tendency for nominal interest rates to follow inflation rates is called the **Fisher effect,** after the early twentieth-century American economist Irving Fisher, who first pointed out the relationship.

Fisher effect the tendency for nominal interest rates to be high when inflation is high and low when inflation is low

---

▪ SUMMARY ▪

- The basic tool for measuring inflation is the *consumer price index,* or CPI. The CPI measures the cost of purchasing a fixed basket of goods and services in any period relative to the cost of the same basket of goods and services in a base year. The *inflation rate* is the annual percentage rate of change in the price level as measured by a *price index* such as the CPI.

- The official U.S. inflation rate, based on the CPI, may overstate the true inflation rate for two reasons: First, it may not adequately reflect improvements in the quality of goods and services. Second, the method of calculating the CPI ignores the fact that consumers can substitute cheaper goods and services for more expensive ones.

- A *nominal quantity* is a quantity that is measured in terms of its current dollar value. Dividing a nominal quantity, such as a family's income or a worker's wage in dollars, by a price index, such as the CPI, expresses that quantity in terms of real purchasing power. This procedure is called *deflating* the nominal quantity. If nominal quantities from two different years are deflated by a common price index, the purchasing power of the two quantities can be compared. To ensure that a nominal payment, such as a Social Security benefit, represents a constant level of real purchasing power, the nominal payment should be increased each year

by a percentage equal to the inflation rate. This method of adjusting nominal payments to maintain their purchasing power is called *indexing.*

- The public sometimes confuses increases in the *relative prices* for specific goods or services with inflation, which is an increase in the general price level. Since the remedies for a change in relative prices are different from the remedies for inflation, this confusion can cause problems.

- Inflation imposes a number of true costs on the economy, including "noise" in the price system; distortions of the tax system; "shoe-leather" costs, which are the real resources that are wasted as people try to economize on cash holdings; unexpected redistributions of wealth; and interference with long-run planning. Because of these costs, most economists agree that sustained economic growth is more likely if inflation is low and stable. *Hyperinflation,* a situation in which the inflation rate is extremely high, greatly magnifies the costs of inflation and is highly disruptive to the economy.

- The *real interest rate* is the annual percentage increase in the purchasing power of a financial asset. It is equal to the *nominal,* or *market, interest rate* minus the inflation rate. When inflation is unexpectedly high, the real interest rate is lower than anticipated, which hurts lenders but benefits borrowers. When inflation is unexpectedly low, lenders benefit and borrowers are hurt. To obtain a given real rate of return, lenders must charge a high nominal interest rate when inflation is high and a low nominal interest rate when inflation is low. The tendency for nominal interest rates to be high when inflation is high and low when inflation is low is called the *Fisher effect*.

■ KEY TERMS ■

consumer price index (CPI) (148)
deflating (a nominal quantity) (152)
deflation (151)
Fisher effect (170)
hyperinflation (165)
indexing (154)

inflation-protected bonds (169)
nominal interest rate (167)
nominal quantity (152)
price index (150)
price level (158)
rate of inflation (150)

real interest rate (167)
real quantity (152)
real wage (153)
relative price (159)

■ REVIEW QUESTIONS ■

1. Explain why changes in the cost of living for any particular individual or family may differ from changes in the official cost-of-living index, the CPI.

2. What is the difference between the *price level* and the *rate of inflation* in an economy?

3. Why is it important to adjust for inflation when comparing nominal quantities (for example, workers' average wages) at different points in time? What is the basic method for adjusting for inflation?

4. Describe how indexation might be used to guarantee that the purchasing power of the wage agreed to in a multi-year labor contract will not be eroded by inflation.

5. Give two reasons why the official inflation rate may understate the "true" rate of inflation. Illustrate by examples.

6. "It's true that unexpected inflation redistributes wealth, from creditors to debtors, for example. But what one side of the bargain loses, the other side gains. So from the perspective of the society as a whole, there is no real cost." Do you agree? Discuss.

7. How does inflation affect the real return on holding cash?

8. True or false: If both the potential lender and the potential borrower correctly anticipate the rate of inflation, inflation will not redistribute wealth from the creditor to the debtor. Explain.

■ PROBLEMS ■

1. Government survey takers determine that typical family expenditures each month in the year designated as the base year are as follows:

   > 20 pizzas at $10 each
   > Rent of apartment, $600 per month
   > Gasoline and car maintenance, $100
   > Phone service (basic service plus 10 long-distance calls), $50

   In the year following the base year, the survey takers determine that pizzas have risen to $11 each, apartment rent is $640, gasoline and maintenance have risen to $120, and phone service has dropped in price to $40.
   a. Find the CPI in the subsequent year and the rate of inflation between the base year and the subsequent year.
   b. The family's nominal income rose by 5 percent between the base year and the subsequent year. Are they worse off or better off in terms of what their income is able to buy?

2. Here are values of the CPI (multiplied by 100) for each year from 1990 to 2000. For each year beginning with 1991, calculate the rate of inflation from the previous year. What happened to inflation rates over the 1990s?

1990	130.7
1991	136.2
1992	140.3
1993	144.5
1994	148.2
1995	152.4
1996	156.9
1997	160.5
1998	163.0
1999	166.6
2000	172.2

3. According to the U.S. Census Bureau (http://www.census.gov/), nominal income for the typical family of four in the United States (median income)was $24,332 in 1980, $32,777 in 1985, $41,451 in 1990, and $62,228 in 2000. In purchasing power terms, how did family income compare in each of those four years? You will need to know that the CPI (multiplied by 100, 1982–1984 = 100) was 82.4 in 1980, 107.6 in 1985, 130.7 in 1990, and 172.2 in 2000. In general terms, how would your answer be affected if the Boskin Commission's conclusions about the CPI were confirmed?

4. A report found that the real entry-level wage for college graduates declined by 8 percent between 1990 and 1997. The nominal entry-level wage in 1997 was $13.65 per hour. Assuming that the findings are correct, what was the nominal entry-level wage in 1990? You will need to use data from Problem 2.

5. Here is a hypothetical income tax schedule, expressed in nominal terms, for the year 2005:

Family income	Taxes due (percent of income)
≤$20,000	10
$20,001–$30,000	12
$30,001–$50,000	15
$50,001–$80,000	20
>$80,000	25

The legislature wants to ensure that families with a given real income are not pushed up into higher tax brackets by inflation. The CPI (times 100) is 175 in 2005 and 185 in 2007. How should the income tax schedule above be adjusted for the year 2007 to meet the legislature's goal?

6. The typical consumer's food basket in the base year 2005 is as follows:

   30 chickens at $3.00 each
   10 hams at $6.00 each
   10 steaks at $8.00 each

   A chicken feed shortage causes the price of chickens to rise to $5.00 each in the year 2006. Hams rise to $7.00 each, and the price of steaks is unchanged.
   a. Calculate the change in the "cost-of-eating" index between 2005 and 2006.
   b. Suppose that consumers are completely indifferent between two chickens and one ham. For this example, how large is the substitution bias in the official "cost-of-eating" index?

7. Here are the actual per-gallon prices for unleaded regular gasoline for June of each year between 1978 and 1986, together with the values of the CPIs for those years. For each year from 1979 to 1986, find the CPI inflation rate and the change in the relative price

of gasoline, both from the previous year. Would it be fair to say that most of the changes in gas prices during this period were due to general inflation, or were factors specific to the oil market playing a role as well?

Year	Gasoline price ($/gallon)	CPI (1982–1984 = 1.00)
1978	0.663	0.652
1979	0.901	0.726
1980	1.269	0.824
1981	1.391	0.909
1982	1.309	0.965
1983	1.277	0.996
1984	1.229	1.039
1985	1.241	1.076
1986	0.955	1.136

8. Repeat Example 6.8 from the text (shoe-leather costs at Woodrow's Hardware). Calculate shoe-leather costs (relative to the original situation, in which Woodrow goes to the bank once a week) assuming that
   a. Inflation is 5 percent rather than 10 percent.
   b. Inflation is 5 percent and Woodrow's trips to the banks cost $2 each.
   c. Inflation remains at 10 percent and a trip to the bank costs $4, but Woodrow needs $10,000 per day to transact with customers.

9. On January 1, 2005, Albert invested $1,000 at 6 percent interest per year for three years. The CPI on January 1, 2005, stood at 100. On January 1, 2006, the CPI (times 100) was 105; on January 1, 2007, it was 110; and on January 1, 2008, the day Albert's investment matured, the CPI was 118. Find the real rate of interest earned by Albert in each of the three years and his total real return over the three-year period. Assume that interest earnings are reinvested each year and themselves earn interest.

10. Frank is lending $1,000 to Sarah for two years. Frank and Sarah agree that Frank should earn a 2 percent real return per year.
    a. The CPI (times 100) is 100 at the time that Frank makes the loan. It is expected to be 110 in one year and 121 in two years. What nominal rate of interest should Frank charge Sarah?
    b. Suppose Frank and Sarah are unsure about what the CPI will be in two years. Show how Frank and Sarah could index Sarah's annual repayments to ensure that Frank gets an annual 2 percent real rate of return.

11.* The Bureau of Labor Statistics has found that the base-year expenditures of the typical consumer break down as follows:

Food and beverages	17.8%
Housing	42.8%
Apparel and upkeep	6.3%
Transportation	17.2%
Medical care	5.7%
Entertainment	4.4%
Other goods, services	5.8%
Total	100.0%

*Problem marked with an asterisk (*) is more difficult.

Suppose that since the base year the prices of food and beverages have increased by 10 percent, the price of housing has increased by 5 percent, and the price of medical care has increased by 10 percent. Other prices are unchanged. Find the CPI for the current year.

▪ ANSWERS TO IN-CHAPTER EXERCISES ▪

6.1 The cost of the family's basket in 2000 remains at $680, as in Table 6.1. If the rent on their apartment falls to $400 in 2005, the cost of reproducing the 2000 basket of goods and services in 2005 is $620 ($400 for rent + $150 for hamburgers + $70 for movie tickets). The CPI for 2005 is accordingly $620/$680, or 0.912. So in this example, the cost of living fell nearly 9 percent between 2000 and 2005.

6.2 To construct your own personal price index, you would need to determine the basket of goods and services that you personally purchased in the base year. Your personal price index in each period would then be defined as the cost of your personal basket in that period relative to its cost in the base year. To the extent that your mix of purchases differs from that of the typical American consumer, your cost-of-living index will differ from the official CPI. For example, if in the base year you spent a higher share of your budget than the typical American on goods and services that have risen relatively rapidly in price, your personal inflation rate will be higher than the CPI inflation rate.

6.3 The percentage changes in the CPI in each year from the previous year are as follows:

1930	$-2.3\% = (0.167 - 0.171)/0.171$
1931	-9.0%
1932	-9.9%
1933	-5.1%

Negative inflation is called deflation. The experience of the 1930s, when prices were falling, contrasts sharply with inflation since 2000.

6.4 Rodriguez's real earnings, in 1982–1984 dollars, were $18 million/1.89, or $9.52 million. In real terms, Rodriguez earned about 64 percent more in 2004 than Bonds did in 2001.

6.5 The real minimum wage in 1950 is $0.75/0.241, or $3.11 in 1982–1984 dollars. The real minimum wage in April 2005 is $5.15/1.946, or $2.65 in 1982–1984 dollars. So the real minimum wage in April 2005 was almost 15 percent less than what it was in 1950.

6.6 The increase in the cost of living between 1950 and April 2005 is reflected in the ratio of the April 2005 CPI to the 1950 CPI, or 1.946/0.241 = 8.07. That is, the cost of living in April 2005 was 8.07 times what it was in 1950. If the minimum wage were indexed to preserve its purchasing power, it would have been 8.07 times higher in April 2005 than in 1950, or 8.07 × $0.75 = $6.05.

6.7 Between April 1980 and April 2005, the price of gasoline increased from $1.26 per gallon to $2.24 per gallon, or by 77.8 percent. During this same period, the CPI increased from 0.810 to 1.946, or by 140.2 percent. Gasoline prices rose less rapidly than the prices of the other goods and services in the CPI. Thus, the relative price of gas fell during this period.

6.8 The real cost of attending this university in 1980 was $8,761/0.824 = $10,632. In 2004 it was $38,297/1.889 = $20,274. Consequently, the relative cost rose by 90.7 percent between 1980 and 2004.

6.9 You should be concerned about the real return on your investment, not your nominal return. To calculate your likely real return, you need to know not only the nominal interest paid on the bonds of the island nation but also the prevailing inflation rate in that country. So your next question should be, "What is the rate of inflation in this country likely to be over the period that I am holding these bonds?"

6.10 The owner of the bond with inflation protection earns a 1.8 percent real interest rate regardless of the level of inflation. If inflation averages 2 percent per year over the next decade, the real rate of return on the bond without inflation protection will be 4.4 − 2 = 2.4 percent. In this case, the person who bought the bond without inflation protection will be better off. If inflation averages 3 percent per year, the real rate of return on the bond without inflation protection will be 4.4 − 3 = 1.4 percent. In this case, the person who bought the inflation-protected bond will be better off. The two bonds will have the same real interest rate (and the two bondholders will be equally well off) if the real interest rate on the bond without inflation protection equals 1.8 percent. This will occur when inflation is 2.6 percent, since 4.4 − 2.6 = 1.8 percent.

6.11 The real rate of return to cash, as with any asset, is the nominal interest rate less the inflation rate. But cash pays no interest; that is, the nominal interest rate on cash is zero. Therefore, the real rate of return on cash is just minus the inflation rate. In other words, cash loses buying power at a rate equal to the rate of inflation. This rate of return depends on the actual rate of inflation and does not depend on whether the rate of inflation is correctly anticipated.

If inflation is high so that the real rate of return on cash is very negative, people will take actions to try to reduce their holdings of cash, such as going to the bank more often. The costs associated with trying to reduce holdings of cash are what economists call shoe-leather costs.

PART

3

THE ECONOMY IN THE LONG RUN

■

For millennia the great majority of the world's inhabitants eked out a spare existence by tilling the soil. Only a small proportion of the population lived above the level of subsistence, learned to read and write, or traveled more than a few miles from their birthplaces. Large cities grew up, serving as imperial capitals and centers of trade, but the great majority of urban populations lived in dire poverty, subject to malnutrition and disease.

Then, about three centuries ago, a fundamental change occurred. Spurred by technological advances and entrepreneurial innovations, a process of economic growth began. Sustained over many years, this growth in the economy's productive capacity has transformed almost every aspect of how we live—from what we eat and wear to how we work and play. What caused this economic growth? And why have some countries enjoyed substantially greater rates of growth than others? As Nobelist Robert E. Lucas Jr. put it in a classic article on economic development, "The consequences for human welfare involved in questions like these are simply staggering: Once one starts to think about them, it is hard to think about anything else." Although most people would attach less significance to these questions than Lucas did, they are undoubtedly of very great importance.

The subject of Part 3 is the behavior of the economy in the long run, including the factors that cause the economy to grow and develop. Chapter 7 begins by tackling directly the causes and consequences of economic growth. A key conclusion of the chapter is that improvements in average labor productivity are the primary source of rising living standards; hence policies to improve living standards should focus on stimulating productivity. Chapter 8 studies long-term trends in the labor market, analyzing the long-run effects of economic growth on real wages and employment opportunities. As the creation of new capital goods is an important factor underlying rising productivity, Chapter 9 examines the processes of saving and capital formation. Chapter 10 introduces the concept of money and examines its relationship to inflation in the long run. In addition, this chapter introduces the Federal Reserve System and describes how the "Fed" controls the money supply to promote economic stability. Chapter 11 discusses the role of banks, bond markets, and stock markets in allocating saving to productive uses, as well as the role of international capital flows, which facilitate the allocation of saving across countries.

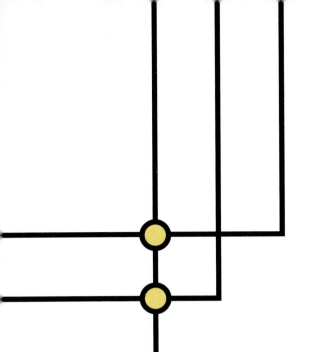

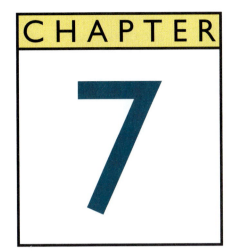

7

ECONOMIC GROWTH, PRODUCTIVITY, AND LIVING STANDARDS

One of us once attended a conference on the effects of economic growth and development on society. A speaker at the conference posed the following question: "Which would you rather be? An ordinary, middle-class American living today, or the richest person in America at the time of George Washington?"

A member of the audience spoke out immediately: "I can answer that question in one word. Dentistry."

The answer drew a laugh, perhaps because it reminded people of George Washington's famous wooden teeth. But it was a good answer. Dentistry in early America—whether the patient was rich or poor—was a primitive affair. Most dentists simply pulled a patient's rotten teeth, with a shot of whiskey for anesthetic.

Other types of medical care were not much better than dentistry. Eighteenth-century doctors had no effective weapons against tuberculosis, typhoid fever, diphtheria, influenza, pneumonia, and other communicable diseases. Such illnesses, now quite treatable, were major killers in Washington's time. Infants and children were particularly susceptible to deadly infectious diseases, especially whooping cough and measles. Even a well-to-do family often lost two or three children to these illnesses. Washington, an unusually large and vigorous man, lived to the age of 67, but the average life expectancy during his era was probably not much more than 40 years.

Would you rather be a rich person living in the eighteenth century or a middle-class person living in the twenty-first century?

Medical care is not the only aspect of ordinary life that has changed drastically over the past two centuries. Author Stephen Ambrose, in his account of the Lewis and Clark expedition, described the limitations of transportation and communication in early America:

> A critical fact in the world of 1801 was that nothing moved faster than the speed of a horse. No human being, no manufactured item, no bushel of wheat, no side of beef (or any beef on the hoof for that matter), no letter, no information, no idea, order, or instruction of any kind moved faster, and, as far as Jefferson's contemporaries were able to tell, nothing ever would.
>
> And except on a racetrack, no horse moved very fast. Road conditions in the United States ranged from bad to abominable, and there weren't very many of them. The best highway in the country ran from Boston to New York; it took a light stagecoach . . . three full days to make the 175-mile journey. The hundred miles from New York to Philadelphia took two full days.[1]

Today New Yorkers can go to Philadelphia by train in an hour and a half. What would George Washington have thought of that? And how would nineteenth-century pioneers, who crossed the continent by wagon train, have reacted to the idea that their great-grandchildren would be able to have breakfast in New York and lunch the same day in San Francisco?

No doubt you can think of other enormous changes in the way average people live, even over the past few decades. Computer technologies and the Internet have changed the ways people work and study in just a few years, for example. Though these changes are due in large part to scientific advances, such discoveries *by themselves* usually have little effect on most people's lives. New scientific knowledge leads to widespread improvements in living standards only when it is commercially applied. Better understanding of the human immune system, for example, has little impact unless it leads to new therapies or drugs. And a new drug will do little to help unless it is affordable to those who need it.

A tragic illustration of this point is the AIDS epidemic in Africa. Although some new drugs will moderate the effects of the virus that causes AIDS, they are so expensive that they are of little practical value in poverty-stricken African nations grappling with the disease. But even if the drugs were affordable, they would have limited benefit without modern hospitals, trained health professionals, and adequate nutrition and sanitation. In short, most improvements in a nation's living standard are the result not just of scientific and technological advances but of an economic system that makes the benefits of those advances available to the average person.

In this chapter we will explore the sources of economic growth and rising living standards in the modern world. We will begin by reviewing the remarkable economic growth in the industrialized countries, as measured by real GDP per person. Since the mid-nineteenth century (and earlier in some countries), a radical transformation in living standards has occurred in these countries. What explains this transformation? The key to rising living standards is a *continuing increase in average labor productivity,* which depends on several factors, from the skills and motivation workers bring to their jobs to the legal and social environment in which they work. We will analyze each of these factors and discuss its implications for government policies to promote growth. We also will discuss the costs of rapid economic growth and consider whether there may be limits to the amount of economic growth a society can achieve.

[1]Stephen E. Ambrose, *Undaunted Courage: Meriwether Lewis, Thomas Jefferson, and the Opening of the American West,* New York: Touchstone (Simon & Schuster), 1996, p. 52.

THE REMARKABLE RISE IN LIVING STANDARDS: THE RECORD

The advances in health care and transportation mentioned in the beginning of this chapter illustrate only a few of the impressive changes that have taken place in people's material well-being over the past two centuries, particularly in industrialized countries like the United States. To study the factors that affect living standards systematically, however, we must go beyond anecdotes and adopt a specific measure of economic well-being in a particular country and time.

In the chapter "Measuring Economic Activity," we introduced the concept of real GDP as a basic measure of the level of economic activity in a country. Recall that, in essence, real GDP measures the physical volume of goods and services produced within a country's borders during a specific period, such as a quarter or a year. Consequently, real GDP *per person* provides a measure of the quantity of goods and services available to the typical resident of a country at a particular time. Although real GDP per person is certainly not a perfect indicator of economic well-being, as we saw in the chapter "Measuring Economic Activity," it is positively related to a number of pertinent variables, such as life expectancy, infant health, and literacy. Lacking a better alternative, economists have focused on real GDP per person as a key measure of a country's living standard and stage of economic development.

Figure 4.2 showed the remarkable growth in real GDP per person that occurred in the United States between 1900 and 2004. For comparison, Table 7.1 shows real GDP per person in eight major countries in selected years from 1870 to 2003. Figure 7.1 displays the same data graphically for five of the eight countries.

The data in Table 7.1 and Figure 7.1 tell a dramatic story. For example, in the United States (which was already a relatively wealthy industrialized country in 1870), real GDP per person grew more than 12-fold between 1870 and 2003. In Japan, real GDP per person grew more than 28 times over the same period. Underlying these statistics is an amazingly rapid process of economic growth and transformation, through which in just a few generations relatively poor agrarian societies became highly industrialized economies—with average standards of living that could scarcely have been imagined in 1870. As Figure 7.1 shows, a significant part of this growth has occurred since 1950, particularly in Japan.

TABLE 7.1
Real GDP per Person in Selected Countries, 1870–2003 (in 2000 dollars)

Country	1870	1913	1950	1979	2003	Annual % change 1870–2003	Annual % change 1950–2003
Australia	5,512	7,236	9,369	17,670	28,312	1.2	2.1
Canada	2,328	5,509	8,906	19,882	29,201	1.9	2.3
France	2,291	4,484	6,164	18,138	26,176	1.8	2.8
Germany	1,152	2,218	4,785	17,222	25,271	2.3	3.2
Italy	2,852	4,018	5,128	16,912	25,458	1.7	3.1
Japan	931	1,763	2,141	16,329	26,636	2.6	4.9
United Kingdom	3,892	5,976	8,709	16,557	26,852	1.5	2.1
United States	2,887	6,852	12,110	22,835	35,488	1.9	2.0

SOURCES: Derived from Angus Maddison, *Phases of Capitalist Development*, Oxford: Oxford University Press, reprinted 1988, Tables A2, B2–B4. Rebased to 2000 and updated to 2003 by the authors using OECD *Quarterly National Accounts*. "Germany" refers to West Germany in 1950 and 1979.

FIGURE 7.1
Real GDP per Person in Five Industrialized Countries, 1870–2003.
Economic growth has been especially rapid since the 1950s, particularly in Japan.

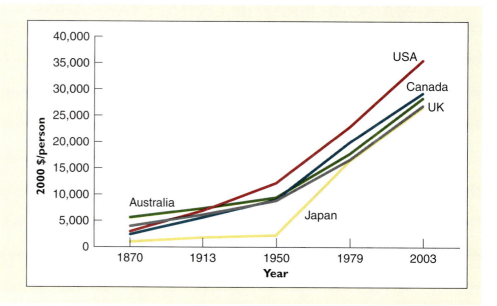

A note of caution is in order. The farther back in time we go, the less precise are historical estimates of real GDP. Most governments did not keep official GDP statistics until after World War II; production records from earlier periods are often incomplete or of questionable accuracy. Comparing economic output over a century or more is also problematic because many goods and services that are produced today were unavailable—indeed, inconceivable—in 1870. How many nineteenth-century horse-drawn wagons, for example, would be the economic equivalent of a BMW 328i automobile or a Boeing 757 jet? Despite the difficulty of making precise comparisons, however, we can say with certainty that the variety, quality, and quantity of available goods and services increased enormously in industrialized countries during the nineteenth and twentieth centuries, a fact reflected in the data on real GDP per capita.

WHY "SMALL" DIFFERENCES IN GROWTH RATES MATTER

The last two columns of Table 7.1 show the annual growth rates of real GDP per person, for both the entire 1870–2003 period and the more recent years, 1950–2003. At first glance, these growth rates don't seem to differ much from country to country. For example, for the period 1870–2003, the highest growth rate is 2.6 percent (Japan) and the lowest is 1.2 percent (Australia). But consider the long-run effect of this seemingly "small" difference in annual growth rates. In 1870, in terms of output per person, Australia was by far the richest of the eight countries listed in Table 7.1, with a real GDP per person nearly six times that of Japan. Yet by 2003 Japan had not just caught up to but exceeded Australia. This remarkable change in economic fortunes is the result of the apparently small difference between a 1.2 percent growth rate and a 2.6 percent growth rate, maintained over 133 years.

The fact that what seem to be small differences in growth rates can have large long-run effects results from what is called the power of compounding, which is often illustrated by *compound interest*.

EXAMPLE 7.1

Compound interest (1)

In 1800 your great-great-grandfather deposited $10.00 in a checking account at 4 percent interest. Interest is compounded annually (so that interest paid at the end of each year receives interest itself in later years). Great-Grandpa's will specified that the account be turned over to his most direct descendant (you) in the year 2005. When you withdrew the funds in that year, how much was the account worth?

The account was worth $10.00 in 1800; $10.00 × 1.04 = $10.40 in 1801; $10.00 × 1.04 × 1.04 = $10.00 × (1.04)^2 = $10.82 in 1802; and so on. Since 205 years elapsed between 1800, when the deposit was made, and the year 2005, when the account was closed, the value of the account in the year 2005 was $10.00 × (1.04)^{205}, or $10.00 × 1.04 to the 205th power. Using a calculator, you will find that $10.00 times 1.04 to the 205th power is $31,033.77—a good return for a $10.00 deposit!

Compound interest—an arrangement in which interest is paid not only on the original deposit but on all previously accumulated interest—is distinguished from *simple interest,* in which interest is paid only on the original deposit. If your great-grandfather's account had been deposited at 4 percent simple interest, it would have accumulated only 40 cents each year (4 percent of the original $10.00 deposit), for a total value of $10.00 + 205 × $0.40 = $92.00 after 205 years. The tremendous growth in the value of his account came from the compounding of the interest—hence the phrase "the power of compound interest."

compound interest the payment of interest not only on the original deposit but on all previously accumulated interest

Compound interest (2)

EXAMPLE 7.2

Refer to Example 7.1. What would your great-grandfather's $10.00 deposit have been worth after 205 years if the annual interest rate had been 2 percent? 6 percent?

At 2 percent interest, the account would be worth $10.00 in 1800; $10.00 × 1.02 = $10.20 in 1801; $10.00 × (1.02)^2 = $10.40 in 1802; and so on. In the year 2005, the value of the account would be $10.00 × (1.02)^{205}, or $579.48. If the interest rate were 6 percent, after 205 years the account would be worth $10.00 × (1.06)^{205}, or $1,540,644.29. Let's summarize the results of Examples 7.1 and 7.2:

Interest rate (%)	Value of $10 after 205 years
2	$579.48
4	$31,033.77
6	$1,540,644.29

The power of compound interest is that even at relatively low rates of interest, a small sum, compounded over a long enough period, can greatly increase in value. A more subtle point, illustrated by this example, is that small differences in interest rates matter a lot. The difference between a 2 percent and a 4 percent interest rate doesn't seem tremendous, but over a long period of time it implies large differences in the amount of interest accumulated on an account. Likewise, the effect of switching from a 4 percent to a 6 percent interest rate is enormous, as our calculations show.[2]

Economic growth rates are similar to compound interest rates. Just as the value of a bank deposit grows each year at a rate equal to the interest rate, so the size of a nation's economy expands each year at the rate of economic growth. This analogy

[2]Economists employ a useful formula for approximating the number of years it will take for an initial amount to double at various growth or interest rates. The formula is 72 divided by the growth or interest rate. Thus, if the interest rate is 2 percent per year, it will take 72/2 = 36 years for the initial sum to double. If the interest rate is 4 percent, it will take 72/4 = 18 years. This formula is a good approximation only for small and moderate interest rates.

suggests that even a relatively modest rate of growth in output per person—say, 1 to 2 percent per year—will produce tremendous increases in average living standard over a long period. And relatively small *differences* in growth rates, as in the case of Australia versus Japan, will ultimately produce very different living standards. Over the long run, then, the rate of economic growth is an extremely important variable. Hence, government policy changes or other factors that affect the long-term growth rate even by a small amount will have a major economic impact.

EXERCISE 7.1

Suppose that real GDP per capita in the United States had grown at 2.6 percent per year, as Japan's did, instead of the actual 1.9 percent per year, from 1870 to 2003. How much larger would real GDP per person have been in the United States in 2003?

ECONOMIC
NATURALIST
7.1

China as Number One?

When your parents were in school in the 1980s, there was a great deal of discussion in the United States about the Japanese economy. Japan's economic growth rate had greatly exceeded that in the United States and Europe since the 1950s. Pundits projected this growth rate into the future and predicted that Japan would have the world's largest output sometime during the twenty first century and would much sooner become the world's most prosperous economy in terms of output per worker. Books like one entitled *Japan as Number One* were best-sellers.

In the latter part of the 1980s, Japan's torrid growth rate cooled off and Japan entered a lengthy recession from which it has not yet fully emerged. Now, however, attention has been diverted to its neighbor, China. Not so long ago, China was one of the poorest countries in the world. In recent decades, however, Chinese economic growth has soared. Now China already produces about half of the entire planet's output of both clothing and cement, and it is also the world's largest producer of coal and steel. It is the world's largest *consumer* of copper, aluminum, and cell phones and the second largest consumer of personal computers.[3] Some observers predict that China will become the world's largest economy sometime during the middle of this century.

Because China also has the world's largest population, its output per person is still much smaller than that in the United States, western Europe, and Japan. As we saw in Example 4.1, China's output per person is only 14 percent as large as that in the United States. In Table 7.2 we list China's share of world population in 2003 as well as its share of world consumption of a variety of items in either 2002 or 2003.

Since China's share of world population is 20.5 percent, its consumption per person exceeds that elsewhere in the world wherever its share of world consumption exceeds 20.5 percent. Thus, for example, China consumes more than twice as much pork per person as the rest of the world, but less than one-fifth as much soda. Even though it consumes less than one-third as many computers per person as the rest of the world, its huge population still makes it the world's second largest consumer of computers.

Will China continue to grow so rapidly? As we have just seen in Examples 7.1 and 7.2, small differences in growth rates have tremendous long-run effects. Will China overtake the United States as the world's largest economy? Will it become the world's most prosperous nation in terms of output per worker? Or will it follow the path of Japan and experience smaller growth in the future? Perhaps more importantly, we should examine how China managed to achieve such extraordinary growth and what other less-developed countries can learn from China's experience.

[3]"Inside the New China," *Fortune*, October 4, 2004.

TABLE 7.2
China's Share of World Population and Consumption, 2002–2003*

Population	20.5%
Consumption of	
Pork	51%
Cigarettes	35
Cotton	33
Fish	32
Steel	27
Televisions	23
Ice cream	19
Washing machines	18
Computers	6
Soda	4

*"Inside the New China," *Fortune,* October 4, 2004. Data for fish are for the year 2001.

WHY NATIONS BECOME RICH: THE CRUCIAL ROLE OF AVERAGE LABOR PRODUCTIVITY

What determines a nation's economic growth rate? To get some insight into this vital question, we will find it useful to express real GDP per person as the product of two terms: average labor productivity and the share of the population that is working.

To do this, let Y equal total real output (as measured by real GDP, for example), N equal the number of employed workers, and POP equal the total population. Then real GDP per person can be written as Y/POP; average labor productivity, or output per employed worker, equals Y/N; and the share of the population that is working is N/POP. The relationship between these three variables is

$$\frac{Y}{POP} = \frac{Y}{N} \times \frac{N}{POP},$$

which, as you can see by canceling out N on the right-hand side of the equation, always holds exactly. In words, this basic relationship is

Real GDP per person = Average labor productivity
$\times$ Share of population employed.

This expression for real GDP per person tells us something very basic and intuitive: The quantity of goods and services that each person can consume depends on (1) how much each worker can produce and (2) how many people (as a fraction of the total population) are working. Furthermore, because real GDP per person equals average labor productivity times the share of the population that is employed, real GDP per person can *grow* only to the extent that there is *growth* in worker productivity and/or the fraction of the population that is employed.

Figures 7.2 and 7.3 show the U.S. figures for the three key variables in the relationship above for the period 1960–2004. Figure 7.2 shows both real GDP per person and real GDP per worker (average labor productivity). Figure 7.3 shows the portion of the entire U.S. population (not just the working-age population) that was employed during that period. Once again, we see that the expansion in output

FIGURE 7.2

Real GDP per Person and Average Labor Productivity in the United States, 1960–2004.

Real output per person in the United States grew 166 percent between 1960 and 2004, and real output per worker (average labor productivity) grew by 105 percent.

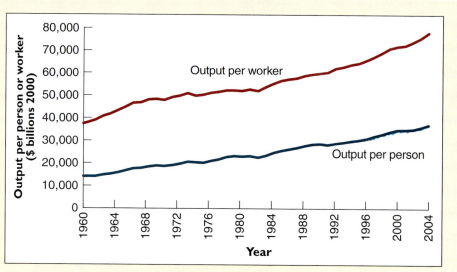

SOURCE: *Economic Report of the President* (http://www.gpoaccess.gov/eop/).

FIGURE 7.3

Share of the U.S. Population Employed, 1960–2004.

The share of the U.S. population holding a job increased from 36 percent in 1960 to 47 percent in 2004.

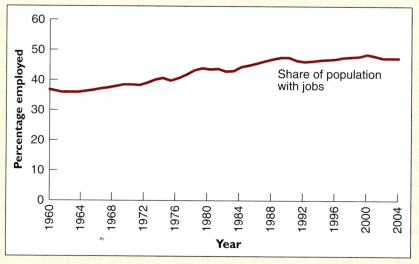

SOURCE: *Economic Report of the President* (http://www.gpoaccess.gov/eop/).

per person in the United States has been impressive. Between 1960 and 2004, real GDP per person in the United States grew by 166 percent. Thus, in 2004, the average American enjoyed about 2½ times as many goods and services as in 1960. Figures 7.2 and 7.3 show that increases in both labor productivity and the share of the population holding a job contributed to this rise in living standard.

Let's look a bit more closely at these two contributing factors, beginning with the share of the population that is employed. As Figure 7.3 shows, between 1960 and 2004, the number of people employed in the United States rose from 36 to 47 percent of the entire population, a remarkable increase. The growing tendency of women to work outside the home (see Economic Naturalist 5.1) was the most important reason for this rise in employment. Another factor leading to higher rates of employment was an increase in the share of the general population that is of working age (ages 16 to 65). The coming of age of the "baby boom" generation, born in the years after World War II, and to a lesser extent the immigration of young workers from other countries, helped cause this growth in the workforce.

Although the rising share of the U.S. population with jobs contributed significantly to the increase in real GDP per person during the past four decades, this trend almost certainly will not continue in the future. Women's participation in the labor force seems unlikely to continue rising at the same rate as in the past four decades. More important, the baby boom generation, now in its prime years of employment, will begin to reach retirement age around the year 2010. As more and more baby boomers retire, the fraction of the population that is employed will begin to drop, probably significantly. In the long run, then, the improvement in living standards brought about by the rising share of Americans with jobs will likely prove transitory.

What about the other factor that determines output per person, average labor productivity? As Figure 7.2 shows, between 1960 and 2004, average labor productivity in the United States increased by 105 percent, accounting for a sizable share of the overall increase in GDP per person. In other periods, the link between average labor productivity and output per person in the United States has often been even stronger, since in most earlier periods the share of the population holding jobs was more stable than it has been recently. (See Figure 4.2 for the behavior of real GDP per person and average labor productivity in the United States over the period 1900–2004.)

This quick look at recent data supports a more general conclusion. *In the long run, increases in output per person arise primarily from increases in average labor productivity.* Furthermore, the more people can produce, the more they can consume. To understand why economies grow, then, we must understand the reasons for increased labor productivity.

RECAP	**ECONOMIC GROWTH AND PRODUCTIVITY**

Real GDP per person, a basic indicator of living standards, has grown dramatically in the industrialized countries. This growth reflects the *power of compound interest:* Even a modest growth rate, if sustained over a long period of time, can lead to large increases in the size of the economy.

Output per person equals average labor productivity times the share of the population that is employed. Since 1960 the share of the U.S. population with jobs has risen significantly, but this variable is likely to decline in coming decades. In the long run, increases in output per person and hence living standards arise primarily from increases in average labor productivity.

THE DETERMINANTS OF AVERAGE LABOR PRODUCTIVITY

What determines the productivity of the average worker in a particular country at a particular time? Popular discussions of this issue often equate worker productivity with the willingness of workers of a given nationality to work hard. Everything else being equal, a culture that promotes hard work certainly tends to increase worker productivity. But intensity of effort alone cannot explain the huge differences in average labor productivity that we observe around the world. For example, average labor productivity in the United States is about 24 times what it is in Indonesia and 100 times what it is in Bangladesh, though there is little doubt that Indonesians and Bangladeshis work very hard.

In this section we will examine six factors that appear to account for the major differences in average labor productivity, both between countries and between generations. Later in the chapter we will discuss how economic policies can influence these factors to spur productivity and growth.

HUMAN CAPITAL

To illustrate the factors that determine average labor productivity, we introduce two prototypical assembly line workers, Lucy and Ethel.

The Everett Collection

How productive are these workers?

EXAMPLE 7.3

Lucy and Ethel on the assembly line

Lucy and Ethel have jobs wrapping chocolate candies and placing them into boxes. Lucy, a novice wrapper, can wrap only 100 candies per hour. Ethel, who has had on-the-job training, can wrap 300 candies per hour. Lucy and Ethel each work 40 hours per week. Find average labor productivity, in terms of candies wrapped per week and candies wrapped per hour, (a) for Lucy, (b) for Ethel, and (c) for Lucy and Ethel as a team.

We have defined average labor productivity in general terms as output per worker. Note, though, that the measurement of average labor productivity depends on the time period that is specified. For example, the data presented in Figure 7.2 tell us how much the average worker produces *in a year*. In this example we are concerned with how much Lucy and Ethel can produce *per hour* of work or *per week* of work. Any one of these ways of measuring labor productivity is equally valid, as long as we are clear about the time unit we are using.

Lucy and Ethel's hourly productivities are given in the problem: Lucy can wrap 100 candies per hour and Ethel can wrap 300. Lucy's weekly productivity is (40 hours/week) × (100 candies wrapped/hour) = 4,000 wrapped candies per week. Ethel's weekly productivity is (40 hours/week) × (300 candies wrapped/hour), or 12,000 candies per week.

Together Lucy and Ethel can wrap 16,000 candies per week. As a team, their average weekly productivity is (16,000 candies wrapped)/(2 weeks of work), or 8,000 candies per week. Their average hourly productivity as a team is (16,000 candies wrapped)/(80 hours of work) = 200 candies per hour. Notice that, taken as a team, the two women's productivity lies midway between their individual productivities.

Ethel is more productive than Lucy because she has had on-the-job training, which has allowed her to develop her candy-wrapping skills to a higher level than Lucy's. Because of her training, Ethel can produce more than Lucy can in a given number of hours.

EXERCISE 7.2

Suppose Ethel attends additional classes in candy wrapping and learns how to wrap 500 candies per hour. Find the output per week and output per hour for Lucy and Ethel, both individually and as a team.

Economists would explain the difference in the two women's performance by saying that Ethel has more human capital than Lucy. *Human capital* comprises the talents, education, training, and skills of workers. Workers with a large stock of human capital are more productive than workers with less training. For example, a secretary who knows how to use a word processing program will be able to type more letters than one who doesn't; an auto mechanic who is familiar with computerized diagnostic equipment will be able to fix engine problems that less well-trained mechanics could not.

ECONOMIC NATURALIST 7.2

Why did West Germany and Japan recover so successfully from the devastation of World War II?

Germany and Japan sustained extensive destruction of their cities and industries during World War II and entered the postwar period impoverished. Yet within 30 years both countries had not only been rebuilt but had become worldwide industrial and economic leaders. What accounts for these "economic miracles"?

Many factors contributed to the economic recovery of West Germany and Japan from World War II, including the substantial aid provided by the United States to Europe under the Marshall Plan and to Japan during the U.S. occupation. Most economists agree, however, that high levels of *human capital* played a crucial role in both countries.

At the end of the war, Germany's population was exceptionally well educated, with a large number of highly qualified scientists and engineers. The country also had (and still does today) an extensive apprentice system that provided on-the-job training to young workers. As a result, Germany had a skilled industrial workforce. In addition, the area that became West Germany benefited substantially from an influx of skilled workers from East Germany and the rest of Soviet-controlled Europe, including 20,000 trained engineers and technicians. Beginning as early as 1949, this concentration of human capital contributed to a major expansion of Germany's technologically sophisticated, highly productive manufacturing sector. By 1960 West Germany was a leading exporter of high-quality manufactured goods, and its citizens enjoyed one of the highest standards of living in Europe.

Japan, which probably sustained greater physical destruction in the war than Germany, also began the postwar period with a skilled and educated labor force. In addition, occupying American forces restructured the Japanese school system and encouraged all Japanese to obtain a good education. Even more so than the Germans, however, the Japanese emphasized on-the-job training. As part of a lifetime employment system, under which workers were expected to stay with the same company their entire career, Japanese firms invested extensively in worker training. The payoff to these investments in human capital was a steady increase in average labor productivity, particularly in manufacturing. By the 1980s Japanese manufactured goods were among the most advanced in the world and Japan's workers among the most skilled.

Although high levels of human capital were instrumental in the rapid economic growth of West Germany and Japan, human capital alone cannot create a high living standard. A case in point is Soviet-dominated East Germany, which had a level of human capital similar to West Germany's after the war but did not enjoy the same economic growth. For reasons we will discuss later in the chapter (see Economic Naturalist 7.5), the communist system imposed by the Soviets utilized East Germany's human capital far less effectively than the economic systems of Japan and West Germany.

Human capital is analogous to physical capital (such as machines and factories) in that it is acquired primarily through the investment of time, energy, and money. For example, to learn how to use a word processing program, a secretary might need to attend a technical school at night. The cost of going to school includes not only the tuition paid but also the *opportunity cost* of the secretary's time spent attending class and studying. The benefit of the schooling is the increase in wages the secretary will earn when the course has been completed. We know by the *cost-benefit principle* that the secretary should learn word processing only if the benefits exceed the costs, including the opportunity costs. In general, then, we would expect to see people acquire additional education and skills when the difference in the wages paid to skilled and unskilled workers is significant.

PHYSICAL CAPITAL

Workers' productivity depends not only on their skills and effort but on the tools they have to work with. Even the most skilled surgeon cannot perform open-heart surgery without sophisticated equipment, and an expert computer programmer is of limited value without a computer. These examples illustrate the importance of *physical capital,* such as factories and machines. More and better capital allows workers to produce more efficiently, as Example 7.4 shows.

EXAMPLE 7.4

Lucy and Ethel get automated

Refer to Example 7.3. Lucy and Ethel's boss acquired an electric candy-wrapping machine, which is designed to be operated by one worker. Using this machine, an untrained worker can wrap 500 candies per hour. What are Lucy and Ethel's hourly and weekly outputs now? Will the answer change if the boss gets a second machine? A third?

Suppose for the sake of simplicity that a candy-wrapping machine must be assigned to one worker only. (This assumption rules out sharing arrangements, in which one worker uses the machine on the day shift and another on the night shift.) If the boss buys just one machine, she will assign it to Lucy. (Why? See Exercise 7.3.) Now Lucy will be able to wrap 500 candies per hour, while Ethel can wrap only 300 per hour. Lucy's weekly output will be 20,000 wrapped candies (40 hours × 500 candies wrapped per hour). Ethel's weekly output is still 12,000 wrapped candies (40 hours × 300 candies wrapped per hour). Together they can now wrap 32,000 candies per week, or 16,000 candies per week each. On an hourly basis, average labor productivity for the two women taken together is 32,000 candies wrapped per 80 hours of work, or 400 candies wrapped per hour—twice their average labor productivity before the boss bought the machine.

With two candy-wrapping machines available, both Lucy and Ethel could use a machine. Each could wrap 500 candies per hour, for a total of 40,000 wrapped candies per week. Average labor productivity for both women taken together would be 20,000 wrapped candies per week, or 500 wrapped candies per hour.

What would happen if the boss purchased a third machine? With only two workers, a third machine would be useless: it would add nothing to either total output or average labor productivity.

EXERCISE 7.3

Using the assumptions made in Examples 7.3 and 7.4, explain why the boss should give the single available candy-wrapping machine to Lucy rather than Ethel. (Hint: Use *the principle of increasing opportunity cost,* introduced in Chapter 3.)

The candy-wrapping machine is an example of a *capital good,* which was defined in the chapter "Measuring Economic Activity" as a long-lived good, which is itself produced and used to produce other goods and services. Capital goods include machines and equipment (such as computers, earthmovers, or assembly lines) as well as buildings (such as factories or office buildings).

Capital goods like the candy-wrapping machine enhance workers' productivity. Table 7.3 summarizes the results from Examples 7.3 and 7.4. For each number of machines the boss might acquire (column 1), Table 7.3 gives the total weekly output of Lucy and Ethel taken together (column 2), the total number of hours worked by the two women (column 3), and average output per hour (column 4), equal to total weekly output divided by total weekly hours.

Table 7.3 demonstrates two important points about the effect of additional capital on output. First, for a given number of workers, adding more capital generally

TABLE 7.3
Capital, Output, and Productivity in the Candy-Wrapping Factory

(1) Number of machines (capital)	(2) Total number of candies wrapped each week (output)	(3) Total hours worked per week	(4) Candies wrapped per hour worked (productivity)
0	16,000	80	200
1	32,000	80	400
2	40,000	80	500
3	40,000	80	500

increases both total output and average labor productivity. For example, adding the first candy-wrapping machine increases weekly output (column 2) by 16,000 candies and average labor productivity (column 4) by 200 candies wrapped per hour.

The second point illustrated by Table 7.3 is that the more capital that is already in place, the smaller the benefits of adding extra capital. Notice that the first machine adds 16,000 candies to total output, but the second machine adds only 8,000. The third machine, which cannot be used since there are only two workers, does not increase output or productivity at all. This result illustrates a general principle of economics, called *diminishing returns to capital*. According to the principle of **diminishing returns to capital,** if the amount of labor and other inputs employed is held constant, then the greater the amount of capital already in use, the less an additional unit of capital adds to production. In the case of the candy-wrapping factory, diminishing returns to capital implies that the first candy-wrapping machine acquired adds more output than the second, which in turn adds more output than the third.

Diminishing returns to capital are a natural consequence of firms' incentive to use each piece of capital as productively as possible. To maximize output, managers will assign the first machine that a firm acquires to the most productive use available, the next machine to the next most productive use, and so on—an illustration of the *principle of increasing opportunity cost,* or *low-hanging-fruit principle* (Chapter 3). When many machines are available, all the highly productive ways of using them already have been exploited. Thus, adding yet another machine will not raise output or productivity by very much. If Lucy and Ethel are already operating two candy-wrapping machines, there is little point to buying a third machine, except perhaps as a replacement or spare.

The implications of Table 7.3 can be applied to the question of how to stimulate economic growth. First, increasing the amount of capital available to the workforce will tend to increase output and average labor productivity. The more adequately equipped workers are, the more productive they will be. Second, the degree to which productivity can be increased by an expanding stock of capital is limited. Because of diminishing returns to capital, an economy in which the quantity of capital available to each worker is already very high will not benefit much from further expansion of the capital stock.

Is there empirical evidence that giving workers more capital makes them more productive? Figure 7.4 shows the relationship between average labor productivity (real GDP per worker) in 1990 and the amount of capital per worker in 15 major countries, including the 8 industrialized countries listed in Table 7.1. The figure shows a strong relationship between the amounts of capital per worker and productivity, consistent with the theory. Note, though, that the relationship between capital and productivity is somewhat weaker for the richest countries. For example, Germany has more capital per worker than the United States, but German workers are less productive than American workers on average. Diminishing returns to capital may help

diminishing returns to capital if the amount of labor and other inputs employed is held constant, then the greater the amount of capital already in use, the less an additional unit of capital adds to production

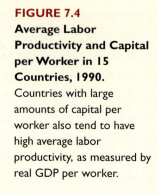

FIGURE 7.4

Average Labor Productivity and Capital per Worker in 15 Countries, 1990.

Countries with large amounts of capital per worker also tend to have high average labor productivity, as measured by real GDP per worker.

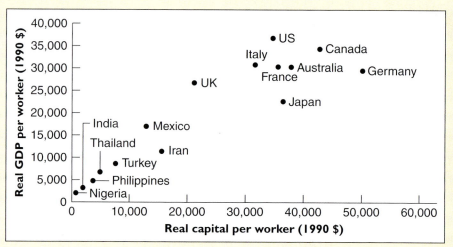

SOURCE: Penn World Tables (www.nber.org). Countries included are those listed in Table 7.1, plus all countries with populations of 40 million or more for which data are available.

to explain the weakening of the relationship between capital and productivity at high levels of capital. In addition, Figure 7.4 does not account for many other differences among countries, such as differences in economic systems or government policies. Thus, we should not expect to see a perfect relationship between the two variables.

LAND AND OTHER NATURAL RESOURCES

Besides capital goods, other inputs to production help to make workers more productive, among them land, energy, and raw materials. Fertile land is essential to agriculture, and modern manufacturing processes make intensive use of energy and raw materials.

In general, an abundance of natural resources increases the productivity of the workers who use them. For example, a farmer can produce a much larger crop in a land-rich country like the United States or Australia than in a country where the soil is poor or arable land is limited in supply. With the aid of modern farm machinery and great expanses of land, today's American farmers are so productive that even though they constitute less than 3 percent of the population, they provide enough food not only to feed the country but to export to the rest of the world.

Although there are limits to a country's supply of arable land, many other natural resources, such as petroleum and metals, can be obtained through international markets. Because resources can be obtained through trade, countries need not possess large quantities of natural resources within their own borders to achieve economic growth. Indeed, a number of countries have become rich without substantial natural resources of their own, including Japan, Hong Kong, Singapore, and Switzerland. Just as important as possessing natural resources is the ability to use them productively—for example, by means of advanced technologies.

TECHNOLOGY

Besides human capital, physical capital, and natural resources, a country's ability to develop and apply new, more productive technologies will help to determine its productivity. Consider just one industry, transportation. Two centuries ago, as suggested by the quote from Stephen Ambrose in the beginning of the chapter, the horse and wagon were the primary means of transportation—a slow and costly method indeed. But in the nineteenth century, technological advances such as the steam engine supported the expansion of riverborne transportation and the development of a national rail network. In the twentieth century, the invention of the internal combustion engine and the development of aviation, supported by the construction of an extensive infrastructure of roads and airports, have produced increasingly rapid, cheap, and reliable transport. Technological change has clearly been a driving force in the transportation revolution.

New technologies can improve productivity in industries other than the one in which they are introduced. Once farmers could sell their produce only in their local communities, for example. Now the availability of rapid shipping and refrigerated transport allows farmers to sell their products virtually anywhere in the world. With a broader market in which to sell, farmers can specialize in those products best suited to local land and weather conditions. Similarly, factories can obtain their raw materials wherever they are cheapest and most abundant, produce the goods they are most efficient at manufacturing, and sell their products wherever they will fetch the best price. Both these examples illustrate *the principle of comparative advantage,* that overall productivity increases when producers concentrate on those activities at which they are relatively most efficient (see Chapter 3).

Numerous other technological developments led to increased productivity, including advances in communication and medicine and the introduction of computer technology. All indications are that the Internet will have a major impact on the U.S. economy, not just in retailing but in many other sectors. In fact, *most economists would probably agree that new technologies are the single most important source of productivity improvement,* and hence of economic growth in general.

However, economic growth does not automatically follow from breakthroughs in basic science. To make the best use of new knowledge, an economy needs entrepreneurs who can exploit scientific advances commercially, as well as a legal and political environment that encourages the practical application of new knowledge.

EXERCISE 7.4

A new kind of wrapping paper has been invented that makes candy-wrapping quicker and easier. The use of this paper *increases* the number of candies a person can wrap by hand by 200 per hour, and the number of candies a person can wrap by machine by 300 per hour. Using the data from Examples 7.3 and 7.4, construct a table like Table 7.3 that shows how this technological advance affects average labor productivity. Do diminishing returns to capital still hold?

Why has U.S. labor productivity grown so rapidly since 1995?

During the 1950s and 1960s, most industrialized countries experienced rapid growth in real GDP and average labor productivity. Between 1947 and 1973, for example, U.S. labor productivity grew by 2.8 percent per year.[4] Between 1973 and 1995, however, labor productivity growth in the United States fell by half, to 1.4 percent per year. Other countries experienced similar productivity slowdowns, and many articles and books were written trying to uncover the reasons. In recent years, however, there has been a rebound in productivity growth, particularly in the United States. Between 1995 and 2004, U.S. labor productivity growth averaged 3.1 percent per year. What caused this resurgence in productivity growth? Can it be sustained?

ECONOMIC NATURALIST 7.3

Economists agree that the pickup in productivity growth was the product of rapid technological progress and increased investment in new information and communication technologies (ICT). Research indicates that productivity has grown rapidly in both those industries that *produce* ICT, such as silicon chips and fiber-optics, and those industries that *use* ICT. The application of these advances had ripple effects in areas ranging from automobile production to retail inventory management. The rapid growth of the Internet, for example, made it possible for consumers to shop and find information online. But it also helped companies improve their efficiency by improving coordination between manufacturers and their

[4]Data refer to labor productivity growth in the nonfarm business sector and can be found at http://data.bls.gov/cgi-bin/dsrv.

suppliers. On the other hand, there has been no acceleration in labor productivity growth in those industries that neither produce nor use much ICT.[5]

Optimists argue that advances in computers, communications, biotechnology, and other ICT fields will allow productivity growth to continue at this elevated rate. Others are more cautious, arguing that the increases in productivity growth from these developments may be temporary rather than permanent. A great deal is riding on which view will turn out to be correct.

ENTREPRENEURSHIP AND MANAGEMENT

entrepreneurs people who create new economic enterprises

The productivity of workers depends in part on the people who help to decide what to produce and how to produce it: entrepreneurs and managers. **Entrepreneurs** are people who create new economic enterprises. Because of the new products, services, technological processes, and production methods they introduce, entrepreneurs are critical to a dynamic, healthy economy. In the late nineteenth and early twentieth centuries, individuals like Henry Ford and Alfred Sloan (automobiles), Andrew Carnegie (steel), John D. Rockefeller (oil), and J. P. Morgan (finance) played central roles in the development of American industry—and, not incidentally, amassed huge personal fortunes in the process. These people and others like them (including contemporary entrepreneurs like Bill Gates) have been criticized for some of their business practices, in some cases with justification. Clearly, though, they and dozens of other prominent business leaders of the past century have contributed significantly to the growth of the U.S. economy. Henry Ford, for example, developed the idea of mass production, which lowered costs sufficiently to bring automobiles within reach of the average American family. Ford began his business in his garage, a tradition that has been maintained by thousands of innovators ever since. Larry Page and Sergey Brin, the co-founders of Google, revolutionized the way college students and many professionals conduct research by developing a method to prioritize the list of Web sites obtained in a search of the Internet.

Entrepreneurship, like any form of creativity, is difficult to teach, although some of the supporting skills, like financial analysis and marketing, can be learned in college or business school. How, then, does a society encourage entrepreneurship? History suggests that the entrepreneurial spirit will always exist; the challenge to society is to channel entrepreneurial energies in economically productive ways. For example, economic policymakers need to ensure that taxation is not so heavy, and regulation not so inflexible, that small businesses—some of which will eventually become big businesses—cannot get off the ground. Sociological factors may play a role as well. Societies in which business and commerce are considered to be beneath the dignity of refined, educated people are less likely to produce successful entrepreneurs (see Economic Naturalist 7.4). In the United States, for the most part, business has been viewed as a respectable activity. Overall, a social and economic milieu that allows entrepreneurship to flourish appears to promote economic growth and rising productivity, perhaps especially so in high-technology eras like our own.

EXAMPLE 7.5

Inventing the Personal Computer

In 1975 Steve Jobs and Steve Wozniak were two 20-year-olds who designed computer games for Atari. They had an idea to make a computer that was smaller and cheaper than the closet-sized mainframes that were then in use. To set up shop in Steve Jobs's parents' garage and buy their supplies, they sold their two most valuable possessions, Jobs's used Volkswagen van and Wozniak's Hewlitt-Packard scientific calculator, for a total of $1,300. The result was the first personal computer, which they named after their new company (and Jobs's favorite fruit): Apple. The rest is history. Clearly, Jobs's

---

[5]Kevin J. Stiroh, "Information Technology and the U.S. Productivity Revival: What Do the Industry Data Say?" *American Economic Review*, 92:1559–1576, December 2002.

and Wozniak's average labor productivity as the inventors of the personal computer was many times what it was when they designed computer games. Creative entrepreneurship can increase productivity just like additional capital or land.

Why did medieval China stagnate economically?

The Sung period in China (A.D. 960–1270) was one of considerable technological sophistication; its inventions included paper, waterwheels, water clocks, gunpowder, and possibly the compass. Yet no significant industrialization occurred, and in subsequent centuries Europe saw more economic growth and technological innovation than China. Why did medieval China stagnate economically?

ECONOMIC NATURALIST 7.4

According to research by economist William Baumol,[6] the main impediment to industrialization during the Sung period was a social system that inhibited entrepreneurship. Commerce and industry were considered low-status activities, not fit for an educated person. In addition, the emperor had the right to seize his subjects' property and to take control of their business enterprises—a right that greatly reduced his subjects' incentives to undertake business ventures. The most direct path to status and riches in medieval China was to go through a system of demanding civil service examinations given by the government every three years. The highest scorers on these national examinations were granted lifetime positions in the imperial bureaucracy, where they wielded much power and often became wealthy, in part through corruption. Not surprisingly, medieval China did not develop a dynamic entrepreneurial class, and consequently its scientific and technological advantages did not translate into sustained economic growth. China's experience shows why scientific advances alone cannot guarantee economic growth; to have economic benefits, scientific knowledge must be commercially applied through new products and new, more efficient means of producing goods and services.

Although entrepreneurship may be more glamorous, managers—the people who run businesses on a daily basis—also play an important role in determining average labor productivity. Managerial jobs span a wide range of positions, from the supervisor of the loading dock to the CEO (chief executive officer) at the helm of a *Fortune* 500 company. Managers work to satisfy customers, deal with suppliers, organize production, obtain financing, assign workers to jobs, and motivate them to work hard and effectively. Such activities enhance labor productivity. For example, in the 1970s and 1980s, Japanese managers introduced new production methods that greatly increased the efficiency of Japanese manufacturing plants. Among them was the *just-in-time* inventory system, in which suppliers deliver production components to the factory just when they are needed, eliminating the need for factories to stockpile components. Japanese managers also pioneered the idea of organizing workers into semi-independent production teams, which allowed workers more flexibility and responsibility than the traditional assembly line. Managers in the United States and other countries studied the Japanese managerial techniques closely and adopted many of them.

THE POLITICAL AND LEGAL ENVIRONMENT

So far we have emphasized the role of the private sector in increasing average labor productivity. But government too has a role to play in fostering improved productivity. One of the key contributions government can make is to provide a *political and legal environment* that encourages people to behave in economically productive ways—to work hard, save and invest wisely, acquire useful information and skills, and provide the goods and services that the public demands.

[6]"Entrepreneurship: Productive, Unproductive, and Destructive," *Journal of Political Economy,* October 1990, pp. 893–921.

One specific function of government that appears to be crucial to economic success is the establishment of *well-defined property rights*. Property rights are well defined when the law provides clear rules for determining who owns what resources (through a system of deeds and titles, for example) and how those resources can be used. Imagine living in a society in which a dictator, backed by the military and the police, could take whatever he wanted, and regularly did so. In such a country, what incentive would you have to raise a large crop or to produce other valuable goods and services? Very little, since much of what you produced would likely be taken away from you. Unfortunately, in many countries of the world today, this situation is far from hypothetical.

Political and legal conditions affect the growth of productivity in other ways, as well. Political scientists and economists have documented the fact that *political instability* can be detrimental to economic growth. This finding is reasonable, since entrepreneurs and savers are unlikely to invest their resources in a country whose government is unstable, particularly if the struggle for power involves civil unrest, terrorism, or guerrilla warfare. On the other hand, a political system that promotes the *free and open exchange of ideas* will speed the development of new technologies and products. For example, some economic historians have suggested that the decline of Spain as an economic power was due in part to the advent of the Spanish Inquisition, which permitted no dissent from religious orthodoxy. Because of the Inquisition's persecution of those whose theories about the natural world contradicted Church doctrine, Spanish science and technology languished, and Spain fell behind more tolerant nations like the Netherlands.

> ### EXERCISE 7.5
>
> **A Bangladeshi worker who immigrates to America is likely to find that his average labor productivity is much higher in the United States than it was at home. The worker is, of course, the same person he was when he lived in Bangladesh. How can the simple act of moving to the United States increase the worker's productivity? What does your answer say about the incentive to immigrate?**

ECONOMIC NATURALIST 7.5

Why did communism fail?

For more than 70 years, from the Russian revolution in 1917 until the collapse of the Soviet Union in 1991, communism was believed by many to pose a major challenge to market-based economic systems. Yet, by the time of the Soviet Union's breakup, the poor economic record of communism had become apparent. Indeed, low living standards in communist countries, compared to those achieved in the West, were a major reason for the popular discontent that brought down the communist system in Europe. Economically speaking, why did communism fail?

The poor growth records of the Soviet Union and other communist countries did not reflect a lack of resources or economic potential. The Soviet Union had a highly educated workforce; a large capital stock; a vast quantity of natural resources, including land and energy; and access to sophisticated technologies. Yet, at the time of its collapse, output per person in the Soviet Union was probably less than one-seventh what it was in the United States.

Most observers would agree that the political and legal environment that established the structure of the communist economic system was a major cause of its ultimate failure. The economic system of the Soviet Union and other communist countries had two main elements: First, the capital stock and other resources were owned by the government rather than by individuals or private corporations. Second, most decisions regarding production and distribution were made and implemented by a government planning agency rather than by individuals and firms interacting through markets. This system performed poorly, we now understand, for several reasons.

One major problem was *the absence of private property rights*. With no ability to acquire a significant amount of private property, Soviet citizens had little incentive to behave in economically productive ways. The owner of an American or Japanese firm is strongly motivated to cut costs and to produce goods that are highly valued by the public, because the owner's income is determined by the firm's profitability. In contrast, the performance of a Soviet firm manager was judged on whether the manager produced the quantities of goods specified by the government's plan—irrespective of the quality of the goods produced or whether consumers wanted them. Soviet managers had little incentive to reduce costs or produce better, more highly valued products, as any extra profits would accrue to the government and not to the manager; nor were there any opportunities for entrepreneurs to start new businesses. Likewise, workers had little reason to work hard or effectively under the communist system, as pay rates were determined by the government planning agency rather than by the economic value of what the workers produced.

A second major weakness of the communist system was the *absence of free markets*. In centrally planned economies, markets are replaced by detailed government plans that specify what should be produced and how. But, as we saw in the example of New York City's food supply (Chapter 3), the coordination of even relatively basic economic activities can be extremely complex and require a great deal of information, much of which is dispersed among many people. In a market system, changes in prices both convey information about the goods and services people want and provide suppliers the incentives to bring these goods and services to market. Indeed, as we know from the *equilibrium principle*, a market in equilibrium leaves individuals with no unexploited opportunities. Central planners in communist countries proved far less able to deal with this complexity than decentralized markets. As a result, under communism consumers suffered constant shortages and shoddy goods.

After the collapse of communism, many formerly communist countries began the difficult transition to a market-oriented economic system. Changing an entire economic system (the most extreme example of a *structural policy*) is a slow and difficult task, and many countries saw economic conditions worsen at first rather than improve. *Political instability* and the absence of a modern *legal framework*, particularly laws applying to commercial transactions, have often hampered the progress of reforms. However, a number of formerly communist countries, including Poland, the Czech Republic, and the former East Germany, have succeeded in implementing Western-style market systems and have begun to achieve significant economic growth.

RECAP	DETERMINANTS OF AVERAGE LABOR PRODUCTIVITY

- Key factors determining average labor productivity in a country include

    The skills and training of workers, called *human capital*.

    The quantity and quality of *physical capital*—machines, equipment, and buildings.

    The availability of land and other *natural resources*.

    The sophistication of the *technologies* applied in production.

    The effectiveness of *management* and *entrepreneurship*.

    The broad *social and legal environment*.

- Labor productivity growth slowed throughout the industrialized world in the 1970s and 1980s. Since 1995, it has rebounded (especially in the United States), largely because of advances in information and communication technology.

BOX 7.1: PRODUCTION FUNCTIONS

Economists often use a mathematical expression called a *production function* to describe the relationship between the amounts of inputs and outputs. In its general form, a production function is written as

$$Y = f(K,L,M,A)$$

where

Y = the amount of output or real GDP

K = the amount of physical capital

L = the amount of labor, adjusted for the level of human capital

M = the amount of available land and other natural resources

A = the level of technology and other factors, such as the effectiveness of management and the social and legal environment

$f(\ )$ is some unspecified functional form

In practice, there are a number of specific functional forms that are used to calculate the level of output. One simple but famous one that involves only Y, K, and L is

$$Y = K^{1/2}L^{1/2} = \sqrt{KL}$$

For example, if $K = 25$ and $L = 100$, $Y = \sqrt{25 \times 100} = \sqrt{2,500} = 50$. This simple production function has several appealing properties, and a slight variant of it fits the aggregate data reasonably well. First, if all the inputs K and L double, output also will double; that is, if $K = 50$ and $L = 200$, $Y = \sqrt{50 \times 200} = \sqrt{10,000} = 100$. Secondly, it exhibits diminishing returns to capital (as well as diminishing returns to labor), so that if we hold the level of labor constant and keep adding more capital, output will rise by smaller and smaller increments. Thus, if L remains equal to 100 and K rises from 25 to 26, output rises from 50 to $\sqrt{26 \times 100} = 50.99$, or by 0.99 unit. If K rises by one more unit to 27, output rises to $\sqrt{27 \times 100} = 51.96$, or by only 0.97 unit.

THE COSTS OF ECONOMIC GROWTH

Both this chapter and the chapter "Measuring Economic Activity" emphasized the positive effects of economic growth on the average person's living standard. But should societies always strive for the highest possible rate of economic growth? The answer is no. Even if we accept for the moment the idea that increased output per person is always desirable, attaining a higher rate of economic growth does impose costs on society.

What are the costs of increasing economic growth? The most straightforward is the cost of creating new capital. We know that by expanding the capital stock we can increase future productivity and output. But, to increase the capital stock, we must divert resources that could otherwise be used to increase the supply of consumer goods. For example, to add more robot-operated assembly lines, a society must employ more of its skilled technicians in building industrial robots and fewer in designing video games. To build new factories, more carpenters and lumber must be assigned to factory construction and less to finishing basements or renovating family rooms. In short, high rates of investment in new capital require people to tighten their belts, consume less, and save more—a real economic cost.

Should a country undertake a high rate of investment in capital goods at the sacrifice of consumer goods? The answer depends on the extent that people are willing and able to sacrifice consumption today to have a bigger economic pie tomorrow. In a country that is very poor, or is experiencing an economic crisis, people may prefer to keep consumption relatively high and savings and investment relatively low. The midst of a thunderstorm is not the time to be putting something aside for a rainy day! But in a society that is relatively well off, people may be more willing to make sacrifices to achieve higher economic growth in the future.

Consumption sacrificed to capital formation is not the only cost of achieving higher growth. In the United States in the nineteenth and early twentieth centuries, periods of rapid economic growth were often times in which many people worked extremely long hours at dangerous and unpleasant jobs. While those workers helped to build the economy that Americans enjoy today, the costs were great in terms of reduced leisure time and, in some cases, workers' health and safety.

Other costs of growth include the cost of the research and development that is required to improve technology and the costs of acquiring training and skill (human capital). The fact that a higher living standard tomorrow must be purchased at the cost of current sacrifices is an example of the *scarcity principle,* that having more of one good thing usually means having less of another. Because achieving higher economic growth imposes real economic costs, we know from the *cost-benefit principle* that higher growth should be pursued only if the benefits outweigh the costs.

PROMOTING ECONOMIC GROWTH

If a society decides to try to raise its rate of economic growth, what are some of the measures that policymakers might take to achieve this objective? Here is a short list of suggestions, based on our discussion of the factors that contribute to growth in average labor productivity and, hence, output per person.

POLICIES TO INCREASE HUMAN CAPITAL

Because skilled and well-educated workers are more productive than unskilled labor, governments in most countries try to increase the human capital of their citizens by supporting education and training programs. In the United States, government provides public education through high school and grants extensive support to post-secondary schools, including technical schools, colleges, and universities. Publicly funded early intervention programs like Head Start also attempt to build human capital by helping disadvantaged children prepare for school. To a lesser degree than some other countries, the U.S. government also funds job training for unskilled youths and retraining for workers whose skills have become obsolete.

Why do almost all countries provide free public education?

All industrial countries provide their citizens free public education through high school, and most subsidize college and other post-secondary schools. Why?

ECONOMIC NATURALIST 7.6

Americans are so used to the idea of free public education that this question may seem odd. But why should the government provide free education when it does not provide even more essential goods and services, such as food or medical care, for free, except to the most needy? Furthermore, educational services can be, and indeed commonly are, supplied and demanded on the private market, without the aid of the government.

An important argument for free or at least subsidized education is that the private demand curve for educational services does not include all the social benefits of education. (Recall the *equilibrium principle* of Chapter 3, which states in part that

Why do almost all countries provide free public education?

a market in equilibrium may not exploit all gains achievable from collective action.) For example, the democratic political system relies on an educated citizenry to operate effectively—a factor that an individual demander of educational services has little reason to consider. From a narrower economic perspective, we might argue that individuals do not capture the full economic returns from their schooling. For example, people with high human capital, and thus high earnings, pay more taxes—funds that can be used to finance government services and aid the less fortunate. Because of income taxation, the private benefit to acquiring human capital is less than the social benefit, and the demand for education on the private market may be less than optimal from society's viewpoint. Similarly, educated people are more likely than others to contribute to technological development, and hence to general productivity growth, which may benefit many other people besides themselves. Finally, another argument for public support of education is that poor people who would like to invest in human capital may not be able to do so because of insufficient income.

The Nobel laureate Milton Friedman, among many economists, suggested that these arguments may justify government grants, called educational *vouchers*, to help citizens purchase educational services in the private sector, but they do *not* justify the government providing education directly, as through the public school system. Defenders of public education, on the other hand, argue that the government should have some direct control over education in order to set standards and monitor quality. What do you think?

POLICIES THAT PROMOTE SAVING AND INVESTMENT

Average labor productivity increases when workers can utilize a sizable and modern capital stock. To support the creation of new capital, government can encourage high rates of saving and investment in the private sector. Many provisions in the U.S. tax code are designed expressly to stimulate households to save and firms to invest. For example, a household that opens an Individual Retirement Account (IRA) is able to save for retirement without paying taxes on either the funds deposited in the IRA or the interest earned on the account. (However, taxes are due when the funds are withdrawn at retirement.) The intent of IRA legislation is to make saving more financially attractive to American households. Similarly, at various times Congress has instituted an investment tax credit, which reduces the tax bills of firms that invest in new capital. Private-sector saving and investment are discussed in greater detail in the chapter "Saving and Capital Formation."

Government can contribute directly to capital formation through *public investment*, or the creation of government-owned capital. Public investment includes the building of roads, bridges, airports, dams, and, in some countries, energy and communications networks. The construction of the U.S. interstate highway system, begun during the administration of President Eisenhower, is often cited as an example of successful public investment. The interstate system substantially reduced long-haul transportation costs in the United States, improving productivity throughout the economy. Today, the web of computers and communications links we call the Internet is having a similar effect. This project, too, received crucial government funding in its early stages. Many research studies have confirmed that government investment in the *infrastructure*, the public capital that supports private-sector economic activities, can be a significant source of growth.

POLICIES THAT SUPPORT RESEARCH AND DEVELOPMENT

Productivity is enhanced by technological progress, which in turn requires investment in research and development (R&D). In many industries, private firms have adequate incentive to conduct research and development activities. There is no need, for example, for the government to finance research for developing a better underarm deodorant. But some types of knowledge, particularly basic scientific knowledge, may have widespread economic benefits that cannot be captured by a single private firm. The developers of the silicon computer chip, for example, were instrumental in creating huge new industries, yet they received only a small portion of the profits flowing from their inventions. Because society in general, rather than the individual inventors, may receive much of the benefit from basic research, government may need to support basic research, as it does through agencies such as the National Science Foundation. The federal government also sponsors a great deal of applied research, particularly in military and space applications. To the extent that national security allows, the government can increase growth by sharing the fruits of such research with the private sector. For example, the Global Positioning System (GPS), which was developed originally for military purposes, is now available in private passenger vehicles, helping drivers find their way.

THE LEGAL AND POLITICAL FRAMEWORK

Although economic growth comes primarily from activities in the private sector, the government plays an essential role in providing the framework within which the private sector can operate productively. We have discussed the importance of secure property rights and a well-functioning legal system, of an economic environment that encourages entrepreneurship, and of political stability and the free and open exchange of ideas. Government policymakers also should consider the potential effects of tax and regulatory policies on activities that increase productivity, such as investment, innovation, and risk taking. Policies that affect the legal and political framework are examples of *structural macroeconomic policies* (see the chapter "Macroeconomics").

THE POOREST COUNTRIES: A SPECIAL CASE?

Radical disparities in living standards exist between the richest and poorest countries of the world (see Table 5.4 for some data). Achieving economic growth in the poorest countries is thus particularly urgent. Are the policy prescriptions of this section relevant to those countries, or are very different types of measures necessary to spur growth in the poorest nations?

To a significant extent, the same factors and policies that promote growth in richer countries apply to the poorest countries as well. Increasing human capital by supporting education and training, increasing rates of saving and investment, investing in public capital and infrastructure, supporting research and development, and encouraging entrepreneurship are all measures that will enhance economic growth in poor countries.

However, to a much greater degree than in richer countries, most poor countries need to improve the legal and political environment that underpins their economies. For example, many developing countries have poorly developed or corrupt legal systems, which discourage entrepreneurship and investment by creating uncertainty about property rights. Taxation and regulation in developing countries are often heavy-handed and administered by inefficient bureaucracies, to the extent that it may take months or years to obtain the approvals needed to start a small business or expand a factory. In many poor countries, excessive government regulation or government ownership of companies prevents markets from operating efficiently to achieve economic growth. For example, government regulation, rather than the market, may determine the allocation of bank credit or the prices for agricultural products. Structural policies that aim to ameliorate these problems are important preconditions for generating growth in the poorest countries. But probably most important—and most difficult, for some countries—is establishing political stability and the rule of law. Without political stability, domestic and foreign savers will be reluctant to invest in the country, and economic growth will be difficult if not impossible to achieve.

Can rich countries help poor countries to develop? Historically, richer nations have tried to help by providing financial aid through loans or grants from individual countries (foreign aid) or by loans made by international agencies, such as the World Bank. Experience has shown, however, that financial aid to countries that do not undertake structural reforms, such as reducing excessive regulation or improving the legal system, is of limited value. To make their foreign aid most effective, rich countries should help poor countries achieve political stability and undertake the necessary reforms to the structure of their economies.

ARE THERE LIMITS TO GROWTH?

Earlier in this chapter, we saw that even relatively low rates of economic growth, if sustained for a long period, will produce huge increases in the size of the economy. This fact raises the question of whether economic growth can continue indefinitely without depleting natural resources and causing massive damage to the global environment. Does the basic truth that we live in a finite world of finite resources imply that, ultimately, economic growth must come to an end?

The concern that economic growth may not be sustainable is not a new one. An influential 1972 book, *The Limits to Growth*,[7] reported the results of computer simulations that suggested that unless population growth and economic expansion were halted, the world would soon be running out of natural resources, drinkable water, and breathable air. This book, and later works in the same vein, raise some fundamental questions that cannot be done full justice here. However, in some ways its conclusions are misleading.

One problem with the "limits to growth" thesis lies in its underlying concept of economic growth. Those who emphasize the environmental limits on growth assume implicitly that economic growth will always take the form of more of what we have now—more smoky factories, more polluting cars, more fast-food restaurants. If that were indeed the case, then surely there would be limits to the growth the planet can sustain. But growth in real GDP does not necessarily take such a form. Increases in real GDP also can arise from new or higher-quality products. For example, not too long ago tennis rackets were relatively simple items made primarily of wood. Today they are made of newly invented synthetic materials and designed for optimum performance using sophisticated computer simulations. Because these new high-tech tennis rackets are more valued by consumers than the old wooden ones, their introduction increased real GDP. Likewise, the introduction of new pharmaceuticals has contributed to economic growth, as have the expanded number of TV channels, digital sound, and Internet-based sales. Thus, economic growth need not take the form of more and more of the same old stuff; it can mean newer, better, and perhaps cleaner and more efficient goods and services.

A second problem with the "limits to growth" conclusion is that it overlooks the fact that increased wealth and productivity expand society's capacity to take measures to safeguard the environment. In fact, the most polluted countries in the world are not the richest but those that are in a relatively early stage of industrialization (see Economic Naturalist 7.7). At this stage countries must devote the bulk of their resources to basic needs—food, shelter, health care—and continued industrial expansion. In these countries, clean air and water may be viewed as a luxury rather than a basic need. In more economically developed countries, where the most basic needs are more easily met, extra resources are available to keep the environment clean. Thus, continuing economic growth may lead to less, not more, pollution.

A third problem with the pessimistic view of economic growth is that it ignores the power of the market and other social mechanisms to deal with scarcity. During the

---

[7]Donella H. Meadows, Dennis L. Meadows, Jørgen Randers, and William W. Behrens III, *The Limits to Growth*, New York: New American Library, 1972.

oil-supply disruptions of the 1970s, newspapers were filled with headlines about the energy crisis and the imminent depletion of world oil supplies. Yet 30 years later, the world's known oil reserves are actually *greater* than they were in the 1970s.[8]

Today's energy situation is so much better than was expected 30 years ago because the market went to work. Reduced oil supplies led to an increase in prices that changed the behavior of both demanders and suppliers. Consumers insulated their homes, purchased more energy-efficient cars and appliances, and switched to alternative sources of energy. Suppliers engaged in a massive hunt for new reserves, opening up major new sources in Latin America, China, and the North Sea. In short, market forces helped society respond effectively to the energy crisis.

In general, shortages in any resource will trigger price changes that induce suppliers and demanders to deal with the problem. Simply extrapolating current economic trends into the future ignores the power of the market system to recognize shortages and make the necessary corrections. Government actions spurred by political pressures, such as the allocation of public funds to preserve open space or reduce air pollution, can be expected to supplement market adjustments.

Despite the shortcomings of the "limits to growth" perspective, most economists would agree that not all the problems created by economic growth can be dealt with effectively through the market or the political process. Probably most important, global environmental problems, such as the possibility of global warming or the on-going destruction of rain forests, are a particular challenge for existing economic and political institutions. Environmental quality is not bought and sold in markets and thus will not automatically reach its optimal level through market processes (recall the *equilibrium principle*). Nor can local or national governments effectively address problems that are global in scope. Unless international mechanisms are established for dealing with global environmental problems, these problems may become worse as economic growth continues.

Why is the air quality so poor in Mexico City?

Developing countries like Mexico, which are neither fully industrialized nor desperately poor, often have severe environmental problems. Why?

ECONOMIC NATURALIST 7.7

One concern about economic growth is that it will cause ever-increasing levels of environmental pollution. Empirical studies show, however, that the relationship between pollution and real GDP per person is more like an inverted U (see Figure 7.5). In other words, as countries move from very low levels of real GDP per person to "middle-income" levels, most measures of pollution tend to worsen, but environmental quality improves as real GDP per person rises even further. One study of the relationship between air quality and real GDP per person found that the level of real GDP per person at which air quality is the worst—indicated by point *A* in Figure 7.5—is roughly equal to the average income level in Mexico.[9] And indeed, the air quality in Mexico City is exceptionally poor, as any visitor to that sprawling metropolis can attest.

That pollution may worsen as a country industrializes is understandable, but why does environmental quality improve when real GDP per person climbs to very high levels? There are a variety of explanations for this phenomenon. Compared to middle-income economies, the richer economies are relatively more concentrated in "clean," high-value services like finance and software production as opposed to pollution-intensive industries like heavy manufacturing. Rich economies are also more

[8]Recent increases in oil prices have again stoked concerns. Recall from Exercise 6.7, however, that the real price of oil actually fell from 1980 to April 2005.

[9]Gene M. Grossman and Alan B. Krueger, "Environmental Impacts of a North American Free Trade Agreement," in Peter Garber, ed., *The Mexico–U.S. Free Trade Agreement*, Cambridge, MA: MIT Press, 1993. See also Grossman and Krueger, "Economic Growth and the Environment," *Quarterly Journal of Economics*, May 1995, pp. 353–78; and World Bank, *World Development Report: Development and the Environment*, 1992.

FIGURE 7.5
The Relationship between Air Pollution and Real GDP per Person.
Empirically, air pollution increases with real GDP per person up to a point and then begins to decline. Maximum air pollution (point *A*) occurs at a level of real GDP per person roughly equal to that of Mexico.

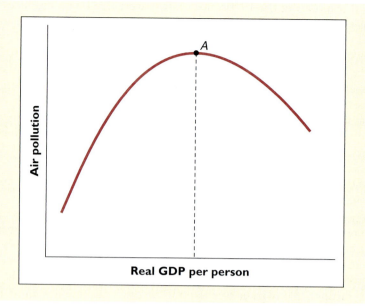

likely to have the expertise to develop sophisticated and cost-effective antipollution technologies. But the main reason the richer economies tend to be cleaner is the same reason that the homes of rich people are generally cleaner and in better condition than the homes of the poor. As income rises above the level necessary to fulfill basic needs, more resources remain to dedicate to "luxuries" like a clean environment (the *scarcity principle*). For the rich family, the extra resources will pay for a cleaning service; for the rich country, they will pay for pollution control devices in factories and on automobiles. Indeed, antipollution laws are generally tougher and more strictly enforced in rich countries than in middle-income and poor countries.

RECAP	**ECONOMIC GROWTH: DEVELOPMENTS AND ISSUES**

- Economic growth has substantial costs, notably the sacrifice of current consumption that is required to free resources for creating new capital and new technologies. Higher rates of growth should be pursued only if the benefits outweigh the costs.

- Policies for promoting economic growth include policies to increase human capital (education and training); policies that promote saving and capital formation; policies that support research and development; and the provision of a legal and political framework within which the private sector can operate productively. Deficiencies in the legal and political framework (for example, official corruption or poorly defined property rights) are a special problem for many developing countries.

- Some have argued that finite resources imply ultimate limits to economic growth. This view overlooks the facts that growth can take the form of better, rather than more, goods and services; that increased wealth frees resources to safeguard the environment; and that political and economic mechanisms exist to address many of the problems associated with growth. However, these mechanisms may not work well when environmental or other problems arising from economic growth are global in scope.

■ SUMMARY ■

- Over the past two centuries, the industrialized nations saw enormous improvements in living standards, as reflected in large increases in real GDP per person. Because of the power of *compound interest*, relatively small differences in growth rates, if continued over long periods, can produce large differences in real GDP per person and average living standards. Thus, the rate of long-term economic growth is an economic variable of critical importance.

- Real GDP per person is the product of average labor productivity (real GDP per employed worker) and the share of the population that is employed. Growth in real GDP per person can occur only through growth in average labor productivity, in the share of the population that is working, or both. In the period since 1960, increases in the share of the U.S. population holding a job contributed significantly to rising real GDP per person. But in the past four decades, as in most periods, the main source of the increase in real GDP per person was rising average labor productivity.

- Among the factors that determine labor productivity are the talents, education, training, and skills of workers, or human capital; the quantity and quality of the physical capital that workers use; the availability of land and other natural resources; the application of technology to the production and distribution of goods and services; the effectiveness of *entrepreneurs* and managers; and the broad social and legal environment. Because of *diminishing returns to capital,* beyond a certain point expansion of the capital stock is not the most effective way to increase average labor productivity. Economists generally agree that new technologies are the most important single source of improvements in productivity.

- In the 1970s and 1980s, the industrial world experienced a slowdown in productivity growth, but productivity growth has rebounded since 1995, largely as a result of advances in information and communication technology.

- Economic growth has costs as well as benefits. Prominent among them is the need to sacrifice current consumption to achieve a high rate of investment in new capital goods; other costs of growing more quickly include extra work effort and the costs of research and development. Thus, more economic growth is not necessarily better; whether increased economic growth is desirable depends on whether the benefits of growth outweigh the costs.

- Among the ways in which government can stimulate economic growth are by adopting policies that encourage the creation of human capital; that promote saving and investment, including public investment in infrastructure; that support research and development, particularly in the basic sciences; and that provide a legal and political framework that supports private-sector activities. The poorest countries, with poorly developed legal, tax, and regulatory systems, are often in the greatest need of an improved legal and political framework and increased political stability.

- Are there limits to growth? Arguments that economic growth must be constrained by environmental problems and the limits of natural resources ignore the fact that economic growth can take the form of increasing quality as well as increasing quantity. Indeed, increases in output can provide additional resources for cleaning up the environment. Finally, the market system, together with political processes, can solve many of the problems associated with economic growth. On the other hand, global environmental problems, which can be handled neither by the market nor by individual national governments, have the potential to constrain economic growth.

■ KEY TERMS ■

compound interest (183)   diminishing returns to capital (191)   entrepreneurs (194)

■ REVIEW QUESTIONS ■

1. What has happened to real GDP per person in the industrialized countries over the past century? What implications does this have for the average person?

2. Why do economists consider growth in average labor productivity to be the key factor in determining long-run living standards?

3. What is *human capital*? Why is it economically important? How is new human capital created?

4. You have employed five workers of varying physical strength to dig a ditch. Workers without shovels have zero productivity in ditchdigging. How should you assign shovels to workers if you don't have enough shovels to go around? How should you assign any additional shovels that you obtain? Using this example, discuss (a) the relationship between the availability of physical capital and average labor productivity and (b) the concept of diminishing returns to capital.

5. What was the cause of the resurgence in U.S. labor productivity growth since 1995? How do we know?

6. Discuss how talented entrepreneurs and effective managers can enhance average labor productivity.

7. What major contributions can the government make to the goal of increasing average labor productivity?

8. Discuss the following statement: "Because the environment is fragile and natural resources are finite, ultimately economic growth must come to an end."

■ PROBLEMS ■

1. Richland's real GDP per person is $10,000, and Poorland's real GDP per person is $5,000. However, Richland's real GDP per person is growing at 1 percent per year and Poorland's is growing at 3 percent per year. Compare real GDP per person in the two countries after 10 years and after 20 years. Approximately how many years will it take Poorland to catch up to Richland?

2. Using the data in Economic Naturalist 7.2, calculate how much higher U.S. labor productivity will be in the year 2024 (relative to 2004) if
   a. productivity continues to grow by 3.1 percent per year.
   b. productivity growth falls to its average rate during the period 1973–1995. (*Note:* You do not need to know the actual values of average labor productivity in any year to solve this problem.)

3. The "graying of America" will substantially increase the fraction of the population that is retired in the decades to come. To illustrate the implications for U.S. living standards, suppose that over the 44 years following 2004 the share of the population that is working returns to its 1960 level, while average labor productivity increases by as much as it did during 1960–2004. Under this scenario, what would be the net change in real GDP per person between 2004 and 2048? The following data will be useful:

	Average labor productivity	**Share of population employed**
1960	$38,034	36.4%
2004	$77,858	47.4%

4. Here are data for Canada, Germany, and Japan on the ratio of employment to population in 1979 and 2003:

	1979	**2003**
Canada	0.44	0.50
Germany	0.33	0.43
Japan	0.48	0.52

Using data from Table 7.1, find average labor productivity for each country in 1979 and in 2003. How much of the increase in output per person in each country over the 1979–2003 period is due to increased labor productivity? To increased employment relative to population?

5. Joanne has just completed high school and is trying to determine whether to go to junior college for two years or go directly to work. Her objective is to maximize the savings she will have in the bank five years from now. If she goes directly to work, she will earn $20,000 per year for each of the next five years. If she goes to junior college, for each of the next two years she will earn nothing—indeed, she will have to borrow $6,000 each year to cover tuition and books. This loan must be repaid in full three years after graduation. If she graduates from junior college, in each of the subsequent three years, her wages will be $38,000 per year. Joanne's total living expenses and taxes, excluding tuition and books, equal $15,000 per year.
   a. Suppose, for simplicity, that Joanne can borrow and lend at 0 percent interest. On purely economic grounds, should she go to junior college or work?

b. Does your answer to part a change if she can earn $23,000 per year with only a high school degree?

c. Does your answer to part a change if Joanne's tuition and books cost $8,000 per year?

d.* Suppose that the interest rate at which Joanne can borrow and lend is 10 percent per year, but other data are as in part a. Savings are deposited at the end of the year they are earned and receive (compound) interest at the end of each subsequent year. Similarly, the loans are taken out at the end of the year in which they are needed, and interest does not accrue until the end of the subsequent year. Now that the interest rate has risen, should Joanne go to college or go to work?

6. The Good'n'Fresh Grocery Store has two checkout lanes and four employees. Employees are equally skilled, and all are able to either operate a register (checkers) or bag groceries (baggers). The store owner assigns one checker and one bagger to each lane. A lane with a checker and a bagger can check out 40 customers per hour. A lane with a checker only can check out 25 customers per hour.

a. In terms of customers checked out per hour, what is total output and average labor productivity for the Good'n'Fresh Grocery Store?

b. The owner adds a third checkout lane and register. Assuming that no employees are added, what is the best way to reallocate the workers to tasks? What is total output and average labor productivity (in terms of customers checked out per hour) now?

c. Repeat part b for the addition of a fourth checkout lane, and a fifth. Do you observe diminishing returns to capital in this example?

7. Harrison, Carla, and Fred are housepainters. Harrison and Carla can paint 100 square feet per hour using a standard paintbrush, and Fred can paint 80 square feet per hour. Any of the three can paint 200 square feet per hour using a roller.

a. Assume Harrison, Carla, and Fred have only paintbrushes at their disposal. What is the average labor productivity, in terms of square feet per painter-hour, for the three painters taken as a team? Assume that the three painters always work the same number of hours.

b. Repeat part a for the cases in which the team has one, two, three, or four rollers available. Are there diminishing returns to capital?

c. An improvement in paint quality increases the area that can be covered per hour (by either brushes or rollers) by 20 percent. How does this technological improvement affect your answers to part b? Are there diminishing returns to capital? Does the technological improvement increase or reduce the economic value of an additional roller?

8. Hester's Hatchery raises fish. At the end of the current season she has 1,000 fish in the hatchery. She can harvest any number of fish that she wishes, selling them to restaurants for $5 apiece. Because big fish make little fish, for every fish that she leaves in the hatchery this year, she will have two fish at the end of next year. The price of fish is expected to be $5 each next year as well. Hester relies entirely on income from current fish sales to support herself.

a. How many fish should Hester harvest if she wants to maximize the growth of her stock of fish from this season to next season?

b. Do you think maximizing the growth of her fish stock is an economically sound strategy for Hester? Why or why not? Relate to the text discussion on the costs of economic growth.

c. How many fish should Hester harvest if she wants to maximize her current income? Do you think this is a good strategy?

d. Explain why Hester is unlikely to harvest either all or none of her fish, but instead will harvest some and leave the rest to reproduce.

9. True or False: For advances in basic science to translate into improvements in standards of living, they must be supported by favorable economic conditions. Discuss, using concrete examples where possible to illustrate your arguments.

10. Write a short essay evaluating the U.S. economy in terms of each of the six determinants of average labor productivity discussed in the text. Are there any areas in which the United States is exceptionally strong, relative to other countries? Areas where the United States is less strong than some other countries? Illustrate your arguments with numbers from the *Statistical Abstract of the United States* (available online at http://www.census. gov/statab/www/) and other sources, as appropriate.

*Problem marked by an asterisk (*) is more difficult.

■ ANSWERS TO IN-CHAPTER EXERCISES ■

7.1 If the United States had grown at the Japanese rate for the period 1870–2003, real GDP per person in 2003 would have been ($2,887) $\times$ $(1.026)^{133}$ = $87,709. Actual GDP per person in the United States in 2003 was $35,488, so at the higher rate of growth, output per person would have been $87,709/$35,488 = 2.47 times higher.

7.2 As before, Lucy can wrap 4,000 candies per week, or 100 candies per hour. Ethel can wrap 500 candies per hour, and working 40 hours weekly she can wrap 20,000 candies per week. Together Lucy and Ethel can wrap 24,000 candies per week. Since they work a total of 80 hours between them, their output per hour as a team is 24,000 candies wrapped per 80 hours = 300 candies wrapped per hour, midway between their hourly productivities as individuals.

7.3 Because Ethel can wrap 300 candies per hour by hand, the benefit of giving Ethel the machine is 500 − 300 = 200 additional candies wrapped per hour. Because Lucy wraps only 100 candies per hour by hand, the benefit of giving Lucy the machine is 400 additional candies wrapped per hour. So the benefit of giving the machine to Lucy is greater than of giving it to Ethel. Equivalently, if the machine goes to Ethel, then Lucy and Ethel between them can wrap 500 + 100 = 600 candies per hour, but if Lucy uses the machine, the team can wrap 300 + 500 = 800 candies per hour. So output is increased by letting Lucy use the machine.

7.4 Now, working by hand, Lucy can wrap 300 candies per hour and Ethel can wrap 500 candies per hour. With a machine, either Lucy or Ethel can wrap 800 candies per hour. As in Exercise 7.3, the benefit of giving a machine to Lucy (500 candies per hour) exceeds the benefit of giving a machine to Ethel (300 candies per hour), so if only one machine is available, Lucy should use it.

The table analogous to Table 7.3 now looks like this:

Relationship of Capital, Output, and Productivity in the Candy-Wrapping Factory

Number of machines (K)	Candies wrapped per week (Y)	Total hours worked (N)	Average hourly labor productivity (Y/N)
0	32,000	80	400
1	52,000	80	650
2	64,000	80	800
3	64,000	80	800

Comparing this table with Table 7.3, you can see that technological advance has increased labor productivity for any value of K, the number of machines available.

Adding one machine increases output by 20,000 candies wrapped per week, adding the second machine increases output by 12,000 candies wrapped per week, and adding the third machine does not increase output at all (because there is no worker available to use it). So diminishing returns to capital still hold after the technological improvement.

7.5 Although the individual worker is the same person he was in Bangladesh, by coming to the United States he gains the benefit of factors that enhance average labor productivity in this country, relative to his homeland. These include more and better capital to work with, more natural resources per person, more advanced technologies, sophisticated entrepreneurs and managers, and a political-legal environment that is conducive to high productivity. It is not guaranteed that the value of the immigrant's human capital will rise (it may not, for example, if he speaks no English and has no skills applicable to the U.S. economy), but normally it will.

Since increased productivity leads to higher wages and living standards, on economic grounds the Bangladeshi worker has a strong incentive to immigrate to the United States if he is able to do so.

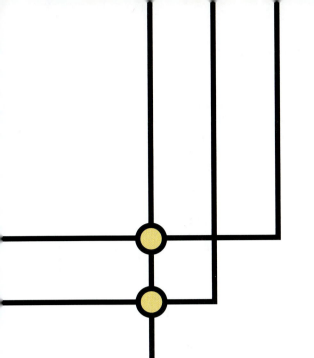

CHAPTER

8

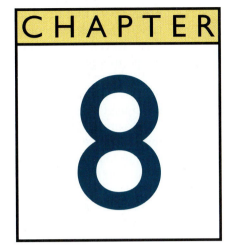

WORKERS, WAGES, AND UNEMPLOYMENT IN THE MODERN ECONOMY

A book by *New York Times* columnist Thomas L. Friedman about the changing world economy, *The Lexus and the Olive Tree*,[1] contains a remarkable photograph. Taken in Jerusalem a few years ago, the photo shows an orthodox Jew, Shimon Biton, praying at the Western Wall, one of Judaism's most sacred places. Mr. Biton's devotions are not unusual—indeed thousands of Jews pray at the Wall every day. What *is* unusual about the photograph is that it shows Mr. Biton holding a cell phone up against the Wall. Through the cell phone, a relative of Mr. Biton's in France is fulfilling his religious obligation to pray "at" the Western Wall.

The photograph nicely illustrates the theme of Friedman's book, that one of the most striking features of the modern world is the close juxtaposition of rapid economic and technological change with traditional values and customs. The photograph suggests that Mr. Biton is quite comfortable combining the traditional and the modern, but as Friedman's book emphasizes, not everyone is so comfortable. In many countries, the conflicting pulls of modernization and traditional ways of life have created enormous social conflicts. Economically, Friedman argues, the powerful forces of modernization have widened the gap between the "haves"—those who can take advantage of rapid technological and economic change—and the "have-nots"—those who are unable or unwilling to do so.

[1]New York: Farrar, Straus, & Giroux, 1999.

AP/World Wide Photos

In the last chapter we examined the remarkable economic growth and increased productivity that have occurred in the industrialized world over the past two centuries. These developments have greatly increased the quantity of goods and services that the economy can produce. But we have not yet discussed how the fruits of economic growth are distributed. Has everyone benefited equally from economic growth and increased productivity? Or, as Friedman's thesis would suggest, is the population divided between those who have caught the "train" of economic modernization, enriching themselves in the process, and those who have been left at the station?

To understand how economic growth and change affect different groups, we must turn to the labor market. Except for retirees and others receiving government support, most people rely almost entirely on wages and salaries to pay their bills and put something away for the future. Hence, it is in the labor market that most people will see the benefits of the economic growth and increasing productivity. This chapter describes and explains some important trends in the labor markets of industrial countries. Using a supply and demand model of the labor market, we focus first on several important trends in real wages and employment. In the second part of the chapter we turn to the problem of unemployment, especially long-term unemployment. We will see that two key factors contributing to recent trends in wages, employment, and unemployment are the *globalization* of the economy, as reflected in the increasing importance of international trade, and ongoing *technological change*. By the end of the chapter, you will better understand the connection between these macroeconomic developments and the economic fortunes of workers and their families.

FIVE IMPORTANT LABOR MARKET TRENDS

In recent decades, at least five trends have characterized the labor markets of the industrialized world. We divide these trends into two groups: those affecting real wages and those affecting employment and unemployment.

TRENDS IN REAL WAGES

1. Over the twentieth century, all industrial countries have enjoyed substantial growth in real wages.

In the United States in 2004, the average worker's yearly earnings could command twice as many goods and services as in 1960 and nearly five times as much as in 1929, just prior to the Great Depression. Similar trends have prevailed in other industrialized countries.

2. Since the early 1970s, however, the rate of real wage growth has slowed.

Though the post–World War II period has seen impressive increases in real wages, the fastest rates of increase occurred during the 1960s and early 1970s. In the 13 years between 1960 to 1973, the buying power of workers' incomes rose at a rate of 2.61 percent per year, a strong rate of increase. But from 1973 to 1996, real yearly earnings grew at only 0.91 percent per year. The good news is that, from 1996 to 2004, real earnings grew at 2.22 percent per year, despite a recession in 2001. Annual earnings growth for the whole 1973–2004 period, at 1.25 percent per year, remained well below what was achieved prior to 1973.

3. Furthermore, recent decades have brought a pronounced increase in wage inequality in the United States.

A growing gap in real wages between skilled and unskilled workers has been of particular concern. Although real earnings per worker doubled between 1960 and 2004, the average real weekly earnings among production workers actually fell, and the real wages of the least-skilled, least-educated workers have declined by as much as 25 to 30 percent according to some studies. At the same time, the best-educated, highest-skilled workers have enjoyed continuing gains in real wages. Data for a recent year showed that, in the United States, the typical worker with an advanced degree beyond college earned almost three times the income of a high school graduate, and four times the income of a worker with less than a high school degree. Many observers worry that the United States is developing a "two-tier" labor market: plenty of good jobs at good wages for the well-educated and highly skilled, but less and less opportunity for those without schooling or skills.

Outside the United States, particularly in western Europe, real wages have grown more rapidly and the trend toward wage inequality has been much less pronounced. But, as we will see, employment trends in Europe have not been as encouraging as in the United States. Let's turn now to the trends in employment and unemployment.

TRENDS IN EMPLOYMENT AND UNEMPLOYMENT

4. In the United States, the number of people with jobs has grown substantially in recent decades.

In 1970, about 57 percent of the over-16 population in the United States had jobs. By 2004, total U.S. employment exceeded 139 million people, more than 62.3 percent of the over-16 population. Between 1980 and 2004, the U.S. economy created 40 million new jobs—an increase in total employment of 40 percent—while the over-16 population grew only 33 percent. Similar job growth has *not* occurred in most other industrialized countries, however. In particular:

5. Western European countries have been suffering high rates of unemployment for almost two decades.

In France, for example, an average of 10.2 percent of the workforce was unemployed over the period 1990–2004, compared to just 5.6 percent in the United States. Figure 8.9, page 232, shows recent unemployment rates in four western European countries. Consistent with the high rates of unemployment, rates of job creation in western Europe have been exceptionally weak.

Given the trend toward increasing wage inequality in the United States and the persistence of high unemployment in Europe, we may conclude that a significant fraction of the industrial world's labor force has not been sharing in the recent economic growth and prosperity. Whereas in the United States the problem takes the form of low and falling real wages for unskilled workers, in Europe work is often simply unavailable for the unskilled and sometimes even for the skilled.

What explains these trends in employment and wages? In the remainder of the chapter, we will show that a supply and demand analysis of the labor market can help to explain these important developments.

RECAP	IMPORTANT LABOR MARKET TRENDS

- Over a long period, average real wages have risen substantially both in the United States and in other industrialized countries.

- Despite the long-term upward trend in real wages, real wage growth has slowed significantly in the United States since the early 1970s.

- In the United States, wage inequality has increased dramatically in recent decades. The real wages of most unskilled workers have actually declined, while the real wages of skilled and educated workers have continued to rise.

- Employment has grown substantially—indeed, much faster than the working-age population—in the United States in recent decades.

- Since about 1980, western European nations have experienced very high rates of unemployment and low rates of job creation.

SUPPLY AND DEMAND IN THE LABOR MARKET

In Chapter 3 we saw how supply and demand analysis can be used to determine equilibrium prices and quantities for individual goods and services. The same approach is equally useful for studying labor market conditions. In the market for labor, the "price" is the wage paid to workers in exchange for their services. The wage is expressed per unit of time, for example, per hour or per year. The "quantity" is the amount of labor firms use, which in this book we will generally measure by number of workers employed. Alternatively, we could state the quantity of labor in terms of the number of hours worked; the choice of units is a matter of convenience.

Who are the demanders and suppliers in the labor market? Firms and other employers demand labor in order to produce goods and services. Virtually all of us supply labor during some phase of our lives. Whenever people work for pay, they are supplying labor services at a price equal to the wage they receive. In this chapter, we will discuss both the supply of and demand for labor, with an emphasis on the demand side of the labor market. Changes in the demand for labor turn out to be key in explaining the aggregate trends in wages and employment described in the preceding section.

The labor market is studied by microeconomists as well as macroeconomists, and both use the tools of supply and demand. However, microeconomists focus on issues such as the determination of wages for specific types of jobs or workers. In this chapter we take the macroeconomic approach and examine factors that affect aggregate, or economywide, trends in employment and wages.

WAGES AND THE DEMAND FOR LABOR

Let's start by thinking about what determines the number of workers employers want to hire at any given wage, that is, the demand for labor. As we will see, the demand for labor depends on both the productivity of labor and the price that the market sets on workers' output. The more productive workers are, or the more valuable the goods and services they produce, the greater the number of workers an employer will want to hire at any given wage.

Table 8.1 shows the relationship between output and the number of workers employed at the Banana Computer Company (BCC), which builds and sells

TABLE 8.1
Production and Marginal Product for Banana Computers

(1) Number of workers	(2) Computers produced per year	(3) Marginal product	(4) Value of marginal product (at \$3,000/computer)
0	0		
1	25	25	\$75,000
2	48	23	69,000
3	69	21	63,000
4	88	19	57,000
5	105	17	51,000
6	120	15	45,000
7	133	13	39,000
8	144	11	33,000

computers. Column 1 of the table shows some different possibilities for the number of technicians BCC could employ in its plant. Column 2 shows how many computers the company can produce each year, depending on the number of workers employed. The more workers, the greater the number of computers BCC can produce. For the sake of simplicity, we will assume that the plant, equipment, and materials the workers use to build computers are fixed quantities.

Column 3 of Table 8.1 shows the *marginal product* of each worker, the extra production that is gained by adding one more worker. Note that each additional worker adds less to total production than the previous worker did. The tendency for marginal product to decline as more and more workers are added is called *diminishing returns to labor.* The principle of **diminishing returns to labor** states that if the amount of capital and other inputs in use is held constant, then the greater the quantity of labor already employed, the less each additional worker adds to production.

The principle of diminishing returns to labor is analogous to the principle of diminishing returns to capital discussed in the previous chapter. The economic basis for these principles is the same—that is, the *principle of increasing opportunity cost,* also known as the *low-hanging-fruit principle.* As we saw in the last chapter, a firm's managers want to use their available inputs in the most productive way possible. Hence, an employer who has one worker will assign that worker to the most productive job. If she hires a second worker, she will assign that worker to the second most productive job. The third worker will be given the third most productive job available, and so on. The greater the number of workers already employed, the lower the marginal product of adding another worker, as shown in Table 8.1.

If BCC computers sell for $3,000 each, then column 4 of Table 8.1 shows the *value of the marginal product* of each worker. The value of a worker's marginal product is the amount of extra revenue that the worker generates for the firm. Specifically, the value of the marginal product of each BCC worker is that worker's marginal product, stated in terms of the number of additional computers produced, multiplied by the price of output, here $3,000 per computer. We now have all the information necessary to find BCC's demand for workers.

diminishing returns to labor if the amount of capital and other inputs in use is held constant, then the greater the quantity of labor already employed, the less each additional worker adds to production

EXAMPLE 8.1

BCC's demand for labor

Suppose that the going wage for computer technicians is $60,000 per year. BCC managers know that this is the wage being offered by all their competitors, so they cannot hire qualified workers for less. How many technicians will BCC hire? What would the answer be if the wage were $50,000 per year?

BCC will hire an extra worker if and only if the value of that worker's marginal product (which equals the extra revenue the worker creates for the firm) exceeds the wage BCC must pay. The going wage for computer technicians, which BCC takes as given, is $60,000 per year. Table 8.1 shows that the value of the marginal product of the first, second, and third workers each exceeds $60,000. Hiring these workers will be profitable for BCC because the extra revenue each generates exceeds the wage that BCC must pay. However, the fourth worker's marginal product is worth only $57,000. If BCC's managers hired a fourth worker, they would be paying $60,000 in extra wages for additional output that is worth only $57,000. Since hiring the fourth worker is a money-losing proposition, BCC will hire only three workers. Thus, the quantity of labor BCC demands when the going wage is $60,000 per year is three technicians.

If the market wage for computer technicians were $50,000 per year instead of $60,000, the fourth technician would be worth hiring, since the value of his marginal product, $57,000, would be $7,000 more than his wages. The fifth technician also would be worth hiring, since the fifth worker's marginal product is worth $51,000—$1,000 more than the going wage. The value of the marginal product of a sixth technician, however, is only $45,000, so hiring a sixth worker would not be profitable. When wages are $50,000 per year, then BCC's labor demand is five technicians.

EXERCISE 8.1

How many workers will BCC hire if the going wage for technicians is $35,000 per year?

The lower the wage a firm must pay, the more workers it will hire. Thus, the demand for labor is like the demand for other goods or services in that the quantity demanded rises as the price (in this case, the wage) falls. Figure 8.1 shows a hypothetical labor demand curve for a firm or industry, with the wage on the vertical axis and employment on the horizontal axis. All else being equal, the higher the wage, the fewer workers a firm or industry will demand.

In our example thus far, we have discussed how labor demand depends on the *nominal*, or dollar, wage. As we explained in the chapter "Measuring the Price Level and Inflation," it is generally more illuminating to examine the real wage, which is the wage expressed in terms of its purchasing power. We shall temporarily hold the general price level constant so that changes in the nominal wage also reflect changes in the real wage.

FIGURE 8.1

The Demand Curve for Labor.

The demand curve for labor is downward-sloping. The higher the wage, the fewer workers employers will hire.

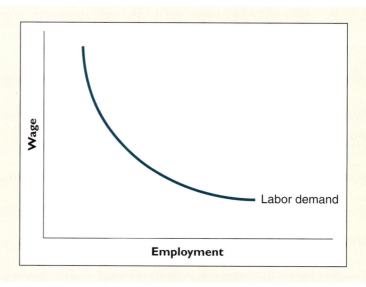

SHIFTS IN THE DEMAND FOR LABOR

The number of workers that BCC will employ at any given real wage depends on the value of their marginal product, as shown in column 4 of Table 8.1. Changes in the economy that increase the value of workers' marginal product will increase the value of extra workers to BCC, and thus BCC's demand for labor at any given real wage. In other words, any factor that raises the value of the marginal product of BCC's workers will shift BCC's labor demand curve to the right.

Two main factors could increase BCC's labor demand: (1) an increase in the price of the company's output (computers) and (2) an increase in the productivity of BCC's workers. Example 8.2 illustrates the first of these possibilities; Example 8.3, the second.

EXAMPLE 8.2   **The price of computers and BCC's demand for labor**

Suppose an increase in the demand for BCC's computers raises the price of its computers to $5,000 each. How many technicians will BCC hire now if the real wage is $60,000 per year? If the real wage is $50,000?

The effect of the increase in computer prices is shown in Table 8.2. Columns 1 to 3 of the table are the same as in Table 8.1. The number of computers a given number of technicians can build (column 2) has not changed; hence, the marginal

TABLE 8.2
Production and Marginal Product for Banana Computers after an Increase in Computer Prices

(1) Number of workers	(2) Computers produced per year	(3) Marginal product	(4) Value of marginal product (at $5,000/computer)
0	0		
		25	$125,000
1	25		
		23	115,000
2	48		
		21	105,000
3	69		
		19	95,000
4	88		
		17	85,000
5	105		
		15	75,000
6	120		
		13	65,000
7	133		
		11	55,000
8	144		

product of particular technicians (column 3) is the same. But because computers can now be sold for $5,000 each instead of $3,000, the *value* of each worker's marginal product has increased by two-thirds (compare column 4 of Table 8.2 with column 4 of Table 8.1).

How does the increase in the price of computers affect BCC's demand for labor? Recall from Example 8.1 that when the price of computers was $3,000 and the going wage for technicians was $60,000, BCC's demand for labor was three workers. But now, with computers selling for $5,000 each, the value of the marginal product of each of the first seven workers exceeds $60,000 (Table 8.2). So, if the real wage of computer technicians is still $60,000, BCC would increase its demand from three workers to seven.

Suppose instead that the going real wage for technicians is $50,000. In Example 8.1, when the price of computers was $3,000 and the wage was $50,000, BCC demanded five workers. But if computers sell for $5,000, we can see from column 4 of Table 8.2 that the value of the marginal product of even the eighth worker exceeds the wage of $50,000. So if the real wage is $50,000, the increase in computer prices raises BCC's demand for labor from five workers to eight.

EXERCISE 8.2

How many workers will BCC hire if the going wage for technicians is $100,000 per year and the price of computers is $5,000? Compare your answer to the demand for technicians at a wage of $100,000 when the price of computers is $3,000.

The general conclusion to be drawn from Example 8.2 is that *an increase in the price of workers' output increases the demand for labor*, shifting the labor demand curve to the right, as shown in Figure 8.2. A higher price for workers' output makes workers more valuable, leading employers to demand more workers at any given real wage.

The second factor that affects the demand for labor is worker productivity. Since an increase in productivity increases the value of a worker's marginal product, it also increases the demand for labor, as Example 8.3 shows.

FIGURE 8.2

A Higher Price of Output Increases the Demand for Labor.

An increase in the price of workers' output increases the value of their marginal product, shifting the labor demand curve to the right.

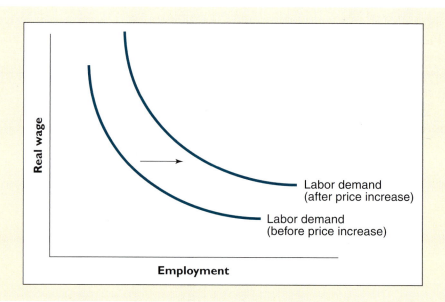

EXAMPLE 8.3

Worker productivity and BCC's demand for labor

Suppose BCC adopts a new technology that reduces the number of components to be assembled, permitting each technician to build 50 percent more machines per year. Assume that the price of computers is $3,000 per machine. How many technicians will BCC hire if the real wage is $60,000 per year?

Table 8.3 shows workers' marginal products and the value of their marginal products after the 50 percent increase in productivity, assuming that computers sell for $3,000 each.

Before the productivity increase, BCC would have demanded three workers at a wage of $60,000 (Table 8.1). After the productivity increase, however, the value of the marginal product of the first six workers exceeds $60,000 (see Table 8.3,

TABLE 8.3

Production and Marginal Product for Banana Computers after an Increase in Worker Productivity

(1) Number of workers	(2) Computers produced per year	(3) Marginal product	(4) Value of marginal product ($3,000/computer)
0	0		
1	37.5	37.5	$112,500
2	72	34.5	103,500
3	103.5	31.5	94,500
4	132	28.5	85,500
5	157.5	25.5	76,500
6	180	22.5	67,500
7	199.5	19.5	58,500
8	216	16.5	49,500

column 4). So at a wage of $60,000, BCC's demand for labor increases from three workers to six.

EXERCISE 8.3

How many workers will BCC hire after the 50 percent increase in productivity if the going wage for technicians is $50,000 per year? Compare this figure to the demand for workers at a $50,000 wage before the increase in productivity.

In general, an increase in worker productivity increases the demand for labor, shifting the labor demand curve to the right, as in Figure 8.3.

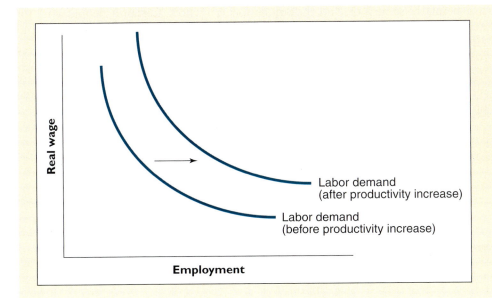

FIGURE 8.3
Higher Productivity Increases the Demand for Labor.
An increase in productivity raises workers' marginal product and—assuming no change in the price of output—the value of their marginal product. Since a productivity increase raises the value of marginal product, employers will hire more workers at any given real wage, shifting the labor demand curve to the right.

THE SUPPLY OF LABOR

We have discussed the demand for labor by employers; to complete the story, we need to consider the supply of labor. The suppliers of labor are workers and potential workers. At any given real wage, potential suppliers of labor must decide if they are willing to work. The total number of people who are willing to work at each real wage is the supply of labor.[2]

Will you clean your neighbor's basement or go to the beach?

You were planning to go to the beach today, but your neighbor asks you to clean out his basement. You like the beach a lot more than fighting cobwebs. Do you take the job?

EXAMPLE 8.4

Unless you are motivated primarily by neighborliness, your answer to this job offer would probably be "It depends on how much my neighbor will pay." You probably would not be willing to take the job for $10 or $20, unless you have a severe and immediate need for cash. But if your neighbor were wealthy and eccentric enough to offer you $500 (to take an extreme example), you would very likely say yes. Somewhere between $20 and the unrealistic figure of $500 is the minimum payment you would be willing to accept to tackle the dirty basement. This minimum payment, the *reservation price* you set for your labor, is the compensation level that leaves you just indifferent between working and not working.

[2]We are still holding the general price level constant, so any increase in the nominal wage also represents an increase in the real wage.

In economic terms, deciding whether to work at any given wage is a straightforward application of the *cost-benefit principle*. The cost to you of cleaning out the basement is the opportunity cost of your time (you would rather be surfing) plus the cost you place on having to work in unpleasant conditions. You can measure this total cost in dollars simply by asking yourself, "What is the minimum amount of money I would take to clean out the basement instead of going to the beach?" The minimum payment that you would accept is the same as your reservation price. The benefit of taking the job is measured by the pay you receive, which will go toward that new DVD player you want. You should take the job only if the promised pay (the benefit of working) exceeds your reservation price (the cost of working).

In this example, your willingness to supply labor is greater the higher the wage. In general, the same is true for the population as a whole. Certainly people work for many reasons, including personal satisfaction, the opportunity to develop skills and talents, and the chance to socialize with coworkers. Still, for most people, income is one of the principal benefits of working, so the higher the real wage, the more willing they are to sacrifice other possible uses of their time. The fact that people are more willing to work when the wage they are offered is higher is captured in the upward slope of the supply curve of labor (see Figure 8.4).

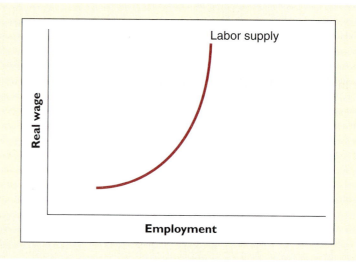

FIGURE 8.4

The Supply of Labor.
The labor supply curve is upward-sloping because, in general, the higher the wage, the more people are willing to work.

Might accepting a job that pays no salary ever be a good career move?

EXERCISE 8.4

You want to make a career in broadcasting. The local radio station is offering an unpaid summer internship that would give you valuable experience. Your alternative to the internship is to earn $3,000 working in a car wash. How would you decide which job to take? Would a decision to take the internship contradict the conclusion that the labor supply curve is upward-sloping?

SHIFTS IN THE SUPPLY OF LABOR

Any factor that affects the quantity of labor offered at a given real wage will shift the labor supply curve. At the macroeconomic level, the most important factor affecting the supply of labor is the size of the working-age population, which is influenced by factors such as the domestic birthrate, immigration and emigration rates, and the ages at which people normally first enter the workforce and retire. All else being equal, an increase in the working-age population raises the quantity of labor supplied at each real wage, shifting the labor supply curve to the right. Changes in the percentage of people of working age who seek employment—for example, as a result of social changes that encourage women to work outside the home—also can affect the supply of labor.

Now that we have discussed both the demand for and supply of labor, we are ready to apply supply and demand analysis to real-world labor markets. But first, try your hand at using supply and demand analysis to answer the following question.

EXERCISE 8.5

Labor unions typically favor tough restrictions on immigration, while employers tend to favor more liberal rules. Why? (*Hint:* How is an influx of potential workers likely to affect real wages?)

RECAP	SUPPLY AND DEMAND IN THE LABOR MARKET

The demand for labor
The extra production gained by adding one more worker is the *marginal product* of that worker. The *value of the marginal product* of a worker is that worker's marginal product times the price of the firm's output. A firm will employ a worker only if the worker's value of marginal product, which is the same as the extra revenue the worker generates for the firm, exceeds the real wage that the firm must pay. The lower the real wage, the more workers the firm will find it profitable to employ. Thus, the labor demand curve, like most demand curves, is downward-sloping.

For a given real wage, any change that increases the value of workers' marginal products will increase the demand for labor and shift the labor demand curve to the right. Examples of factors that increase labor demand are an increase in the price of workers' output and an increase in productivity.

The supply of labor
An individual is willing to supply labor if the real wage that is offered is greater than the opportunity cost of the individual's time. Generally, the higher the real wage, the more people are willing to work. Thus, the labor supply curve, like most supply curves, is upward-sloping.

For a given real wage, any factor that increases the number of people available and willing to work increases the supply of labor and shifts the labor supply curve to the right. Examples of facts that increase labor supply include an increase in the working-age population or an increase in the share of the working-age population seeking employment.

EXPLAINING THE TRENDS IN REAL WAGES AND EMPLOYMENT

We are now ready to analyze the important trends in real wages and employment discussed earlier in the chapter. We will do so in a series of Economic Naturalist boxes.

Why have real wages increased by so much in the industrialized countries?

As we discussed, real annual earnings in the United States have quadrupled since 1929, and other industrialized countries have experienced similar gains. These increases have greatly improved the standard of living of workers in these countries. Why have real wages increased by so much in the United States and other industrialized countries?

The large increase in real wages results from the sustained growth in productivity experienced by the industrialized countries during the twentieth century. (Figure 4.2, page 100, shows the growth of output per worker in the United States

ECONOMIC NATURALIST 8.1

FIGURE 8.5

An Increase in Productivity Raises the Real Wage.

An increase in productivity raises the demand for labor, shifting the labor demand curve from D to D'. The real wage rises from w to w', and employment rises from N to N'.

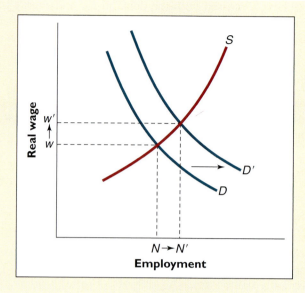

since 1900.) As illustrated by Figure 8.5, increased productivity raises the demand for labor, increasing employment and the real wage.

Of the factors contributing to productivity growth in the industrialized countries, two of the most important were (1) the dramatic technological progress that occurred during the twentieth century and (2) large increases in capital, which provided workers with more and better tools with which to work. Labor supply increased during the century as well, of course (not shown in the diagram). However, the increases in labor demand, driven by rapidly expanding productivity, have been so great as to overwhelm the depressing effect on real wages of increased labor supply.

ECONOMIC NATURALIST 8.2

Since the 1970s, real wage growth in the United States has slowed, while employment has expanded rapidly. What accounts for these trends?

With the exception of the period since the late 1990s, rates of real wage growth after 1973 in the United States have been significantly lower than in previous decades. But over much of the recent period, the economy has created new jobs at a record rate. What accounts for these trends?

Let's begin with the slowdown in real wage growth since the early 1970s. Supply and demand analysis tells us that a slowdown in real wage growth must result from slower growth in the demand for labor, more rapid growth in the supply of labor, or both. On the demand side, recall from the last chapter that since the early 1970s the United States and other industrialized nations have experienced a slowdown in productivity growth. Thus, one possible explanation for the slowdown in the growth of real wages since the early 1970s is the decline in the pace of productivity gains.

Some evidence for a relationship between productivity and real wages is given in Table 8.4, which shows the average annual growth rates in labor productivity and real annual earnings for each decade since 1960. You can see that the growth in productivity decade by decade corresponds closely to the growth in real earnings. Particularly striking is the rapid growth of both productivity and wages during the 1960s. Since the 1970s, growth in both productivity and real wages has been significantly slower, although some improvement is apparent after 1990.

Table 8.4 also shows that real wage growth has lagged productivity growth since 2000. Slow real wage growth during this period may be the result of the weak

TABLE 8.4
Growth Rates in Productivity and Real Earnings

	Annual Growth Rate (%)	
	Productivity	Real earnings
1960–1970	2.34	2.90
1970–1980	0.81	0.78
1980–1990	1.42	1.13
1990–2000	1.82	2.06
2000–2004	2.08	1.02

SOURCE: *Economic Report of the President*, 2005 (http://www.gpoaccess.gov/eop). Productivity is real GDP divided by civilian employment; real earnings equal total compensation of employees divided by civilian employment and deflated by the GDP deflator.

labor market that followed the recession of 2001; if so, then real wage growth can be expected to catch up to productivity growth as the labor market returns to normal.

While the effects of the slowdown in productivity on the demand for labor are an important reason for declining real wage growth, they can't be the whole story. We know this because, with labor supply held constant, slower growth in labor demand would lead to reduced rates of employment growth, as well as reduced growth in real wages. But job growth in the United States has been rapid in recent decades. Large increases in employment in the face of slow growth of labor demand can be explained only by simultaneous increases in the supply of labor (see Exercise 8.6).

Labor supply in the United States does appear to have grown rapidly recently. As we saw in the chapter "Measuring Economic Activity," for example, increased participation in the labor market by women has increased the U.S. supply of labor since the mid-1970s. Other factors, including the coming of age of the baby boomers and high rates of immigration, also help to explain the increase in the supply of labor. The combination of slower growth in labor demand (the result of the productivity slowdown) and accelerated growth in labor supply (the result of increased participation by women in the workforce, together with other factors) helps to explain why real wage growth has been sluggish for many years in the United States, even as employment has grown rapidly.

What about the future? As we saw in the previous chapter, labor supply growth is likely to slow in the coming decades as the baby boomers retire and the percentage of women in the labor force stabilizes. Productivity has recently grown more quickly, reflecting the benefits of new technologies, among other factors (the chapter "Economic Growth, Productivity, and Living Standards"). Especially if the recent productivity trend continues, there seems to be a good chance that workers will see healthy gains in real wages in the years to come.

EXERCISE 8.6

According to Economic Naturalist 8.2, relatively weak growth in productivity and relatively strong growth in labor supply after about 1973 can explain (1) the slowdown in real wage growth and (2) the more rapid expansion in employment after about 1973. Show this point graphically by drawing two supply and demand diagrams of the labor market, one corresponding to the period 1960–1972 and the other to 1973–2000 (the period ending just before the 2001 recession). Assuming that productivity growth was strong but labor supply growth was modest during 1960–1972, show that we would expect to see rapid real wage growth but only moderate

> growth in employment in that period. Now apply the same analysis to 1973–2000, assuming that productivity growth is weaker but labor supply growth stronger than in 1960–1972. What do you predict for growth in the real wage and employment in 1973–2000 relative to the earlier period?

INCREASING WAGE INEQUALITY: THE EFFECTS OF GLOBALIZATION

Another important trend in U.S. labor markets is increasing inequality in wages, especially the tendency for the wages of the less-skilled and less-educated to fall further and further behind those of better-trained workers. We next discuss two reasons for this increasing inequality: (1) globalization and (2) technological change.

Why has the gap between the wages of skilled and unskilled workers widened in recent years? (1) Globalization

ECONOMIC NATURALIST 8.3

In recent years, the real wages of more highly skilled and educated workers have continued to rise, while the real wages of less-skilled workers have stagnated or even declined. Does the "globalization" of the world economy have anything to do with this trend?

Many commentators have blamed the increasing divergence between the wages of skilled and unskilled workers on the phenomenon of "globalization." This popular term refers to the fact that to an increasing extent, the markets for many goods and services are becoming international, rather than national or local in scope. While Americans have long been able to buy products from all over the world, the ease with which goods and services can cross borders is increasing rapidly. In part this trend is the result of international trade agreements, such as the North American Free Trade Agreement (NAFTA), which reduced taxes on goods and services traded among Canada, the United States, and Mexico. However, technological advances such as the Internet also have promoted globalization. A recent TV commercial showed a small auto parts manufacturer in Texas bidding over the Internet for a contract from a Japanese auto firm.

The main economic benefit of globalization is increased specialization and the efficiency that it brings. Instead of each country trying to produce everything its citizens consume, each can concentrate on producing those goods and services at which it is relatively most efficient. As implied by the *principle of comparative advantage* (Chapter 2), the result is that consumers of all countries enjoy a greater variety of goods and services, of better quality and at lower prices, than they would without international trade.

The effects of globalization on the *labor* market are mixed, however, which explains why many politicians opposed free trade agreements. Expanded trade means that consumers stop buying certain goods and services from domestic producers and switch to foreign-made products. Consumers would not make this switch unless the foreign products were better, cheaper, or both, so expanded trade clearly makes them better off. But the workers and firm owners in the domestic industries that lose business may well suffer from the increase in foreign competition.

The effects of increasing trade on the labor market can be analyzed using Figure 8.6. The figure contrasts the supply and demand for labor in two different industries: (a) textiles and (b) computer software. Imagine that, initially, there is little or no international trade in these two goods. Without trade, the demand for workers in each industry is indicated by the curves marked $D_{textiles}$ and $D_{software}$, respectively. Wages and employment in each industry are determined by the intersection of the demand curves and the labor supply curves in each industry. As we have drawn the figure, initially, the real wage is the same in both industries, equal to w. Employment is $N_{textiles}$ in textiles and $N_{software}$ in software.

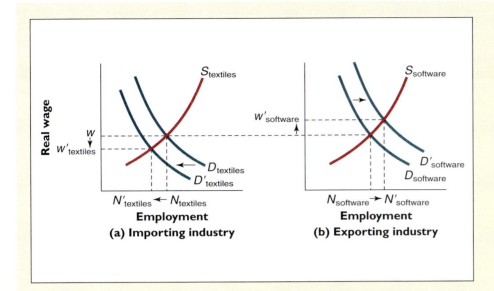

FIGURE 8.6
The Effect of Globalization on the Demand for Workers in Two Industries.
Initially, real wages in the two industries are equal at w. After an increase in trade, (a) demand for workers in the importing industry (textiles) declines, lowering real wages and employment, while (b) demand for workers in the exporting industry (software) increases, raising real wages and employment in that industry.

What will happen when this economy is opened up to trade, perhaps because of a free trade agreement? Under the agreement, countries will begin to produce for export those goods or services at which they are relatively more efficient and to import goods or services that they are relatively less efficient at producing. Suppose the country in this example is relatively more efficient at producing software than manufacturing textiles. With the opening of trade, the country gains new foreign markets for its software and begins to produce for export as well as for domestic use. Meanwhile, because the country is relatively less efficient at producing textiles, consumers begin to purchase foreign-made textiles, which are cheaper or of higher quality, instead of the domestic product. In short, software becomes an exporting industry and textiles an importing industry.

These changes in the demand for domestic products are translated into changes in the demand for labor. The opening of export markets increases the demand for domestic software, raising its price. The higher price for domestic software, in turn, raises the value of the marginal products of software workers, shifting the labor demand curve in the software industry to the right, from $D_{software}$ to $D'_{software}$ in Figure 8.6(b). Wages in the software industry rise, from w to $w'_{software}$, and employment in the industry rises as well. In the textile industry the opposite happens. Demand for domestic textiles falls as consumers switch to imports. The price of domestic textiles falls with demand, reducing the value of the marginal product of textile workers and hence the demand for their labor, to $D'_{textiles}$ in Figure 8.6(a). Employment in the textile industry falls, and the real wage falls as well, from w to $w'_{textiles}$.

In sum, Figure 8.6 shows how globalization can contribute to increasing wage inequality. Initially, we assumed that software workers and textile workers received the same wage. However, the opening up of trade raised the wages of workers in the "winning" industry (software) and lowered the wages of workers in the "losing" industry (textiles), increasing inequality.

In practice, the tendency of trade to increase wage inequality may be even worse than depicted in the example, because the great majority of the world's workers, particularly those in developing countries, have relatively low skill levels. Thus, when industrialized countries like the United States open up trade with developing countries, the domestic industries that are likely to face the toughest international competition are those that use mostly low-skilled labor. Conversely, the industries that are likely to do the best in international competition are those that employ mostly skilled workers. Thus, increased trade may lower the wages of those workers who are already poorly paid and increase the wages of those who are well paid.

The fact that increasing trade may exacerbate wage inequality explains some of the political resistance to globalization, but in general it does not justify attempts to reverse the trend. Increasing trade and specialization is a major source of improvement in living standards, both in the United States and abroad, so trying to stop the process is counterproductive. Indeed, the economic forces behind globalization—primarily, the desire of consumers for better and cheaper products and of producers for new markets—are so powerful that the process would be hard to stop even if government officials were determined to do so.

Rather than trying to stop globalization, helping the labor market to adjust to the effects of globalization is probably a better course. To a certain extent, indeed, the economy will adjust on its own. Figure 8.6 showed that, following the opening to trade, real wages and employment fall in (a) textiles and rise in (b) software. At that point, wages and job opportunities are much more attractive in the software industry than in textiles. Will this situation persist? Clearly, there is a strong incentive for workers who are able to do so to leave the textile industry and seek employment in the software industry.

worker mobility the movement of workers between jobs, firms, and industries

The movement of workers between jobs, firms, and industries is called **worker mobility.** In our example, worker mobility will tend to reduce labor supply in textiles and increase it in software, as workers move from the contracting industry to the growing one. This process will reverse some of the increase in wage inequality by raising wages in textiles and lowering them in software. It also will shift workers from a less competitive sector to a more competitive sector. To some extent, then, the labor market can adjust on its own to the effects of globalization.

Of course, there are many barriers to a textile worker becoming a software engineer. So there also may be a need for *transition aid* to workers in the affected sectors. Ideally, such aid helps workers train for and find new jobs. If that is not possible or desirable—say, because a worker is nearing retirement—transition aid can take the form of government payments to help the worker maintain his or her standard of living. Because trade and specialization increase the total economic pie, the "winners" from globalization can afford the taxes necessary to finance aid and still enjoy a net benefit from increased trade.

INCREASING WAGE INEQUALITY: TECHNOLOGICAL CHANGE

A second source of increasing wage inequality is ongoing technological change that favors more highly skilled or educated workers. Economic Naturalist 8.4 examines the effect of technological change on the labor market.

ECONOMIC NATURALIST 8.4

Why has the gap between the wages of less-skilled and higher-skilled workers widened in recent years? (2) Technological change

How has the pattern of technological change contributed to increasing inequality of wages?

As we have seen, new scientific knowledge and the technological advances associated with it are a major source of improved productivity and economic growth. Increases in worker productivity are in turn a driving force behind wage increases and higher average living standards. In the long run and on average, technological progress is undoubtedly the worker's friend.

This sweeping statement is not true at all times and in all places, however. Whether a particular technological development is good for a particular worker depends on the effect of that innovation on the worker's value of marginal product and, hence, on his or her wage. For example, at one time the ability to add numbers rapidly and accurately was a valuable skill; a clerk with that skill could expect advancement and higher wages. However, the invention and mass production of the electronic calculator has rendered human calculating skills less valuable, to the detriment of those who have that skill.

History is replete with examples of workers who opposed new technologies out of fear that their skills would become less valuable. In England in the early nineteenth century, rioting workmen destroyed newly introduced labor-saving machinery. The name of the workers' reputed leader, Ned Ludd, has been preserved in the term *Luddite,* meaning a person who is opposed to the introduction of new technologies. The same theme appears in American folk history in the tale of John Henry, the mighty pile-driving man who died in an attempt to show that a human could tunnel into a rock face more quickly than a steam-powered machine.

How do these observations bear on wage inequality? According to some economists, many recent technological advances have taken the form of **skill-biased technological change,** that is, technological change that affects the marginal product of higher-skilled workers differently from that of lower-skilled workers. Specifically, technological developments in recent decades appear to have favored more-skilled and educated workers. Developments in automobile production are a case in point. The advent of mass production techniques in the 1920s provided highly paid work for several generations of relatively low-skilled autoworkers. But in recent years automobile production, like the automobiles themselves, has become considerably more sophisticated. The simplest production jobs have been taken over by robots and computer-controlled machinery, which require skilled operatives who know how to use and maintain the new equipment. Consumer demands for luxury features and customized options also has raised the automakers' demand for highly skilled craftsmen. Thus, in general, the skill requirements for jobs in automobile production have risen. Similarly, few office workers today can escape the need to use computer applications, such as word processing and spreadsheets. And in many places, elementary school teachers are expected to know how to set up a Web page or use the Internet.

Figure 8.7 illustrates the effects of technological change that favors skilled workers. Figure 8.7(a) shows the market for unskilled workers; Figure 8.7(b) shows the market for skilled workers. The demand curves labeled $D_{unskilled}$ and $D_{skilled}$ show the demand for each type of worker before a skill-biased technological change. Wages and employment for each type of worker are determined by the intersection of the demand and supply curves in each market. Figure 8.7 shows that,

skill-biased technological change technological change that affects the marginal products of higher-skilled workers differently from those of lower-skilled workers

Unimpressed by new technology

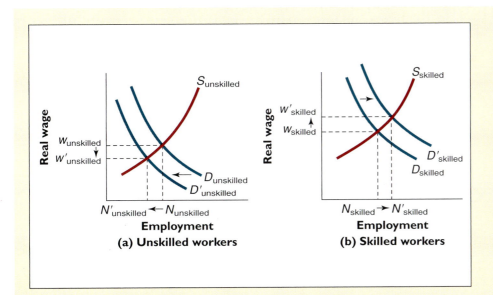

(a) Unskilled workers

(b) Skilled workers

FIGURE 8.7
The Effect of Skill-Biased Technological Change on Wage Inequality.
The figure shows the effects of a skill-biased technological change that increases the marginal product of skilled workers and reduces the marginal product of unskilled workers. The resulting increase in the demand for skilled workers raises their wages (b), while the decline in demand for unskilled workers reduces their wages (a). Wage inequality increases.

even before the technological change, unskilled workers received lower real wages than skilled workers ($w_{\text{unskilled}} < w_{\text{skilled}}$), reflecting the lower marginal products of the unskilled.

Now suppose that a new technology—computer-controlled machinery, for example—is introduced. This technological change is biased toward skilled workers, which means that it raises their marginal productivity relative to unskilled workers. We will assume in this example that the new technology also lowers the marginal productivity of unskilled workers, perhaps because they are unable to use the new technology, but all that is necessary for our conclusions is that they benefit less than skilled workers. Figure 8.7 shows the effect of this change in marginal products. In part (b) the increase in the marginal productivity of skilled workers raises the demand for those workers; the demand curve shifts rightward to D'_{skilled}. Accordingly, the real wages and employment of skilled workers also rise. In contrast, because they have been made less productive by the technological change, the demand for unskilled workers shifts leftward to $D'_{\text{unskilled}}$ [Figure 8.7(a)]. Lower demand for unskilled workers reduces their real wages and employment.

In summary, this analysis supports the conclusion that technological change that is biased in favor of skilled workers will tend to increase the wage gap between the skilled and unskilled. Empirical studies have confirmed the role of skill-biased technological change in recent increases in wage inequality.

Because new technologies that favor skilled workers increase wage inequality, should government regulators act to block them? As in the case of globalization, most economists would argue against trying to block new technologies, since technological advances are necessary for economic growth and improved living standards. If the Luddites had somehow succeeded in preventing the introduction of labor-saving machinery in Great Britain, economic growth and development over the past few centuries might have been greatly reduced.

The remedies for the problem of wage inequalities caused by technological change are similar to those for wage inequalities caused by globalization. First among them is worker mobility. As the pay differential between skilled and unskilled work increases, unskilled workers will have a stronger incentive to acquire education and skills, to everyone's benefit. A second remedy is transition aid. Government policymakers should consider programs that will help workers to retrain if they are able, or provide income support if they are not.

RECAP	EXPLAINING THE TRENDS IN REAL WAGES AND EMPLOYMENT

- The long-term increase in real wages enjoyed by workers in industrial countries results primarily from large productivity gains, which have raised the demand for labor. Technological progress and an expanded and modernized capital stock are two important reasons for these long-term increases in productivity.
- The slowdown in real wage growth that began in the 1970s resulted in part from the slowdown in productivity growth (and, hence, the slower growth in labor demand) that occurred at about the same time. Increased labor supply, arising from such factors as the increased participation of women and the coming of age of the baby boom generation, depressed real wages further while also expanding employment. In the latter part of the 1990s, resurgence in productivity growth was accompanied by an increase in real wage growth.
- Both globalization and skill-biased technological change contribute to wage inequality. Globalization raises the wages of workers in exporting industries by raising the demand for those workers, while reducing the wages of workers in importing industries. Technological change that favors more-skilled workers

increases the demand for such workers, and hence their wages, relative to the wages of less-skilled workers.

Attempting to block either globalization or technological change is not the best response to the problem of wage inequality. To some extent, worker mobility (movement of workers from low-wage to high-wage industries) will offset the inequality created by these forces. Where mobility is not practical, transition aid—government assistance to workers whose employment prospects have worsened—may be the best solution.

UNEMPLOYMENT

The concept of the unemployment rate was introduced in the chapter "Measuring Economic Activity." To review, government survey takers classify adults as employed (holding a job), unemployed (not holding a job, but looking for one), or not in the labor force (not holding a job and not looking for one—retirees, for example). The labor force consists of the employed and the unemployed. The unemployment rate is the percentage of the labor force that is unemployed.

Unemployment rates differ markedly from country to country. In the United States, unemployment rates reached historic lows in 2000—slightly above 4 percent of the labor force—although U.S. rates rose to 6 percent in the 2001 recession. (Figure 5.3, page 139, shows the U.S. unemployment rate since 1960.) In Canada and many western European countries, unemployment rates for many years have been two to three times the U.S. rate. In Europe, unemployment is exceptionally high among young people. Supposedly, high school guidance counselors in Britain once gave high school seniors a pamphlet titled "Leaving School: How to Apply for Unemployment Benefits."

As we saw in the chapter "Measuring Economic Activity," a high unemployment rate has serious economic, psychological, and social costs. Understanding the causes of unemployment and finding ways to reduce it are therefore major concerns of macroeconomists. In the remainder of this chapter, we discuss the causes and costs of three types of unemployment, and we also will consider some features of labor markets that may exacerbate the problem.

TYPES OF UNEMPLOYMENT AND THEIR COSTS

Economists have found it useful to think of unemployment as being of three broad types: *frictional* unemployment, *structural* unemployment, and *cyclical* unemployment. Each type of unemployment has different causes and imposes different economic and social costs.

Frictional Unemployment

The function of the labor market is to match available jobs with available workers. If all jobs and workers were the same, or if the set of jobs and workers were static and unchanging, this matching process would be quick and easy. But the real world is more complicated. In practice, both jobs and workers are highly *heterogeneous*. Jobs differ in their location, in the skills they require, in their working conditions and hours, and in many other ways. Workers differ in their career aspirations, their skills and experience, their preferred working hours, their willingness to travel, and so on.

The real labor market is also *dynamic*, or constantly changing and evolving. On the demand side of the labor market, technological advances, globalization, and changing consumer tastes spur the creation of new products, new firms, and even new industries, while outmoded products, firms, and industries disappear. Thus CD players have replaced record players, and word processors have replaced typewriters. As a result of this upheaval, new jobs are constantly being created, while some old jobs cease to be viable. The workforce in a modern economy is equally dynamic. People move, gain new skills, leave the labor force for a time to rear children or go back to school, and even change careers.

Because the labor market is heterogeneous and dynamic, the process of matching jobs with workers often takes time. For example, a software engineer who loses or quits her job in Silicon Valley may take weeks or even months to find an appropriate new job. In her search she will probably consider alternative areas of software development or even totally new challenges. She also may want to think about different regions of the country in which software companies are located, such as North Carolina's Research Triangle or New York City's Silicon Alley. During the period in which she is searching for a new job, she is counted as unemployed.

frictional unemployment the short-term unemployment associated with the process of matching workers with jobs

Short-term unemployment that is associated with the process of matching workers with jobs is called **frictional unemployment.** The *costs* of frictional unemployment are low and may even be negative; that is, frictional unemployment may be economically beneficial. First, frictional unemployment is short-term, so its psychological effects and direct economic losses are minimal. Second, to the extent that the search process leads to a better match between worker and job, a period of frictional unemployment is actually productive, in the sense that it leads to higher output over the long run. Indeed, a certain amount of frictional unemployment seems essential to the smooth functioning of a rapidly changing, dynamic economy.

Structural Unemployment

structural unemployment the long-term and chronic unemployment that exists even when the economy is producing at a normal rate

A second major type of unemployment is **structural unemployment,** or the long-term and chronic unemployment that exists even when the economy is producing at a normal rate. Several factors contribute to structural unemployment. First, a *lack of skills, language barriers,* or *discrimination* keeps some workers from finding stable, long-term jobs. Migrant farmworkers and unskilled construction workers who

"The one single thought that sustains me is that the fundamentals are good."

find short-term or temporary jobs from time to time, but never stay in one job for very long, fit the definition of chronically unemployed.

Second, economic changes sometimes create a *long-term mismatch* between the skills some workers have and the available jobs. The U.S. steel industry, for example, has declined over the years, while the computer industry has grown rapidly. Ideally, steelworkers who lose their jobs would be able to find new jobs in computer firms (worker mobility), so their unemployment would only be frictional in nature. In practice, of course, many ex-steelworkers lack the education, ability, or interest necessary to work in the computer industry. Since their skills are no longer in demand, these workers may drift into chronic or long-term unemployment.

Finally, structural unemployment can result from *structural features of the labor market* that act as barriers to employment. Examples of such barriers include unions and minimum wage laws, both of which may keep wages above their market-clearing level, creating unemployment. We will discuss some of these structural features shortly.

The *costs* of structural unemployment are much higher than those of frictional unemployment. Because structurally unemployed workers do little productive work over long periods, their idleness causes substantial economic losses both to the unemployed workers and to society. Structurally unemployed workers also lose out on the opportunity to develop new skills on the job, and their existing skills wither from disuse. Long spells of unemployment are also much more difficult for workers to handle psychologically than the relatively brief spells associated with frictional unemployment.

Cyclical Unemployment

The third type of unemployment occurs during periods of recession (that is, periods of unusually low production) and is called **cyclical unemployment.** The sharp peaks in unemployment shown in Figure 5.3 reflect the cyclical unemployment that occurs during recessions. Increases in cyclical unemployment, although they are relatively short-lived, are associated with significant declines in real GDP and are therefore quite costly economically. We will study cyclical unemployment in more detail later in the chapters dealing with booms and recessions.

cyclical unemployment the extra unemployment that occurs during periods of recession

In principle, frictional, structural, and cyclical unemployment add up to the total unemployment rate. In practice, sharp distinctions often cannot be made between the different categories, so any breakdown of the total unemployment rate into the three types of unemployment is necessarily subjective and approximate.

IMPEDIMENTS TO FULL EMPLOYMENT

In discussing structural unemployment, we mentioned that structural features of the labor market may contribute to long-term and chronic unemployment. Let's discuss a few of those features.

Minimum Wage Laws[3]

The federal government and most states have minimum wage laws, which prescribe the lowest hourly wage that employers may pay to workers. Basic supply and demand analysis shows that if the minimum wage law has any effect at all, it must raise the unemployment rate. Figure 8.8 shows why. The figure shows the demand and supply curves for low-skilled workers, to whom the minimum wage is most relevant. The market-clearing real wage, at which the quantity of labor demanded equals the quantity of labor supplied, is w, and the corresponding level of employment of low-skilled workers is N. Now suppose there is a legal minimum wage w_{min} that exceeds the market-clearing wage w, as shown in Figure 8.8. At the minimum wage, the number of people who want jobs, N_B, exceeds the number of workers

[3]Minimum wages are also discussed in the chapter "Labor Markets, Poverty, and Income Distribution."

FIGURE 8.8

A Legal Minimum Wage May Create Unemployment.

If the minimum wage w_{min} exceeds the market-clearing wage w for low-skilled workers, it will create unemployment equal to the difference between the number of people who want to work at the minimum wage, N_B, and the number of people that employers are willing to hire, N_A.

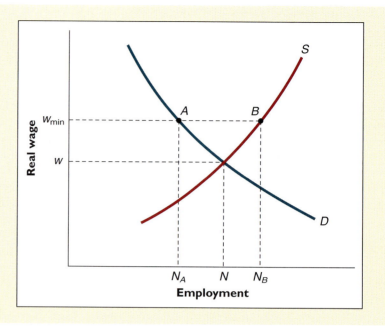

that employers are willing to hire, N_A. The result is unemployment in the amount $N_B - N_A$, also equal to the length of the line segment AB in the figure. If there were no minimum wage, this unemployment would not exist, since the labor market would clear at wage w.

If minimum wages create unemployment, why are they politically popular? A minimum wage creates two classes of workers: those who are lucky enough to find jobs at the minimum wage and those who are shut out because the minimum wage exceeds the market-clearing wage. Workers who do find jobs at the minimum wage will earn more than they would have otherwise, because the minimum wage is higher than the market-clearing wage. If the minimum wage were put to a vote, the number of workers who benefit from the legislation, and who could thus be expected to support it, might well exceed the number of workers who are hurt by it. In creating groups of "winners" and "losers," minimum wage legislation resembles rent control legislation (see Chapter 3). But like rent controls, minimum wages create economic inefficiency. Thus, other methods of attacking poverty, such as direct grants to the working poor, might prove more effective.

Labor Unions

Labor unions are organizations that negotiate with employers on behalf of workers. Among the issues that unions negotiate, which are embodied in the contracts they draw up with employers, are the wages workers earn, rules for hiring and firing, the duties of different types of workers, working hours and conditions, and procedures for resolving disputes between workers and employers. Unions gain negotiating power by their power to call a strike—that is, to refuse work until a contract agreement has been reached.

Through the threat of a strike, a union can usually get employers to agree to a wage that is higher than the market-clearing wage. Thus, Figure 8.8 could represent conditions in a unionized industry if w_{min} is interpreted as the union wage instead of the legal minimum wage. As in the case of a minimum wage, a union wage that is higher than the market-clearing wage leads to unemployment, in the amount $N_B - N_A$ in Figure 8.8. Furthermore, a high union wage creates a trade-off similar to the one created by a minimum wage. Those workers who are lucky enough to get jobs as union members will be paid more than they would be otherwise.

Unfortunately, their gain comes at the expense of other workers who are unemployed as a result of the artificially high union wage.

Are labor unions good for the economy? That is a controversial, emotionally charged question. Early in the twentieth century, some employers who faced little local competition for workers—coal-mining companies in Appalachia, for example—exploited their advantage by forcing workers to toil long hours in dangerous conditions for low pay. Through bitter and sometimes bloody confrontations with these companies, labor organizations succeeded in eliminating many of the worst abuses. Unions also point with pride to their historic political role in supporting progressive labor legislation, such as laws that banned child labor. Finally, union leaders often claim to increase productivity and promote democracy in the workplace by giving workers some voice in the operations of the firm.

Opponents of unions, while acknowledging that these organizations may have played a positive role in the past, question their value in a modern economy. Today, more and more workers are professionals or semiprofessionals, rather than production workers, so they can move relatively easily from firm to firm. Indeed, many labor markets have become national or even international, so today's workers have numerous potential employers. Thus, the forces of competition—the fact that employers must persuade talented workers to work for them—should provide adequate protection for workers. Indeed, opponents would argue that unions are becoming increasingly self-defeating, since firms that must pay artificially high union wages and abide by inflexible work rules will not be able to compete in a global economy. The ultimate effect of such handicaps will be the failure of unionized firms and the loss of union jobs. Indeed, unions are in decline in the United States and now represent 12.5 percent of the workforce—a large fraction of which are government workers, such as public school teachers and the police.

Unemployment Insurance

Another structural feature of the labor market that may increase the unemployment rate is the availability of *unemployment insurance,* or government transfer payments to unemployed workers. Unemployment insurance provides an important social benefit in that it helps the unemployed to maintain a decent standard of living while they are looking for a job. But because its availability allows the unemployed to search longer or less intensively for a job, it may lengthen the average amount of time the typical unemployed worker is without a job.

Most economists would argue that unemployment insurance should be generous enough to provide basic support to the unemployed but not so generous as to remove the incentive to actively seek work. Thus, unemployment insurance should last for only a limited time, and its benefits should not be as high as the income a worker receives when working.

Other Government Regulations

Besides minimum wage legislation, many other government regulations bear on the labor market. They include *health and safety regulations,* which establish the safety standards employers must follow, and rules that prohibit racial or gender-based discrimination in hiring. Many of these regulations are beneficial. In some cases, however, the costs of complying with regulations may exceed the benefits they provide. Further, to the extent that regulations increase employer costs and reduce productivity, they depress the demand for labor, lowering real wages and contributing to unemployment. For maximum economic efficiency, legislators should use the *cost-benefit criterion* when deciding what regulations to impose on the labor market.

The points raised in this section can help us to understand one of the important labor market trends discussed earlier in the chapter, namely, the persistence of high unemployment in western Europe.

ECONOMIC
NATURALIST
8.5

Why are unemployment rates so high in western Europe?

For more than two decades, unemployment has been exceptionally high in the major countries of western Europe, as Figure 8.9 shows. In 2004, for example, the unemployment rate was 8.1 percent in Italy, 9.8 percent in France, and 9.8 percent in Germany, compared with a U.S. unemployment rate of only 5.5 percent. In the 1950s, 1960s, and 1970s, western Europe consistently enjoyed very low unemployment rates. Why has European unemployment been so stubbornly high for the past two decades?

One explanation for the high unemployment in major western European countries is the existence of structural "rigidities" in their labor markets. Relative to the United States, European labor markets are highly regulated. European governments set rules in matters ranging from the number of weeks of vacation workers must receive to the reasons for which a worker can be dismissed. Minimum wages in Europe are high, and unemployment benefits are much more generous than in the United States. European unions are also far more powerful than those in the United States; their wage agreements are often extended by law to all firms in the industry, whether or not they are unionized. This lack of flexibility in labor markets—which some observers refer to as *Eurosclerosis*—causes higher frictional and structural unemployment.

FIGURE 8.9

Unemployment Rates in Western Europe, 1980–2004.

In the major western European countries, unemployment rates have been high for more than two decades.

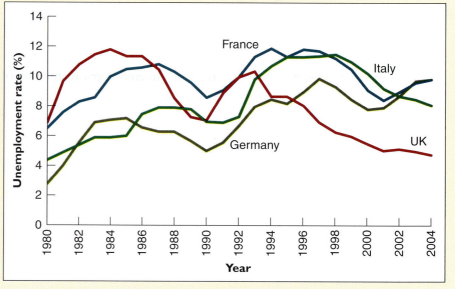

SOURCE: Standardized unemployment rates, Bureau of Labor Statistics (http://www.stats.bls.gov).

If European labor markets are so dysfunctional, why has serious European unemployment emerged only in the past two decades? One explanation turns on the increasing pace of *globalization* and *skill-biased technological change*. As we saw, these two factors decrease the demand for less-skilled labor relative to the demand for skilled labor. In the United States, falling demand has depressed the wages of the less skilled, increasing wage inequality. But in western Europe, high minimum wages, union contracts, generous unemployment insurance, and other factors may have created a floor for the wage that firms could pay or that workers would accept. As the marginal productivity of the less skilled dropped below that floor, firms no longer found it profitable to employ those workers, swelling the ranks of the unemployed. Thus, the combination of labor market rigidity and the declining marginal productivity of low-skilled workers may be responsible for the European unemployment problem.

Evidence for the idea that inflexible labor markets have contributed to European unemployment comes from the United Kingdom, where the government of Prime Minister Margaret Thatcher instituted a series of reforms beginning in the early 1980s. Britain has since largely deregulated its labor market so that it functions much more like that in the United States. Figure 8.9 shows that unemployment in Britain has gradually declined and is now lower than in other western European countries. Labor market reforms like those in Britain are examples of *structural policies*.

RECAP	UNEMPLOYMENT

Economists distinguish among three broad types of unemployment. *Frictional unemployment* is the short-term unemployment that is associated with the process of matching workers with jobs. *Structural unemployment* is the long-term or chronic unemployment that occurs even when the economy is producing at a normal rate. *Cyclical unemployment* is the extra unemployment that occurs during periods of recession. Frictional unemployment may be economically beneficial, as improved matching of workers and jobs may increase output in the long run. Structural and cyclical unemployment impose heavy economic costs on workers and society, as well as psychological costs on workers and their families.

Structural features of the labor market may cause structural unemployment. Examples of such features are legal minimum wages or union contracts that set wages above market-clearing levels; unemployment insurance, which allows unemployed workers to search longer or less intensively for a job; and government regulations that impose extra costs on employers. Regulation of the labor market is not necessarily undesirable, but it should be subject to the cost-benefit criterion. Heavy labor market regulation and high unionization rates in western Europe help to explain the persistence of high unemployment rates in those countries.

■ SUMMARY ■

- For the average person, the most tangible result of economic growth and increasing productivity is the availability of "good jobs at good wages." Over the long run, the U.S. economy has for the most part delivered on this promise, as both real wages and employment have grown strongly. But while growth in employment has recently been rapid, two worrisome trends dog the U.S. labor market: a slowdown since the early 1970s in the growth of real wages and increasing wage inequality. Western Europe has experienced less wage inequality but significantly higher rates of unemployment than the United States.

- Trends in real wages and employment can be studied using a supply and demand model of the labor market. If we hold the general price level constant, the productivity of labor and the price of workers' output determine the demand for labor. Employers will hire workers only as long as the value of the marginal product of the last worker hired equals or exceeds the wage the firm must pay. Because of *diminishing returns to labor*, the more workers a firm employs, the less

additional product will be obtained by adding yet another worker. The lower the going wage, the more workers will be hired; that is, the demand for labor curve slopes downward. Economic changes that increase the value of labor's marginal product, such as an increase in the price of workers' output or an increase in productivity, shift the labor demand curve to the right. Conversely, changes that reduce the value of labor's marginal product shift the labor demand curve to the left.

- The supply curve for labor shows the number of people willing to work at any given real wage. Since more people will work at a higher real wage, the supply curve is upward-sloping. An increase in the working-age population, or a social change that promotes labor market participation (like increased acceptance of women in the labor force) will raise labor supply and shift the labor supply curve to the right.

- Improvements in productivity, which raise the demand for labor, account for the bulk of the increase in U.S. real wages over the last century. The slowdown in real wage growth that has occurred in recent decades is the result of slower growth in labor demand, which was caused in turn by a slowdown in the rate of productivity improvement, and of more rapid growth in labor supply. Rapid growth in labor supply, caused by such factors as immigration and increased labor force participation by women, also has contributed to the continued expansion of employment. Recently, there has been some improvement in the rate of growth of productivity and real wages.

- Two reasons for the increasing wage inequality in the United States are economic globalization and *skill-biased technological change*. Both have increased the demand for, and hence the real wages of, relatively skilled and educated workers. Attempting to block globalization and technological change is counterproductive, however, since both factors are essential to economic growth and increased productivity. To some extent, the movement of workers from lower-paying to higher-paying jobs or industries (*worker mobility*) will counteract the trend toward wage inequality. A policy of providing transition aid and training for workers with obsolete skills is a more useful response to the problem.

- There are three broad types of unemployment: frictional, structural, and cyclical. *Frictional unemployment* is the short-term unemployment associated with the process of

matching workers with jobs in a dynamic, heterogeneous labor market. *Structural unemployment* is the long-term and chronic unemployment that exists even when the economy is producing at a normal rate. It arises from a variety of factors, including language barriers, discrimination, structural features of the labor market, lack of skills, or long-term mismatches between the skills workers have and the available jobs. *Cyclical unemployment* is the extra unemployment that occurs during periods of recession. The costs of frictional unemployment are low, as it tends to be brief and to create more productive matches between workers and jobs. But structural unemployment, which is often long term, and cyclical unemployment, which is associated with significant reductions in real GDP, are relatively more costly.

- Structural features of the labor market that may contribute to unemployment include minimum wage laws, which discourage firms from hiring low-skilled workers; labor unions, which can set wages above market-clearing levels; unemployment insurance, which reduces the incentives of the unemployed to find work quickly; and other government regulations, which—although possibly conferring benefits—increase the costs of employing workers. The labor market "rigidity" created by government regulations and union contracts is more of a problem in western Europe than in the United States, which may account for Europe's high unemployment rates.

◾ KEY TERMS ◾

cyclical unemployment (229)
diminishing returns to labor (213)

frictional unemployment (228)
skill-biased technological change (225)

structural unemployment (228)
worker mobility (224)

◾ REVIEW QUESTIONS ◾

1. List and discuss the five important labor market trends given in the first section of the chapter. How do these trends either support or qualify the proposition that increasing labor productivity leads to higher standards of living?

2. Alice is very skilled at fixing manual typewriters. Would you expect her high productivity to result in a high real wage for her? Why or why not?

3. Acme Corporation is considering hiring Jane Smith. Based on her other opportunities in the job market, Jane has told Acme that she will work for them for $40,000 per year. How should Acme determine whether to employ her?

4. Why have real wages risen by so much in the United States in the past century? Why did real wage growth

slow for 25 years beginning in the early 1970s? What has been happening to real wages recently?

5. What are two major factors contributing to increased inequality in wages? Briefly, why do these factors raise wage inequality? Contrast possible policy responses to increasing inequality in terms of their effects on economic efficiency.

6. List three types of unemployment and their causes. Which of these types is economically and socially the least costly? Explain.

7. Describe some of the structural features of European labor markets that have helped to keep European unemployment rates high. If these structural features create unemployment, why don't European governments just eliminate them?

■ PROBLEMS ■

1. Data on the average earnings of people of different education levels are available from the Bureau of the Census (try online at http://www.census.gov/population/socdemo/education/tableA-3.txt). Using these data, prepare a table showing the earnings of college graduates relative to high school graduates and of college graduates relative to those with less than a high school degree. Show the data for the latest year available, for every fifth year going back to the earliest data available. What are the trends in relative earnings?

2. Production data for Bob's Bicycle Factory are as follows:

Number of workers	Bikes assembled/day
1	10
2	18
3	24
4	28
5	30

   Other than wages, Bob has costs of $100 (for parts and so on) for each bike assembled.
   a. Bikes sell for $130 each. Find the marginal product and the value of the marginal product for each worker (don't forget about Bob's cost of parts).
   b. Make a table showing Bob's demand curve for labor.
   c. Repeat part b for the case in which bikes sell for $140 each.
   d. Repeat part b for the case in which worker productivity increases by 50 percent. Bikes sell for $130 each.

3. The marginal product of a worker in a lightbulb factory equals $30 - N$ bulbs per hour, where N is the total number of workers employed. Lightbulbs sell for $2 each, and there are no costs to producing them other than labor costs.
   a. The going hourly wage for factory workers is $20 per hour. How many workers should the factory manager hire? What if the wage is $30 per hour?
   b. Graph the factory's demand for labor.
   c. Repeat part b for the case in which lightbulbs sell for $3 each.
   d. Suppose the supply of factory workers in the town in which the lightbulb factory is located is 20 workers (in other words, the labor supply curve is vertical at 20 workers). What will be the equilibrium real wage for factory workers in the town if lightbulbs sell for $2 each? If they sell for $3 each?

4. How would each of the following likely affect the real wage and employment of unskilled workers on an automobile plant assembly line?
   a. Demand for the type of car made by the plant increases.
   b. A sharp increase in the price of gas causes many commuters to switch to mass transit.
   c. Because of alternative opportunities, people become less willing to do factory work.
   d. The plant management introduces new assembly-line methods that increase the number of cars unskilled workers can produce per hour while reducing defects.
   e. Robots are introduced to do most basic assembly-line tasks.
   f. The workers unionize.

5. How would each of the following factors be likely to affect the economywide supply of labor?
   a. The mandatory retirement age is increased.
   b. Increased productivity causes real wages to rise.
   c. War preparations lead to the institution of a national draft, and many young people are called up.
   d. More people decide to have children (consider both short-run and long-run effects).
   e. Social Security benefits are made more generous.

6. Either skilled or unskilled workers can be used to produce a small toy. The marginal product of skilled workers, measured in terms of toys produced per day, equals

$200 - N^s$, where N^s is the number of skilled workers employed. Similarly, the marginal product of unskilled workers is $100 - N^u$, where N^u is the number of unskilled workers employed. The toys sell for $3 each.

a. Assume that there are 100 skilled workers and 50 unskilled workers available (and the labor supply curves for each group are vertical). In dollars, what will be the equilibrium wage for each type of worker? (*Hint:* What are the marginal products and the values of marginal product for each type of worker when all workers are employed?)

b. Electronic equipment is introduced that increases the marginal product of skilled workers (who can use the equipment) to $300 - N^s$. The marginal products of unskilled workers are unaffected. Now what are the equilibrium wages for the two groups?

c. Suppose that unskilled workers find it worthwhile to acquire skills when the wage differential between skilled and unskilled workers is $300 per day or greater. Following the introduction of the electronic equipment, how many unskilled workers will become skilled? (*Hint:* How many workers would have to shift from the unskilled to the skilled category to make the equilibrium difference in wages precisely equal to $300 per day?) What are equilibrium wages for skilled and unskilled workers after some unskilled workers acquire training?

7. An economy with no foreign trade produces sweaters and dresses. There are 14 workers in the sweater industry and 26 workers in the dress industry. The marginal product of workers in the sweater industry, measured in sweaters produced per day, is $20 - NS$, where NS is the number of workers employed in the sweater industry. The marginal product of workers in the dress industry, measured in dresses produced per day, is $30 - ND$, where ND is the number of workers employed in the dress industry.

a. Initially, sweaters sell for $40 apiece and dresses are $60 apiece. Find the equilibrium wage in each industry.

b. The economy opens up to trade. Foreign demand for domestically produced sweaters is strong, raising the price of sweaters to $50 each. But foreign competition reduces demand for domestically produced dresses so that they now sell for $50 each. Assuming that workers cannot move between industries, what are wages in each industry now? Who has been hurt and who has been helped by the opening up to trade?

c. Now suppose that workers can move freely from one industry to the other, and will always move to the industry that pays the higher wage. In the long run, how many of the 40 workers in the economy will be in each industry? What wages will they receive? In the long run, are domestic workers hurt or helped by the opening up to foreign trade? Assume that sweaters and dresses continue to sell for $50.

8. For each of the following scenarios, state whether the unemployment is frictional, structural, or cyclical. Justify your answer.

a. Ted lost his job when the steel mill closed down. He lacks the skills to work in another industry and so has been unemployed over a year.

b. Alice was laid off from her job at the auto plant because the recession reduced the demand for cars. She expects to get her job back when the economy picks up.

c. Lance is an unskilled worker who works for local moving companies during their busy seasons. The rest of the year he is unemployed.

d. Gwen had a job as a clerk but quit when her husband was transferred to another state. She looked for a month before finding a new job that she liked.

e. Tao looked for a job for six weeks after finishing college. He turned down a couple of offers because they didn't let him use the skills he had acquired in college, but now he has a job in the area that he trained for.

f. Karen, a software engineer, lost her job when the start-up company she was working for went bankrupt. She interviewed at five companies before accepting a new job in another firm in the same industry.

9. The demand for and supply of labor in a certain industry are given by the equations

$$N^d = 400 - 2w$$

$$N^s = 240 + 2w$$

where N^d is the number of workers employers want to hire, N^s is the number of people willing to work, and both labor demand and labor supply depend on the real wage w, which is measured in dollars per day.

a. Find employment and the real wage in labor market equilibrium.

b. Suppose the minimum wage is $50 per day. Find employment and unemployment. Is anyone made better off by the minimum wage? Worse off? In answering the last part of the question, consider not only workers but employers and other people in the society, such as consumers and taxpayers.

c. Repeat part b except now assume that a union contract requires that workers be paid $60 per day.

d. Repeat part b but, instead of a minimum wage, suppose there is an unemployment benefit that pays $50 per day. Workers are indifferent between earning a wage of $50 per day and remaining unemployed and collecting the benefit.

e. Repeat part b, assuming that the minimum wage is $50 per day. However, assume that the cost of complying with government regulations on workplace safety reduces labor demand to $N^d = 360 - 2w$.

10. The *Economic Report of the President* (ERP), put out annually by the President's Council of Economic Advisers, is available in the library or online (http://www.gpoaccess.gov/eop). ERP includes both useful articles on recent economic developments and a statistical section that provides historical data on many macro variables.

From the ERP or some other source, find data for the nonrecession year 2005 on the percentage of the unemployed who were out of work less than 5 weeks, between 5 and 14 weeks, and over 26 weeks. What do these data suggest about the relative importance of frictional and structural unemployment in the economy when the economy is not in recession?

Compare the data you found for the most recent year to similar data for the recession years 1981–1982, 1990–1991, and 2001. How do recessions change the proportion of unemployment that is short term and long term?

■ ANSWERS TO IN-CHAPTER EXERCISES ■

8.1 The value of the marginal product of the seventh worker is $39,000, and the value of the marginal product of the eighth worker is $33,000. So the seventh but not the eighth worker is profitable to hire at a wage of $35,000.

8.2 With the computer price at $5,000, it is profitable to hire three workers at a wage of $100,000, since the third worker's value of marginal product ($105,000) exceeds $100,000, but the fourth worker's value of marginal product ($95,000) is less than $100,000. At a computer price of $3,000, we can refer to Table 8.1 to find that not even the first worker has a value of marginal product as high as $100,000, so at that computer price, BCC will hire no workers. In short, at a wage of $100,000, the increase in the computer price raises the demand for technicians from zero to three.

8.3 The seventh but not the eighth worker's value of marginal product exceeds $50,000 (Table 8.3), so it is profitable to hire seven workers if the going wage is $50,000. From Table 8.1, before the increase in productivity, the first five workers have values of marginal product greater than $50,000, so the demand for labor at a given wage of $50,000 is five workers. Thus, the increase in productivity raises the quantity of labor demanded at a wage of $50,000 from five workers to seven workers.

8.4 Even though you are receiving no pay, the valuable experience you gain as an intern is likely to raise the pay you will be able to earn in the future, so it is an investment in human capital. You also find working in the radio station more enjoyable than working in a car wash, presumably. To decide which job to take, you should ask yourself, "Taking into account both the likely increase in my future earnings and my greater enjoyment from working in the radio station, would I be willing to pay $3,000 to work in the radio station rather than in the car wash?" If the answer is yes, then you should work in the radio station, otherwise you should go to the car wash.

A decision to work in the radio station does not contradict the idea of an upward-sloping labor supply curve, if we are willing to think of the total compensation for that job as including not just cash wages but such factors as the value of the training that you receive. Your labor supply curve is still upward-sloping in the sense that the greater the value you place on the internship experience, the more likely you are to accept the job.

8.5 Immigration to a country raises labor supply—indeed, the search for work is one of the most powerful factors drawing immigrants in the first place. As shown in the accompanying figure, an increase in labor supply will tend to lower the wages that employers have to pay (from w to w'), while raising overall employment (from N to N'). Because of its tendency to reduce real wages, labor unions generally oppose large-scale immigration, while employers support it.

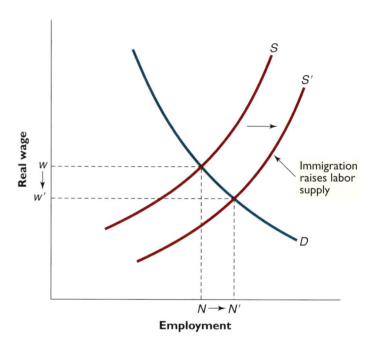

Although the figure shows the overall, or aggregate, supply of labor in the economy, the specific effects of immigration on wages depend on the skills and occupations of the immigrants. Current U.S. immigration policy makes the reunification of families the main reason for admitting immigrants, and for the most part immigrants are not screened by their education or skills. The United States also has a good deal of illegal immigration, made up largely of people looking for economic opportunity. These two factors create a tendency for new immigrants to the United States to be relatively low-skilled. Since immigration tends to increase the supply of unskilled labor by relatively more, it depresses wages of domestic low-skilled workers more than it does the wages of domestic high-skilled workers. Some economists, such as George Borjas of Harvard University, have argued that low-skilled immigration is another important factor reducing the wages of less-skilled workers relative to workers with greater skills and education. Borjas argues that the United States should adopt the approach used by Canada and give preference to potential immigrants with relatively higher levels of skills and education.

8.6 Part (a) of the accompanying figure shows the labor market in 1960–1972; part (b) shows the labor market in 1973–2000. For comparability, we set the initial labor supply (S) and demand (D) curves the same in both parts, implying the same initial values of the real wage (w) and employment (N). In part (a) we show the effects of a large increase in labor demand (from D to D'), the result of rapid productivity growth, and a relatively small increase in labor supply (from S to S'). The real wage rises to w' and employment rises to N'. In part (b) we observe the effects of a somewhat smaller increase in labor demand (from D to D'') and a larger increase in labor supply (from S to S''). Part (b), corresponding to the 1973–2000 period, shows a smaller increase in the real wage and a larger increase in employment than part (a), corresponding to 1960–1972. These results are consistent with actual developments in the U.S. labor market over these two periods.

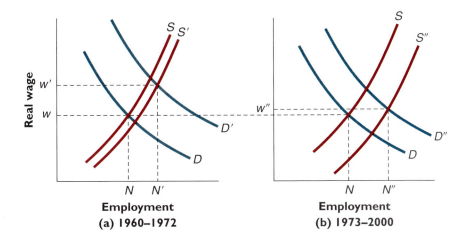

(a) 1960–1972   (b) 1973–2000

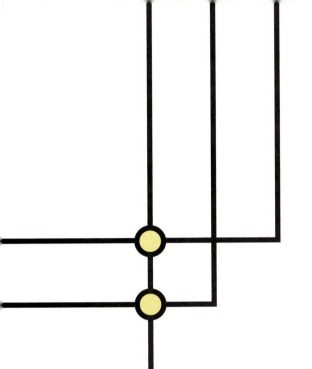

9

SAVING AND
CAPITAL FORMATION

O n your mother's or father's knee you probably heard the fable of the ant and the grasshopper. All summer the ant worked hard laying up food for the winter. The grasshopper mocked the ant's efforts and contented himself with basking in the sunshine, ignoring the ant's earnest warnings. When winter came the ant was well-fed, while the grasshopper starved. Moral: When times are good, the wise put aside something for the future.

Of course, there is also the modern ending to the fable, in which the grasshopper breaks his leg by tripping over the anthill, sues the ant for negligence, and ends up living comfortably on the ant's savings. (Nobody knows what happened to the ant.) Moral: Saving is risky; live for today.

The pitfalls of modern life notwithstanding, saving is important, both to individuals and to nations. People need to save to provide for their retirement and for other future needs, such as their children's education or a new home. An individual's or a family's savings also can provide a crucial buffer in the event of an economic emergency, such as the loss of a job or unexpected medical bills. At the national level, the production of new capital goods—factories, equipment, and housing—is an important factor promoting economic growth and higher living standards. As we will see in this chapter, the resources necessary to produce new capital come primarily from a nation's collective saving.

Because adequate saving is so important both to ensuring families' financial security and creating new capital goods, many people have expressed concern about the low saving rate of American households. Figure 9.1 shows the U.S. household saving rate (the percentage of after-tax household income that is saved) since 1960. Never very high by international standards, the U.S.

household saving rate declined sharply in the mid-1980s and fell again in the mid-1990s, reaching 1.8 percent of household disposable income in 2004.

FIGURE 9.1

Household Saving Rate in the United States, 1960–2004.

The U.S. household saving rate, declining since the mid-1980s, fell to 1.8 percent in 2004.

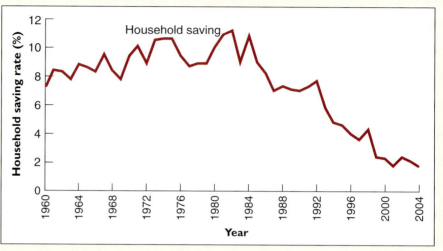

SOURCE: Bureau of Economic Analysis (http://www.bea.gov/).

What was the significance of this precipitous decline? Alarmists saw the data as evidence of "grasshopperish" behavior, and a threat to Americans' future prosperity. The reality, as we will see, is more complex. Many American families do save very little, a choice that is likely to exact a toll on their economic well-being in the long run. On the other hand, household saving is only one part of the total saving of the U.S. economy, as businesses and governments also save. In fact, the total saving of the U.S. economy, called *national saving*, has not declined significantly in recent years. Thus, if the United States is suffering a "savings shortfall," it is much less severe than might be suggested by the figures on household saving only.

In this chapter we will look at saving and its links to the formation of new capital. We begin by defining the concepts of saving and wealth and exploring the connection between them. We will consider why people choose to save, rather than spending all their income. We then turn to national saving—the collective saving of households, businesses, and government. Because national saving determines the capacity of an economy to create new capital, it is the more important measure of saving from a macroeconomic perspective.

We next discuss capital formation. Most decisions to invest in new capital are made by firms. As we will see, a firm's decision to invest is in many respects analogous to its decision about whether to increase employment; firms will choose to expand their capital when the benefits of doing so exceed the costs. We end the chapter by showing how national saving and capital formation are related, using a supply and demand approach.

SAVING AND WEALTH

saving current income minus spending on current needs

saving rate saving divided by income

In general, the **saving** of an economic unit—whether a household, a business, a university, or a nation—may be defined as its *current income* minus its *spending on current needs*. For example, if Consuelo earns $300 per week, spends $280 weekly on living expenses such as rent, food, clothes, and entertainment, and deposits the remaining $20 in the bank, her saving is $20 per week. The **saving rate** of any economic unit is its saving divided by its income. Since Consuelo saves $20 of her weekly income of $300, her saving rate is $20/$300, or 6.7 percent.

The saving of an economic unit is closely related to its **wealth,** or the value of its assets minus its liabilities. **Assets** are anything of value that one *owns*, either *financial* or *real*. Examples of financial assets that you or your family might own include cash, a checking account, stocks, and bonds. Examples of real assets include a home or other real estate, jewelry, consumer durables like cars, and valuable collectibles. **Liabilities,** on the other hand, are the debts one *owes*. Examples of liabilities are credit card balances, student loans, and mortgages.

By comparing an economic unit's assets and liabilities, economists calculate that unit's wealth, also called its *net worth*. This comparison is done using a list of assets and liabilities on a particular date, called a **balance sheet.**

Consuelo constructs her balance sheet

To take stock of her financial position on January 1, 2005, Consuelo lists her assets and liabilities on that date in a balance sheet. The result is shown in Table 9.1. What is Consuelo's wealth?

> *wealth* the value of *assets* minus *liabilities*
>
> *assets* anything of value that one *owns*
>
> *liabilities* the debts one *owes*
>
> *balance sheet* a list of an economic unit's assets and liabilities on a specific date

EXAMPLE 9.1

TABLE 9.1
Consuelo's Balance Sheet on January 1, 2005

Assets		Liabilities	
Cash	$ 80	Student loan	$3,000
Checking account	1,200	Credit card balance	250
Shares of stock	1,000		
Car (market value)	3,500		
Furniture (market value)	500		
Total	**$6,280**		**$3,250**
		Net worth	**$3,030**

Consuelo's financial assets are the cash in her wallet, the balance in her checking account, and the current value of some shares of stock her parents gave her. Together her financial assets are worth $2,280. She also lists $4,000 in real assets, the sum of the market values of her car and her furniture. Consuelo's total assets, both financial and real, come to $6,280. Her liabilities are the student loan she owes the bank and the balance due on her credit card, which total $3,250. Consuelo's wealth, or net worth, on January 1, 2005, is the value of her assets ($6,280) minus the value of her liabilities ($3,250), or $3,030.

EXERCISE 9.1

What would Consuelo's net worth be if her student loan were for $6,500 rather than $3,000? Construct a new balance sheet for her.

Saving and wealth are related, because saving contributes to wealth. To understand this relationship better, we must distinguish between *stocks* and *flows*.

STOCKS AND FLOWS

Saving is an example of a **flow,** a measure that is defined *per unit of time*. For example, Consuelo's saving is $20 *per week*. Wealth, in contrast, is a **stock,** a measure that is defined *at a point in time*. Consuelo's wealth of $3,030, for example, is her wealth on a particular date—January 1, 2005.

> *flow* a measure that is defined *per unit of time*
>
> *stock* a measure that is defined *at a point in time*

The flow of saving increases the stock of wealth in the same way that the flow of water through the faucet increases the amount of water in the tub.

To visualize the difference between stocks and flows, think of water running into a bathtub. The amount of water in the bathtub at any specific moment—for example, 40 gallons at 7:15 p.m.—is a stock, because it is measured at a specific point in time. The rate at which the water flows into the tub—for example, 2 gallons per minute—is a flow, because it is measured per unit of time. In many cases, a flow is the *rate of change* in a stock: If we know that there are 40 gallons of water in the tub at 7:15 p.m., for example, and that water is flowing in at 2 gallons per minute, we can easily determine that the stock of water will be changing at the rate of 2 gallons per minute and will equal 42 gallons at 7:16 p.m., 44 gallons at 7:17 p.m., and so on, until the bathtub overflows.

EXERCISE 9.2

Continuing the example of the bathtub: If there are 40 gallons of water in the tub at 7:15 p.m. and water is being *drained* at the rate of 3 gallons per minute, what will be the stock and flow at 7:16 p.m.? At 7:17 p.m.? Does the flow still equal the rate of change in the stock?

The relationship between saving (a flow) and wealth (a stock) is similar to the relationship between the flow of water into a bathtub and the stock of water in the tub in that the *flow* of saving causes the *stock* of wealth to change at the same rate. Indeed, as Example 9.2 illustrates, every dollar that a person saves adds a dollar to his or her wealth.

EXAMPLE 9.2

The link between saving and wealth

Consuelo saves $20 per week. How does this saving affect her wealth on January 8, 2005? Does the change in her wealth depend on whether Consuelo uses her saving to accumulate assets or to pay down her liabilities?

Consuelo could use the $20 she saved during the first week in January to increase her assets—for example, by adding the $20 to her checking account—or to reduce her liabilities—for example, by paying down her credit card balance. Suppose she adds the $20 to her checking account, increasing her assets on January 8, 2005, by $20. Since her liabilities are unchanged, her wealth also increases by $20, to $3,050 (see Table 9.1).

If Consuelo decides to use the $20 she saved during the first week in January to pay down her credit card balance, she reduces it from $250 to $230. That action would reduce her liabilities by $20, leaving her assets unchanged. Since wealth equals assets minus liabilities, reducing her liabilities by $20 increases her wealth by $20, to $3,050. Thus, saving $20 per week raises Consuelo's stock of wealth on January 8, 2005, by $20, regardless of whether she uses her saving to increase her assets or reduce her liabilities.

The close relationship between saving and wealth explains why saving is so important to an economy. Higher rates of saving today lead to faster accumulation of wealth, and the wealthier a nation is, the higher its standard of living. Thus, a high rate of saving today contributes to an improved standard of living in the future.

CAPITAL GAINS AND LOSSES

Though saving increases wealth, it is not the only factor that determines wealth. Wealth also can change because of changes in the values of the real or financial assets one owns. Suppose Consuelo's shares of stock rise in value during January, from $1,000 to $1,500. This increase in the value of Consuelo's stock raises her total assets by $500 without affecting her liabilities. As a result, Consuelo's wealth on February 1, 2005, rises by $500, from $3,030 to $3,530 (see Table 9.2).

TABLE 9.2
Consuelo's Balance Sheet on February 1, 2005, after an Increase in the Value of Her Stocks

Assets		Liabilities	
Cash	$ 80	Student loan	$3,000
Checking account	1,200	Credit card balance	250
Shares of stock	1,500		
Car (market value)	3,500		
Furniture (market value)	500		
Total	**$6,780**		**$3,250**
		Net worth	**$3,530**

Changes in the value of existing assets are called **capital gains** when an asset's value increases and **capital losses** when an asset's value decreases. Just as capital gains increase wealth, capital losses decrease wealth. Capital gains and losses are not counted as part of saving, however. Instead, the change in a person's wealth during any period equals the saving done during the period plus capital gains or minus capital losses during that period. In terms of an equation,

capital gains increases in the value of existing assets

capital losses decreases in the values of existing assets

$$\text{Change in wealth} = \text{Saving} + \text{Capital gains} - \text{Capital losses}.$$

EXERCISE 9.3

How would each of the following actions or events affect Consuelo's *saving* and her *wealth*?

a. Consuelo deposits $20 in the bank at the end of the week as usual. She also charges $50 on her credit card, raising her credit card balance to $300.

b. Consuelo uses $300 from her checking account to pay off her credit card bill.

c. Consuelo's old car is recognized as a classic. Its market value rises from $3,500 to $4,000.

d. Consuelo's furniture is damaged and as a result falls in value from $500 to $200.

Capital gains and losses can have a major effect on one's overall wealth, as Economic Naturalist 9.1 illustrates.

The bull market and household wealth

On the whole, Americans felt very prosperous during the 1990s: Measures of household wealth during this period showed enormous gains. Yet, as Figure 9.1 shows, saving by U.S. households was quite low throughout those years. How did American households increase their wealth in the 1990s while saving very little?

During the 1990s an increasing number of Americans acquired stocks, either directly through purchases or indirectly through their pension and retirement funds. At the same time, stock prices rose at record rates (see Figure 9.2). The strongly rising "bull market," which increased the prices of most stocks, enabled many

ECONOMIC NATURALIST 9.1

Americans to enjoy significant capital gains and increased wealth without saving much, if anything. Indeed, some economists argued that the low household saving rate of the 1990s is partially *explained* by the bull market; because capital gains increased household wealth by so much, many people saw no need to save.

The stock market peaked in early 2000 and stock prices fell quite sharply over the following two years. It is interesting that U.S. households did not choose to save more in 2000 and in subsequent years (Figure 9.1), despite the decline in their stock market wealth. One explanation is that an even larger component of household wealth—the value of privately owned homes—rose significantly in 2000–2004, partly offsetting the effect of the decline in stock values on household wealth.

FIGURE 9.2

The Bull Market of the 1990s.

Stock prices rose sharply during the 1990s, greatly increasing the wealth of households that held stocks. This figure shows the Standard & Poor's 500 index of stock prices, divided by the CPI to correct for inflation, for the period 1960–2004. Stock prices peaked in 2000, and then fell sharply until reaching a trough in early 2003.

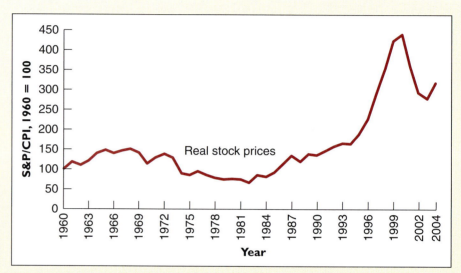

SOURCE: Economic Report of the President (http://www.gpoaccess.gov/eop/).

We have seen how saving is related to the accumulation of wealth. To understand why people choose to save, however, we need to examine their motives for saving.

RECAP	SAVING AND WEALTH

In general, *saving* is current income minus spending on current needs. *Wealth* is the value of assets—anything of value that one owns—minus liabilities—the debts one owes. Saving is measured per unit of time (for example, dollars per week) and thus is a *flow*. Wealth is measured at a point in time and thus is a *stock*. In the same way the flow of water through the faucet increases the stock of water in a bathtub, the flow of saving increases the stock of wealth.

Wealth also can be increased by *capital gains* (increases in the value of existing assets) or reduced by *capital losses* (decreases in asset values). The capital gains afforded stockholders by the bull market of the 1990s allowed many families to increase their wealth significantly while doing very little saving.

WHY DO PEOPLE SAVE?

Why do people save part of their income instead of spending everything they earn? Economists have identified at least three broad reasons for saving. First, people save to meet certain long-term objectives, such as a comfortable retirement. By putting away part of their income during their working years, they can live better after retirement than they would if they had to rely solely on Social Security and their company pensions. Other long-term objectives might include college tuition for one's children and the purchase of a new home or car. Since many of these needs occur at fairly predictable stages in one's life, economists call this type of saving **life-cycle saving.**

A second reason to save is to protect oneself and family against unexpected setbacks—the loss of a job, for example, or a costly health problem. Personal financial advisors typically suggest that families maintain an emergency reserve (a "rainy-day fund") equal to three to six months' worth of income. Saving for protection against potential emergencies is called **precautionary saving.**

life-cycle saving saving to meet long-term objectives, such as retirement, college attendance, or the purchase of a home

precautionary saving saving for protection against unexpected setbacks, such as the loss of a job or a medical emergency

"Fortunately, you have the life savings of a man three times your age."

A third reason to save is to accumulate an estate to leave to one's heirs, usually one's children but possibly a favorite charity or other worthy cause. Saving for the purpose of leaving an inheritance, or bequest, is called **bequest saving.** Bequest saving is done primarily by people at the higher end of the income ladder. But because these people control a large share of the nation's wealth, bequest saving is an important part of overall saving.

bequest saving saving done for the purpose of leaving an inheritance

To be sure, people usually do not mentally separate their saving into these three categories; rather, all three reasons for saving motivate most savers to varying degrees. The Economic Naturalist 9.2 shows how the three reasons for saving can explain household saving behavior in Japan.

Household saving in Japan

After World War II Japanese households increased their saving rates to 15–25 percent of their income, an unusually high rate. Although cultural factors often were cited as a reason for the high Japanese propensity to save, saving rates in Japan were much lower before World War II. Moreover, household saving rates in Japan have declined since 1990 (although they remain higher than those in the United States). Why did the Japanese save so much until about 1990, and why have Japanese saving rates declined somewhat since then?

ECONOMIC NATURALIST 9.2

Among the reasons for saving we discussed, *life-cycle* reasons are probably the most important determinants of saving in Japan. The Japanese have long life expectancies, and many retire relatively early. With a long period of retirement to finance, Japanese families must save a great deal during their working years. When the working age population was a high percentage of the total population, the overall saving rate was high. As the baby boom generation reached the age of retirement and the Japanese fertility rate declined, so too has the Japanese saving rate declined.[1]

Other factors also help to explain the changes in Japanese saving rates. Down payment requirements on houses are high in Japan compared to other countries. Before 1990, land and housing prices in Japan were extremely high, so that young people had to save a great deal or borrow their parents' savings to buy their first homes. After the Japanese real estate market crashed at the beginning of the 1990s, however, land and housing prices fell so young people do not need to save as much as before.

Studies also have found that *bequest saving* is important in Japan. Many older people live with their children after retirement. In return for support and attention during their later years, parents feel they must provide substantial inheritances for their children.

Precautionary saving is probably lower in Japan than in some other countries, however. Although Japan's recent economic troubles have reduced the practice of *lifetime employment*, Japanese firms still make extensive use of the system, which essentially guarantees a job for life to workers who join a firm after graduating from college. This type of job security, coupled with Japan's traditionally low unemployment rate, reduces the need for precautionary saving.

Although most people are usually motivated to save for at least one of the three reasons we have discussed, the amount they choose to save may depend on the economic environment. One economic variable that is quite significant in saving decisions is the real interest rate.

SAVING AND THE REAL INTEREST RATE

Most people don't save by putting cash in a mattress. Instead, they make financial investments that they hope will provide a good return on their saving. For example, a checking account may pay interest on the account balance. More sophisticated financial investments, such as government bonds or shares of stock in a corporation (see the chapter "Financial Markets and International Capital Flows"), also pay returns in the form of interest payments, dividends, or capital gains. High returns are desirable, of course, because the higher the return, the faster one's savings will grow.

The rate of return that is most relevant to saving decisions is the *real interest rate*, denoted r. Recall from the chapter "Measuring the Price Level and Inflation" that the real interest rate is the rate at which the real purchasing power of a financial asset increases over time. The real interest rate equals the market, or nominal, interest rate (i) minus the inflation rate (π).

The real interest rate is relevant to savers because it is the "reward" for saving. Suppose you are thinking of increasing your saving by $1,000 this year, which you can do if you give up your habit of eating out once a week. If the real interest rate is 5 percent, then in a year your extra saving will give you extra purchasing power of $1,050, measured in today's dollars. But if the real interest rate were 10 percent, your sacrifice of $1,000 this year would be rewarded by $1,100 in purchasing power next year. Obviously, all else being equal, you would be more willing to save today if you knew the reward next year would be greater. In either case the *cost* of the extra saving—giving up your weekly night out—is the same. But the *benefit* of the extra saving, in terms of increased purchasing power next year, is higher if the real interest rate is 10 percent rather than 5 percent.

[1]Maiko Koga, "The Decline of the Saving Rate and the Demographic Effects," Bank of Japan Research and Statistics Department, November 2004.

EXAMPLE 9.3

By how much does a high savings rate enhance a family's future living standard?

The Spends and the Thrifts are similar families, except that the Spends save 5 percent of their income each year and the Thrifts save 20 percent. The two families began to save in 1980 and plan to continue to save until their respective breadwinners retire in the year 2015. Both families earn $40,000 a year in real terms in the labor market, and both put their savings in a mutual fund that has yielded a real return of 8 percent per year, a return they expect to continue into the future. Compare the amount that the two families consume in each year from 1980 to 2015, and compare the families' wealth at retirement.

In the first year, 1980, the Spends saved $2,000 (5 percent of their $40,000 income) and consumed $38,000 (95 percent of $40,000). The Thrifts saved $8,000 in 1980 (20 percent of $40,000) and hence consumed only $32,000 in that year, $6,000 less than the Spends. In 1981, the Thrifts' income was $40,640, the extra $640 representing the 8 percent return on their $8,000 savings. The Spends saw their income grow by only $160 (8 percent of their savings of $2,000) in 1981. With an income of $40,640, the Thrifts consumed $32,512 in 1981 (80 percent of $40,640) compared to $38,152 (95 percent of $40,160) for the Spends. The consumption gap between the two families, which started out at $6,000, thus fell to $5,640 after one year.

Because of the more rapid increase in the Thrifts' wealth and hence interest income, each year the Thrifts' income grew faster than the Spends'; each year the Thrifts continued to save 20 percent of their higher incomes compared to only 5 percent for the Spends. Figure 9.3 shows the paths followed by the consumption spending of the two families. You can see that the Thrifts' consumption, though starting at a lower level, grows relatively more quickly. By 1995 the Thrifts had overtaken the Spends, and from that point onward, the amount by which the Thrifts outspent the Spends grew with each passing year. Even though the Spends continued to consume 95 percent of their income each year, their income grew so slowly that by 2000, they were consuming nearly $3,000 a year less than the Thrifts ($41,158 a year versus $43,957). And by the time the two families retire, in 2015, the Thrifts will be consuming more than $12,000 per year more than the Spends ($55,774 versus $43,698). Even more striking is the difference between the retirement nest eggs of the two families. Whereas the Spends will enter retirement with total accumulated savings of just over $77,000, the Thrifts will have more than $385,000, five times as much.

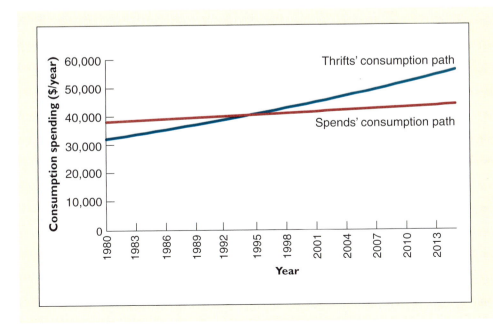

FIGURE 9.3
Consumption Trajectories of the Thrifts and the Spends.
The figure shows consumption spending in each year by two families, the Thrifts and the Spends. Because the Thrifts save more than the Spends, their annual consumption spending rises relatively more quickly. By the time of retirement in the year 2015, the Thrifts are both consuming significantly more each year than the Spends and also have a retirement nest egg that is five times larger.

These dramatic differences depend in part on the assumption that the real rate of return is 8 percent—lower than the actual return to mutual funds since 1980 but still a relatively high rate of return from a historical perspective. On the other hand, the Spend family in our example actually saves more than typical U.S. households, many of which carry $5,000 or more in credit card debt at high rates of interest and have no significant savings at all. The point of the example, which remains valid under alternative assumptions about the real interest rate and saving rates, is that, because of the power of compound interest, a high rate of saving pays off handsomely in the long run.

"Someday, son, all this will be mine."

While a higher real interest rate increases the reward for saving, which tends to strengthen people's willingness to save, another force counteracts that extra incentive. Recall that a major reason for saving is to attain specific goals: a comfortable retirement, a college education, or a first home. If the goal is a specific amount—say, $25,000 for a down payment on a home—then a higher rate of return means that households can save *less* and still reach their goal, because funds that are put aside will grow more quickly. For example, to accumulate $25,000 at the end of five years, at a 5 percent interest rate a person would have to save about $4,309 per year. At a 10 percent interest rate, reaching the $25,000 goal would require saving only about $3,723 per year. To the extent that people are *target savers* who save to reach a specific goal, higher interest rates actually decrease the amount they need to save.

In sum, a higher real interest rate has both positive and negative effects on saving—a positive effect because it increases the reward for saving and a negative effect because it reduces the amount people need to save each year to reach a given target. Empirical evidence suggests that, in practice, higher real interest rates lead to modest increases in saving.

SAVING, SELF-CONTROL, AND DEMONSTRATION EFFECTS

The reasons for saving we just discussed are based on the notion that people are rational decision makers who will choose their saving rates to maximize their welfare over the long run. Yet many psychologists, and some economists, have argued instead that people's saving behavior is based as much on psychological as on economic factors. For example, psychologists stress that many people lack the *self-control* to do what they know is in their own best interest. People smoke or eat greasy food, despite the known long-term health risks. Similarly, they may have good intentions about saving but lack the self-control to put aside as much as they ought to each month.

One way to strengthen self-control is to remove temptations from the immediate environment. A person who is trying to quit smoking will make a point of not having cigarettes in the house, and a person with a weight problem will avoid going to a bakery. Similarly, a person who is not saving enough might arrange to use a payroll savings plan, through which a predetermined amount is deducted from each paycheck and set aside in a special account from which withdrawals are not permitted until retirement. Making saving automatic and withdrawals difficult eliminates the temptation to spend all of current earnings or squander accumulated savings. Payroll savings plans have helped many people to increase the amount that they save for retirement or other purposes.

An implication of the self-control hypothesis is that consumer credit arrangements that make borrowing and spending easier may reduce the amount that people save. For example, in recent years banks have encouraged people to borrow against the *equity* in their homes, that is, the value of the home less the value of the outstanding mortgage. Such financial innovations, by increasing the temptation to spend, may have reduced the household saving rate. The increased availability of credit cards with high borrowing limits is another temptation.

Downward pressure on the saving rate also may occur when additional spending by some consumers stimulates additional spending by others. Such *demonstration effects* arise when people use the spending of others as a yardstick by which to measure the adequacy of their own living standards. For example, a family in an upper-middle-class American suburb in which the average house has 3,000 square feet of living space might regard a 1,500-square-foot house as being uncomfortably small—too cramped, for example, to entertain friends in the manner to which community members have become accustomed. In contrast, a similar family living in a low-income neighborhood might find the very same house luxuriously large.

The implication of demonstration effects for saving is that families who live among others who consume more than they do may be strongly motivated to increase their own consumption spending. When satisfaction depends in part on *relative* living standards, an upward spiral may result in which household spending is higher, and saving lower, than would be best for either the individual families involved or for the economy as a whole.

Why do U.S. households save so little?

Household saving in the United States, which has always been comparatively low, has fallen even further in the past decade (Figure 9.1). Surveys show that a significant fraction of American households live from paycheck to paycheck with very little saving. Why do U.S. households save so little?

ECONOMIC NATURALIST 9.3

Economists do not agree on the reasons for low household saving in the United States, although many hypotheses have been suggested.

One possible reason for low saving is the availability of generous government assistance to the elderly. From a *life-cycle* perspective, an important motivation for saving is to provide for retirement. In general, the U.S. government provides a less comprehensive "social safety net" than other industrialized countries; that is, it offers relatively fewer programs to assist people in need. To the extent that the U.S. government does provide income support, however, it is heavily concentrated on the older segment of the population. Together the Social Security and Medicare programs, both of which are designed primarily to assist retired people, constitute a major share of the federal government's expenditures. These programs have been very successful; indeed they have virtually wiped out poverty among the elderly. To the extent that Americans believe that the government will ensure them an adequate living standard in retirement, however, their incentive to save for the future is reduced.

Another important life-cycle objective is buying a home. We have seen that the Japanese must save a great deal to purchase a home because of high house prices and down payment requirements. The same is true in many other countries. But in the United States, with its highly developed financial system, people can buy homes with down payments of 10 percent or less of the purchase price. The ready availability of mortgages with low or even no down payments reduces the need to save for the purchase of a home.

What about *precautionary saving*? Unlike Japan and Europe, which had to rebuild after World War II, the United States has not known sustained economic hardship since the Great Depression of the 1930s (which fewer and fewer Americans are alive to remember). Perhaps the nation's prosperous past has led Americans to be more confident about the future and hence less inclined to save for economic emergencies than other people, even though the United States does not offer the level of employment security found in Japan or in Europe.

U.S. household saving is not only low by international standards, it has been declining. The good performance of the stock market in the 1990s along with continuing increases in the prices of family homes probably help to explain this savings decline (see Economic Naturalist 9.1). As long as Americans enjoy capital gains, they see their wealth increase almost without effort, and their incentive to save is reduced.

Psychological factors also may explain Americans' saving behavior. For example, unlike in most countries, U.S. homeowners can easily borrow against their home equity. This ability, made possible by the highly developed U.S. financial markets, may exacerbate *self-control* problems by increasing the temptation to spend. Finally, *demonstration effects* may have depressed saving in recent decades. The last chapter discussed the phenomenon of increasing wage inequality, which has improved the relative position of more skilled and educated workers. Increased spending by households at the top of the earnings scale on houses, cars, and other consumption goods may have led those just below them to spend more as well, and so on. Middle-class families that were once content with medium-priced cars may now feel they need Volvos and BMWs to keep up with community standards. To the extent that demonstration effects lead families to spend beyond their means, they reduce their saving rate.

RECAP	**WHY DO PEOPLE SAVE?**

Motivations for saving include saving to meet long-term objectives such as retirement (*life-cycle saving*), saving for emergencies (*precautionary saving*), and saving to leave an inheritance or bequest (*bequest saving*). The amount that people save also depends on macroeconomic factors, such as the real interest rate. A higher real interest rate stimulates saving by increasing the reward for saving, but it also can depress saving by making it easier for savers to reach a specific savings target. On net, a higher real interest rate appears to lead to modest increases in saving.

Psychological factors also may affect saving rates. If people have *self-control* problems, then financial arrangements (such as automatic payroll deductions) that make it more difficult to spend will increase their saving. People's saving decisions also may be influenced by *demonstration effects,* as when people feel compelled to spend at the same rate as their neighbors, even though they may not be able to afford to do so.

NATIONAL SAVING AND ITS COMPONENTS

Thus far we have been examining the concepts of saving and wealth from the individual's perspective. But macroeconomists are interested primarily in saving and wealth for the country as a whole. In this section we will study *national saving,* or the aggregate saving of the economy. National saving includes the saving of business firms and the government as well as that of households. Later in the chapter we will examine the close link between national saving and the rate of capital formation in an economy.

THE MEASUREMENT OF NATIONAL SAVING

To define the saving rate of a country as a whole, we will start with a basic accounting identity that was introduced in the chapter "Measuring Economic Activity." According to this identity, for the economy as a whole, production (or income) must equal total expenditure. In symbols, the identity is

$$Y = C + I + G + NX,$$

where Y stands for either production or aggregate income (which must be equal), C equals consumption expenditure, I equals investment spending, G equals government purchases of goods and services, and NX equals net exports.

For now, let's assume that net exports (NX) are equal to zero, which would be the case if a country did not trade at all with other countries or if its exports and imports were always balanced. (We also discuss the foreign sector in the chapter "International Trade.") With net exports set at zero, the condition that output equals expenditure becomes

$$Y = C + I + G.$$

To determine how much saving is done by the nation as a whole, we can apply the general definition of saving. As for any other economic unit, a nation's saving equals its *current income* less its *spending on current needs*. The current income of the country as a whole is its GDP, or Y, that is, the value of the final goods and services produced within the country's borders during the year.

Identifying the part of total expenditure that corresponds to the nation's spending on current needs is more difficult than identifying the nation's income. The component of aggregate spending that is easiest to classify is investment spending I. We know that investment spending—the acquisition of new factories, equipment, and other capital goods, as well as residential construction—is done to expand the economy's future productive capacity or provide more housing for the future, not to satisfy current needs. So investment spending clearly is *not* part of spending on current needs.

Deciding how much of consumption spending by households, C, and government purchases of goods and services, G, should be counted as spending on current needs is less straightforward. Certainly most consumption spending by households—on food, clothing, utilities, entertainment, and so on—is for current needs. But consumption spending also includes purchases of long-lived *consumer durables*, such as cars, furniture, and appliances. Consumer durables are only partially used up during the current year; they may continue to provide service, in fact, for years after their purchase. So household spending on consumer durables is a combination of spending on current needs and spending on future needs.

As with consumption spending, most government purchases of goods and services are intended to provide for current needs. However, like household purchases, a portion of government purchases is devoted to the acquisition or construction of long-lived capital goods, such as roads, bridges, schools, government buildings, and military hardware. And like consumer durables, these forms of *public capital* are only partially used up during the current year; most will provide useful services far into the future. So, like consumption spending, government purchases are in fact a mixture of spending on current needs and spending on future needs.

In its official data, the government has begun to distinguish investment in public capital from the rest of government purchases. Nevertheless, this is a relatively small portion of the total, and determining precisely how much of spending is for current needs and how much is for future needs is extremely difficult. For simplicity's sake, in this book we will follow the traditional practice of treating *all* of both consumption expenditures (C) and government purchases (G) as spending on current needs. But keep in mind that because consumption spending and government purchases do in fact include some spending for future rather than current needs, treating all of C and G as spending on current needs will understate the true amount of national saving.

If we treat all consumption spending and government purchases as spending on current needs, then the nation's saving is its income Y less its spending on current needs, $C + G$. So we can define **national saving** S as

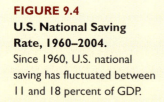
national saving the saving of the entire economy, equal to GDP less consumption expenditures and government purchases of goods and services, or $Y - C - G$

$$S = Y - C - G. \tag{9.1}$$

Figure 9.4 shows the U.S. national saving rate (national saving as a percentage of GDP) for the years 1960 through 2004. Since 1960 the U.S. national saving rate has fluctuated between 11 and 18 percent. Like household saving, national saving declined somewhat over time, though by comparing Figures 9.4 and 9.1 you can see that the decline in national saving has been far more modest. Furthermore, unlike household saving, national saving recovered in the latter 1990s. As we will see next, the reason for these differences between the behavior of national saving and household saving is that saving done by business firms and, for a while, by the government has been substantial.

FIGURE 9.4

U.S. National Saving Rate, 1960–2004.
Since 1960, U.S. national saving has fluctuated between 11 and 18 percent of GDP.

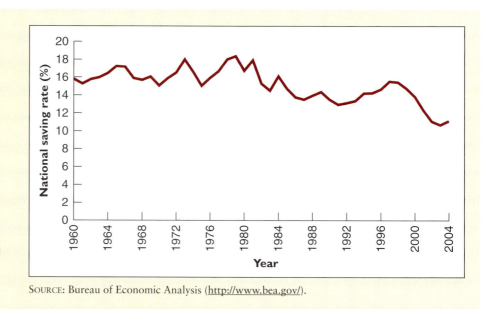

SOURCE: Bureau of Economic Analysis (http://www.bea.gov/).

PRIVATE AND PUBLIC COMPONENTS OF NATIONAL SAVING

To understand national saving better, let's examine its two major components: private saving and public saving. Private saving is the amount households and businesses save from private-sector income. Public saving is the amount governments save from public-sector income. Although the private sector's total income from the production of goods and services is Y, it must pay taxes from this income and it collects additional amounts from the government in the form of *transfer payments* and *interest* paid to individuals and institutions who hold government bonds. **Transfer payments** are payments the government makes to the public for which it receives no

transfer payments payments the government makes to the public for which it receives no current goods or services in return

current goods or services in return. Social Security benefits, welfare payments, farm support payments, and pensions to government workers are transfer payments.

Subtracting transfers and government interest payments from total taxes yields the net amount paid by the private sector to the government—the amount it pays to the government minus the amount it receives from the government. We call this amount *net taxes*, which we label T:

$$T = \text{Total taxes} - \text{Transfer payments} - \text{Government interest payments}.$$

Private saving is the amount of the private sector's after-tax income that is not spent on current consumption expenditures. Private saving $S_{private}$ is therefore equal to total private income from the production of goods and services minus net taxes minus consumption, or

$$S_{private} = Y - T - C.$$

private saving the saving of the private sector of the economy is equal to the after-tax income of the private sector minus consumption expenditures $(Y - T - C)$; private saving can be further broken down into household saving and business saving

Private saving can be further broken down into saving done by households and business firms. *Household saving*, also called *personal saving*, is saving done by families and individuals. Household saving corresponds to the familiar image of families putting aside part of their incomes each month, and it is the focus of much attention in the news media. But businesses are important savers as well—indeed business saving makes up the bulk of private saving in the United States. Businesses use the revenues from their sales to pay workers' salaries and other operating costs, to pay taxes, and to provide dividends to their shareholders. The funds remaining after these payments have been made are equal to *business saving*. A business firm's savings are available for the purchase of new capital equipment or the expansion of its operations. Alternatively, a business can put its savings in the bank for future use.

Public saving is the amount of the public sector's income that is not spent on current needs. The public sector includes state and local governments as well as the federal government. Public sector income is merely net taxes T. Government spending on current needs is equal to government purchases G (remember that, for the sake of simplicity, we are ignoring the investment portion of government purchases). Thus, we calculate public saving S_{public} as

$$S_{public} = T - G.$$

public saving the saving of the government sector is equal to net tax payments minus government purchases $(T - G)$

If we add public and private saving together, we can derive the expression for total national saving that appears in Equation 9.1 in another way:

$$S_{private} + S_{public} = (Y - T - C) + (T - G) = Y - C - G = S \qquad (9.2)$$

This equation confirms that national saving S is the sum of private saving and public saving. Since private saving can be broken down in turn into household and business saving, we see that national saving is made up of the saving of three groups: households, businesses, and the government.

PUBLIC SAVING AND THE GOVERNMENT BUDGET

Although the idea that households and businesses can save is familiar to most people, the fact that the government also can save is less widely understood. Public saving is closely linked to the government's decisions about spending and taxing. Governments finance the bulk of their spending by taxing the private sector. If taxes and spending in a given year are equal, the government is said to have a *balanced budget*. If in any given year the amount that the government collects in taxes is greater than the amount it spends, the difference is called the **government budget surplus**. When a government has a surplus, it uses the extra funds to pay down its

government budget surplus the excess of government tax collections over government spending $(T - G)$; the government budget surplus equals public saving

outstanding debt to the public. Algebraically, the government budget surplus may be written as $T - G$, or net tax collections minus government purchases.

If the algebraic expression for the government budget surplus, $T - G$, looks familiar, that is because it is also the definition of public saving. Thus, *public saving is identical to the government budget surplus*. In other words, when the government collects more in taxes than it spends, public saving will be positive. In the year 2000, for example, the federal government had the largest budget surplus in history. Example 9.4 illustrates the relationships among public saving, the government budget surplus, and national saving in that year.

EXAMPLE 9.4

Government saving

Following are data on U.S. government revenues and expenditures for 2000, in billions of dollars. Calculate (a) the federal government's budget surplus, (b) the budget surplus or deficit of state and local governments, and (c) the contribution of the government sector to national saving.

Federal government:	
Receipts	2,053.8
Expenditures	1,864.4
State and local governments:	
Receipts	1,319.5
Expenditures	1,269.5

SOURCE: Economic Report of the President (http://www.gpoaccess.gov/eop/).

The federal government's receipts minus its expenditures were 2,053.8 − 1,864.4 = 189.4, so the federal government ran a budget surplus of $189.4 billion in 2000. State and local government receipts minus expenditures were 1,319.5 − 1,269.5 = 50.0, so state and local governments ran a collective budget surplus of $50.0 billion. The budget surplus of the entire government sector—that is, the federal surplus plus the state and local surplus—was 189.4 + 50.0 = 239.4, or $239.4 billion. So the contribution of the government sector to U.S. national saving in 2000 was $239.4 billion.

government budget deficit the excess of government spending over tax collections ($G - T$)

If, on the other hand, the government spends more than it collects in taxes, public saving will be negative. In this circumstance, we speak about the **government budget deficit,** which is the amount by which spending exceeds taxes and is calculated by $G - T$.[2] If the government runs a deficit, it must make up the difference by borrowing from the public by issuing new government bonds.

Although the government had a budget surplus of $239.4 billion in the year 2000, it subsequently ran budget deficits. By the year 2004, the budget deficit had grown to $412.3 billion. The box below provides more details.

Federal government:	
Receipts	1,974.8
Expenditures	2,381.3
State and local governments:	
Receipts	1,581.7
Expenditures	1,587.5

SOURCE: Bureau of Economic Analysis (http://www.bea.gov).

[2]Note that a budget deficit of $100 billion is the same as a budget surplus of −$100 billion.

The federal government's receipts minus expenditures were 1,974.8 − 2,381.3 = −406.5 in 2004. Since expenditures were greater than receipts, the federal government ran a budget deficit of $406.5 billion. State and local government receipts minus expenditures were 1,581.7 − 1,587.5 = −5.8, so state and local governments ran a collective budget deficit of $5.8 billion. The entire government sector ran a deficit of $406.5 billion + $5.8 billion = $412.3 billion. The government sector's contribution to national saving therefore, was negative and equal to −$412.3 billion.

There were three main reasons for this dramatic turnaround in the government budget. First, government receipts fell because of the recession that began in 2001. During a recession incomes fall. Since many taxes are based on income, during a recession tax receipts also fall or rise more slowly than expected. The second reason was the reduction in tax rates enacted by President Bush and Congress during the president's first term. Finally, government expenditures rose dramatically between 2000 and 2004, in large part as a result of the wars in Iraq and Afghanistan and expenditures by the Department of Homeland Security in response to the terrorist attack on September 11, 2001.[3]

Figure 9.4 showed the U.S. national saving rate since 1960. Figure 9.5 shows the behavior since 1960 of the three components of national saving: household saving, business saving, and public saving, each measured as a percentage of GDP. Note that business saving played a major role in national saving during these years, while the role of household saving was relatively modest. As we saw in Figure 9.1, household saving has been declining since the mid-1980s.

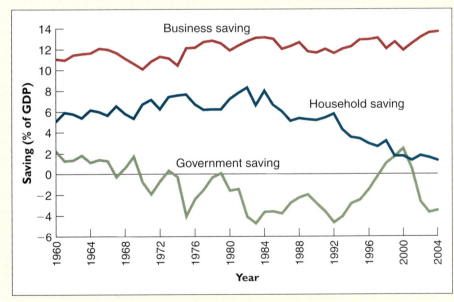

SOURCE: Bureau of Economic Analysis (http://www.bea.gov/).

FIGURE 9.5

The Three Components of National Saving, 1960–2004.

Of the three components of national saving, business saving is the most important. Household saving has declined since the mid-1980s. Government saving has generally been negative, except in the 1960s and for a brief period in the late 1990s.

The contribution of public saving has varied considerably over time. Until about 1970, the federal, state, and local governments typically ran a combined surplus, making a positive contribution to national saving. But by the late 1970s, public saving had turned negative, reflecting large budget deficits, particularly at the federal level. For the next two decades, the government was a net drain on national saving except for a brief period in the late 1990s.

[3]William G. Gale and Peter R. Orszag, "Bush Administration Tax Policy: Revenue and Budget Effects," *Tax Notes*, October 4, 2004, pp. 105–118.

IS LOW HOUSEHOLD SAVING A PROBLEM?

Figure 9.1 showed that saving by U.S. households, never high by international standards, fell substantially during the 1990s. This decline in the household saving rate received much attention from the news media. Is the United States' low household saving rate as much of a problem as the press suggests?

From a macroeconomic perspective, the problem posed by low household saving has probably been overstated. The key fact often overlooked in media reports is that national saving, not household saving, determines the capacity of an economy to invest in new capital goods and to achieve continued improvement in living standards. Although household saving is low, saving by business firms has been significant. Furthermore, during the 1990s, public saving increased as federal government budgets moved from deficit toward surplus. Until 2002 U.S. national saving had been reasonably stable, despite the sharp decline in the household saving rate shown in Figure 9.1. Indeed, although the U.S. national saving rate has typically been low compared to those of other industrialized countries, it had been sufficient to allow the United States to become one of the world's most productive economies. Since 2002, however, large federal budget deficits (implying negative public saving) have contributed to a decline in the U.S. national saving rate.

From a microeconomic perspective, the low household saving rate does signal a problem, which is the large and growing inequality in wealth among U.S. households. Saving patterns tend to increase this inequality, since the economically better-off households tend not only to save more but, as business owners or shareholders, are also the ultimate beneficiaries of the saving done by businesses. In contrast, lower-income families, many of whom save very little and do not own a business or shares in a corporation, have accumulated very little wealth—in many cases, their life savings are less than $5,000. These households have little protection against setbacks such as chronic illness or job loss and must rely almost entirely on government support programs such as Social Security to fund their retirement. For this group, the low household saving rate is definitely a concern.

This inequality has been exacerbated by the run-up in home prices in the early part of this decade. Many middle- and upper-income households who do not save a large portion of their income have nevertheless accumulated considerable wealth as the values of their homes have risen. When they sell their homes to move to smaller houses or apartments after they retire, they will be able to realize a substantial capital gain (provided housing prices do not fall) that will help finance their retirement. Lower-income people who do not own their own homes will not enjoy this advantage.

RECAP	**NATIONAL SAVING AND ITS COMPONENTS**

- *National saving,* the saving of the nation as a whole, is defined by $S = Y - C - G$, where Y is GDP, C is consumption spending, and G is government purchases of goods and services. National saving is the sum of public saving and private saving: $S = S_{private} + S_{public}$.

- *Private saving,* the saving of the private sector, is defined by $S_{private} = Y - T - C$, where T is net tax payments. Private saving can be broken down further into household saving and business saving.

- *Public saving,* the saving of the government, is defined by $S_{public} = T - G$. Public saving equals the government budget surplus, $T - G$. When the government budget is in surplus, government saving is positive; when the government budget is in deficit, public saving is negative.

INVESTMENT AND CAPITAL FORMATION

From the point of view of the economy as a whole, the importance of national saving is that it provides the funds needed for investment. Investment—the creation of new capital goods and housing—is critical to increasing average labor productivity and improving standards of living.

What factors determine whether and how much firms choose to invest? Firms acquire new capital goods for the same reason they hire new workers: They expect that doing so will be profitable. We saw in the last chapter that the profitability of employing an extra worker depends primarily on two factors: the cost of employing the worker and the value of the worker's marginal product. In the same way, firms' willingness to acquire new factories and machines depends on the expected *cost* of using them and the expected *benefit*, equal to the value of the marginal product that they will provide.

Should Larry buy a riding lawn mower?

EXAMPLE 9.5

Larry is thinking of going into the lawn care business. He can buy a $4,000 riding mower by taking out a loan at 6 percent annual interest. With this mower and his own labor, Larry can net $6,000 per summer, after deduction of costs such as gasoline and maintenance. Of the $6,000 net revenues, 20 percent must be paid to the government in taxes. Assume that Larry could earn $4,400 after taxes by working in an alternative job. Assume also that the lawn mower can always be resold for its original purchase price of $4,000. Should Larry buy the lawn mower?

To decide whether to invest in the capital good (the lawn mower), Larry should compare the financial benefits and costs. With the mower he can earn revenue of $6,000, net of gasoline and maintenance costs. However, 20 percent of that, or $1,200, must be paid in taxes, leaving Larry with $4,800. Larry could earn $4,400 after taxes by working at an alternative job, so the financial benefit to Larry of buying the mower is the difference between $4,800 and $4,400, or $400; $400 is the value of the marginal product of the lawn mower.

Since the mower does not lose value over time and since gasoline and maintenance costs have already been deducted, the only remaining cost Larry should take into account is the interest on the loan for the mower. Larry must pay 6 percent interest on $4,000, or $240 per year. Since this financial cost is less than the financial benefit of $400, the value of the mower's marginal product, Larry should buy the mower.

Larry's decision might change if the costs and benefits of his investment in the mower change, as Example 9.6 shows.

Should Larry buy a riding lawn mower? (continued)

EXAMPLE 9.6

With all other assumptions the same as in Example 9.5, decide whether Larry should buy the mower:

a. If the interest rate is 12 percent rather than 6 percent.

b. If the purchase price of the mower is $7,000 rather than $4,000.

c. If the tax rate on Larry's net revenues is 25 percent rather than 20 percent.

d. If the mower is less efficient than Larry originally thought so that his net revenues will be $5,500 rather than $6,000.

In each case, Larry must compare the financial costs and benefits of buying the mower.

a. If the interest rate is 12 percent, then the interest cost will be 12 percent of $4,000, or $480, which exceeds the value of the mower's marginal product ($400). Larry should not buy the mower.

b. If the cost of the mower is $7,000, then Larry must borrow $7,000 instead of $4,000. At 6 percent interest, his interest cost will be $420—too high to justify the purchase, since the value of the mower's marginal product is $400.

c. If the tax rate on net revenues is 25 percent, then Larry must pay 25 percent of his $6,000 net revenues, or $1,500, in taxes. After taxes, his revenues from mowing will be $4,500, which is only $100 more than he could make working at an alternative job. Furthermore, the $100 will not cover the $240 in interest that Larry would have to pay. So again, Larry should not buy the mower.

d. If the mower is less efficient than originally expected so that Larry can earn net revenues of only $5,500, Larry will be left with only $4,400 after taxes—the same amount he could earn by working at another job. So in this case, the value of the mower's marginal product is zero. At any interest rate greater than zero, Larry should not buy the mower.

EXERCISE 9.4

Repeat Example 9.5, but assume that, over the course of the year, wear and tear reduces the resale value of the lawn mower from $4,000 to $3,800. Should Larry buy the mower?

The examples involving Larry and the lawn mower illustrate the main factors firms must consider when deciding whether to invest in new capital goods. On the cost side, two important factors are the *price of capital goods* and the *real interest rate*. Clearly, the more expensive new capital goods are, the more reluctant firms will be to invest in them. Buying the mower was profitable for Larry when its price was $4,000, but not when its price was $7,000.

Why is the real interest rate an important factor in investment decisions? The most straightforward case is when a firm has to borrow (as Larry did) to purchase its new capital. The real interest rate then determines the real cost to the firm of paying back its debt. Since financing costs are a major part of the total cost of owning and operating a piece of capital, much as mortgage payments are a major part of the cost of owning a home, increases in the real interest rate make the purchase of capital goods less attractive to firms, all else being equal.

Even if a firm does not need to borrow to buy new capital—say, because it has accumulated enough profits to buy the capital outright—the real interest rate remains an important determinant of the desirability of an investment. If a firm does not use its profits to acquire new capital, most likely it will use those profits to acquire financial assets such as bonds, which will earn the firm the real rate of interest. If the firm uses its profits to buy capital rather than to purchase a bond, it forgoes the opportunity to earn the real rate of interest on its funds. Thus, the real rate of interest measures the *opportunity cost* of a capital investment. Since an increase in the real interest rate raises the opportunity cost of investing in new capital, it lowers the willingness of firms to invest, even if they do not literally need to borrow to finance new machines or equipment.

On the benefit side, the key factor in determining business investment is the *value of the marginal product* of the new capital, which should be calculated net of both operating and maintenance expenses and taxes paid on the revenues the capital generates. The value of the marginal product is affected by several factors. For example, a technological advance that allows a piece of capital to produce more goods and services would increase the value of its marginal product, as would lower taxes on the revenues produced by the new capital. An increase in the price of the good or service that the capital is used to produce will also increase the value of the marginal product and, hence, the desirability of the investment. For example, if the going price for lawn-mowing services were to rise, then all else being equal, investing in the mower would become more profitable for Larry.

Why has investment in computers increased so much in recent decades?

ECONOMIC NATURALIST 9.4

Since about 1980, investment in new computer systems by U.S. firms has risen sharply (see Figure 9.6). Purchases of new computers and software by firms now exceed 2.5 percent of GDP and amount to about 24 percent of all private nonresidential investment. Why has investment in computers increased so much?

Investment in computers has increased by much more than other types of investment. Hence, the factors that affect all types of investment (such as the real interest rate and the tax rate) are not likely to be responsible for the boom. The two main causes of increased investment in computers appear to be the declining price of computing power and the increase in the value of the marginal product of computers. In recent years, the price of computing power has fallen at a precipitous rate. An industry rule of thumb is that the amount of computing power that is obtainable at a given price doubles every 18 months. As the price of computing power falls, an investment in computers becomes more and more likely to pass the *cost-benefit* test.

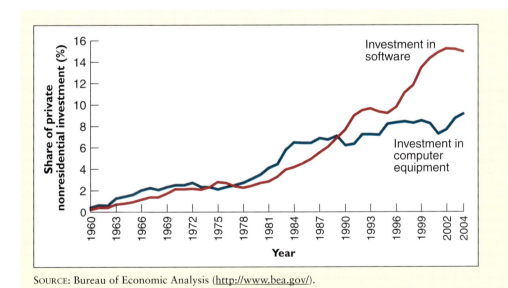

SOURCE: Bureau of Economic Analysis (http://www.bea.gov/).

FIGURE 9.6

Investment in Computers and Software, 1960-2004. Investment in computer equipment and software since 1960 shown as a percentage of private nonresidential investment. Computer-related investments by U.S. firms have risen significantly since 1980.

On the benefit side, for some years after the beginning of the computer boom, economists were unable to associate the technology with significant productivity gains. Defenders of investment in computer systems argued that the improvements in goods and services computers create are particularly hard to measure. How does one quantify the value to consumers of 24-hour-a-day access to cash or of the ability to make airline reservations online? Critics responded that the expected benefits of the computer revolution may have proved illusory because of problems such as user-unfriendly software and poor technical training. However, U.S. productivity has increased noticeably in recent years (see the chapter "Economic Growth, Productivity, and Living Standards"), and many people are now crediting the improvement to investment in computers and computer-related technologies like the Internet. As more firms become convinced that computers do add significantly to productivity and profits, the boom in computer investment can be expected to continue.

RECAP	FACTORS THAT AFFECT INVESTMENT

Any of the following factors will increase the willingness of firms to invest in new capital:

1. A decline in the price of new capital goods.

2. A decline in the real interest rate.

3. Technological improvement that raises the marginal product of capital.

4. Lower taxes on the revenues generated by capital.

5. A higher relative price for the firm's output.

SAVING, INVESTMENT, AND FINANCIAL MARKETS

Saving and investment are determined by different forces. Ultimately, though, in an economy without international borrowing and lending, national saving must equal investment. The supply of saving (by households, firms, and the government) and the demand for saving (by firms that want to purchase or construct new capital) are equalized through the workings of *financial markets*. Figure 9.7 illustrates this process. Quantities of national saving and investment are measured on the horizontal axis; the real interest rate is shown on the vertical axis. As we will see, in the market for saving, the real interest rate functions as the "price."

FIGURE 9.7
The Supply of and Demand for Saving.
Saving is supplied by households, firms, and the government and demanded by borrowers wishing to invest in new capital goods. The supply of saving (S) increases with the real interest rate, and the demand for saving by investors (I) decreases with the real interest rate. In financial market equilibrium, the real interest rate takes the value that equates the quantity of saving supplied and demanded.

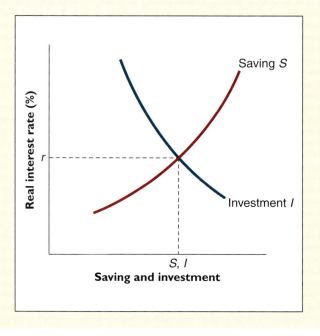

In the figure the supply of saving is shown by the upward-sloping curve marked S. This curve shows the quantity of national saving that households, firms, and the government are willing to supply at each value of the real interest rate. The saving curve is upward-sloping because empirical evidence suggests that increases in the real interest rate stimulate saving. The demand for saving is given by the downward-sloping curve marked I. This curve shows the quantity of investment in new capital that firms would choose and hence the amount they would need to borrow in financial markets, at each value of the real interest rate. Because higher real interest rates raise the cost of borrowing and reduce firms' willingness to invest, the demand for saving curve is downward-sloping.

Putting aside the possibility of borrowing from foreigners (discussed in the chapter "International Trade"), a country can invest only those resources that its savers make available. In equilibrium, then, desired investment (the demand for saving) and desired national saving (the supply of saving) must be equal. As Figure 9.7 suggests, desired saving is equated with desired investment through adjustments in the real interest rate, which functions as the "price" of saving. The movements of the real interest rate clear the market for saving in much the same way that the price of apples clears the market for apples. In Figure 9.7, the real interest rate that clears the market for saving is r, the real interest rate that corresponds to the intersection of the supply and demand curves.

The forces that push the real interest rate toward its equilibrium level are similar to the forces that lead to equilibrium in any other supply and demand situation. Suppose, for example, that the real interest rate exceeded r. At a higher real interest rate, savers would provide more funds than firms would want to invest. As lenders (savers) competed among themselves to attract borrowers (investors), the real interest rate would be bid down. The real interest rate would fall until it equaled r, the only interest rate at which both borrowers and lenders are satisfied, and no opportunities are left unexploited in the financial market (recall Chapter 3's *equilibrium principle*). What would happen if the real interest rate were *lower* than r?

Changes in factors *other than the real interest rate* that affect the supply of or demand for saving will shift the curves, leading to a new equilibrium in the financial market. Changes in the real interest rate cannot shift the supply or demand curves, just as a change in the price of apples cannot shift the supply or demand for apples, because the effects of the real interest rate on saving are already incorporated in the slopes of the curves. A few examples will illustrate the use of the supply and demand model of financial markets.

The effects of new technology

EXAMPLE 9.7

Exciting new technologies have been introduced in recent years, ranging from the Internet to new applications of genetics. A number of these technologies appear to have great commercial potential. How does the introduction of new technologies affect saving, investment, and the real interest rate?

The introduction of any new technology with the potential for commercial application creates profit opportunities for those who can bring the fruits of the technology to the public. In economists' language, the technical breakthrough raises the marginal product of new capital. Figure 9.8 shows the effects of a technological

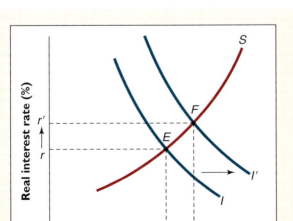

FIGURE 9.8
The Effects of a New Technology on National Saving and Investment.
A technological breakthrough raises the marginal product of new capital goods, increasing desired investment and the demand for saving. The real interest rate rises, as do national saving and investment.

breakthrough, with a resulting increase in the marginal product of capital. At any given real interest rate, an increase in the marginal product of capital makes firms more eager to invest. Thus, the advent of the new technology causes the demand for saving to shift upward and to the right, from I to I'.

At the new equilibrium point F, investment and national saving are higher than before, as is the real interest rate, which rises from r to r'. The rise in the real interest rate reflects the increased demand for funds by investors as they race to apply the new technologies. Because of the incentive of higher real returns, saving increases as well. Indeed, the real interest rate in the United States was relatively high in the late 1990s (Figure 6.2), as was the rate of investment, reflecting the opportunities created by new technologies.

Example 9.8 examines the effect of changing fiscal policies on the market for saving.

EXAMPLE 9.8   **An increase in the government budget deficit**

Suppose the government increases its spending without raising taxes, thereby increasing its budget deficit (or reducing its budget surplus). How will this decision affect national saving, investment, and the real interest rate?

National saving includes both private saving (saving by households and businesses) and public saving, which is equivalent to the government budget surplus. An increase in the government budget deficit (or a decline in the surplus) reduces public saving. Assuming that private saving does not change, the reduction in public saving will reduce national saving as well.

Figure 9.9 shows the effect of the increased government budget deficit on the market for saving and investment. At any real interest rate, a larger deficit reduces

FIGURE 9.9

The Effects of an Increase in the Government Budget Deficit on National Saving and Investment.

An increase in the government budget deficit reduces the supply of saving, raising the real interest rate and lowering investment. The tendency of increased government deficits to reduce investment in new capital is called *crowding out*.

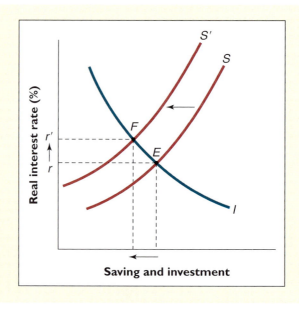

national saving, causing the saving curve to shift to the left, from S to S'. At the new equilibrium point F, the real interest rate is higher at r', and both national saving and investment are lower. In economic terms, the government has dipped further into the pool of private savings to borrow the funds to finance its budget deficit. The government's extra borrowing forces investors to compete for a smaller quantity of available saving, driving up the real interest rate. The higher real interest rate makes investment less attractive, assuring that investment will decrease along with national saving.

The tendency of government budget deficits to reduce investment spending is called **crowding out.** Reduced investment spending implies slower capital formation, and thus lower economic growth, as we saw in the chapter "Economic Growth, Productivity, and Living Standards." This adverse effect of budget deficits on economic growth is a key reason that economists advise governments to minimize their deficits.

crowding out the tendency of increased government deficits to reduce investment spending

EXERCISE 9.5

Suppose the general public becomes more "grasshopper-like" and less "ant-like" in their saving decisions, becoming less concerned about saving for the future. How will the change in public attitudes affect the country's rate of capital formation and economic growth?

How can we increase national saving?

Most policymakers recognize that the United States would eventually benefit from higher national saving rates. The government could increase public saving by reducing budget deficits, either by decreasing government spending or by increasing taxes. For political reasons, however, a rapid reduction of the government budget deficit may be difficult to achieve. Alternatively, increasing the incentives for households and firms to save would increase private saving. Some economists, for example, believe that the federal income tax should be scrapped in favor of a federal consumption tax. A consumption tax would be similar to the sales tax collected in most states, wherein people are taxed only when they spend. Taxing the portion of income that is consumed but not the portion that is saved would increase the incentive to save. Other economists favor further reductions in the tax rates on dividends and capital gains beyond those passed during George W. Bush's first term as president. These tax cuts would increase the after-tax rate of return to saving and thereby promote additional private saving. If private saving rises by more than the immediate loss in tax revenues, national saving also will rise.

ECONOMIC NATURALIST 9.5

At the national level, high saving rates lead to greater investment in new capital goods and thus higher standards of living. At the individual or family level, a high saving rate promotes the accumulation of wealth and the achievement of economic security. In this chapter, we have studied some of the factors that underlie saving and investment decisions. The next two chapters will look more closely at how savers hold their wealth and at how the financial system allocates the pool of available saving to the most productive investment projects.

■ SUMMARY ■

- In general, *saving* equals current income minus spending on current needs; the *saving rate* is the percentage of income that is saved. *Wealth*, or net worth, equals the market value of assets (real or financial items of value) minus liabilities (debts). Saving is a *flow*, being measured in dollars per unit of time; wealth is a *stock*, measured in dollars at a point in time. As the amount of water in a bathtub changes according to the rate at which water flows in, the stock of wealth increases at the saving rate. Wealth also increases if the value of existing assets rises (*capital gains*) and decreases if the value of existing assets falls (*capital losses*).

- Individuals and households save for a variety of reasons, including *life-cycle* objectives, as saving for retirement or a new home; the need to be prepared for an emergency (*precautionary saving*); and the desire to leave an inheritance (*bequest saving*). The amount people save also is affected by the real interest rate, which is the "reward" for saving. Evidence suggests that higher real interest rates lead to modest increases in saving. Saving also can be affected by psychological factors, such as the degree of self-control and the desire to consume at the level of one's neighbors (demonstration effects).

- The saving of an entire country is *national saving S*. National saving is defined by $S = Y - C - G$, where Y represents total output or income, C equals consumption spending, and G equals government purchases of goods and services. National saving can be broken up into private saving, or $Y - T - C$, and public saving, or $T - G$, where T stands for taxes paid to the government less transfer payments and interest paid by the government to the private sector. Private saving can be further broken down into household saving and business saving. In the United States, the bulk of private saving is done by businesses.

- Public saving is equivalent to the government budget surplus, $T - G$; if the government runs a budget deficit, then public saving is negative. The U.S. national saving rate is low relative to other industrialized countries, but it is higher and more stable than U.S. household saving.

- Investment is the purchase or construction of new capital goods, including housing. Firms will invest in new capital goods if the benefits of doing so outweigh the costs. Two factors that determine the cost of investment are the price of new capital goods and the real interest rate. The higher the real interest rate, the more expensive it is to borrow, and the less likely firms are to invest. The benefit of investment is the value of the marginal product of new capital, which depends on factors such as the productivity of new capital goods, the taxes levied on the revenues they generate, and the relative price of the firm's output.

- In the absence of international borrowing or lending, the supply of and demand for national saving must be equal. The supply of national saving depends on the saving decisions of households and businesses and the fiscal policies of the government (which determine public saving). The demand for saving is the amount business firms want to invest in new capital. The real interest rate, which is the "price" of borrowed funds, changes to equate the supply of and demand for national saving. Factors that affect the supply of or demand for saving will change saving, investment, and the equilibrium real interest rate. For example, an increase in the government budget deficit will reduce national saving and investment and raise the equilibrium real interest rate. The tendency of government budget deficits to reduce investment is called *crowding out*.

■ KEY TERMS ■

assets (243)	government budget deficit (256)	public saving (255)
balance sheet (243)	government budget surplus (255)	saving (242)
bequest saving (247)	liabilities (243)	saving rate (242)
capital gains (245)	life-cycle saving (247)	stock (243)
capital losses (245)	national saving (254)	transfer payments (254)
crowding out (265)	precautionary saving (247)	wealth (243)
flow (243)	private saving (255)	

■ REVIEW QUESTIONS ■

1. Explain the relationship between saving and wealth, using the concepts of flows and stocks. Is saving the only means by which wealth can increase? Explain.

2. Give three basic motivations for saving. Illustrate each with an example. What other factors would psychologists cite as being possibly important for saving?

3. Define *national saving*, relating your definition to the general concept of saving. Why does the standard U.S. definition of national saving potentially understate the true amount of saving being done in the economy?

4. Household saving rates in the United States are very low. Is this fact a problem for the U.S. economy? Why or why not?

5. Why do increases in real interest rates reduce the quantity of saving demanded? (*Hint:* Who are the "demanders" of saving?)

6. Name one factor that could increase the supply of saving and one that could increase the demand for saving. Show the effects of each on saving, investment, and the real interest rate.

■ PROBLEMS ■

1. a. Corey has a mountain bike worth $300, a credit card debt of $150, $200 in cash, a Sandy Koufax baseball card worth $400, $1,200 in a checking account, and an electric bill due for $250. Construct Corey's balance sheet and calculate his net worth. For each remaining part, explain how the event affects Corey's assets, liabilities, and wealth.

b. Corey goes to a baseball card convention and finds out that his baseball card is a worthless forgery.

c. Corey uses $150 from his paycheck to pay off his credit card balance. The remainder of his earnings is spent.

d. Corey writes a $150 check on his checking account to pay off his credit card balance. Of the events in the previous three parts, which, if any, corresponds to saving on Corey's part?

2. State whether each of the following is a stock or a flow, and explain.

a. The gross domestic product.

b. National saving.

c. The value of the U.S. housing stock on January 1, 2005.

d. The amount of U.S. currency in circulation as of this morning.

e. The government budget deficit.

f. The quantity of outstanding government debt on January 1, 2005.

3. Ellie and Vince are a married couple, both with college degrees and jobs. How would you expect each of the following events to affect the amount they save each month? Explain your answers in terms of the basic motivations for saving.

a. Ellie learns she is pregnant.

b. Vince reads in the paper about possible layoffs in his industry.

c. Vince had hoped that his parents would lend financial assistance toward the couple's planned purchase of a house, but he learns that they can't afford it.

d. Ellie announces that she would like to go to law school in the next few years.

e. A boom in the stock market greatly increases the value of the couple's retirement funds.

f. Vince and Ellie agree that they would like to leave a substantial amount to local charities in their wills.

4. Individual retirement accounts, or IRAs, were established by the U.S. government to encourage saving. An individual who deposits part of current earnings in an IRA does not have to pay income taxes on the earnings deposited, nor are any income taxes charged on the interest earned by the funds in the IRA. However, when the funds are withdrawn from the IRA, the full amount withdrawn is treated as income and is taxed at the individual's current income tax rate. In contrast, an individual depositing in a non-IRA account has to pay income taxes on the funds deposited and on interest earned in each year but does not have to pay taxes on withdrawals from the account. Another feature of IRAs that is different from a standard saving account is that funds deposited in an IRA cannot be withdrawn prior to retirement, except upon payment of a substantial penalty.

a. Greg, who is five years from retirement, receives a $10,000 bonus at work. He is trying to decide whether to save this extra income in an IRA account or in a regular savings account. Both accounts earn 5 percent nominal interest, and Greg is in the 30 percent tax bracket in every year (including his retirement year). Compare the amounts that Greg will have in five years under each of the two saving strategies, net of all taxes. Is the IRA a good deal for Greg?

b. Would you expect the availability of IRAs to increase the amount that households save? Discuss in light of (1) the response of saving to changes in the real interest rate and (2) psychological theories of saving.

5. In each part that follows, use the economic data given to find national saving, private saving, public saving, and the national saving rate.

a. Household saving = 200   Business saving = 400
Government purchases of goods and services = 100
Government transfers and interest payments = 100
Tax collections = 150   GDP = 2,200

b. GDP = 6,000   Tax collections = 1,200
Government transfers and interest payments = 400
Consumption expenditures = 4,500
Government budget surplus = 100

c. Consumption expenditures = 4,000   Investment = 1,000
Government purchases = 1,000   Net exports = 0
Tax collections = 1,500
Government transfers and interest payments = 500

6. Obtain a recent copy of the *Survey of Current Business,* published by the Bureau of Economic Analysis, in the library or online at http://www.bea.doc.gov/bea/pubs.htm. In the national data portion of the *Survey,* find nominal data on GDP, consumption, government purchases of goods and services, total government expenditures, and total government receipts for the most recent complete year available (see Tables 1.1 and 3.1). Calculate national saving, private saving, public saving, and the national saving rate. How does the government's contribution to national saving in the most recent period compare to 2004? (See the data for 2004 in the text.)

7. Ellie and Vince are trying to decide whether to purchase a new home. The house they want is priced at $200,000. Annual expenses such as maintenance, taxes, and insurance equal 4 percent of the home's value. If properly maintained, the house's real value is not expected to change. The real interest rate in the economy is 6 percent, and Ellie and Vince can qualify to borrow the full amount of the purchase price (for simplicity, assume no down payment) at that rate. Ignore the fact that mortgage interest payments are tax-deductible in the United States.
   a. Ellie and Vince would be willing to pay $1,500 monthly rent to live in a house of the same quality as the one they are thinking about purchasing. Should they buy the house?
   b. Does the answer to part a change if they are willing to pay $2,000 monthly rent?
   c. Does the answer to part a change if the real interest rate is 4 percent instead of 6 percent?
   d. Does the answer to part a change if the developer offers to sell Ellie and Vince the house for $150,000?
   e. Why do home-building companies dislike high interest rates?

8. The builder of a new movie theater complex is trying to decide how many screens she wants. Below are her estimates of the number of patrons the complex will attract each year, depending on the number of screens available.

Number of screens	Total number of patrons
1	40,000
2	75,000
3	105,000
4	130,000
5	150,000

   After paying the movie distributors and meeting all other noninterest expenses, the owner expects to net $2.00 per ticket sold. Construction costs are $1,000,000 per screen.
   a. Make a table showing the value of marginal product for each screen from the first through the fifth. What property is illustrated by the behavior of marginal products?
   b. How many screens will be built if the real interest rate is 5.5 percent?
   c. If the real interest rate is 7.5 percent?
   d. If the real interest rate is 10 percent?
   e. If the real interest rate is 5.5 percent, how far would construction costs have to fall before the builder would be willing to build a five-screen complex?

9. For each of the following scenarios, use supply and demand analysis to predict the resulting changes in the real interest rate, national saving, and investment. Show all your diagrams.
   a. The legislature passes a 10 percent investment tax credit. Under this program, for every $100 that a firm spends on new capital equipment, it receives an extra $10 in tax refunds from the government.
   b. A reduction in military spending moves the government's budget from deficit into surplus.
   c. A new generation of computer-controlled machines becomes available. These machines produce manufactured goods much more quickly and with fewer defects.

d. The government raises its tax on corporate profits. Other tax changes also are made, such that the government's deficit remains unchanged.

e. Concerns about job security raise precautionary saving.

f. New environmental regulations increase firms' costs of operating capital.

■ ANSWERS TO IN-CHAPTER EXERCISES ■

9.1 If Consuelo's student loan were for $6,500 instead of $3,000, her liabilities would be $6,750 (the student loan plus the credit card balance) instead of $3,250. The value of her assets, $6,280, is unchanged. In this case, Consuelo's wealth is negative, since assets of $6,280 less liabilities of $6,750 equals −$470. Negative wealth or net worth means one owes more than one owns.

9.2 If water is being drained from the tub, the flow is negative, equal to −3 gallons per minute. There are 37 gallons in the tub at 7:16 p.m. and 34 gallons at 7:17 p.m. The rate of change of the stock is −3 gallons per minute, which is the same as the flow.

9.3 a. Consuelo has set aside her usual $20, but she has also incurred a new liability of $50. So her net saving for the week is *minus* $30. Since her assets (her checking account) have increased by $20 but her liabilities (her credit card balance) have increased by $50, her wealth also has declined by $30.

b. In paying off her credit card bill, Consuelo reduces her assets by $300 by drawing down her checking account and reduces her liabilities by the same amount by reducing her credit card balance to zero. Thus, there is no change in her wealth. There is also no change in her saving (note that Consuelo's income and spending on current needs have not changed).

c. The increase in the value of Consuelo's car raises her assets by $500. So her wealth also rises by $500. Changes in the value of existing assets are not treated as part of saving, however, so her saving is unchanged.

d. The decline in the value of Consuelo's furniture is a capital loss of $300. Her assets and wealth fall by $300. Her saving is unchanged.

9.4 The loss of value of $200 over the year is another financial cost of owning the mower, which Larry should take into account in making his decision. His total cost is now $240 in interest costs plus $200 in anticipated loss of value of the mower (known as depreciation), or $440. This exceeds the value of marginal product, $400, and so now Larry should not buy the mower.

9.5 Household saving is part of national saving. A decline in household saving, and hence national saving, at any given real interest rate shifts the saving supply curve to the left. The results are as in Figure 9.9. The real interest rate rises and the equilibrium values of national saving and investment fall. Lower investment is the same as a lower rate of capital formation, which would be expected to slow economic growth.

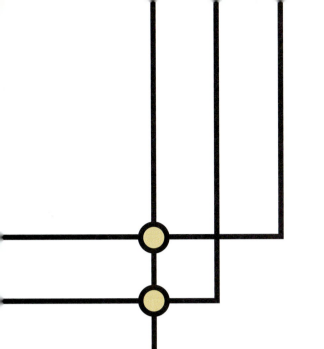

MONEY, PRICES, AND THE FEDERAL RESERVE

The Aztec people, who dominated central Mexico until the coming of the Spanish in the sixteenth century, are perhaps best remembered today for their elaborate ceremonies that culminated in human sacrifice. But the Aztec Empire also had a sophisticated economic system, which included active trade not only in a wide variety of agricultural goods—such as corn, tomatoes, and peanuts—but also in manufactured items, including jewelry, sandals, cloaks, baskets, alcohol, and weapons. Slaves and captives—some designated for sacrifice—also were bought and sold. Trade was carried out in local markets, notably in the Aztec capital city, located where Mexico City now stands, and over long distances, as far north as present-day Arizona, for example.[1]

Despite ample supplies of gold, the Aztecs did not use metallic coins to carry out their market transactions, as most European peoples did. Instead, they often used chocolate or, more specifically, cacao "beans" (the seeds of the cacao plant). Prices of goods or services were quoted in cacao beans, in much the same way that today we quote prices in terms of dollars. Cacao beans also could be used to purchase goods, to pay for a service, or to make change—for example, to balance a transaction when a good of greater value was traded for one of lesser value. For larger items, prices were quoted in terms of bags of approximately 24,000 cacao beans, although large purchases might actually be paid for with something easier to carry than bags of cacao beans, such as woven cloaks.

[1]See Jack Weatherford, *The History of Money: From Sandstone to Cyberspace*, New York: Crown Publishers, 1997, for a discussion of the use of money in many economies from the ancients to the present day.

money any asset that can be used in making purchases

Cacao beans were, for the Aztecs, a form of money. In everyday language, people use the word *money* to mean "income" or "wealth," as in "That job pays good money" or "I wish I had as much money as she does." Economists, however, give a much more specific meaning to the term. To the economist, **money** is any asset that can be used in making purchases.

Common examples of money in the modern world are currency and coin. A checking account balance represents another asset that can be used in making payments (as when you write a check to pay for your weekly groceries) and so is also counted as money. In contrast, shares of stock, for example, cannot be used directly in most transactions. Stock must first be sold—that is, converted into cash or a checking account deposit—before further transactions, such as buying your groceries, can be made.

Historically, a wide variety of objects have been used as money, including not only cacao beans but also gold and silver coins, shells, beads, feathers, and, on the Island of Yap, large, immovable boulders. Prior to the use of metallic coins, by far the most common form of money was the cowrie, a type of shell found in the South Pacific. Cowries were used as money in some parts of Africa until very recently, being officially accepted for payment of taxes in Uganda until the beginning of the twentieth century. Today money can be virtually intangible, as in the case of your checking account balance, which exists only in the form of an entry in your bank's computer.

In this chapter we discuss the role of money in modern economies: why it is important, how it is measured, how it is created. Money plays a major role in everyday economic transactions but, as we will see, it is also quite important at the macro level. For example, as we mentioned in the chapter "Macroeconomics," one of the three main types of macroeconomic policy, monetary policy, relates primarily to decisions about how much money should be allowed to circulate in the economy. In the United States, monetary policy is made by the Federal Reserve, the nation's central bank. Because the Federal Reserve, or Fed, determines the nation's money supply, this chapter also introduces the Fed and discusses the main policy tool at its disposal. Finally, the chapter discusses the important relationship between the amount of money in circulation and the rate of inflation in an economy.

MONEY AND ITS USES

medium of exchange an asset used in purchasing goods and services

barter the direct trade of goods or services for other goods or services

Why do people use money? Money has three principal uses: a *medium of exchange*, a *unit of account*, and a *store of value*.

Money serves as a **medium of exchange** when it is used to purchase goods and services, as when you pay cash for a newspaper or write a check to cover your utilities bill. This is perhaps money's most crucial function. Think about how complicated daily life would become if there were no money. Without money, all economic transactions would have to be in the form of **barter**, which is the direct trade of goods or services for other goods or services.

Barter is highly inefficient because it requires that each party to a trade has something that the other party wants, a so-called double coincidence of wants. For example, under a barter system, a musician could get her dinner only by finding someone willing to trade food for a musical performance. Finding such a match of needs, where each party happens to want exactly what the other person has to offer, would be difficult to do on a regular basis. In a world with money, the musician's problem is considerably simpler. First, she must find someone who is willing to pay money for her musical performance. Then, with the money received, she can purchase the food and other goods and services that she needs. In a society that uses money, it is not necessary that the person who wants to hear music and the person willing to provide food to the musician be one and the same. In other words, there need not be a double coincidence of wants for trades of goods and services to take place.

© Catherine Karnow/CORBIS

In a world without money, she could eat only by finding someone willing to trade food for a musical performance.

By eliminating the problem of having to find a double coincidence of wants in order to trade, the use of money in a society permits individuals to specialize in producing particular goods or services, as opposed to having every family or village produce most of what it needs. Specialization greatly increases economic efficiency and material standards of living, as we discussed in Chapter 2 (*the principle of comparative advantage*). This usefulness of money in making transactions explains why savers hold money, even though money generally pays a low rate of return. Cash, for example, pays no interest at all, and the balances in checking accounts usually pay a lower rate of interest than could be obtained in alternative financial investments.

Money's second function is as a *unit of account*. As a **unit of account,** money is the basic yardstick for measuring economic value. In the United States virtually all prices—including the price of labor (wages) and the prices of financial assets, such as shares of General Motors stock—are expressed in dollars. Expressing economic values in a common unit of account allows for easy comparisons. For example, grain can be measured in bushels and coal in tons, but to judge whether 20 bushels of grain is economically more or less valuable than a ton of coal, we express both values in dollar terms. The use of money as a unit of account is closely related to its use as a medium of exchange; because money is used to buy and sell things, it makes sense to express prices of all kinds in money terms.

As a **store of value,** its third function, money is a way of holding wealth. For example, the miser who stuffs cash in his mattress or buries gold coins under the old oak tree at midnight is holding wealth in money form. Likewise, if you regularly keep a balance in your checking account, you are holding part of your wealth in the form of money. Although money is usually the primary medium of exchange or unit of account in an economy, it is not the only store of value. There are numerous other ways of holding wealth, such as owning stocks, bonds, or real estate.

For most people, money is not a particularly good way to hold wealth, apart from its usefulness as a medium of exchange. Unlike government bonds and other types of financial assets, most forms of money pay no interest, and there is always the risk of cash being lost or stolen. However, cash has the advantage of being anonymous and difficult to trace, making it an attractive store of value for smugglers, drug dealers, and others who want their assets to stay out of the view of the Internal Revenue Service.

unit of account a basic measure of economic value

store of value an asset that serves as a means of holding wealth

Private money: Ithaca Hours and LETS

Since money is such a useful tool, why is money usually issued only by governments? Are there examples of privately issued money?

ECONOMIC NATURALIST 10.1

Money is usually issued by the government, not private individuals, but in part this reflects legal restrictions on private money issuance. Where the law allows, private moneys do sometimes emerge.[2] For example, privately issued currencies circulate in more than 30 U.S. communities. In Ithaca, New York, a private currency known as "Ithaca Hours" has circulated since 1991. Instituted by town resident Paul Glover, each Ithaca Hour is equivalent to $10, the average hourly wage of workers in the county. The bills, printed with specially developed inks to prevent counterfeiting, honor local people and the environment. An estimated 1,600 individuals and businesses have earned and spent Hours. Founder Paul Glover argues that the use of Hours, which can't be spent elsewhere, induces people to do more of their shopping in the local economy.

A more high-tech form of private money is associated with computerized trading systems called LETS, for local electronic trading system. These are quite popular in Australia, New Zealand, and Great Britain (the United States has about 10 of them). Participants in a LETS post a list of goods and services they would like to buy or sell. When transactions are made, the appropriate number of "computer credits" is

---

[2]Barbara A. Good, "Private Money: Everything Old Is New Again," Federal Reserve Bank of Cleveland, *Economic Commentary,* April 1, 1998.

subtracted from the buyer's account and added to the seller's account. People are allowed to have negative balances in their accounts, so participants have to trust other members not to abuse the system by buying many goods and services and then quitting. LETS credits exist in the computer only and are never in the form of paper or metal. In this respect, LETS may foreshadow the electronic monetary systems of the future.

What do Ithaca Hours and LETS credits have in common? By functioning as a medium of exchange, each facilitates trade within a community.

MEASURING MONEY

How much money, defined as financial assets usable for making purchases, is there in the U.S. economy at any given time? This question is not simple to answer because in practice it is not easy to draw a clear distinction between those assets that should be counted as money and those that should not. Dollar bills are certainly a form of money, and a van Gogh painting certainly is not. However, brokerage firms now offer accounts that allow their owners to combine financial investments in stocks and bonds with check-writing and credit card privileges. Should the balances in these accounts, or some part of them, be counted as money? It is difficult to tell.

Economists skirt the problem of deciding what is and isn't money by using several alternative definitions of money, which vary in how broadly the concept of money is defined. A relatively "narrow" definition of the amount of money in the U.S. economy is called M1. **M1** is the sum of currency outstanding and balances held in checking accounts. A broader measure of money, called **M2**, includes all the assets in M1 plus some additional assets that are usable in making payments, but at greater cost or inconvenience than currency or checks. Table 10.1 lists the components of M1 and M2 and also gives the amount of each type of asset outstanding as of April 2005. For most purposes, however, it is sufficient to think of money as the sum of currency outstanding and balances in checking accounts, or M1.

M1 sum of currency outstanding and balances held in checking accounts

M2 All the assets in M1 plus some additional assets that are usable in making payments but at greater cost or inconvenience than currency or checks

TABLE 10.1
Components of M1 and M2, April 2005

M1		**1,361.0**
Currency	704.3	
Demand deposits	325.8	
Other checkable deposits	323.4	
Travelers' checks	7.5	
M2		**6,481.5**
M1	1,361.0	
Savings deposits	3,544.7	
Small-denomination time deposits	868.8	
Money market mutual funds	707.0	

NOTES: Billions of dollars, adjusted for seasonal variations. In M1, currency refers to cash and coin. Demand deposits are non-interest-bearing checking accounts, and "other checkable deposits" includes checking accounts that bear interest. M2 includes all the components of M1, balances in savings accounts, "small-denomination" (under $100,000) deposits held at banks for a fixed term, and money market mutual funds (MMMFs). MMMFs are organizations that sell shares, use the proceeds to buy safe assets (like government bonds), and often allow their shareholders some check-writing privileges.

SOURCE: Federal Reserve Bank of St. Louis, FRED database, http://www.stlouisfed.org/fred2/, or Federal Reserve release H.6.

Note that credit card balances are not included in either M1 or M2 even though people increasingly use credit cards to pay for many of their purchases, including food, clothing, cars, and even college tuition. The main reason credit card balances are not included in the money supply is that they do not represent part of people's wealth. Indeed, a credit card charge of $1,000 represents an obligation to pay someone else $1,000.

RECAP	**MONEY AND ITS USES**

Money is any asset that can be used in making purchases, such as currency or a checking account. Money serves as a *medium of exchange* when it is used to purchase goods and services. The use of money as a medium of exchange eliminates the need for *barter* and the difficulties of finding a "double coincidence of wants." Money also serves as a *unit of account* and a *store of value.*

In practice, two basic measures of money are M1 and M2. M1, a more narrow measure, is made up primarily of currency and balances held in checking accounts. The broader measure, M2, includes all the assets in M1 plus some additional assets usable in making payments.

COMMERCIAL BANKS AND THE CREATION OF MONEY

What determines the amount of money in the economy? If the economy's supply of money consisted entirely of currency, the answer would be simple: The supply of money would just be equal to the value of the currency created and circulated by the government. However, as we have seen, in modern economies the money supply consists not only of currency but also of deposit balances held by the public in commercial banks. Commercial banks are privately owned firms that accept deposits from individuals and businesses and use those deposits to make loans. There are literally thousands of commercial banks in the United States, and together they comprise the private banking system.

The determination of the money supply in a modern economy depends in part on the behavior of commercial banks and their depositors. To see how, we will use the example of a fictional country, the Republic of Gorgonzola. Initially, we assume, Gorgonzola has no commercial banking system. To make trading easier and eliminate the need for barter, the government directs the central bank of Gorgonzola to put into circulation a million identical paper notes, called guilders. The central bank prints the guilders and distributes them to the populace. At this point the Gorgonzolan money supply is a million guilders.

However, the citizens of Gorgonzola are unhappy with a money supply made up entirely of paper guilders, since the notes may be lost or stolen. In response to the demand for safekeeping of money, some Gorgonzolan entrepreneurs set up a system of commercial banks. At first, these banks are only storage vaults where people can deposit their guilders. When people need to make a payment, they can either physically withdraw their guilders or, more conveniently, write a check on their account. Checks give the banks permission to transfer guilders from the account of the person paying by check to the account of the person to whom the check is made out. With a system of payments based on checks, the paper guilders need never leave the banking system, although they flow from one bank to another as a depositor of one bank makes a payment to a depositor in another bank. Deposits do not pay interest in this economy; indeed, the banks can make a profit only by charging depositors fees in exchange for safeguarding their cash.

Let's suppose for now that people prefer bank deposits to cash and so deposit all of their guilders with the commercial banks. With all guilders in the vaults of banks, the balance sheet of all of Gorgonzola's commercial banks taken together is as shown in Table 10.2.

TABLE 10.2
Consolidated Balance Sheet of Gorgonzolan Commercial Banks (Initial)

Assets		Liabilities	
Currency	1,000,000 guilders	Deposits	1,000,000 guilders

The *assets* of the commercial banking system in Gorgonzola are the paper guilders sitting in the vaults of all the individual banks. The banking system's *liabilities* are the deposits of the banks' customers, since checking account balances represent money owed by the banks to the depositors.

Cash or similar assets held by banks are called **bank reserves.** In this example, bank reserves, for all the banks taken together, equal 1,000,000 guilders—the currency listed on the asset side of the consolidated balance sheet. Banks hold reserves to meet depositors' demands for cash withdrawals or to pay checks drawn on their depositors' accounts. In this example, the bank reserves of 1,000,000 guilders equal 100 percent of banks' deposits, which are also 1,000,000 guilders. A situation in which bank reserves equal 100 percent of bank deposits is called **100 percent reserve banking.**

Bank reserves are held by banks in their vaults, rather than circulated among the public, and thus are *not* counted as part of the money supply. However, bank deposit balances, which can be used in making transactions, *are* counted as money. So, after the introduction of "safekeeper" banks in Gorgonzola, the money supply, equal to the value of bank deposits, is 1,000,000 guilders, which is the same as it was prior to the introduction of banks.

After a while, to continue the story, the commercial bankers of Gorgonzola begin to realize that keeping 100 percent reserves against deposits is not necessary. True, a few guilders flow in and out of the typical bank as depositors receive payments or write checks, but for the most part the stacks of paper guilders just sit there in the vaults, untouched and unused. It occurs to the bankers that they can meet the random inflow and outflow of guilders to their banks with reserves that are less than 100 percent of their deposits. After some observation, the bankers conclude that keeping reserves equal to only 10 percent of deposits is enough to meet the random ebb and flow of withdrawals and payments from their individual banks. The remaining 90 percent of deposits, the bankers realize, can be lent out to borrowers to earn interest.

So the bankers decide to keep reserves equal to 100,000 guilders, or 10 percent of their deposits. The other 900,000 guilders they lend out at interest to Gorgonzolan cheese producers who want to use the money to make improvements to their farms. After the loans are made, the balance sheet of all of Gorgonzola's commercial banks taken together has changed, as shown in Table 10.3.

bank reserves cash or similar assets held by commercial banks for the purpose of meeting depositor withdrawals and payments

100 percent reserve banking a situation in which banks' reserves equal 100 percent of their deposits

TABLE 10.3
Consolidated Balance Sheet of Gorgonzolan Commercial Banks after One Round of Loans

Assets		Liabilities	
Currency (= reserves)	100,000 guilders	Deposits	1,000,000 guilders
Loans to farmers	900,000 guilders		

After the loans are made, the banks' reserves of 100,000 guilders no longer equal 100 percent of the banks' deposits of 1,000,000 guilders. Instead, the **reserve-deposit ratio,** which is bank reserves divided by deposits, is now equal to 100,000/1,000,000, or 10 percent. A banking system in which banks hold fewer reserves than deposits so that the reserve-deposit ratio is less than 100 percent is called a **fractional-reserve banking system.**

Notice that 900,000 guilders have flowed out of the banking system (as loans to farmers) and are now in the hands of the public. But we have assumed that private citizens prefer bank deposits to cash for making transactions. So ultimately people will redeposit the 900,000 guilders in the banking system. After these deposits are made, the consolidated balance sheet of the commercial banks is as in Table 10.4.

reserve-deposit ratio bank reserves divided by deposits

fractional-reserve banking system a banking system in which bank reserves are less than deposits so that the reserve-deposit ratio is less than 100 percent

TABLE 10.4
Consolidated Balance Sheet of Gorgonzolan Commercial Banks after Guilders Are Redeposited

Assets		Liabilities	
Currency (= reserves)	1,000,000 guilders	Deposits	1,900,000 guilders
Loans to farmers	900,000 guilders		

Notice that bank deposits, and hence the economy's money supply, now equal 1,900,000 guilders. In effect, the existence of the commercial banking system has permitted the creation of new money. These deposits, which are liabilities of the banks, are balanced by assets of 1,000,000 guilders in reserves and 900,000 guilders in loans owed to the banks.

The story does not end here. On examining their balance sheets, the bankers are surprised to see that they once again have "too many" reserves. With deposits of 1,900,000 guilders and a 10 percent reserve-deposit ratio, they need only 190,000 guilders in reserves. But they have 1,000,000 guilders in reserves— 810,000 too many. Since lending out their excess guilders is always more profitable than leaving them in the vault, the bankers proceed to make another 810,000 guilders in loans. Eventually these loaned-out guilders are redeposited in the banking system, after which the consolidated balance sheet of the banks is as shown in Table 10.5.

TABLE 10.5
Consolidated Balance Sheet of Gorgonzolan Commercial Banks after Two Rounds of Loans and Redeposits

Assets		Liabilities	
Currency (= reserves)	1,000,000 guilders	Deposits	2,710,000 guilders
Loans to farmers	1,710,000 guilders		

Now the money supply has increased to 2,710,000 guilders, equal to the value of bank deposits. Despite the expansion of loans and deposits, however, the bankers find that their reserves of 1,000,000 guilders *still* exceed the desired level of 10 percent of deposits, which are 2,710,000 guilders. And so yet another round of lending will take place.

EXERCISE 10.1

Determine what the balance sheet of the banking system of Gorgonzola will look like after a third round of lending to farmers and redeposits of guilders into the commercial banking system. What is the money supply at that point?

The process of expansion of loans and deposits will only end when reserves equal 10 percent of bank deposits, because as long as reserves exceed 10 percent of deposits, the banks will find it profitable to lend out the extra reserves. Since reserves at the end of every round equal 1,000,000 guilders, for the reserve-deposit ratio to equal 10 percent, total deposits must equal 10,000,000 guilders. Further, since the balance sheet must balance, with assets equal to liabilities, we know as well that at the end of the process, loans to cheese producers must equal 9,000,000 guilders. If loans equal 9,000,000 guilders, then bank assets, the sum of loans and reserves (1,000,000 guilders), will equal 10,000,000 guilders, which is the same as bank liabilities (bank deposits). The final consolidated balance sheet is as shown in Table 10.6.

TABLE 10.6
Final Consolidated Balance Sheet of Gorgonzolan Commercial Banks

Assets		Liabilities	
Currency (= reserves)	1,000,000 guilders	Deposits	10,000,000 guilders
Loans to farmers	9,000,000 guilders		

The money supply, which is equal to total deposits, is 10,000,000 guilders at the end of the process. We see that the existence of a fractional-reserve banking system has multiplied the money supply by a factor of 10, relative to the economy with no banks or the economy with 100 percent reserve banking. Put another way, with a 10 percent reserve-deposit ratio, each guilder deposited in the banking system can "support" 10 guilders worth of deposits.

To find the money supply in this example more directly, we observe that deposits will expand through additional rounds of lending as long as the ratio of bank reserves to bank deposits exceeds the reserve-deposit ratio desired by banks. When the actual ratio of bank reserves to deposits equals the desired reserve-deposit ratio, the expansion stops. So ultimately, deposits in the banking system satisfy the following relationship:

$$\frac{\text{Bank reserves}}{\text{Bank deposits}} = \text{Desired reserve-deposit ratio.}$$

This equation can be rewritten to solve for bank deposits:

$$\text{Bank deposits} = \frac{\text{Bank reserves}}{\text{Desired reserve-deposit ratio}}. \tag{10.1}$$

In Gorgonzola, since all the currency in the economy flows into the banking system, bank reserves equal 1,000,000 guilders. The reserve-deposit ratio desired by banks is 0.10. Therefore, using Equation 10.1, we find that bank deposits equal (1,000,000 guilders)/0.10, or 10 million guilders, the same answer we found in the consolidated balance sheet of the banks, Table 10.6.

EXERCISE 10.2

Find deposits and the money supply in Gorgonzola if the banks' desired reserve-deposit ratio is 5 percent rather than 10 percent. What if the total amount of currency circulated by the central bank is 2,000,000 guilders and the desired reserve-deposit ratio remains at 10 percent?

THE MONEY SUPPLY WITH BOTH CURRENCY AND DEPOSITS

In the example of Gorgonzola, we assumed that all money is held in the form of deposits in banks. In reality, of course, people keep only part of their money holdings in the form of bank accounts and hold the rest in the form of currency. Fortunately, allowing for the fact that people hold both currency and bank deposits does not greatly complicate the determination of the money supply, as Example 10.1 shows.

The money supply with both currency and deposits

EXAMPLE 10.1

Suppose that the citizens of Gorgonzola choose to hold a total of 500,000 guilders in the form of currency and to deposit the rest of their money in banks. Banks keep reserves equal to 10 percent of deposits. What is the money supply in Gorgonzola?

The money supply is the sum of currency in the hands of the public and bank deposits. Currency in the hands of the public is given as 500,000 guilders. What is the quantity of bank deposits? Since 500,000 of the 1,000,000 guilders issued by the central bank are being used by the public in the form of currency, only the remaining 500,000 guilders is available to serve as bank reserves. We know that deposits equal bank reserves divided by the reserve-deposit ratio, so deposits are 500,000 guilders/0.10 = 5,000,000 guilders. The total money supply is the sum of currency in the hands of the public (500,000 guilders) and bank deposits (5,000,000 guilders), or 5,500,000 guilders.

We can write a general relationship that captures the reasoning of Example 10.1. First, let's write out the fact that the money supply equals currency plus bank deposits:

Money supply = Currency held by the public + Bank deposits.

We also know that bank deposits equal bank reserves divided by the reserve-deposit ratio that is desired by commercial banks (Equation 10.1). Using that relationship to substitute for bank deposits in the expression for the money supply, we get

$$\text{Money supply} = \text{Currency held by public} + \frac{\text{Bank reserves}}{\text{Desired reserve-deposit ratio}}. \quad (10.2)$$

We can use Equation 10.2 to confirm our answer to Example 10.1. In that example, currency held by the public is 500,000 guilders, bank reserves are 500,000 guilders, and the desired reserve-deposit ratio is 0.10. Plugging these values into Equation 10.2, we get that the money supply equals 500,000 + 500,000/0.10 = 5,500,000, the same answer we found before.

The money supply at Christmas

EXAMPLE 10.2

During the Christmas season, people choose to hold unusually large amounts of currency for shopping. With no action by the central bank, how would this change in currency holding affect the national money supply?

To illustrate with a numerical example, suppose that initially bank reserves are 500, the amount of currency held by the public is 500, and the desired reserve-deposit ratio in the banking system is 0.2. Inserting these values into Equation 10.2, we find that the money supply equals 500 + 500/0.2 = 3,000.

Now suppose that because of Christmas shopping needs, the public increases its currency holdings to 600 by withdrawing 100 from commercial banks. These withdrawals reduce bank reserves to 400. Using Equation 10.2, we find now that the money supply is 600 + 400/0.2 = 2,600. So the public's increased holdings of currency have caused the money supply to drop, from 3,000 to 2,600. The reason for the drop is that with a reserve-deposit ratio of 20 percent, every dollar in the vaults of banks can "support" $5 of deposits and hence $5 of money supply. However, the same dollar in the hands of the public becomes $1 of currency, contributing only $1 to the total money supply. So when the public withdraws cash from the banks, the overall money supply declines. (We will see in the next section, however, that in practice the central bank has means to offset the impact of the public's actions on the money supply.)

RECAP	COMMERCIAL BANKS AND THE CREATION OF MONEY

- Part of the money supply consists of deposits in private commercial banks. Hence, the behavior of commercial banks and their depositors helps to determine the money supply.

- Cash or similar assets held by banks are called *bank reserves*. In modern economies, banks' reserves are less than their deposits, a situation called *fractional-reserve banking*. The ratio of bank reserves to deposits is called the *reserve-deposit ratio*; in a fractional-reserve banking system, this ratio is less than 1.

- The portion of deposits not held as reserves can be lent out by the banks to earn interest. Banks will continue to make loans and accept deposits as long as the reserve-deposit ratio exceeds its desired level. This process stops only when the actual and desired reserve-deposit ratios are equal. At that point, total bank deposits equal bank reserves divided by the desired reserve-deposit ratio, and the money supply equals the currency held by the public plus bank deposits (see Equation 10.2).

THE FEDERAL RESERVE SYSTEM

Federal Reserve System (or Fed) the central bank of the United States

For participants in financial markets and the average citizen as well, one of the most important branches of the government is the **Federal Reserve System,** often called the **Fed.** The Fed is the *central bank* of the United States. Like central banks in other countries, the Fed has two main responsibilities.

First, it is responsible for monetary policy, which means that the Fed determines how much money circulates in the economy. As we will see in later chapters, changes in the supply of money can affect many important macroeconomic variables, including interest rates, inflation, unemployment, and exchange rates. Because of its ability to affect key variables, particularly financial variables such as interest rates, financial market participants pay close attention to Fed actions and announcements. As a necessary first step in understanding how Fed policies have the effects that they do, in this chapter we will focus on the basic question of how the Fed affects the supply of money, leaving for later the explanation of why changes in the money supply affect the economy.

Second, along with other government agencies, the Federal Reserve bears important responsibility for the oversight and regulation of financial markets. The Fed also plays a major role during periods of crisis in financial markets. To lay the groundwork for discussing how the Fed carries out its responsibilities, we first briefly review the history and structure of the Federal Reserve System.

THE HISTORY AND STRUCTURE OF THE FEDERAL RESERVE SYSTEM

The Federal Reserve System was created by the Federal Reserve Act, passed by Congress in 1913, and began operations in 1914. Like all central banks, the Fed is a government agency. Unlike commercial banks, which are private businesses whose principal objective is making a profit, central banks like the Fed focus on promoting public goals such as economic growth, low inflation, and the smooth operation of financial markets.

"I'm sorry, sir, but I don't believe you know us well enough to call us the Fed."

The Federal Reserve Act established a system of 12 regional Federal Reserve banks, each associated with a geographical area called a Federal Reserve district. Congress hoped that the establishment of Federal Reserve banks around the country would ensure that different regions were represented in the national policymaking process. In fact, the regional Feds regularly assess economic conditions in their districts and report this information to policymakers in Washington. Regional Federal Reserve banks also provide various services, such as check-clearing services, to the commercial banks in their district.

Board of Governors the leadership of the Fed, consisting of seven governors appointed by the president to staggered 14-year terms

At the national level, the leadership of the Federal Reserve System is provided by its **Board of Governors.** The Board of Governors, together with a large professional staff, is located in Washington, D.C. The Board consists of seven governors, who are appointed by the president of the United States, subject to confirmation by the Senate, to 14-year terms. The terms are staggered so that one governor comes up for reappointment every other year. The president also appoints one of these Board members to serve as chairman of the Board of Governors for a term of four years. The Fed chairman, along with the secretary of the Treasury, is probably one of the two most powerful economic policymakers in the U.S. government, after the president. Recent chairmen, such as Paul Volcker and Alan Greenspan, have been highly regarded and influential.

Federal Open Market Committee (or FOMC) the committee that makes decisions concerning monetary policy

Decisions about monetary policy are made by a 12-member committee called the **Federal Open Market Committee** (or **FOMC**). The FOMC consists of the seven Fed governors, the president of the Federal Reserve Bank of New York, and four of the presidents of the other regional Federal Reserve banks, who serve on a rotating basis. The FOMC meets approximately eight times a year to review the state of the economy and to determine monetary policy.

CONTROLLING THE MONEY SUPPLY WITH OPEN-MARKET OPERATIONS

The Fed's primary responsibility is making monetary policy, which involves decisions about the appropriate size of the nation's money supply. As we saw in the previous section, central banks in general, and the Fed in particular, do not control the money supply directly. Nevertheless, they can control the money supply indirectly in several ways. In this chapter we discuss the most important of these, called *open-market operations.* In the chapter "Stabilizing the Economy," we discuss two other methods the Fed can use to change the money supply: lending at the discount window and changing reserve requirements.

Suppose that the Fed wants to increase bank reserves, with the ultimate goal of increasing bank deposits and the money supply. To accomplish this, the Fed buys financial assets, usually government bonds, from the public. A bond is a piece of paper representing a loan. You may have received a bond as a present for graduating from high school, a confirmation, or a bar mitzvah. People purchase bonds when they are making a loan to the government. In return, bond owners usually receive periodic interest payments from the government until the loan is repaid. Bond owners may choose to keep their bond until the loan is repaid or they can sell it to someone else.[3]

To simplify the actual procedure a bit, think of the Fed as buying bonds that the public had originally purchased from the government and paying the public for these bonds with newly printed money. Assuming that the public is already holding all the currency that it wants, they will deposit the cash they receive as payment for their bonds in commercial banks. Thus, the reserves of the commercial banking system will increase by an amount equal to the value of the bonds purchased by the Fed. The increase in bank reserves will lead in turn, through the process of lending and redeposit of funds described in the previous section, to an expansion of bank deposits and the money supply, as summarized by Equation 10.2. The Fed's purchase of government bonds from the public, with the result that bank reserves and the money supply are increased, is called an **open-market purchase.**

open-market purchase the purchase of government bonds from the public by the Fed for the purpose of increasing the supply of bank reserves and the money supply

To reduce bank reserves and hence the money supply, the Fed reverses the procedure. It sells some of the government bonds that it holds (acquired in previous open-market purchases) to the public. Assume that the public pays for the bonds by writing checks on their accounts in commercial banks. Then, when the Fed presents the checks to the commercial banks for payment, reserves equal in value to the

[3]A more complete description of bonds is presented in the next chapter.

government bonds sold by the Fed are transferred from the commercial banks to the Fed. The Fed retires these reserves from circulation, lowering the supply of bank reserves and, hence, the overall money supply. The sale of government bonds by the Fed to the public for the purpose of reducing bank reserves and hence the money supply is called an **open-market sale.** Open-market purchases and sales together are called **open-market operations.** Open-market operations are the most convenient and flexible tool that the Federal Reserve has for affecting the money supply and are employed on a regular basis.

open-market sale the sale by the Fed of government bonds to the public for the purpose of reducing bank reserves and the money supply

open-market operations open-market purchases and open-market sales

Increasing the money supply by open-market operations

EXAMPLE 10.3

In a particular economy, currency held by the public is 1,000 shekels, bank reserves are 200 shekels, and the desired reserve-deposit ratio is 0.2. What is the money supply? How is the money supply affected if the central bank prints 100 shekels and uses this new currency to buy government bonds from the public? Assume that the public does not wish to change the amount of currency it holds.

As bank reserves are 200 shekels and the reserve-deposit ratio is 0.2, bank deposits must equal 200 shekels/0.2, or 1,000 shekels. The money supply, equal to the sum of currency held by the public and bank deposits, is therefore 2,000 shekels, a result you can confirm using Equation 10.2.

The open-market purchase puts 100 more shekels into the hands of the public. We assume that the public continues to want to hold 1,000 shekels in currency, so they will deposit the additional 100 shekels in the commercial banking system, raising bank reserves from 200 to 300 shekels. As the desired reserve-deposit ratio is 0.2, multiple rounds of lending and redeposit will eventually raise the level of bank deposits to 300 shekels/0.2, or 1,500 shekels. The money supply, equal to 1,000 shekels held by the public plus bank deposits of 1,500 shekels, equals 2,500 shekels. So the open-market purchase of 100 shekels, by raising bank reserves by 100 shekels, has increased the money supply by 500 shekels. Again, you can confirm this result using Equation 10.2.

EXERCISE 10.3

Continuing Example 10.3, suppose that instead of an open-market purchase of 100 shekels, the central bank conducts an open-market sale of 50 shekels' worth of government bonds. What happens to bank reserves, bank deposits, and the money supply?

THE FED'S ROLE IN STABILIZING FINANCIAL MARKETS: BANKING PANICS

Besides controlling the money supply, the Fed also has the responsibility (together with other government agencies) of ensuring that financial markets operate smoothly. Indeed, the creation of the Fed in 1913 was prompted by a series of financial market crises that disrupted both the markets themselves and the U.S. economy as a whole. The hope of the Congress was that the Fed would be able to eliminate or at least control such crises.

Historically, in the United States, *banking panics* were perhaps the most disruptive type of recurrent financial crisis. In a **banking panic,** news or rumors of the imminent bankruptcy of one or more banks leads bank depositors to rush to withdraw their funds. Next, we will discuss banking panics and the Fed's attempts to control them.

Why do banking panics occur? An important factor that helps make banking panics possible is the existence of fractional-reserve banking. In a fractional-reserve

banking panic an episode in which depositors, spurred by news or rumors of the imminent bankruptcy of one or more banks, rush to withdraw their deposits from the banking system banking system, like that of the United States and all other industrialized countries, bank reserves are less than deposits, which means that banks do not keep enough cash on hand to pay off their depositors if they were all to decide to withdraw their deposits. Normally this is not a problem, as only a small percentage of depositors attempt to withdraw their funds on any given day. But if a rumor circulates that one or more banks are in financial trouble and may go bankrupt, depositors may panic, lining up to demand their money. Since bank reserves are less than deposits, a sufficiently severe panic could lead even financially healthy banks to run out of cash, forcing them into bankruptcy and closure.

The Federal Reserve was established in response to a particularly severe banking panic that occurred in 1907. The Fed was equipped with two principal tools to try to prevent or moderate banking panics. First, the Fed was given the power to supervise and regulate banks. It was hoped that the public would have greater confidence in banks, and thus be less prone to panic, if people knew that the Fed was keeping a close watch on bankers' activities. Second, the Fed was allowed to make loans to banks. The idea was that, during a panic, banks could borrow cash from the Fed with which to pay off depositors, avoiding the need to close.

No banking panics occurred between 1914, when the Fed was established, and 1930. However, between 1930 and 1933, the United States experienced the worst and most protracted series of banking panics in its history. Economic historians agree that much of the blame for this panic should be placed on the Fed, which neither appreciated the severity of the problem nor acted aggressively enough to contain it.

ECONOMIC
NATURALIST
10.2

The banking panics of 1930–1933 and the money supply

The worst banking panics ever experienced in the United States occurred during the early stages of the Great Depression, between 1930 and 1933. During this period, approximately one-third of the banks in the United States were forced to close. This near-collapse of the banking system was probably an important reason that the Depression was so severe. With many fewer banks in operation, it was very difficult for small businesses and consumers during the early 1930s to obtain credit. Another important effect of the banking panics was to greatly reduce the nation's money supply. Why should banking panics reduce the national money supply?

During a banking panic, people are afraid to keep deposits in a bank because of the risk that the bank will go bankrupt and their money will be lost (this was prior to the introduction of federal deposit insurance, discussed below). During the 1930–1933 period, many bank depositors withdrew their money from banks, holding currency instead. These withdrawals reduced bank reserves. Each extra dollar of currency held by the public adds $1 to the money supply; but each extra dollar of bank reserves translates into several dollars of money supply, because in a fractional-reserve banking system each dollar of reserves can "support" several dollars in bank deposits. Thus, the public's withdrawals from banks, which increased currency holdings by the public but reduced bank reserves by an equal amount, led to a net decrease in the total money supply (currency plus deposits).

In addition, fearing banking panics and the associated withdrawals by depositors, banks increased their desired reserve-deposit ratios, which reduced the quantity of deposits that could be supported by any given level of bank reserves. This change in reserve-deposit ratios also tended to reduce the money supply.

Data on currency holdings by the public, the reserve-deposit ratio, bank reserves, and the money supply for selected dates are shown in Table 10.7. Notice the increase over the period in the amount of currency held by the public and in the reserve-deposit ratio, as well as the decline in bank reserves after 1930. The last column shows that the U.S. money supply dropped by about one-third between December 1929 and December 1933.

TABLE 10.7
Key U.S. Monetary Statistics, 1929–1933

	Currency held by public	Reserve-deposit ratio	Bank reserves	Money supply
December 1929	3.85	0.075	3.15	45.9
December 1930	3.79	0.082	3.31	44.1
December 1931	4.59	0.095	3.11	37.3
December 1932	4.82	0.109	3.18	34.0
December 1933	4.85	0.133	3.45	30.8

NOTE: Data on currency, the monetary base, and the money supply are in billions of dollars.

SOURCE: Milton Friedman and Anna J. Schwartz, *A Monetary History of the United States, 1863–1960,* Princeton, N.J.: Princeton University Press, 1963, Table A-1.

Using Equation 10.2, we can see that increases in currency holdings by the public and increases in the reserve-deposit ratio both tend to reduce the money supply. These effects were so powerful in 1930–1933 that the nation's money supply, shown in the fourth column of Table 10.7, dropped precipitously, even though currency holdings and bank reserves, taken separately, actually rose during the period.

EXERCISE 10.4

Using the data from Table 10.7, confirm that the relationship between the money supply and its determinants is consistent with Equation 10.2. Would the money supply have fallen in 1931–1933 if the public had stopped withdrawing deposits after December 1930 so that currency held by the public had remained at its December 1930 level?

EXERCISE 10.5

According to Table 10.7, the U.S. money supply fell from $44.1 billion to $37.3 billion over the course of 1931. The Fed did use open-market purchases during 1931 to replenish bank reserves in the face of depositor withdrawals. Find (a) the quantity of reserves that the Fed injected into the economy in 1931 and (b) the quantity of reserves the Fed would have had to add to the economy to keep the money supply unchanged from 1930, assuming that public currency holdings and reserve-deposit ratios for each year remained as reported in the table. Why has the Fed been criticized for being too timid in 1931?

When the Fed failed to stop the banking panics of the 1930s, policymakers decided to look at other strategies for controlling panics. In 1934 Congress instituted a system of deposit insurance. Under a system of **deposit insurance,** the government guarantees depositors—specifically, under current rules, those with deposits of less than $100,000—that they will get their money back even if the bank goes bankrupt. Deposit insurance eliminates the incentive for people to withdraw their deposits when rumors circulate that the bank is in financial trouble, which nips panics in the bud. Indeed, since deposit insurance was instituted, the United States has had no significant banking panics.

Unfortunately, deposit insurance is not a perfect solution to the problem of banking panics. An important drawback is that when deposit insurance is in force, depositors know they are protected no matter what happens to their bank, and they

deposit insurance a system under which the government guarantees that depositors will not lose any money even if their bank goes bankrupt

become completely unconcerned about whether their bank is making prudent loans. This situation can lead to reckless behavior by banks or other insured intermediaries. For example, during the 1980s, many savings and loan associations in the United States went bankrupt, in part because of reckless lending and financial investments. Like banks, savings and loans have deposit insurance, so the U.S. government had to pay savings and loan depositors the full value of their deposits. This action ultimately cost U.S. taxpayers hundreds of billions of dollars. To try to prevent such occurrences, the Federal Reserve and other government regulators examine banks to make sure they are lending prudently.

MONEY AND PRICES

From a macroeconomic perspective, a major reason that control of the supply of money is important is that, *in the long run, the amount of money circulating in an economy and the general level of prices are closely linked*. Indeed, it is virtually unheard of for a country to experience high, sustained inflation without a comparably rapid growth in the amount of money held by its citizens. The link between money growth and inflation for nine countries in Latin America during the period 1995–2004 is illustrated in Figure 10.1. Although the relationship is somewhat loose, countries with higher rates of money growth clearly tend to have higher rates of inflation, and this relationship has been found in other countries and in other periods. The economist Milton Friedman summarized the inflation–money relationship by saying, "Inflation is always and everywhere a monetary phenomenon." We will see later that, over short periods, inflation can arise from sources other than an increase in the supply of money. But over a longer period, and particularly for more severe inflations, Friedman's dictum is certainly correct: The rate of inflation and the rate of growth of the money supply are closely related.

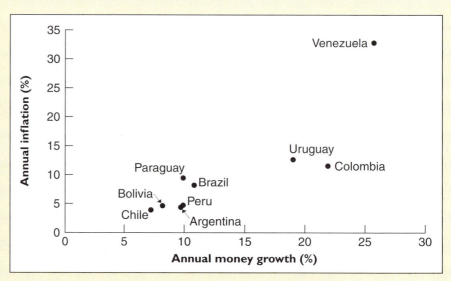

FIGURE 10.1

Inflation and Money Growth in Latin America, 1995–2004.

Latin American countries with higher rates of growth in their money supplies also tended to have higher rates of inflation between 1995 and 2004. (The data for Paraguay end in 2003.)

SOURCE: International Monetary Fund, *International Financial Statistics*.

The existence of a close link between money supply and prices should make intuitive sense. Imagine a situation in which the available supply of goods and services is approximately fixed. Then the more cash (say, dollars) that people hold, the more they will be able to bid up the prices of the fixed supply of goods and services. Thus, a large money supply relative to the supply of goods and services (too much money chasing too few goods) tends to result in high prices. Likewise, a rapidly *growing* supply of money will lead to quickly *rising* prices—that is, inflation.

VELOCITY

To explore the relationship of money growth and inflation in a bit more detail, it is useful to introduce the concept of *velocity*. In economics, **velocity** is a measure of the speed at which money changes hands in transactions involving final goods and services. For example, a given dollar bill might pass from your hand to the grocer's when you buy a quart of milk. The same dollar may then pass from the grocer to a new car dealer when your grocer buys a car, and then from the car dealer to her doctor in exchange for medical services. The more quickly money circulates from one person to the next, the higher its velocity. More formally, velocity is defined as the number of times per year the typical dollar in the money supply is used to buy final goods or services, according to the following formula:

$$\text{Velocity} = \frac{\text{Nominal GDP}}{\text{Money stock}}.$$

velocity a measure of the speed at which money changes hands in transactions involving final goods and services, or, equivalently, nominal GDP divided by the stock of money. Numerically, $V = (P \times Y)/M$, where V is velocity, $P \times Y$ is nominal GDP, and M is the money supply whose velocity is being measured

Let V stand for velocity and let M stand for the particular money stock being considered (for example, M1 or M2). Nominal GDP (a measure of the total value of transactions) equals the price level P times real GDP (Y). Using this notation, we can write the definition of velocity as

$$V = \frac{P \times Y}{M}. \tag{10.3}$$

The higher this ratio, the faster the "typical" dollar is circulating.

The velocity of money in the U.S. economy

EXAMPLE 10.4

In the United States in 2004, M1 was $1,373.5 billion, M2 was $6,430.7 billion, and nominal GDP was $11,734.3 billion. Find the velocity of M1 and of M2 for that year.

Using Equation 10.3, velocity for M1 is given by

$$V = \frac{\$11,734.3 \text{ billion}}{\$1,373.5 \text{ billion}} = 8.54.$$

Similarly, velocity for M2 was

$$V = \frac{\$11,734.3 \text{ billion}}{\$6,430.7 \text{ billion}} = 1.82.$$

You can see that the velocity of M1 is higher than that of M2. This makes sense: Because the components of M1, such as cash and checking accounts, are used more frequently for transactions, each dollar of M1 "turns over" more often than the average dollar of M2.

A variety of factors determine velocity. A leading example is advances in payment technologies, such as the introduction of credit cards and debit cards or the creation of networks of automatic teller machines (ATMs). These new technologies and payment methods have allowed people to carry out their daily business while holding less cash, and thus have tended to increase velocity over time.

MONEY AND INFLATION IN THE LONG RUN

We can use the definition of velocity to see how money and prices are related in the long run. First, rewrite the definition of velocity, Equation 10.3, by multiplying both sides of the equation by the money stock M. This yields

$$M \times V = P \times Y. \tag{10.4}$$

quantity equation money times velocity equals nominal GDP; $M \times V = P \times Y$

Equation 10.4, a famous relationship in economics, is called, for historical reasons, the *quantity equation*. The **quantity equation** states that money times velocity equals nominal GDP. Because the quantity equation is simply a rewriting of the definition of velocity, Equation 10.3, it always holds exactly.

The quantity equation is historically important because late nineteenth and early twentieth-century monetary economists, such as Yale's Irving Fisher, used this relationship to theorize about the relationship between money and prices. We can do the same thing here. To keep things simple, imagine that velocity V is determined by current payment technologies and thus is approximately constant over the period we are considering. Likewise, suppose that real output Y is approximately constant. If we use a bar over a variable to indicate that the variable is constant, we can rewrite the quantity equation as

$$M \times \overline{V} = P \times \overline{Y}, \tag{10.5}$$

where we are treating $\overline{V}$ and $\overline{Y}$ as fixed numbers.

Now look at Equation 10.5 and imagine that for some reason the Federal Reserve increases the money supply M by 10 percent. Because $\overline{V}$ and $\overline{Y}$ are assumed to be fixed, Equation 10.5 can continue to hold only if the price level P also rises by 10 percent. That is, according to the quantity equation, a 10 percent increase in the money supply M should cause a 10 percent increase in the price level P, that is, an inflation of 10 percent.

The intuition behind this conclusion is the one we mentioned at the beginning of this section. If the quantity of goods and services Y is approximately constant (and assuming that velocity V also is constant), an increase in the supply of money will lead people to bid up the prices of the available goods and services. Thus, high rates of money growth will tend to be associated with high rates of inflation, which is exactly what we observed in Figure 10.1.

If high rates of money growth lead to inflation, why do countries allow their money supplies to rise quickly? Usually, rapid rates of money growth are the result of large government budget deficits. Particularly in developing countries or countries suffering from war or political instability, governments sometimes find that they cannot raise sufficient taxes or borrow enough from the public to cover their expenditures. In this situation, the government's only recourse may be to print new money and use this money to pay its bills. If the resulting increase in the amount of money in circulation is large enough, the result will be inflation.

RECAP	**MONEY AND PRICES**

- A high rate of money growth generally leads to inflation. The larger the amount of money in circulation, the higher the public will bid up the prices of available goods and services.

- *Velocity* measures the speed at which money circulates in payments for final goods and services; equivalently it is equal to nominal GDP divided by the stock of money. A numerical value for velocity can be obtained from the equation $V = (P \times Y)/M$, where V is velocity, $P \times Y$ is nominal GDP, and M is the money supply.

- The *quantity equation* states that money times velocity equals nominal GDP, or, in symbols, $M \times V = P \times Y$. The quantity equation is a restatement of the definition of velocity and thus always holds. If velocity and output are approximately constant, the quantity equation implies that a given percentage increase in the money supply leads to the same percentage increase in the price level. In other words, the rate of growth of the money supply equals the rate of inflation.

BOX 10.1: APPROXIMATING THE PERCENTAGE CHANGE OF A PRODUCT

In Equation 10.5 we assumed that V and Y were constant and showed that the percentage change in M would then equal the rate of inflation, which is the percentage change in P. If V and Y are not constant, one can still make some interesting inferences about the connection between changes in the money stock and inflation. According to the quantity equation (Equation 10.4), $MV = PY$. Since this relationship is always true by definition, it is an identity. Consequently, any time the left-hand side MV changes by a specific amount or by a specific percentage, the right-hand side PY must change by the same amount or by the same percentage. Thus:

$$\% \text{ change in } MV = \% \text{ change in } PY. \qquad (10.6)$$

Economists often use a simple approximation to disaggregate the percentage changes in Equation 10.6. The percentage change in the product of two (or more) variables is approximately equal to the sum of the percentage changes in each of the variables, as long as those percentage changes are relatively small. Using this approximation, we can rewrite Equation 10.6 as

$$\% \text{ change in } M + \% \text{ change in } V \approx \% \text{ change in } P + \% \text{ change in } Y, \quad (10.7)$$

where the mathematical symbol $\approx$ means " is approximately equal to."

Suppose, for example, the money supply M grows by 4 percent per year, velocity V grows by 1 percent per year, and real GDP Y grows by 3 percent per year. If we insert these values into Equation 10.7, we obtain

$$4\% + 1\% \approx \% \text{ change in } P + 3\%.$$

We can solve this to obtain the approximate rate of inflation:

$$\% \text{ change in } P \approx 4\% + 1\% - 3\% = 2\%.$$

Indeed, whenever any three percentage changes in Equation 10.7 are known, one can use Equation 10.7 to solve for the fourth percentage change. Economists use this "percentage change rule" in a variety of applications.

■ SUMMARY ■

- *Money* is any asset that can be used in making purchases, such as currency and checking account balances. Money has three main functions: It is a *medium of exchange*, which means that it can be used in transactions. It is a *unit of account*, in that economic values are typically measured in units of money (e.g., dollars). And it is a *store of value*, a means by which people can hold wealth. In practice, it is difficult to measure the money supply, since many assets have some moneylike features. A relatively narrow measure of money is M1, which includes currency and checking accounts. A broader measure of money, M2, includes all the assets in M1 plus additional assets that are somewhat less convenient to use in transactions than those included in M1.

- Because bank deposits are part of the money supply, the behavior of commercial banks and of bank depositors affects the amount of money in the economy. A key factor is the *reserve-deposit ratio* chosen by banks. *Bank reserves* are cash or similar assets held by commercial banks, for the purpose of meeting depositor withdrawals and payments. The reserve-deposit ratio is bank reserves divided by deposits in banks. A banking system in which all deposits are held as reserves practices *100 percent reserve banking.* Modern banking systems have reserve-deposit ratios less than 100 percent, and are called *fractional-reserve banking systems.*

- Commercial banks create money through multiple rounds of lending and accepting deposits. This process of lending and increasing deposits comes to an end when banks' reserve-deposit ratios equal their desired levels. At that point, bank deposits equal bank reserves divided by the desired reserve-deposit ratio. The money supply equals currency held by the public plus deposits in the banking system.

- The central bank of the United States is called the *Federal Reserve System,* or the Fed for short. The Fed's two main responsibilities are making monetary policy, which means determining how much money will circulate in the economy, and overseeing and regulating financial markets, especially banks. Created in 1914, the Fed is headed by a *Board of Governors* made up of seven governors appointed by the president. One of these seven governors is appointed chairman. The *Federal Open Market Committee,* which meets about eight times a year to determine monetary policy, is made up of the seven governors and five of the presidents of the regional Federal Reserve banks.

- The Fed can affect the money supply indirectly in several ways. In the most important of these, called *open-market operations,* the Fed buys or sells government securities in exchange for currency held by banks or the public.

- One of the original purposes of the Federal Reserve was to help eliminate or control banking panics. A *banking panic* is an episode in which depositors, spurred by news or rumors of the imminent bankruptcy of one or more banks, rush to withdraw their deposits from the banking system. Because banks do not keep enough reserves on hand to pay off all depositors, even a financially healthy bank can run out of cash during a panic and be forced to close. The Federal Reserve failed to contain banking panics during the Great Depression, which led to sharp declines in the money supply. The adoption of a system of *deposit insurance* in the United States eliminated banking panics. A disadvantage of deposit insurance is that if banks or other insured intermediaries make bad loans or financial investments, the taxpayers may be responsible for covering the losses.

- In the long run, the rate of growth of the money supply and the rate of inflation are closely linked because a larger amount of money in circulation allows people to bid up the prices of existing goods and services. *Velocity* measures the speed at which money circulates in payments for final goods and services; equivalently, it is equal to nominal GDP divided by the stock of money. Velocity is defined by the equation $V = (P \times Y)/M$, where V is velocity, $P \times Y$ is nominal GDP, and M is the money supply. The definition of velocity can be rewritten as the *quantity equation,* $M \times V = P \times Y$. The quantity equation shows that, if velocity and output are constant, a given percentage increase in the money supply will lead to the same percentage increase in the price level.

■ KEY TERMS ■

bank reserves (276)
banking panic (283)
barter (272)
Board of Governors of the Federal
   Reserve System (282)
deposit insurance (285)
Federal Open Market Committee
   (FOMC) (282)

Federal Reserve System (the Fed) (280)
fractional-reserve banking
   system (277)
M1 (274)
M2 (274)
medium of exchange (272)
money (272)
100 percent reserve banking (276)

open-market operations (283)
open-market purchase (282)
open-market sale (283)
quantity equation (288)
reserve-deposit ratio (277)
store of value (273)
unit of account (273)
velocity (287)

■ REVIEW QUESTIONS ■

1. What is *money*? Why do people hold money even though it pays a lower return than other financial assets?

2. Suppose that the public switches from doing most of its shopping with currency to using checks instead. If the Fed takes no action, what will happen to the national money supply? Explain.

3. The Fed wants to reduce the U.S. money supply. Describe what it would do, and explain how this action would accomplish the Fed's objective.

4. What is a *banking panic*? Prior to the introduction of deposit insurance, why might even a bank that had made sound loans have reason to fear a panic?

5. Define *velocity*. How has the introduction of new payment technologies, such as ATM machines, affected velocity? Explain.

6. Use the quantity equation to explain why money growth and inflation tend to be closely linked.

■ PROBLEMS ■

1. During World War II, an Allied soldier named Robert Radford spent several years in a large German prisoner-of-war camp. At times more than 50,000 prisoners were held in the camp, with some freedom to move about within the compound. Radford later wrote an account of his experiences. He described how an economy developed in the camp, in which prisoners traded food, clothing, and other items. Services, such as barbering, also were exchanged. Lacking paper money, the prisoners began to use cigarettes (provided monthly by the Red Cross) as money. Prices were quoted, and payments made, using cigarettes.

   a. In Radford's POW camp, how did cigarettes fulfill the three functions of money?

   b. Why do you think the prisoners used cigarettes as money, as opposed to other items of value such as squares of chocolate or pairs of boots?

   c. Do you think a nonsmoking prisoner would have been willing to accept cigarettes in exchange for a good or service in Radford's camp? Why or why not?

2. Obtain recent data on M1, M2, and their components. (For an online source, see Table 10.1.) By what percentage have the two monetary aggregates grown over the past year? Which components of the two aggregates have grown the most quickly?

3. Redo the example of Gorgonzola in the text (see Tables 10.2 to 10.6), assuming that (a) initially, the Gorgonzolan central bank puts 5,000,000 guilders into circulation, and (b) commercial banks desire to hold reserves of 20 percent of deposits. As in the text, assume that the public holds no currency. Show the consolidated balance sheets of Gorgonzolan commercial banks after the initial deposits (compare to Table 10.2), after one round of loans (compare to Table 10.3), after the first redeposit of guilders (compare to Table 10.4), and after two rounds of loans and redeposits (Table 10.5). What are the final values of bank reserves, loans, deposits, and the money supply?

4. a. Bank reserves are 100, the public holds 200 in currency, and the desired reserve-deposit ratio is 0.25. Find deposits and the money supply.

   b. The money supply is 500, and currency held by the public equals bank reserves. The desired reserve-deposit ratio is 0.25. Find currency held by the public and bank reserves.

   c. The money supply is 1,250, of which 250 is currency held by the public. Bank reserves are 100. Find the desired reserve-deposit ratio.

5. When a central bank increases bank reserves by $1, the money supply rises by more than $1. The amount of extra money created when the central bank increases bank reserves by $1 is called the *money multiplier.*

   a. Explain why the money multiplier is generally greater than 1. In what special case would it equal 1?

   b. The initial money supply is $1,000, of which $500 is currency held by the public. The desired reserve-deposit ratio is 0.2. Find the increase in money supply associated with increases in bank reserves of $1, $5, and $10. What is the money multiplier in this economy?

   c. Find a general rule for calculating the money multiplier.

   d. Suppose the Fed wanted to reduce the money multiplier, perhaps because it believes that change would give it more precise control over the money supply. What action could the Fed take to achieve its goal?

6. Refer to Table 10.7. Suppose that the Fed had decided to set the U.S. money supply in December 1932 and in December 1933 at the same value as in December 1930. Assuming that the values of currency held by the public and the reserve-deposit ratio had remained as given in the table, by how much more should the Fed have increased bank reserves at each of those dates to accomplish that objective?

7. Suppose real GDP is $8 trillion, nominal GDP is $10 trillion, M1 is $2 trillion, and M2 is $5 trillion.

   a. Find velocity for M1 and for M2.

   b. Show that the quantity equation holds for both M1 and M2.

8. You are given the following hypothetical data for 2007 and 2008:

	2007	2008
Money supply	1,000	1,050
Velocity	8.0	8.0
Real GDP	12,000	12,000

a. Find the price level for 2007 and 2008. What is the rate of inflation between the two years?
b. What is the rate of inflation between 2007 and 2008 if the money supply in 2008 is 1,100 instead of 1,050?
c. What is the rate of inflation between 2007 and 2008 if the money supply in 2008 is 1,100 and output in 2008 is 12,600?

■ ANSWERS TO IN-CHAPTER EXERCISES ■

10.1 Table 10.5 shows the balance sheet of banks after two rounds of lending and redeposits. At that point, deposits are 2,710,000 guilders and reserves are 1,000,000 guilders. Since banks have a desired reserve-deposit ratio of 10 percent, they will keep 271,000 guilders (10 percent of deposits) as reserves and lend out the remaining 729,000 guilders. Loans to farmers are now 2,439,000 guilders. Eventually the 729,000 guilders lent to the farmers will be redeposited into the banks, giving the banks deposits of 3,439,000 guilders and reserves of 1,000,000 guilders. The balance sheet is as shown in the accompanying table.

Assets		Liabilities	
Currency (= reserves)	1,000,000 guilders	Deposits	3,439,000 guilders
Loans to farmers	2,439,000 guilders		

Notice that assets equal liabilities. The money supply equals deposits, or 3,439,000 guilders. Currency held in the banks as reserves does not count in the money supply.

10.2 Because the public holds no currency, the money supply equals bank deposits, which in turn equal bank reserves divided by the reserve-deposit ratio (Equation 10.1). If bank reserves are 1,000,000 and the reserve-deposit ratio is 0.05, then deposits equal 1,000,000/0.05 = 20,000,000 guilders, which is also the money supply. If bank reserves are 2,000,000 guilders and the reserve-deposit ratio is 0.10, then the money supply and deposits are again equal to 20,000,000 guilders, or 2,000,000/0.10.

10.3 If the central bank sells 50 shekels of government bonds in exchange for currency, the immediate effect is to reduce the amount of currency in the hands of the public by 50 shekels. To restore their currency holding to the desired level of 1,000 shekels, the public will withdraw 50 shekels from commercial banks, reducing bank reserves from 200 shekels to 150 shekels. The desired reserve-deposit ratio is 0.2, so ultimately deposits must equal 150 shekels in reserves divided by 0.2, or 750 shekels. (Note that to contract deposits, the commercial banks will have to "call in" loans, reducing their loans outstanding.) The money supply equals 1,000 shekels in currency held by the public plus 750 shekels in deposits, or 1,750 shekels. Thus the open-market purchase has reduced the money supply from 2,000 to 1,750 shekels.

10.4 Verify directly for each date in Table 10.7 that

$$\text{Money supply} = \text{Currency} + \frac{\text{Bank reserves}}{\text{Desired reserve-deposit ratio}}.$$

For example, for December 1929, we can check that 45.9 = 3.85 + 3.15/0.075.

Suppose that the currency held by the public in December 1933 had been 3.79, as in December 1930, rather than 4.85, and that the difference ($4.85 - 3.79 = 1.06$) had been left in the banks. Then bank reserves in December 1933 would have been $3.45 + 1.06 = 4.51$, and the money supply would have been $3.79 + 4.51/0.133 = 37.7$. So the money supply would still have fallen between 1930 and 1933 if people had not increased their holdings of currency, but only by about half as much.

10.5 Over the course of 1931, currency holdings by the public rose by $0.80 billion but bank reserves fell overall by only $0.20 billion. Thus, the Fed must have replaced $0.60 billion of lost reserves during the year through open-market purchases.

Currency holdings at the end of 1931 were $4.59 billion. To have kept the money supply at the December 1930 value of $44.1 billion, the Fed would have had to ensure that bank deposits equaled $44.1 billion $-$ $4.59 billion, or $39.51 billion. As the reserve-deposit ratio in 1931 was 0.095, this would have required bank reserves of $0.095 \times$ $39.51 billion, or $3.75 billion, compared to the actual value in December 1931 of $3.11 billion. Thus, to keep the money supply from falling, the Fed would have had to increase bank reserves by $0.64 billion more than it did. The Fed has been criticized for increasing bank reserves by only about half what was needed to keep the money supply from falling.

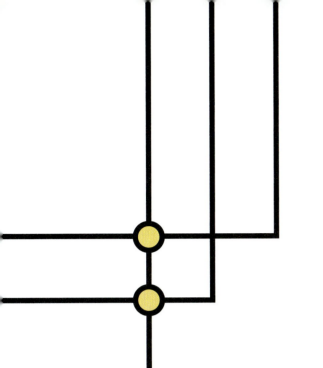

FINANCIAL MARKETS AND INTERNATIONAL CAPITAL FLOWS

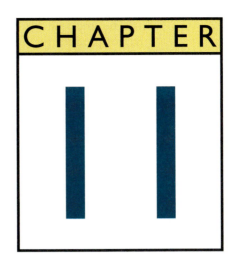

A television ad for an online trading company showed an office worker, call him Ed, sitting in front of his computer. Instead of working, Ed is checking the prices of the stocks he bought over the Internet. Suddenly his eyes widen, as on the computer screen a graph shows the price of his stock shooting up like a rocket. With a whoop, Ed heads down to his boss's office, delivers a few well-chosen insults, and quits his job. Unfortunately, when Ed returns to his desk to pack up his belongings, the computer screen shows that the price of his stock has fallen as quickly as it rose. The last we hear of Ed are his futile attempts to convince his boss that he was only kidding.

Ed's story is not a bad metaphor for the behavior of U.S. financial markets in the years around the turn of the millennium. The 1990s were a boom period in the United States, with strong economic growth, record low unemployment rates, and almost nonexistent inflation. This prosperity was mirrored in the spectacular performance of the stock market. In 1999 the Dow Jones index, a popular measure of stock prices, broke 10,000 and then 11,000 for the first time—almost triple the value of the index five years earlier. Prices of stocks of start-up companies, particularly high-technology and Internet companies, rose to stunning levels, making billionaires of some entrepreneurs still in their twenties. Nor were the benefits of rising stock prices confined to the very rich or the very nerdy. Stock ownership among the general population—including both direct ownership of stocks and

Would investors have spent $5.3 billion to build the Shoreham Nuclear Power Plant if they had known that regulators would never certify it as safe enough to operate?

indirect ownership through mutual funds and pension plans—reached record levels. The stock market boom, however, was not sustained. High-tech companies did not produce the profits that their investors had hoped for, and stock prices began to drop. Many start-up companies saw their stock become nearly worthless, and the values of even established companies fell by one-third or more.

During periods such as the 1990s, people often begin to think of the stock market as a place to gamble and, maybe, to strike it rich. Some people do get rich playing the market, and some people, like Ed and many real-life investors in stocks in recent years, lose everything. But the stock market, as well as other financial markets, plays a crucial role in the economy that is not shared by the gambling establishments in Las Vegas or Atlantic City. That role is to ensure that national saving is devoted to the most productive uses.

In the chapter "Saving and Capital Formation," we discussed the importance of national saving. Under most circumstances, a high rate of national saving permits a high rate of capital formation, which both economic logic and experience predict will tend to increase labor productivity and living standards. However, creating new capital does not *guarantee* a richer and more productive economy. History is full of examples of "white elephants," capital projects in which millions, and even billions, of dollars were invested with little economic benefit: nuclear power plants that were never opened, massive dams whose main effect was to divert water supplies and disrupt the local agriculture, new technologies that just didn't work as planned.

A healthy economy not only saves adequately but also invests those savings in a productive way. In market economies, like that of the United States, channeling society's savings into the best possible capital investments is the role of the financial system: banks, stock markets, bond markets, and other financial markets and institutions. For this reason, many economists have argued that the development of well-functioning financial markets is a crucial precursor to sustained economic growth. In the first part of this chapter, we discuss some major financial markets and institutions and their role in directing saving to productive uses.

Many of the people who purchased stock in U.S. companies during the roller-coaster years of the late 1990s and early 2000s were foreigners, looking to the United States for investment opportunities. More broadly, in the modern world, saving often flows across national boundaries, as savers purchase financial assets in countries other than their own and borrowers look abroad for sources of financing. Flows of funds between lenders and borrowers located in different countries are referred to as *international capital flows*. We discuss the international dimension of saving and capital formation in the second part of the chapter. As we will see, for many countries, including the United States, foreign savings provide an important supplement to domestic savings as a means of financing the formation of new capital.

THE FINANCIAL SYSTEM AND THE ALLOCATION OF SAVING TO PRODUCTIVE USES

We have emphasized the importance of high rates of saving and capital formation for economic growth and increased productivity. High rates of saving and investment by themselves are not sufficient, however. A case in point is the former Soviet Union, which had very high rates of saving and investment but often used its resources very inefficiently, for example, by constructing massive but poorly designed factories that produced inferior goods at high cost. A successful economy not only saves but also uses its savings wisely by applying these limited funds to the investment projects that seem likely to be the most productive.

In the Soviet Union, a centralized bureaucracy made decisions about the allocation of saving to alternative uses. Because the bureaucrats in Moscow had relatively poor information and because they allowed themselves to be influenced by noneconomic considerations such as political favoritism, they often made poor decisions. In a market economy like that of the United States, in contrast, savings are allocated by means of a decentralized, market-oriented financial system. The U.S. financial system consists both of financial institutions, like banks, and financial markets, such as bond markets and stock markets.

The financial system of countries like the United States improves the allocation of savings in at least two distinct ways. First, the financial system provides *information* to savers about which of the many possible uses of their funds are likely to prove most productive and hence pay the highest return. By evaluating the potential productivity of alternative capital investments, the financial system helps to direct savings to its best uses. Second, financial markets help savers to *share the risks* of individual investment projects. Sharing of risks protects individual savers from bearing excessive risk, while at the same time making it possible to direct savings to projects, such as the development of new technologies, which are risky but potentially very productive as well.

In this section, we briefly discuss three key components of the financial system: the banking system, the bond market, and the stock market. In doing so, we elaborate on the role of the financial system as a whole in providing information about investment projects and in helping savers to share the risks of lending.

THE BANKING SYSTEM

As we discussed in the last chapter, the U.S. banking system consists of thousands of commercial banks that accept deposits from individuals and businesses and use those deposits to make loans. Banks are the most important example of a class of institutions called **financial intermediaries,** firms that extend credit to borrowers using funds raised from savers. Other examples of financial intermediaries are savings and loan associations and credit unions.

financial intermediaries firms that extend credit to borrowers using funds raised from savers

Why are financial intermediaries such as banks, which "stand between" savers and investors, necessary? Why don't individual savers just lend directly to borrowers who want to invest in new capital projects? The main reason is that, through specialization, banks and other intermediaries develop a *comparative advantage* in evaluating the quality of borrowers—the information-gathering function that we referred to a moment ago. Most savers, particularly small savers, do not have the time or the knowledge to determine for themselves which borrowers are likely to use the funds they receive most productively. In contrast, banks and other intermediaries have gained expertise in performing the information-gathering activities necessary for profitable lending, including checking out the borrower's background, determining whether the borrower's business plans make sense, and monitoring the borrower's activities during the life of the loan. Because banks specialize in evaluating potential borrowers, they can perform this function at a much lower cost, and with better results, than individual savers could on their own. Banks also reduce the costs of gathering information about potential borrowers by pooling the savings of many individuals to make large loans. Each large loan needs to be evaluated only once, by the bank, rather than separately by each of the hundreds of individuals whose savings may be pooled to make the loan.

Banks help savers by eliminating their need to gather information about potential borrowers and by directing their savings toward higher-return, more-productive investments. Banks help borrowers as well, by providing access to credit that might otherwise not be available. Unlike a *Fortune* 500 corporation, which typically has many ways to raise funds, a small business that wants to buy a copier or remodel its offices will have few options other than going to a bank. Because the bank's lending officer has developed expertise in evaluating small-business loans, and even may have an ongoing business relationship with the small-business owner, the bank will be able to gather the information it needs to make the loan at a reasonable cost. Likewise, consumers who want to borrow to finish a basement or add a room to a

"O.K., folks, let's move along. I'm sure you've all seen someone qualify for a loan before."

house will find few good alternatives to a bank. In sum, banks' expertise at gathering information about alternative lending opportunities allows them to bring together small savers looking for good uses for their funds, and small borrowers with worthwhile investment projects.

In addition to being able to earn a return on their savings, a second reason that people hold bank deposits is to make it easier to make payments. Most bank deposits allow the holder to write a check against them or draw on them using a debit card or ATM card. For many transactions, paying by check or debit card is more convenient than using cash. For example, it is safer to send a check through the mail than to send cash, and paying by check gives you a record of the transaction, whereas a cash payment does not. We discussed the role of banks in the creation of money in the previous chapter.

ECONOMIC NATURALIST 11.1

How has the banking crisis in Japan affected the Japanese economy?

During the 1980s, real estate and stock prices soared in Japan. Japanese banks made many loans to real estate developers, and the banks themselves acquired stock in corporations. (Unlike in the United States, in Japan it is legal for commercial banks to own stock.) However, in the early 1990s, land prices plummeted in Japan, leading many bank borrowers to default on their loans. Stock prices also came down sharply, reducing the value of banks' shareholdings. The net result was that most Japanese banks fell into severe financial trouble, with many large banks near bankruptcy. What was the effect of this crisis, which lasted more than a decade, on the Japanese economy?

Relative to the United States, which has more developed stock and bond markets, Japan has traditionally relied very heavily on banks to allocate its savings. Thus, when the severe financial problems of the banks prevented them from operating normally, many borrowers found it unusually difficult to obtain credit—a situation known as a "credit crunch." Smaller borrowers such as small- and medium-sized businesses had been particularly dependent on banks for credit and thus suffered disproportionately.

The Japanese economy, after many years of robust growth, suffered a severe recession throughout the 1990s. Many factors contributed to this sharp slowdown. However, the virtual breakdown of the banking system certainly did not help the situation, as credit shortages interfered with smaller firms' ability to make capital investments and, in some cases, to purchase raw materials and pay workers. The Japanese government recognized the problem but responded very slowly, in large part out of reluctance to bear the high costs of returning the banks to a healthy financial condition. In recent years, the health of the Japanese banking system appears to have improved significantly, although problems remain and the Japanese economy has not returned to its earlier high rate of growth.

BONDS AND STOCKS

Large and well-established corporations that wish to obtain funds for investment will sometimes go to banks. Unlike the typical small borrower, however, a larger firm usually has alternative ways of raising funds, notably through the corporate bond market and the stock market. We first discuss some of the mechanics of bonds and stocks, then return to the role of bond and stock markets in allocating saving.

Bonds A bond is a legal promise to repay a debt. These repayments typically consist of two parts. First, the **principal amount,** which is the amount originally lent, is paid at some specific date in the future, called the **maturation date.** Second, the owner of the bond, called the *bondholder,* receives regular interest, or **coupon payments,** until the bond's maturation date. For example, a bond may have a principal amount of $1,000 payable on January 1, 2025, and annual coupon payments of $50. These coupon payments are also equal to the principal amount times the **coupon rate,** where the coupon rate is the interest rate promised when the bond is issued. (The coupon rate therefore is also equal to the annual coupon payment divided by the principal.) In the example in the text, the principal is $1,000 and the coupon rate is 5 percent, resulting in annual coupon payments of (.05)($1,000), or $50.

Corporations and governments frequently raise funds by issuing bonds and selling them to savers. The coupon rate that a newly issued bond must promise in order to be attractive to savers depends on a number of factors, including the bond's term, its credit risk, and its tax treatment. The *term* of a bond is the length of time until the bond's maturation date, which can range from 30 days to 30 years or more. The annual coupon rates on long-term (30-year) bonds generally exceed those on short-term (1-year) bonds because lenders require higher coupon rates (and, hence, higher annual coupon payments) to lend for a long term. *Credit risk* is the risk that the borrower will go bankrupt and thus not repay the loan. A borrower that is viewed as risky will have to pay a higher coupon rate to compensate lenders for taking the chance of losing all or part of their financial investment. For example, so-called high-yield bonds, less formally known as "junk bonds," are bonds issued by firms judged to be risky by credit-rating agencies; these bonds pay higher coupon rates than bonds issued by companies thought to be less risky.

Bonds also differ in their *tax treatment.* For example, interest paid on bonds issued by local governments, called *municipal bonds,* is exempt from federal taxes, whereas interest on other types of bonds is treated as taxable income. Because of this tax advantage, lenders are willing to accept a lower coupon rate on municipal bonds.

Bond owners are not required to hold their bonds until their maturation dates. They are always free to sell their bonds in the *bond market,* an organized market run by professional bond traders. The market value of a particular bond at any given point in time is called the *price* of the bond. The price of a bond can be greater than, less than, or equal to the principal amount of the bond, depending on

bond a legal promise to repay a debt, usually including both the principal amount and regular interest payments

principal amount the amount originally lent

maturation date the date at which the principal will be repaid

coupon payments regular interest payments made to the bondholder

coupon rate the interest rate promised when a bond is issued; the annual coupon payments are equal to the coupon rate times the principal amount of the bond

how the current or prevailing interest rate in financial markets compares with the interest rate at the time the bond was issued. The close relationship between the price of a bond and the current interest rate is illustrated by Example 11.1.

EXAMPLE 11.1

Bond prices and interest rates

On January 1, 2006, Tanya purchases a newly issued, two-year government bond with a principal amount of $1,000 for a price of $1,000. The coupon rate on the bond is 5 percent, paid annually, reflecting the prevailing interest rates on January 1, 2006. Hence, Tanya, or whoever owns the bond at the time, will receive a coupon payment of $50 (5 percent of $1,000) on January 1, 2007. The owner of the bond will receive another coupon payment of $50 on January 1, 2008, at which time she also will receive repayment of the principal amount of $1,000.

On January 1, 2007, after receiving her first year's coupon payment, Tanya decides to sell her bond to raise the funds to take a vacation. She offers her bond for sale in the bond market. The buyer of the bond will receive $1,050 on January 1, 2008, representing the second coupon payment of $50, plus repayment of the $1,000 principal. How much can Tanya expect to get for her "used" bond? The answer depends on the prevailing interest rate in the bond market when she sells her bond on January 1, 2007.

Suppose first that, on January 1, 2007, when Tanya takes her bond to the bond market, the prevailing interest rate on newly issued one-year bonds has risen to 6 percent. Thus, someone who buys a new one-year bond on January 1, 2007, with a 6 percent coupon rate for $1,000 will receive $1,060 on January 1, 2008 ($1,000 principal repayment plus a $60 coupon payment). Would that person also be willing to pay Tanya the $1,000 Tanya paid for her bond? No. Note that the coupon payment on Tanya's "used" bond does not rise when interest rates rise but remains equal to $50. Consequently, the purchaser of Tanya's "used" bond will only receive $1,050 on January 1, 2008, when the bond matures. In order to sell her "used" bond, Tanya will have to reduce the price below $1,000. This example illustrates the fact that *bond prices and interest rates are inversely related*. When the interest rate being paid on newly issued bonds rises, the price financial investors are willing to pay for existing bonds falls.

How much would the price for Tanya's "used" bond have to fall? Recall that the person who buys the newly issued one-year bond on January 1, 2007, for $1,000 will receive $1,060 on January 1, 2008. This $60 gain represents a 6 percent return on the price he paid. That person will buy Tanya's "used" bond only if Tanya's bond also will give him a 6 percent return. The price for Tanya's bond that allows the purchaser to earn a 6 percent return must satisfy the equation

$$\text{Bond price} \times 1.06 = \$1,050.$$

Solving the equation for the bond price, we find that Tanya's bond will sell for $1,050/1.06, or just under $991. To check this result, note that on January 1, 2008, the purchaser of the bond will receive $1,050, or $59 more than he paid on January 1, 2007. His rate of return is $59/$991, or 6 percent, as expected.

What if the prevailing interest rate had instead fallen to 4 percent? When prevailing interest rates fall, bond prices rise. The price of Tanya's "used" bond would rise until it, too, gave a return of 4 percent. At that point, the price of Tanya's bond would satisfy the relationship

$$\text{Bond price} \times 1.04 = \$1,050,$$

implying that the price of her bond would rise to $1,050/1.04, or almost $1,010.

Finally, what happens if the interest rate when Tanya wants to sell is 5 percent, the same as it was when she originally bought the bond? You should show that in this case the bond would sell at its original price of $1,000.

EXERCISE 11.1

Three-year government bonds are issued with a principal amount (sometimes called the *face value*) of $1,000 and an annual coupon rate of 7 percent. Thus, the owner will receive three coupon payments of (0.07)($1,000) = $70 at the end of each year. One year prior to the maturation date of these bonds, a newspaper headline reads, "Bad Economic News Causes Prices of Bonds to Plunge," and the story reveals that these three-year bonds have fallen in price to $960. What has happened to prevailing interest rates? What is the one-year interest rate at the time of the newspaper story?

Issuing bonds is one means by which a corporation or a government can obtain funds from savers. Another important way of raising funds, but one restricted to corporations, is by issuing stock to the public.

Stocks   A share of **stock** (or *equity*) is a claim to partial ownership of a firm. For example, if a corporation has 1 million shares of stock outstanding, ownership of one share is equivalent to ownership of one-millionth of the company. Stockholders receive returns on their financial investment in two forms. First, stockholders receive a regular payment called a **dividend** for each share of stock they own. Dividends are determined by the firm's management and usually depend on the firm's recent profits. Second, stockholders receive returns in the form of *capital gains* when the price of their stock increases (we discussed capital gains and losses in the chapter "Saving and Capital Formation").

stock (or equity) a claim to partial ownership of a firm

dividend a regular payment received by stockholders for each share that they own

Prices of stocks are determined through trading on a stock exchange, such as the New York Stock Exchange. A stock's price rises and falls as the demand for the stock changes. Demand for stocks in turn depends on factors such as news about the prospects of the company. For example, the stock price of a pharmaceutical company that announces the discovery of an important new drug is likely to rise on the announcement, even if actual production and marketing of the drug is some time away, because financial investors expect the company to become more profitable in the future. Example 11.2 illustrates numerically some key factors that affect stock prices.

How much should you pay for a share of FortuneCookie.com?

EXAMPLE 11.2

You have the opportunity to buy shares in a new company called FortuneCookie.com, which plans to sell gourmet fortune cookies over the Internet. Your stockbroker estimates that the company will pay $1.00 per share in dividends a year from now, and that in a year the market price of the company will be $80.00 per share. Assuming that you accept your broker's estimates as accurate, what is the most that you should be willing to pay today per share of FortuneCookie.com? How does your answer change if you expect a $5.00 dividend? If you expect a $1.00 dividend but an $84.00 stock price in one year?

Based on your broker's estimates, you conclude that in one year each share of FortuneCookie.com you own will be worth $81.00 in your pocket—the $1.00 dividend plus the $80.00 you could get by reselling the stock. Finding the maximum price you would pay for the stock today therefore boils down to asking how much would you invest today to have $81.00 a year from today. Answering this question in turn requires one more piece of information, which is the expected rate of return that you require in order to be willing to buy stock in this company.

How would you determine your required rate of return to hold stock in FortuneCookie.com? For the moment, let's imagine that you are not too worried about the potential riskiness of the stock, either because you think that it is a "sure thing" or because you are a devil-may-care type who is not bothered by risk. In that case, your required rate of return to hold FortuneCookie.com should be about the same as you can get on other financial investments, such as government bonds. The available return on other financial investments gives the *opportunity cost* of your funds. So, for example, if the interest rate currently being offered by government bonds is 6 percent, you should be willing to accept a 6 percent return to hold FortuneCookie.com as well. In that case, the maximum price you would pay today for a share of FortuneCookie.com satisfies the equation

$$\text{Stock price} \times 1.06 = \$81.00.$$

This equation defines the stock price you should be willing to pay if you are willing to accept a 6 percent return over the next year. Solving this equation yields stock price = $81.00/1.06 = $76.42. If you buy FortuneCookie.com for $76.42, then your return over the year will be ($81.00 − $76.42)/$76.42 = $4.58/$71.42 = 6 percent, which is the rate of return you required to buy the stock.

If instead the dividend is expected to be $5.00, then the total benefit of holding the stock in one year, equal to the expected dividend plus the expected price, is $5.00 + $80.00, or $85.00. Assuming again that you are willing to accept a 6 percent return to hold FortuneCookie.com, the price you are willing to pay for the stock today satisfies the relationship stock price × 1.06 = $85.00. Solving this equation for the stock price yields stock price = $85.00/1.06 = $80.19. Comparing this price with that in the previous case, we see that a higher expected dividend in the future increases the value of the stock today. That's why good news about the future prospects of a company—such as the announcement by a pharmaceutical company that it has discovered a useful new drug—affects its stock price immediately.

If the expected future price of the stock is $84.00, with the dividend at $1.00, then the value of holding the stock in one year is once again $85.00, and the calculation is the same as the previous one. Again, the price you should be willing to pay for the stock is $80.19.

These examples show that an increase in the future dividend or in the future expected stock price raises the stock price today, whereas an increase in the return a saver requires to hold the stock lowers today's stock price. Since we expect required returns in the stock market to be closely tied to market interest rates, this last result implies that increases in interest rates tend to depress stock prices as well as bond prices.

Our examples also took the future stock price as given. But what determines the future stock price? Just as today's stock price depends on the dividend shareholders expect to receive this year and the stock price a year from now, the stock price a year from now depends on the dividend expected for next year and the stock price two years from now, and so on. Ultimately, then, today's stock price is affected not only by the dividend expected this year but future dividends as well. A company's ability to pay dividends depends on its earnings. If a company's earnings are expected to increase rapidly in the future, its future dividends will probably grow too. Thus, as we noted in the example of the pharmaceutical company that announces the discovery of a new drug, news about future earnings—even earnings quite far in the future—is likely to affect a company's stock price immediately.

EXERCISE II.2

As in Example II.2, you expect a share of FortuneCookie.com to be worth $80.00 per share in one year, and also to pay a dividend of $1.00 in one year. What should you be willing to pay for the stock today if the prevailing interest rate, equal to your required rate of return, is 4 percent? What if the interest rate is 8 percent? In general, how would you expect stock prices to react if economic news arrives that implies that interest rates will rise in the very near future?

In Example 11.2 we assumed that you were willing to accept a return of 6 percent to hold FortuneCookie.com, the same return that you could get on a government bond. However, financial investments in the stock market are quite risky in that returns to holding stocks can be highly variable and unpredictable. For example, although you expect a share of FortuneCookie.com to be worth $80.00 in one year, you also realize that there is a chance it might sell as low as $50.00 or as high as $110.00 per share. Most financial investors dislike risk and unpredictability and thus have a higher required rate of return for holding risky assets like stocks than for holding relatively safe assets like government bonds. The difference between the required rate of return to hold risky assets and the rate of return on safe assets, like government bonds, is called the **risk premium**. Example 11.3 illustrates the effect of financial investors' dislike of risk on stock prices.

risk premium the rate of return that financial investors require to hold risky assets minus the rate of return on safe assets

Riskiness and stock prices

EXAMPLE 11.3

Continuing Example 11.2, suppose that FortuneCookie.com is expected to pay a $1.00 dividend and have a market price of $80.00 per share in one year. The interest rate on government bonds is 6 percent per year. However, to be willing to hold a risky asset like a share of FortuneCookie.com, you require an expected return four percentage points higher than the rate paid by safe assets like government bonds (a risk premium of 4 percent). Hence you require a 10 percent expected return to hold FortuneCookie.com. What is the most you would be willing to pay for the stock now? What do you conclude about the relationship between perceived riskiness and stock prices?

As a share of FortuneCookie.com is expected to pay $81.00 in one year and the required return is 10 percent, we have stock price × 1.10 = $81.00. Solving for the stock price, we find the price to be $81.00/1.10 = $73.64, less than the price of $76.42 we found when there was no risk premium and the required rate of return was 6 percent (Example 11.2). We conclude that financial investors' dislike of risk, and the resulting risk premium, lowers the prices of risky assets like stocks.

RECAP	FACTORS AFFECTING STOCK PRICES

1. An increase in expected future dividends or in the expected future market price of a stock raises the current price of the stock.

2. An increase in interest rates, implying an increase in the required rate of return to hold stocks, lowers the current price of stocks.

3. An increase in perceived riskiness, as reflected in an increase in the risk premium, lowers the current price of stocks.

BOND MARKETS, STOCK MARKETS, AND THE ALLOCATION OF SAVINGS

Like banks, bond markets and stock markets provide a means of channeling funds from savers to borrowers with productive investment opportunities. For example, a corporation that is planning a capital investment but does not want to borrow from a bank has two other options: It can issue new bonds, to be sold to savers in the bond market, or it can issue new shares in itself, which are then sold in the stock market. The proceeds from the sales of new bonds or stocks are then available to the firm to finance its capital investment.

How do stock and bond markets help to ensure that available savings are devoted to the most productive uses? As we mentioned earlier, two important functions served by these markets are gathering information about prospective borrowers and helping savers to share the risks of lending.

The informational role of bond and stock markets Savers and their financial advisors know that to get the highest possible returns on their financial investments, they must find the potential borrowers with the most profitable opportunities. This knowledge provides a powerful incentive to scrutinize potential borrowers carefully.

For example, companies considering a new issue of stocks or bonds know that their recent performance and plans for the future will be carefully studied by professional analysts on Wall Street and other financial investors. If the analysts and other potential purchasers have doubts about the future profitability of the firm, they will offer a relatively low price for the newly issued shares or they will demand a high interest rate on newly issued bonds. Knowing this, a company will be reluctant to go to the bond or stock market for financing unless its management is confident that it can convince financial investors that the firm's planned use of the funds will be profitable. Thus, the ongoing search by savers and their financial advisors for high returns leads the bond and stock markets to direct funds to the uses that appear most likely to be productive.

Risk sharing and diversification Many highly promising investment projects are also quite risky. The successful development of a new drug to lower cholesterol could create billions of dollars in profits for a drug company, for example; but if the drug turns out to be less effective than some others on the market, none of the development costs will be recouped. An individual who lent his or her life savings to help finance the development of the anticholesterol drug might enjoy a handsome return but also takes the chance of losing everything. Savers are generally reluctant to take large risks, so without some means of reducing the risk faced by each saver, it might be very hard for the company to find the funds to develop the new drug.

diversification the practice of spreading one's wealth over a variety of different financial investments to reduce overall risk

Bond and stock markets help reduce risk by giving savers a means to *diversify* their financial investments. **Diversification** is the practice of spreading one's wealth over a variety of different financial investments to reduce overall risk. The idea of diversification follows from the adage that "you shouldn't put all your eggs in one basket." Rather than putting all of his or her savings in one very risky project, a financial investor will find it much safer to allocate a small amount of savings to each of a large number of stocks and bonds. That way, if some financial assets fall in value, there is a good chance that others will rise in value, with gains offsetting losses. Example 11.4 illustrates the benefits of diversification.

EXAMPLE 11.4

The benefits of diversification

Vikram has $200 to invest and is considering two stocks, the Smith Umbrella Company and the Jones Suntan Lotion Company. Suppose the price of one share of each stock is $100. The umbrella company will turn out to be the better investment if the weather is rainy, but the suntan lotion company will be the better investment if the weather is sunny. In Table 11.1, we illustrate the amounts by which the price of one share of each stock will change and how this depends on the weather.

TABLE 11.1
Changes in the Stock Price of Two Companies

Actual weather	Increase in Stock Price per Share	
	Smith Umbrella Co.	Jones Suntan Lotion Co.
Rainy	+$10	Unchanged
Sunny	Unchanged	+$10

According to Table 11.1, the price of one share of Smith Umbrella Co. stock will rise by $10 (from $100 to $110) if it rains but will remain unchanged if the weather is sunny. The price of one share of Jones Suntan Co. stock, on the other hand, is expected to rise by $10 (from $100 to $110) if it is sunny but will remain unchanged if there is rain.

Suppose the chance of rain is 50 percent, and the chance of sunshine is 50 percent. How should Vikram invest his $200? If Vikram were to invest all his $200 in Smith Umbrella, he could buy two shares. Half of the time it will rain and each share will rise by $10, for a total gain of $20. Half of the time, however, it will be sunny, in which case the stock price will remain unchanged. Thus, his average gain will be 50 percent (or one-half) times $20 plus 50 percent times $0, which is equal to $10.

If, however, Vikram invested all of his $200 in Jones Suntan Lotion Company, he could again buy two shares for $100 each. Each share would rise by $10 if the weather is sunny (for a total gain of $20) and remain unchanged if the weather is rainy. Since it will be sunny half the time, the average gain will be 50 percent times $20 plus 50 percent times $0, or $10.

Although Vikram can earn an *average* gain of $10 if he puts all of his money into either stock, investing in only one stock is quite risky, since his actual gain varies widely depending on whether there is rain or shine. Can Vikram *guarantee* himself a gain of $10, avoiding the uncertainty and risk? Yes, all he has to do is buy one share of each of the two stocks. If it rains, he will earn $10 on his Smith Umbrella stock and nothing on his Jones Suntan stock. If it's sunny, he will earn nothing on Smith Umbrella but $10 on Jones Suntan. Rain or shine, he is guaranteed to earn $10—without risk.

The existence of bond markets and stock markets makes it easy for savers to diversify by putting a small amount of their savings into each of a wide variety of different financial assets, each of which represents a share of a particular company or investment project. From society's point of view, diversification makes it possible for risky but worthwhile projects to obtain funding, without individual savers having to bear too much risk.

For the typical person, a particularly convenient way to diversify is to buy bonds and stocks indirectly through mutual funds. A **mutual fund** is a financial intermediary that sells shares in itself to the public, then uses the funds raised to buy a wide variety of financial assets. Holding shares in a mutual fund thus amounts to owning a little bit of many different financial assets, which helps to achieve diversification. The advantage of mutual funds is that it is usually less costly and time-consuming to buy shares in one or two mutual funds than to buy many different stocks and bonds directly. Over the past decade, mutual funds have become increasingly popular in the United States.

mutual fund a financial intermediary that sells shares in itself to the public, then uses the funds raised to buy a wide variety of financial assets

Why did the U.S. stock market rise sharply in the 1990s, then fall in the new millennium?

Stock prices soared during the 1990s in the United States. The Standard & Poor's 500 index, which summarizes the stock price performance of 500 major companies, rose 60 percent between 1990 and 1995, then more than doubled between 1995 and 2000. However, in the first two years of the new millennium, this index lost nearly half its value. Why did the U.S. stock market boom in the 1990s and bust in the 2000s?

ECONOMIC NATURALIST
11.2

The prices of stocks depend on their purchasers' expectations about future dividends and stock prices and on the rate of return required by potential stockholders. The required rate of return in turn equals the interest rate on safe assets plus the risk premium. In principle, a rise in stock prices could be the result of increased optimism about future dividends, a fall in the required return, or some combination.

Probably both factors contributed to the boom in stock prices in the 1990s. Dividends grew rapidly in the 1990s, reflecting the strong overall performance of the U.S. economy. Encouraged by the promise of new technologies, many financial investors expected future dividends to be even higher.

There is also evidence that the risk premium that people required to hold stocks fell during the 1990s, thereby lowering the total required return and raising stock prices. One possible explanation for a decline in the risk premium in the 1990s is increased diversification. During that decade, the number and variety of mutual funds available increased markedly. Millions of Americans invested in these funds, including many who had never owned stock before or had owned stock in only a few companies. This increase in diversification for the typical stock market investor may have lowered the perceived risk of holding stocks (because she could now own stocks by buying mutual funds), which in turn reduced the risk premium and raised stock prices. An alternative explanation is that investors simply underestimated the riskiness inherent in the economy and, consequently, in the stock market. To the extent that investors underestimated the riskiness of stocks, the risk premium may have fallen to an unrealistically low level.

After 2000 both of these favorable factors reversed. The growth in dividends was disappointing to stockholders, in large part because many high-tech firms did not prove as profitable as had been hoped. An additional blow was a series of corporate accounting scandals in 2002, in which it became known that some large firms had taken illegal or unethical actions to make their profits seem larger than in fact they were. A number of factors, including a recession, a major terrorist attack, and the accounting scandals, also increased stockholders' concerns about the riskiness of stocks, so that the risk premium they required to hold stocks rose from its 1990s lows. The combination of lower expected dividends and a higher premium for risk sent stock prices sharply downward. Only in 2003, when the economy began to grow more rapidly, did stock prices begin to recover.

INTERNATIONAL CAPITAL FLOWS

Our discussion thus far has focused on financial markets operating within a given country, such as the United States. However, economic opportunities are not necessarily restricted by national boundaries. The most productive use of a U.S. citizen's savings might be located far from U.S. soil, in helping to build a factory in Thailand or starting a small business in Poland. Likewise, the best way for a Brazilian saver to diversify her assets and reduce her risks could be to hold bonds and stocks from a number of different countries. Over time, extensive financial markets have developed to permit cross-border borrowing and lending. Financial markets in which borrowers and lenders are residents of different countries are called *international financial markets*.

International financial markets differ from domestic financial markets in at least one important respect: Unlike a domestic financial transaction, an international financial transaction is subject to the laws and regulations of at least two countries, the country that is home to the lender and the country that is home to the borrower. Thus, the size and vitality of international financial markets depend on the degree of political and economic cooperation among countries. For example, during the relatively peaceful decades of the late nineteenth and early twentieth centuries, international financial markets were remarkably highly developed. Great Britain, at the time the world's dominant economic power, was a major international lender, dispatching its savings for use around the globe. However, during the turbulent years 1914–1945, two world wars and the Great Depression substantially reduced both international finance and international trade in goods and services. The extent of international finance and trade returned to the levels achieved in the late nineteenth century only in the 1980s.

In thinking about international financial markets, it is useful to understand that lending is economically equivalent to acquiring a real or financial asset, and borrowing is economically equivalent to selling a real or financial asset. For example, savers lend to companies by purchasing stocks or bonds, which are financial assets for the lender and financial liabilities for the borrowing firms. Similarly, lending to a government is accomplished in practice by acquiring a government bond—a financial asset for the lender and a financial liability for the borrower, in this case the government. Savers also can provide funds by acquiring real assets such as land; if I purchase a parcel of land from you, though I am not making a loan in the usual sense, I am providing you with funds that you can use for consuming or investing. In lieu of interest or dividends from a bond or a stock, I receive the rental value of the land that I purchased.

Purchases or sales of real and financial assets across international borders (which are economically equivalent to lending and borrowing across international borders) are known as **international capital flows.** From the perspective of a particular country, say the United States, purchases of domestic (U.S.) assets by foreigners are called **capital inflows;** purchases of foreign assets by domestic (U.S.) households and firms are called **capital outflows.** To remember these terms, it may help to keep in mind that capital inflows represent funds "flowing in" to the country (foreign savers buying domestic assets), while capital outflows are funds "flowing out" of the country (domestic savers buying foreign assets). The difference between the two flows is expressed as **net capital inflows**—capital inflows minus capital outflows—or *net capital outflows*—capital outflows minus capital inflows. Although one can look at net capital flows in either direction, we shall focus on net capital inflows, which, once again, are equal to foreign purchases of domestic assets (which bring funds into the country) minus domestic purchases of foreign assets (which send funds out of the country). Note that capital inflows and outflows are *not* counted as exports or imports, because they refer to the purchase of existing real and financial assets rather than currently produced goods and services.

From a macroeconomic perspective, international capital flows play two important roles. First, they allow countries whose productive investment opportunities are greater than domestic savings to fill in the gap by borrowing from abroad. Second, they allow countries to run trade imbalances—situations in which the country's exports of goods and services do not equal its imports of goods and services. The rest of this chapter discusses these key roles. We begin by analyzing the important link between international capital flows and trade imbalances.

CAPITAL FLOWS AND THE BALANCE OF TRADE

In the chapter "Measuring Economic Activity," we introduced the term *net exports* (*NX*), the value of a country's exports less the value of its imports. An equivalent term for the value of a country's exports less the value of its imports is the **trade balance.** Because exports need not equal imports in each quarter or year, the trade balance (or net exports) need not always equal zero. If the trade balance is positive in a particular period so that the value of exports exceeds the value of imports, a country is said to have a **trade surplus** for that period equal to the value of its exports minus the value of its imports. If the trade balance is negative, with imports greater than exports, the country is said to have a **trade deficit** equal to the value of its imports minus the value of its exports.

Figure 11.1 shows the components of the U.S. trade balance since 1960 (see Figure 4.5 for data extending back to 1900). The blue line represents U.S. exports as a percentage of GDP; the red line, U.S. imports as a percentage of GDP. When exports exceed imports, the vertical distance between the two lines gives the U.S. trade surplus as a percentage of GDP. When imports exceed exports, the vertical distance between the two lines represents the U.S. trade deficit. Figure 11.1 shows

international capital flows purchases or sales of real and financial assets across international borders

capital inflows purchases of domestic assets by foreign households and firms

capital outflows purchases of foreign assets by domestic households and firms

net capital inflows capital inflows minus capital outflows

trade balance (or net exports) the value of a country's exports less the value of its imports in a particular period (quarter or year)

trade surplus when exports exceed imports, the difference between the value of a country's exports and the value of its imports in a given period

trade deficit when imports exceed exports, the difference between the value of a country's imports and the value of its exports in a given period

FIGURE 11.1

The U.S. Trade Balance, 1960–2004.

This figure shows U.S. exports and imports as a percentage of GDP. Since the late 1970s, the United States has run a trade deficit, with imports exceeding exports.

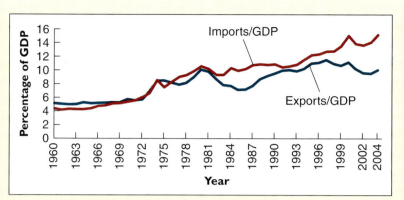

SOURCE: Bureau of Economic Analysis (http://www.bea.gov).

first that international trade has become an increasingly important part of the U.S. economy in the past several decades. In 1960, only 5.1 percent of U.S. GDP was exported, and the value of imports equaled 4.3 percent of U.S. GDP. In 2004, by comparison, 10.0 percent of U.S. production was sold abroad, and imports amounted to 15.2 percent of U.S. GDP. Second, the figure shows that since the late 1970s, the United States has consistently run trade deficits, frequently equal to 2 percent or more of GDP. Why has the U.S. trade balance been in deficit for so long? We will answer that question later in this section.

The trade balance represents the difference between the value of goods and services exported by a country and the value of goods and services imported by the country. Net capital inflows represent the difference between purchases of domestic assets by foreigners and purchases of foreign assets by domestic residents. There is a precise and very important link between these two imbalances, which is that in any given period, *the trade balance and net capital inflows sum to zero.* For future reference, let's write this relationship as an equation:

$$NX + KI = 0, \tag{11.1}$$

where NX is the trade balance (the same as net exports) and we use KI to stand for net capital inflows. The relationship given by Equation 11.1 is an identity, meaning that it is true by definition.

To see why Equation 11.1 holds, consider what happens when (for example) a U.S. resident purchases an imported good, say a Japanese automobile priced at $20,000. Suppose the U.S. buyer pays by check so that the Japanese car manufacturer now holds $20,000 in an account in a U.S. bank. What will the Japanese manufacturer do with this $20,000? Basically, there are two possibilities.

First, the Japanese company may use the $20,000 to buy U.S.-produced goods and services, such as U.S.-manufactured car parts or Hawaiian vacations for its executives. In this case, the United States has $20,000 in exports to balance the $20,000 automobile import. Because exports equal imports, the U.S. trade balance is unaffected by these transactions (for these transactions, $NX = 0$). And because no assets are bought or sold, there are no capital inflows or outflows ($KI = 0$). So under this scenario, the condition that the trade balance plus net capital inflows equals zero, as stated in Equation 11.1, is satisfied.

Alternatively, the Japanese car producer might use the $20,000 to acquire U.S. assets, such as a U.S. Treasury bond or some land adjacent to its plant in Tennessee. In this case, the United States compiles a trade deficit of $20,000, because the $20,000 car import is not offset by an export ($NX = -\$20,000$). But there is a corresponding capital inflow of $20,000, reflecting the purchase of a U.S. asset by the

Japanese ($KI = \$20,000$). So once again the trade balance and net capital inflows sum to zero, and Equation 11.1 is satisfied.[1]

In fact, there is a third possibility, which is that the Japanese car company might swap its dollars to some other party outside the United States. For example, the company might trade its dollars to another Japanese firm or individual in exchange for Japanese yen. However, the acquirer of the dollars would then have the same two options as the car company—to buy U.S. goods and services or acquire U.S. assets—so that the equality of net capital inflows and the trade deficit would continue to hold.

EXERCISE 11.3

A U.S. saver purchases a $20,000 Japanese government bond. Explain why Equation 11.1 is satisfied no matter what the Japanese government does with the $20,000 it receives for its bond.

THE DETERMINANTS OF INTERNATIONAL CAPITAL FLOWS

Capital inflows, recall, are purchases of domestic assets by foreigners, while capital outflows are purchases of foreign assets by domestic residents. For example, capital inflows into the United States include foreign purchases of items such as the stocks and bonds of U.S. companies, U.S. government bonds, and real assets such as land or buildings owned by U.S. residents. Why would foreigners want to acquire U.S. assets, and, conversely, why would Americans want to acquire assets abroad?

The basic factors that determine the attractiveness of any asset, either domestic or foreign, are *return* and *risk*. Financial investors seek high real returns; thus, with other factors (such as the degree of risk and the returns available abroad) held constant, a higher real interest rate in the home country promotes capital inflows by making domestic assets more attractive to foreigners. By the same token, a higher real interest rate in the home country reduces capital outflows by inducing domestic residents to invest their savings at home. Thus, all else being equal, a higher real interest rate at home increases net capital inflows. Conversely, a low real interest rate at home tends to reduce net capital inflows (by increasing net capital outflows), as financial investors look abroad for better opportunities. Figure 11.2 shows the relationship between a country's net capital inflows and the real rate of interest prevailing in that country. When the domestic real interest rate is high, net capital inflows are positive (foreign purchases of domestic assets exceed domestic purchases of foreign assets). But when the real interest rate is low, net capital inflows are negative (that is, the country experiences net capital outflows).

The effect of risk on capital flows is the opposite of the effect of the real interest rate. For a given real interest rate, an increase in the riskiness of domestic assets reduces net capital inflows, as foreigners become less willing to buy the home country's assets, and domestic savers become more inclined to buy foreign assets. For example, political instability, which increases the risk of investing in a country, tends to reduce net capital inflows. Figure 11.3 shows the effect of an increase in risk on capital flows: At each value of the domestic real interest rate, an increase in risk reduces net capital inflows, shifting the capital inflows curve to the left.

EXERCISE 11.4

For given real interest rate and riskiness in the home country, how would you expect net capital inflows to be affected by an increase in real interest rates abroad? Show your answer graphically.

---

[1] If the Japanese company simply left the $20,000 in the U.S. bank, it would still count as a capital inflow, since the deposit would still be a U.S. asset acquired by foreigners.

FIGURE 11.2

Net Capital Inflows and the Real Interest Rate.

Holding constant the degree of risk and the real returns available abroad, a high real interest rate in the home country will induce foreigners to buy domestic assets, increasing capital inflows. A high real rate in the home country also reduces the incentive for domestic savers to buy foreign assets, reducing capital outflows. Thus, all else being equal, the higher the domestic real interest rate r, the higher will be net capital inflows KI.

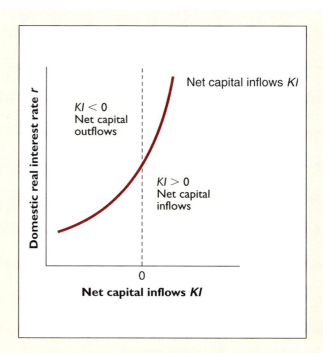

FIGURE 11.3

An Increase in Risk Reduces Net Capital Inflows.

An increase in the riskiness of domestic assets, arising, for example, from an increase in political instability, reduces the willingness of foreign and domestic savers to hold domestic assets. The supply of capital inflows declines at each value of the domestic real interest rate, shifting the KI curve to the left.

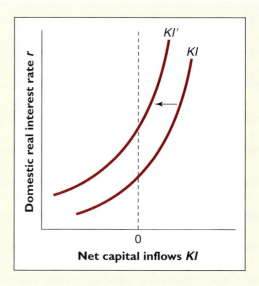

SAVING, INVESTMENT, AND CAPITAL INFLOWS

International capital flows have a close relationship to domestic saving and investment. As we will see next, capital inflows augment the domestic saving pool, increasing the funds available for investment in physical capital, while capital outflows reduce the amount of saving available for investment. Thus capital inflows can help to promote economic growth within a country, and capital outflows to restrain it.

To derive the relationship among capital inflows, saving, and investment, recall from the chapter "Measuring Economic Activity" that total output or income Y must always equal the sum of the four components of expenditure: consumption (C), investment (I), government purchases (G), and net exports (NX). Writing out this identity, we have

$$Y = C + I + G + NX.$$

Next, we subtract $C + G + NX$ from both sides of the identity to obtain

$$Y - C - G - NX = I.$$

In the chapter "Saving and Capital Formation," we saw that national saving S is equal to $Y - C - G$. If we make this substitution in the preceding equation, we obtain

$$S - NX = I. \tag{11.2}$$

Now recall that Equation 11.1 describes the relationship between the trade balance NX and net capital inflows KI. In particular, the trade balance plus capital inflows equals zero, or $NX + KI = 0$. This also can be written as $KI = -NX$. If we make this substitution in the above equation, we find that

$$S + KI = I. \tag{11.3}$$

Equation 11.3, a key result, says that the sum of national saving S and net capital inflows from abroad KI must equal domestic investment in new capital goods, I. In other words, in an open economy, the pool of saving available for domestic investment includes not only national saving (the saving of the domestic private and public sectors) but funds from savers abroad as well.

The chapter "Saving and Capital Formation" introduced the saving-investment diagram, which shows that in a closed economy, the supply of saving must equal the demand for saving. A similar diagram applies to an open economy, except that the supply of saving in an open economy includes net capital inflows as well as domestic saving. Figure 11.4 shows the open-economy version of the saving-investment diagram. The domestic real interest rate is shown on the vertical axis and saving and investment flows on the horizontal axis. As in a closed economy, the downward-sloping curve I shows the demand for funds by firms that want to make capital investments. The curve marked $S + KI$, shows the total supply of saving, including *both* domestic saving S and net capital inflows from abroad KI. Since a higher domestic real interest rate increases both domestic saving and net capital inflows, the $S + KI$ curve is upward-sloping. As Figure 11.4 shows, the equilibrium

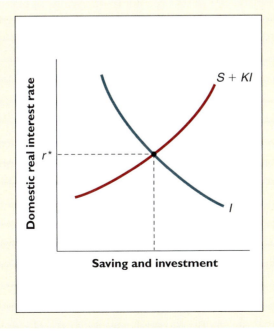

FIGURE 11.4

The Saving-Investment Diagram for an Open Economy.

The total supply of saving in an open economy is the sum of national saving S and net capital inflows KI. An increase in the domestic real interest rate will increase both S and KI. The domestic demand for saving for purposes of capital investment is shown by the curve labeled I. The equilibrium real interest rate r^* sets the total supply of saving, including capital inflows, equal to the domestic demand for saving.

real interest rate in an open economy, r^*, is the level that sets the total amount of saving supplied (including net capital inflows from abroad) equal to the amount of saving demanded for purposes of domestic capital investment.

Figure 11.4 also indicates how net capital inflows can benefit an economy. A country that attracts significant amounts of foreign capital flows will have a larger pool of total saving and, hence, both a lower real interest rate and a higher rate of investment in new capital than it otherwise would. The United States and Canada both benefited from large inflows of capital in the early stages of their economic development, as do many developing countries today. Because capital inflows tend to react very sensitively to risk, an implication is that countries that are politically stable and safeguard the rights of foreign investors will attract more foreign capital and thus grow more quickly than countries without those characteristics.

Although capital inflows are generally beneficial to the countries that receive them, they are not costless. Countries that finance domestic capital formation primarily by capital inflows face the prospect of paying interest and dividends to the foreign financial investors from whom they have borrowed. A number of developing countries have experienced *debt crises*, arising because the domestic investments they made with foreign funds turned out poorly, leaving them insufficient income to pay what they owed their foreign creditors. An advantage to financing domestic capital formation primarily with domestic saving is that the returns from the country's capital investments accrue to domestic savers rather than flowing abroad.

ECONOMIC NATURALIST 11.3

Why did the Argentine economy collapse in 2001–2002?

Argentina, with a wealth of natural resources and an educated population, has long been among the most prosperous economies of Latin America. However, in 2001–2002 the country faced a severe economic crisis. Political dissatisfaction reached so high a level that Argentines rioted in the streets of Buenos Aires, and the country had five different presidents within a span of a few months. Why did the Argentine economy collapse in 2001–2002?

Because Argentina is a developing economy with extensive human and natural resources, investments in new capital goods in that country could potentially be very profitable. However, Argentina's national saving rate is among the lowest in Latin America. To make up the difference between the demand for investment (new capital goods) and the domestic supply of saving, Argentina borrowed extensively from abroad, that is, capital inflows to Argentina were large. These capital inflows helped Argentina to invest more and grow more quickly than it otherwise might have. However, the rapid capital inflows also implied that, over time, Argentina was building up a large debt to foreigners. Foreigners remained willing to lend to Argentina so long as they expected to earn good returns on their loans.

Unfortunately, in the late 1990s, the situation in Argentina took a turn for the worse. In 1998, following a three-year growth boom, the Argentine economy slowed considerably. Moreover, partly as a result of the slowing economy, which reduced tax receipts and raised the public's demands for government services, the government budgetary situation worsened. The central government of Argentina, which had a budget surplus of over 2 percent of GDP in 1993, began to run large deficits. Free-spending provincial and city governments ran deficits of their own, which exacerbated the nation's fiscal problem.

The increased government budget deficits reduced Argentina's national saving, increasing the need to borrow abroad. But at the same time that Argentina's borrowing needs were rising, foreign lenders began to worry that the country—with its slowing economy, high debt burden, and worsening government budget deficits—was a much riskier location for investment than they had thought. Increased risk reduces the supply of capital inflows (see Figure 11.3) and thus also reduces the total pool of saving available; the result is a higher domestic interest rate, lower domestic investment, and hence a weakening economy. As the economy continued to weaken, and government budgets worsened, foreign lenders became so pessimistic about Argentina that they would lend only at very high interest rates, if at all. Ultimately Argentina was unable to repay even the interest on its foreign debt and was forced to default (refuse to pay). At that point the country became essentially unable to borrow abroad at any price. Investment in Argentina collapsed, real interest rates soared, and Argentina was forced to negotiate with government-sponsored agencies, such as the International Monetary Fund, to obtain loans to rebuild its economy. During the past few years, the Argentine economy has recovered, but the government has refused to repay all of its foreign debt.

THE SAVING RATE AND THE TRADE DEFICIT

We have seen that a country's exports and imports do not necessarily balance in each period. Indeed, the United States has run a trade deficit, with its imports exceeding exports, for many years. What causes trade deficits? Stories in the media sometimes claim that trade deficits occur because a country produces inferior goods that no one wants to buy or because other countries impose unfair trade restrictions on imports. Despite the popularity of these explanations, however, there is little support for them in either economic theory or evidence. For example, the United States has a large trade deficit with China, but no one would claim U.S. goods are generally inferior to Chinese goods. And many developing countries have significant trade deficits even though they, rather than their trading partners, tend to impose the more stringent restrictions on trade.

Economists argue that, rather than the quality of a country's exports or the existence of unfair trade restrictions, *a low rate of national saving is the primary cause of trade deficits.*

We have already seen the relationship between national saving and the trade balance in Equation 11.2, $S - NX = I$, which we rewrite as

$$S - I = NX. \qquad (11.4)$$

According to Equation 11.4, if we hold domestic investment (I) constant, a high rate of national saving S implies a high level of net exports NX, while a low level of national saving implies a low level of net exports. Furthermore, if a country's national saving is less than its investment, or $S < I$, then Equation 11.4 implies that net exports NX will be negative. That is, the country will have a trade deficit. The conclusion from Equation 11.4 is that, holding domestic investment constant, low national saving tends to be associated with a trade deficit ($NX < 0$), and high national saving is associated with a trade surplus ($NX > 0$).

Why does a low rate of national saving tend to be associated with a trade deficit? A country with a low national saving rate is one in which households and the government have high spending rates, relative to domestic income and production. Since part of the spending of households and the government is devoted to imported goods, we would expect a low-saving, high-spending economy to have a high volume of imports. Furthermore, a low-saving economy consumes a large proportion of its domestic production, reducing the quantity of goods and services available for export. With high imports and low exports, a low-saving economy will experience a trade deficit.

A country with a trade deficit also must be receiving capital inflows, as we have seen. (Equation 11.1 tells us that if a trade deficit exists so that $NX < 0$, then it must be true that $KI > 0$—net capital inflows are positive.) Is a low national saving rate also consistent with the existence of net capital inflows? The answer is yes. A country with a low national saving rate will not have sufficient saving of its own to finance domestic investment. Thus, there likely will be many good investment opportunities in the country available to foreign savers, leading to capital inflows. Equivalently, a shortage of domestic saving will tend to drive up the domestic real interest rate, which attracts capital flows from abroad.

We conclude that a low rate of national saving tends to create a trade deficit, as well as to promote the capital inflows that must accompany a trade deficit. Economic Naturalist 11.4 illustrates this effect for the case of the United States.

ECONOMIC NATURALIST 11.4

Why is the U.S. trade deficit so large?

As shown by Figure 11.1, U.S. trade was more or less in balance until the mid-1970s. Since the late 1970s, however, the United States has run large trade deficits, particularly in the mid-1980s and since the latter part of the 1990s. Indeed, in 2004 the trade deficit equaled 5.2 percent of U.S. GDP. Why is the U.S. trade deficit so large?

Figure 11.5 shows national saving, investment, and the trade balance for the United States from 1960 to 2004 (all measured relative to GDP). Note that the trade balance has been negative since the late 1970s, indicating a trade deficit. Note also that trade deficits correspond to periods in which investment exceeds national saving, as required by Equation 11.4.

U.S. national saving and investment were roughly in balance in the 1960s and early 1970s, and, hence, the U.S. trade balance was close to zero during that period. However, U.S. national saving fell sharply during the late 1970s and 1980s. One factor that contributed to the decline in national saving was the large government deficits of the era (see the chapter "Saving and Capital Formation"). Because investment did not decline as much as saving, the U.S. trade deficit ballooned in the 1980s, coming under control only when investment fell during the recession of 1990–1991. Saving and investment both recovered during the 1990s, but in the latter part of the 1990s, national saving dropped again. This time the federal government was not at fault, since its budget showed a healthy surplus. Rather, the fall in national saving reflected a decline in private saving, the result of a powerful upsurge in consumption spending. Much of the increase in consumption spending was for imported goods and services, which increased the trade deficit. In 2002, however, the federal government again began to have large budget deficits. This reduced national saving even more and led to a record trade deficit in 2004.

FIGURE 11.5

National Saving, Investment, and the Trade Balance in the United States, 1960–2004.

Since the 1970s, U.S. national saving has fallen below domestic investment, implying a significant trade deficit.

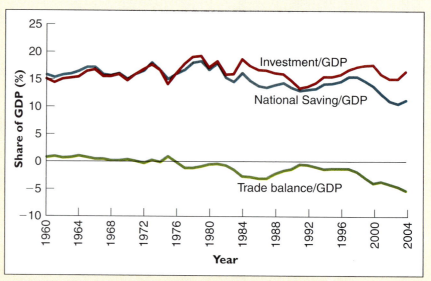

SOURCE: Bureau of Economic Analysis (http://www.bea.gov).

Is the U.S. trade deficit a problem? The trade deficit implies that the United States is relying heavily on foreign saving, and net capital inflows to finance its domestic capital formation. These foreign loans must ultimately be repaid with interest. If the foreign savings are well invested and the U.S. economy grows, repayment will not pose a problem. However, if economic growth in the United States slackens, repaying the foreign lenders will impose an economic burden in the future.

"But we're not just talking about buying a car—we're talking about confronting this country's trade deficit with Japan."

RECAP	INTERNATIONAL CAPITAL FLOWS AND THE BALANCE OF TRADE

- Purchases or sales of assets across borders are called *international capital flows*. If a person, firm, or government in (say) the United States borrows from abroad, we say that there is a capital inflow into the United States. In this case, foreign savers are acquiring U.S. assets. If a person, firm, or government in the United States lends to someone abroad, thereby acquiring a foreign asset, we say that there has been a capital outflow from the United States to the foreign country. Net capital inflows to a given country equal capital inflows minus outflows.

- If a country imports more goods and services than it exports, it must borrow abroad to cover the difference. Likewise, a country that exports more than it imports will lend the difference to foreigners. Thus, as a matter of accounting, the trade balance *NX* and net capital inflows *KI* must sum to zero in every period.

- The funds available for domestic investment in new capital goods equal the sum of domestic saving and net capital inflows from abroad. The higher the return and the lower the risk of investing in the domestic country, the greater will be the capital inflows from abroad. Capital inflows benefit an economy by providing more funds for capital investment, but they can become a burden if the returns from investing in new capital goods are insufficient to pay back the foreign lenders.

- An important cause of a trade deficit is a low national saving rate. A country that saves little and spends a lot will tend to import a greater quantity of goods and services than it is able to export. At the same time, the country's low saving rate implies a need for more foreign borrowing to finance domestic investment spending.

To this point in the book, we have discussed a variety of issues relating to the long-run performance of the economy, including economic growth, the sources of increasing productivity and improved living standards, the determination of real wages, and the determinants of saving and capital formation. Beginning with the next chapter, we will take a more short-run perspective, examining first the causes of recessions and booms in the economy and then turning to policy measures that can be used to affect these fluctuations.

▪ SUMMARY ▪

- Besides balancing saving and investment in the aggregate, financial markets and institutions play the important role of allocating saving to the most productive investment projects. The financial system improves the allocation of saving in two ways: First, it provides information to savers about which of the many possible uses of their funds are likely to prove must productive, and hence pay the highest return. For example, *financial intermediaries* such as banks develop expertise in evaluating prospective borrowers, making it unnecessary for small savers to do that on their own. Similarly, stock and bond analysts evaluate the business prospects of a company issuing shares of stock or bonds, which determines the price the stock will sell for or the interest rate the company will have to offer on its bond. Second, financial markets help savers share the risks of lending by permitting them to *diversify* their financial investments. Individual savers often hold stocks through *mutual funds,* a type of financial intermediary that reduces risk by holding many different financial assets. By reducing the risk faced by any one saver, financial markets allow risky but potentially very productive projects to be funded.

- Corporations that do not wish to borrow from banks can obtain financing by issuing bonds or stocks. A *bond* is a legal promise to repay a debt, including both the *principal amount* and regular interest or coupon payments. The prices of existing bonds decline when interest rates rise. A share of *stock* is a claim to partial ownership of a firm. The price of a stock depends positively on the *dividend* the stock is expected to pay and on the expected future price of the stock and negatively on the rate of return required by financial investors to hold the stock. The required rate of return in turn is the sum of the return on safe assets and the additional return required to compensate financial investors for the riskiness of stocks, called the *risk premium.*

- The *trade balance,* or net exports, is the value of a country's exports less the value of its imports in a particular period. Exports need not equal imports in each period. If exports exceed imports, the difference is called a *trade surplus,* and if imports exceed exports, the difference is called a *trade deficit.* Trade takes place in assets as well as goods and services. Purchases of domestic assets (real or financial) by foreigners are called *capital inflows,* and purchases of foreign assets by domestic savers are called *capital outflows.*

- *Net capital inflows* are equal to capital inflows minus capital outflows, or foreign purchases of domestic assets minus domestic purchases of foreign assets. Because imports that are not financed by sales of exports must be financed by sales of assets, the trade balance and net capital inflows sum to zero.

- The higher the real interest rate in a country, and the lower the risk of investing there, the higher its net capital inflows. The availability of capital inflows expands a country's pool of saving, allowing for more domestic investment and increased growth. A drawback to using capital inflows to finance domestic capital formation is that the returns to capital (interest and dividends) accrue to foreign financial investors rather than domestic residents.

- A low rate of national saving is the primary cause of trade deficits. A low-saving, high-spending country is likely to import more than a high-saving country. It also consumes more of its domestic production, leaving less for export. Finally, a low-saving country is likely to have a high real interest rate, which attracts net capital inflows. Because the sum of the trade balance and net capital inflows is zero, a high level of net capital inflows always accompanies a large trade deficit.

▪ KEY TERMS ▪

bond (299)
capital inflows (307)
capital outflows (307)
coupon payments (299)
coupon rate (299)
diversification (304)

dividend (301)
financial intermediaries (297)
international capital flows (307)
maturation date (299)
mutual fund (305)
net capital inflows (307)

principal amount (299)
risk premium (303)
stock (or equity) (301)
trade balance (307)
trade deficit (307)
trade surplus (307)

■ REVIEW QUESTIONS ■

1. Give two ways that the financial system helps to improve the allocation of savings. Illustrate with examples.

2. Arjay plans to sell a bond that matures in one year and has a principal value of $1,000. Can he expect to receive $1,000 in the bond market for the bond? Explain.

3. Suppose you are much less concerned about risk than the typical person. Are stocks a good financial investment for you? Why or why not?

4. Stock prices surge, but the prices of government bonds remain stable. What can you infer from the behavior of bond prices about the possible causes of the increase in stock values?

5. From the point of view of a given country, say, Spain, give an example of a capital inflow and a capital outflow.

6. How are capital inflows or outflows related to domestic investment in new capital goods?

7. Explain with examples why, in any period, a country's net capital inflows equal its trade deficit.

8. How would increased political instability in a country likely affect capital inflows, the domestic real interest rate, and investment in new capital goods? Show graphically.

■ PROBLEMS ■

1. Simon purchases a bond, newly issued by the Amalgamated Corporation, for $1,000. The bond pays $60 to its holder at the end of the first and second years and pays $1,060 upon its maturity at the end of the third year.
   a. What are the principal amount, the term, the coupon rate, and the coupon payment for Simon's bond?
   b. After receiving the second coupon payment (at the end of the second year), Simon decides to sell his bond in the bond market. What price can he expect for his bond if the one-year interest rate at that time is 3 percent? 8 percent? 10 percent?
   c. Can you think of a reason that the price of Simon's bond after two years might fall below $1,000, even though the market interest rate equals the coupon rate?

2. Shares in Brothers Grimm, Inc., manufacturers of gingerbread houses, are expected to pay a dividend of $5.00 in one year and to sell for $100 per share at that time. How much should you be willing to pay today per share of Grimm:
   a. If the safe rate of interest is 5 percent and you believe that investing in Grimm carries no risk?
   b. If the safe rate of interest is 10 percent and you believe that investing in Grimm carries no risk?
   c. If the safe rate of interest is 5 percent but your risk premium is 3 percent?
   d. Repeat parts a to c, assuming that Grimm is not expected to pay a dividend but the expected price is unchanged.

3. Your financial investments consist of U.S. government bonds maturing in 10 years and shares in a start-up company doing research in pharmaceuticals. How would you expect each of the following news items to affect the value of your assets? Explain.
   a. Interest rates on newly issued government bonds rise.
   b. Inflation is forecasted to be much lower than previously expected (*Hint:* Recall the Fisher effect from the chapter "Demand.") Assume for simplicity that this information does *not* affect your forecast of the dollar value of the pharmaceutical company's future dividends and stock price.
   In parts c to f, interest rates on newly issued government bonds are assumed to remain unchanged.
   c. Large swings in the stock market increase financial investors' concerns about market risk.
   d. The start-up company whose stock you own announces the development of a valuable new drug. However, the drug will not come to market for at least five years.
   e. The pharmaceutical company announces that it will not pay a dividend next year.
   f. The federal government announces a system of price controls on prescription drugs.

4. You have $1,000 to invest and are considering buying some combination of the shares of two companies, DonkeyInc and ElephantInc. Shares of DonkeyInc will pay a

10 percent return if the Democrats are elected, an event you believe to have a 40 percent probability; otherwise the shares pay a zero return. Shares of ElephantInc will pay 8 percent if the Republicans are elected (a 60 percent probability), zero otherwise. Either the Democrats or the Republicans will be elected.

a. If your only concern is maximizing your average expected return, with no regard for risk, how should you invest your $1,000?

b. What is your expected return if you invest $500 in each stock? (*Hint:* Consider what your return will be if the Democrats win and if the Republicans win, then weight each outcome by the probability that event occurs.)

c. The strategy of investing $500 in each stock does *not* give the highest possible average expected return. Why might you choose it anyway?

d. Devise an investment strategy that guarantees at least a 4.4 percent return, no matter which party wins.

e. Devise an investment strategy that is riskless, that is, one in which the return on your $1,000 does not depend at all on which party wins.

5. From the Web site of the Bureau of Economic Analysis, http://www.bea.gov, find data on the components of nominal GDP for the most recent quarter available and for the previous two complete years. Find net exports, national saving (which can be derived from the relationship $S = Y - C - G$), and gross private domestic investment for the period, and verify that they satisfy the relationship $S - I = NX$. How has the U.S. trade balance changed over the past two years as a percentage of GDP? Are the changes attributable to changes in the national saving rate, the rate of investment, or both?

6. How do each of the following transactions affect (1) the trade surplus or deficit and (2) capital inflows or outflows for the United States? Show that in each case the identity that the trade balance plus net capital inflows equals zero applies.

a. A U.S. exporter sells software to Israel. She uses the Israeli shekels received to buy stock in an Israeli company.

b. A Mexican firm uses proceeds from its sale of oil to the United States to buy U.S. government debt.

c. A Mexican firm uses proceeds from its sale of oil to the United States to buy oil drilling equipment from a U.S. firm.

d. A Mexican firm receives U.S. dollars from selling oil to the United States. A French firm accepts the dollars as payment for drilling equipment. The French firm uses the dollars to buy U.S. government debt.

e. A British financial investor writes a check on his bank account in New York to purchase shares of General Motors stock (GM is a U.S. company).

7. Use a diagram like Figure 11.4 to show the effects of each of the following on the real interest rate and capital investment of a country that is a net borrower from abroad.

a. Investment opportunities in the country improve owing to new technologies.

b. The government budget deficit rises.

c. Domestic citizens decide to save more.

d. Foreign investors believe that the riskiness of lending to the country has increased.

8. A country's domestic supply of saving, domestic demand for saving for purposes of capital formation, and supply of net capital inflows are given by the following equations:

$$S = 1,500 + 2,000r,$$

$$I = 2,000 - 4,000r,$$

$$KI = -100 + 6,000r.$$

a. Assuming that the market for saving and investment is in equilibrium, find national saving, net capital inflows, domestic investment, and the real interest rate.

b. Repeat part a, assuming that desired national saving declines by 120 at each value of the real interest rate. What effect does a reduction in domestic saving have on net capital inflows?

c. Concern about the economy's macroeconomic policies causes capital inflows to fall sharply so that now $KI = -700 + 6,000r$. Repeat part a. What does a reduction in capital inflows do to domestic investment and the real interest rate?

■ ANSWERS TO IN-CHAPTER EXERCISES ■

11.1 Since bond prices fell, interest rates must have risen. To find the interest rate, note that bond investors are willing to pay only $960 today for a bond that will pay back $1,070 (a coupon payment of $70 plus the principal amount of $1,000) in one year. To find the one-year return, divide $1,070 by $960 to get 1.115. Thus, the interest rate must have risen to 11.5 percent.

11.2 The share of stock will be worth $81.00 in one year—the sum of its expected future price and the expected dividend. At an interest rate of 4 percent, its value today is $81.00/1.04 = $77.88. At an interest rate of 8 percent, the stock's current value is $81.00/1.08 = $75.00. Recall from Example 11.2 that when the interest rate is 6 percent, the value of a share of FortuneCookie.com is $76.42. Since higher interest rates imply lower stock values, news that interest rates are about to rise should cause the stock market to fall.

11.3 The purchase of the Japanese bond is a capital outflow for the United States, or $KI = -\$20,000$. The Japanese government now holds $20,000. What will it do with these funds? There are basically three possibilities. First, it might use the funds to purchase U.S. goods and services (military equipment, for example). In that case, the U.S. trade balance equals $+\$20,000$, and the sum of the trade balance and capital inflows is zero. Second, the Japanese government might acquire U.S. assets, for example, deposits in U.S. banks. In that case, a capital inflow to the United States of $20,000 offsets the original capital outflow. Both the trade balance and net capital outflows individually are zero, and so their sum is zero.

Finally, the Japanese government might use the $20,000 to purchase non-U.S. goods, services, or assets—oil from Saudi Arabia, for example. But then the non-U.S. recipient of the $20,000 is holding the funds, and it has the same options that the Japanese government did. Eventually, the funds will be used to purchase U.S. goods, services, or assets, satisfying Equation 11.1. Indeed, even if the recipient holds onto the funds (in cash, or as a U.S. bank deposit), that would still count as a capital inflow to the United States, as U.S. dollars or accounts in a U.S. bank are U.S. assets acquired by foreigners.

11.4 An increase in the real interest rate abroad increases the relative attractiveness of foreign financial investments to both foreign and domestic savers. Net capital inflows to the home country will fall at each level of the domestic real interest rate. The supply curve of net capital inflows shifts left, as in Figure 11.3.

4

THE ECONOMY IN THE SHORT RUN

A sign in Redwood City, California, boasts that the Bay Area town has the world's best climate. Redwood City's mean annual temperature and rainfall are similar to that of many other U.S. cities, so on what basis do Redwood City's boosters make their claim? The weather in Redwood City is attractive to many people because it varies so little over the year, being almost equally comfortable and temperate in winter and in summer. A city with the same average yearly temperature as Redwood City, but where the winters are freezing and the summers unbearably hot, would not be nearly so pleasant a place to live.

An analogous idea applies to the performance of the economy. As we saw, over a period of decades or more, the economy's average rate of growth is the crucial determinant of average living standards. But short-term fluctuations of the economy's growth rate around its long-run average matter for economic welfare as well. In particular, periods of slow or negative economic growth, known as *recessions,* may create significant economic hardship and dissatisfaction. In Part 4 we will explore the causes of short-term fluctuations in key economic variables, including output, unemployment, and inflation, and we will discuss the options available to government policymakers for stabilizing the economy.

Chapter 12 provides some necessary background for our study of short-term fluctuations by describing their key characteristics and reviewing the historical record of fluctuations in the U.S. economy. In Chapters 13 through 16, we develop a framework for the analysis of short-term fluctuations and the alternative policy responses. Chapter 13 shows how fluctuations in spending, or *aggregate demand,* may lead to short-run fluctuations in output and employment. That chapter also explains how changes in fiscal policy—policies relating to government spending and taxation—can be used to stabilize spending and output. Chapter 14 focuses on monetary policy, a second tool for stabilizing output and employment. Chapter 15 incorporates inflation into the analysis, discussing both the sources of inflation and the policies that can be used to control it. Finally, Chapter 16 extends the analysis and discusses the practices and pitfalls of macroeconomic policymaking in more detail.

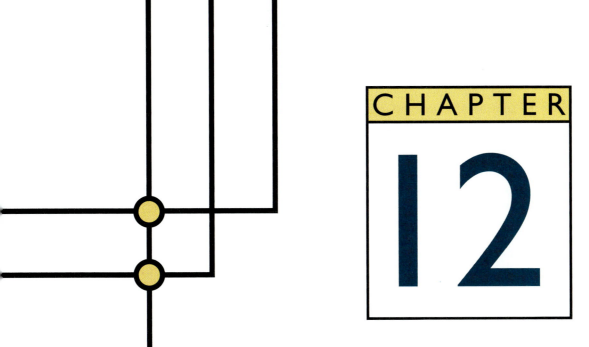

CHAPTER

12

SHORT-TERM
ECONOMIC FLUCTUATIONS:
AN INTRODUCTION

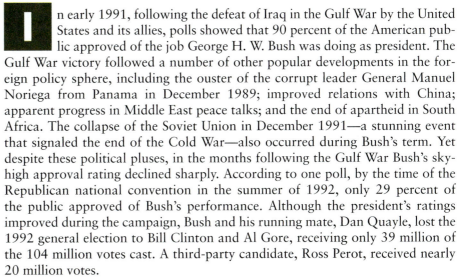

In early 1991, following the defeat of Iraq in the Gulf War by the United States and its allies, polls showed that 90 percent of the American public approved of the job George H. W. Bush was doing as president. The Gulf War victory followed a number of other popular developments in the foreign policy sphere, including the ouster of the corrupt leader General Manuel Noriega from Panama in December 1989; improved relations with China; apparent progress in Middle East peace talks; and the end of apartheid in South Africa. The collapse of the Soviet Union in December 1991—a stunning event that signaled the end of the Cold War—also occurred during Bush's term. Yet despite these political pluses, in the months following the Gulf War Bush's sky-high approval rating declined sharply. According to one poll, by the time of the Republican national convention in the summer of 1992, only 29 percent of the public approved of Bush's performance. Although the president's ratings improved during the campaign, Bush and his running mate, Dan Quayle, lost the 1992 general election to Bill Clinton and Al Gore, receiving only 39 million of the 104 million votes cast. A third-party candidate, Ross Perot, received nearly 20 million votes.

What caused this turnaround in (the first) President Bush's political fortunes? Despite his high marks from voters in foreign policy, the president's domestic economic policies were widely viewed as ineffective. Bush received much criticism for breaking his campaign pledge not to raise taxes. More important, the economy weakened significantly in 1990–1991, then recovered only slowly. Although inflation was low, by mid-1992 unemployment had reached 7.8 percent of the labor force—2.5 percentage points higher than in the first year of Bush's term, and the highest level since 1984. A sign in Democratic candidate Bill Clinton's campaign headquarters summarized Clinton's strategy for winning the White House: "It's the economy, stupid." Clinton realized the importance of the nation's economic problems and pounded away at the Republican administration's inability to pull the country out of the doldrums. Clinton's focus on the economy was the key to his election.

Clinton's ability to parlay criticism of economic conditions into electoral success is not unusual in U.S. political history. Weakness in the economy played a decisive role in helping Franklin D. Roosevelt to beat Herbert Hoover in 1932, John F. Kennedy to best Richard Nixon in 1960, and Ronald Reagan to defeat Jimmy Carter in 1980. President George W. Bush found the political popularity he enjoyed after ousting the Taliban from Afghanistan in 2001 eroded by an economic downturn and a slow subsequent recovery—although, unlike his father, he succeeded in winning reelection. On the other hand, strong economic conditions often have helped incumbent presidents (or the incumbent's party) to retain office, including Nixon in 1972, Reagan in 1984, and Clinton in 1996. Indeed, a number of empirical studies have suggested that economic performance in the year preceding the election is among the most important determinants of whether an incumbent president is likely to win reelection.

In the preceding part, we discussed the factors that determine long-run economic growth. Over the broad sweep of history, those factors determine the economic success of a society. Indeed, over a span of 30, 50, or 100 years, relatively small differences in the rate of economic growth can have an enormous effect on the average person's standard of living. But even though the economic "climate" (long-run economic conditions) is the ultimate determinant of living standards, changes in the economic "weather" (short-run fluctuations in economic conditions) are also important. A good long-run growth record is not much consolation to a worker who has lost her job due to a recession. The bearing that short-term macroeconomic performance has on election results is one indicator of the importance the average person attaches to it.

In this part of the book, we study short-term fluctuations in economic activity, commonly known as *recessions* and *expansions*. We will start, in this chapter, with some background on the history and characteristics of these economic ups and downs. However, the main focus of this part is the *causes* of short-term fluctuations, as well as the available *policy responses*. Because the analysis of short-term economic fluctuations can become complex and even controversial, we will proceed in a step-by-step fashion. In this chapter we will introduce a basic—and oversimplified—model of booms and recessions, which we will refer to as the *basic Keynesian model* in honor of its principal originator, the British economist John Maynard Keynes. The basic Keynesian model focuses on the components of aggregate spending, such as consumption spending by households and investment spending by firms, and the effects of changes in spending on total real GDP.

Though this model is a useful starting point, it does not address some key issues. First, and perhaps most important, the basic Keynesian model has little to say about the determinants of inflation. Second, because it focuses on the very short run, this model does not give adequate attention to the economy's own natural tendency to eliminate deviations from full employment over the longer run. Because the basic Keynesian model does not take into account the "self-correcting" tendencies of the economy, it tends to overstate the need for government intervention to offset fluctuations. In the next two chapters, we will add new features to the model to make it more realistic. By the end of this part, we will have discussed the major causes of short-term economic fluctuations, as well as the options policymakers have in responding to them.

Herbert Hoover
© CORBIS

Jimmy Carter
© David Rubinger/CORBIS

George Bush
© Wally McNamee/CORBIS

Victims of recession.

RECESSIONS AND EXPANSIONS

As background to the study of short-term economic fluctuations, let's review the historical record of the fluctuations in the U.S. economy. Figure 12.1 shows the path of real GDP in the United States since 1920. (Figure 4.1, page 100, provides an even longer data series.) As you can see, the growth path of real GDP is not always smooth; the bumps and wiggles correspond to short periods of faster or slower growth.

A period in which the economy is growing at a rate significantly below normal is called a **recession** or a *contraction*. An extremely severe or protracted recession is called a **depression.** You should be able to pick out the Great Depression in Figure 12.1, particularly the sharp initial decline between 1929 and 1933. But you also can see that the U.S. economy was volatile in the mid-1970s and the early 1980s, with serious recessions in 1973–1975 and 1981–1982. A moderate recession (but not moderate enough for the first President Bush) occurred in 1990–1991. The next recession did not begin for another 10 years, the longest period without a recession in U.S. history. It, too, was short and relatively mild, beginning in March 2001 and ending eight months later.

recession (or contraction) a period in which the economy is growing at a rate significantly below normal

depression a particularly severe or protracted recession

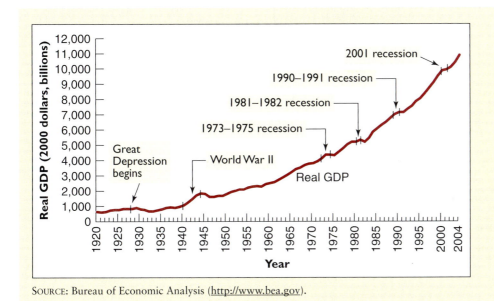

FIGURE 12.1
Fluctuations in U.S. Real GDP, 1920–2004.
Real GDP does not grow smoothly but has speedups (expansions or booms) and slowdowns (recessions or depressions). Note the contraction from 1929 to 1933 (the first phase of the Great Depression), the boom in 1941–1945 (World War II), and the recessions of 1973–1975, 1981–1982, 1990–1991, and 2001.

Source: Bureau of Economic Analysis (http://www.bea.gov).

An informal definition of a recession, often cited by reporters, is a period during which real GDP falls for at least two consecutive quarters. This definition is not a bad rule of thumb, as real GDP usually does fall during recessions. However, many economists would argue that periods in which real GDP growth is well below normal, though not actually negative, should be counted as recessions. Indeed, real GDP fell in only one quarter during the 2001 recession. Another problem with relying on GDP figures for dating recessions is that GDP data can be substantially revised, sometimes years after the fact. In practice, when trying to determine whether a recession is in progress, economists look at a variety of economic data, not just GDP.

Table 12.1 lists the beginning and ending dates of U.S. recessions since 1929, as well as the *duration* (length, in months) of each. The table also gives the highest unemployment rate recorded during each recession and the percentage change in real GDP. (Ignore the last column of the table for now.) The beginning of a recession is called the **peak,** because it represents the high point of economic activity prior to a downturn. The end of a recession, which marks the low point of economic activity prior to a recovery, is called the **trough.** The dates of peaks and troughs reported in Table 12.1 were determined by the National Bureau of Economic Research (NBER), a nonprofit organization of economists that has been a major source of research on short-term economic fluctuations since its founding in 1920. In

peak the beginning of a recession; the high point of economic activity prior to a downturn

trough the end of a recession; the low point of economic activity prior to a recovery

Economic Naturalist 12.1 we describe the data and methods the NBER uses in identifying different phases of the business cycle. The NBER is not a government agency, but it is usually treated by the news media and the government as the "official" arbiter of the dates of peaks and troughs.

"Please stand by for a series of tones. The first indicates the official end of the recession, the second indicates prosperity, and the third the return of the recession."

TABLE 12.1
U.S. Recessions since 1929

Peak date (beginning)	Trough date (end)	Duration (months)	Highest unemployment rate (%)	Change in real GDP (%)	Duration of subsequent expansion (months)
Aug. 1929	Mar. 1933	43	24.9	−28.8	50
May 1937	June 1938	13	19.0	−5.5	80
Feb. 1945	Oct. 1945	8	3.9	−8.5	37
Nov. 1948	Oct. 1949	11	5.9	−1.4	45
July 1953	May 1954	10	5.5	−1.2	39
Aug. 1957	Apr. 1958	8	6.8	−1.7	24
Apr. 1960	Feb. 1961	10	6.7	2.3	106
Dec. 1969	Nov. 1970	11	5.9	0.1	36
Nov. 1973	Mar. 1975	16	8.5	−1.1	58
Jan. 1980	July 1980	6	7.6	−0.3	12
July 1981	Nov. 1982	16	9.7	−2.1	92
July 1990	Mar. 1991	8	7.5	−0.9	120
Mar. 2001	Nov. 2001	8	5.8	0.8	

NOTES: Unemployment rate is the annual rate. Peak and trough dates from the National Bureau of Economic Research. Unemployment and real GDP data from *Historical Statistics of the United States* and the *Economic Report of the President*. Unemployment rate is the annual rate for the trough year or the subsequent year, whichever is higher. Change in annual real GDP is measured from the peak year to the trough year, except that the entry for the 1945 recession is the 1945–1946 change in real GDP, the entry for the 1980 recession is the 1979–1980 change, and the entry for 2001 is the 2000–2001 change.

SOURCES: Peak and trough dates, National Bureau of Economic Research; unemployment and real GDP, *Historical Statistics of the United States* and *Economic Report of the President*.

Table 12.1 shows that since 1929, by far the longest and most severe recession in the United States was the 43-month economic collapse that began in August 1929 and lasted until March 1933, initiating what became known as the Great Depression. Between 1933 and 1937, the economy grew fairly rapidly, so technically the period was not a recession, although unemployment remained very high at close to 20 percent of the workforce. In 1937–1938, the nation was hit by another significant recession. Full economic recovery from the Depression did not come until U.S. entry into World War II at the end of 1941. The economy boomed from 1941 to 1945 (see Figure 12.1), reflecting the enormous wartime production of military equipment and supplies.

In sharp contrast to the 1930s, U.S. recessions since World War II have generally been short—between 6 and 16 months, from peak to trough. As Table 12.1 shows, the two most severe postwar recessions, 1973–1975 and 1981–1982, lasted just 16 months. And, though unemployment rates during those two recessions were quite high by today's standards, they were low compared to the Great Depression. Since 1982 the U.S. economy has experienced only two relatively mild recessions: in 1990–1991 and in 2001. Although recent recessions have not been among the worst that Americans have experienced, they warn us to guard against overconfidence. Prosperity and economic stability can never be guaranteed.

The opposite of a recession is an **expansion**—a period in which the economy is growing at a rate that is significantly *above* normal. A particularly strong and protracted expansion is called a **boom.** In the United States, strong expansions occurred during 1933–1937, 1961–1969, 1982–1990, and 1991–2001, with exceptionally strong growth during 1995–2000 (see Figure 12.1). On average, expansions have been much longer than recessions. The final column of Table 12.1 shows the duration, in months, of U.S. expansions since 1929. As you can see in the table, the 1961–1969 expansion lasted 106 months; the 1982–1990 expansion, 92 months. The longest expansion of all began in March 1991, at the trough of the 1990–1991 recession. This expansion lasted 120 months, a full 10 years, until a new recession began in March 2001.

expansion a period in which the economy is growing at a rate significantly above normal

boom a particularly strong and protracted expansion

Calling the 2001 recession

The Business Cycle Dating Committee of the National Bureau of Economic Research determined that a recession, the first in 10 years, began in March 2001. What led the committee to choose that date?

ECONOMIC NATURALIST 12.1

As of the beginning of 2001, there had been no "official" recession in the United States since the one that began in July 1990 and ended in March 1991. As mentioned above, this 10-year period without a recession was the longest expansion in U.S. history. However, the economy weakened considerably during the latter part of 2000 and in the spring and summer of 2001. A further blow was the terrorist attacks of September 11, 2001, which caused the loss of many jobs both in the affected areas and (because people became afraid to travel) in industries such as airlines and hotels. Because of the increased likelihood that a recession had begun, the six economists who form the Business Cycle Dating Committee—the group within the National Bureau of Economic Research that actually determines recession dates—found themselves called upon for the first time in a decade.

The determination of whether and when a recession has begun involves intensive statistical analysis, mixed in with a significant amount of human judgment. The Business Cycle Dating Committee typically relies heavily on a small set of statistical indicators that measure the overall strength of the economy. The committee prefers indicators that are available monthly, because they are available quickly and may provide relatively precise information about the timing of peaks and troughs. Four of the most important indicators used by the committee are

- Industrial production, which measures the output of factories and mines.

- Total sales in manufacturing, wholesale trade, and retail trade.

- Nonfarm employment (the number of people at work outside of agriculture).

- Real after-tax income received by households, excluding transfers like Social Security payments.

Each of these indicators measures a different aspect of the economy. Because their movements tend to coincide with the overall movements in the economy, they are called *coincident indicators.*

Normally the coincident indicators move more or less together; during the 2001 recession they did not. Industrial production and sales in the manufacturing sector began to decline as early as September 2000. This early weakness in manufacturing reflected slow sales of information technology (computers, software, communications devices, and the like) following the collapse of the "dot-com bubble" in the stock market during 2000. (The values of high-tech stocks fell by two-thirds or more during the year.) However, the weakness in manufacturing was not immediately reflected in the economy as a whole, as both employment and personal income grew strongly in the fall of 2000. Employment did not start to decline until around March 2001, and real personal income continued to grow into the fall of 2001.

The failure of the coincident indicators to move closely together made the committee's job difficult. The committee ultimately chose the date of the peak, or beginning of the recession, to be March 2001, the month in which nonfarm employment began to decline. A rationale for their choice is that recessions are supposed to reflect declines in the entire economy, not just a few specific sectors. It might be argued that the decline in nonfarm employment in March 2001 (which counts people at work in the entire economy, outside of agriculture) was the first clear indication that the slowdown that had begun in the high-tech sector had spread to the broader economy.

EXERCISE 12.1

Update Table 12.1 using the National Bureau of Economic Research Web site (go to http://www.nber.org and click on *business cycle dates*). According to the NBER, is the U.S. economy currently in recession or expansion? How much time has elapsed since the last peak or trough? Explore the NBER Web site to find additional useful information about current conditions in the U.S. economy.

SOME FACTS ABOUT SHORT-TERM ECONOMIC FLUCTUATIONS

Although Figure 12.1 and Table 12.1 show only twentieth-century data, periods of expansion and recession have been a feature of industrial economies since at least the late eighteenth century. Karl Marx and Friedrich Engels referred to these fluctuations, which they called "commercial crises," in their Communist Manifesto of 1848. In the United States, economists have been studying short-term fluctuations for at least a century. The traditional term for these fluctuations is *business cycles,* and they are still often referred to as *cyclical fluctuations.* Neither term is accurate though; as Figure 12.1 shows, economic fluctuations are not "cyclical" at all in the sense that they recur at predictable intervals, but instead are *irregular in their length and severity.* This irregularity makes the dates of peaks and troughs extremely hard to predict, despite the fact that professional forecasters have devoted a great deal of effort and brainpower to the task.

Expansions and recessions usually are not limited to a few industries or regions but, as noted in Economic Naturalist 12.1, are *felt throughout the economy.* Indeed, the largest fluctuations may have a *global impact.* For instance, the Great Depression of the 1930s affected nearly all the world's economies, and the 1973–1975 and 1981–1982 recessions also were widely felt outside the United States. When East Asia

Recessions are very difficult to forecast.

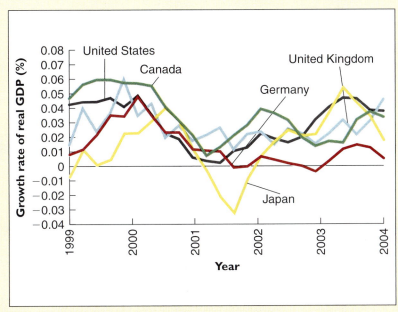

SOURCE: International Monetary Fund (http://www.imf.org).

FIGURE 12.2

Real GDP Growth in Five Major Countries, 1999–2004.

Quarterly growth rates (measured as the change in real GDP over the past four quarters) for five major industrialized countries show that all the countries except Japan enjoyed rapid GDP growth in 1999 and 2000. (Japan has been growing slowly for more than a decade.) The 2001 recession was reflected in falling growth rates in all of the major countries, with recovery beginning in 2002.

suffered a major slowdown in the late 1990s, the effects of that slowdown spilled over into many other regions (although not so much the United States).

Even a relatively moderate recession, like the one that occurred in 2001, can have global effects. Figure 12.2, which shows growth rates of real GDP over the period 1999–2004 for Canada, Germany, Japan, the United Kingdom, and the United States, illustrates this point. You can see that—except for Japan, which has performed poorly since the early 1990s—all the countries experienced relatively strong growth in 1999 and 2000. The 2001 recession lowered growth rates in all of the countries, with recovery beginning in 2002.

Unemployment is a key indicator of short-term economic fluctuations. The unemployment rate typically rises sharply during recessions and recovers (although more slowly) during expansions. Figure 5.3 on page 139 shows the U.S. unemployment rate since 1960. You should be able to identify the recessions that began in 1960, 1969, 1973, 1981, 1990, and 2001 by noting the sharp peaks in the unemployment rate in those years. Recall from the chapter "Workers, Wages, and Unemployment in the Modern Economy" that the part of unemployment that is associated with recessions is called *cyclical unemployment*. Beyond this increase in unemployment, labor market conditions generally worsen during recessions. For example, during recessions, real wages grow more slowly, workers are less likely to receive promotions or bonuses, and new entrants to the labor force (such as college graduates) have a much tougher time finding attractive jobs.

Generally, industries that produce *durable goods,* such as cars, houses, and capital equipment, are more affected than others by recessions and booms. In contrast, industries that provide *services* and *nondurable goods* like food are much less sensitive to short-term fluctuations. Thus, an automobile worker or a construction worker is far more likely to lose his or her job in a recession than is a barber or a baker.

Like unemployment, *inflation* follows a typical pattern in recessions and expansions, though it is not so sharply defined. Figure 12.3 shows the U.S. inflation rate since 1960; in the figure, periods of recession are indicated by shaded vertical bars. As you can see, recessions tend to be followed soon after by a decline in the rate of inflation. For example, the recession of 1981–1982 was followed by a sharp reduction in inflation. Furthermore, many—though not all—postwar recessions

Unemployment among construction workers rises substantially during recessions.

FIGURE 12.3

U.S. Inflation, 1960–2004.
U.S. inflation since 1960 is measured by the change in the CPI, and periods of recession are indicated by the shaded vertical bars. Note that inflation declined following the recessions of 1960–1961, 1969–1970, 1973–1975, 1981–1982, 1990–1991, and 2001, and rose prior to many of those recessions.

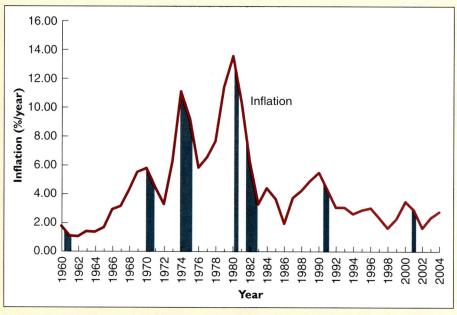

SOURCE: Economic Report of the President (http://gpoaccess.gov/eop).

have been preceded by increases in inflation, as Figure 12.3 shows. The behavior of inflation during expansions and recessions will be discussed more fully in the chapter "Inflation, Aggregate Supply, and Aggregate Demand."

RECAP	RECESSIONS, BOOMS, AND THEIR CHARACTERISTICS

- A recession is a period in which output is growing more slowly than normal. An expansion, or boom, is a period in which output is growing more quickly than normal.

- The beginning of a recession is called the peak, and its end (which corresponds to the beginning of the subsequent expansion) is called the trough.

- The sharpest recession in the history of the United States was the initial phase of the Great Depression in 1929–1933. Severe recessions also occurred in 1973–1975 and 1981–1982. Two relatively mild recessions occurred in 1990–1991 and 2001.

- Short-term economic fluctuations (recessions and expansions) are irregular in length and severity, and thus are difficult to predict.

- Expansions and recessions have widespread (and sometimes global) impacts, affecting most regions and industries.

- Unemployment rises sharply during a recession and falls, usually more slowly, during an expansion.

- Durable goods industries are more affected by expansions and recessions than other industries. Services and nondurable goods industries are less sensitive to ups and downs in the economy.

- Recessions tend to be followed by a decline in inflation and are often preceded by an increase in inflation.

OUTPUT GAPS AND CYCLICAL UNEMPLOYMENT

If policymakers are to respond appropriately to recessions and expansions, and economists are to study them, knowing whether a particular economic fluctuation is "big" or "small" is essential. Intuitively, a "big" recession or expansion is one in which output and the unemployment rate deviate significantly from their normal or trend levels. In this section we will attempt to be more precise about this idea by introducing the concept of the *output gap*, which measures how far output is from its normal level at a particular time. We also will revisit the idea of *cyclical unemployment,* or the deviation of unemployment from its normal level. Finally, we will examine how these two concepts are related.

POTENTIAL OUTPUT AND THE OUTPUT GAP

The concept of potential output is a useful starting point for thinking about the measurement of expansions and recessions. **Potential output,** also called *potential GDP* or *full-employment output,* is the maximum sustainable amount of output (real GDP) that an economy can produce. Note that *potential output* is not simply the maximum amount of output. Because capital and labor can be utilized at greater-than-normal rates for limited periods of time, a country's actual output can temporarily exceed its potential output. These greater-than-normal utilization rates, however, cannot be sustained indefinitely, partly because workers cannot work overtime every week and machinery occasionally must be shut down for maintenance and repairs. Potential output is not a fixed number but grows over time, reflecting increases in both the amounts of available capital and labor and their productivity. We discussed the sources of growth in potential output (the economy's productive capacity) in the chapter "Economic Growth, Productivity, and Living Standards." We will use the symbol Y^* to signify the economy's potential output at a given point in time.

Why does a nation's output sometimes grow quickly and sometimes slowly, as shown for the United States in Figure 12.1? Logically, there are two possibilities: First, changes in the rate of output growth may reflect *changes in the rate at which the country's potential output is increasing.* For example, unfavorable weather conditions, such as a severe drought, would reduce the rate of potential output growth in an agricultural economy, and a decline in the rate of technological innovation might reduce the rate of potential output growth in an industrial economy. Under the assumption that the country is using its resources at normal rates, so that actual output equals potential output, a significant slowdown in potential output growth would tend to result in recession. Similarly, new technologies, increased capital investment, or a surge in immigration that swells the labor force could produce unusually brisk growth in potential output, and hence an economic boom.

Undoubtedly, changes in the rate of growth of potential output are part of the explanation for expansions and recessions. In the United States, for example, the economic boom of the second half of the 1990s was propelled in part by new information technologies, such as the Internet. And the severe slowdown in Japan during the decade of the 1990s reflected in part a reduction in the growth of potential output, arising from factors such as slower growth in the Japanese labor force and capital stock. When changes in the rate of GDP growth reflect changes in the growth rate of potential output, the appropriate policy responses are those discussed in the chapter "Economic Growth, Productivity, and Living Standards." In particular, when a recession results from slowing growth in potential output, the government's best response is to try to promote saving, investment, technological innovation, human capital formation, and other activities that support growth.

A second possible explanation for short-term economic fluctuations is that *actual output does not always equal potential output.* For example, potential output may be growing normally, but for some reason the economy's capital and labor resources may not be fully utilized, so that actual output is significantly below the level of potential

potential output, Y* (or potential GDP or full-employment output) the maximum sustainable amount of output (real GDP) that an economy can produce

output. This low level of output, resulting from underutilization of economic resources, would generally be interpreted as a recession. Alternatively, capital and labor may be working much harder than normal—firms may put workers on overtime, for example—so that actual output expands beyond potential output, creating a boom.

At any point in time, the difference between potential output and actual output is called the **output gap**. Recalling that Y^* is the symbol for potential output and that Y stands for actual output (real GDP), we can express the output gap as $Y^* - \overline{Y}$. A positive output gap—when actual output is below potential and resources are not being fully utilized—is called a **recessionary gap**. A negative output gap—when actual output is above potential and resources are being utilized at above-normal rates—is referred to as an **expansionary gap**.

Policymakers generally view both recessionary gaps and expansionary gaps as problems. It is not difficult to see why a recessionary gap is bad news for the economy: When there is a recessionary gap, capital and labor resources are not being fully utilized, and output and employment are below maximum sustainable levels. This is the sort of situation that poses problems for politicians' reelection prospects, as discussed in this chapter's introduction. In addition to the fact that it is unsustainable, an expansionary gap is considered a problem by policymakers for a more subtle reason: What's wrong, after all, with having higher output and employment, even if it is temporary? A prolonged expansionary gap is problematic because, when faced with a demand for their products that significantly exceeds their sustainable capacity, firms tend to raise prices. Thus, an expansionary gap typically results in increased inflation, which reduces the efficiency of the economy in the longer run. (We discuss the genesis of inflation in more detail in the chapter "Inflation, Aggregate Supply, and Aggregate Demand.")

output gap, $Y^* - Y$ the difference between the economy's potential output and its actual output at a point in time

recessionary gap a positive output gap, which occurs when potential output exceeds actual output ($Y^* > Y$)

expansionary gap a negative output gap, which occurs when actual output is higher than potential output ($Y > Y^*$)

"Ed, this is Art Simbley over at Hollis, Bingham, Cotter & Krone. What did you get for thirty-four across, 'Persian fairy,' four letters?"

Thus, whenever an output gap exists, whether it is recessionary or expansionary, policymakers have an incentive to try to eliminate the gap by returning actual output to potential. In the next four chapters we will discuss both how output gaps arise and the tools that policymakers have for *stabilizing* the economy—that is, bringing actual output into line with potential output.

THE NATURAL RATE OF UNEMPLOYMENT AND CYCLICAL UNEMPLOYMENT

Whether recessions arise because of slower growth in potential output or because actual output falls below potential, they bring bad times. In either case, output falls (or at least grows more slowly), implying reduced living standards. Recessionary output gaps are particularly frustrating for policymakers, however, because they imply that the economy has the *capacity* to produce more, but for some reason available resources are not being fully utilized. Recessionary gaps are *inefficient* in that they unnecessarily reduce the total economic pie, making the typical person worse off.

An important indicator of the low utilization of resources during recessions is the unemployment rate. In general, a *high* unemployment rate means that labor resources are not being fully utilized, so that output has fallen below potential (a recessionary gap). By the same logic, an unusually *low* unemployment rate suggests that labor is being utilized at an unsustainably high rate, so that actual output exceeds potential output (an expansionary gap).

To better understand the relationship between the output gap and unemployment, recall from the chapter "Workers, Wages, and Unemployment in the Modern Economy" the three broad types of unemployment: frictional unemployment, structural unemployment, and cyclical unemployment. *Frictional unemployment* is the short-term unemployment that is associated with the matching of workers and jobs. Some amount of frictional unemployment is necessary for the labor market to function efficiently in a dynamic, changing economy. *Structural unemployment* is the long-term and chronic unemployment that occurs even when the economy is producing at its normal rate. Structural unemployment often results when workers' skills are outmoded and do not meet the needs of employers—so, for example, steelworkers may become structurally unemployed as the steel industry goes into a long-term decline, unless those workers can retrain to find jobs in growing industries. Finally, *cyclical unemployment* is the extra unemployment that occurs during periods of recession. Unlike cyclical unemployment, which is present only during recessions, frictional unemployment and structural unemployment are always present in the labor market, even when the economy is operating normally. Economists call the part of the total unemployment rate that is attributable to frictional and structural unemployment the **natural rate of unemployment.** Put another way, the natural rate of unemployment is the unemployment rate that prevails when cyclical unemployment is zero, so that the economy has neither a recessionary nor an expansionary output gap. We will denote the natural rate of unemployment as u^*.

Cyclical unemployment, which is the difference between the total unemployment rate and the natural rate, thus can be expressed as $u - u^*$, where u is the actual unemployment rate and u^* denotes the natural rate of unemployment. In a recession, the actual unemployment rate u exceeds the natural unemployment rate u^*, so cyclical unemployment, $u - u^*$, is positive. When the economy experiences an expansionary gap, in contrast, the actual unemployment rate is lower than the natural rate, so that cyclical unemployment is negative. Negative cyclical unemployment corresponds to a situation in which labor is being used at an unsustainably high level, so that actual unemployment has dipped below its usual frictional and structural levels.

natural rate of unemployment, u^* the part of the total unemployment rate that is attributable to frictional and structural unemployment; equivalently, the unemployment rate that prevails when cyclical unemployment is zero, so that the economy has neither a recessionary nor an expansionary output gap

Why has the natural rate of unemployment in the United States apparently declined?

According to the Congressional Budget Office, which regularly estimates the natural rate of unemployment in the United States, the natural rate has fallen steadily since about 1979, from 6.3 percent of the labor force to about 5.2 percent.[1] Some economists, noting that unemployment remained close to 4 percent for several years

ECONOMIC NATURALIST 12.2

---

[1]Congressional Budget Office, *Economic and Budget Outlook: Fiscal Years 2006 to 2015*, January 2005, available online at http://www.cbo.gov/.

around the turn of the millennium, have argued for an even lower natural rate, perhaps as low as 4.5 percent. Why is the U.S. natural rate of unemployment apparently so much lower today than it was 20 years ago?

The natural rate of unemployment may have fallen because of reduced frictional unemployment, reduced structural unemployment, or both. A variety of ideas have been advanced to explain declines in both types of unemployment. One promising suggestion is based on the changing age structure of the U.S. labor force.[2] The average age of U.S. workers is rising, reflecting the aging of the baby boom generation. Indeed, over the past 25 years, the share of the labor force aged 16–24 has fallen from about 25 percent to about 15 percent. Since young workers are more prone to unemployment than older workers, the aging of the labor force may help to explain the overall decline in unemployment.

Why are young workers more likely to be unemployed? Compared to teenagers and workers in their twenties, older workers are much more likely to hold long-term, stable jobs. In contrast, younger workers tend to hold short-term jobs, perhaps because they are not ready to commit to a particular career, or because their time in the labor market is interrupted by schooling or military service. Because they change jobs more often, younger workers are more prone than others to frictional unemployment. They also have fewer skills, on average, than older workers, so they may experience more structural unemployment. As workers age and gain experience, however, their risk of unemployment declines.

Another possible explanation for the declining natural rate of unemployment is that labor markets have become more efficient at matching workers with jobs, thereby reducing both frictional and structural unemployment. For example, agencies that arrange temporary help have become much more commonplace in the United States in recent years. Although the placements these agencies make are intended to be temporary, they often become permanent when an employer and worker discover that a particularly good match has been made. Online job services, which allow workers to search for jobs nationally and even internationally, also are becoming increasingly important. By reducing the time people must spend in unemployment and by creating more lasting matches between workers and jobs, temporary help agencies, online job services, and similar innovations may have reduced the natural rate of unemployment.[3]

OKUN'S LAW

Okun's law each extra percentage point of cyclical unemployment is associated with about a 2 percentage point increase in the output gap, measured in relation to potential output

What is the relationship between an output gap and the amount of cyclical unemployment in the economy? We have already observed that by definition, cyclical unemployment is positive when the economy has a recessionary gap, negative when there is an expansionary gap, and zero when there is no output gap. A more quantitative relationship between cyclical unemployment and the output gap is given by a rule of thumb called *Okun's law*, after Arthur Okun, one of President Kennedy's chief economic advisers. According to **Okun's law**, each extra percentage point of cyclical unemployment is associated with about a 2 percentage point increase in the output gap, measured in relation to potential output.[4] So, for example, if cyclical unemployment increases from 1 percent to 2 percent of the labor force, the recessionary gap will increase from 2 percent to 4 percent of potential GDP. Example 12.1 illustrates further.

---

[2]See Robert Shimer, "Why Is the U.S. Unemployment Rate So Much Lower?" in B. Bernanke and J. Rotemberg, eds., *NBER Macroeconomics Annual*, 1998.

[3]For a detailed analysis of factors affecting the natural rate, see Lawrence Katz and Alan Krueger, "The High-Pressure U.S. Labor Market of the 1990s," *Brookings Papers on Economic Activity*, 1:1–88, 1999.

[4]Mathematically, Okun's law can be expressed as $(Y^* - Y)/Y^* = 2(u - u^*)$. This relationship between unemployment and output has weakened over time. When Arthur Okun first formulated his law in the 1960s, he suggested that each extra percentage point of unemployment was associated with about a 3 percentage point increase in the output gap.

Okun's law and the output gap in the U.S. economy

EXAMPLE 12.1

Following are the actual unemployment rate, the natural unemployment rate, and potential GDP (in billions of chained 2000 dollars) for the U.S. economy in four selected years.

Year	u	u^*	Y^*
1982	9.7%	6.1%	5,584
1991	6.8	5.8	7,305
1998	4.5	5.2	8,950
2002	5.8	5.2	10,342

SOURCES: Unemployment rate: http://www.bls.gov. Natural unemployment rate and potential GDP: Congressional Budget Office, (http://www.cbo.gov/Spreadsheet/6060_Table2-2.xls).

In 1982 cyclical unemployment, $u - u^*$, was 9.7% − 6.1%, or 3.6 percent of the labor force. According to Okun's law, the output gap for that year would be twice that percentage, or 7.2 percent of potential output. Since potential output was estimated to be $5,584 billion, the value of the output gap for that year was 7.2% × $5,584 billion, or $402 billion.[5]

In 1991 cyclical unemployment was 6.8% − 5.8%, or 1.0 percent of the labor force. According to Okun's law, the output gap for 1991 would be twice 1.0 percent, or 2.0 percent of potential GDP. Since potential GDP in 1991 was $7,305 billion, the output gap in that year should have been 2.0% × $7,305, or $146 billion.

Both 1982 and 1991 were recession years, so the output gaps were recessionary gaps. In contrast, 1998 was a year of expansion, in which unemployment was below the natural rate and the economy experienced an expansionary gap. Cyclical unemployment in 1998 was 4.5% − 5.2%, or −0.7 percent. The output gap in 1998 therefore should have been about −1.4 percent of the potential GDP of $8,950 billion, or −$125 billion. In other words, in 1998 actual GDP was about $125 billion greater than potential GDP.

The year 2002 followed a recession year, so the economy was still experiencing a recessionary gap. In 2002 cyclical unemployment was 5.8% − 5.2%, or 0.6 percent of the labor force. According to Okun's law, the output gap for 2002 would be 1.2 percent of the potential GDP of $10,342, or $124 billion.

EXERCISE 12.2

In the first quarter of 2005, the U.S. unemployment rate was 5.3 percent. Assume the natural rate of unemployment was 5.2 percent. By what percentage did actual GDP differ from potential GDP in the first quarter of 2005?

The output losses sustained in recessions, calculated according to Okun's law, can be quite significant. In Example 12.1 we found the U.S. output gap in 1982 to be $402 billion. The U.S. population in 1982 was about 230 million. Hence, the output loss per person in that year equaled the total output gap of $402 billion divided by 230 million people, or $1,748—about $7,000 for a family of four in 2000 dollars. This calculation implies that output gaps and cyclical unemployment may have significant costs—a conclusion that justifies the concern that the public and policymakers have about recessions.

[5]Economists use a variety of methods to estimate potential output. One way is to use a production function (see page 198), together with data on the amount of capital and labor available, to estimate how much the economy is able to produce on a sustained basis.

**ECONOMIC
NATURALIST
12.3**

Why did the Federal Reserve take measures to slow down the economy in 1999 and 2000?

As noted in the chapters "Macroeconomics" and "Money, Prices, and the Federal Reserve," monetary policy decisions of the Federal Reserve—actions that change the level of the nation's money supply—affect the performance of the U.S. economy. Why did the Federal Reserve take measures to slow down the economy in 1999 and 2000?

Throughout the 1990s, cyclical unemployment in the United States fell dramatically, becoming negative sometime in 1997, according to Congressional Budget Office estimates. Okun's law indicates that growing negative cyclical unemployment rates signal an increasing expansionary gap (illustrated in Example 12.1), and with it an increased risk of future inflation.

In 1997 and 1998 the Federal Reserve argued that the inflationary pressures typically caused by rapidly expanding output and falling unemployment rates were being offset by productivity gains and international competition, leaving inflation rates lower than expected. Because inflation remained low during this period—despite a small but growing expansionary gap—the Federal Reserve did little to eliminate the gap.

However, as the actual unemployment rate continued to fall throughout 1999 and early 2000 the expansionary gap continued to widen, causing the Federal Reserve to grow increasingly concerned about the growing imbalance between actual and potential GDP and the threat of increasing inflation. In response, the Federal Reserve took actions in 1999 and 2000 to slow the growth of output and bring actual and potential output closer into alignment (we will give more details about how the Fed can do this in the chapters "Stabilizing the Economy" and "Inflation, Aggregate Supply, and Aggregate Demand"). The Fed's actions helped to "promote overall balance in the economy"[6] and restrain inflation throughout 2000. By early 2001, however, the U.S. economy stalled and fell into recession (a topic analyzed in Economic Naturalist 13.2), leading the Federal Reserve to reverse course and take policy measures aimed at eliminating the growing *recessionary* gap.

RECAP	OUTPUT GAPS, CYCLICAL UNEMPLOYMENT, AND OKUN'S LAW

- Potential output is the maximum sustainable amount of output (real GDP) that an economy can produce. The output gap, $Y^* - Y$, is the difference between potential output Y^* and actual output Y. When actual output is below potential, the resulting output gap is called a recessionary gap. When actual output is above potential, the difference is called an expansionary gap. A recessionary gap reflects a waste of resources, while an expansionary gap threatens to ignite inflation; hence, policymakers have an incentive to try to eliminate both types of output gaps.

- The natural rate of unemployment u^* is the sum of the frictional and structural unemployment rates. It is the rate of unemployment that is observed when the economy is operating at a normal level, with no output gap.

- Cyclical unemployment, $u - u^*$, is the difference between the actual unemployment rate u and the natural rate of unemployment u^*. Cyclical unemployment is positive when there is a recessionary gap, negative when there is an expansionary gap, and zero when there is no output gap.

- Okun's law relates cyclical unemployment and the output gap. According to this rule of thumb, each percentage point increase in cyclical unemployment is associated with about a 2 percentage point increase in the output gap, measured in relation to potential output.

[6]Testimony of Chairman Alan Greenspan, *The Federal Reserve's semiannual report on the economy and monetary policy*, Committee on Banking and Financial Services, U.S. House of Representatives February 17, 2000. Available online at http://www.federalreserve.gov/boarddocs/hh/2000/February/Testimony.htm.

WHY DO SHORT-TERM FLUCTUATIONS OCCUR? A PREVIEW AND A PARABLE

What causes periods of recession and expansion? In the preceding section, we discussed two possible reasons for slowdowns and speedups in real GDP growth. First, growth in potential output itself may slow down or speed up, reflecting changes in the growth rates of available capital and labor and in the pace of technological progress. Second, even if potential output is growing normally, actual output may be higher or lower than potential output—that is, expansionary or recessionary output gaps may develop. Earlier in this book, we discussed some of the reasons that growth in potential output can vary, and the options that policymakers have for stimulating growth in potential output. But we have not yet addressed the question of how output gaps can arise or what policymakers should do in response. The causes and cures of output gaps will be a major topic of the next four chapters. Here is a brief preview of the main conclusions of those chapters:

1. In a world in which prices adjusted immediately to balance the quantities supplied and demanded for all goods and services, output gaps would not exist. However, for many goods and services, the assumption that prices will adjust immediately is not realistic. Instead, many firms adjust the prices of their output only periodically. In particular, rather than changing prices with every variation in demand, firms tend to adjust to changes in demand in the short run by varying the quantity of output they produce and sell. This type of behavior is known as "meeting the demand" at a preset price.

2. Because in the short run firms tend to meet the demand for their output at preset prices, changes in the amount that customers decide to spend will affect output. When total spending is low for some reason, output may fall below potential output; conversely, when spending is high, output may rise above potential output. In other words, *changes in economywide spending are the primary cause of output gaps.* Thus, government policies can help to eliminate output gaps by influencing total spending. For example, the government can affect total spending directly simply by changing its own level of purchases.

3. Although firms tend to meet demand in the short run, they will not be willing to do so indefinitely. If customer demand continues to differ from potential output, firms will eventually adjust their prices to eliminate output gaps. If demand exceeds potential output (an expansionary gap), firms will raise their prices aggressively, spurring inflation. If demand falls below potential output (a recessionary gap), firms will raise their prices less aggressively or even cut prices, reducing inflation.

4. Over the longer run, price changes by firms eliminate any output gap and bring production back into line with the economy's potential output. Thus, the economy is "self-correcting" in the sense that it operates to eliminate output gaps over time. Because of this self-correcting tendency, in the long run actual output equals potential output, so that output is determined by the economy's productive capacity rather than by the rate of spending. In the long run, total spending influences only the rate of inflation.

These ideas will become clearer as we proceed through the next chapters. Before plunging into the details of the analysis, though, let's consider an example that illustrates the links between spending and output in the short and long run.

Al's ice cream store produces gourmet ice cream on the premises and sells it directly to the public. What determines the amount of ice cream that Al produces on a daily basis? The productive capacity, or potential output, of the shop is one important factor. Specifically, Al's potential output of ice cream depends on the amount of capital (number of ice cream makers) and labor (number of workers) that he employs, and on the productivity of that capital and labor. Although Al's potential output usually changes rather slowly, on occasion it can fluctuate significantly—for example, if an ice cream maker breaks down or Al contracts the flu.

The main source of day-to-day variations in Al's ice cream production, however, is not changes in potential output but fluctuations in the demand for ice cream by the public. Some of these fluctuations in spending occur predictably over the course of the day (more demand in the afternoon than in the morning, for example), the week (more demand on weekends), or the year (more demand in the summer). Other changes in demand are less regular—more demand on a hot day than a cool one, or when a parade is passing by the store. Some changes in demand are hard for Al to interpret: For example, a surge in demand for rocky road ice cream on one particular Tuesday could reflect a permanent change in consumer tastes, or it might just be a random, one-time event.

How should Al react to these ebbs and flows in the demand for ice cream? The basic supply-and-demand model that we introduced in Chapter 3, if applied to the market for ice cream, would predict that the price of ice cream should change with every change in the demand for ice cream. For example, prices should rise just after the movie theater next door to Al's shop lets out on Friday night, and they should fall on unusually cold, blustery days, when most people would prefer a hot cider to an ice cream cone. Indeed, taken literally, the supply and demand model of Chapter 3 predicts that ice cream prices should change almost moment to moment. Imagine Al standing in front of his shop like an auctioneer, calling out prices in an effort to determine how many people are willing to buy at each price!

Of course, we do not expect to see this behavior by an ice cream store owner. Price setting by auction does in fact occur in some markets, such as the market for grain or the stock market, but it is not the normal procedure in most retail markets, such as the market for ice cream. Why this difference? The basic reason is that sometimes the economic benefits of hiring an auctioneer and setting up an auction exceed the costs of doing so, and sometimes they do not. In the market for grain, for example, many buyers and sellers gather together in the same place at the same time to trade large volumes of standardized goods (bushels of grain). In that kind of situation, an auction is an efficient way to determine prices and balance the quantities supplied and demanded. In an ice cream store, by contrast, customers come in by twos and threes at random times throughout the day. Some want shakes, some cones, and some sodas. With small numbers of customers and a low sales volume at any given time, the costs involved in selling ice cream by auction are much greater than the benefits of allowing prices to vary with demand.

So how does Al, the ice cream store manager, deal with changes in the demand for ice cream? Observation suggests that he begins by setting prices based on the best information he has about the demand for his product and the costs of production. Perhaps he prints up a menu or makes a sign announcing the prices. Then, over a period of time, he will keep his prices fixed and serve as many customers as want to buy (up to the point where he runs out of ice cream or room in the store at these prices). This behavior is what we call "meeting the demand" at preset prices, and it implies that *in the short run*, the amount of ice cream Al produces and sells is determined by the demand for his products.

However, *in the long run*, the situation is quite different. Suppose, for example, that Al's ice cream earns a citywide reputation for its freshness and flavor. Day after day Al observes long lines in his store. His ice cream maker is overtaxed, as are his employees and his table space. There can no longer be any doubt that at current prices, the quantity of ice cream the public wants to consume exceeds what Al is able and willing to supply on a normal basis (his potential output). Expanding the store is an attractive possibility, but not one (we assume) that is immediately feasible. What will Al do?

Certainly one thing Al can do is raise his prices. At higher prices, Al will earn higher profits. Moreover, raising ice cream prices will bring the quantity of ice cream demanded closer to Al's normal production capacity—his potential output.

Indeed, when the price of Al's ice cream finally rises to its equilibrium level, the shop's actual output will equal its potential output. Thus, over the long run, ice cream prices adjust to their equilibrium level, and the amount that is sold is determined by potential output.

This example illustrates in a simple way the links between spending and output—except, of course, that we must think of this story as applying to the whole economy, not to a single business. The key point is that there is an important difference between the short run and the long run. In the short run, producers often choose not to change their prices, but rather to meet the demand at preset prices. Because output is determined by demand, in the short run total spending plays a central role in determining the level of economic activity. Thus, Al's ice cream store enjoys a boom on an unusually hot day, when the demand for ice cream is strong, while an unseasonably cold day brings an ice cream recession. But in the long run, prices adjust to their market-clearing levels, and output equals potential output. Thus, the quantities of inputs and the productivity with which they are used are the primary determinants of economic activity in the long run, as we saw in the chapter "Economic Growth, Productivity, and Living Standards." Although total spending affects output in the short run, in the long run its main effects are on prices.

Why did the Coca-Cola Company test a vending machine that "knows" when the weather is hot?

ECONOMIC NATURALIST 12.4

According to the *New York Times* (October 28, 1999, p. C1), the Coca-Cola Company has quietly tested a soda vending machine that includes a temperature sensor. Why would Coca-Cola want a vending machine that "knows" when the weather is hot?

When the weather is hot, the demand for refreshing soft drinks rises, increasing their market-clearing price. To take advantage of this variation in consumer demand, the vending machines that Coca-Cola tested were equipped with a computer chip that gave them the capability to raise soda prices automatically when the temperature climbs. The company's chairman and chief executive, M. Douglas Ivester, described in an interview how the desire for a cold drink increases during a sports championship final held in the summer heat. "So it is fair that it should be more expensive," Mr. Ivester was quoted as saying. "The machine will simply make this process automatic." Company officials suggested numerous other ways in which vending machine prices could be made dependent on demand. For example, machines could be programmed to reduce prices during off-peak hours or at low-traffic machines.

In traditional vending machines, cold drinks are priced in a way analogous to the way Al prices his ice cream: A price is set, and demand is met at the preset price until the machine runs out of soda. The weather-sensitive vending machine illustrates how technology may change pricing practices in the future. Indeed, increased computing power and access to the Internet already have allowed some firms, such as airline companies, to change prices almost continuously in response to variations in demand. Conceivably, the practice of meeting demand at a preset price may someday be obsolete.

On the other hand, Coca-Cola's experiments with "smart" vending machines also illustrate the barriers to fully flexible pricing in practice. First, the new vending machines are more costly than the standard model. In deciding whether to use them, the company must decide whether the extra profits from variable pricing justify the extra cost of the machines. Second, in early tests, many consumers reacted negatively to the new machines, complaining that they take unfair advantage of thirsty customers. In practice, customer complaints and concerns about "fairness" make companies less willing to vary prices sensitively with changing demand.

■ SUMMARY ■

- Real GDP does not grow smoothly. Periods in which the economy is growing at a rate significantly below normal are called *recessions;* periods in which the economy is growing at a rate significantly above normal are called *expansions.* A severe or protracted recession, like the long decline that occurred between 1929 and 1933, is called a *depression,* while a particularly strong expansion is called a *boom.*

- The beginning of a recession is called the *peak,* because it represents the high point of economic activity prior to a downturn. The end of a recession, which marks the low point of economic activity prior to a recovery, is called the *trough.* Since World War II, U.S. recessions have been much shorter on average than booms, lasting between 6 and 16 months. The longest boom period in U.S. history began with the end of the 1990–1991 recession in March 1991, ending exactly 10 years later in March 2001 when a new recession began.

- Short-term economic fluctuations are irregular in length and severity, and are thus hard to forecast. Expansions and recessions are typically felt throughout the economy and may even be global in scope. Unemployment rises sharply during recessions, while inflation tends to fall during or shortly after a recession. Durable goods industries tend to be particularly sensitive to recessions and booms, whereas services and nondurable goods industries are less sensitive.

- *Potential output,* also called potential GDP or full-employment output, is the maximum sustainable amount of output (real GDP) that an economy can produce. The difference between potential output and actual output is the *output gap.* When output is below potential, the gap is called a *recessionary gap;* when output is above potential, the difference is called an *expansionary gap.* Recessions can occur either because potential output is growing unusually slowly or because actual output is below potential. Because recessionary gaps represent wasted resources and expansionary gaps threaten to create inflation, policymakers have an incentive to try to eliminate both types of gap.

- The *natural rate of unemployment* is the part of the total unemployment rate that is attributable to frictional and structural unemployment. Equivalently, the natural rate of unemployment is the rate of unemployment that exists when the output gap is zero. Cyclical unemployment, the part of unemployment that is associated with recessions and expansions, equals the total unemployment rate less the natural unemployment rate. Cyclical unemployment is related to the output gap by *Okun's law,* which states that each extra percentage point of cyclical unemployment is associated with about a 2 percentage point increase in the output gap, measured in relation to potential output.

- In the next several chapters, our study of recessions and expansions will focus on the role of economywide spending. If firms adjust prices only periodically, and in the meantime produce enough output to meet demand, then fluctuations in spending will lead to fluctuations in output over the short run. During that short-run period, government policies that influence aggregate spending may help to eliminate output gaps. In the long run, however, firms' price changes will eliminate output gaps—that is, the economy will "self-correct"—and total spending will influence only the rate of inflation.

■ KEY TERMS ■

boom (327)
depression (325)
expansion (327)
expansionary gap (332)
natural rate of unemployment,
   u^* (333)

Okun's law (334)
output gap, $Y^* - Y$ (332)
peak (325)
potential output, Y^* (or potential
GDP or full-employment
output) (331)

recession (or contraction) (325)
recessionary gap (332)
trough (325)

■ REVIEW QUESTIONS ■

1. Define *recession* and *expansion.* What are the beginning and ending points of a recession called? In the postwar United States, which have been longer on average: recessions or expansions?

2. Why is the traditional term *business cycles* a misnomer? How does your answer relate to the ease or difficulty of forecasting peaks and troughs?

3. Which firm is likely to see its profits reduced the most in a recession: an automobile producer, a manufacturer of boots and shoes, or a janitorial service? Which is likely to see its profits reduced the least? Explain.

4. How is each of the following likely to be affected by a recession: the natural unemployment rate, the cyclical un-

employment rate, the inflation rate, the poll ratings of the president?

5. Define *potential output*. Is it possible for an economy to produce an amount greater than potential output? Explain.

6. True or false: All recessions are the result of output gaps. Explain.

7. True or false: When output equals potential output, the unemployment rate is zero. Explain.

8. If the natural rate of unemployment is 5 percent, what is the total rate of unemployment if output is 2 percent below potential output? What if output is 2 percent above potential output?

■ PROBLEMS ■

1. Using Table 12.1, find the average duration, the minimum duration, and the maximum duration of expansions in the United States since 1929. Are expansions getting longer or shorter on average over time? Is there any tendency for long expansions to be followed by long recessions?

2. From the homepage of the Bureau of Economic Analysis (http://www.bea.gov/bea/dn1.htm) obtain quarterly data for U.S. real GDP from the last three recessions: 1981–1982, 1990–1991, and 2001.
   a. How many quarters of negative real GDP growth occurred in each recession?
   b. Which, if any, of the recessions satisfied the informal criterion that a recession must have two consecutive quarters of negative GDP growth?

3. Given below are data on real GDP and potential GDP for the United States for the years 1999–2003, in billions of 2000 dollars. For each year, calculate the output gap as a percentage of potential GDP and state whether the gap is a recessionary gap or an expansionary gap. Also calculate the year-to-year growth rates of real GDP. Can you identify the recession that occurred during this period?

Year	Real GDP	Potential GDP
1999	$ 9,470	$ 9,281
2000	$ 9,817	$ 9,634
2001	$ 9,891	$ 9,991
2002	$10,049	$10,342
2003	$10,321	$10,677

SOURCE: Potential GDP: Congressional Budget Office; real GDP, http://www.bea.gov.

4. From the homepage of the Bureau of Labor Statistics (http://www.stats.bls.gov/), obtain the most recent available data on the unemployment rate for workers aged 16–19 and workers aged 20 or over. How do they differ? What are some of the reasons for the difference? How does this difference relate to the decline in the overall natural rate of unemployment since 1980?

5. Using Okun's law, fill in the four pieces of missing data in the table below. The data are hypothetical.

Year	Real GDP	Potential GDP	Natural unemployment rate (%)	Actual unemployment rate (%)
2006	7,840	8,000	(a)	6
2007	8,100	(b)	5	5
2008	(c)	8,200	4.5	4
2009	8,415	8,250	5	(d)

■ ANSWERS TO IN-CHAPTER EXERCISES ■

12.1 Answers will vary, depending on when the data are obtained.

12.2 The actual unemployment rate in the first quarter of 2005 exceeded the natural rate by 0.1 percent, so by Okun's law actual output fell below potential output by $2 \times 0.1 = 0.2\%$ of potential output (a recessionary gap).

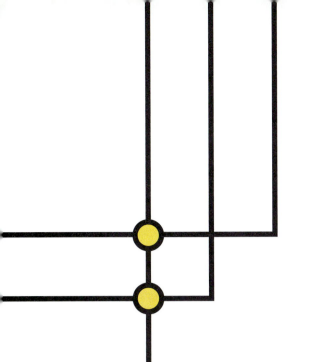

SPENDING AND OUTPUT

IN THE SHORT RUN

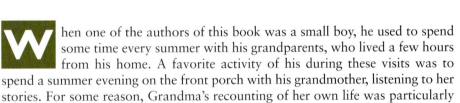

When one of the authors of this book was a small boy, he used to spend some time every summer with his grandparents, who lived a few hours from his home. A favorite activity of his during these visits was to spend a summer evening on the front porch with his grandmother, listening to her stories. For some reason, Grandma's recounting of her own life was particularly fascinating to her grandson.

Grandma had spent the early years of her marriage in New England, during the worst part of the Great Depression. In one of her reminiscences, she remarked that at that time, in the mid-1930s, it had been a satisfaction to her to be able to buy her children a new pair of shoes every year. In the small town where she and her family lived, many children had to wear their shoes until they fell apart, and a few unlucky boys and girls went to school barefoot. Her grandson thought this was scandalous: "Why didn't their parents just buy them new shoes?" he demanded.

"They couldn't," said Grandma. "They didn't have the money. Most of the fathers had lost their jobs because of the Depression."

"What kind of jobs did they have?"

"They worked in the shoe factories, which had to close down."

"Why did the factories close down?"

"Because," Grandma explained, "nobody had any money to buy shoes."

The grandson was only six or seven years old at the time, but even he could see that there was something badly wrong with Grandma's logic. On the one side were boarded-up shoe factories and shoe workers with no jobs; on the other, children without shoes. Why couldn't the shoe factories just open and produce

the shoes the children so badly needed? He made his point quite firmly, but Grandma just shrugged and said it didn't work that way.

The story of the closed-down shoe factories illustrates in a microcosm the cost to society of a recessionary gap. In an economy with a recessionary gap, available resources, which in principle could be used to produce valuable goods and services, are instead allowed to lie fallow. This waste of resources lowers the economy's output and economic welfare, compared to its potential.

Grandma's account also suggests how such an unfortunate situation might come about. Suppose factory owners and other producers, being reluctant to accumulate unsold goods on their shelves, produce just enough output to satisfy the demand for their products. And suppose that, for some reason, the public's willingness or ability to spend declines. If spending declines, factories will respond by cutting their production (because they don't want to produce goods they can't sell) and by laying off workers who are no longer needed. And because the workers who are laid off will lose most of their income—a particularly serious loss in the 1930s, in the days before government-sponsored unemployment insurance was common—they must reduce their own spending. As their spending declines, factories will reduce their production again, laying off more workers, who in turn reduce their spending— and so on, in a vicious circle. In this scenario, the problem is not a lack of productive capacity—the factories have not lost their ability to produce—but rather *insufficient spending* to support the normal level of production.

The idea that a decline in aggregate spending may cause output to fall below potential output was one of the key insights of John Maynard Keynes, a highly influential British economist of the first half of the twentieth century. Box 13.1 gives

© Bettmann/CORBIS

BOX 13.1: JOHN MAYNARD KEYNES AND THE KEYNESIAN REVOLUTION

John Maynard Keynes (1883–1946), perhaps the most influential economist of the twentieth century, was a remarkable individual who combined a brilliant career as an economic theorist with an active life in diplomacy, finance, journalism, and the arts. Keynes (pronounced "canes") first came to prominence at the end of World War I when he attended the Versailles peace conference as a representative of the British Treasury. He was appalled by the shortsightedness of the diplomats at the conference, particularly their insistence that the defeated Germans make huge compensatory payments (called reparations) to the victorious nations. In his widely read book *The Economic Consequences of the Peace* (1919), Keynes argued that the reparations imposed on Germany were impossibly large, and that attempts to extract the payments would prevent Germany's economic recovery and perhaps lead to another war. Unfortunately for the world, he turned out to be right.

In the period between the two world wars, Keynes held a professorship at Cambridge, where his father had taught economics. Keynes's early writings had been on mathematics and logic, but after his experience in Versailles, he began to work primarily on economics, producing several well-regarded books. He developed an imposing intellectual reputation, editing Great Britain's leading scholarly journal in economics, writing articles for newspapers and magazines, advising the government, and playing a major role in the political and economic debates of the day. On the side, Keynes made fortunes both for himself and for King's College (a part of Cambridge University) by speculating in international currencies and commodities. He was also an active member of the Bloomsbury Group, a circle of leading artists, performers, and writers that included E. M. Forster and Virginia Woolf. In 1925 Keynes married the glamorous Russian ballerina Lydia Lopokova. Theirs was by all

a brief account of Keynes's life and ideas. The goal of this chapter is to present a theory, or model, of how recessions and expansions may arise from fluctuations in aggregate spending, along the lines first suggested by Keynes. This model, which we call the *basic Keynesian model,* is also known as the *Keynesian cross,* after the diagram that is used to illustrate the theory. In the body of the chapter, we will emphasize a numerical and graphical approach to the basic Keynesian model, although an algebraic solution to the simple model is presented in Appendix A which provides an algebraic analysis to the more general model.

We will begin with a brief discussion of the key assumptions of the basic Keynesian model. We will then turn to the important concept of total, or aggregate, *planned spending* in the economy. We will show how, in the short run, the rate of aggregate spending helps to determine the level of output, which can be greater than or less than potential output. In other words, depending on the level of spending, the economy may develop an output gap. "Too little" spending leads to a recessionary output gap, while "too much" creates an expansionary output gap.

An implication of the basic Keynesian model is that government policies that affect the level of spending can be used to reduce or eliminate output gaps. Policies used in this way are called *stabilization policies.* Keynes himself argued for the active use of fiscal policy—policy relating to government spending and taxes—to eliminate output gaps and stabilize the economy. In the latter part of this chapter, we will show why Keynes thought fiscal policy could help to stabilize the economy, and we will discuss the usefulness of fiscal policy as a stabilization tool.

As we mentioned in the previous chapter, the basic Keynesian model is not a complete or entirely realistic model of the economy, since it applies only to the

accounts a very successful marriage, and Keynes devoted significant energies to managing his wife's career and promoting the arts in Britain.

Like other economists of the time, Keynes struggled to understand the Great Depression that gripped the world in the 1930s. His work on the problem led to the publication in 1936 of *The General Theory of Employment, Interest, and Money.* In *The General Theory,* Keynes tried to explain how economies can remain at low levels of output and employment for protracted periods. He stressed a number of factors, most notably that aggregate spending may be too low to permit full employment during such periods. Keynes recommended increases in government spending as the most effective way to increase aggregate spending and restore full employment.

The General Theory is a difficult book, reflecting Keynes's own struggle to understand the complex causes of the Depression. In retrospect, some of *The General Theory*'s arguments seem unclear or even inconsistent. Yet the book is full of fertile ideas, many of which had a worldwide impact and eventually led to what has been called the *Keynesian revolution.* Over the years, many economists have added to or modified Keynes's conception, to the point that Keynes himself, were he alive today, probably would not recognize much of what is now called *Keynesian economics.* But the ideas that insufficient aggregate spending can lead to recession and that government policies can help to restore full employment are still critical to Keynesian theory.

In 1937 a heart attack curtailed Keynes's activities, but he remained an important figure on the world scene. In 1944 he led the British delegation to the international conference in Bretton Woods, New Hampshire, which established the key elements of the postwar international monetary and financial system, including the International Monetary Fund and the World Bank. Keynes died in 1946.

relatively short period during which firms do not adjust their prices but instead meet the demand forthcoming at preset prices. Furthermore, by treating prices as fixed, the basic Keynesian model presented in this chapter does not address the determination of inflation. Nevertheless, this model is an essential building block of leading current theories of short-run economic fluctuations and stabilization policies. In subsequent chapters, we will extend the basic Keynesian model to incorporate inflation and other important features of the economy.

THE KEYNESIAN MODEL'S CRUCIAL ASSUMPTION: FIRMS MEET DEMAND AT PRESET PRICES

The basic Keynesian model is built on a key assumption, highlighted in Box 13.2. This assumption is that firms do not continuously change their prices as supply and demand conditions change. Rather, over short periods, firms tend to keep their prices fixed and *meet the demand* that is forthcoming at those prices.[1] As we will see, the assumption that firms vary their production in order to meet demand at preset prices implies that fluctuations in spending will have powerful effects on the nation's real GDP.

> **BOX 13.2: KEY ASSUMPTION OF THE BASIC KEYNESIAN MODEL**
>
> **In the short run, firms meet the demand for their products at preset prices.**
>
> Firms do not respond to every change in the demand for their products by changing their prices. Instead, they typically set a price for some period, then *meet the demand* at that price. By "meeting the demand," we mean that firms produce just enough to satisfy their customers at the prices that have been set.

The assumption that, over short periods of time, firms meet the demand for their products at preset prices is generally realistic. Think of the stores where you shop. The price of a pair of jeans does not fluctuate from moment to moment according to the number of customers who enter the store or the latest news about the price of denim. Instead, the store posts a price and sells jeans to any customer who wants to buy at that price, at least until the store runs out of stock. Similarly, the corner pizza restaurant may leave the price of its large pie unchanged for months or longer, allowing its pizza production to be determined by the number of customers who want to buy at the preset price.

menu costs the costs of changing prices

Firms do not normally change their prices frequently because doing so would be costly. Economists refer to the costs of changing prices as **menu costs**. In the case of the pizza restaurant, the menu cost is literally just that—the cost of printing up a new menu when prices change. Similarly, the clothing store faces the cost of remarking all its merchandise if the manager changes prices. But menu costs also may include other kinds of costs—for example, the cost of doing a market survey to determine what price to charge and the cost of informing customers about price changes. Economic Naturalist 13.1 discusses how technology may affect menu costs in the future.

Menu costs will not prevent firms from changing their prices indefinitely. As we saw in the case of Al's ice cream store (see the last chapter), too great an imbalance between demand and supply, as reflected by a difference between sales and potential output, will eventually lead firms to change their prices. If no one is buying jeans, for example, at some point the clothing store will mark down its jeans prices. Or if the pizza restaurant becomes the local hot spot, with a line of customers stretching out

---

[1]Obviously, firms can only meet the forthcoming demand up to the point where they reach the limit of their capacity to produce. For that reason, the Keynesian analysis of this chapter is relevant only when producers have unused capacity.

the door, eventually the manager will raise the price of a large pie. Like many other economic decisions, the decision to change prices reflects a cost-benefit comparison: Prices should be changed if the benefit of doing so—the fact that sales will be brought more nearly in line with the firm's normal production capacity—outweighs the menu costs associated with making the change. As we have stressed, the basic Keynesian model developed in this chapter ignores the fact that prices will eventually adjust, and therefore should be interpreted as applying to the short run.

Will new technologies eliminate menu costs?

Thanks to new technologies, changing prices and informing customers about price changes is becoming increasingly less costly. Will technology eliminate menu costs as a factor in price setting?

ECONOMIC NATURALIST 13.1

Keynesian theory is based on the assumption that costs of changing prices, which economists refer to as menu costs, are sufficiently large to prevent firms from adjusting prices immediately in response to changing market conditions. However, in many industries, new technologies have eliminated or greatly reduced the direct costs of changing prices. For example, the use of bar codes to identify individual products, together with scanner technologies, allows a grocery store manager to change prices with just a few keystrokes, without having to change the price label on each can of soup or loaf of bread. Airlines use sophisticated computer software to implement complex pricing strategies, under which two travelers on the same flight to Milwaukee may pay very different fares, depending on whether they are business or vacation travelers and on how far in advance their flights were booked. Online retailers, such as booksellers, have the ability to vary their prices by type of customer and even by individual customer, while other Internet-based companies, such as eBay and Priceline, allow for negotiation over the price of each individual purchase. As described in Economic Naturalist 12.4, the Coca-Cola company experimented with a vending machine that automatically varied the price of a soft drink according to the outdoor temperature, charging more when the weather is hot.

Will these reductions in the direct costs of changing prices make the Keynesian theory, which assumes that firms meet demand at preset prices, less relevant to the real world? This is certainly a possibility that macroeconomists must take into account. However, it is unlikely that new technologies will completely eliminate the costs of changing prices anytime soon. Gathering the information about market conditions needed to set the profit-maximizing price—including the prices charged by competitors, the costs of producing the good or service, and the likely demand for the product—will remain costly for firms. Another cost of changing prices is the use of valuable managerial time and attention needed to make informed pricing decisions. A more subtle cost of changing prices—particularly raising prices—is that doing so may lead regular customers to rethink their choice of suppliers and decide to search for a better deal elsewhere.

"You thought we would offer lower fares? How insensitive."

PLANNED AGGREGATE EXPENDITURE

In the Keynesian theory discussed in this chapter, output at each point in time is determined by the amount that people throughout the economy want to spend—what we will refer to as *planned aggregate expenditure*. Specifically, **planned aggregate expenditure *(PAE)*** is total planned spending on final goods and services.

The four components of spending on final goods and services were introduced in the chapter "Measuring Economic Activity":

1. *Consumer expenditure*, or simply *consumption* (C), is spending by domestic households on final goods and services. Examples of consumer expenditure are spending on food, clothes, and entertainment and on consumer durable goods like automobiles and furniture.

planned aggregate expenditure (PAE)

total planned spending on final goods and services

2. *Investment* (*I*) is spending by domestic firms on new capital goods, such as office buildings, factories, and equipment. Spending on new houses and apartment buildings (residential investment) and increases in inventories (inventory investment) also are included in investment.[2]

3. *Government purchases* (*G*) is spending by domestic governments (federal, state, and local) on goods and services. Examples of government purchases include new schools and hospitals, military hardware, equipment for the space program, and the services of government employees, such as soldiers, police, and government office workers. Recall from the chapter "Measuring Economic Activity" that *transfer payments,* such as social security benefits and unemployment insurance, and interest on the government debt are *not* included in government purchases. Transfer payments and interest contribute to aggregate expenditure only at the point when they are spent by their recipients (for example, when a recipient of a Social Security check uses the funds to buy food, clothing, or other consumption goods).

4. *Net exports* (*NX*) equals exports minus imports. Exports are sales of domestically produced goods and services to foreigners. Imports are purchases by domestic residents of goods and services produced abroad which have been included in *C*, *I*, and *G* but must now be subtracted because they do not represent domestic production. Net exports therefore represent the net demand for domestic goods and services by foreigners.

Together, these four types of spending—by households, firms, the government, and the rest of the world—sum to total, or aggregate, spending.

PLANNED SPENDING VERSUS ACTUAL SPENDING

In the Keynesian model, output is determined by planned aggregate expenditure, or planned spending, for short. Could *planned* spending ever differ from *actual* spending? The answer is yes. The most important case is that of a firm that sells either less or more of its product than expected. As was noted in the chapter "Measuring Economic Activity," additions to the stocks of goods sitting in a firm's warehouse are treated in official government statistics as inventory investment by the firm. In effect, government statisticians assume that the firm buys its unsold output from itself; they then count those purchases as part of the firm's investment spending.[3]

Suppose, then, that a firm's actual sales are less than expected, so that part of what it had planned to sell remains in the warehouse. In this case, the firm's actual investment, including the unexpected increases in its inventory, is greater than its planned investment, which did not include the added inventory. Suppose we agree to let *I*^*p* equal the firm's planned investment, including planned inventory investment. A firm that sells less of its output than planned, and therefore adds more to its inventory than planned, will find that its actual investment (including unplanned inventory investment) exceeds its planned investment, so that $I > I^p$.

What about a firm that sells more of its output than expected? In that case, the firm will add less to its inventory than it planned, so actual investment will be less than planned investment, or $I < I^p$. Example 13.1 gives a numerical illustration.

---

[2]In everyday conversations, people often use the term "investment" to mean *financial* investment, for example, the purchase of stocks or bonds. As we discussed earlier, we use "investment" here to mean spending on new capital goods, such as factories, housing, and equipment, which is not the same as financial investment. This distinction is important to keep in mind.

[3]For the purposes of measuring GDP, treating unsold output as being purchased by its producer has the advantage of ensuring that actual production and actual expenditure are equal.

Actual and planned investment

EXAMPLE 13.1

The Fly-by-Night Kite Company produces $5,000,000 worth of kites during the year. It expects sales of $4,800,000 for the year, leaving $200,000 worth of kites to be stored in the warehouse for future sale. During the year, Fly-by-Night adds $1,000,000 in new production equipment as part of an expansion plan. Find Fly-by-Night's actual investment I and its planned investment I^p if actual kite sales turn out to be $4,600,000. What if sales are $4,800,000? What if they are $5,000,000?

Fly-by-Night's planned investment I^p equals its purchases of new production equipment ($1,000,000) plus its planned additions to inventory ($200,000), for a total of $1,200,000 in planned investment. The company's planned investment does not depend on how much it actually sells.

If Fly-by-Night sells only $4,600,000 worth of kites, it will add $400,000 in kites to its inventory instead of the $200,000 worth originally planned. In this case, actual investment equals the $1,000,000 in new equipment plus the $400,000 in inventory investment, so $I = \$1,400,000$. We see that when the firm sells less output than planned, actual investment exceeds planned investment ($I > I^p$).

If Fly-by-Night has $4,800,000 in sales, then it will add $200,000 in kites to inventory, just as planned. In this case, actual and planned investment are the same:

$$I = I^p = \$1,200,000.$$

Finally, if Fly-by-Night sells $5,000,000 worth of kites, it will have no output to add to inventory. Its inventory investment will be zero, and its total actual investment (including the new equipment) will equal $1,000,000, which is less than its planned investment of $1,200,000 ($I < I^p$).

Because firms that are meeting the demand for their product or service at pre-set prices cannot control how much they sell, their actual investment (including inventory investment) may well differ from their planned investment. However, for households, the government, and foreign purchasers, we may reasonably assume that actual spending and planned spending are the same. Thus, from now on we will assume that, for consumption, government purchases, and net exports, actual spending equals planned spending.

With these assumptions, we can define planned aggregate expenditure by the following equation:

$$PAE = C + I^p + G + NX. \qquad (13.1)$$

Equation 13.1 says that planned aggregate expenditure is the sum of planned spending by households, firms, governments, and foreigners. We use a superscript p to distinguish planned investment spending by firms, I^p, from actual investment spending, I. However, because planned spending equals actual spending for households, the government, and foreigners, we do not need to use superscripts for consumption, government purchases, or net exports.

HEY, BIG SPENDER! CONSUMER SPENDING AND THE ECONOMY

The largest component of planned aggregate expenditure—nearly two-thirds of total spending—is consumption spending, denoted C. As already mentioned, consumer spending includes household purchases of goods, such as groceries and clothing; services, such as health care, concerts, and college tuition; and consumer durables, such as cars, furniture, and home computers. Thus, consumers' willingness to spend affects sales and profitability in a wide range of industries. (Households' purchases of new homes are classified as investment, rather than consumption; but home purchases represent another channel through which household decisions affect total spending.)

What determines how much people plan to spend on consumer goods and services in a given period? While many factors are relevant, a particularly important determinant of the amount people plan to consume is their after-tax, or *disposable*, income. All else being equal, households and individuals with higher disposable incomes will consume more than those with lower disposable incomes. Keynes himself stressed the importance of disposable income in determining household consumption decisions, claiming a "psychological law" that people would tie their spending closely to their incomes.

Recall from the chapter "Saving and Capital Formation" that the disposable income of the private sector is the total production of the economy, Y, less net taxes (taxes minus transfers), or T. So we can assume that consumption spending (C) increases as disposable income $(Y - T)$ increases. As already mentioned, other factors also may affect consumption, such as the real interest rate, also discussed in the chapter "Saving and Capital Formation." For now we will ignore those other factors, returning to some of them later.

A general equation that captures the link between consumption and the private sector's disposable income is

$$C = \overline{C} + mpc(Y - T). \tag{13.2}$$

consumption function the relationship between consumption spending and its determinants, in particular, disposable (after-tax) income.

This equation, which we will dissect in a moment, is known as the *consumption function*. The **consumption function** relates consumption spending to its determinants, in particular, disposable (after-tax) income.

Let's look at the consumption function, Equation 13.2, more carefully. The right side of the equation contains two terms, $\overline{C}$ and $mpc(Y - T)$. The first term, $\overline{C}$, is a constant term in the equation that is intended to capture factors *other than disposable income* that affect consumption. For example, suppose consumers were to become more optimistic about the future, so that they desire to consume more and save less at any given level of their current disposable incomes. An increase in desired consumption at any given level of disposable income would be represented in the consumption function as an increase in the term $\overline{C}$.

wealth effect the tendency of changes in asset prices to affect households' wealth and thus their spending on consumption goods

We can imagine other factors that may affect the term $\overline{C}$ in the consumption function. Suppose, for example, that there is a boom in the stock market or a sharp increase in home prices, making consumers feel wealthier and hence more inclined to spend, for a given level of current disposable income. This effect could be captured by assuming that $\overline{C}$ increases. Likewise, a fall in home prices or stock prices that made consumers feel poorer and less inclined to spend would be represented by a decrease in $\overline{C}$. Economists refer to the effect of changes in asset prices on households' wealth and, hence, their consumption spending as the **wealth effect** of changes in asset prices.

What effect did the 2000–2002 decline in U.S. stock market values have on consumption spending?

From March 2000 to October 2002, the U.S. stock market suffered a 49 percent drop in value as measured by the Standard and Poor's 500 stock index, a widely referenced benchmark of U.S. stock performance. What effect did this decline in U.S. stock market values have on consumption spending?

According to MIT economist James Poterba, U.S. households owned roughly $13.3 trillion of corporate stock in 2000.[4] If households' stock market holdings

ECONOMIC
NATURALIST
13.2

---

[4]"The Stock Market and the Consumer," Hoover Institution Weekly Essays, November 6, 2000. Online at http://www-hoover.stanford.edu/pubaffairs/we/current/poterba_1100.html.

reflect those of the Standard and Poor's stock index, the 49 percent drop in the value of the stock market wiped out approximately $6.5 trillion of household wealth in two years. According to economic models based on historical experience, a dollar's decrease in household wealth reduces consumer spending by 3 to 7 cents per year, so the reduction in stock market wealth had the potential to reduce overall consumer spending by $195 billion to $455 billion, a drop of approximately 3 to 7 percent. Yet, real consumption spending continued to rise from 2000 through 2002. Why did this happen?

Despite the start of a recession in March 2001, overall consumption spending remained strong during 2000–2002 for a variety of reasons. As Economic Naturalist 12.1 points out, consumers' real after-tax income continued to grow into the fall of 2001, helping to maintain strong consumer spending despite the drop in the stock market. Furthermore, throughout 2001 and into early 2002, the Federal Reserve significantly reduced interest rates (how the Federal Reserve does this will be discussed in the next chapter). A reduction in interest rates helps to promote consumer spending, especially on "big-ticket" items such as automobiles, by reducing consumers' borrowing costs. Finally, housing prices rose significantly during this period, increasing consumers' housing wealth and partially offsetting their decline in stock-related wealth. Data on repeat house sales that measure the price of individual houses that are sold and resold over time indicate that housing prices rose by 20.1 percent between the first quarter of 2000 and the third quarter of 2002.[5] Since the total market value of household real estate was about $12 trillion in 2000,[6] house appreciation added about $2.4 trillion to household wealth, offsetting about 37 percent of the decline in stock market wealth during this period.

The second term on the right side of Equation 13.2, $mpc(Y - T)$, reflects the effect of disposable income, $Y - T$, on consumption. The parameter mpc, a fixed number, is called the *marginal propensity to consume*. The **marginal propensity to consume** *(mpc)* is the amount by which consumption rises when current disposable income rises by one dollar. Presumably, if people receive an extra dollar of income, they will consume part of the dollar and save the rest. In other words, their consumption will increase, but by less than the full dollar of extra income. Thus, it is realistic to assume that the marginal propensity to consume is greater than 0 (an increase in income leads to an increase in consumption) but less than 1 (the increase in consumption will be less than the full increase in income). Mathematically, we can summarize these assumptions as $0 < mpc < 1$.

Figure 13.1 shows a hypothetical consumption function, with consumption spending (C) on the vertical axis and disposable income (Y − T) on the horizontal axis. The intercept of the consumption function on the vertical axis equals exogenous consumption $\overline{C}$, and the slope of the consumption function equals the marginal propensity to consume, *mpc*.

To see how this consumption function fits reality, compare Figure 13.1 to Figure 13.2, which shows the relationship between aggregate real consumption expenditures and real disposable income in the United States for the period 1960–2004. Figure 13.2, a type of diagram called a *scatter plot*, shows aggregate real consumption on the vertical axis and aggregate real disposable income on the horizontal axis. Each point on the graph corresponds to a year between 1960 and 2004 (selected years are indicated in the figure). The position of each point is determined by the combination of consumption and disposable income associated with that year. As you can see, there is indeed a close relationship between

marginal propensity to consume (mpc) the amount by which consumption rises when disposable income rises by one dollar. We assume that $0 < mpc < 1$

[5]U.S. Office of Federal Housing Enterprise Oversight (OFHEO), http://www.ofheo.gov. House prices continued to rise at an even greater rate after 2002.
[6]Federal Reserve Board, *Flow of Funds Accounts of the United States*, http://www.federalreserve.gov.

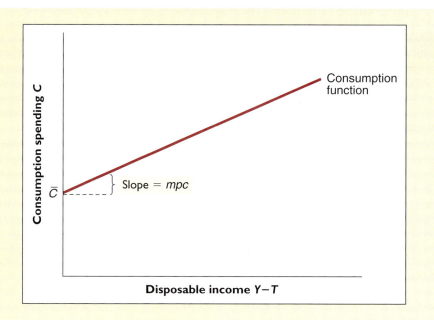

FIGURE 13.1

A Consumption Function.

The consumption function relates households' consumption spending, C, to disposable income, Y − T. The vertical intercept of this consumption function is the exogenous component of consumption, $\bar{C}$, and the slope of the line equals the marginal propensity to consume, mpc.

aggregate consumption and disposable income: Higher disposable income implies higher consumption.

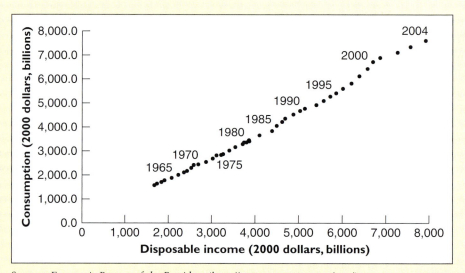

FIGURE 13.2

The U.S. Consumption Function, 1960–2004.

Each point on this figure represents a combination of aggregate real consumption and aggregate real disposable income for a specific year between 1960 and 2004. Note the strong positive relationship between consumption and disposable income.

SOURCE: *Economic Report of the President* (http://www.gpoaccess.gov/eop/).

PLANNED AGGREGATE EXPENDITURE AND OUTPUT

Thinking back to Grandma's reminiscences, recall that an important element of her story involved the links among production, income, and spending. As the shoe factories in Grandma's town reduced production, the incomes of both factory workers and factory owners fell. Workers' incomes fell as the number of hours of work per week were reduced (a common practice during the Depression), as workers were laid off, or as wages were cut. Factory owners' income fell as profits declined. Reduced incomes, in turn, forced both workers and factory owners to curtail their spending—which led to still lower production and further reductions in income. This vicious circle led the economy further and further into recession.

The logic of Grandma's story has two key elements: (1) declines in production (which imply declines in the income received by producers) lead to reduced spending and (2) reductions in spending lead to declines in production and income. In this section, we look at the first part of the story, the effects of production and income on spending. We return later in this chapter to the effects of spending on production and income.

Why do changes in production and income affect planned aggregate spending? The consumption function, which relates consumption to disposable income, is the basic source of this relationship. Because consumption spending C is a large part of planned aggregate spending, and because consumption depends on output Y, aggregate spending as a whole depends on output. Example 13.2 illustrates this relationship numerically.

Linking planned aggregate expenditure to output   **EXAMPLE 13.2**

In a particular economy, the consumption function is

$$C = 620 + 0.8(Y - T),$$

so that the intercept term in the consumption function $\overline{C}$ equals 620, and the marginal propensity to consume *mpc* equals 0.8. Also, suppose that we are given that planned investment spending $I^P = 220$, government purchases $G = 300$, net exports $NX = 20$, and taxes $T = 250$.

Write a numerical equation linking planned aggregate expenditure *PAE* to output Y. How does planned spending change when output and, hence, income change?

Recall the definition of planned aggregate expenditure, Equation 13.1:

$$PAE = C + I^P + G + NX$$

To find a numerical equation for planned aggregate expenditure, we need to find numerical expressions for each of its four components. The first component of spending, consumption, is defined by the consumption function, $C = 620 + 0.8(Y - T)$. Since taxes $T = 250$, we can substitute for T to write the consumption function as $C = 620 + 0.8(Y - 250)$. Now plug this expression for C into the definition of planned aggregate expenditure above to get

$$PAE = \left[620 + 0.8(Y - 250)\right] + I^P + G + NX,$$

where we have just replaced C by its value as determined by the consumption function. Similarly, we can substitute the given numerical values of planned investment I^P, government purchases G, and net exports NX into the definition of planned aggregate expenditure to get

$$PAE = \left[620 + 0.8(Y - 250)\right] + 220 + 300 + 20.$$

To simplify this equation, first note that $0.8(Y - 250) = 0.8Y - 200$, then add all the terms that don't depend on output Y. The result is

$$PAE = (620 - 200 + 220 + 300 + 20) + 0.8Y$$

$$= 960 + 0.8Y.$$

The final expression shows the relationship between planned aggregate expenditure and output in this numerical example. Note that, according to this equation, a $1 increase in Y leads to an increase in *PAE* of (0.8)($1), or 80 cents. The reason for this is that the marginal propensity to consume, *mpc*, in this example is 0.8. Hence, a $1 increase in income raises consumption spending by 80 cents. Since consumption is a component of total planned spending, total spending rises by 80 cents as well.

The solution to Example 13.2 illustrates a general point: Planned aggregate expenditure can be divided into two parts, a part that depends on output (Y) and a part that is independent of output. The portion of planned aggregate expenditure that is independent of output is called **autonomous expenditure.** In Example 13.2, autonomous expenditure is the constant term in the equation for planned aggregate expenditure, or 960. This portion of planned spending, being a fixed number, does not vary when output varies. By contrast, the portion of planned aggregate expenditure that depends on output (Y) is called **induced expenditure.** In Example 13.2, induced expenditure equals $0.8Y$, the second term in the expression for planned aggregate expenditure. Note that the numerical value of induced expenditure depends, by definition, on the numerical value taken by output. Autonomous expenditure and induced expenditure together equal planned aggregate expenditure.

autonomous expenditure the portion of planned aggregate expenditure that is independent of output

induced expenditure the portion of planned aggregate expenditure that depends on output Y

RECAP	PLANNED AGGREGATE EXPENDITURE

- Planned aggregate expenditure (PAE) is total planned spending on final goods and services. The four components of planned spending are consumer expenditure (C), planned investment (I^p), government purchases (G), and net exports (NX). Planned investment differs from actual investment when firms' sales are different from what they expected, so that additions to inventory (a component of investment) are different from what firms anticipated.

- The largest component of aggregate expenditure is consumer expenditure, or simply consumption. Consumption depends on disposable, or after-tax, income, according to a relationship known as the consumption function, stated algebraically as $C = \overline{C} + mpc(Y - T)$.

- The constant term in the consumption function, $\overline{C}$, captures factors other than disposable income that affect consumer spending. For example, an increase in housing or stock prices that makes households wealthier and thus more willing to spend—an effect called the wealth effect—could be captured by an increase in $\overline{C}$. The slope of the consumption function equals the marginal propensity to consume, mpc, where $0 < mpc < 1$. This is the amount by which consumption rises when disposable income rises by one dollar.

- Increases in output Y, which imply equal increases in income, cause consumption to rise. As consumption is part of planned aggregate expenditure, planned spending depends on output as well. The portion of planned aggregate expenditure that depends on output is called induced expenditure. The portion of planned aggregate expenditure that is independent of output is autonomous expenditure.

SHORT-RUN EQUILIBRIUM OUTPUT

short-run equilibrium output the level of output at which output Y equals planned aggregate expenditure PAE; short-run equilibrium output is the level of output that prevails during the period in which prices are predetermined

Now that we have defined planned aggregate expenditure and seen how it is related to output, the next task is to see how output itself is determined. Recall the assumption of the basic Keynesian model: In the short run, producers leave prices at preset levels and simply meet the demand that is forthcoming at those prices. In other words, during the short-run period in which prices are preset, firms produce an amount that is equal to planned aggregate expenditure. Accordingly, we define **short-run equilibrium output** as the level of output at which output Y equals planned aggregate expenditure PAE:

$$Y = PAE. \tag{13.3}$$

Short-run equilibrium output is the level of output that prevails during the period in which prices are predetermined.

We can find the short-run equilibrium output in three ways. First, we can use a table to compute the level of output at which $Y - PAE = 0$. Second, we can use a graph called the *Keynesian cross*. Finally, we can use algebra. Although we focus on the first two in this chapter, an optional box on page 358 illustrates the use of algebra to solve the simple model in Example 13.2, and Appendix A to this chapter uses algebra to solve the more general model.

First, we use the data in Table 13.1 to find the equilibrium level of output for the economy described in Example 13.2. Column 2 of Table 13.1 lists the levels of planned aggregate expenditure (PAE) for the different levels of output given in column 1. Recall that in Example 13.2, planned spending is determined by the equation

$$PAE = 960 + 0.8Y.$$

TABLE 13.1
Numerical Determination of Short-Run Equilibrium Output

(1) Output Y	(2) Planned aggregate expenditure PAE = 960 + 0.8Y	(3) Y − PAE	(4) Y = PAE?
4,000	4,160	−160	No
4,200	4,320	−120	No
4,400	4,480	−80	No
4,600	4,640	−40	No
4,800	4,800	0	**Yes**
5,000	4,960	40	No
5,200	5,120	80	No

Thus, for example when $Y = 4,000$, $PAE = 960 + 0.8(4,000) = 4,160$. Because consumption rises with output, total planned spending (which includes consumption) rises also. But if you compare columns 1 and 2, you will see that when output rises by 200, planned spending rises by only 160. That is because the marginal propensity to consume in this economy is 0.8, so that each dollar in added income raises consumption and planned spending by 80 cents.

Again, short-run equilibrium output is the level of output at which $Y = PAE$, or, equivalently, $Y - PAE, = 0$. At this level of output, actual investment will equal planned investment and there will be no tendency for output to change. Looking at Table 13.1, we can see there is only one level of output that satisfies that condition, $Y = 4,800$. At that level, output and planned aggregate expenditure are precisely equal, so that producers are just meeting the demand for their goods and services.

In this economy, what would happen if output differed from its equilibrium value of 4,800? Suppose, for example, that output were 4,000. Looking at the second column of Table 13.1, you can see that when output is 4,000, planned aggregate expenditure equals $960 + 0.8(4,000)$, or 4,160. Thus, if output is 4,000, firms are not producing enough to meet the demand. They will find that as sales exceed the amounts they are producing, their inventories of finished goods are being depleted by 160 per year, and that actual investment (including inventory investment) is less than planned investment. Under the assumption that firms are committed to meeting their customers' demand, firms will respond by expanding their production.

Would expanding production to 4,160, the level of planned spending firms faced when output was 4,000, be enough? The answer is no, because of induced expenditure. That is, as firms expand their output, aggregate income (wages and profits) rises with it, which in turn leads to higher levels of consumption. Indeed, if output expands to 4,160, planned spending will increase as well, to 960 + 0.8(4,160), or 4,288. So an output level of 4,160 will still be insufficient to meet demand. As Table 13.1 shows, output will not be sufficient to meet planned aggregate expenditure until it expands to its short-run equilibrium value of 4,800.

What if output were initially greater than its equilibrium value—say, 5,000? From Table 13.1, we can see that when output equals 5,000, planned spending equals only 4,960—less than what firms are producing. So at an output level of 5,000, firms will not sell all they produce, and they will find that their merchandise is piling up on store shelves and in warehouses (actual investment, including inventory investment, is greater than planned investment). In response, firms will cut their production runs. As Table 13.1 shows, they will have to reduce production to its equilibrium value of 4,800 before output just matches planned spending.

EXERCISE 13.1

Construct a table like Table 13.1 for an economy like the one we have been working with, assuming that the consumption function is $C = 820 + 0.7(Y - T)$ and that $I^P = 600$, $G = 600$, $NX = 200$, and $T = 600$.

   What is short-run equilibrium output in this economy? (*Hint:* Try using values for output above 5,000.)

Short-run equilibrium output also can be determined graphically, as Example 13.3 shows.

EXAMPLE 13.3

Finding short-run equilibrium output (graphical approach)

Using a graphical approach, find short-run equilibrium output for the economy described in Example 13.2.

Figure 13.3 shows the graphical determination of short-run equilibrium output for the economy described in Example 13.2. Output Y is plotted on the horizontal axis and planned aggregate expenditure PAE on the vertical axis. The figure contains

FIGURE 13.3

Determination of Short-Run Equilibrium Output (Keynesian Cross).

The 45° line represents the short-run equilibrium condition $Y = PAE$. The line $PAE = 960 + 0.8Y$, referred to as the expenditure line, shows the relationship of planned aggregate expenditure to output. Short-run equilibrium output (4,800) is determined at the intersection of the two lines, point E. This type of diagram is known as a Keynesian cross.

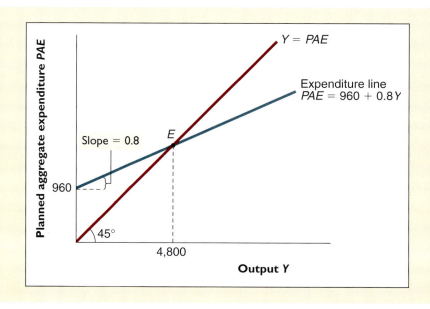

two lines, one of which is a 45° line extending from the origin. In general, a 45° line from the origin includes the points at which the variable on the vertical axis equals the variable on the horizontal axis. Hence, in this case, the 45° line represents the equation $Y = PAE$. Since short-run equilibrium output must satisfy the equation $Y = PAE$, the combination of output and spending that satisfies this condition must lie somewhere on the 45° line in Figure 13.3.

The second line in Figure 13.3, less steep than the 45° line, shows the relationship between planned aggregate expenditure PAE and output Y. Because it summarizes how planned spending depends on output, we will call this line the *expenditure line*. In this example, we know that the relationship between planned aggregate expenditure and output (the equation for the expenditure line) is

$$PAE = 960 + 0.8Y.$$

According to this equation, when $Y = 0$, the value of PAE is 960. Thus, 960 is the intercept of the expenditure line, as shown in Figure 13.3. Notice that *the intercept of the expenditure line equals autonomous expenditure*, a result that will always hold. The slope of the line relating aggregate demand to output is 0.8, the value of the coefficient of output in the equation $PAE = 960 + 0.8Y$. Where does the number 0.8 come from? (*Hint:* What determines by how much aggregate spending increases when output rises by a dollar?)

Only one point in Figure 13.3 is consistent with *both* the definition of short-run equilibrium output, $Y = PAE$, and the given relationship between planned spending and output, $PAE = 960 + 0.8Y$. That point is the intersection of the two lines, point E. At point E, short-run equilibrium output equals 4,800, which is the same value that we obtained using Table 13.1 and by a direct numerical solution. At points to the right of E, output exceeds planned aggregate expenditure. Hence, to the right of point E, firms will be producing more than they can sell, which will lead them to reduce their rate of production. By contrast, to the left of point E, planned aggregate spending exceeds output. In that region, firms will not be producing enough to meet demand, and they will tend to increase their production. Only at point E, where output equals 4,800, will firms be producing enough to just satisfy planned spending on goods and services.

The diagram in Figure 13.3 is often called the *Keynesian cross*, after its characteristic shape. The Keynesian cross shows graphically how short-run equilibrium output is determined in a world in which producers meet demand at predetermined prices.

EXERCISE 13.2

Use a Keynesian cross diagram to show graphically the determination of short-run equilibrium output for the economy described in Exercise 13.1. What are the intercept and the slope of the expenditure line?

PLANNED SPENDING AND THE OUTPUT GAP

We are now ready to use the basic Keynesian model to show how insufficient spending can lead to a recession. To illustrate the effects of spending changes on output, we will continue to work with the economy introduced in Example 13.2. We have shown that in this economy, short-run equilibrium output equals 4,800. Let's now make the additional assumption that potential output in this economy also equals 4,800, or $Y^* = 4,800$, so that initially there is no output gap. Starting from this position of full employment, Example 13.4 shows how a fall in planned aggregate expenditure can lead to a recession.

BOX 13.3: USING ALGEBRA TO SOLVE EXAMPLE 13.2

In this optional box, we use algebra to solve the simple model presented in Example 13.2. In Appendix A to this chapter, we use algebra to solve a more general model.

The equilibrium level of output in the simple Keynesian model occurs when output Y is equal to planned aggregate expenditure PAE. Planned aggregate expenditure $PAE = C + I^p + G + NX$. By making the appropriate substitutions for C, I^p, G, and NX in Example 13.2, we found that $PAE = 960 + 0.8Y$. Consequently, we can find the equilibrium level of output by solving the equation

$$Y = 960 + 0.8Y \qquad (13.4)$$

Subtracting $0.8Y$ from both sides of Equation 13.4 yields

$$0.2Y = 960 \qquad (13.5)$$

Dividing both sides of Equation 13.5 by 0.2, we obtain

$$Y = 960/0.2 = 4,800$$

Thus, the equilibrium level of output is 4,800.

EXAMPLE 13.4

A fall in planned spending leads to a recession

For the economy introduced in Example 13.2, we have found that short-run equilibrium output Y equals 4,800. Assume also that potential output Y^* equals 4,800, so that the output gap $Y^* - Y$ equals zero.

Suppose, though, that consumers become more pessimistic about the future, so that they begin to spend less at every level of current disposable income. We can capture this change by assuming that $\overline{C}$, the constant term in the consumption function, falls to a lower level. To be specific, suppose that $\overline{C}$ falls by 10 units, which in turn implies a decline in autonomous expenditure of 10 units. What is the effect of this reduction in planned spending on the economy?

We can see the effects of the decline in consumer spending on the economy using the Keynesian cross diagram. Figure 13.4 shows the original short-run

FIGURE 13.4

A Decline in Planned Spending Leads to a Recession.

A decline in consumers' willingness to spend at any current level of disposable income reduces planned autonomous expenditure and shifts the expenditure line down. The short-run equilibrium point drops from E to F, reducing output and opening up a recessionary gap.

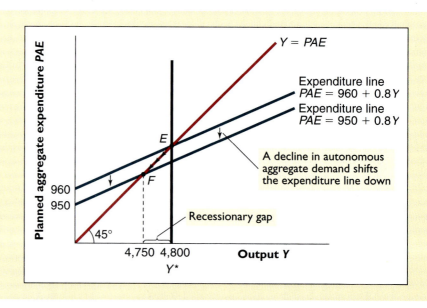

equilibrium point of the model (E), at the intersection of the 45° line, along which $Y = PAE$, and the original expenditure line, representing the equation $PAE = 960 + 0.8Y$. As before, the initial value of short-run equilibrium output is 4,800, which we have now assumed also corresponds to potential output Y^*. But what happens if $\overline{C}$ declines by 10, reducing autonomous expenditure by 10 as well?

Originally, autonomous expenditure in this economy was 960, so a decline of 10 units causes it to fall to 950. Instead of the economy's planned spending being described by the equation $PAE = 960 + 0.8Y$, as initially, it is now given by $PAE = 950 + 0.8Y$. What does this change imply for the graph in Figure 13.4? Since the intercept of the expenditure line (equal to autonomous expenditure) has decreased from 960 to 950, the effect of the decline in consumer spending will be to shift the expenditure line down in parallel fashion, by 10 units. Figure 13.4 indicates this downward shift in the expenditure line. The new short-run equilibrium point is at point F, where the new, lower expenditure line intersects the 45° line.

Point F is to the left of the original equilibrium point E, so we can see that output and spending have fallen from their initial levels. Since output at point F is lower than potential output, 4,800, we see that the fall in consumer spending has resulted in a recessionary gap in the economy. More generally, starting from a situation of full employment (where output equals potential output), any decline in autonomous expenditure leads to a recession.

Numerically, how large is the recessionary gap in Figure 13.4? To answer this question, we can use Table 13.2, which is in the same form as Table 13.1. The key difference is that in Table 13.2 planned aggregate expenditure is given by $PAE = 950 + 0.8Y$, rather than by $PAE = 960 + 0.8Y$, as in Table 13.1.

TABLE 13.2
Determination of Short-Run Equilibrium Output after a Fall in Spending

(1) Output Y	(2) Planned aggregate expenditure PAE = 950 + 0.8Y	(3) Y − PAE	(4) Y = PAE?
4,600	4,630	−30	No
4,650	4,670	−20	No
4,700	4,710	−10	No
4,750	4,750	0	**Yes**
4,800	4,790	10	No
4,850	4,830	20	No
4,900	4,870	30	No
4,950	4,910	40	No
5,000	4,950	50	No

As in Table 13.1, the first column of the table shows alternative possible values of output Y, and the second column shows the levels of planned aggregate expenditure PAE implied by each value of output in the first column. Notice that 4,800, the value of short-run equilibrium output found in Table 13.1, is no longer an equilibrium; when output is 4,800, planned spending is 4,790, so output and planned spending are not equal. As the table shows, following the decline in planned aggregate expenditure, short-run equilibrium output is 4,750, the only value of output for which $Y = PAE$. Thus, a drop of 10 units in autonomous expenditure has led to a

50-unit decline in short-run equilibrium output. If full-employment output is 4,800, then the recessionary gap shown in Figure 13.4 is $4,800 - 4,750 = 50$ units.

EXERCISE 13.3

In the economy described in Example 13.4, we found a recessionary gap of 50, relative to potential output of 4,800. Suppose that in this economy, the natural rate of unemployment u^* is 5 percent. What will the actual unemployment rate be after the recessionary gap appears? (*Hint:* Recall Okun's law from the last chapter.)

Example 13.4 showed that a decline in autonomous expenditure, arising from a decreased willingness of consumers to spend, causes short-run equilibrium output to fall and opens up a recessionary gap. The same conclusion applies to declines in autonomous expenditure arising from other sources. Suppose, for example, that firms become disillusioned with new technologies and cut back their planned investment in new equipment. In terms of the model, this reluctance of firms to invest can be interpreted as a decline in planned investment spending I^p. Under our assumption that planned investment spending is given and does not depend on output, planned investment is part of autonomous expenditure. So a decline in planned investment spending depresses autonomous expenditure and output, in precisely the same way that a decline in the autonomous part of consumption spending does. Similar conclusions apply to declines in other components of autonomous expenditure, such as government purchases and net exports, as we will see in later applications.

EXERCISE 13.4

Repeat the analysis of Example 13.4, except assume that consumers become *more* rather than less confident about the future. As a result, $\overline{C}$ rises by 10 units, which in turn raises autonomous expenditure by 10 units. Show graphically that this increase in consumers' willingness to spend leads to an expansionary output gap. Find the numerical value of the expansionary output gap.

"These are hard times for retailers, so we should show them our support in every way we can."

Why was the deep Japanese recession of the 1990s bad news for the rest of East Asia?

During the 1990s, Japan suffered a prolonged economic slump. Japan's economic problems were a major concern not only of the Japanese but of policymakers in other East Asian countries, such as Thailand and Singapore. Why did East Asian policymakers worry about the effects of the Japanese slump on their own economies?

ECONOMIC NATURALIST 13.3

Although the economies of Japan and its East Asian neighbors are intertwined in many ways, one of the most important links is through trade. Much of the economic success of East Asia has been based on the development of export industries, and over the years Japan has been the most important customer for East Asian goods. When the economy slumped in the 1990s, Japanese households and firms reduced their purchases of imported goods sharply. This fall in demand dealt a major blow to the export industries of other East Asian countries.

Not just the owners and workers of export industries were affected, though; as wages and profits in export industries fell, so did domestic spending in the East Asian nations. The declines in domestic spending reduced sales at home as well as abroad, further weakening the East Asian economies. In terms of the model, the decline in exports to Japan reduced net exports NX, and thus autonomous expenditure, in East Asian countries. The fall in autonomous expenditure led to a recessionary gap, much like that shown in Figure 13.4.

Japan is not the only country whose economic ups and downs have had a major impact on its trading partners. Because the United States is the most important trading partner of both Canada and Mexico, the U.S. recession that began in 2001 (see Economic Naturalist 13.4) led to declining exports and recessions in Canada and Mexico as well. East Asia, which exports high-tech goods to the United States, also was hurt by the U.S recession, with GDP in countries such as Singapore dropping sharply. Economic growth rebounded throughout most of East Asia after 2001, largely because of increased demand for exports to the United States and China.

What caused the 2001 recession in the United States?

According to the National Bureau of Economic Research, a recession began in the United States in March 2001—the first U.S. recession in 10 years (see Economic Naturalist 12.1 for a discussion of the NBER's "call"). What caused the 2001 recession in the United States?

ECONOMIC NATURALIST 13.4

Consumer spending is nearly two-thirds of aggregate expenditure, so it should not be surprising that most recessions involve significant reductions in spending by households. In this respect, the 2001 recession in the United States was quite unusual, as consumer spending remained fairly strong throughout most of the downturn (see Economic Naturalist 13.2). Instead, this recession can be attributed primarily to a steep drop in investment spending by firms.

Why did investment expenditures fall? The period between 1995 and 2000 had been one of high rates of investment and rapid growth in the U.S. economy, fueled in large part by optimism about new technologies such as the Internet, fiber optics, and genetic engineering. However, by mid-2000 it was becoming apparent that some of the new technologies would not be as profitable as had been hoped. The prices of shares in high-tech companies fell sharply during the year and corporations cut back their investments in computers, software, telecommunications equipment, and the like. Although at first the decline was concentrated in the high-tech sector, the slowdown spread to other parts of the economy. Total employment peaked and began to decline in March 2001.

An additional shock occurred on September 11, 2001, when terrorist attacks destroyed the World Trade Center in New York City and inflicted heavy damage on the Pentagon in Washington, D.C. People became afraid to travel, and the demand for air travel, hotel rooms, and tourist services plummeted, worsening the downturn. However, consumers regained confidence surprisingly quickly—for example, spurred by generous rebates, they purchased a record number of automobiles during October. Increased government spending on security and defense also raised planned aggregate expenditure by the end of the year, and the recession ended in November. The economy rebounded in 2002, although employment did not surpass its prerecession peak until 2004.

THE MULTIPLIER

In Example 13.4, earlier in the chapter, we analyzed a case in which the initial decline in consumer spending (as measured by the fall in $\overline{C}$) was only 10 units, and yet short-run equilibrium output fell by 50 units. Why did a relatively modest initial decline in consumer spending lead to a much larger fall in output?

The reason the impact on output was greater than the initial change in spending is the "vicious circle" effect suggested by Grandma's reminiscences about the Great Depression. Specifically, a fall in consumer spending not only reduces the sales of consumer goods directly; it also reduces the incomes of workers and owners in the industries that produce consumer goods. As their incomes fall, these workers and capital owners reduce their spending, which reduces the output and incomes of *other* producers in the economy. And these reductions in income lead to still further cuts in spending. Ultimately, these successive rounds of declines in spending and income may lead to a decrease in planned aggregate expenditure and output that is significantly greater than the change in spending that started the process.

income-expenditure multiplier
the effect of a one-unit increase in autonomous expenditure on short-run equilibrium output; for example, a multiplier of 5 means that a 10-unit decrease in autonomous expenditure reduces short-run equilibrium output by 50 units

The effect on short-run equilibrium output of a one-unit increase in autonomous expenditure is called the **income-expenditure multiplier,** or the *multiplier* for short. In the economy of Example 13.4, the multiplier is 5. That is, each 1-unit change in autonomous expenditure leads to a 5-unit change in short-run equilibrium output in the same direction (or, as we saw in Example 13.4, a 10-unit change in autonomous expenditure leads to a 50-unit change in short-run equilibrium output). The idea that a change in spending may lead to a significantly larger change in short-run equilibrium output is a key feature of the basic Keynesian model.

What determines how large the multiplier will be? An important factor is the marginal propensity to consume out of disposable income *mpc*. If the *mpc* is large, then falls in income will cause people to reduce their spending sharply, and the multiplier effect will then also be large. If the marginal propensity to consume is small, then people will not reduce spending so much when income falls, and the multiplier also will be small. Appendix B to this chapter provides more details on the multiplier in the basic Keynesian model, including a formula that allows us to calculate the value of the multiplier under specific assumptions about the economy.

RECAP	FINDING SHORT-RUN EQUILIBRIUM OUTPUT

- Short-run equilibrium output is the level of output at which output equals planned aggregate expenditure, or, in symbols, $Y = PAE$. For a specific sample economy, short-run equilibrium output can be solved for numerically, as in Table 13.1, or graphically.

- The graphical solution is based on a diagram called the Keynesian cross. The Keynesian cross diagram includes two lines: a 45° line that represents the condition $Y = PAE$ and the expenditure line, which shows the relationship of planned aggregate expenditure to output. Short-run equilibrium output is determined at the intersection of the two lines. If short-run equilibrium output differs from potential output, an output gap exists.

■ Increases in autonomous expenditure shift the expenditure line upward, increasing short-run equilibrium output; decreases in autonomous expenditure shift the expenditure line downward, leading to declines in short-run equilibrium output. Decreases in autonomous expenditure that drive actual output below potential output are a source of recessions.

■ Generally, a one-unit change in autonomous expenditure leads to a larger change in short-run equilibrium output, reflecting the working of the income-expenditure multiplier. The multiplier arises because a given initial increase in spending raises the incomes of producers, which leads them to spend more, raising the incomes and spending of other producers, and so on.

STABILIZING PLANNED SPENDING: THE ROLE OF FISCAL POLICY

According to the basic Keynesian model, inadequate spending is an important cause of recessions. To fight recessions—at least, those caused by insufficient demand rather than slow growth of potential output—policymakers must find ways to stimulate planned spending. Policies that are used to affect planned aggregate expenditure, with the objective of eliminating output gaps, are called **stabilization policies**. Policy actions intended to increase planned spending and output are called **expansionary policies**; expansionary policy actions are normally taken when the economy is in recession. It is also possible, as we have seen, for the economy to be "overheated," with output greater than potential output (an expansionary gap). The risk of an expansionary gap, as we will see in more detail later, is that it may lead to an increase in inflation. To offset an expansionary gap, policymakers will try to reduce spending and output. **Contractionary policies** are policy actions intended to reduced planned spending and output.

The two major tools of stabilization policy are *monetary policy* and *fiscal policy*. Recall that monetary policy refers to decisions about the size of the money supply, whereas fiscal policy refers to decisions about the government's budget—how much the government spends and how much tax revenue it collects. In the remainder of this chapter, we will focus on how fiscal policy can be used to influence spending in the basic Keynesian model. Monetary policy will be discussed in the next two chapters. In the final chapter of Part 4, we discuss both monetary and fiscal policy in greater detail and highlight some practical issues that arise in formulating macroeconomic policy.

GOVERNMENT PURCHASES AND PLANNED SPENDING

Decisions about government spending represent one of the two main components of fiscal policy, the other being decisions about taxes and transfer payments. As was mentioned earlier (see Box 13.1), Keynes himself felt that changes in government purchases were probably the most effective tool for reducing or eliminating output gaps. His basic argument was straightforward: Government purchases of goods and services, being a component of planned aggregate expenditure, directly affect total spending. If output gaps are caused by too much or too little total spending, then the government can help to guide the economy toward full employment by changing its own level of spending. Keynes's views seemed to be vindicated by the events of the 1930s, notably the fact that the Depression did not finally end until governments greatly increased their military spending in the latter part of the decade.

Example 13.5 shows how increased government purchases of goods and services can help to eliminate a recessionary gap. (The effects of government spending on transfer programs, such as unemployment benefits, are a bit different. We will return to that case shortly.)

stabilization policies
government policies that are used to affect planned aggregate expenditure, with the objective of eliminating output gaps

expansionary policies
government policy actions intended to increase planned spending and output

contractionary policies
government policy actions designed to reduce planned spending and output

EXAMPLE 13.5 **An increase in the government's purchases eliminates a recessionary gap**

In Example 13.4, we found that a drop of 10 units in consumer spending creates a recessionary gap of 50 units. How can the government eliminate the output gap and restore full employment by changing its purchases of goods and services G?

In Example 13.4, we found that planned aggregate expenditure was given by the equation $PAE = 960 + 0.8Y$, so that autonomous expenditure equaled 960. The 10-unit drop in $\overline{C}$ implied a 10-unit drop in autonomous expenditure, to 950. Because the multiplier in that sample economy equaled 5, this 10-unit decline in autonomous expenditure resulted in turn in a 50-unit decline in short-run equilibrium output.

To offset the effects of the consumption decline, the government would have to restore autonomous expenditure to its original value, 960. Under our assumption that government purchases are simply given and do not depend on output, government purchases are part of autonomous expenditure, and changes in government purchases change autonomous expenditure one-for-one. Thus, to increase autonomous expenditure from 950 to 960, the government should simply increase its purchases by 10 units (for example, by increasing spending on military defense or road construction). According to the basic Keynesian model, this increase in government purchases should return autonomous expenditure and, hence, output to their original levels.

The effect of the increase in government purchases is shown graphically in Figure 13.5. After the 10-unit decline in the autonomous component of consumption spending $\overline{C}$, the economy is at point F, with a 50-unit recessionary gap. A 10-unit increase in government purchases raises autonomous expenditure by 10 units, raising the intercept of the expenditure line by 10 units and causing the expenditure line to shift upward in parallel fashion. The economy returns to point E, where short-run equilibrium output equals potential output ($Y = Y^* = 4,800$) and the output gap has been eliminated.

FIGURE 13.5

An Increase in Government Purchases Eliminates a Recessionary Gap.

After a 10-unit decline in the autonomous part of consumer spending $\overline{C}$, the economy is at point F, with a recessionary gap of 50 (see Figure 13.4). A 10-unit increase in government purchases raises autonomous expenditure by 10 units, shifting the expenditure line back to its original position and raising the equilibrium point from F to E. At point E, where output equals potential output ($Y = Y^* = 4,800$), the output gap has been eliminated.

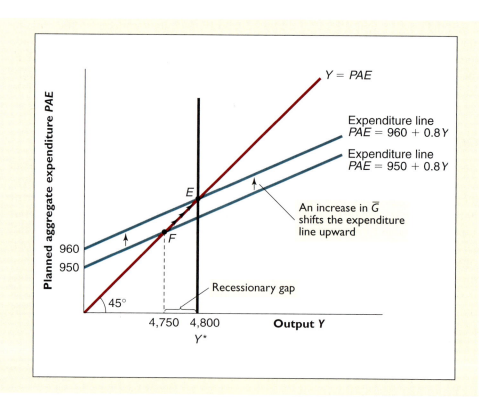

EXERCISE 13.5

In Exercise 13.4, you considered the case in which consumers become more rather than less confident, leading to an expansionary output gap. Discuss how a change in government purchases could be used to eliminate this output gap. Show your analysis graphically.

To this point we have been considering the effect of fiscal policy on a hypothetical economy. Economic Naturalists 13.5 and 13.6 illustrate the application of fiscal policy in real economies.

Why is Japan building roads nobody wants to use?

A few years ago Japanese officials decided to build a 160-mile-long toll road on the northern island of Hokkaido. Thus far, the costs of the road have been about $60 million per mile. Very few drivers use the road, largely because an existing highway that runs parallel to the new toll road is free. Officials tried to attract drivers by offering prizes and running promotional contests. Though the campaign succeeded in increasing the average number of cars on the road to 862 per day, the route is still the least-used highway in Japan.[7] Why is Japan building roads nobody wants to use?

ECONOMIC NATURALIST 13.5

As noted in Economic Naturalist 13.3, Japan spent the 1990s in a deep slump. In response, the Japanese government periodically initiated large spending programs to try to stimulate the economy. Indeed, during the 1990s, the Japanese government spent more than $1 trillion on public works projects. More than $10 billion was spent on the Tokyo subway system alone, an amount so far over budget that subway tokens will have to cost an estimated $9.50 each if the investment is ever to be recouped. (Even more frustrating to passengers, the subway does not run in a complete circle, requiring them to make inconvenient transfers to traverse the city.) Other examples of government spending programs include the construction of multimillion-dollar concert halls in small towns, elaborate tunnels where simple roads would have been adequate, and the digging up and relaying of cobblestone sidewalks. Despite all this spending, the Japanese slump has dragged on.

The basic Keynesian model implies that increases in government spending such as those undertaken in Japan should help to increase output and employment. Japanese public works projects do appear to have stimulated the economy, though not enough to pull Japan out of recession. Why has Japan's fiscal policy proved inadequate to the task? Some critics have argued that the Japanese government was unconscionably slow in initiating the fiscal expansion, and that when spending was finally increased, it was simply not enough, relative to the size of the Japanese economy and the depth of the recession. Another possibility, which lies outside the basic Keynesian model, is that the wasteful nature of much of the government spending demoralized Japanese consumers, who realized that as taxpayers they would at some point be responsible for the costs incurred in building roads nobody wants to use. Reduced consumer confidence implies reduced consumption spending, which, to some extent, may have offset the stimulus from government spending. Very possibly, more productive investments of Japanese public funds would have had a greater impact on aggregate expenditure (by avoiding the fall in consumer confidence); certainly, they would have had a greater long-term benefit in terms of increasing the potential output of the economy.

Does military spending stimulate the economy?

An antiwar poster from the 1960s bore the message "War is good business. Invest your son." War itself poses too many economic and human costs to be good business, but military spending could be a different matter. According to the basic Keynesian

ECONOMIC NATURALIST 13.6

[7]*New York Times*, November 25, 1999, p. A1.

FIGURE 13.6

U.S. Military Expenditures as a Share of GDP, 1940–2004.

Military expenditures as a share of GDP rose during World War II, the Korean War, the Vietnam War, and the Reagan military buildup of the early 1980s. Increased military spending is generally associated with an expanding economy and declining unemployment. The shaded areas indicate periods of recession.

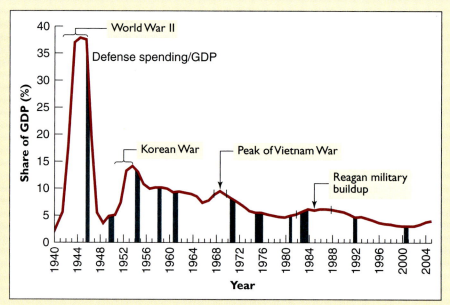

SOURCE: *Economic Report of the President* (http://www.gpoaccess.gov/eop/).

model, increases in planned aggregate expenditure resulting from stepped-up government purchases may help bring an economy out of a recession or depression. Does military spending stimulate aggregate demand? Figure 13.6 shows U.S. military spending as a share of GDP from 1940 to 2004. The shaded areas in the figure correspond to periods of recession as shown in Table 12.1. Note the spike that occurred during World War II (1941–1945), when military spending reached nearly 38 percent of U.S. GDP, as well as the surge during the Korean War (1950–1953). Smaller increases in military spending relative to GDP occurred at the peak of the Vietnam War in 1967–1969, during the Reagan military buildup of the 1980s, and during the wars in Afghanistan and Iraq.

Figure 13.6 provides some support for the idea that expanded military spending tends to promote growth in aggregate demand. The clearest case is the World War II era, during which massive military spending helped the U.S. economy to recover from the Great Depression. The U.S. unemployment rate fell from 17.2 percent of the workforce in 1939 (when defense spending was less than 2 percent of GDP) to 1.2 percent in 1944 (when defense spending was greater than 37 percent of GDP). Two brief recessions, in 1945 and 1948–1949, followed the end of the war and the sharp decline in military spending. At the time, though, many people feared that the war's end would bring a resumption of the Great Depression, so the relative mildness of the two postwar recessions was something of a relief.

Increases in defense spending during the post–World War II period also were associated with economic expansions. The Korean War of 1950–1953 occurred simultaneously with a strong expansion, during which the unemployment rate dropped from 5.9 percent in 1949 to 2.9 percent in 1953. A recession began in 1954, the year after the armistice was signed, though military spending had not yet declined much. Economic expansions also occurred during the Vietnam-era military buildup in the 1960s and the Reagan buildup of the 1980s. Finally, on a smaller scale, increased government spending for homeland security and the wars in Afghanistan and Iraq probably contributed to the relative mildness of the U.S. recession in 2001 and the strength of the subsequent recovery. These episodes support the idea that increases in government purchases—in this case, of weapons, other military supplies, and the services of military personnel—can help to stimulate the economy.

"Your majesty, my voyage will not only forge a new route to the spices of the East but also create over three thousand new jobs."

TAXES, TRANSFERS, AND AGGREGATE SPENDING

Besides making decisions about government purchases of goods and services, fiscal policymakers also determine the level and types of taxes to be collected and transfer payments to be made. (Transfer payments, recall, are payments made by the government to the public, for which no current goods or services are received. Examples of transfer payments are unemployment insurance benefits, Social Security benefits, and income support payments to farmers. Once again, transfer payments are *not* included in government purchases of goods and services.) The basic Keynesian model implies that, like changes in government purchases, changes in the level of taxes or transfers can be used to affect planned aggregate expenditure and thus eliminate output gaps.

Unlike changes in government purchases, however, changes in taxes or transfers do not affect planned spending directly. Instead they work indirectly, by changing disposable income in the private sector. Recall that disposable income is equal to $Y - T$, where T represents *net taxes*. Net taxes, in turn, are equal to taxes minus transfers. Consequently, net taxes will fall by one unit if *either* taxes are cut by one *or* transfers are increased by one. According to the consumption function, when disposable income rises, households should spend more. Thus, a tax cut or increase in transfers should increase planned aggregate expenditure. Likewise, an increase in taxes or a cut in transfers, by lowering households' disposable income, will tend to lower planned spending. Example 13.6 illustrates the effects of a tax cut on spending and output.

Using a tax cut to close a recessionary gap

EXAMPLE 13.6

In Example 13.4, we found that in our hypothetical economy, an initial drop in consumer spending of 10 units creates a recessionary gap of 50 units. Example 13.5 showed that this recessionary gap could be eliminated by a 10-unit increase in government purchases. Suppose that, instead of increasing government purchases, fiscal policymakers decided to stimulate consumer spending by changing the level of tax collections. By how much should they change taxes to eliminate the output gap?

A common first guess at the answer to this problem is that policymakers should cut taxes by 10, but that guess is not correct. Let's see why.

The source of the recessionary gap in Example 13.4 is the reduction that households made in their consumption spending by 10 units at each level of output Y—that is, the constant term $\overline{C}$ in the consumption function is assumed to have fallen 10 units. To eliminate this recessionary gap, the change in taxes must induce households to increase their consumption spending by 10 units at each output level.

However, if taxes T are cut by 10 units, raising disposable income $Y - T$ by 10 units, consumption at each level of output Y will increase by only 8 units.

Why? The reason is that the marginal propensity to consume out of disposable income in our example is 0.8, so that consumption spending increases by only 0.8 times the amount of the tax cut. (The rest of the tax cut is saved.) An increase in autonomous expenditure of eight units is not enough to return output to its full-employment level, in this example.

To raise consumption spending by 10 units at each level of output, fiscal policy-makers must instead cut taxes by 12.5 units. This will raise the level of disposable income, $Y - T$, by 12.5 units at each level of output Y. Consequently, consumption will increase by the marginal propensity to consume times the increase in disposable income, or by $0.8(12.5) = 10$. Thus, a tax cut of 12.5 will spur households to increase their consumption by 10 units at each level of output.

These changes are illustrated in Table 13.3 using the model of the economy in Example 13.2 and the drop in consumer spending from Example 13.4. Following the initial 10-unit drop in consumer spending, the equilibrium level of output fell to 4,750. When net taxes are equal to their initial level of 250, column 3 illustrates that disposable income equals $4{,}750 - 250 = 4{,}500$. After the drop in consumer spending, the consumption function becomes $C = 610 + 0.8(Y - T)$. Thus, when $Y = 4{,}750$ and $T = 250$, consumption will equal $610 + 0.8(4{,}750 - 250) = 610 + 0.8(4{,}500) = 4{,}210$, as shown in column 4. If taxes are cut by 12.5 to 237.5, disposable income at that level of output will rise by 12.5 to $4{,}750 - 237.5 = 4{,}512.5$. Consumption at that level of output will rise by $0.8(12.5) = 10$ so that $C = 610 + 0.8(4{,}750 - 237.5) = 4{,}220$. This increase will just offset the initial 10-unit decrease in $\overline{C}$ and will bring the economy back to full employment.

TABLE 13.3
Initial Effect of a Reduction in Taxes of 12.5

(1) Output Y	(2) Net taxes T	(3) Disposable income $Y - T$	(4) Consumption $610 + 0.8(Y - T)$
4,750	250	4,500	4,210
4,750	237.5	4,512.5	4,220

Note that since T refers to *net taxes*, or taxes less transfers, the same result could be obtained by increasing transfer payments by 12.5 units. Because households spend 0.8 times any increase in transfer payments they receive, this policy also would raise consumption spending by 10 units at any level of output.

Graphically, the effect of the tax cut is identical to the effect of the increase in government purchases, shown in Figure 13.5. Because it leads to a 10-unit increase in consumption at any level of output, the tax cut shifts the expenditure line up by 10 units. Equilibrium is attained at point E in Figure 13.5, where output again equals potential output.[8]

EXERCISE 13.6

In a particular economy, a 20-unit increase in planned investment moved the economy from an initial situation with no output gap to a situation with an expansionary gap. Describe two ways in which fiscal policy could be used to offset this expansionary gap. Assume the marginal propensity to consume equals 0.5.

[8]Note that the final level of consumption will rise above 4,220. When output returns to 4,800, $C = 610 + 0.8(4{,}800 - 237.5) = 4{,}260$.

Why did the federal government send out millions of $300 and $600 checks to households in 2001?

On May 25, 2001, Congress passed the Economic Growth and Tax Relief Reconciliation Act (EGTRRA) of 2001, which President George W. Bush signed on June 7. The EGTRRA made significant cuts in income tax rates and also provided for one-time tax rebate checks of up to $300 for individual taxpayers and up to $600 for married taxpayers filing a joint return. Millions of families received these checks in August and September of 2001, with payments totaling about $38 billion. Why did the federal government send out these checks?

Although the 2001 recession was not officially "declared" until November 2001 (when the National Bureau of Economic Research announced that the recession had begun in March), there was clear evidence by the spring of 2001 that the economy was slowing. Congress and the president hoped that by sending tax rebate checks to households, they could stimulate spending and perhaps avoid recession. In retrospect, the timing of the tax rebate was quite good, since the economy and consumer confidence were further buffeted by the terrorist attacks on New York City and Washington on September 11, 2001.

Did the tax rebates have their intended effect of stimulating consumer spending? In a recent study, economists found that households spent about two-thirds of their rebates within six months of receiving them.[9] This suggests that the rebate had a substantial effect on consumer spending, which held up remarkably well during the last quarter of 2001 and into 2002.

ECONOMIC NATURALIST 13.7

RECAP	FISCAL POLICY AND PLANNED SPENDING

Fiscal policy includes two general tools for affecting total spending and eliminating output gaps: (1) changes in government purchases and (2) changes in taxes or transfer payments. An increase in government purchases increases autonomous expenditure by an equal amount. A reduction in taxes or an increase in transfer payments increases autonomous expenditure by an amount equal to the marginal propensity to consume times the reduction in taxes or increase in transfers. The ultimate effect of a fiscal policy change on short-run equilibrium output equals the change in autonomous expenditure times the multiplier. Accordingly, if the economy is in recession, an increase in government purchases, a cut in taxes, or an increase in transfers can be used to stimulate spending and eliminate the recessionary gap.

[9]David S. Johnson, Jonathan A. Parker, and Nicholas S. Souleles, *Household Expenditure and the Income Tax Rebates of 2001*, National Bureau of Economic Research Working Paper 10,784, September 2004.

FISCAL POLICY AS A STABILIZATION TOOL: THREE QUALIFICATIONS

The basic Keynesian model might lead you to think that precise use of fiscal policy can eliminate output gaps. But as is often the case, the real world is more complicated than economic models suggest. We close the chapter with three qualifications about the use of fiscal policy as a stabilization tool.

FISCAL POLICY AND THE SUPPLY SIDE

We have focused on the use of fiscal policy to affect planned aggregate expenditure. However, most economists would agree that *fiscal policy may affect potential output as well as planned aggregate expenditure.* On the spending side, for example, investments in public capital, such as roads, airports, and schools, can play a major role in the growth of potential output, as we discussed in the chapter "Economic Growth, Productivity, and Living Standards." On the other side of the ledger, tax and transfer programs may well affect the incentives, and thus the economic behavior, of households and firms. Some critics of the Keynesian theory have gone so far as to argue that the *only* effects of fiscal policy that matter are effects on potential output. This was essentially the view of the so-called *supply-siders,* a group of economists and journalists whose influence reached a high point during the first Reagan term (1981–1985). We will examine these arguments in greater detail in the chapter "Inflation, Aggregate Supply, and Aggregate Demand." Most economists now agree that fiscal policy affects *both* planned spending *and* potential output.

THE PROBLEM OF DEFICITS

A second consideration for fiscal policymakers thinking about stabilization policies is *the need to avoid large and persistent budget deficits.* Recall from the chapter "Saving and Capital Formation" that the government's budget deficit is the excess of government spending over tax collections. Sustained government deficits can be harmful because they reduce national saving, which in turn reduces investment in new capital goods—an important source of long-run economic growth. The need to keep deficits under control may make increasing spending or cutting taxes to fight a slowdown a less attractive option, both economically and politically. For example, Japan has substantially increased government spending over the past decade in its attempts to stimulate its lagging economy (see Economic Naturalist 13.5). The Japanese government's budget deficit has in the process become so large that the Japanese prime minister ruled out additional fiscal stimulus until the deficit can be brought under better control.

THE RELATIVE INFLEXIBILITY OF FISCAL POLICY

The third qualification about the use of fiscal policy is that *fiscal policy is not always flexible enough to be useful for stabilization.* Our examples have implicitly assumed that the government can change spending or taxes relatively quickly in order to eliminate output gaps. In reality, changes in government spending or taxes must usually go through a lengthy legislative process, which reduces the ability of fiscal policy to respond in a timely way to economic conditions. For example, budget and tax changes proposed by the president must typically be submitted to Congress 18 months or more before they go into effect. Another factor that limits the flexibility of fiscal policy is that fiscal policymakers have many other objectives besides stabilizing aggregate spending, from ensuring an adequate national defense to providing income support to the poor. What happens if, say, the need to strengthen the national defense requires an increase in government spending, but the need to contain planned aggregate expenditure requires a decrease in government spending? Such conflicts can be difficult to resolve through the political process.

This lack of flexibility means that fiscal policy is less useful for stabilizing spending than the basic Keynesian model suggests. Nevertheless, most economists view fiscal policy as an important stabilizing force, for two reasons. The first is the presence of **automatic stabilizers,** provisions in the law that imply *automatic* increases in government spending or decreases in taxes when real output declines. For example, some government spending is earmarked as "recession aid"; it flows to communities automatically when the unemployment rate reaches a certain level. Taxes and transfer payments also respond automatically to output gaps: When GDP declines, income tax collections fall (because households' taxable incomes fall) while unemployment insurance payments and welfare benefits rise—all without any explicit action by Congress. These automatic changes in government spending and tax collections help to increase planned spending during recessions and reduce it during expansions, without the delays inherent in the legislative process.

The second reason that fiscal policy is an important stabilizing force is that although fiscal policy may be difficult to change quickly, it may still be useful for dealing with prolonged episodes of recession. The Great Depression of the 1930s and the Japanese slump of the 1990s are two cases in point. However, because of the relative lack of flexibility of fiscal policy, in modern economies aggregate spending is more usually stabilized through monetary policy. The stabilizing role of monetary policy is the subject of the next chapter.

automatic stabilizers
provisions in the law that imply *automatic* increases in government spending or decreases in taxes when real output declines

■ SUMMARY ■

- The basic Keynesian model shows how fluctuations in planned aggregate expenditure, or total planned spending, can cause actual output to differ from potential output. Too little spending leads to a recessionary output gap; too much spending creates an expansionary output gap. This model relies on the crucial assumption that firms do not respond to every change in demand by changing prices. Instead, they typically set a price for some period, then meet the demand forthcoming at that price. Firms do not change prices continually because changing prices entails costs, called *menu costs.*

- *Planned aggregate expenditure* is total planned spending on final goods and services. The four components of total spending are consumption, investment, government purchases, and net exports. Planned and actual consumption, government purchases, and net exports are generally assumed to be the same. Actual investment may differ from planned investment, because firms may sell a greater or lesser amount of their production than they expected. If firms sell less than they expected, for example, they are forced to add more goods to inventory than anticipated. And because additions to inventory are counted as part of investment, in this case actual investment (including inventory investment) is greater than planned investment.

- Consumption is related to disposable, or after-tax, income by a relationship called the *consumption function.* The

amount by which desired consumption rises when disposable income rises by one dollar is called the *marginal propensity to consume (mpc).* The marginal propensity to consume is always greater than zero but less than one (that is, $0 < mpc < 1$).

- An increase in real output raises planned aggregate expenditure, since higher output (and, equivalently, higher income) encourages households to consume more. Planned aggregate expenditure can be broken down into two components: autonomous expenditure and induced expenditure. *Autonomous expenditure* is the portion of planned spending that is independent of output; *induced expenditure* is the portion of spending that depends on output.

- In the period in which prices are fixed, *short-run equilibrium output* is the level of output that just equals planned aggregate expenditure. Short-run equilibrium can be determined numerically by a table that compares alternative values of output and the planned spending implied by each level of output. Short-run equilibrium output also can be determined graphically in a Keynesian cross diagram, drawn with planned aggregate expenditure on the vertical axis and output on the horizontal axis. The Keynesian cross contains two lines: an expenditure line, which relates planned aggregate expenditure to output, and a 45° line, which represents the condition that short-run equilibrium output equals planned aggregate expenditure. Short-run equilibrium output is determined at the point at which these two lines intersect.

- Changes in autonomous expenditure will lead to changes in short-run equilibrium output. In particular, if the economy is initially at full employment, a fall in autonomous expenditure will create a recessionary gap and a rise in autonomous expenditure will create an expansionary gap. The amount by which a one-unit increase in autonomous expenditure raises short-run equilibrium output is called the *multiplier.* An increase in autonomous expenditure not only raises spending directly; it also raises the incomes of producers, who in turn increase their spending, and so on. Hence the multiplier is greater than one; that is, a one-dollar increase in autonomous expenditure tends to raise short-run equilibrium output by more than one dollar.

- To eliminate output gaps and restore full employment, the government employs *stabilization policies.* The two major types of stabilization policy are monetary policy and fiscal policy. Stabilization policies work by changing planned aggregate expenditure and, hence, short-run equilibrium output. For example, an increase in government purchases raises autonomous expenditure directly, so it can be used to reduce or eliminate a recessionary gap. Similarly, a cut in taxes or an increase in transfer payments increases the public's disposable income, raising consumption spending at each level of output by an amount equal to the marginal propensity to consume times the cut in taxes or increase in transfers. Higher consumer spending, in turn, raises short-run equilibrium output.

- Three qualifications must be made to the use of fiscal policy as a stabilization tool. First, fiscal policy may affect potential output as well as aggregate spending. Second, large and persistent government budget deficits reduce national saving and growth; the need to keep deficits under control may limit the use of expansionary fiscal policies. Finally, because changes in fiscal policy must go through a lengthy legislative process, fiscal policy is not always flexible enough to be useful for short-run stabilization. However, *automatic stabilizers*—provisions in the law that imply automatic increases in government spending or reductions in taxes when output declines—can overcome the problem of legislative delays to some extent and contribute to economic stability.

■ KEY TERMS ■

automatic stabilizers (371)
autonomous expenditure (354)
consumption function (350)
contractionary policies (363)
expansionary policies (363)

income-expenditure multiplier (362)
induced expenditure (354)
marginal propensity to consume (*mpc*) (351)
menu costs (346)

planned aggregate expenditure (*PAE*) (347)
short-run equilibrium output (354)
stabilization policies (363)
wealth effect (350)

■ REVIEW QUESTIONS ■

1. What is the key assumption of the basic Keynesian model? Explain why this assumption is needed if one is to accept the view that aggregate spending is a driving force behind short-term economic fluctuations.

2. Give an example of a good or service whose price changes very frequently and one whose price changes relatively infrequently. What accounts for the difference?

3. Define *planned aggregate expenditure* and list its components. Why does planned spending change when output changes?

4. Explain how planned spending and actual spending can differ. Illustrate with an example.

5. Sketch a graph of the consumption function, labeling the axes of the graph. Discuss the economic meaning of (a) a movement from left to right along the graph of the consumption function and (b) a parallel upward shift of the consumption function. Give an example of a factor that could lead to a parallel upward shift of the consumption function.

6. Sketch the Keynesian cross diagram. Explain in words the economic significance of the two lines graphed in the diagram. Given only this diagram, how could you determine autonomous expenditure, induced expenditure, the marginal propensity to consume, and short-run equilibrium output?

7. Using the Keynesian cross diagram, illustrate the main cause of the 2001 recession discussed in Economic Naturalist 13.4.

8. Define the *multiplier.* In economic terms, why is the multiplier greater than one?

9. The government is considering two alternative policies, one involving increased government purchases of 50 units, the other involving a tax cut of 50 units. Which policy will stimulate planned aggregate expenditure by more? Why?

10. Discuss three reasons why the use of fiscal policy to stabilize the economy is more complicated than suggested by the basic Keynesian model.

▪ PROBLEMS ▪

1. Acme Manufacturing is producing $4,000,000 worth of goods this year and expects to sell its entire production. It also is planning to purchase $1,500,000 in new equipment during the year. At the beginning of the year, the company has $500,000 in inventory in its warehouse. Find actual investment and planned investment if
   a. Acme actually sells $3,850,000 worth of goods.
   b. Acme actually sells $4,000,000 worth of goods.
   c. Acme actually sells $4,200,00 worth of goods.

   Assuming that Acme's situation is similar to that of other firms, in which of these three cases is output equal to short-run equilibrium output?

2. Data on before-tax income, taxes paid, and consumption spending for the Simpson family in various years are given below.

Before-tax income ($)	Taxes paid ($)	Consumption spending ($)
25,000	3,000	20,000
27,000	3,500	21,350
28,000	3,700	22,070
30,000	4,000	23,600

   a. Graph the Simpsons' consumption function and find their household's marginal propensity to consume.
   b. How much would you expect the Simpsons to consume if their income was $32,000 and they paid taxes of $5,000?
   c. Homer Simpson wins a lottery prize. As a result, the Simpson family increases its consumption by $1,000 at each level of after-tax income. ("Income" does not include the prize money.) How does this change affect the graph of their consumption function? How does it affect their marginal propensity to consume?

3. An economy is described by the following equations:

$$C = 1,800 + 0.6(Y - T)$$
$$I^p = 900$$
$$G = 1,500$$
$$NX = 100$$
$$T = 1,500$$
$$Y^* = 9,000$$

   a. Find a numerical equation linking planned aggregate expenditure to output.
   b. Find autonomous expenditure and induced expenditure in this economy.

4. For the economy described in problem 3:
   a. Construct a table like Table 13.1 to find short-run equilibrium output. Consider possible values for short-run equilibrium output ranging from 8,200 to 9,000.
   b. Show the determination of short-run equilibrium output for this economy using the Keynesian cross diagram.
   c. What is the output gap for this economy? If the natural rate of unemployment is 4 percent, what is the actual unemployment rate for this economy (use Okun's law)?

5. For the economy described in problem 3, find the effect on short-run equilibrium output of
   a. An increase in government purchases from 1,500 to 1,600.
   b. A decrease in tax collections from 1,500 to 1,400 (leaving government purchases at their original value).
   c. A decrease in planned investment spending from 900 to 800.

Take as given that the multiplier for this economy is 2.5. If you have studied Appendix B in this chapter, show why this is so.

6. An economy is initially at full employment, but a decrease in planned investment spending (a component of autonomous expenditure) pushes the economy into recession. Assume that the *mpc* of this economy is 0.75 and that the multiplier is 4.
   a. How large is the recessionary gap after the fall in planned investment?
   b. By how much would the government have to change its purchases to restore the economy to full employment?
   c. Alternatively, by how much would the government have to change taxes?
   d.*Suppose that the government's budget is initially in balance, with government spending equal to taxes collected. A balanced-budget law forbids the government from running a deficit. Is there anything that fiscal policymakers could do to restore full employment in this economy, assuming they do not want to violate the balanced-budget law?

7. An economy is described by the following equations:

$$C = 40 + 0.8(Y - T)$$
$$I^p = 70$$
$$G = 120$$
$$NX = 10$$
$$T = 150$$
$$Y^* = 580$$

The multiplier in this economy is 5.

   a. Find a numerical equation relating planned aggregate expenditure to output.
   b. Construct a table to find the value of short-run equilibrium output. (*Hint:* The economy is fairly close to full employment.)
   c. By how much would government purchases have to change in order to eliminate any output gap? By how much would taxes have to change? Show the effects of these fiscal policy changes in a Keynesian cross diagram.
   d. Repeat part c assuming that $Y^* = 630$.

8.*For the following economy, find autonomous expenditure, the multiplier, short-run equilibrium output, and the output gap. By how much would autonomous expenditure have to change to eliminate the output gap?

$$C = 3,000 + 0.5(Y - T)$$
$$I^p = 1,500$$
$$G = 2,500$$
$$NX = 200$$
$$T = 2,000$$
$$Y^* = 12,000$$

9.*An economy has zero net exports. Otherwise, it is identical to the economy described in problem 7.
   a. Find short-run equilibrium output.
   b. Economic recovery abroad increases the demand for the country's exports; as a result, *NX* rises to 100. What happens to short-run equilibrium output?
   c. Repeat part b, but this time assume that foreign economies are slowing, reducing the demand for the country's exports, so that $NX = -100$. (A negative value of net exports means that exports are less than imports.)
   d. How do your results help to explain the tendency of recessions and expansions to spread across countries?

---

*Problems marked by an asterisk (*) are more difficult.

10.*This problem illustrates the workings of automatic stabilizers. Suppose that the components of planned spending in an economy are as described in Appendix A: $C = \overline{C} + mpc(Y - T)$, $I^p = \overline{I}$, $G = \overline{G}$, and $NX = \overline{NX}$. However, suppose that, realistically, taxes are not fixed but depend on income. Specifically, we assume

$$T = tY,$$

where t is the fraction of income paid in taxes (the tax rate). As we will see in this problem, a tax system of this sort serves as an automatic stabilizer, because taxes collected automatically fall when incomes fall.

   a. Find an algebraic expression for short-run equilibrium output in this economy.
   b. Find an algebraic expression for the multiplier, that is, the amount that output changes when autonomous expenditure changes by one unit. Compare the expression you found to the formula for the multiplier when taxes are fixed. Show that making taxes proportional to income reduces the multiplier.
   c. Explain how reducing the size of the multiplier helps to stabilize the economy, holding constant the typical size of fluctuations in the components of autonomous expenditure.
   d. Suppose $\overline{C} = 500$, $\overline{I} = 1{,}500$, $\overline{G} = 2{,}000$, $\overline{NX} = 0$, $mpc = 0.8$, and $t = 0.25$. Calculate numerical values for short-run equilibrium output and the multiplier.

■ ANSWERS TO IN-CHAPTER EXERCISES ■

13.1 First we need to find an equation that relates planned aggregate expenditure PAE to output Y. We start with the definition of planned aggregate expenditure and then substitute the numerical values given in the problem:

$$
\begin{aligned}
PAE &= C + I^p + G + NX \\
&= \left[\overline{C} + mpc(Y - T)\right] + I^p + G + NX \\
&= \left[820 + 0.7(Y - 600)\right] + 600 + 600 + 200 \\
&= 1{,}800 + 0.7Y.
\end{aligned}
$$

Using this relationship, we construct a table analogous to Table 13.1. Some trial and error is necessary to find an appropriate range of guesses for output (column 1).

Determination of Short-Run Equilibrium Output

(1) Output Y	(2) Planned aggregate expenditure PAE = 1,800 + 0.7Y	(3) Y − PAE	(4) Y = PAE?
5,000	5,300	−300	No
5,200	5,440	−240	No
5,400	5,580	−180	No
5,600	5,720	−120	No
5,800	5,860	−60	No
6,000	6,000	0	**Yes**
6,200	6,140	60	No
6,400	6,280	120	No
6,600	6,420	180	No

Short-run equilibrium output equals 6,000, as that is the only level of output that satisfies the condition $Y = PAE$.

*Problems marked by an asterisk (*) are more difficult.

13.2 The graph shows the determination of short-run equilibrium output, $Y = 6,000$. The intercept of the expenditure line is 1,800 and its slope is 0.7. Notice that the intercept equals autonomous expenditure and the slope equals the marginal propensity to consume.

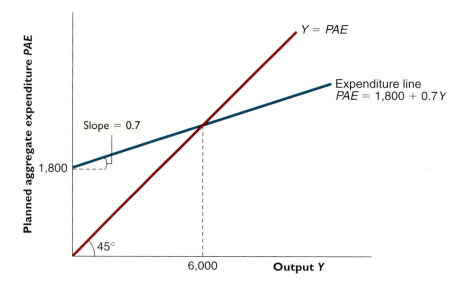

13.3 This problem is an application of Okun's law, introduced in the last chapter. The recessionary gap in this example is 50/4,800, or about 1.04 percent, of potential output. By Okun's law, cyclical unemployment is one-half the percentage size of the output gap, or 0.52 percent. As the natural rate of unemployment is 5 percent, total unemployment rate after the recessionary gap appears will be approximately 5.52 percent.

13.4 This exercise is just the reverse of Example 13.4. An increase in $\overline{C}$ of 10 units raises autonomous expenditure and hence the intercept of the expenditure line by 10 units. The expenditure line shifts up, in parallel fashion, by 10 units, leading to an increase in output and an expansionary output gap. As output falls by 50 units in Example 13.4, it rises by 50 units, to 4,850, in the case analyzed here. To verify that short-run equilibrium output equals 4,850, note that an increase of 10 units in autonomous expenditure implies that PAE rises from $960 + 0.8Y$ to $970 + 0.8Y$. When $Y = 4,850$, then $PAE = 970 + 0.8(4,850) = 4,850$, so that we have $Y = PAE$.

13.5 In Exercise 13.4 we saw that a 10-unit increase in $\overline{C}$ increases autonomous expenditure and hence the intercept of the expenditure line by 10 units. The expenditure line shifts upward, in parallel fashion, by 10 units, leading to an expansionary output gap. To offset this gap, the government should reduce its purchases by 10 units, returning autonomous expenditure to its original level. The expenditure line shifts back down to its original position, restoring output to its initial full-employment level. The graph is just the reverse of Figure 13.5, with the expenditure line being shifted up by the increase in consumption and down by the offsetting reduction in government purchases.

13.6 The 20-unit increase in planned investment is a 20-unit increase in autonomous expenditure, which will lead to an even greater increase in short-run equilibrium output. To offset the 20-unit increase in autonomous expenditure by means of fiscal policy, the government can reduce its purchases by 20 units. Alternatively, it could raise taxes (or cut transfers) to reduce consumption spending. Since the $mpc = 0.5$, to reduce consumption spending by 20 units at each level of output, the government will need to increase taxes (or reduce transfers) by 40 units. At each level of output, a 40-unit tax increase will reduce disposable income by 40 units and cause consumers to reduce their spending by $0.5 \times 40 = 20$ units, as needed to eliminate the expansionary output gap.

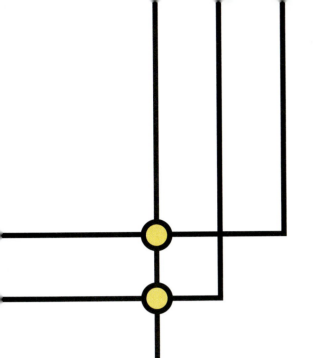

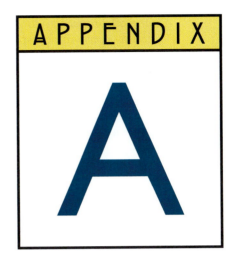

AN ALGEBRAIC SOLUTION OF THE BASIC KEYNESIAN MODEL

This chapter has shown how to solve the basic Keynesian model numerically and graphically, using the Keynesian cross diagram. In this appendix, we will show how to find a more general algebraic solution for short-run equilibrium output in the basic Keynesian model. This solution has the advantage of showing clearly the links between short-run equilibrium output, the multiplier, and autonomous expenditure. The general method also can be applied when we make changes to the basic Keynesian model, as we will see in following chapters.

The model we will work with is the same one presented in the main part of the chapter. Start with the definition of planned aggregate expenditure, Equation 13.1:

$$PAE = C + I^p + G + NX. \qquad (13.1)$$

Equation 13.1 says that planned aggregate expenditure is the sum of the four types of planned spending: consumption spending by households C; planned investment spending by firms I^p; government purchases G; and net exports purchased by foreigners NX.

The first component of planned aggregate expenditure, consumption spending, is determined by the *consumption function*, Equation 13.2:

$$C = \overline{C} + mpc(Y - T). \qquad (13.2)$$

The consumption function says that consumption spending increases when disposable (after-tax) income $Y - T$ increases. Each dollar increase in disposable income raises consumption spending by *mpc* dollars, where *mpc*, known as the *marginal propensity to consume*, is a number between 0 and 1. Other factors affecting consumption spending are captured by the term $\overline{C}$. For example, a boom in the stock market that leads consumers to spend more at each level of disposable income (a *wealth effect*) would be represented as an increase in $\overline{C}$.

As in the body of the chapter, we assume that planned investment, government purchases, net exports, and net tax collections are simply given numbers. A variable whose value is fixed and given from outside the model is called an *exogenous* variable; so, in other words, we are assuming that planned investment, government purchases, net exports, and net tax collections are exogenous variables. Using an overbar to denote the given value of an exogenous variable, we can write this assumption as

$$I^p = \overline{I} \qquad \text{Planned investment,}$$
$$G = \overline{G} \qquad \text{Government purchases,}$$
$$NX = \overline{NX} \qquad \text{Net exports,}$$
$$T = \overline{T} \qquad \text{Net taxes (taxes less transfers).}$$

So, for example, $\overline{I}$ is the given value of planned investment spending, as determined outside the model. In our examples, we will set $\overline{I}$ and the other exogenous variables equal to some particular number.

Our goal is to solve algebraically for *short-run equilibrium output*, the level of output that prevails during the period in which prices are predetermined. The first step is to relate planned aggregate expenditure *PAE* to output *Y*. Starting with the definition of planned aggregate expenditure (Equation 13.1), use the consumption function (Equation 13.2) to substitute for consumption spending *C* and replace I^p, *G*, *NX*, and *T* with their exogenous values. With these substitutions, planned aggregate expenditure can be written as

$$PAE = \left[\overline{C} - mpc(Y - \overline{T})\right] + \overline{I} + \overline{G} + \overline{NX}.$$

Rearranging this equation to separate the terms that do and do not depend on output *Y*, we get

$$PAE = \left[\overline{C} - mpc\overline{T} + \overline{I} + \overline{G} + \overline{NX}\right] + mpcY. \qquad (13A.1)$$

Equation 13A.1 is an important equation, because it shows the relationship between planned aggregate expenditure *PAE* and output *Y*. The bracketed term on the right side of the equation represents *autonomous expenditure*, the part of planned spending that does not depend on output. The term *mpcY* represents *induced expenditure*, the part of planned spending that does depend on output. Equation 13A.1 is also the equation that describes the *expenditure line* in the Keynesian cross diagram; it shows that the intercept of the expenditure line equals autonomous expenditure and the slope of the expenditure line equals the marginal propensity to consume.

We can illustrate how Equation 13A.1 works numerically by using Example 13.2 in the text. That example assumed the following numerical values: $\overline{C} = 620$, $\overline{I} = 220$, $\overline{G} = 300$, $\overline{NX} = 20$, $\overline{T} = 250$, and *mpc* = 0.8. Plugging these values into Equation 13A.1 and simplifying, we get

$$PAE = 960 + 0.8Y,$$

which is the same answer we found in Example 13.2. Autonomous expenditure in this example equals 960, and induced expenditure equals 0.8*Y*.

The second step in solving for short-run equilibrium output begins with the definition of short-run equilibrium output (Equation 13.3):

$$Y = PAE.$$

Remember that short-run equilibrium output is the value of output at which output equals planned aggregate expenditure. Using Equation 13A.1 to substitute for *PAE* in the definition of short-run equilibrium output, we get

$$Y = [\overline{C} - mpc\overline{T} + \overline{I} + \overline{G} + \overline{NX}] + mpcY.$$

The value of Y that solves this equation is the value of short-run equilibrium output. To solve for Y, group all terms involving Y on the left side of the equation:

$$Y - mpcY = [\overline{C} - mpc\overline{T} + \overline{I} + \overline{G} + \overline{NX}]$$

or

$$Y(1 - mpc) = [\overline{C} - mpc\overline{T} + \overline{I} + \overline{G} + \overline{NX}].$$

Dividing both sides of the equation by $(1 - mpc)$ gives

$$Y = \left(\frac{1}{1 - mpc}\right)[\overline{C} - mpc\overline{T} + \overline{I} + \overline{G} + \overline{NX}]. \qquad (13A.2)$$

Equation 13A.2 gives short-run equilibrium output for our model economy in terms of the exogenous values $\overline{C}, \overline{I}, \overline{G}, \overline{NX}$, and $\overline{T}$ and the marginal propensity to consume, mpc. We can use this formula to solve for short-run equilibrium output in specific numerical examples. For example, suppose that we once again plug in the numerical values assumed in Example 13.2: $\overline{C} = 620$, $\overline{I} = 220$, $\overline{G} = 300$, $\overline{NX} = 20, \overline{T} = 250$, and $mpc = 0.8$. We get

$$Y = \left(\frac{1}{1 - 0.8}\right)[620 - 0.8(250) + 220 + 300 + 20] = \frac{1}{0.2}(960) = 5(960) = 4,800,$$

which is the same answer we found more laboriously using Table 13.1.

EXERCISE 13A.1

Use Equation 13A.2 to find short-run equilibrium output for the economy described in Exercise 13.1 in the text. What are the intercept and the slope of the expenditure line?

Equation 13A.2 shows clearly the relationship between autonomous expenditure and short-run equilibrium output. Autonomous expenditure is the first term on the right side of Equation 13A.1, equal to $\overline{C} - mpc\overline{T} + \overline{I} + \overline{G} + \overline{NX}$. The equation shows that a one-unit increase in autonomous expenditure increases short-run equilibrium output by $1/(1 - mpc)$ units. In other words, we can see from Equation 13A.2 that the *multiplier* for this model equals $1/(1 - mpc)$. Further discussion of the multiplier is given in the second appendix to the chapter.

■ ANSWERS TO IN-APPENDIX EXERCISE ■

13A.1 The equation describing short-run equilibrium output is

$$Y = \left(\frac{1}{1 - mpc}\right)(\overline{C} - mpc\overline{T} + \overline{I} + \overline{G} + \overline{NX}). \qquad (13A.2)$$

Using data from Exercise 13.1, set $\overline{C} = 820$, $mpc = 0.7$, $\overline{I} = 600$, $\overline{G} = 600$, $\overline{NX} = 200$, and $\overline{T} = 600$. Plugging these values into Equation 13A.2, we get

$$Y = \left(\frac{1}{1 - 0.7}\right)[820 - 0.7(600 + 600 + 600 + 200)] = 3.33 \times 1,800 = 6,000,$$

which is the same result obtained in Exercise 13.1.

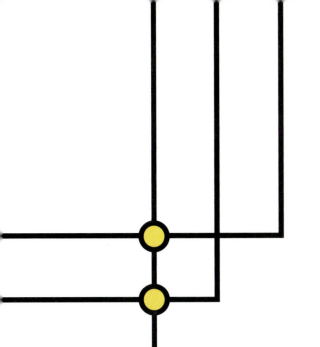

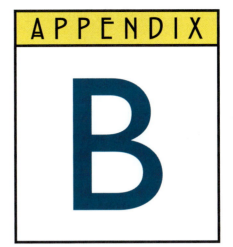
THE MULTIPLIER IN THE BASIC KEYNESIAN MODEL

This appendix builds on Example 13.4 in the text to give a more complete explanation of the *income-expenditure multiplier* in the basic Keynesian model. In Example 13.4, we saw that a drop in autonomous expenditure of 10 units caused a decline in short-run equilibrium output of 50 units, five times as great as the initial change in spending. Hence, the multiplier in this example is 5.

To see why this multiplier effect occurs, note that the initial decrease of 10 in consumer spending (more precisely, in the constant term of the consumption function, $\bar{C}$) in Example 13.4 has two effects. First, the fall in consumer spending directly reduces planned aggregate expenditure by 10 units. Second, the fall in spending also reduces by 10 units the incomes of producers (workers and firm owners) of consumer goods. Under the assumption of Example 13.4 that the marginal propensity to consume is 0.8, the producers of consumer goods will therefore reduce *their* consumption spending by 8, or 0.8 times their income loss of 10. This reduction in spending cuts the income of *other* producers by 8 units, leading them to reduce their spending by 6.4, or 0.8 times their income loss of 8. These income reductions of 6.4 lead still other producers to cut their spending by 5.12, or 0.8 times 6.4, and so on. In principle, this process continues indefinitely, although after many rounds of spending and income reductions, the effects become quite small.

When all these "rounds" of income and spending reductions are added, the *total* effect on planned spending of the initial reduction of 10 in consumer spending is

$$10 + 8 + 6.4 + 5.12 + \cdots.$$

The three dots indicate that the series of reductions continues indefinitely. The total effect of the initial decrease in consumption also can be written as

$$10[1 + 0.8 + (0.8)^2 + (0.8)^3 + \cdots].$$

This expression highlights the fact that the spending that takes place in each round is 0.8 times the spending in the previous round (0.8), because that is the marginal propensity to consume out of the income generated by the previous round of spending.

A useful algebraic relationship, which applies to any number x greater than 0 but less than 1, is

$$1 + x + x^2 + x^3 + \cdots = \frac{1}{1 - x}.$$

If we set $x = 0.8$, this formula implies that the total effect of the decline in consumption spending on aggregate demand and output is

$$10\left(\frac{1}{1 - 0.8}\right) = 10\left(\frac{1}{0.2}\right) = 10 \times 5 = 50.$$

This answer is consistent with our earlier calculation, which showed that short-run equilibrium output fell by 50 units, from 4,800 to 4,750.

By a similar analysis, we also can find a general algebraic expression for the multiplier in the basic Keynesian model. Recalling that mpc is the marginal propensity to consume out of disposable income, we know that a one-unit increase in autonomous expenditure raises spending and income by one unit in the first round; by $mpc \times 1 = mpc$ units in the second round; by $mpc \times mpc = mpc^2$ units in the second round; by $mpc \times mpc^2 = mpc^3$ units in the third round; and so on. Thus, the total effect on short-run equilibrium output of a one-unit increase in autonomous expenditure is given by

$$1 + mpc + mpc^2 + mpc^3 + \cdots.$$

Applying the algebraic formula given above, and recalling that $0 < mpc < 1$, we can rewrite this expression as $1/(1 - mpc)$. Thus, in a basic Keynesian model with a marginal propensity to consume of mpc, the multiplier equals $1/(1 - mpc)$, the same result found in Appendix A to this chapter. Note that if $mpc = 0.8$, then $1/(1 - mpc) = 1/(1 - 0.8) = 5$, which is the same value of the multiplier we found numerically above.

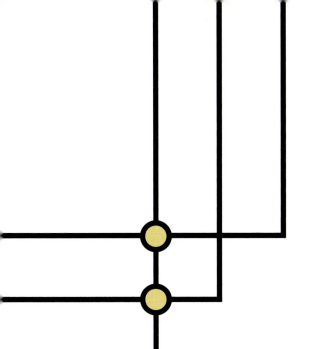

STABILIZING THE ECONOMY: THE ROLE OF THE FED

Financial market participants and commentators go to remarkable lengths to try to predict the actions of the Federal Reserve. For a while, the CNBC financial news program *Squawk Box* reported regularly on what the commentators called the Greenspan Briefcase Indicator. The idea was to spot the Fed chairman at that time, Alan Greenspan, on his way to meet with the Federal Open Market Committee, the group that determines U.S. monetary policy. If Greenspan's briefcase was packed full, presumably with macroeconomic data and analyses, the guess was that the Fed planned to change interest rates. A slim briefcase meant no change in rates was likely.

"It was right 17 out of the first 20 times," the program's anchor Mark Haines noted, "but it has a built-in self-destruct mechanism, because Greenspan packs his [own] briefcase. He can make it wrong or right. He has never publicly acknowledged the indicator, but we have reason to believe that he knows about it. We have to consider the fact that he wants us to stop doing it because the last two times the briefcase has been wrong, and that's disturbing."[1]

The Briefcase Indicator is but one example of the close public scrutiny that the chairman of the Federal Reserve and other monetary policymakers face. Every speech, every congressional testimony, every interview from a member of the Board of Governors is closely analyzed for clues about the future course of monetary policy. The reason for the intense public interest in the Federal Reserve's decisions about monetary policy—and especially the level of interest rates—is that those decisions have important implications both for financial markets and for the economy in general.

[1]Robert H. Frank, "Safety in Numbers," *New York Times Magazine*, November 28, 1999, p. 35.

In this chapter, we examine the workings of monetary policy, one of the two major types of *stabilization policy*. (The other type, fiscal policy, was discussed in the last chapter.) As we saw in that chapter, stabilization policies are government policies that are meant to influence planned aggregate expenditure, with the goal of eliminating output gaps. Both types of stabilization policy, monetary and fiscal, are important and have been useful at various times. However, monetary policy, which can be changed quickly by a decision of the Federal Reserve's Federal Open Market Committee (FOMC), is more flexible and responsive than fiscal policy, which can be changed only by legislative action by Congress. Under normal circumstances, therefore, monetary policy is used more actively in the United States than fiscal policy to help stabilize the economy.

We will begin this chapter by discussing how the Fed uses its ability to control the money supply to influence the level of interest rates. We then turn to the economic effects of changes in interest rates. Building on our analysis of the basic Keynesian model in the last chapter, we will see that, in the short run, monetary policy works by affecting planned spending and thus short-run equilibrium output. We will defer discussion of the other major effect of monetary policy actions, that is, changes in the rate of inflation, until the next chapter. In the chapter "The Practice and Pitfalls of Macroeconomic Policy," we will analyze monetary and fiscal policy in even greater detail and discuss some of the intricacies and pitfalls of macroeconomic policymaking.

THE FEDERAL RESERVE AND INTEREST RATES

When we introduced the Federal Reserve System in the chapter "Money, Prices, and the Federal Reserve," we focused on the Fed's control of the *money supply*, that is, the quantity of currency and checking accounts held by the public. Determining the nation's money supply is the primary task of monetary policymakers. But if you follow the economic news regularly, you may find the idea that the Fed's job is to control the money supply a bit foreign, because the news media nearly always focus on the Fed's decisions about *interest rates*. Indeed, the announcement the Fed makes after each meeting of the Federal Open Market Committee nearly always concerns its plan for a particular short-term interest rate, called the *federal funds rate* (more on the federal funds rate later).

Actually, there is no contradiction between the two ways of looking at monetary policy—as control of the money supply or as the setting of interest rates. As we will see in this section, the Fed changes the money supply to control the nominal interest rate. Thus, controlling the money supply and controlling the nominal interest rate are two sides of the same coin: Any value of the money supply chosen by the Fed implies a specific setting for the nominal interest rate, and vice versa. The reason for this close connection is that the nominal interest rate is effectively the "price" of holding money (or, more accurately, its opportunity cost). So, by controlling the quantity of money supplied to the economy, the Fed also controls the "price" of holding money (the nominal interest rate).

To better understand how the Fed determines interest rates, we will look first at the market for money, beginning with the demand side of that market. We will see that given the demand for money by the public, the Fed can control interest rates by changing the amount of money it supplies. Later we will show how the Fed uses control of interest rates to influence planned spending and the state of the economy.

THE DEMAND FOR MONEY

Recall from the chapter "Money, Prices, and the Federal Reserve" that *money* refers to the set of assets, such as cash and checking accounts, that are usable in transactions. Money is also a store of value, like stocks, bonds, or real estate—in other words, a type of financial asset. As a financial asset, money is a way of holding wealth.

Anyone who has some wealth must determine the *form* in which he or she wishes to hold that wealth. For example, if Louis has wealth of $10,000, he could, if he wished, hold all $10,000 in cash. Or he could hold $5,000 of his wealth in the form of cash and $5,000 in government bonds. Or he could hold $1,000 in cash, $2,000 in a checking account, $2,000 in government bonds, and $5,000 in rare stamps. Indeed, there are thousands of different real and financial assets to choose from, all of which can be held in different amounts and combinations, so Louis's choices are virtually infinite. The decision about the forms in which to hold one's wealth is called the **portfolio allocation decision.**

What determines the particular mix of assets that Louis or another wealth holder will choose? All else being equal, people generally prefer to hold assets that they expect to pay a high *return* and do not carry too much *risk*. They also may try to reduce the overall risk they face through *diversification*—that is, by owning a variety of different assets.[2] Many people own some real assets, such as a car or a home, because they provide services (transportation or shelter) and often a financial return (an increase in value, as when the price of a home rises in a strong real estate market).

Here we do not need to analyze the entire portfolio allocation decision, but only one part of it—namely, the decision about how much of one's wealth to hold in the form of *money* (cash and checking accounts). The amount of wealth an individual chooses to hold in the form of money is that individual's **demand for money,** sometimes called an individual's *liquidity preference.* So if Louis decided to hold his entire $10,000 in the form of cash, his demand for money would be $10,000. But if he were to hold $1,000 in cash, $2,000 in a checking account, $2,000 in government bonds, and $5,000 in rare stamps, his demand for money would be only $3,000—that is, $1,000 in cash plus the $2,000 in his checking account.

portfolio allocation decision *the decision about the forms in which to hold one's wealth*

demand for money *the amount of wealth an individual chooses to hold in the form of money*

Consuelo's demand for money

EXAMPLE 14.1

Example 9.1 presented the balance sheet of an individual named Consuelo (see Table 9.1). What is her demand for money? If Consuelo wanted to increase her money holdings by $100, how could she do so? What if she wanted to reduce her money holdings by $100?

Looking back at Table 9.1, p. 243, we see that Consuelo's balance sheet shows five different asset types: cash, a checking account, shares of stock, a car, and furniture. Of these assets, the first two (the cash and the checking account) are forms of money. As shown in Table 9.1, Consuelo's money holdings consist of $80 in cash and $1,200 in her checking account. Thus, Consuelo's demand for money—the amount of wealth she chooses to hold in the form of money—is $1,280.

There are many different ways in which Consuelo could increase her money holdings, or demand for money, by $100. She could sell $100 worth of stock and deposit the proceeds in the bank. That action would leave the total value of her assets and her wealth unchanged (because the decrease in her stockholdings would be offset by the increase in her checking account) but would increase her money holdings by $100. Another possibility would be to take a $100 cash advance on her credit card. That action would increase both her money holdings and her assets by $100 but would also increase her liabilities—specifically, her credit card balance—by $100. Once again, her total wealth would not change, though her money holdings would increase.

To reduce her money holdings, Consuelo need only use some of her cash or checking account balance to acquire a nonmoney asset or pay down a liability. For example, if she were to buy an additional $100 of stock by writing a check against her bank account, her money holdings would decline by $100. Similarly, writing a check to reduce her credit card balance by $100 would reduce her money holdings by $100. You can confirm that though her money holdings decline, in neither case does Consuelo's total wealth change.

[2]The chapter "Financial Markets and International Capital Flows" discusses risk, return, and diversification in more detail.

How much money should an individual (or household) choose to hold? Application of the *cost-benefit principle* tells us that an individual should increase his or her money holdings only so long as the extra benefit of doing so exceeds the extra cost. As we saw in the chapter "Money, Prices, and the Federal Reserve," the principal *benefit* of holding money is its usefulness in carrying out transactions. Consuelo's shares of stock, her car, and her furniture are all valuable assets, but she cannot use them to buy groceries or pay her rent. She can make routine payments using cash or her checking account, however. Because of its usefulness in daily transactions, Consuelo will almost certainly want to hold some of her wealth in the form of money. Furthermore, if Consuelo is a high-income individual, she will probably choose to hold more money than someone with a lower income would, because she is likely to spend more and carry out more transactions than the low-income person.

Consuelo's benefit from holding money is also affected by the technological and financial sophistication of the society she lives in. For example, in the United States, developments such as credit cards, debit cards, and ATM machines have generally reduced the amount of money people need to carry out routine transactions, decreasing the public's demand for money at given levels of income. In the United States in 1960, for example, money holdings in the form of cash and checking account balances (the monetary aggregate M1) were about 28 percent of GDP. By 2004 that ratio had fallen to about 12 percent of GDP.

Although money is an extremely useful asset, there is also a cost to holding money—more precisely, an opportunity cost—that arises from the fact that most forms of money pay little or no interest. Cash pays zero interest, and most checking accounts pay either no interest or very low rates. For the sake of simplicity, we will just assume that *the nominal interest rate on money is zero*. In contrast, most alternative assets, such as bonds or stocks, pay a positive nominal return. A bond, for example, pays a fixed amount of interest each period to the holder, while stocks pay dividends and also may increase in value (capital gains).

The cost of holding money arises because, in order to hold an extra dollar of wealth in the form of money, a person must reduce by one dollar the amount of wealth held in the form of higher-yielding assets, such as bonds or stocks. The *opportunity cost* of holding money is measured by the interest rate that could have been earned if the person had chosen to hold interest-bearing assets instead of money. All else being equal, the higher the nominal interest rate, the higher the opportunity cost of holding money, and hence the less money people will choose to hold.

We have been talking about the demand for money by individuals, but businesses also hold money to carry out transactions with customers and to pay workers and suppliers. The same general factors that determine individuals' money demand also affect the demand for money by businesses. That is, in choosing how much money to hold, a business, like an individual, will compare the benefits of holding money for use in transactions with the opportunity cost of holding a non-interest-bearing asset. Although we will not differentiate between the money held by individuals and the money held by businesses in discussing money demand, you should be aware that in the U.S. economy, businesses hold a significant portion—more than half—of the total money stock. Example 14.2 illustrates the determination of money demand by a businessowner.

Innovations such as ATM machines have reduced the amount of money that people need to hold for routine transactions.

© Royalty-Free/CORBIS/MGH-DIL

EXAMPLE 14.2   How much money should Kim's restaurants hold?

Kim owns several successful restaurants. Her accountant informs her that on the typical day, her restaurants are holding a total of $50,000 in cash on the premises. The accountant points out that if Kim's restaurants reduced their cash holdings, Kim could use the extra cash to purchase interest-bearing government bonds.

The accountant proposes two methods of reducing the amount of cash Kim's restaurants hold. First, she could increase the frequency of cash pickups by her armored car service. The extra service would cost $500 annually but would allow

Kim's restaurants to reduce their average cash holding to $40,000. Second, in addition to the extra pickups, Kim could employ a computerized cash management service to help her keep closer tabs on the inflows and outflows of cash at her restaurants. The service costs $700 a year, but the accountant estimates that, together with more frequent pickups, the more efficient cash management provided by the service could help Kim reduce average cash holdings at her restaurants to $30,000.

The interest rate on government bonds is 6 percent. How much money should Kim's restaurants hold? What if the interest rate on government bonds is 8 percent?

Kim's restaurants need to hold cash to carry out their normal business, but holding cash also has an opportunity cost, which is the interest those funds could be earning if they were held in the form of government bonds instead of zero-interest cash. As the interest rate on government bonds is 6 percent, each $10,000 by which Kim can reduce her restaurants' money holdings yields an annual benefit of $600 (6 percent of $10,000).

If Kim increases the frequency of pickups by her armored car service, reducing the restaurants' average money holdings from $50,000 to $40,000, the benefit will be the additional $600 in interest income that Kim will earn. The cost is the $500 charged by the armored car company. Since the benefit exceeds the cost, Kim should purchase the extra service and reduce the average cash holdings at her restaurants to $40,000.

Should Kim go a step further and employ the cash management service as well? Doing so would reduce average cash holdings at the restaurants from $40,000 to $30,000, which has a benefit in terms of extra interest income of $600 per year. However, this benefit is less than the cost of the cash management service, which is $700 per year. So Kim should *not* employ the cash management service and instead should maintain average cash holdings in her restaurants of $40,000.

If the interest rate on government bonds rises to 8 percent, then the benefit of each $10,000 reduction in average money holdings is $800 per year (8 percent of $10,000) in extra interest income. In this case, the benefit of employing the cash management service, $800, exceeds the cost of doing so, which is $700. So Kim should employ the service, reducing the average cash holdings of her business to $30,000. The example shows that a higher nominal interest rate on alternative assets reduces the quantity of money demanded.

EXERCISE 14.1

The interest rate on government bonds falls from 6 percent to 4 percent. How much cash should Kim's restaurants hold now?

MACROECONOMIC FACTORS THAT AFFECT THE DEMAND FOR MONEY

In any household or business, the demand for money will depend on a variety of individual circumstances. For example, a high-volume retail business that serves thousands of customers each day will probably choose to have more money on hand than a legal firm that bills clients and pays employees monthly. But while individuals and businesses vary considerably in the amount of money they choose to hold, three macroeconomic factors affect the demand for money quite broadly: the nominal interest rate, real output, and the price level. As we see next, the nominal interest rate affects the cost of holding money throughout the economy, while real output and the price level affect the benefits of money.

- *The nominal interest rate (i).* We have seen that the interest rate paid on alternatives to money, such as government bonds, determines the opportunity cost of holding money. The higher the prevailing nominal interest rate, the greater the opportunity cost of holding money, and hence the less money individuals and businesses will demand.

What do we mean by *the* nominal interest rate? As we have discussed, there are thousands of different assets, each with its own interest rate (rate of return). So can we really talk about *the* nominal interest rate? The answer is that, while there are many different assets, each with its own corresponding interest rate, the rates on those assets tend to rise and fall together. This is to be expected, because if the interest rates on some assets were to rise sharply while the rates on other assets declined, financial investors would flock to the assets paying high rates and refuse to buy the assets paying low rates. So, although there are many different interest rates in practice, speaking of the general level of interest rates usually does make sense. In this book, when we talk about *the* nominal interest rate, what we have in mind is some average measure of interest rates. This simplification is one more application of the macroeconomic concept of *aggregation,* introduced in the chapter "Macroeconomics."

The nominal interest rate is a macroeconomic factor that affects the cost of holding money. A macroeconomic factor that affects the *benefit* of holding money is

- *Real income or output (Y).* An increase in aggregate real income or output—as measured, for example, by real GDP—raises the quantity of goods and services that people and businesses want to buy and sell. When the economy enters a boom, for example, people do more shopping and stores have more customers. To accommodate the increase in transactions, both individuals and businesses need to hold more money. Thus higher real output raises the demand for money.

A second macroeconomic factor affecting the benefit of holding money is

- *The price level (P).* The higher the prices of goods and services, the more dollars (or yen, or euros) are needed to make a given set of transactions. Thus, a higher price level is associated with a higher demand for money.

Today, when a couple of teenagers go out for a movie and snacks on Saturday night, they need probably five times as much cash as their parents did 25 years ago. Because the prices of movie tickets and popcorn have risen steeply over 25 years, more money (that is, more dollars) is needed to pay for a Saturday night date than in the past. By the way, the fact that prices are higher today does *not* imply that people are worse off today than in the past, because nominal wages and salaries also have risen substantially. In general, however, higher prices do imply that people need to keep a greater number of dollars available, in cash or in a checking account.

THE MONEY DEMAND CURVE

For the purposes of monetary policymaking, economists are most interested in the aggregate, or economywide, demand for money. The interaction of the aggregate demand for money, determined by the public, and the supply of money, which is set by the Fed, determines the nominal interest rate that prevails in the economy.

money demand curve Shows the relationship between the aggregate quantity of money demanded M and the nominal interest rate i; because an increase in the nominal interest rate increases the opportunity cost of holding money, which reduces the quantity of money demanded, the money demand curve slopes down

The economywide demand for money can be represented graphically by the *money demand curve* (see Figure 14.1). The **money demand curve** relates the aggregate quantity of money demanded M to the nominal interest rate i. The quantity of money demanded M is a nominal quantity, measured in dollars (or yen, or euros, depending on the country). Because an increase in the nominal interest rate increases the opportunity cost of holding money, which reduces the quantity of money demanded, the money demand curve slopes down.

If we think of the nominal interest rate as the "price" (more precisely, the opportunity cost) of money and the amount of money people want to hold as the "quantity," the money demand curve is analogous to the demand curve for a good or service. As with a standard demand curve, the fact that a higher price of money leads people to demand less of it is captured in the downward slope of the demand

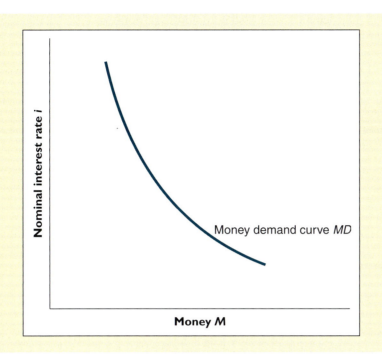

FIGURE 14.1

The Money Demand Curve.

The money demand curve relates the economywide demand for money to the nominal interest rate. Because an increase in the nominal interest rate raises the opportunity cost of holding money, the money demand curve slopes down.

curve. Furthermore, as in a standard demand curve, changes in factors other than the price of money (the nominal interest rate) can cause the demand curve for money to shift. For a given nominal interest rate, any change that makes people want to hold more money will shift the money demand curve to the right, and any change that makes people want to hold less money will shift the money demand curve to the left. We have already identified two macroeconomic factors other than the nominal interest rate that affect the economywide demand for money: real output and the price level. Because an increase in either of these variables increases the demand for money, it shifts the money demand curve rightward, as shown in Figure 14.2. Similarly, a fall in real output or the general price level reduces money demand, shifting the money demand curve leftward.

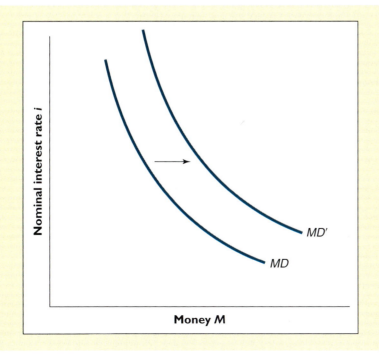

FIGURE 14.2

A Shift in the Money Demand Curve.

At a given nominal interest rate, any change that makes people want to hold more money—such as an increase in the general price level or in real GDP—will shift the money demand curve to the right.

The money demand curve also may shift in response to other changes that affect the cost or benefit of holding money, such as the technological and financial advances we mentioned earlier. For example, the introduction of ATM machines reduced the amount of money people choose to hold and thus shifted the economywide money demand curve to the left. Economic Naturalist 14.1 describes another potential source of shifts in the demand for money, holdings of U.S. dollars by foreigners.

ECONOMIC
NATURALIST
14.1

Why does the average Argentine hold more U.S. dollars than the average U.S. citizen?

Estimates are that the value of U.S. dollars circulating in Argentina exceeds $1,000 per person, which is higher than the per capita dollar holdings in the United States. A number of other countries, including those that once belonged to the former Soviet Union, also hold large quantities of dollars. In all, as much as $300 billion in U.S. currency—more than half the total amount issued—may be circulating outside the borders of the United States. Why do Argentines and other non-U.S. residents hold so many dollars?

U.S. residents and businesses hold dollars primarily for transaction purposes, rather than as a store of value. As a store of value, interest-bearing bonds and dividend-paying stocks are a better choice for Americans than zero-interest money. But this is not necessarily the case for the citizens of other countries, particularly nations that are economically or politically unstable. Argentina, for example, endured many years of high and erratic inflation in the 1970s and 1980s, which sharply eroded the value of financial investments denominated in Argentine pesos. Lacking better alternatives, many Argentines began saving in the form of U.S. currency, which they correctly believed to be more stable in value than peso-denominated assets.

Argentina's use of dollars became officially recognized in 1990. In that year, the country instituted a new monetary system, called a currency board, under which U.S. dollars and Argentine pesos by law traded freely one for one. Under the currency board system, Argentines became accustomed to carrying U.S. dollars in their wallets for transaction purposes, along with pesos. However, in 2001 Argentina's monetary problems returned with a vengeance, as the currency board system broke down, the peso plummeted in value relative to the dollar, and inflation returned. Consequently, the Argentinian demand for dollars increased during the next few years.

Some countries, including a number formed as a result of the breakup of the Soviet Union, have endured not only high inflation but political instability and uncertainty as well. In a politically volatile environment, citizens face the risk that their savings, including their bank deposits, will be confiscated or heavily taxed by the government. Often they conclude that a hidden cache of U.S. dollars is the safest way to hold wealth. Indeed, an estimated $1 million in 100-dollar bills can be stored in a suitcase. The ability to hold such wealth in a relatively small container is one reason why international criminals, most notably drug dealers, allegedly hold so many 100-dollar bills. Now that the European currency, the euro, which is worth more than $1, can be held in the form of a 500-euro banknote, it has been suggested that drug dealers and other cash-hoarders may switch to holding 500-euro bills in even smaller suitcases. If they do, the demand for dollars would decline.

RECAP	**MONEY DEMAND**

- For the economy as a whole, the demand for money is the amount of wealth that individuals, households, and businesses choose to hold in the form of money. The opportunity cost of holding money is measured by the nominal interest rate i, which is the return that could be earned on alternative assets such as bonds. The benefit of holding money is its usefulness in transactions.

- Increases in real GDP (Y) or the price level (P) raise the nominal volume of transactions and thus the economywide demand for money. The demand for money also is affected by technological and financial innovations, such as the introduction of ATM machines, that affect the costs or benefits of holding money.

- The money demand curve relates the economywide demand for money to the nominal interest rate. Because an increase in the nominal interest rate raises the opportunity cost of holding money, the money demand curve slopes downward.

- Changes in factors other than the nominal interest rate that affect the demand for money can shift the money demand curve. For example, increases in real GDP or the price level raise the demand for money, shifting the money demand curve to the right, whereas decreases shift the money demand curve to the left.

THE SUPPLY OF MONEY AND MONEY MARKET EQUILIBRIUM

Where there is demand, can supply be far behind? As we have seen, the *supply* of money is controlled by the central bank—in the United States, the Federal Reserve, or Fed. The Fed's primary tool for controlling the money supply is *open-market operations*. For example, to increase the money supply, the Fed can use newly created money to buy government bonds from the public (an open-market purchase), which puts the new money into circulation.

Figure 14.3 shows the demand for and the supply of money in a single diagram. The nominal interest rate is on the vertical axis, and the nominal quantity of money (in dollars) is on the horizontal axis. As we have seen, because a higher nominal interest rate increases the opportunity cost of holding money, the money demand

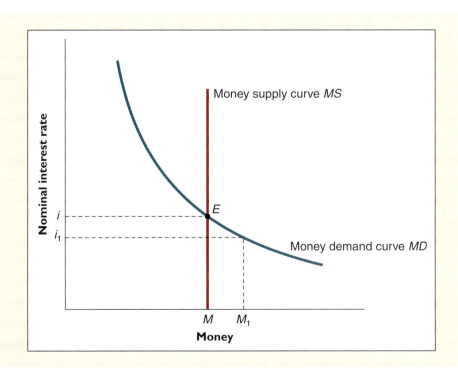

FIGURE 14.3

Equilibrium in the Market for Money.
Equilibrium in the market for money occurs at point *E*, where the demand for money by the public equals the amount of money supplied by the Federal Reserve. The equilibrium nominal interest rate, which equates the supply of and demand for money, is *i*.

curve slopes downward. And because the Fed fixes the supply of money, we have drawn the *money supply curve* as a vertical line that intercepts the horizontal axis at the quantity of money chosen by the Fed, denoted M.

As in standard supply and demand analysis, equilibrium in the market for money occurs at the intersection of the supply and demand curves, shown as point E in Figure 14.3. The equilibrium amount of money in circulation, M, is simply the amount of money the Fed chooses to supply. The equilibrium nominal interest rate i is the interest rate at which the quantity of money demanded by the public, as determined by the money demand curve, equals the fixed supply of money made available by the Fed.

To understand how the market for money reaches equilibrium, it may be helpful to recall the relationship between interest rates and the market price of bonds that was introduced in Example 11.1 on page 300. As we saw in that example, the prices of existing bonds are *inversely related* to the current interest rate. Higher interest rates imply lower bond prices, and lower interest rates imply higher bond prices. With this relationship between interest rates and bond prices in mind, let's ask what happens if, say, the nominal interest rate is initially below the equilibrium level in the market for money—for example, at a value such as i_1 in Figure 14.3. At that interest rate, the public's demand for money is M_1, which is greater than the actual amount of money in circulation, equal to M. How will the public—households and firms—react if the amount of money they hold is less than they would like? To increase their holdings of money, people will try to sell some of the interest-bearing assets they hold, such as bonds. But if everyone is trying to sell bonds and there are no willing buyers, then all the attempt to reduce bond holdings will achieve is to drive down the price of bonds, in the same way that a glut of apples will drive down the price of apples.

A fall in the price of bonds, however, is equivalent to an increase in interest rates. Thus, the public's collective attempt to increase its money holdings by selling bonds and other interest-bearing assets, which has the effect of lowering bond prices, also implies higher market interest rates. As interest rates rise, the quantity of money demanded by the public will decline (represented by a right-to-left movement along the money demand curve), as will the desire to sell bonds. Only when the interest rate reaches its equilibrium value, i in Figure 14.3, will people be content to hold the quantities of money and other assets that are actually available in the economy.

EXERCISE 14.2

Describe the adjustment process in the market for money if the nominal interest rate is initially above rather than below its equilibrium value. What happens to the price of bonds as the money market adjusts toward equilibrium?

HOW THE FED CONTROLS THE NOMINAL INTEREST RATE

We began this section by noting that the public and the press usually talk about Fed policy in terms of decisions about the nominal interest rate rather than the money supply. Indeed, Fed policymakers themselves usually describe their plans in terms of a specific value for the interest rate. We now have the necessary background to understand how the Fed translates the ability to determine the economy's money supply into control of the nominal interest rate.

Figure 14.3 showed that the nominal interest rate is determined by equilibrium in the market for money. Let's suppose that for some reason the Fed decides to lower the interest rate. As we will see, to lower the interest rate, the Fed must increase the supply of money, which, as we saw in the chapter "Money, Prices, and the Federal Reserve," is usually accomplished by using newly created money to purchase government bonds from the public (an open-market purchase).

Figure 14.4 shows the effects of such an increase in the money supply by the Fed. If the initial money supply is M, then equilibrium in the money market occurs at point E in the figure, and the equilibrium nominal interest rate is i. Now suppose the Fed, by means of open-market purchases of bonds, increases the money supply to M'. This increase in the money supply shifts the vertical money supply curve to the right, which shifts the equilibrium in the money market from point E to point F (see Figure 14.4). Note that at point F the equilibrium nominal interest rate has declined, from i to i'. The nominal interest rate must decline if the public is to be persuaded to hold the extra money that has been injected into the economy.

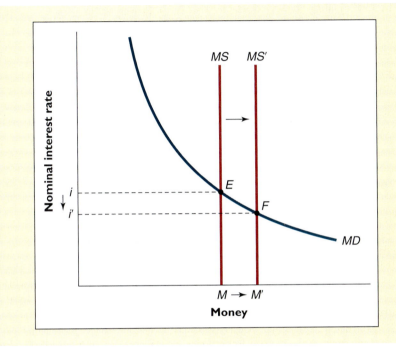

FIGURE 14.4

The Fed Lowers the Nominal Interest Rate. The Fed can lower the equilibrium nominal interest rate by increasing the supply of money. For the given money demand curve, an increase in the money supply from M to M' shifts the equilibrium point in the money market from E to F, lowering the equilibrium nominal interest rate from i to i'.

To understand what happens in financial markets when the Fed expands the money supply, recall once again the inverse relationship between interest rates and the price of bonds. To increase the money supply, the Fed typically buys government bonds from the public. However, if households and firms are initially satisfied with their asset holdings, they will be willing to sell bonds only at a price that is higher than the initial price. That is, the Fed's bond purchases will drive up the price of bonds in the open market. But we know that higher bond prices imply lower interest rates. Thus, the Fed's bond purchases lower the prevailing nominal interest rate.

A similar scenario unfolds if the Fed decides to raise interest rates. To raise interest rates, the Fed must *reduce* the money supply. Reduction of the money supply may be accomplished by an open-market sale—the sale of government bonds to the public in exchange for money.[3] (The Fed keeps a large inventory of government bonds, acquired through previous open-market purchases, for use in open-market operations.) But in the attempt to sell bonds on the open market, the Fed will drive down the price of bonds. Given the inverse relationship between the price of bonds and the interest rate, the fall in bond prices is equivalent to a rise in the interest rate.

---

[3]The sale of existing government bonds by the Federal Reserve in an open-market sale should not be confused with the sale of newly issued government bonds by the Treasury when it finances government budget deficits. Whereas open-market sales reduce the money supply, Treasury sales of new bonds do not affect the money supply. The difference arises because the Federal Reserve does not put the money it receives in an open-market sale back into circulation, leaving less money for the public to hold. In contrast, the Treasury puts the money it receives from selling newly issued bonds back into circulation as it purchases goods and services.

In terms of money demand and money supply, the higher interest rate is necessary to persuade the public to hold less money.

As Figures 14.3 and 14.4 illustrate, control of the interest rate is not separate from control of the money supply. If Fed officials choose to set the nominal interest rate at a particular level, they can do so only by setting the money supply at a level consistent with the target interest rate. The Fed *cannot* set the interest rate and the money supply independently, since for any given money demand curve, a particular interest rate implies a particular size of the money supply, and vice versa.

Since monetary policy actions can be expressed in terms of either the interest rate or the money supply, why does the Fed (and almost every other central bank) choose to communicate its policy decisions to the public by referring to the nominal interest rate rather than the money supply? One reason, as we will see shortly, is that the main effects of monetary policy on both the economy and financial markets are exerted through interest rates. Consequently, the interest rate is often the best summary of the overall impact of the Fed's actions. Another reason for focusing on interest rates is that they are more familiar to the public than the money supply. Finally, interest rates can be monitored continuously in the financial markets, which makes the effects of Fed policies on interest rates easy to observe. By contrast, measuring the amount of money in the economy requires collecting data on bank deposits, with the consequence that several weeks may pass before policymakers and the public know precisely how Fed actions have affected the money supply.

What's so important about the federal funds rate?

ECONOMIC NATURALIST 14.2

federal funds rate the interest rate that commercial banks charge each other for very short-term (usually overnight) loans; because the Fed frequently sets its policy in terms of the federal funds rate, this rate is closely watched in financial markets

Although thousands of interest rates and other financial data are easily available, the interest rate that is perhaps most closely watched by the public, politicians, the media, and the financial markets is the *federal funds rate*. What is the federal funds rate, and why is it so important?

The **federal funds rate** is the interest rate commercial banks charge each other for very short-term (usually overnight) loans. For example, a bank that has insufficient reserves to meet its legal reserve requirements (see the chapter "Money, Prices, and the Federal Reserve") might borrow reserves for a few days from a bank that has extra reserves. Despite its name, the federal funds rate is not an official government interest rate and is not connected to the federal government.

Because the market for loans between commercial banks is tiny compared to some other financial markets, such as the market for government bonds, one might expect the federal funds rate to be of little interest to anyone other than the managers of commercial banks. But enormous attention is paid to this interest rate, because over most of the past 40 years, the Fed has expressed its policies in terms of the federal funds rate. Indeed, at the close of every meeting of the Federal Open Market Committee, the Fed announces whether the federal funds rate will be increased, decreased, or left unchanged. The Fed also may indicate the likely direction of future changes in the federal funds rate. Thus, more than any other financial variable, changes in the federal funds rate indicate the Fed's plans for monetary policy.

Why does the Fed choose to focus on this particular nominal interest rate over all others? As we saw in the chapter "Money, Prices, and the Federal Reserve," in practice the Fed affects the money supply through its control of bank reserves. Because open-market operations directly affect the supply of bank reserves, the Fed's control over the federal funds rate is particularly tight. If, for example, the Fed wants the federal funds rate to fall, it conducts open-market purchases, which increase reserves, until the federal funds rate falls to the new desired level. However, if Fed officials chose to do so, they could probably signal their intended policies just as effectively in terms of another short-term nominal interest rate, such as the rate on short-term government debt.

Figure 14.5 shows the behavior of the federal funds rate from January 1970 through August 2005. As you can see, the Fed has allowed this interest rate to vary considerably in response to economic conditions. Later in the chapter, we will consider two specific episodes in which the Fed changed the federal funds rate in response to an economic slowdown.

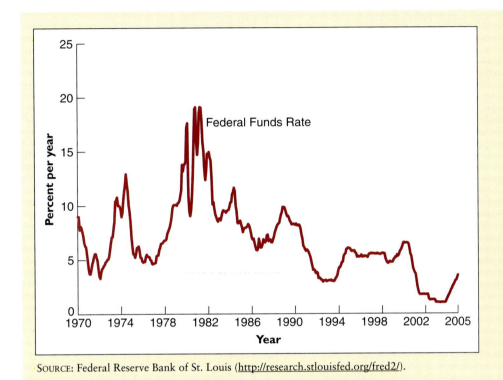

FIGURE 14.5

The Federal Funds Rate, 1970–2005.

The federal funds rate is the interest rate commercial banks charge each other for short-term loans. It is closely watched because the Fed expresses its policies in terms of the federal funds rate. The Fed has allowed the federal funds rate to vary considerably in response to economic conditions.

SOURCE: Federal Reserve Bank of St. Louis (http://research.stlouisfed.org/fred2/).

A SECOND WAY THE FED CONTROLS THE MONEY SUPPLY: DISCOUNT WINDOW LENDING

Although the Fed controls the money supply, and hence the federal funds rate, primarily by using open-market operations, it can change the money supply with two other tools, but it does so much less frequently. One tool is called *discount window lending.* Recall from the chapter "Money, Prices, and the Federal Reserve" that the cash or assets held by a commercial bank for the purpose of meeting depositor withdrawals are called its reserves. Its desired amount of reserves is equal to its deposits multiplied by the desired reserve-deposit ratio, as implied by Equation 10.1. When an individual commercial bank has insufficient reserves, it may choose to borrow reserves from the Fed. For historical reasons, lending of reserves by the Federal Reserve to commercial banks is called **discount window lending.** The interest rate that the Fed charges commercial banks that borrow reserves is called the **discount rate.** Loans of reserves by the Fed directly increase the quantity of reserves in the banking system, leading ultimately to increases in bank deposits and the money supply. Be careful not to confuse the discount rate and the federal funds rate. The discount rate is the interest rate commercial banks pay to the Fed; the federal funds rate is the interest rate commercial banks charge each other for short-term loans. The discount rate, also known as the *primary credit rate,* is normally set one percentage point above the federal funds rate.

discount window lending the lending of reserves by the Federal Reserve to commercial banks

discount rate (*also known as the primary credit rate*) the interest rate that the Fed charges commercial banks to borrow reserves

A THIRD WAY OF CONTROLLING THE MONEY SUPPLY: CHANGING RESERVE REQUIREMENTS

As Equation 10.2 illustrated, the economy's money supply depends on three factors: the amount of currency the public chooses to hold, the supply of bank reserves, and the reserve-deposit ratio maintained by commercial banks. The reserve-deposit ratio is equal to total bank reserves divided by total deposits. As we saw in the chapter "Money, Prices, and the Federal Reserve," if banks kept all of their deposits as reserves, the reserve-deposit ratio would be 100 percent, and banks would not make any loans. As banks lend out more of their deposits, the reserve-deposit ratio falls.

Within a certain range, commercial banks are free to set the reserve-deposit ratio they want to maintain. However, Congress granted the Fed the power to set minimum values of the reserve-deposit ratio for commercial banks. The legally required values of the reserve-deposit ratio set by the Fed are called **reserve requirements.**

reserve requirements set by the Fed, the minimum values of the ratio of bank deposits that commercial banks are allowed to maintain

Changes in reserve requirements can be used to affect the money supply, although the Fed does not usually use them in this way. For example, suppose that commercial banks are maintaining a legally mandated minimum 3 percent reserve-deposit ratio. If the Fed wants to expand the money supply, it could reduce required reserves to, say, 2 percent of deposits. This would allow banks to lend a greater portion of their deposits and keep a smaller percentage of deposits as required reserves. If banks wanted to make new loans, these new loans would generate additional deposits, as we saw in the chapter "Money, Prices, and the Federal Reserve." A decline in the economywide reserve-deposit ratio would therefore cause the money supply to rise.

Suppose, on the other hand, the Fed wanted to contract the money supply. If the Fed raised required reserves to, say, 5 percent of deposits, commercial banks would need to raise their reserve-deposit ratio to at least 5 percent. This would lead to a contraction of loans and deposits, which would decrease the money supply.

CAN THE FED CONTROL THE REAL INTEREST RATE?

Through its control of the money supply, the Fed can control the economy's *nominal* interest rate. But many important economic decisions, such as the decisions to save and invest, depend on the *real* interest rate. To affect those decisions, the Fed must exert some control over the real interest rate.

Most economists believe that the Fed can control the real interest rate, at least for some period. To see why, recall the definition of the real interest rate from the chapter "Measuring the Price Level and Inflation":

$$r = i - \pi.$$

The real interest rate r equals the nominal interest rate i minus the rate of inflation π. As we have seen, the Fed can control the nominal interest rate quite precisely through its ability to determine the money supply. Furthermore, inflation appears to change relatively slowly in response to changes in policy or economic conditions, for reasons we will discuss in the next chapter. Because inflation tends to adjust slowly, actions by the Fed to change the nominal interest rate generally lead the real interest rate to change by about the same amount.

The idea that the Fed can set the real interest rate appears to contradict the analysis in the chapter "Saving and Capital Formation," which concluded that the real interest rate is determined by the condition that national saving must equal investment in new capital goods. *This apparent contradiction is rooted in a difference in the time frame being considered.* Because inflation does not adjust quickly, the Fed can control the real interest rate over the short run. In the long run, however—that is, over periods of several years or more—the inflation rate and other economic variables will adjust, and the balance of saving and investment will determine the real interest rate. Thus, the Fed's ability to influence consumption and investment spending through its control of the real interest rate is strongest in the short run.

In discussing the Fed's control over interest rates, we also should return to a point mentioned earlier in this chapter: In reality, not just one but many thousands of interest rates are seen in the economy. Because interest rates tend to move together (allowing us to speak of *the* interest rate), an action by the Fed to change the federal funds rate generally causes other interest rates to change in the same direction. However, the tendency of other interest rates (such as the long-term government bond rate or the rate on bonds issued by corporations) to move in the same direction as the federal funds rate is only a tendency, not an exact relationship. In practice, then, the Fed's control of other interest rates may be somewhat less precise than its control of the federal funds rate—a fact that complicates the Fed's policymaking.

RECAP	**THE FEDERAL RESERVE AND INTEREST RATES**

- In the market for money, the money demand curve slopes downward, reflecting the fact that a higher nominal interest rate increases the opportunity cost of holding money and thus reduces the amount of money people want to hold. The money supply curve is vertical at the quantity of money that the Fed chooses to supply. The equilibrium nominal interest rate i is the interest rate at which the quantity of money demanded by the public equals the fixed supply of money made available by the Fed.

- The Federal Reserve controls the nominal interest rate by changing the supply of money. An open-market purchase of government bonds increases the money supply and lowers the equilibrium nominal interest rate. An increase in discount window lending or a reduction in reserve requirements will have the same effect. Conversely, an open-market sale of bonds reduces the money supply and increases the nominal interest rate, as will a decrease in discount window lending or an increase in reserve requirements. The Fed can prevent changes in the demand for money from affecting the nominal interest rate by adjusting the quantity of money supplied appropriately. The Fed typically expresses its policy intentions in terms of a specific nominal interest rate, the federal funds rate.

- Because inflation is slow to adjust, in the short run, the Fed can control the real interest rate (equal to the nominal interest rate minus the inflation rate) as well as the nominal interest rate. In the long run, however, the real interest rate is determined by the balance of saving and investment.

THE EFFECTS OF FEDERAL RESERVE ACTIONS ON THE ECONOMY

Now that we have seen how the Fed can influence interest rates (both nominal and real), we can consider how monetary policy can be used to eliminate output gaps and stabilize the economy. The basic idea is relatively straightforward. As we will see in this section, planned aggregate expenditure is affected by the level of the real interest rate prevailing in the economy. Specifically, a lower real interest rate encourages higher planned spending by households and firms, while a higher real interest rate reduces spending. By adjusting the real interest rate, the Fed can move planned spending in the desired direction. Under the assumption of the basic Keynesian model that firms produce just enough goods and services to meet the demand for their output, the Fed's stabilization of planned spending leads to stabilization of aggregate output and employment as well. In this section we will first explain how planned aggregate expenditure is related to the real interest rate. Then we will show how the Fed can use changes in the real interest rate to fight a recession or inflation.

PLANNED AGGREGATE EXPENDITURE AND THE REAL INTEREST RATE

In the last chapter, we saw how planned spending is affected by changes in real output Y. Changes in output affect the private sector's disposable income $(Y - T)$, which in turn influences consumption spending—a relationship captured by the consumption function.

A second variable that has potentially important effects on aggregate expenditure is the real interest rate r. In our discussion of saving and investment in the chapter "Financial Markets and International Capital Flows," we saw that the real interest rate influences the behavior of both households and firms.

For households, the effect of a higher real interest rate is to increase the reward for saving, which leads households to save more.[4] At a given level of income, households can save more only if they consume less. Thus, saying that a higher real interest rate *increases* saving is the same as saying that a higher real interest rate *reduces* consumption spending at each level of income. The idea that higher real interest rates reduce household spending makes intuitive sense. Think, for example, about people's willingness to buy consumer durables, such as automobiles or furniture. Purchases of consumer durables, which are part of consumption spending, are often financed by borrowing from a bank, credit union, or finance company. When the real interest rate rises, the monthly finance charges associated with the purchase of a car or a piano are higher, and people become less willing or able to make the purchase. Thus, a higher real interest rate reduces people's willingness to spend on consumer goods, holding constant disposable income and other factors that affect consumption.

Besides reducing consumption spending, a higher real interest rate also discourages firms from making capital investments. As in the case of a consumer thinking of buying a car or a piano, when a rise in the real interest rate increases financing costs, firms may reconsider their plans to invest. For example, upgrading a computer system may be profitable for a manufacturing firm when the cost of the system can be financed by borrowing at a real interest rate of 3 percent. However, if the real interest rate rises to 6 percent, doubling the cost of funds to the firm, the same upgrade may not be profitable and the firm may choose not to invest. We also should remember that residential investment—the building of houses and apartment buildings—is also part of investment spending. Higher interest rates, in the form of higher mortgage rates, certainly discourage this kind of investment spending as well.

The conclusion is that, at any given level of output, *both consumption spending and planned investment spending decline when the real interest rate increases.* Conversely, a fall in the real interest rate tends to stimulate consumption and investment spending by reducing financing costs. Example 14.3 is a numerical illustration of how planned aggregate expenditure can be related to the real interest rate and output.

When the real interest rate rises, financing a new car becomes more expensive and fewer cars are purchased.

---

[4]Because a higher real interest rate also reduces the amount households must put aside to reach a given savings target, a higher real interest rate could theoretically increase or decrease saving. However, empirical evidence suggests that higher real interest rates have a modest positive effect on saving.

Planned aggregate expenditure and the real interest rate   **EXAMPLE 14.3**

In a certain economy, the components of planned spending are given by

$$C = 640 + 0.8(Y - T) - 400r,$$
$$I^P = 250 - 600r,$$
$$G = 300,$$
$$NX = 20,$$
$$T = 250.$$

Find the relationship of planned aggregate expenditure to the real interest rate r and output Y in this economy. Find autonomous expenditure and induced expenditure.

This example is similar to Example 13.2, except that now the real interest rate r is allowed to affect both consumption and planned investment. For example, the final term in the equation describing consumption, $-400r$, implies that a 1 percentage point (0.01) increase in the real interest rate, from 4 percent to 5 percent—that is, from .04 to .05—reduces consumption spending by $400(0.01) = 4$ units. Similarly, the final term in the equation for planned investment tells us that in this example, a 1 percentage point increase in the real interest rate lowers planned investment by $600(0.01) = 6$ units. Thus, the overall effect of a 1 percentage point increase in the real interest rate is to lower planned aggregate expenditure by 10 units, the sum of the effects on consumption and investment. As in the earlier examples, disposable income $(Y - T)$ is assumed to affect consumption spending through a marginal propensity to consume of 0.8 (see the first equation), and government purchases G, net exports NX, and taxes T are assumed to be fixed numbers.

To find a numerical equation that describes the relationship of planned aggregate expenditure (PAE) to output, we can begin as in the last chapter with the general definition of planned aggregate expenditure:

$$PAE = C + I^P + G + NX.$$

Substituting for the four components of expenditure, using the equations describing each type of spending, we get

$$PAE = \left[640 + 0.8(Y - 250) - 400r\right] + \left[250 - 600r\right] + 300 + 20.$$

The first term in brackets on the right side of this equation is the expression for consumption, using the fact that taxes $T = 250$; the second bracketed term is planned investment; and the last two terms correspond to the assumed numerical values of government purchases and net exports. If we simplify this equation and group together the terms that do not depend on output Y and the terms that do depend on output, we get

$$PAE = \left[(640 - 0.8 \times 250 - 400r) + (250 - 600r) + 300 + 20\right] + 0.8Y,$$

or, simplifying further,

$$PAE = \left[1{,}010 - 1{,}000r\right] + 0.8Y. \tag{14.1}$$

In Equation 14.1, the term in brackets is *autonomous expenditure*, the portion of planned aggregate expenditure that does not depend on output. *Notice that in this example autonomous expenditure depends on the real interest rate r.* Induced expenditure, the portion of planned aggregate expenditure that does depend on output, equals $0.8Y$ in this example.

EXAMPLE 14.4

The real interest rate and short-run equilibrium output

In the economy described in Example 14.3, the real interest rate r is set by the Fed to equal 0.05 (5 percent). Find short-run equilibrium output.

We found in Example 14.3 that, in this economy, planned aggregate expenditure is given by Equation 14.1. We are given that the Fed sets the real interest rate at 5 percent. Setting $r = 0.05$ in Equation 14.1 gives

$$PAE = \left[1{,}010 - 1{,}000 \times (0.05)\right] + 0.8Y.$$

Simplifying, we get

$$PAE = 960 + 0.8Y.$$

So, when the real interest rate is 5 percent, autonomous expenditure is 960 and induced expenditure is $0.8Y$. Short-run equilibrium output is the level of output that equals planned aggregate spending. To find short-run equilibrium output, we could now apply the tabular method used in the last chapter, comparing alternative values of output with the planned aggregate expenditure at that level of output. Short-run equilibrium output would be determined as the value of output such that output just equals spending, or

$$Y = PAE.$$

However, conveniently, when we compare this example with Example 13.2 in the last chapter, we see that the equation for planned aggregate expenditure, $PAE = 960 + 0.8Y$, is identical to what we found there. Thus, Table 13.1, which we used to solve Example 13.2, applies to this example as well, and we get the same answer for short-run equilibrium output, which is $Y = 4{,}800$.

Short-run equilibrium output also can be found graphically, using the Keynesian cross diagram from the last chapter. Again, since the equation for planned aggregate output is the same as in Example 13.2, Figure 13.3 applies equally well here.

EXERCISE 14.3

For the economy described in Example 14.4, suppose the Fed sets the real interest rate at 3 percent rather than at 5 percent. Find short-run equilibrium output. (*Hint:* Consider values between 4,500 and 5,500.)

THE FED FIGHTS A RECESSION

We have seen that the Fed can control the real interest rate, and that the real interest rate in turn affects planned spending and short-run equilibrium output. Putting these two results together, we can see how Fed actions may help to stabilize the economy.

Suppose the economy faces a recessionary gap—a situation in which real output is below potential output, and planned spending is "too low." To fight a recessionary gap, the Fed should reduce the real interest rate, stimulating consumption and investment spending. According to the theory we have developed, this increase in planned spending will cause output to rise, restoring the economy to full employment. Example 14.5 illustrates this point by extending Example 14.4.

EXAMPLE 14.5

The Fed fights a recession

For the economy described in Example 14.4, suppose potential output Y^* equals 5,000. As before, the Fed has set the real interest rate equal to 5 percent. At that real interest rate, what is the output gap? What should the Fed do to eliminate the output gap and restore full employment? You are given that the multiplier in this economy is 5.

In Example 14.4 we showed that with the real interest rate at 5 percent, short-run equilibrium output for this economy is 4,800. Potential output is 5,000, so the output gap $(Y - Y^*)$ equals $5,000 - 4,800 = 200$. Because actual output is below potential, this economy faces a recessionary gap.

To fight the recession, the Fed should lower the real interest rate, raising aggregate expenditure until output reaches 5,000, the full-employment level. That is, the Fed's objective is to increase output by 200. Because the multiplier equals 5, to increase output by 200, the Fed must increase autonomous expenditure by $200/5 = 40$ units. By how much should the Fed reduce the real interest rate to increase autonomous expenditure by 40 units? Autonomous expenditure in this economy is $[1,010 - 1,000r]$, as you can see from Equation 14.1, so that each percentage point reduction in r increases autonomous expenditure by $1,000 \times (0.01) = 10$ units. To increase autonomous expenditure by 40, then, the Fed should lower the real interest rate by 4 percentage points, from 5 percent to 1 percent.

In summary, to eliminate the recessionary gap of 200, the Fed should lower the real interest rate from 5 percent to 1 percent. Notice that the Fed's decrease in the real interest rate increases short-run equilibrium output, as economic logic suggests.

The Fed's recession-fighting policy is shown graphically in Figure 14.6. The reduction in the real interest rate raises planned spending at each level of output, shifting the expenditure line upward. When the real interest rate equals 1 percent, the expenditure line intersects the $Y = PAE$ line at $Y = 5,000$, so that output and potential output are equal.

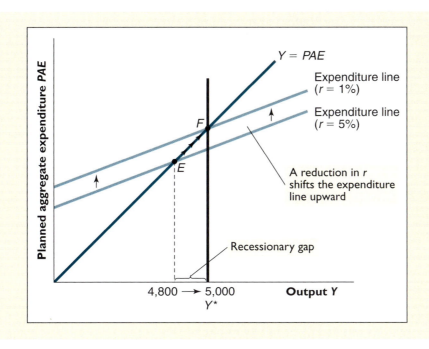

FIGURE 14.6
The Fed Fights a Recession.
When the real interest rate is 5 percent, the expenditure line intersects the $Y = PAE$ line at point E. At that point, output is 4,800, below the economy's potential output of 5,000 (a recessionary gap of 200). If the Fed reduces the real interest rate to 1 percent, stimulating consumption and investment spending, the expenditure line will shift upward. At the new point of intersection F, output will equal potential output at 5,000.

EXERCISE 14.4

Continuing Example 14.5, suppose that potential output is 4,850 rather than 5,000. By how much should the Fed cut the real interest rate to restore full employment? You may take as given that the multiplier is 5.

How did the Fed respond to recession and the terror attacks in 2001?

The U.S. economy began slowing in the fall of 2000, with investment in high-tech equipment falling particularly sharply (see Economic Naturalist 13.4). According to the National Bureau of Economic Research, a recession began in March 2001. To make matters worse, on September 11, 2001, terrorist attacks on New York City and Washington shocked the nation and led to serious problems in the travel and financial industries, among others. How did the Federal Reserve react to these events?

The Fed first began to respond to growing evidence of an economic slow-down at the end of the year 2000. At the time, the federal funds rate stood at about 6.5 percent (see Figure 14.5). The Fed's most dramatic move was a surprise cut of 0.5 percentage point in the funds rate in January 2001, between regularly scheduled meetings of the Federal Open Market Committee. Further rate cuts followed, and by July the funds rate was below 4 percent. By summer's end, however, there was still considerable uncertainty about the likely severity of the economic slowdown.

The picture changed suddenly on September 11, 2001, when the terror attacks on the World Trade Center and the Pentagon killed almost 3,000 people. The terrorist attacks imposed great economic as well as human costs. The physical damage in lower Manhattan was in the billions of dollars, and many offices and businesses in the area had to close. The Fed, in its role as supervisor of the financial system, worked hard to assist in the restoration of normal operations in the financial district of New York City. (The Federal Reserve Bank of New York, which actually conducts open-market operations, is only a block from the site of the World Trade Center.) The Fed also tried to ease financial conditions by temporarily lowering the federal funds rate to as low as 1.25 percent, in the week following the attack.

In the weeks and months following September 11, the Fed turned its attention from the direct impact of the attack to the possible indirect effects on the U.S. economy. The Fed was worried that consumers, nervous about the future, would severely cut back their spending; together with the ongoing weakness in investment, a fall in consumption spending could sharply worsen the recession. To stimulate spending, the Fed continued to cut the federal funds rate.

By the time the recession officially ended in November 2001, the funds rate was at 2.0 percent, 4.5 percentage points lower than a year earlier. A number of factors made the 2001 recession relatively short and mild, including President Bush's tax cuts (see Economic Naturalist 13.7), and increased government expenditures for homeland security and defense. Nevertheless, most economists agree that the Fed's quick actions helped to moderate the impact of the recession and the September 11 attacks.

THE FED FIGHTS INFLATION

To this point we have focused on the problem of stabilizing output, without considering inflation. In the next chapter, we will see how ongoing inflation can be incorporated into our analysis. For now we will simply note that one important cause of inflation is an expansionary output gap—a situation in which planned spending, and hence actual output, exceeds potential output. When an expansionary gap exists, firms find that the demand for their output exceeds their normal rate of production. Although firms may be content to meet this excess demand at previously determined prices for some time, if the high demand persists, they ultimately will raise their prices, spurring inflation.

Because an expansionary gap tends to lead to inflation, the Fed moves to eliminate expansionary gaps as well as recessionary gaps. The procedure for getting rid of an expansionary gap—a situation in which output is "too high" relative to potential output—is the reverse of that for fighting a recessionary gap, a situation in which output is "too low." As we have seen, the cure for a recessionary gap is to reduce the real interest rate, an action that stimulates planned spending and increases output. The cure for an expansionary gap is to *raise* the real interest rate, which reduces consumption and planned investment by raising the cost of borrowing. The resulting fall in planned spending leads in turn to a decline in output and to a reduction in inflationary pressures.

The Fed fights inflation

EXAMPLE 14.6

For the economy studied in Examples 14.4 and 14.5, assume that potential output is 4,600 rather than 5,000. At the initial real interest rate of 5 percent, short-run equilibrium output is 4,800, so this economy has an expansionary gap of 200. How should the Fed change the real interest rate to eliminate this gap?

In Example 14.5 we were told that the multiplier in this economy is 5. Hence, to reduce total output by 200, the Fed needs to reduce autonomous expenditure by $200/5 = 40$ units. From Equation 14.1, we know that autonomous expenditure in this economy is $[1,010 - 1,000r]$, so that each percentage point (0.01) increase in the real interest rate lowers autonomous expenditure by 10 units ($1,000 \times 0.01$). We conclude that to eliminate the inflationary gap, the Fed should raise the real interest rate by 4 percentage points (0.04), from 5 percent to 9 percent. The higher real interest rate will reduce planned aggregate expenditure and output to the level of potential output, 4,600, eliminating inflationary pressures.

The effects of the Fed's inflation-fighting policy are shown in Figure 14.7. With the real interest rate at 5 percent, the expenditure line intersects the $Y = PAE$ line at point E in the figure, where output equals 4,800. To reduce planned spending and output, the Fed raises the real interest rate to 9 percent. The higher real interest rate slows consumption and investment spending, moving the expenditure line downward. At the new equilibrium point G, actual output equals potential output at 4,600. The Fed's raising the real interest rate—a contractionary policy action—has thus eliminated the expansionary output gap, and with it, the threat of inflation.

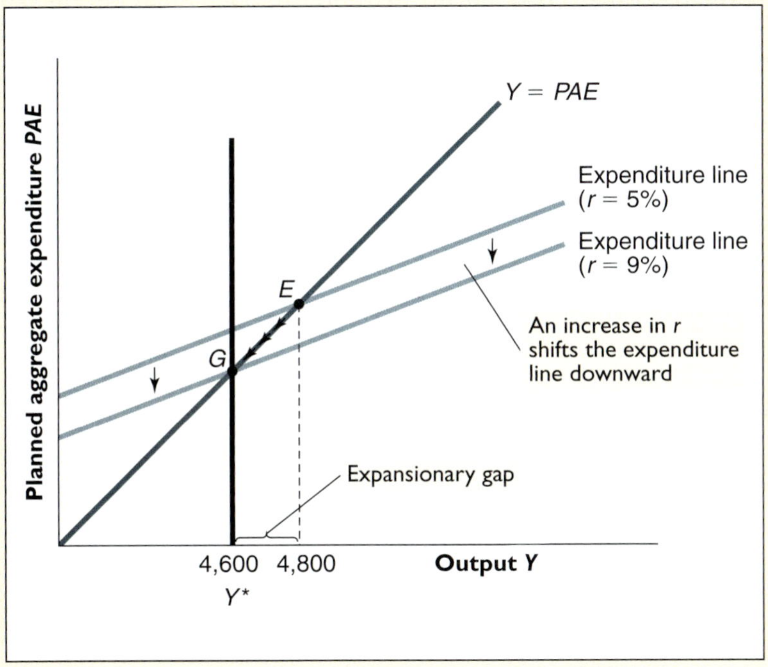

FIGURE 14.7
The Fed Fights Inflation.
When the real interest rate is 5 percent, the expenditure line intersects the $Y = PAE$, or 45°, line at point E, where short-run equilibrium output equals 4,800. If potential output is 4,600, an expansionary output gap of 200 exists. If the Fed raises the real interest rate to 9 percent, reducing planned aggregate expenditure, the expenditure line shifts downward. At the new intersection point G, actual output equals potential output at 4,600, and the expansionary gap is eliminated.

"Personally, I liked this roller coaster a lot better before the Federal Reserve Board got hold of it."

ECONOMIC NATURALIST 14.4

Why did the Fed raise interest rates in 2004 and 2005?

The Fed began tightening monetary policy in June 2004 when it increased the federal funds rate from 1.0 to 1.25 percent. It continued to tighten by raising the federal funds rate by one-quarter percent at each successive meeting of the Federal Open Market Committee. By August 2005, after more than a year of tightening, the federal funds rate was 3.50 percent. Why did the Fed begin increasing the funds rate in 2004?

Because the recovery that began in November 2001 was slower than normal and marked by weak job growth, the Fed kept reducing the funds rate until it reached 1.0 percent in June 2003. Once the recovery took hold, however, this very low rate was no longer necessary. While employment had not risen as much during the recovery as it had in previous recoveries, real GDP grew at a rate of nearly 6 percent during the second half of 2003 and by 4.4 percent in 2004. Furthermore, by June 2004 the unemployment rate had fallen to 5.6 percent, not far above most estimates of the natural rate of unemployment. Although inflation began to rise in 2004, most of the increase was due to the sharp run-up in oil prices, and the rate of inflation excluding energy remained low. Nevertheless, the Fed began to raise the federal funds rate in order to prevent the emergence of an expansionary gap, which would result in higher inflation. Thus, the Fed's rate increases could be viewed as a preemptive strike against future inflation. Had the Fed waited until an expansionary gap appeared, a significant inflation problem could have emerged, and the Fed might have had to raise the federal funds rate by even more than it did.

The Fed's interest rate policies affect the economy as a whole, but they have a particularly important effect on financial markets. The introduction to this chapter noted the tremendous lengths financial market participants will go to in an attempt to anticipate Federal Reserve policy changes. Economic Naturalist 14.5 illustrates the type of information financial investors look for, and why it is so important to them.

Why does news of inflation hurt the stock market?

Financial market participants watch data on inflation extremely closely. A report that inflation is increasing or is higher than expected often causes stock prices to fall sharply. Why does bad news about inflation hurt the stock market?

Investors in the financial markets worry about inflation because of its likely impact on Federal Reserve policy. Financial investors understand that the Fed, when

ECONOMIC NATURALIST 14.5

faced with signs of an expansionary gap, is likely to raise interest rates in an attempt to reduce planned spending and "cool down" the economy. This type of contractionary policy action hurts stock prices in two ways. First, it slows down economic activity, reducing the expected sales and profits of companies whose shares are traded in the stock market. Lower profits, in turn, reduce the dividends those firms are likely to pay their shareholders.

Second, higher real interest rates reduce the value of stocks by increasing the required return for holding stocks. We saw in the chapter "Financial Markets and International Capital Flows" that an increase in the return financial investors require in order to hold stocks lowers current stock prices. Intuitively, if interest rates rise, interest-bearing alternatives to stocks such as newly issued government bonds will become more attractive to investors, reducing the demand for, and hence the price of, stocks.

"Interest rates gyrated wildly today, on rumors that the Federal Reserve Board would be replaced by the cast of 'Saturday Night Live.'"

Should the Federal Reserve respond to changes in stock prices?

ECONOMIC NATURALIST 14.6

Many credit the Federal Reserve and its chairman at the time, Alan Greenspan, for effective monetary policymaking that set the stage for sustained economic growth and rising asset prices throughout the 1990s, in particular the second half of the decade. Between January 1995 and March 2000, the S&P 500 stock market index rose from a value of 459 to 1,527, a phenomenal 233 percent increase in just over five years, as the U.S. economy enjoyed a record-long business cycle expansion. Indeed, the stock market's strong, sustained rise helped to fuel additional consumer spending, which in turn promoted further economic expansion.

However, as stock prices fell sharply in the two years after their March 2000 peak, some people questioned whether the Federal Reserve should have preemptively raised interest rates to constrain investors' "irrational exuberance."[5] In this view, overly optimistic investor sentiment led to a speculative run-up in stock prices that eventually burst in 2000 as investors began to realize that firms' earnings could not support the stock prices that were being paid. Earlier intervention by the Federal Reserve, critics argued, would have slowed down the dramatic increase in stock prices and therefore could have prevented the resulting stock market "crash" and the

[5]Fed Chairman Alan Greenspan mentioned the possibility of "irrational exuberance" driving investor behavior in a December 5, 1996, speech, which is available online at http://www.federalreserve.gov/boarddocs/speeches/1996/19961205.htm.

resulting loss of consumer wealth. As this chapter makes clear, the Federal Reserve's primary focus is on reducing output gaps and keeping inflation low. Should the Fed also respond to changing stock prices when it makes decisions about monetary policy?

At a symposium in August 2002, Alan Greenspan defended the Fed's monetary policymaking performance in the late 1990s, pointing out that it is very difficult to identify asset bubbles—surges in prices of assets to unsustainable levels— "until after the fact—that is, when its bursting confirm(s) its existence."[6] Even if such a speculative bubble could be identified, Greenspan noted, the Federal Reserve could have done little—short of "inducing a substantial contraction in economic activity"—to prevent investors' speculation from driving up stock prices. Indeed, Greenspan claimed, "the notion that a well-timed incremental tightening could have been calibrated to prevent the late 1990s bubble is almost surely an illusion." Rather, the Federal Reserve was focusing as early as 1999 on policies that would "mitigate the fallout when it occurs and, hopefully, ease the transition to the next expansion."[7]

Greenspan's remarks highlight two basic problems with using monetary policy to address "bubbles" in asset markets. First, doing so presupposes that the Federal Reserve is better than financial-market professionals at identifying when asset prices are inappropriately high, relative to the asset's underlying value. In practice, however, the Fed does not have information about the stock market that is not also available to private-sector investors. Second, even if the Fed were sure that a "bubble" existed, monetary policy is not a very good tool for addressing the problem. The Fed could try to lower stock prices by raising the federal funds rate and slowing the economy. But if this policy led to a recession and rising unemployment, the outcome would be precisely the one that the Fed was trying to avoid in the first place. For these reasons, although the Fed monitors conditions in the stock market, when setting monetary policy it focuses on inflation, spending, and output, rather than stock prices themselves. Not all economists agree with the Fed's approach, however, and the debate continues.

THE FED'S MONETARY POLICY REACTION FUNCTION

The Fed attempts to stabilize the economy and keep inflation low by manipulating the real interest rate. When an expansionary gap exists, so that inflation threatens to become a problem, the Fed restrains spending by raising the real interest rate. When the economy faces a recessionary gap and inflation falls, the Fed reduces the real interest rate in order to stimulate spending. Economists sometimes find it convenient to model the behavior of the Fed in terms of a *policy reaction function*. In general, a **policy reaction function** describes how the action a policymaker takes depends on the state of the economy.

policy reaction function describes how the action a policymaker takes depends on the state of the economy

One example of a monetary policy reaction function, which we will use in the next few chapters, is

$$r = r^* + g(\pi - \pi^*) \tag{14.2}$$

where

r = the actual real interest rate set by the Fed (the "real interest rate")

r^* = the Fed's long-run target for the real interest rate (the "target real interest rate")

---

[6] The text of Greenspan's speech is available online at http://www.federalreserve.gov/boarddocs/speeches/2002/20020830/default.htm.

[7] *The Federal Reserve's Semiannual Report on Monetary Policy*, testimony of Chairman Alan Greenspan before the Committee on Banking and Financial Services, U.S. House of Representatives, July 22, 1999. Available online at http://www.federalreserve.gov/boarddocs/hh/1999/July/Testimony.htm.

π = the actual inflation rate (the "inflation rate")

π^* = the Fed's long-run target for the inflation rate (the "target inflation rate")

g = a positive number chosen by the Fed.

According to Equation 14.2, the Fed sets the actual real interest rate r equal to its target real interest rate r^* plus some portion of the amount by which actual inflation π exceeds the Fed's target inflation rate π^*. When the actual inflation rate π equals the Fed's long-run **target inflation rate** π^*, the term in parentheses will equal zero, and the actual real interest rate set by the Fed, r, will equal its long-run **target real interest rate**, r^*. When actual inflation exceeds the long-run target inflation rate, $\pi > \pi^*$, and the term in parentheses will be positive. When this happens, Equation 14.2 shows that the real interest rate will exceed its long-run target ($r > r^*$). Finally, when actual inflation is less than the long-run inflation target, $\pi < \pi^*$, and the term in parentheses will be negative. When this happens, Equation 14.2 indicates that the Fed will set the real interest rate below its long-run target real interest rate ($r < r^*$).

We refer to r^* and π^* as *long-run* targets because they are generally determined by long-run considerations. As we will discuss further in the chapter "The Practice and Pitfalls of Macroeconomic Policy," the Fed will generally try to set its target for the real interest rate at the level that sets saving equal to investment.[8] Likewise, as we will see later, the Fed chooses its target inflation rate at a level that helps to achieve the best long-run economic performance. Although π^* represents the Fed's long-run target for inflation, in the short run, (actual) inflation π need not equal the target inflation rate π^*. Thus, as Equation 14.2 implies, in the short run, the real interest rate r need not equal its target r^* either. For now, we shall take both r^* and π^* as given, fixed numbers. Note, also, that the two targets r^* and π^* will generally be different numbers.

One simple numerical example of the monetary policy reaction function described in Equation 14.2 is

$$r = 0.04 + 1.0(\pi - 0.02).$$

In this example, the target real interest rate r^* is 0.04, or 4 percent; the target inflation rate π^* is 0.02, or 2 percent; and the value of g is 1.0. If actual inflation π is equal to its target rate of 2 percent, the expression in parentheses is equal to zero and the Fed sets the real interest rate equal to its real interest rate target of 4 percent, as indicated in the third line of Table 14.1. The other numbers in Table 14.1 show how the Fed changes the real interest rate in response to inflation rising above or falling below the target inflation rate.

Suppose an expansionary gap begins to "overheat" the economy and push up inflation. If inflation rises to 0.03, that is, to 3 percent, the Fed increases the (actual) real interest rate to 5 percent. On the other hand, if inflation falls to 1 percent, the

target inflation rate the Fed's long-run goal for inflation

target real interest rate the Fed's long-run goal for the real interest rate

TABLE 14.1

A Monetary Policy Reaction Function for the Fed

Rate of inflation, π	Real interest rate set by Fed, r
0.00 (= 0%)	0.02 (= 2%)
0.01	0.03
0.02	0.04
0.03	0.05
0.04	0.06

[8]The chapter "Saving and Capital Formation" discussed how the real interest rate is related to the market for saving and investment.

FIGURE 14.8

An Example of a Fed Monetary Policy Reaction Function.

This hypothetical example of a monetary policy reaction function for the Fed shows the (actual) real interest rate the Fed sets in response to any given value of the inflation rate. The upward slope captures the idea that the Fed raises the (actual) real interest rate when inflation rises. The numerical values in the figure are from Table 14.1.

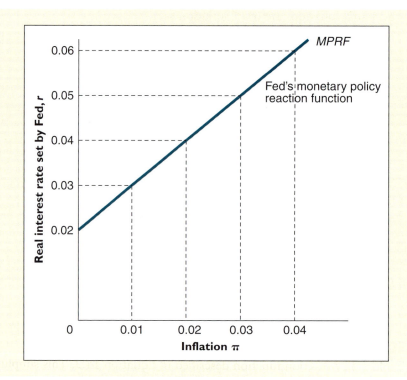

Fed reduces the (actual) real interest rate to 3 percent. The graph of this policy reaction function is presented in Figure 14.8. The vertical axis of the graph shows the (actual) real interest rate chosen by the Fed; the horizontal axis shows the rate of inflation. The upward slope of the monetary policy reaction function captures the idea that the Fed reacts to increases in inflation by raising the real interest rate.

We also can draw the more general monetary policy reaction function given by Equation 14.2 by recalling that $r = r^*$ whenever $\pi = \pi^*$, in which case $g(\pi - \pi^*) = 0$. When actual inflation is at the target rate of inflation, the Fed will set the real interest rate equal to its target real interest rate. (In our preceding numerical example, this occurred when $\pi = \pi^* = 2$ percent and $r^* = 4$ percent.) This is illustrated by point A in Figure 14.9. If inflation rises above the Fed's inflation target, however, Equation 14.2 indicates that the Fed responds by increasing the real interest rate above its target for the real interest rate. Furthermore,

FIGURE 14.9

A General Monetary Policy Reaction Function.

In this more general example, the target real interest rate is given by r^* and the target inflation rate is π^*. When (actual) inflation π is equal to the target rate of inflation π^*, the Fed sets the real interest rate r equal to its target real interest rate r^*. When inflation rises above its target, the Fed increases the real interest rate r above r^*. The slope of the line is equal to the parameter g.

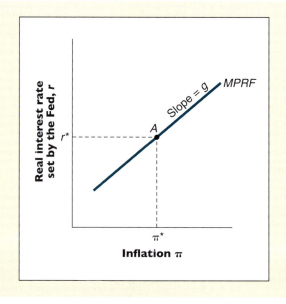

Equation 14.2 indicates that whenever inflation rises by one percentage point above its target, the Fed increases the real interest rate by g percentage points, so the slope of this policy reaction function is g. In our preceding numerical example, the value of g was 1.0, but the value of g can be 0.5, 1.5, or some other positive number.

How does the Fed determine its monetary policy reaction function? In practice the process is a complex one, involving a combination of statistical analysis of the economy and human judgment. Although we will discuss this process more fully in the chapter "The Practice and Pitfalls of Macroeconomic Policy," one useful insight into the process can be drawn even from the simplified policy reaction function shown in Table 14.1 and Figures 14.8 and 14.9. The value of g in the monetary policy reaction function contains information about how aggressively the Fed plans to pursue its inflation target. To illustrate, suppose the Fed's monetary policy reaction function was very flat (that is, suppose the value of g was small). In this case, the Fed changes the real interest rate rather modestly in response to increases or decreases in inflation. We would then conclude that the Fed does not intend to be very aggressive in its attempts to offset movements in inflation away from the target level. In contrast, suppose the reaction function slopes steeply upward because g is big. In this second case, a given change in inflation elicits a large adjustment of the real interest rate by the Fed. We would then say that the Fed plans to be quite aggressive in responding to changes in inflation.

In principle, any number of economic variables, from stock prices to the value of the dollar in terms of the Japanese yen, could affect Fed policy and thus appear in the monetary policy reaction function. In the next two chapters, we will adopt the simple policy reaction function described in Equation 14.2. This simplification will not change our main results in any significant way. Furthermore, as we will see, this policy reaction function captures the most important aspect of Fed behavior—namely, its tendency to raise the actual real interest rate when inflation is rising and to reduce it when inflation is falling. Rising inflation usually occurs when the economy is "overheated" and experiencing an expansionary gap. Similarly, falling inflation usually occurs when the economy is sluggish and experiencing a recessionary gap. Consequently, our simple monetary policy reaction function implicitly includes the size of any output gap (since this will affect actual inflation), even though the gap is not explicitly included as a separate variable.

RECAP	**MONETARY POLICY AND THE ECONOMY**

An increase in the real interest rate reduces both consumption spending and planned investment spending. Through its control of the real interest rate, the Fed is thus able to influence planned spending and short-run equilibrium output. To fight a recession (a recessionary output gap), the Fed should lower the real interest rate, stimulating planned spending and output. Conversely, to fight the threat of inflation (an expansionary output gap), the Fed should raise the real interest rate, reducing planned spending and output.

The Fed's monetary policy reaction function relates its policy action (specifically, its setting of the real interest rate) to the state of the economy. For the sake of simplicity, we consider a policy reaction function in which the (actual) real interest rate set by the Fed depends only on the Fed's real interest rate target and the extent to which the (actual) rate of inflation differs from the Fed's inflation rate target. In the short run, inflation may be more or less than the Fed's inflation target, implying that in the short run the real interest rate also may be greater or less than the Fed's target for the real interest rate. Because the Fed raises the real interest rate whenever inflation rises above the Fed's inflation target (in order to restrain spending), the Fed's monetary policy reaction is upward-sloping. The Fed's policy reaction function contains information about the central bank's inflation target and real interest rate target, as well as the aggressiveness with which it intends to pursue its inflation target.

ECONOMIC NATURALIST 14.7

What is the Taylor rule?

Equation 14.2 describes a monetary policy reaction function in which the real interest rate set by the Fed depends on the target real interest rate and the extent to which the inflation rate differs from the Fed's target inflation rate. In reality, however, the Fed can respond to a number of economic factors so that there are many possible monetary policy reaction functions. Perhaps the most famous is the one proposed in 1993 by economist John Taylor, which is now known as the Taylor rule. After examining historical data, Taylor suggested that his simple rule provided a remarkably accurate description of the actual behavior of the Fed.[9] What is the Taylor rule? Does the Fed always follow it?

Taylor's "rule" was simply a monetary policy reaction function in which he added the size of the output gap as a third determinant of the real interest rate set by the Fed:

$$r = 0.02 + 0.5(\pi - 0.02) - \frac{0.5(Y^* - Y)}{Y^*}.$$

According to the Taylor rule, the target real interest rate is 0.02, or 2 percent; the Fed's target rate of inflation is also 2 percent; and the value of g is 0.5. If inflation rises from 2 percent (0.02) to 3 percent (0.03), or by 1 percentage point (0.01), the Taylor rule implies that the Fed will increase the real interest rate by $0.5 \times 0.01 = 0.005$, or by 0.5 percentage points. $Y^* - Y$ is the current output gap (the difference between potential and actual output). Thus, $(Y^* - Y)/Y^*$ is the output gap relative to potential output, or the output gap expressed as a percentage of potential output. If inflation is equal to the target rate of inflation and actual output is equal to potential output, the terms in both parentheses equal zero, and the Fed sets the real interest rate equal to its target real interest rate of 2 percent.[10] If, however, a recessionary gap equal to a fraction 0.01 (or 1%) of potential output develops, the Fed will *reduce* the real interest rate by 0.5 percentage points (that is, by 0.005). Taylor's rule also describes the subsequent behavior of the Fed under Chairman Alan Greenspan reasonably accurately. Thus, the Taylor rule is a real-world example of a policy reaction function.

Although the Taylor rule has worked well as a description of the Fed's behavior, we reiterate that it is not a rule in any legal sense. The Fed is perfectly free to deviate from it and does so when circumstances warrant. Still, the Taylor rule provides a useful benchmark for assessing and predicting the Fed's actions.

EXERCISE 14.5

This exercise asks you to apply the Taylor rule. Suppose inflation is 3 percent and the output gap is zero. According to the Taylor rule, at what value should the Fed set the real interest rate? The nominal interest rate? Suppose the Fed were to receive new information showing that there is a 1 percent recessionary gap (inflation is still 3 percent). According to the Taylor rule, how should the Fed change the real interest rate, if at all?

■ SUMMARY ■

- Monetary policy is one of two types of stabilization policy, the other being fiscal policy. Although the Federal Reserve operates by controlling the money supply, the media's attention nearly always focuses on the Fed's decisions about interest rates, not the money supply. There is no contradiction between these two ways of looking at monetary policy,

---

[9]John Taylor, "Discretion versus Policy Rules in Practice." *Carnegie-Rochester Conference Series on Public Policy,* 1993, pp. 195–227.

[10]As we discussed earlier, the Fed controls the real interest rate by adjusting the nominal interest rate. If inflation is 2 percent and the Fed wants to set the real interest rate equal to 2 percent, it will change the money supply until the nominal interest rate is $2 + 2 = 4$ percent.

however, as the Fed's ability to control the money supply is the source of its ability to control interest rates.

- The nominal interest rate is determined in the market for money, which has both a demand side and a supply side. For the economy as a whole, the *demand for money* is the amount of wealth households and businesses choose to hold in the form of money (such as cash or checking accounts). The demand for money is determined by a comparison of cost and benefits. The opportunity cost of holding money, which pays either zero interest or very low interest, is the interest that could have been earned by holding interest-bearing assets instead of money. Because the nominal interest rate measures the opportunity cost of holding a dollar in the form of money, an increase in the nominal interest rate reduces the quantity of money demanded. The benefit of money is its usefulness in carrying out transactions. All else being equal, an increase in the volume of transactions increases the demand for money. At the macroeconomic level, an increase in the price level or in real GDP increases the dollar volume of transactions, and thus the demand for money.

- The *money demand curve* relates the aggregate quantity of money demanded to the nominal interest rate. Because an increase in the nominal interest rate increases the opportunity cost of holding money, which reduces the quantity of money demanded, the money demand curve slopes down. Factors other than the nominal interest rate that affect the demand for money will shift the demand curve to the right or left. For example, an increase in the price level or real GDP increases the demand for money, shifting the money demand curve to the right.

- The Federal Reserve determines the supply of money through the use of open-market operations. The supply curve for money is vertical at the value of the money supply set by the Fed. Money market equilibrium occurs at the nominal interest rate at which money demand equals the money supply. The Fed can reduce the nominal interest rate by increasing the money supply (shifting the money supply curve to the right) or increase the nominal interest rate by reducing the money supply (shifting the money supply curve to the left). The nominal interest rate that the Fed targets most closely is the *federal funds rate*, which is the rate commercial banks charge each other for very short-term loans.

- In addition to open-market purchases and sales, the Federal Reserve has two other tools that it can use to change the money supply. The first involves changes in discount window lending, which occur when commercial banks borrow additional reserves from the Fed. The second involves changes in reserve requirements, which are the minimum values of the reserve-deposit ratio that commercial banks are required to maintain. However, the Fed uses these two additional tools infrequently to change the money supply.

- In the short run, the Fed can control the real interest rate as well as the nominal interest rate. Recall that the real interest rate equals the nominal interest rate minus the inflation rate. Because the inflation rate adjusts relatively slowly, the Fed can change the real interest rate by changing the nominal interest rate. In the long run, the real interest rate is determined by the balance of saving and investment (see the chapter "Saving and Capital Formation").

- The Federal Reserve's actions affect the economy because changes in the real interest rate affect planned spending. For example, an increase in the real interest rate raises the cost of borrowing, reducing consumption and planned investment. Thus, by increasing the real interest rate, the Fed can reduce planned spending and short-run equilibrium output. Conversely, by reducing the real interest rate, the Fed can stimulate planned aggregate expenditure and thereby raise short-run equilibrium output. The Fed's ultimate objectives are to eliminate output gaps and maintain low inflation. To eliminate a recessionary output gap, the Fed will lower the real interest rate. To eliminate an expansionary output gap, the Fed will raise the real interest rate.

- A *policy reaction function* describes how the action a policymaker takes depends on the state of the economy. For example, a monetary policy reaction function for the Fed could illustrate how the actual real interest rate set by the Fed depends on its real interest rate target and the extent to which inflation differs from the Fed's target rate of inflation.

■ KEY TERMS ■

demand for money (385)
discount rate (395)
discount window lending (395)
federal funds rate (394)

money demand curve (388)
policy reaction function (406)
portfolio allocation decision (385)

reserve requirements (396)
target inflation rate (407)
target real interest rate (407)

■ REVIEW QUESTIONS ■

1. What is the *demand for money*? How does the demand for money depend on the nominal interest rate? On the price level? On income? Explain in terms of the costs and benefits of holding money.

2. Show graphically how the Fed controls the nominal interest rate. Can the Fed control the real interest rate?

3. What effect does an open-market purchase of bonds by the Fed have on nominal interest rates? Discuss in terms of (a) the effect of the purchase on bond prices and (b) the effect of the purchase on the supply of money.

4. You hear a news report that employment growth is lower than expected. How do you expect that report to affect market interest rates? Explain. (*Hint:* Assume that Fed policymakers have access to the same data that you do.)

5. Why does the real interest rate affect planned aggregate expenditure? Give examples.

6. The Fed faces a recessionary gap. How would you expect it to respond? Explain step by step how its policy change is likely to affect the economy.

7. The Fed decides to take a *contractionary* policy action. What would you expect to happen to the nominal interest rate, the real interest rate, and the money supply? Under what circumstances would this type of policy action most likely be appropriate?

8. Define *policy reaction function*. Sketch a policy reaction function relating the Fed's setting of the real interest rate to inflation.

▪ PROBLEMS ▪

1. During the heavy Christmas shopping season, sales of retail stores, online sales firms, and other merchants rise significantly.
   a. What would you expect to happen to the money demand curve during the Christmas season? Show graphically.
   b. If the Fed took no action, what would happen to nominal interest rates around Christmas?
   c. In fact, nominal interest rates do not change significantly in the fourth quarter of the year, due to deliberate Fed policy. Explain and show graphically how the Fed can ensure that nominal interest rates remain stable around Christmas.

2. The following table shows Uma's estimated annual benefits of holding different amounts of money:

Average money holdings ($)	Total benefit ($)
500	35
600	47
700	57
800	65
900	71
1,000	75
1,100	77
1,200	77

   a. How much money will Uma hold on average if the nominal interest rate is 9 percent? 5 percent? 3 percent? Assume that she wants her money holding to be a multiple of $100. (*Hint:* Make a table comparing the extra benefit of each additional $100 in money holdings with the opportunity cost, in terms of forgone interest, of additional money holdings.)
   b. Graph Uma's money demand curve for interest rates between 1 percent and 12 percent.

3. How would you expect each of the following to affect the economywide demand for money? Explain.
   a. Competition among brokers forces down the commission charge for selling holdings of bonds or stocks.
   b. Grocery stores begin to accept credit cards in payment.
   c. Financial investors become concerned about increasing riskiness of stocks.
   d. Online banking allows customers to check balances and transfer funds between checking and mutual fund investments 24 hours a day.
   e. The economy enters a boom period.
   f. Political instability increases in developing nations.

4. Suppose the economywide demand for money is given by $P(0.2Y - 25,000i)$. The price level P equals 3.0, and real output Y equals 10,000. At what value should the Fed set the nominal money supply if
   a. It wants to set the nominal interest rate at 4 percent?
   b. It wants to set the nominal interest rate at 6 percent?

5. An economy is described by the following equations:

$$C = 2,600 + 0.8(Y - T) - 10,000r,$$
$$I^P = 2,000 - 10,000r,$$
$$G = 1,800,$$
$$NX = 0,$$
$$T = 3,000.$$

The real interest rate, expressed as a decimal, is 0.10 (that is, 10 percent). Find a numerical equation relating planned aggregate expenditure to output. Using a table or other method, solve for short-run equilibrium output. Show your result graphically using the Keynesian cross diagram.

6. For the economy described in problem 5 above:
   a. Potential output Y^* equals 12,000. What real interest rate should the Fed set to bring the economy to full employment? You may take as given that the multiplier for this economy is 5.
   b. Repeat part a for the case in which potential output $Y^* = 9,000$.
   c.* Show that the real interest rate you found in part a sets national saving at potential output, defined as $Y^* - C - G$, equal to planned investment, I^P. This result shows that the real interest rate must be consistent with equilibrium in the market for saving when the economy is at full employment.

7.* Here is another set of equations describing an economy:

$$C = 14,400 + 0.5(Y - T) - 40,000r,$$
$$I^P = 8,000 - 20,000r,$$
$$G = 7,000,$$
$$NX = -1,800,$$
$$T = 8,000,$$
$$Y^* = 40,000.$$

   a. Find a numerical equation relating planned aggregate expenditure to output and to the real interest rate.
   b. At what value should the Fed set the real interest rate to eliminate any output gap? (*Hint:* Set output Y equal to the value of potential output given above in the equation you found in part a. Then solve for the real interest rate that also sets planned aggregate expenditure equal to potential output.)

8. Suppose the Fed follows the following monetary policy reaction function:

$$r = 0.01 + 0.5(\pi - 0.03)$$

   a. What is the Fed's real interest rate target?
   b. What is the Fed's inflation rate target?
   c. Draw this policy reaction on a graph and indicate the value of its slope.
   d. Find the real interest rate and the nominal interest rate that the Fed will set when actual inflation is 3 percent.
   e. Find the real interest rate and the nominal interest rate that the Fed will set when actual inflation is 5 percent.

*Problems marked with an asterisk (*) are more difficult.

9. By law, the Federal Reserve must report twice each year to Congress about monetary policy and the state of the economy. When the Monetary Policy Report is presented, it is customary for the Fed chairman to testify before Congress, to update legislators on the economic situation.

Obtain a copy of the most recent Monetary Policy Report from the Fed's Web page http://www.federalreserve.gov/ (click "Monetary Policy" and follow the links). In the period covered by the testimony, did monetary policy ease, tighten, or remain neutral? What principal developments in the economy led the Fed to take the actions that it did?

▪ ANSWERS TO IN-CHAPTER EXERCISES ▪

14.1 At 4 percent interest, the benefit of each $10,000 reduction in cash holdings is $400 per year (4% × $10,000). In this case, the cost of the extra armored car service, $500 a year, exceeds the benefit of reducing cash holdings by $10,000. Kim's restaurants should therefore continue to hold $50,000 in cash. Comparing this result with Example 14.2, you can see that the demand for money by Kim's restaurants is lower, the higher the nominal interest rate.

14.2 If the nominal interest rate is above its equilibrium value, then people are holding more money than they would like. To bring their money holdings down, they will use some of their money to buy interest-bearing assets such as bonds.

If everyone is trying to buy bonds, however, the price of bonds will be bid up. An increase in bond prices is equivalent to a fall in market interest rates. As interest rates fall, people will be willing to hold more money. Eventually interest rates will fall enough that people are content to hold the amount of money supplied by the Fed, and the money market will be in equilibrium.

14.3 If $r = 0.03$, then consumption is $C = 640 + 0.8(Y - 250) - 400(0.03) = 428 + 0.8Y$, and planned investment is $I^P = 250 - 600(0.03) = 232$. Planned aggregate expenditure is given by

$$PAE = C + I^P + G + NX$$
$$= (428 + 0.8Y) + 232 + 300 + 20$$
$$= 980 + 0.8Y.$$

To find short-run equilibrium output, we can construct a table analogous to Table 14.1. As usual, some trial and error is necessary to find an appropriate range of guesses for output (column 1).

Determination of Short-Run Equilibrium Output

(1) Output Y	(2) Planned aggregate expenditure PAE = 980 + 0.8Y	(3) Y − PAE	(4) Y = PAE?
4,500	4,580	−80	No
4,600	4,660	−60	No
4,700	4,740	−40	No
4,800	4,820	−20	No
4,900	4,900	0	**Yes**
5,000	4,980	20	No
5,100	5,060	40	No
5,200	5,140	60	No
5,300	5,220	80	No
5,400	5,300	100	No
5,500	5,380	120	No

Short-run equilibrium output equals 4,900, as that is the only level of output that satisfies the condition $Y = PAE$.

The answer can be obtained more quickly by simply setting $Y = PAE$ and solving for short-run equilibrium output Y. Remembering that $PAE = 980 + 0.8Y$ and substitution for PAE, we get

$$Y = 980 + 0.8Y$$
$$Y(1 - 0.8) = 980$$
$$Y = 5 \times 980 = 4,900.$$

So lowering the real interest rate from 5 percent to 3 percent increases short-run equilibrium output from 4,800 (as found in Example 14.4) to 4,900.

If you have read Appendix B to the preceding chapter on the multiplier, there is yet another way to find the answer. Using that appendix, we can determine that the multiplier in this model is 5, since $1/(1 - mpc) = 1/(1 - 0.8) = 5$. Each percentage point reduction in the real interest rate increases consumption by 4 units and planned investment by 6 units, for a total impact on planned spending of 10 units per percentage point reduction. Reducing the real interest rate by 2 percentage points, from 5 percent to 3 percent, thus increases autonomous expenditure by 20 units. Because the multiplier is 5, an increase of 20 in autonomous expenditure raises short-run equilibrium output by $20 \times 5 = 100$ units, from the value of 4,800 we found in Example 14.4 to the new value of 4,900.

14.4 When the real interest rate is 5 percent, output is 4,800. Each percentage point reduction in the real interest rate increases autonomous expenditure by 10 units. Since the multiplier in this model is 5, to raise output by 50 units, the real interest rate should be cut by 1 percentage point, from 5 percent to 4 percent. Increasing output by 50 units, to 4,850, eliminates the output gap.

14.5 If $\pi = 0.03$ and the output gap is zero, we can plug these values into the Taylor rule to obtain

$$r = 0.02 + 0.5(0.03 - 0.02) - 0.5(0) = 0.02 + 0.005 = 0.025 = 2.5\%.$$

So the real interest rate implied by the Taylor rule when inflation is 3 percent and the output gap is zero is 2.5 percent. The nominal interest rate equals the real rate plus the inflation rate, or $2.5\% + 3\% = 5.5\%$.

If there is a recessionary gap of 1 percent of potential output, the Taylor rule formula becomes

$$r = 0.02 + 0.5(0.03 - 0.02) - 0.5(0.01) = 0.02 + 0.5(0.01) - 0.5(0.01)$$
$$= 0.02 = 2\%$$

The nominal interest rate implied by the Taylor rule in this case is the 2 percent real rate plus the 3 percent inflation rate, or $2 + 3 = 5$ percent. So the Taylor rule has the Fed lowering the real interest rate when the economy goes into recession, which is both sensible and realistic.

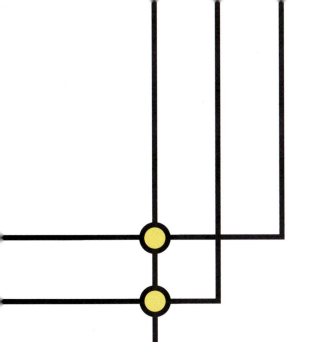

MONETARY POLICY IN THE BASIC KEYNESIAN MODEL

This appendix extends the algebraic analysis of the basic Keynesian model that was presented in Appendix A to the last chapter to include the role of monetary policy. The main difference from that appendix is that in this analysis, the real interest rate is allowed to affect planned spending. We will not describe the supply and demand for money algebraically but will simply assume that the Fed can set the real interest rate r at any level it chooses.

The real interest rate affects consumption and planned investment. To capture these effects, we will modify the equations for those two components of spending as follows:

$$C = \overline{C} + mpc(Y - T) - ar,$$

$$I^P = \overline{I} - br.$$

The first equation is the consumption function with an additional term, equal to $-ar$. Think of a as a fixed number, greater than zero, that measures the strength of the interest rate effect on consumption. Thus, the term $-ar$ captures the idea that when the real interest rate r rises, consumption declines by a times the increase in the interest rate. Likewise, the second equation adds the term $-br$ to the equation for planned investment spending. The parameter b is a fixed positive number that measures how strongly changes in the real interest rate affect planned investment; for example, if the real interest rate r rises, planned investment is assumed to decline by b times the increase in the real interest rate. We continue to assume that government purchases, taxes, and net exports are exogenous variables, so that $G = \overline{G}$, $T = \overline{T}$, and $NX = \overline{NX}$.

To solve for short-run equilibrium output, we start as usual by finding the relationship of planned aggregate expenditure to output. The definition of planned aggregate expenditure is

$$PAE = C + I^P + G + NX.$$

Substituting the modified equations for consumption and planned investment into this definition, along with the exogenous values of government spending, net exports, and taxes, we get

$$PAE = \left[\overline{C} + mpc(Y - \overline{T}) - ar\right] + \left[\overline{I} - br\right] + \overline{G} + \overline{NX}.$$

The first term in brackets on the right side describes the behavior of consumption, and the second bracketed term describes planned investment. Rearranging this equation in order to group together terms that depend on the real interest rate and terms that depend on output, we find

$$PAE = \left[\overline{C} - mpc\overline{T} + \overline{I} + \overline{G} + \overline{NX}\right] - (a + b)r + mpcY.$$

This equation is similar to Equation 13A.1, in Appendix A to the last chapter, except that it has an extra term, $-(a + b)r$, on the right side. This extra term captures the idea that an increase in the real interest rate reduces consumption and planned investment, lowering planned spending. Notice that the term $-(a + b)r$ is part of autonomous expenditure, since it does not depend on output. Since autonomous expenditure determines the intercept of the expenditure line in the Keynesian cross diagram, changes in the real interest rate will shift the expenditure line up (if the real interest rate decreases) or down (if the real interest rate increases).

To find short-run equilibrium output, we use the definition of short-run equilibrium output to set $Y = PAE$ and solve for Y:

$$Y = PAE$$
$$= \left[\overline{C} - mpc\overline{T} + \overline{I} + \overline{G} + \overline{NX}\right] - (a + b)r + mpcY$$
$$Y(1 - mpc) = \left[\overline{C} - mpc\overline{T} + \overline{I} + \overline{G} + \overline{NX}\right] - (a + b)r$$
$$Y = \left(\frac{1}{1 - mpc}\right)\left[(\overline{C} - mpc\overline{T} + \overline{I} + \overline{G} + \overline{NX}) - (a + b)r\right]. \qquad (14A.1)$$

Equation 14A.1 shows that short-run equilibrium output once again equals the multiplier, $1/(1 - mpc)$, times autonomous expenditure, $\overline{C} - mpc\overline{T} + \overline{I} + \overline{G} + \overline{NX} - (a + b)r$. Autonomous expenditure in turn depends on the real interest rate r. The equation also shows that the impact of a change in the real interest rate on short-run equilibrium output depends on two factors: (1) the effect of a change in the real interest rate on consumption and planned investment, which depends on the magnitude of $(a + b)$, and (2) the size of the multiplier, $1/(1 - mpc)$, which relates changes in autonomous expenditure to changes in short-run equilibrium output. The larger the effect of the real interest rate on planned spending, and the larger the multiplier, the more powerful will be the effect of a given change in the real interest rate on short-run equilibrium output.

To check Equation 14A.1, we can use it to resolve Example 14.4 (see page 400). In that example, we are given $\overline{C} = 640$, $\overline{I} = 250$, $\overline{G} = 300$, $\overline{NX} = 20$, $\overline{T} = 250$, $mpc = 0.8$, $a = 400$, and $b = 600$. The real interest rate set by the Fed is 5 percent, or 0.05. Substituting these values into Equation 14A.1 and solving, we obtain

$$Y = \left(\frac{1}{1 - 0.8}\right)\left[640 - 0.8 \times 250 + 250 + 300 + 20 - (400 + 600) \times 0.05\right]$$
$$= 5 \times 960 = 4,800$$

This is the same result we found in Example 14.4.

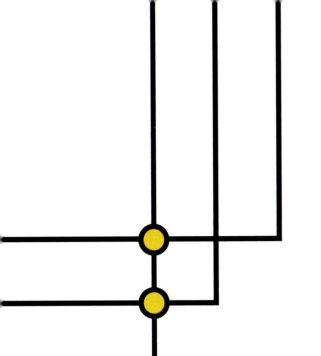

INFLATION, AGGREGATE SUPPLY, AND AGGREGATE DEMAND

During the summer and fall of 1996, Federal Reserve chairman Alan Greenspan was under increasing pressure by many economists to increase interest rates. The unemployment rate was falling and stood below 5.5 percent, generally considered to be the natural unemployment rate at that time. The rapid pace of economic growth suggested that an expansionary gap would soon appear, which meant that inflation would not be far behind. These economists urged Greenspan to increase the federal funds rate to slow the economy and prevent a possible surge in inflation.

Yet Greenspan was unconvinced. He thought he saw evidence of new economic developments that would permit the rapid growth to continue without increased inflation. If he was right, an aggressive increase in interest rates was not only unnecessary but could damage the economy. What did Greenspan see? Did the Fed raise interest rates in 1996? What happened to output and inflation? We will discuss Greenspan's decision later in this chapter (in Economic Naturalist 15.3), but first we need to introduce the basic framework for understanding inflation and the policies used to control it.

In the previous two chapters we made the assumption that firms are willing to meet the demand for their products at preset prices. When firms simply produce what is demanded, the level of planned aggregate expenditure determines the nation's real GDP. If the resulting level of short-run equilibrium output is lower than potential output, a recessionary output gap develops, and if the resulting level of output exceeds potential output, the economy experiences an expansionary gap. As we saw in the previous two chapters, policymakers can attempt to eliminate output gaps by taking actions that affect the level of autonomous expenditure, such as changing the level of government spending or taxes (fiscal policy) or using the Fed's control of the money supply to change the real interest rate (monetary policy).

The basic Keynesian model is useful for understanding the role of spending in the short-run determination of output, but it is too simplified to provide a fully realistic description of the economy. The main shortcoming of the basic Keynesian model is that it does not explain the behavior of *inflation*. Indeed, the model represents a special case in which prices are constant and inflation is zero. Although firms may meet demand at preset prices for a time, as assumed in the basic Keynesian model, prices do *not* remain fixed indefinitely. Indeed, sometimes they may rise quite rapidly—the phenomenon of high inflation—imposing significant costs on the economy in the process. In this chapter, we will extend the basic Keynesian model to allow for ongoing inflation. As we will show, the extended model can be conveniently represented by a new diagram, called the *aggregate demand–aggregate supply diagram*. Using this extended analysis, we will be able to show how macroeconomic policies affect inflation as well as output, illustrating in the process the difficult trade-offs policymakers sometimes face. We will emphasize numerical and graphical analysis of output and inflation in the body of the chapter. The appendix at the end of the next chapter presents an algebraic treatment.

aggregate demand (AD) curve shows the relationship between short-run equilibrium output Y and the rate of inflation π; the name of the curve reflects the fact that short-run equilibrium output is determined by, and equals, total planned spending in the economy; increases in inflation reduce planned spending and short-run equilibrium output, so the aggregate demand curve is downward-sloping

INFLATION, SPENDING, AND OUTPUT: THE AGGREGATE DEMAND CURVE

To begin incorporating inflation into the model, our first step is to introduce a new relationship, called the *aggregate demand curve*, which is shown graphically in Figure 15.1. The **aggregate demand (AD) curve** shows the relationship between short-run equilibrium output Y and the rate of inflation, denoted π. The name of the curve reflects the fact that, as we have seen, short-run equilibrium output is determined by total planned spending, or demand, in the economy. Indeed, by definition, short-run equilibrium output *equals* planned aggregate expenditure, so

FIGURE 15.1

The Aggregate Demand Curve.

The aggregate demand curve *AD* shows the relationship between short-run equilibrium output Y and the rate of inflation π. Because short-run equilibrium output equals planned spending, the *AD* curve also shows the relationship between inflation and planned spending. The downward slope of the *AD* curve implies that an increase in inflation reduces short-run equilibrium output.

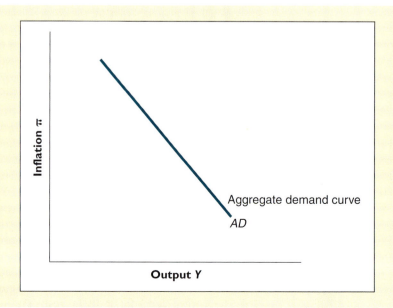

Aggregate demand curve
AD

Inflation π

Output Y

that we could just as well say that the *AD* curve shows the relationship between inflation and spending.[1]

We will see shortly that, all else being equal, *an increase in the rate of inflation tends to reduce short-run equilibrium output.* Therefore, in a diagram showing inflation π on the vertical axis and output Y on the horizontal axis (Figure 15.1), the aggregate demand curve is downward-sloping.[2] Note that we refer to the *AD* "curve," even though the relationship is drawn as a straight line in Figure 15.1. In general, the *AD* curve can be either straight or curving.

Why does higher inflation lead to a lower level of planned spending and short-run equilibrium output? As we will see next, one important reason is the Fed's response to increases in inflation.

INFLATION, THE FED, AND THE *AD* CURVE

One of the primary responsibilities of the Fed, or any central bank, is to maintain a low and stable rate of inflation. For example, in recent years, the Fed has tried to keep inflation in the United States in the range of 2 to 3 percent. By keeping inflation low, the central bank tries to avoid the costs high inflation imposes on the economy.

What can the Fed do to keep inflation low and stable? As we have already mentioned, one situation that is likely to lead to increased inflation is an expansionary output gap, in which short-run equilibrium output exceeds potential output. When output is above potential output, firms must produce at above-normal capacity to meet the demands of their customers. Like Al's ice cream store, described in the chapter "Short-Term Economic Fluctuations," firms may be willing to do this for a time. But eventually they will adjust to the high level of demand by raising prices, contributing to inflation. To control inflation, then, the Fed needs to dampen planned spending and output when they threaten to exceed potential output.

How can the Fed avoid a situation of economic "overheating," in which spending and output exceed potential output? As we saw in the previous chapter, the Fed can act to reduce autonomous expenditure, and hence short-run equilibrium output, by raising the real interest rate. This behavior by the Fed is a key factor that underlies the link between inflation and output that is summarized by the aggregate demand curve. When inflation is high—that is, when inflation is above the Fed's target inflation rate—the Fed responds by raising the real interest rate (as implied by the Fed's monetary *policy reaction function*, introduced in the last chapter).[3] The increase in the real interest rate reduces consumption and investment spending (autonomous expenditure) and hence reduces short-run equilibrium output. Because higher inflation leads, through the Fed's actions, to a reduction in output, the aggregate demand (*AD*) curve is downward-sloping, as Figure 15.1 shows. We can summarize this chain of reasoning symbolically as follows:

$$\pi \uparrow \Rightarrow r \uparrow \Rightarrow \text{autonomous expenditure} \downarrow \Rightarrow Y \downarrow \qquad (AD \text{ curve})$$

where, recall, π is inflation, r is the real interest rate, and Y is output.

---

[1]It is important to distinguish the aggregate demand curve from the expenditure line, introduced as part of the Keynesian cross diagram in the chapter "Spending and Output in the Short Run." The upward-sloping expenditure line shows the relationship between planned aggregate expenditure and output. Again, the aggregate demand (*AD*) curve shows the relationship between short-run equilibrium output (which equals planned spending) and inflation.

[2]Economists sometimes define the aggregate demand curve as the relationship between aggregate demand and the *price level*, rather than inflation, which is the *rate of change* of the price level. The definition used here both simplifies the analysis and yields results more consistent with real-world data. For a comparison of the two approaches, see David Romer, "Keynesian Macroeconomics without the LM Curve," *Journal of Economic Perspectives,* Spring 2000, pp. 149–170. The graphical analysis used in this chapter follows closely the approach recommended by Romer.

[3]Recall from our earlier discussion that the Fed uses a nominal interest rate to announce its intentions. According to the policy reaction function, the Fed increases the real interest rate when inflation rises. It does this by acting to increase the nominal interest rate by more than the increase in inflation.

FIGURE 15.2

The Aggregate Demand Curve and the Monetary Policy Reaction Function.
(a) With the Fed's target real interest rate r^* and target inflation rate π^* held fixed, the Fed will respond to an increase in inflation from π_1 to π_2 by increasing the real interest rate from r_1 to r_2. This increase in r will create a movement along the monetary policy reaction function, from point A to point B. (b) The increase in the real interest rate will reduce the equilibrium level of output, leading to a movement along the aggregate demand curve, from point A to point B. Thus, higher inflation causes the Fed to increase r, which reduces output.

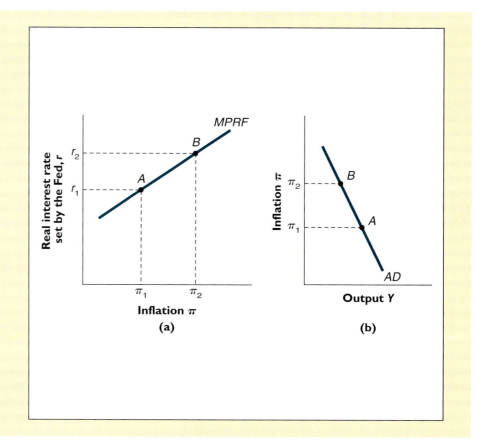

These changes are illustrated in Figure 15.2. In Figure 15.2(a), we have redrawn the Fed's monetary policy reaction function from Figure 14.9. With the Fed's target real interest rate r^* and target inflation rate π^* held fixed, an increase in inflation from π_1 to π_2 will cause the Fed to raise the real interest rate from r_1 to r_2. The increase in the real interest rate will create a movement along the monetary policy reaction function, from point A to point B. In Figure 15.2(b), the increase in the real interest rate will create a similar movement along the aggregate demand curve, again from point A to point B.

OTHER REASONS FOR THE DOWNWARD SLOPE OF THE *AD* CURVE

Although we focus here on the behavior of the Fed as the source of the *AD* curve's downward slope, there are other channels through which higher inflation reduces planned spending and thus short-run equilibrium output. Hence, the downward slope of the *AD* curve does not depend on the Fed behaving in the particular way just described.

One additional reason for the downward slope of the *AD* curve is the effect of inflation on the *real value of money* held by households and businesses. At high levels of inflation, the purchasing power of money held by the public declines rapidly. This reduction in the public's real wealth may cause households to restrain consumption spending, reducing short-run equilibrium output.

A second channel by which inflation may affect planned spending is through *distributional effects*. Studies have found that people who are less well off are often hurt more by inflation than wealthier people are. For example, retirees on fixed incomes and workers receiving the minimum wage (which is set in dollar terms) lose buying power when prices are rising rapidly. Less affluent people are also likely to be relatively unsophisticated in making financial investments and hence less able than wealthier citizens to protect their savings against inflation.

People at the lower end of the income distribution tend to spend a greater percentage of their disposable income than do wealthier individuals. Thus, if a burst of inflation redistributes resources from relatively high-spending, less affluent households toward relatively high-saving, more affluent households, overall spending may decline.

A third connection between inflation and aggregate demand arises because higher rates of inflation generate *uncertainty* for households and businesses. When inflation is high, people become less certain about what things will cost in the future, and uncertainty makes planning more difficult. In an uncertain economic environment, both households and firms may become more cautious, reducing their spending as a result.

A final link between inflation and total spending operates through the *prices of domestic goods and services sold abroad*. As we will see in the chapter "Exchange Rates and the Open Economy," the foreign price of domestic goods depends in part on the rate at which the domestic currency, such as the dollar, exchanges for foreign currencies, such as the British pound. However, for constant rates of exchange between currencies, a rise in domestic inflation causes the prices of domestic goods in foreign markets to rise more quickly. As domestic goods become relatively more expensive to prospective foreign purchasers, export sales decline. Net exports are part of aggregate expenditure, and so once more we find that increased inflation is likely to reduce spending. All these factors contribute to the downward slope of the *AD* curve, together with the behavior of the Fed.

SHIFTS OF THE AGGREGATE DEMAND CURVE

The downward slope of the aggregate demand, or *AD*, curve shown in Figure 15.1 reflects the fact that *all other factors held constant*, a higher level of inflation will lead to lower planned spending and thus lower short-run equilibrium output. Again, a principal reason higher inflation reduces planned spending and output is that the Fed tends to react to increases in inflation by raising the real interest rate, which in turn reduces consumption and planned investment, two important components of planned aggregate expenditure.

However, even if inflation is held constant, various factors can affect planned spending and short-run equilibrium output. Graphically, as we will see in this section, these factors will cause the *AD* curve to shift. Specifically, for a given level of inflation, if there is a change in the economy that *increases* short-run equilibrium output, the *AD* curve will shift to the *right*. If, on the other hand, the change *reduces* short-run equilibrium output at each level of inflation, the *AD* curve will shift to the *left*. We will focus on two sorts of changes in the economy that shift the aggregate demand curve: (1) *exogenous* changes in spending, which are changes in spending caused by factors other than output or interest rates, and (2) changes in the Fed's monetary policy, as reflected in a shift in the Fed's monetary policy reaction function.

Changes in Spending

We have seen that planned aggregate expenditure depends both on output (through the consumption function) and on the real interest rate (which affects both consumption and planned investment). However, many factors other than output or the real interest rate can affect planned spending. For example, at given levels of output and the real interest rate, fiscal policy affects the level of government purchases, and changes in consumer confidence can affect consumption spending. Likewise, new technological opportunities may lead firms to increase their planned investment, and an increased willingness of foreigners to purchase domestic goods will raise net exports. We will refer to changes in planned spending that are not caused by changes in output or the real interest rate as *exogenous* changes in spending.

FIGURE 15.3

Effect of an Increase in Exogenous Spending.

The *AD* curve is seen both *before* (AD) and *after* (AD') an increase in exogenous spending—specifically, an increase in consumption spending resulting from a rise in the stock market. If the inflation rate and the real interest rate set by the Fed are held constant, an increase in exogenous spending raises short-run equilibrium output. As a result, the *AD* curve will shift to the right, from *AD* to *AD'*.

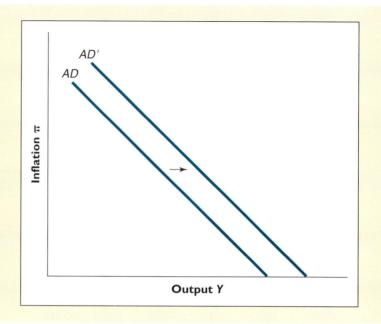

For a given inflation rate (and thus for a given real interest rate set by the Fed), an exogenous increase in spending raises short-run equilibrium output, for the reasons we have discussed in the past two chapters. Because it increases output at each level of inflation, *an exogenous increase in spending shifts the AD curve to the right*. This result is illustrated graphically in Figure 15.3. Imagine, for example, that a rise in the stock market makes consumers more willing to spend (the wealth effect). Then, for each level of inflation, aggregate spending and short-run equilibrium output will be higher, a change that is shown as a shift of the *AD* curve to the right, from *AD* to *AD'*.

Similarly, at a given inflation rate, an exogenous decline in spending—for example, a fall in government purchases resulting from a more restrictive fiscal policy—causes short-run equilibrium output to fall. We conclude that *an exogenous decrease in spending shifts the AD curve to the left*.

EXERCISE 15.1

Determine how the following events will affect the *AD* curve:

a. Due to widespread concerns about future weakness in the economy, businesses reduce their spending on new capital.

b. The federal government reduces income taxes.

Changes in the Fed's Target Inflation Rate

Recall that the Fed's monetary policy reaction function describes how the Fed sets the real interest rate at each level of inflation. The monetary policy reaction function is determined from Equation 14.2 as

$$r = r^* + g(\pi - \pi^*).$$

Suppose for now that the Fed's target real interest rate r^* and its target inflation rate π^* are held constant. This equation for the Fed's monetary policy reaction function then implies that the Fed will raise the actual real interest rate r in response to an increase in inflation π. Furthermore, the parameter g implies that every time inflation rises by an additional percentage point, the Fed will raise the real interest rate

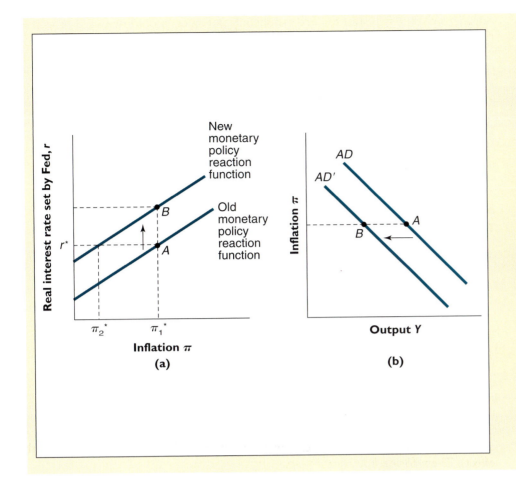

FIGURE 15.4

A Shift in the Fed's Monetary Policy Reaction Function.

The Fed chooses a "tighter" monetary policy by reducing its target inflation rate and setting the real interest rate at a higher level than usual for each given rate of inflation. Graphically, this change corresponds to an upward (or leftward) shift in the Fed's monetary policy reaction function (a). This change to a tighter monetary policy shifts the AD curve to the left (b). If a protracted recession led the Fed to increase its target inflation rate and set a lower real interest rate at each level of inflation, the Fed's monetary policy reaction function would shift downward (rightward) and the AD curve would shift to the right.

by g percentage points. The Fed's adjustment of the real interest rate in response to changes in inflation is an important reason that the AD curve is downward-sloping, as we already have seen. In particular, changes in the real interest rate r in response to changes in the inflation rate π result in movements along the AD curve, as in Figure 15.2, and not in a shift of the AD curve. Under normal circumstances, the Fed generally follows a stable monetary policy reaction function with constant values of r^* and π^*, implying that the Fed's normal actions do not shift the AD curve.

Sometimes, however, the Fed switches to a tighter or easier monetary policy than normal for a particular rate of inflation. In that event, the Fed changes its target inflation rate, and both the monetary policy reaction function and the aggregate demand curve will shift. For example, Figure 15.4 illustrates what happens when the Fed reduces its target inflation rate.

Suppose the economy is initially at point A in both graphs, and inflation π is initially equal to its target π_1^*. Thus, the Fed initially sets $r = r^*$ when $\pi = \pi_1^*$. If the Fed chooses a tighter monetary policy, it *reduces* its target inflation rate to π_2^*. The Fed will now set the real interest rate r equal to its target real interest rate r^* when (actual) inflation is equal to its new lower target inflation rate π_2^*. This change in π^* will shift the monetary policy reaction function in Figure 15.4(a) upward (to the left). At the initial level of inflation, the Fed will raise the real interest rate r to point B on the new monetary policy reaction function even though r^* has not changed. The increase in r will reduce planned expenditure and the short-run equilibrium output at the initial rate of inflation. In summary, an upward (leftward) shift of the Fed's monetary policy reaction function leads the AD curve to shift to the left, to AD' in Figure 15.4(b).

Conversely, if the nation is experiencing an unusually severe and protracted recession, the Fed may choose a looser monetary policy by raising its target inflation rate. This change will shift the Fed's monetary policy reaction downward or to the right. The reduction in the real interest rate at the initial rate of inflation would lead to higher levels of expenditure and short-run equilibrium output. Therefore, a downward (rightward) shift in the Fed's monetary policy reaction function shifts the *AD* curve right.

As we will see in the next chapter, the monetary policy reaction function also will shift if the Fed changes its target real interest rate r^*. Throughout this chapter, however, we will assume that the Fed's target real interest rate r^* remains unchanged. Consequently, in this chapter, shifts in the Fed's monetary policy reaction function occur only when the Fed changes its target inflation rate π^*.

SHIFTS OF THE AD CURVE VERSUS MOVEMENTS ALONG THE AD CURVE

Let's end this section by reviewing and summarizing the important distinction between *movements along* the *AD* curve and *shifts* of the *AD* curve.

The downward slope of the *AD* curve captures the inverse relationship between inflation, on the one hand, and short-run equilibrium output, on the other. As we have seen, a rise in the inflation rate leads the Fed to raise the real interest rate, according to its monetary policy reaction function. The higher real interest rate, in turn, depresses planned spending and hence lowers short-run equilibrium output. The downward slope of the *AD* curve embodies this relationship among inflation, spending, and output. Hence, changes in the inflation rate, and the resulting changes in the real interest rate and short-run equilibrium output resulting from movements along a stationary monetary policy reaction function, are represented by *movements along* the *AD* curve. In particular, as long as the Fed sets the real interest rate in accordance with a fixed monetary policy reaction function, changes in the real interest rate will *not* shift the *AD* curve.

These changes are summarized as follows:

Figure 15.2
(no change in π^*): $\pi \uparrow \Rightarrow$ Movement along a stationary monetary $\Rightarrow r \uparrow \Rightarrow$ Movement along a stationary aggregate policy reaction function   demand curve

However, any factor that changes the short-run equilibrium level of output *at a given level of inflation* will *shift* the *AD* curve—to the right if short-run equilibrium output increases, or to the left if short-run equilibrium output decreases. We have identified two factors that can shift the *AD* curve: exogenous changes in spending (that is, changes in spending that are not caused by changes in output or the real interest rate) and changes in the Fed's inflation rate target. (Remember, we will postpone discussing changes in r^* until the next chapter.) An exogenous increase in spending increases short-run equilibrium output at every level of inflation, hence shifting the *AD* curve to the right.

Figure 15.3: Exogenous increase in spending $\Rightarrow$ Shift in aggregate demand curve to the right

The aggregate demand curve also will shift to the right if the Fed *raises* its inflation target, as in Exercise 15.2, which is the opposite of Figure 15.4.

EXERCISE 15.2

Draw the appropriate monetary policy reaction functions and aggregate demand curves and explain what happens when the Fed increases its inflation target.

An increase in the Fed's inflation rate target would shift the Fed's monetary policy reaction function down (right) and also would shift the AD curve right.

Exercise 15.2   Shift in monetary policy   Shift in the
(opposite of: Increase in $\pi^* \Rightarrow$ reaction function $\Rightarrow$ aggregate demand
Figure 15.4)   to the right   curve to the right

Conversely, an exogenous decline in spending or a reduction in the Fed's inflation rate target (as in Figure 15.4) decreases short-run equilibrium output at every level of inflation, shifting the AD curve to the left.

The key to determining whether action by the Federal Reserve has shifted the AD curve is to think about the Fed's targets. When the Fed responds to inflation by changing the real interest rate but does not change its inflation target, the economy moves along a stationary AD curve. On the other hand, when the Fed shifts its monetary policy function by changing its inflation target, the AD curve also will shift in the same direction.

EXERCISE 15.3

What is the difference, if any, between the following?

a. An upward (leftward) shift in the Fed's monetary policy reaction function.

b. A response by the Fed to higher inflation, for a given monetary policy reaction function.

How does each scenario affect the AD curve?

RECAP	THE AGGREGATE DEMAND (AD) CURVE

■ The AD curve shows the relationship between short-run equilibrium output and inflation. Higher inflation leads the Fed to raise the real interest rate, which reduces autonomous expenditure and thus short-run equilibrium output. Therefore, the AD curve slopes downward.

■ The AD curve also may slope downward because (1) higher inflation reduces the real value of money held by the public, reducing wealth and spending; (2) inflation redistributes resources from less affluent people, who spend a high percentage of their disposable income, to more affluent people, who spend a smaller percentage of disposable income; (3) higher inflation creates greater uncertainty in planning for households and firms, reducing their spending; and (4) for a constant rate of exchange between the dollar and other currencies, rising prices of domestic goods and services reduce foreign sales and hence net exports (a component of aggregate spending).

■ If the Fed does not change its target inflation rate, the Fed's monetary policy reaction function will not shift and changes in inflation correspond to movements *along* the AD curve; they do not *shift* the AD curve.

■ An exogenous increase in spending raises short-run equilibrium output at each value of inflation, and so shifts the AD curve to the right. Exogenous increases in spending result from increases in $\overline{C}, \overline{I}, \overline{G},$ and $\overline{NX}$, or a decrease in $\overline{T}$. Conversely, an exogenous decrease in spending shifts the AD curve to the left.

■ A change to an easier monetary policy, as reflected by an increase in the Fed's target inflation rate and a downward (rightward) shift in its monetary policy reaction function, shifts the *AD* curve to the right. A change to a tighter, more anti-inflationary monetary policy, as reflected by a decrease in the Fed's target inflation rate and an upward (leftward) shift in the Fed's monetary policy reaction function, shifts the *AD* curve to the left.

INFLATION AND AGGREGATE SUPPLY

Thus far in this chapter, we have focused on how changes in inflation affect spending and short-run equilibrium output, a relationship captured by the *AD* curve. But we have not yet discussed how inflation itself is determined. From the chapter "Money, Prices, and the Federal Reserve," we know that in the long run, inflation is determined primarily by the growth of the money supply. In the rest of this chapter, however, we will examine the main factors that determine the inflation rate in modern industrial economies in the short, medium, and long run, as well as the options that policymakers have to control inflation. In doing so, we will introduce a useful diagram for analyzing the behavior of output and inflation, called the *aggregate demand–aggregate supply diagram*.

Physicists have noted that a body will tend to keep moving at a constant speed and direction unless it is acted upon by some outside force—a tendency they refer to as *inertia*. Applying this concept to economics, many observers have noted that inflation seems to be inertial, in the sense that it tends to remain roughly constant as long as the economy is at full employment and there are no external shocks to the price level. In the first part of this section, we will discuss why inflation behaves in this way.

However, just as a physical object will change speed if it is acted on by outside forces, so various economic forces can change the rate of inflation. Later in this section, we will discuss three factors that can cause the inflation rate to change. The first is the presence of an *output gap*: Inflation tends to rise when there is an expansionary output gap and to fall when there is a recessionary output gap. The second factor that can affect the inflation rate is a shock that directly affects prices, which we will refer to as an *inflation shock*. A large increase in the price of imported oil, for example, raises the price of gasoline, heating oil, and other fuels, as well as of goods made with oil or services using oil. Finally, the third factor that directly affects the inflation rate is a *shock to potential output*, or a sharp change in the level of potential output—a natural disaster that destroyed a significant portion of a country's factories and businesses is one extreme example. Together, inflationary shocks and shocks to potential output are known as *aggregate supply shocks*.

INFLATION INERTIA

In low-inflation industrial economies like that of the United States today, inflation tends to change relatively slowly from year to year, a phenomenon that is sometimes referred to as *inflation inertia*. If the rate of inflation in one year is 2 percent, it may be 3 percent or even 4 percent in the next year. But unless the nation experiences very unusual economic conditions, inflation is unlikely to rise to 6 percent or 8 percent or fall to −2 percent in the following year. This relatively sluggish behavior contrasts sharply with the behavior of economic variables such as stock or commodity prices, which can change rapidly from day to day. For example, oil prices might well rise by 20 percent over the course of a year and then fall 20 percent over the next year. Yet since about 1992, the U.S. inflation rate has generally remained in the range of 2–3 percent per year.

Why does inflation tend to adjust relatively slowly in modern industrial economies? To answer this question, we must consider two closely related factors that play an important role in determining the inflation rate: the behavior of the public's *inflation expectations* and the existence of *long-term wage and price contracts*.

First, consider the public's expectations about inflation. In negotiating future wages and prices, both buyers and sellers take into account the rate of inflation they expect to prevail in the next few years. As a result, today's *expectations* of future inflation may help to determine the future inflation rate. Suppose, for example, that office worker Fred and his boss Colleen agree that Fred's performance this past year justifies an increase of 2 percent in his real wage for next year. What *nominal*, or dollar, wage increase should they agree on? If Fred believes that inflation is likely to be 3 percent over the next year, he will ask for a 5 percent increase in his nominal wage to obtain a 2 percent increase in his real wage. If Colleen agrees that inflation is likely to be 3 percent, she should be willing to go along with a 5 percent nominal increase, knowing that it implies only a 2 percent increase in Fred's real wage. Thus, the rate at which Fred and Colleen *expect* prices to rise affects the rate at which at least one price—Fred's nominal wage—*actually* rises.

A similar dynamic affects the contracts for production inputs other than labor. For example, if Colleen is negotiating with her office supply company, the prices she will agree to pay for next year's deliveries of copy paper and staples will depend on what she expects the inflation rate to be. If Colleen anticipates that the price of office supplies will not change relative to the prices of other goods and services, and that the general inflation rate will be 3 percent, then she should be willing to agree to a 3 percent increase in the price of office supplies. On the other hand, if she expects the general inflation rate to be 6 percent, then she will agree to pay 6 percent more for copy paper and staples next year, knowing that a nominal increase of 6 percent implies no change in the price of office supplies relative to other goods and services.

Economywide, then, the higher the expected rate of inflation, the more nominal wages and the cost of other inputs will tend to rise. But if wages and other costs of production grow rapidly in response to expected inflation, firms will have to raise their prices rapidly as well in order to cover their costs. Thus, a high rate of expected inflation tends to lead to a high rate of actual inflation. Similarly, if expected inflation is low, leading wages and other costs to rise relatively slowly, actual inflation should be low as well.

EXERCISE 15.4

Assume that employers and workers agree that real wages should rise by 2 percent next year.

a. **If inflation is expected to be 2 percent next year, what will happen to nominal wages next year?**

b. **If inflation is expected to be 4 percent next year, rather than 2 percent, what will happen to nominal wages next year?**

c. **Use your answers from parts a and b to explain how an increase in expected inflation will tend to affect the following year's actual rate of inflation.**

The conclusion that actual inflation is partially determined by expected inflation raises the question of what determines inflation expectations. To a great extent, people's expectations are influenced by their recent experience. If inflation has been low and stable for some time, people are likely to expect it to continue to be low. But if inflation has recently been high, people will expect it to continue to be high. If inflation has been unpredictable, alternating between low and high levels, the public's expectations will likewise tend to be volatile, rising or falling with news or rumors about economic conditions or economic policy.

Figure 15.5 illustrates schematically how low and stable inflation may tend to be self-perpetuating. As the figure shows, if inflation has been low for some time, people will continue to expect low inflation. Increases in nominal wages and other production costs thus will tend to be small. If firms raise prices only by enough to cover costs, then actual inflation will be low, as expected. This low actual rate in turn will promote low expected inflation, perpetuating the "virtuous circle." The same logic applies in reverse in an economy with high inflation: A persistently high inflation rate leads the public to expect high inflation, resulting in higher increases in nominal wages and other production costs. This in turn contributes to a high rate of actual inflation, and so on in a vicious circle. This role of inflation expectations in the determination of wage and price increases helps to explain why inflation often seems to adjust slowly.

FIGURE 15.5

A Virtuous Circle of Low Inflation and Low Expected Inflation.

Low inflation leads people to expect low inflation in the future. As a result, they agree to accept small increases in wages and in the prices of the goods and services they supply, which keeps inflation—and expected inflation—low. In a similar way, high inflation leads people to expect high inflation, which in turn tends to produce high inflation.

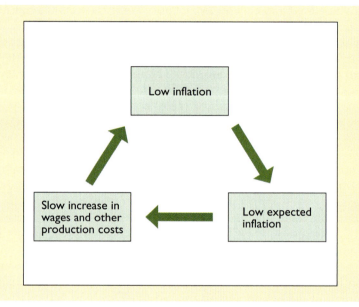

The role of inflation expectations in the slow adjustment of inflation is strengthened by a second key element, the existence of *long-term wage and price contracts*. Union wage contracts, for example, often extend for three years into the future. Likewise, contracts that set the prices manufacturing firms pay for parts and raw materials often cover several years. Long-term contracts serve to "build in" wage and price increases that depend on inflation expectations at the time the contracts were signed. For example, a union negotiating in a high-inflation environment is much more likely to demand a rapid increase in nominal wages over the life of the contract than would a union in an economy in which prices are stable.

To summarize, in the absence of external shocks, inflation tends to remain relatively stable over time—at least in low-inflation industrial economies like that of the United States. In other words, inflation is *inertial* (or as some people put it, "sticky"). Inflation tends to be inertial for two main reasons. The first is the behavior of people's expectations of inflation. A low inflation rate leads people to expect low inflation in the future, which results in reduced pressure for wage and price increases. Similarly, a high inflation rate leads people to expect high inflation in the future, resulting in more rapid increases in wages and prices. The effects of expectations are reinforced by the existence of long-term wage and price contracts, which is the second reason inflation tends to be stable over time. Long-term contracts tend to build in the effects of people's inflation expectations.

Although the rate of inflation tends to be inertial, it does of course change over time. We next discuss a key factor causing the inflation rate to change.

EXERCISE 15.5

Based on Figure 15.5, discuss why the Federal Reserve has a strong incentive to maintain a low inflation rate in the economy.

THE OUTPUT GAP AND INFLATION

An important factor influencing the rate of inflation is the output gap, or the difference between potential output and actual output ($Y^* - Y$). We have seen that, in the short run, firms will meet the demand for their output at previously determined prices. For example, Al's ice cream shop will serve ice cream to any customer who comes into the shop at the prices posted behind the counter. The level of output that is determined by the demand at preset prices is called *short-run equilibrium output*.

At a particular time, the level of short-run equilibrium output may happen to equal the economy's long-run productive capacity, or potential output. But that is not necessarily the case. Output may exceed potential output, giving rise to an expansionary gap, or it may fall short of potential output, producing a recessionary gap. Let's consider what happens to inflation in each of these three possible cases: no output gap, an expansionary gap, and a recessionary gap.

If actual output equals potential output, then by definition there is no output gap. When the output gap is zero, firms are satisfied, in the sense that their sales equal their maximum sustainable production rates. As a result, firms have no incentive either to reduce or increase their prices *relative* to the prices of other goods and services. However, the fact that firms are satisfied with their sales does *not* imply that inflation—the rate of change in the overall price level—is zero.

To see why, let's go back to the idea of inflation inertia. Suppose that inflation has recently been steady at 3 percent per year, so that the public has come to expect an inflation rate of 3 percent per year. If the public's inflation expectations are reflected in the wage and price increases agreed to in long-term contracts, then firms will find their labor and materials costs are rising at 3 percent per year. To cover their costs, firms will need to raise their prices by 3 percent per year. Note that if all firms are raising their prices by 3 percent per year, the *relative* prices of various goods and services in the economy—say, the price of ice cream relative to the price of a taxi ride—will not change. Nevertheless, the economywide rate of inflation equals 3 percent, the same as in previous years. We conclude that, *if the output gap is zero, the rate of inflation will tend to remain the same.*

Suppose instead that an expansionary gap exists, so that most firms' sales exceed their maximum sustainable production rates. As we might expect in situations in which the quantity demanded exceeds the quantity firms desire to supply, firms will ultimately respond by trying to increase their relative prices. To do so, they will increase their prices by *more* than the increase in their costs. If all firms behave this way, then the general price level will begin to rise more rapidly than before. Thus, *when an expansionary gap exists, the rate of inflation will tend to increase.*

Finally, if a recessionary gap exists, firms will be selling an amount less than their capacity to produce, and they will have an incentive to cut their relative prices so they can sell more. In this case, firms will raise their prices less than needed to cover fully their increases in costs, as determined by the existing inflation rate. As a result, *when a recessionary gap exists, the rate of inflation will tend to decrease.* These important results are summarized in Box 15.1.

BOX 15.1: THE OUTPUT GAP AND INFLATION

Relationship of output to potential output		Behavior of inflation
1. No output gap $Y = Y^*$	→	Inflation remains unchanged
2. Expansionary gap $Y > Y^*$	→	Inflation rises $\pi\uparrow$
3. Recessionary gap $Y < Y^*$	→	Inflation falls $\pi\downarrow$

EXAMPLE 15.1

Spending changes and inflation

In the previous two chapters, we saw that changes in spending can create expansionary or recessionary gaps. Therefore, based on the discussion above, we can conclude that changes in spending also lead to changes in the rate of inflation. If the economy is currently operating at potential output, what effect will a fall in consumer confidence that makes consumers less willing to spend at each level of disposable income have on the rate of inflation in the economy?

A decrease in exogenous consumption spending, C, for a given level of inflation, output, and real interest rates, reduces aggregate expenditures and short-run equilibrium output. If the economy was originally operating at potential output, the reduction in consumption will cause a recessionary gap, since actual output, Y, will now be less than potential output, Y^*. As indicated above, when $Y < Y^*$, the rate of inflation will tend to fall because firms' sales fall short of maximum sustainable production rates, leading them to slow down the rate at which they increase their prices.

EXERCISE 15.6

Suppose that firms become optimistic about the future and decide to increase their investment in new capital. What effect will this have on the rate of inflation, assuming that the economy is currently operating at potential output?

THE AGGREGATE DEMAND–AGGREGATE SUPPLY DIAGRAM

The adjustment of inflation in response to an output gap can be shown conveniently in a diagram. Figure 15.6, drawn with inflation π on the vertical axis and real output Y on the horizontal axis, is an example of an *aggregate demand–aggregate supply diagram*, or *AD-AS diagram* for short. The diagram has three elements, one of which is the downward-sloping *AD* curve, introduced earlier in the chapter. Recall that the *AD* curve shows how planned aggregate spending, and hence short-run equilibrium output, depends on the inflation rate. The second element is a vertical line marking the economy's potential output Y^*. Because potential output represents the economy's long-run productive capacity, we will refer to this vertical line as the **long-run aggregate supply line**, or *LRAS* line. The third element in Figure 15.6, and a new one, is the *short-run aggregate supply line*, labeled *SRAS* in the diagram. The **short-run aggregate supply (SRAS) line** is a horizontal line that shows the current rate of inflation in the economy, which in the figure is labeled π. We can think of the current rate of inflation as having been determined by past expectations of inflation and past pricing decisions. The short-run aggregate supply line is horizontal because, in the short run, producers supply whatever output is demanded at preset prices.

long-run aggregate supply (LRAS) line a vertical line showing the economy's potential output Y^*

short-run aggregate supply (SRAS) line a horizontal line showing the current rate of inflation, as determined by past expectations and pricing decisions

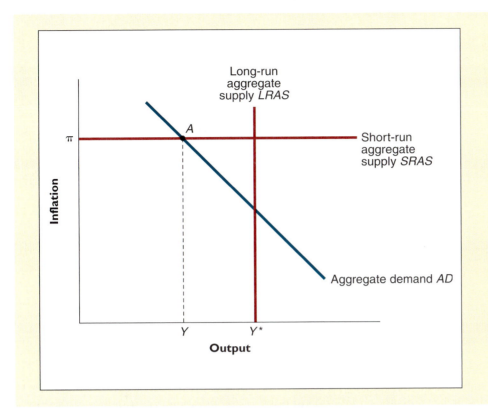

FIGURE 15.6
The Aggregate Demand–Aggregate Supply (AD-AS) Diagram. This diagram has three elements: the *AD* curve, which shows how short-run equilibrium output depends on inflation; the long-run aggregate supply (*LRAS*) line, which marks the economy's potential output Y*: and the short-run aggregate supply (*SRAS*) line, which shows the current value of inflation π. Short-run equilibrium output, which is equal to Y here, is determined by the intersection of the *AD* curve and the *SRAS* line (point A). Because actual output Y is less than potential output Y*, this economy has a recessionary gap.

The *AD-AS* diagram can be used to determine the level of output prevailing at any particular time. As we have seen, the inflation rate at any moment is given directly by the position of the *SRAS* line—for example, current inflation equals π in Figure 15.6. To find the current level of output, recall that the *AD* curve shows the level of short-run equilibrium output at any given rate of inflation. Since the inflation rate in this economy is π, we can infer from Figure 15.6 that short-run equilibrium output must equal Y, which corresponds to the intersection of the *AD* curve and the *SRAS* line (point A in the figure). Notice that in Figure 15.6, short-run equilibrium output Y is smaller than potential output Y*, so there is a recessionary gap in this economy.

The intersection of the *AD* curve and the *SRAS* line (point A in Figure 15.6) is referred to as the point of *short-run equilibrium* in this economy. When the economy is in **short-run equilibrium,** inflation equals the value determined by past expectations and past pricing decisions, and output equals the level of short-run equilibrium output that is consistent with that inflation rate.

Although the economy may be in short-run equilibrium at point A in Figure 15.6, it will not remain there. The reason is that at point A, the economy is experiencing a recessionary gap (output is less than potential output, as indicated by the *LRAS* line). As we have just seen, when a recessionary gap exists, firms are not selling as much as they would like to and so they slow down the rate at which they increase their prices. Eventually, the low level of aggregate demand that is associated with a recessionary gap causes the inflation rate to fall.

The adjustment of inflation in response to a recessionary gap is shown graphically in Figure 15.7. As inflation declines, the *SRAS* line moves downward. Because of inflation inertia (caused by the slow adjustment of the public's inflation expectations and the existence of long-term contracts), inflation adjusts downward only gradually. The *SRAS* line, for example, may shift from *SRAS* to *SRAS₂* to *SRAS₃*. It will continue to shift down as long as a recessionary gap exists. Thus, the *SRAS* line will move downward until it intersects the *AD* curve at point B in Figure 15.7. At that point, actual output equals potential output and the recessionary gap has been

short-run equilibrium a situation in which inflation equals the value determined by past expectations and pricing decisions and output equals the level of short-run equilibrium output that is consistent with that inflation rate; graphically, short-run equilibrium occurs at the intersection of the *AD* curve and the *SRAS* line

FIGURE 15.7

The Adjustment of Inflation When a Recessionary Gap Exists.

At the initial short-run equilibrium point A, a recessionary gap exists, which puts downward pressure on inflation. As inflation gradually falls, the SRAS line moves downward gradually until it reaches SRAS_Final, and actual output equals potential output (point B). Once the recessionary gap has been eliminated, inflation stabilizes at π', and the economy settles into long-run equilibrium at the intersection of AD, LRAS, and SRAS_Final (point B).

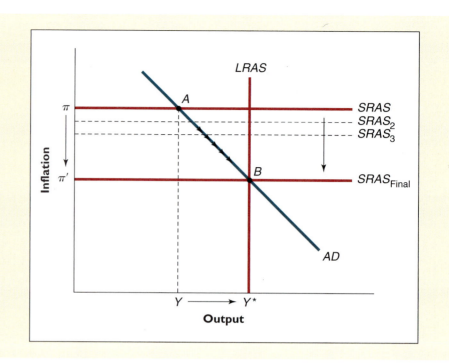

long-run equilibrium a situation in which actual output equals potential output and the inflation rate is stable; graphically, long-run equilibrium occurs when the AD curve, the SRAS line, and the LRAS line all intersect at a single point

eliminated. Consequently, the final *SRAS* line is labeled *SRAS*_Final. Because there is no further pressure on inflation at point *B*, the inflation rate stabilizes at the lower level. A situation like that represented by point *B* in Figure 15.7, in which the inflation rate is stable and actual output equals potential output, is referred to as **long-run equilibrium** of the economy. Long-run equilibrium occurs when the *AD* curve, the *SRAS* line, and the *LRAS* line all intersect at a single point.

Figure 15.7 illustrates the important point that when a recessionary gap exists, inflation will tend to fall. It also shows that as inflation declines, short-run equilibrium output rises, increasing gradually from *Y* to *Y** as the short-run equilibrium point moves down the *AD* curve. The source of this increase in output is the behavior of the Federal Reserve, which lowers the real interest rate as inflation falls, stimulating aggregate demand. Falling inflation stimulates spending and output in other ways, such as by reducing uncertainty.[4] As output rises, cyclical unemployment, which by Okun's law is proportional to the output gap, also declines. This process of falling inflation, falling real interest rates, rising output, and falling unemployment continues until the economy reaches full employment at point *B* in Figure 15.7, the economy's long-run equilibrium point.

What happens if instead of a recessionary gap, the economy has an expansionary gap, with output greater than potential output? An expansionary gap would cause the rate of inflation to *rise*, as firms respond to high demand by raising their prices more rapidly than their costs are rising. In graphical terms, an expansionary gap would cause the *SRAS* line to move upward over time. Inflation and the *SRAS* line would continue to rise until the economy reached long-run equilibrium, with actual output equal to potential output. This process is illustrated in Figure 15.8. Initially, the economy is in short-run equilibrium at point *A*, where *Y* > *Y** (an expansionary gap). The expansionary gap causes inflation to rise over time; graphically, the short-run aggregate supply line moves upward, from *SRAS* to *SRAS*_2 and then to *SRAS*_3. As the *SRAS* line rises, short-run equilibrium output falls—the result of the Fed's tendency to increase the real interest rate when inflation rises. Eventually the *SRAS* line reaches *SRAS*_Final, where it intersects the *AD* curve and the *LRAS* line

---

[4]Our explanation for the downward slope of the *AD* curve, earlier in the chapter, described some of these other factors.

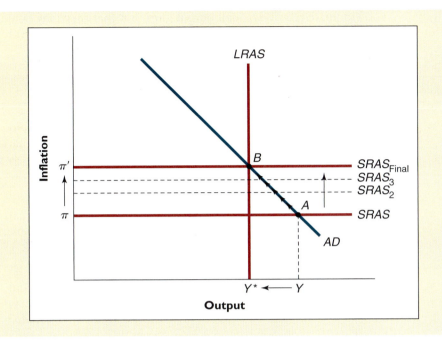

FIGURE 15.8
The Adjustment of Inflation When an Expansionary Gap Exists. At the initial short-run equilibrium point A, an expansionary gap exists. Inflation rises gradually (the SRAS line moves upward) and output falls. The process continues until the economy reaches long-run equilibrium at point B, where inflation stabilizes and the output gap is eliminated.

at point B. This is the point at which the economy reaches long-run equilibrium, with no output gap and stable inflation.

THE SELF-CORRECTING ECONOMY

Our analysis of Figures 15.7 and 15.8 makes an important general point: The economy tends to be *self-correcting* in the long run. In other words, given enough time, output gaps tend to disappear without changes in monetary or fiscal policy (other than the change in the real interest rate embodied in the Fed's policy reaction function). Expansionary output gaps are eliminated by rising inflation, while recessionary output gaps are eliminated by falling inflation. This result contrasts sharply with the basic Keynesian model, which does not include a self-correcting mechanism. The difference in results is explained by the fact that the basic Keynesian model concentrates on the short-run period, during which prices do not adjust, and does not take into account the changes in prices and inflation that occur over a longer period.

Does the economy's tendency to self-correct imply that aggressive monetary and fiscal policies are not needed to stabilize output? The answer to this question depends crucially on the *speed* with which the self-correction process takes place. If self-correction takes place very slowly, so that actual output differs from potential for protracted periods, then active use of monetary and fiscal policy can help to stabilize output. But if self-correction is rapid, then active stabilization policies are probably not justified in most cases, given the lags and uncertainties that are involved in policymaking in practice. Indeed, if the economy returns to full employment quickly, then attempts by policymakers to stabilize spending and output may end up doing more harm than good, for example, by causing actual output to "overshoot" potential output.

The speed with which a particular economy corrects itself depends on a variety of factors, including the prevalence of long-term contracts and the efficiency and flexibility of product and labor markets. (For a case study, see the comparison of U.S. and European labor markets in the chapter "Workers, Wages, and Unemployment in the Modern Economy.") However, a reasonable conclusion is that the greater the initial output gap, the longer the economy's process of self-correction will take. This observation suggests that stabilization policies should not be used actively to try to eliminate relatively small output gaps, but that they may be quite useful in remedying large gaps—for example, when the unemployment rate is exceptionally high.

RECAP	**AD-AS AND THE SELF-CORRECTING ECONOMY**

- The economy is in short-run equilibrium when inflation equals the value determined by past expectations and pricing decisions, and output equals the level of short-run equilibrium output that is consistent with that inflation rate. Graphically, short-run equilibrium occurs at the intersection of the *AD* curve and the *SRAS* line.

- The economy is in long-run equilibrium when actual output equals potential output (there is no output gap) and the inflation rate is stable. Graphically, long-run equilibrium occurs when the *AD* curve, the *SRAS* line, and the *LRAS* line intersect at a common point.

- Inflation adjusts gradually to bring the economy into long-run equilibrium (a phenomenon called the economy's self-correcting tendency). Inflation rises to eliminate an expansionary gap and falls to eliminate a recessionary gap. Graphically, the *SRAS* line moves up or down as needed to bring the economy into long-run equilibrium.

- The more rapid the self-correction process, the less need for active stabilization policies to eliminate output gaps. In practice, policymakers' attempts to eliminate output gaps are more likely to be helpful when the output gap is large than when it is small.

SOURCES OF INFLATION

We have seen that inflation can rise or fall in response to an output gap. But what creates the output gaps that give rise to changes in inflation? And are there factors besides output gaps that can affect the inflation rate? In this section we use the *AD-AS* diagram to explore the ultimate sources of inflation. We first discuss how excessive growth in aggregate spending can spur inflation, then turn to factors operating through the supply side of the economy.

EXCESSIVE AGGREGATE SPENDING

One important source of inflation in practice is excessive aggregate spending—or, in more colloquial terms, "too much spending chasing too few goods." Example 15.2 illustrates.

EXAMPLE 15.2

Military buildups and inflation

Wars and military buildups are sometimes associated with increased inflation. Explain why, using the *AD-AS* diagram. Can the Fed do anything to prevent the increase in inflation caused by a military buildup?

Wars and military buildups are potentially inflationary because increased spending on military hardware raises total demand relative to the economy's productive capacity. In the face of rising sales, firms increase their prices more quickly, raising the inflation rate.

The two panels of Figure 15.9 illustrate this process. Looking first at Figure 15.9(a), suppose that the economy is initially in long-run equilibrium at point *A*, where the aggregate demand curve *AD* intersects both the short-run and long-run

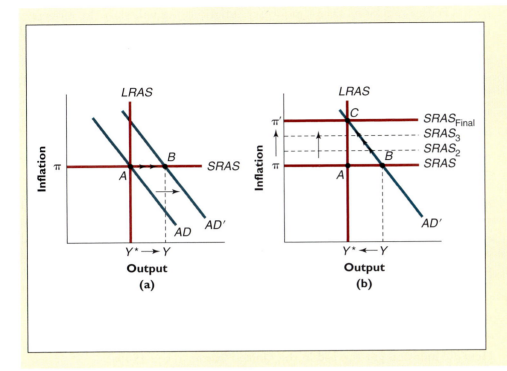

FIGURE 15.9

War and Military Buildup as a Source of Inflation. (a) An increase in military spending shifts the *AD* curve to the right, from *AD* to *AD′*. At the new short-run equilibrium point *B*, actual output has risen above potential output *Y**, creating an expansionary gap. (b) This gap leads to rising inflation, shown as an upward movement of the *SRAS* line, from *SRAS*, eventually to *SRAS*$_{Final}$. At the new long-run equilibrium point *C*, actual output has fallen back to the level of potential output, but at π' inflation is higher than it was originally.

aggregate supply lines, *SRAS* and *LRAS,* respectively. Point *A* is a long-run equilibrium point, with output equal to potential output and stable inflation. Now suppose that the government decides to spend more on armaments. Increased military spending is an increase in government purchases *G*, an exogenous increase in spending. We saw earlier that, for a given level of inflation, an exogenous increase in spending raises short-run equilibrium output, shifting the *AD* curve to the right. Figure 15.9(a) shows the aggregate demand curve shifting rightward, from *AD* to *AD′*, as the result of increased military expenditure. The economy moves to a new, short-run equilibrium at point *B*, where *AD′* intersects *SRAS*. Note that at point *B* actual output has risen above potential, to *Y > Y**, creating an expansionary gap. Because inflation is inertial and does not change in the short run, the immediate effect of the increase in government purchases is only to increase output, just as we saw in the Keynesian cross analysis of the chapter "Spending and Output in the Short Run."

The process doesn't stop there, however, because inflation will not remain the same indefinitely. At point *B* an expansionary gap exists, so inflation will gradually begin to increase. Figure 15.9(b) shows this increase in inflation as a shift of the *SRAS* line from its initial position to successively higher levels and eventually to *SRAS*$_{Final}$. When inflation has risen to π', enough to eliminate the output gap (point *C*), the economy is back in long-run equilibrium. We see now that the increase in output created by the military buildup was only temporary. In the long run, actual output has returned to the level of potential output, but at a higher rate of inflation.

Since output has returned to its original level while government spending has increased, some other component of spending must now be lower than it was originally. Indeed, as we move from point *B* to point *C* along the *AD′* curve, the Fed is raising the real interest rate in response to higher inflation. As a result, investment will fall. In the chapter "Saving and Capital Formation," we called this phenomenon the crowding out of investment in the long run, following an increase in government spending.

Does the Fed have the power to prevent the increased inflation that is induced by a rise in military spending? The answer is yes. We saw earlier that a decision by the Fed to reduce its target monetary inflation rate will shift the monetary policy reaction function upward (left) and the *AD* curve to the left. So if the Fed aggressively tightens monetary policy (shifts its reaction function) as the military buildup proceeds, it can reverse the rightward shift of the *AD* curve caused by increased government spending. Offsetting the rightward shift of the *AD* curve in turn avoids the development of an expansionary gap, with its inflationary consequences. The Fed's policy works because the higher real interest rate it sets at each level of inflation acts to reduce consumption and investment spending. The reduction in private spending offsets the increase in demand by the government, eliminating—or at least moderating—the inflationary impact of the military purchases.

We should not conclude, by the way, that avoiding the inflationary consequences of a military buildup makes the buildup costless to society. When the Fed reduces its target inflation rate, it increases the real interest rate more rapidly than in Figure 15.9. Consequently, the economy moves back to Y^* more rapidly, and consumption and investment are also reduced to their final levels more rapidly. The private sector must give up some resources so that more of the nation's output can be devoted to military purposes. This reduction in resources reduces both current living standards (by reducing consumption) and future living standards (by reducing investment).

ECONOMIC NATURALIST 15.1

How did inflation get started in the United States in the 1960s?

In the United States from 1959 through 1963, inflation hovered around 1 percent per year. Beginning in 1964, however, inflation began to rise, reaching nearly 6 percent in 1970. Why did inflation become a problem in the United States in the 1960s?

Increases in government spending, plus the failure of the Federal Reserve to act to contain inflation, appear to explain most of the increase in inflation during the 1960s. On the fiscal side, military expenditures increased dramatically in the latter part of the decade, as the war in Vietnam escalated. Defense spending rose from $50.6 billion, or about 7.4 percent of GDP, in 1965 to $81.9 billion, or 9.4 percent of GDP, in 1968, and it remained at a high level for some years. To appreciate the size of this military buildup relative to the size of the economy, note that the *increase* in military spending alone between 1965 and 1968 was about 2 percent of GDP. In contrast, in 2001 the *total* U.S. defense budget was a little over 3 percent of GDP. Moreover, at about the same time as the wartime military buildup, government spending on social programs—reflecting the impact of President Lyndon Johnson's Great Society and War on Poverty initiatives—also increased dramatically.

These government-induced increases in total spending contributed to an economic boom. Indeed, the 1961–1969 economic expansion was the longest in history at the time, being surpassed only recently by the long expansion of the 1990s. However, an expansionary gap developed and eventually inflation began to rise, as would have been predicted by the analysis in Example 15.2.

An interesting contrast exists between these effects of the 1960s military buildup and those of the 1980s buildup under President Reagan, which did not lead to an increase in inflation. One important difference between the two eras was the behavior of the Federal Reserve. As we saw in Example 15.2, the Fed can offset the inflationary impact of increased government spending by fighting inflation more aggressively (shifting its monetary policy reaction function upward). Except for a brief attempt in 1966, the Federal Reserve generally did not try actively to offset inflationary pressures during the 1960s. That failure may have been simply a miscalculation, or it may have reflected a reluctance to take the politically unpopular step of slowing the economy during a period of great political turmoil. But in the early 1980s, under Paul Volcker, the Federal Reserve acted vigorously to contain inflation. As a result, inflation actually declined in the 1980s, despite the military buildup.

EXERCISE 15.7

In Example 15.1 we found that a decline in consumer spending tends to reduce the rate of inflation. Using the *AD-AS* diagram, illustrate the short-run and long-run effects of a fall in consumer spending on inflation. How does the decline in spending affect output in the short run and in the long run?

"I told you the Fed should have tightened."

Whereas output gaps cause gradual changes in inflation, on occasion an economic shock can cause a relatively rapid increase or decrease in inflation. Such jolts to prices, which we call *inflation shocks,* are the subject of the next section.

INFLATION SHOCKS

In late 1973, at the time of the Yom Kippur War between Israel and a coalition of Arab nations, the Organization of Petroleum-Exporting Countries (OPEC) dramatically cut its supplies of crude oil to the industrialized nations, quadrupling world oil prices. The sharp increase in oil prices was quickly transferred to the price of gasoline, heating oil, and goods and services that were heavily dependent on oil, such as air travel. The effects of the oil price increase, together with agricultural shortages that increased the price of food, contributed to a significant rise in the overall U.S. inflation rate in 1974.[5]

The increase in inflation in 1974 is an example of what is referred to as an *inflation shock.* An **inflation shock** is a sudden change in the normal behavior of inflation, unrelated to the nation's output gap. An inflation shock that causes an increase in inflation, like the large rise in oil prices in 1973, is called an *adverse* inflation shock. An inflation shock that reduces inflation, such as the sharp decline in oil prices that occurred in 1986, is called a *favorable* inflation shock. Economic Naturalist 15.2 gives more details on the economic effects of inflation shocks.

OPEC's 1973–1974 cutback in oil production created long lines, rising prices, and frayed tempers at the gas pump.

inflation shock a sudden change in the normal behavior of inflation, unrelated to the nation's output gap

---

[5]In the chapter "Measuring the Price Level and Inflation," we distinguished between relative price changes (changes in the prices of individual goods) and inflation (changes in the overall price level). In the 1973–1974 episode, changes in the prices of individual categories of goods, such as energy and food, were sufficiently large and pervasive that the overall price level was significantly affected. Thus, these relative price changes carried an inflationary impact as well.

**ECONOMIC
NATURALIST
15.2**

Why did inflation escalate in the United States in the 1970s?

Having risen in the second half of the 1960s, inflation continued to rise in the 1970s. Already at 6.2 percent in 1973, inflation jumped to 11.0 percent in 1974. After subsiding from 1974 to 1978, it began to rise again in 1979, to 11.4 percent, and reached 13.5 percent in 1980. Why did inflation increase so much in the 1970s?

We have already described the quadrupling of oil prices in late 1973 and the sharp increases in agricultural prices at about the same time, which together constituted an adverse inflation shock. A second inflation shock occurred in 1979, when the turmoil of the Iranian Revolution restricted the flow of oil from the Middle East and doubled oil prices yet again.

Figure 15.10 shows the effects of an adverse inflation shock on a hypothetical economy. Before the inflation shock occurs, the economy is in long-run equilibrium at point A, at the intersection of AD, LRAS, and SRAS. At point A actual output is equal to potential output Y^*, and the inflation rate is stable at π. However, an adverse inflation shock directly increases inflation, so that the SRAS line shifts rapidly upward to SRAS'. A new short-run equilibrium is established at point B, where SRAS' intersects the aggregate demand curve AD. In the wake of the inflation shock, inflation rises to π' and output falls, from Y^* to Y'. Thus, an inflation shock creates the worst possible scenario: higher inflation coupled with a recessionary gap. The combination of inflation and recession has been referred to as *stagflation*, or stagnation plus inflation. The U.S. economy experienced a stagflation in 1973–1975, after the first oil shock, and again in 1980, after the second oil shock.

FIGURE 15.10

The Effects of an Adverse Inflation Shock.

Starting from long-run equilibrium at point A, an adverse inflation shock directly raises current inflation, causing the SRAS line to shift upward to SRAS'. At the new short-run equilibrium, point B, inflation has risen to π' and output has fallen to Y', creating a recessionary gap. If the Fed does nothing, eventually the economy will return to point A, restoring the original inflation rate but suffering a long recession in the process. The Fed could ease monetary policy by shifting down its monetary policy reaction function, shifting the AD curve to AD' and restoring full employment more quickly at point C. The cost of this strategy is that inflation remains at its higher level.

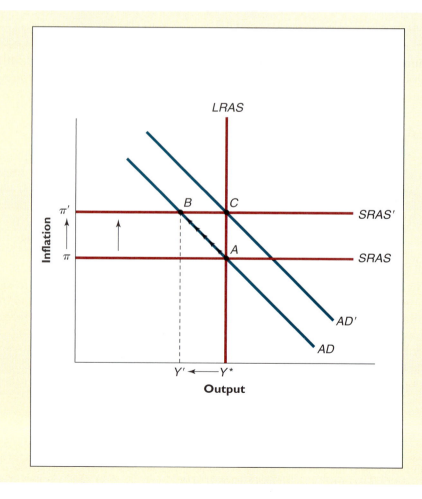

As we discuss in more detail in the next chapter, an adverse inflation shock creates a dilemma for macroeconomic policymakers. Suppose monetary and fiscal policies were left unchanged following an inflationary shock. Soon after the inflation shock, the economy would reach its short-run equilibrium at point B in Figure 15.10, with higher inflation. Because of the recessionary gap that exists at point B, eventually inflation would begin to drift downward, until finally the recessionary gap is eliminated. Graphically, this decline in inflation would be represented by a downward movement of the $SRAS$ line, from $SRAS'$ back to $SRAS$. Inflation would stop declining only when long-run equilibrium is restored, at point A in the figure, where inflation is at its original level of π and output equals potential output.

Although a "do-nothing" policy approach would ultimately eliminate both the output gap and the surge in inflation, it also would put the economy through a protracted recession. Consequently, policymakers might opt to eliminate the recessionary gap more quickly by pursuing a more expansionary fiscal policy or by choosing an easier monetary policy (more precisely, by raising the target inflation rate and thereby shifting the monetary policy reaction function down). An increase in the Fed's target inflation rate, for example, would shift the AD curve to the right, from AD to AD', taking the economy to a new long-run equilibrium, point C in Figure 15.10. This expansionary policy would help to restore output to the full-employment level more quickly, but as Figure 15.10 shows, it also would allow inflation to stabilize at the new, higher level.

In the 1970s, though U.S. policymakers tried to strike a balance between stabilizing output and containing inflation, the combination of recession and increased inflation hobbled the economy.

In the chapter "Money, Prices, and the Federal Reserve," we discussed the long-run relationship between inflation and money growth. The example of an inflation shock shows that inflation does not always originate from excessive money growth; it can arise from a variety of factors. However, our analysis also shows that, in the absence of monetary easing, inflation that arises from factors such as inflation shocks eventually will die away. By contrast, *sustained* inflation requires that monetary policy remain easy, that is, policymakers allow the money supply to rise rapidly. In this respect, our analysis of this chapter is consistent with the earlier long-run analysis, which concluded that sustained inflation is possible only if monetary policy is sufficiently expansionary.

EXERCISE 15.8

Inflation shocks also can be beneficial for the economy, such as when oil prices declined in the late 1990s. What effect would a decrease in oil prices have on output and inflation?

SHOCKS TO POTENTIAL OUTPUT

In analyzing the effects of increased oil prices on the U.S. economy in the 1970s, we assumed that potential output was unchanged in the wake of the shock. However, the sharp rise in oil prices during that period probably affected the economy's potential output as well. As oil prices rose, for example, many companies retired less energy-efficient equipment or scrapped older "gas-guzzling" vehicles. A smaller capital stock implies lower potential output.

If the increases in oil prices did reduce potential output, their inflationary impact would have been compounded. Figure 15.11 illustrates the effects on the economy of a sudden decline in potential output. For the sake of simplicity, the figure includes only the effects of the reduction in potential output, and not the direct effect of the inflation shock. (Problem 7 at the end of the chapter asks you to combine the two effects.)

Suppose once again that the economy is in long-run equilibrium at point A. Then potential output falls unexpectedly, from Y^* to $Y^{*\prime}$, shifting the long-run

FIGURE 15.11

The Effects of a Shock to Potential Output.

The economy is in long-run equilibrium at point *A* when a decline in potential output, from *Y** to *Y**', creates an expansionary gap. Inflation rises, and the short-run aggregate supply line shifts upward from *SRAS* to *SRAS'*. A new long-run equilibrium is reached at point *B*, where actual output equals the new, lower level of potential output, *Y**', and inflation has risen to *π'*. Because it is the result of a fall in potential output, the decline in output is permanent.

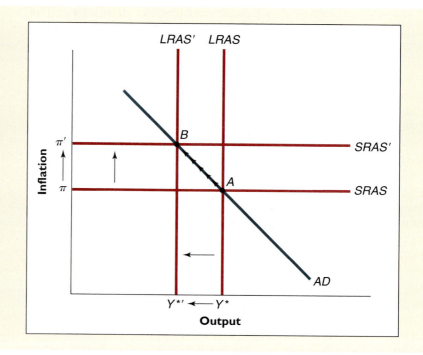

aggregate supply shock either an inflation shock or a shock to potential output; adverse aggregate supply shocks of both types reduce output and increase inflation

aggregate supply line leftward from *LRAS* to *LRAS'*. After this decline in potential output, is the economy still in long-run equilibrium at point *A*? The answer is no, because output now exceeds potential output at that point. In other words, an expansionary gap has developed. This gap reflects the fact that although planned spending has not changed, the capacity of firms to supply goods and services has been reduced.

As we have seen, an expansionary gap leads to rising inflation. In Figure 15.11, increasing inflation is represented by an upward movement of the *SRAS* line. Eventually the short-run aggregate supply line reaches *SRAS'*, and the economy reaches a new long-run equilibrium at point *B*. (Why is point *B* a long-run, and not just a short-run, equilibrium?) At that point, output has fallen to the new, lower level of potential output, *Y**', and inflation has risen to *π'*.

Sharp changes in potential output and inflation shocks are both referred to as **aggregate supply shocks.** As we have seen, an adverse aggregate supply shock of either type leads to lower output and higher inflation, and therefore poses a difficult challenge for policymakers. A difference between the two types of aggregate supply shocks is that the output losses associated with an adverse inflation shock are temporary (because the economy self-corrects and will ultimately return to its initial level of potential output), but those associated with a fall in potential output are permanent (output remains lower even after the economy has reached a new long-run equilibrium).

Was Greenspan right in 1996?

ECONOMIC NATURALIST 15.3

In the introduction to this chapter, we described the Fed's dilemma in 1996. Although the unemployment rate was falling below what many economists considered to be the natural rate of unemployment at that time, Alan Greenspan believed that the economy could continue to grow without stoking inflation. Because he did not see inflation as a threat, despite the rapid rate of economic growth, Geenspan did not support an increase in interest rates to slow the economy. Consequently, the Fed did not increase interest rates. Was it the right decision? What did Greenspan see?

Prior to becoming chairman of the Fed, Greenspan had his own economic consulting company. In that capacity, he had acquired a reputation for his knowledge of the economy and his ability to dissect economic data to discover trends not obvious to others. He continued his practice of painstaking data analysis when he went to the Fed.

During the summer and fall of 1996, Greenspan was puzzled. Although most people thought the economy was operating close to full employment, both price and wage inflation were lower than they had been at full employment in the past. Furthermore, though companies did not seem to be raising their prices, corporate profits were surging. Putting these and other clues together, Greenspan concluded that productivity must be rising rapidly. Higher productivity reduces firms' costs and allows them to increase profits even if they don't increase prices. Indeed, businesspeople in a range of industries were reporting productivity gains resulting from business restructuring and expanded capital investment. Since the official government data did not indicate substantial increases in productivity, Greenspan asked economists at the Fed to examine the official data in greater detail.

What they found was puzzling. When they used the official government data to construct detailed productivity data for each industry, some of the results didn't seem to make sense. The industry data, for example, implied that productivity in many service-producing industries had risen very slowly and had actually *fallen* in several industries. Given the substantial improvements in communications and information technology (see Economic Naturalist 7.3), these results were implausible. As reported in the minutes of the September 24, 1996 meeting of the Federal Reserve Open Market Committee, "this result . . . suggested considerable error in estimating output and prices for many services. Consequently, it was likely that actual productivity growth was higher than the current measures indicated."[6]

The economists' analysis convinced Greenspan that substantial but as yet unmeasured gains in productivity had increased productive capacity in many industries and in the economy as a whole. Consequently, potential output was higher than people had thought. With potential output higher, the economy could continue to grow without generating an expansionary gap or higher inflation. An increase in the federal funds rate was not necessary.

History tells us that Greenspan was right. As we discussed in Economic Naturalist 7.3 during the latter part of the 1990s, the U.S. economy benefited from a large, positive shock to potential output. The main contributing factor was impressive technological advance, particularly in computers, software, and communications. These advances were reflected in more rapid productivity growth and an increase in potential output. And productivity gains from the adoption of new information technology propelled the economy without exacerbating inflation.

As Table 15.1 shows, real GDP growth during the 1995–2000 period was 4.1 percent per year, significantly higher than the average growth rate over the previous decade; and unemployment averaged only 4.8 percent, also significantly better than the prior decade. Despite this rapid economic growth, inflation during 1995–2000 averaged only 2.5 percent per year. Furthermore, average annual growth of output per hour worked accelerated from 1.5 percent during the 1985–1995 period to 2.5 percent during 1995–2000.

TABLE 15.1
U.S. Macroeconomic Data, Annual Averages, 1985–2000

Years	% Growth in real GDP	Unemployment rate (%)	Inflation rate (%)	Productivity growth (%)
1985–1995	2.8	6.3	3.5	1.5
1995–2000	4.1	4.8	2.5	2.5

SOURCE: *Economic Report of the President* (http://www.gpoaccess/gov/eop).

[6]Minutes from the Federal Reserve's September 24, 1996, meeting (http://www.federalreserve.gov/FOMC/minutes/19960924.htm).

Graphically, the effects of a positive shock to potential output are just the reverse of those seen in Figure 15.11, which shows the effects of an adverse shock. A positive shock to potential output causes the *LRAS* line to shift right, leading in the short run to a recessionary gap (output is lower than the new, higher level of potential output). Inflation declines, reflected in a downward movement of the *SRAS* line. In the new, long-run equilibrium, output is higher and inflation lower than initially. These results are consistent with the U.S. experience of the latter part of the 1990s. As Greenspan said in a January 2000 speech to the Economic Club of New York, "When we look back at the 1990s . . . (w)e may conceivably conclude . . . (that) the American economy was experiencing a once-in-a-century acceleration of innovation, which propelled forward productivity, output, corporate profits, and stock prices at a pace not seen in generations, if ever."

EXERCISE 15.9

What if productivity hadn't increased in the late 1990s? How would the economy have been different in 2000?

RECAP	SOURCES OF INFLATION

- Inflation may result from excessive spending, which creates an expansionary output gap and puts upward pressure on prices. For example, a military buildup that raises government purchases sharply may cause the economy to overheat. However, monetary policy or fiscal policy can be used to offset excessive spending, preventing higher inflation from emerging.
- Inflation also may arise from an aggregate supply shock, either an inflation shock or a shock to potential output. An inflation shock is a sudden change in the normal behavior of inflation, unrelated to the nation's output gap. An example of an inflation shock is a run-up in energy and food prices large enough to raise the overall price level. An inflation shock creates stagflation, a combination of recession and higher inflation.
- Stagflation poses a difficult dilemma for policymakers. If they take no action, eventually inflation will subside and output will recover, but in the interim, the economy may suffer a protracted period of recession. If they use monetary or fiscal policy to increase aggregate demand, they will shorten the recession but also may lock in the higher level of inflation.
- A shock to potential output is a sharp change in potential output. Like an adverse inflation shock, an adverse shock to potential output results in both higher inflation and lower output. Because lower potential output implies that productive capacity has fallen, however, output does not recover following a shock to potential output, as it eventually does following an inflation shock.

FISCAL POLICY AND THE SUPPLY SIDE

In this chapter and in the chapter "Spending and Output in the Short Run," we focused on the role of fiscal policy—government spending and taxes—in the determination of aggregate expenditure and aggregate demand. We have seen, for example, that increased government spending or lower taxes can expand the economy by increasing aggregate expenditure. However, most economists agree that fiscal policies affect the economy's productive capacity, or potential output, as well as planned aggregate expenditure. In general, a **supply-side policy** is a policy that affects potential output (the "supply side" of the economy). As we discuss here, fiscal policies are often supply-side policies in this sense.

supply-side policy a policy that affects potential output

For example, government expenditures on public capital increase aggregate spending, as we have already discussed. However, they also may increase the economy's potential output. The interstate highway system, begun under President Eisenhower, is a case in point: By lowering the costs of long-distance transportation, interstate highways made the U.S. economy more productive and increased potential output. Thus, spending on public capital may be a supply-side policy as well as influence on aggregate demand.

Government tax and transfer programs affect the incentives, and thus the economic behavior, of households and firms. To the extent that changes in behavior in turn affect potential output, tax and transfer programs also have supply-side effects. A lower tax rate on interest income (as opposed to all income), for example, may increase people's willingness to save for the future, as we saw in the chapter "Saving and Capital Formation." Although greater saving implies lower consumption expenditures and thus weaker aggregate demand in the short run, greater saving also leads to more investment in the long run and a faster rate of capital formation in the economy. As a result, potential output and aggregate supply will grow more rapidly.

Tax and transfer policies also affect potential output by affecting the supply of labor. For example, lower tax rates on earnings may increase potential output by inducing people to work more hours. To illustrate, suppose that Tom earns $10 per hour before taxes and his tax rate is 40 percent. Thus, for each hour he works, Tom earns $10; pays 40 percent of $10, or $4, in taxes; and takes home $6 in after-tax earnings. Tom's situation is depicted in the first line of Table 15.2. Now suppose his tax rate is reduced to 30 percent. If Tom's before-tax wage rate remains equal to $10, his taxes on each hour of work fall to 30 percent of $10, or $3, and he takes home $7 in after-tax earnings, as illustrated in the second line of Table 15.2. Consequently, a *reduction* in Tom's tax rate from 40 percent to 30 percent *increases* his after-tax wage from $6 to $7 per hour.

TABLE 15.2
The Effects of a Reduction in Tax Rates on Tom's After-Tax Wage Rates

Pre-tax wage	Tax rate	Taxes paid	After-tax wage
$10	40% (= 0.40)	$4	$6
$10	30% (= 0.30)	$3	$7

Reductions in tax rates may increase the number of hours people want to work and reduce the amount of time they want to spend at home watching television and doing chores because the *opportunity cost* of watching television has risen. Tom's opportunity cost of watching an additional hour of television is equal to the amount of after-tax earnings he could have earned during that hour, which has risen from $6 to $7.

According to the cost-benefit principle, individuals make decisions by comparing the extra benefits with the extra costs. In examining the effects of tax rates on economic incentives, therefore, economists focus on people's **marginal tax rate** which is the tax rate on the *marginal* or extra dollar of income, or the amount by which taxes rise when before-tax income rises by one dollar. Someone's marginal tax rate can differ considerably from his **average tax rate,** which is calculated by dividing his total taxes by his total before-tax income to obtain the percentage of before-tax income he pays in taxes.

marginal tax rate the amount by which taxes rise when before-tax income rises by one dollar

average tax rate total taxes divided by total before-tax income

Although there was no difference between Tom's marginal and average tax rates in Table 15.2, this is not true for most people, as we show in Exercise 15.10. In 2004 total taxes collected by federal, state, and local governments were about

27 percent of U.S. GDP and many of these taxes, such as property taxes, do not depend on income. As Economic Naturalist 15.4 illustrates, however, most Americans face marginal tax rates on their incomes that are greater than 27 percent.

EXERCISE 15.10

Suppose Tom pays no taxes on the first $10,000 of his income. Suppose, however, he has to pay taxes of 20 percent on any *additional* income. Thus, if he earns $11,000, he pays .20($11,000 − $10,000) = $200 in taxes. Similarly, if he earns $15,000 he pays .20($15,000 − $10,000) = $1,000 in taxes. Calculate Tom's average and marginal tax rates if he earns $5,000, $11,000, and $15,000.

ECONOMIC
NATURALIST
15.4

Estimating your marginal tax rate

Recall that a person's marginal tax rate is the amount by which her taxes rise when her before-tax income rises by one dollar. Calculating one's marginal tax rate can be difficult because there are many taxes that depend directly on income, such as federal income taxes, state income taxes, and Social Security, Disability, and Medicare taxes. Calculating some of these taxes can be complicated and depends upon family composition, sources of income (wages, interest, dividends, etc.), medical expenses, and many other details.

Nevertheless, you can estimate your marginal tax rate at several Internet Web sites. Table 15.3 lists the marginal tax rates from one popular Web site for a single, self-employed person with no dependents at various income levels.

TABLE 15.3
Marginal Tax Rates Faced by a Self-Employed Single Person in the United States, 2005

Pre-tax earnings	Marginal tax rate
$ 10,000	28%
25,000	32
50,000	42
100,000	36
250,000	41
$500,000	42

ASSUMPTIONS: All income is earned income, and there are no itemized deductions. Taxes include federal and state income taxes, as well as Social Security, Disability, and Medicare taxes. The marginal state income tax rate, which differs among states, is assumed to be 3 percent on income between $10,000 and $50,000, 4 percent on income between $50,000 and $100,000, and 5 percent on income above $100,000.

SOURCE: http://www.smartmoney.com/tax/filing/index.cfm?story=marginal.

Note that the marginal tax rate in every case in Table 15.3 is greater than the average economywide tax rate of 27 percent.[7] Note also that the marginal tax rate actually falls between $50,000 and $100,000. Although the marginal federal income tax rates increase with income, the marginal Social Security and Medicare tax

---

[7]Marginal tax rates for families with children are more difficult to calculate because of the earned income tax credit, which subsidizes low-income workers with children. If one treats the credit as a negative tax, the marginal tax rate for low-income families with children is often negative, and many Web sites that calculate marginal tax rates, like Smart Money's, do not account for the tax credit. On the other hand, if one counts as a tax the reduction in government transfer payments and benefits (such as food stamps, welfare benefits, and Medicaid) that low-income families lose when they earn additional income, their marginal tax rates can often exceed 50 percent.

rate falls after one earns more than about $90,000 per year, and most Americans pay more in Social Security taxes than they do in federal income taxes.[8]

EXERCISE 15.11

Go to the Web site listed in Table 15.3 and estimate your own marginal tax rate.

Changes in marginal tax rates may affect other aspects of the labor supply decision besides the number of hours worked. For example, consider a student's decision about whether to invest the time and money necessary to become a doctor. From an economic perspective, the return to that investment in human capital is the extra income that the student will be able to earn as a doctor, relative to what he or she might earn without a medical degree. If the marginal tax rate on earnings is high, the economic incentive to become a doctor will be lower, and the student may decide not to make that investment. Likewise, a lower marginal tax rate increases the incentive for people to be entrepreneurial and to take risks—for example, by starting their own companies—since they know that they will be able to keep a larger portion of the returns to their efforts. As we discussed in the chapter "Economic Growth, Productivity, and Living Standards," entrepreneurship is an important source of economic growth.

In Figure 15.12 we illustrate one scenario in which a cut in marginal tax rates increases both aggregate demand and aggregate supply. As before, the tax cut shifts the aggregate demand curve to the right, from *AD* to *AD'*. Now, however, the tax cut also increases potential output so the long-run aggregate supply line also shifts to the right. As a result, real output will increase in both the short run and the long run. Whether the rate of inflation also will increase depends on the relative size of

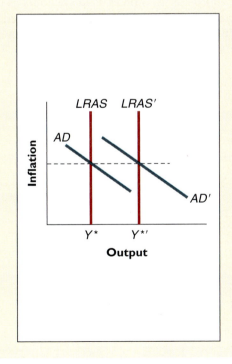

FIGURE 15.12
The Potential Effects of Tax Rate Reductions on Both Aggregate Demand and Aggregate Supply.
The economy begins in long-run equilibrium at point *A*. A reduction in tax rates shifts the aggregate demand curve to the right, from *AD* to *AD'*. It also may increase potential output from *Y** to *Y*'*. This is represented by a shift in the long-run aggregate supply line from *LRAS* to *LRAS'*. Output will definitely rise. In the long run, inflation may rise, fall, or remain unchanged, depending on the relative magnitudes of the shifts in *AD* and *LRAS*.

[8]Since the data in Table 15.3 refer to self-employed individuals, they include Social Security, Disability, and Medicare taxes of 15.3 percent on all earned income below about $90,000 and 2.9 percent on all earned income above that amount. Although the employers of workers who are not self-employed are responsible for paying half of these taxes, most economists agree that employees effectively pay both the employee and employer portions of the tax. The tax rate calculations do not account for the fact that some (but not all) of the extra Social Security taxes people pay will result in greater Social Security benefits when they retire.

the two shifts. For simplicity, we have drawn them so that inflation remains constant, but this need not be the case.

Although economists agree that tax rates affect economic behavior, the magnitude and sometimes even the direction of the effects can be controversial. In our earlier example, we showed that a decline in Tom's tax rate implies an increase in his after-tax wage rate. As we mentioned, the increase in Tom's after-tax wage gives him an incentive to work more hours and to watch less television, because the opportunity cost of watching television instead of working has risen. On the other hand, the reduction in Tom's tax rate also might increase his after-tax wage to such an extent that he may feel that he can afford to work even fewer hours and still pay his bills.[9] Empirical studies of the labor market suggest that the responsiveness of an individual's labor supply to changes in taxes depends on many factors, including age, sex, marital status, and education. For example, married women have traditionally been more likely to move in and out of the labor force and appear to be more responsive to changes in after-tax wages than are their husbands, who have historically tended to remain in the labor market on a full-time basis even when tax rates change.

While many Americans may be dismayed by what they consider to be high taxes, Europeans generally have considerably higher marginal tax rates. In Economic Naturalist 15.5, we examine the claim that the higher marginal tax rates in Europe are responsible for the fact that the typical European works many fewer hours each year than the typical American.

ECONOMIC NATURALIST 15.5

Why do Americans work more hours than Europeans?

The average American works many more hours than the average Western European. Not only is the average workweek longer in America, but Americans generally take fewer vacations, have fewer holidays, retire later, and experience less unemployment than Europeans. As indicated in Table 15.4, during the period 1993–1996, the average American worked 100/64 = 1.56 times as many hours as the average Italian, or 56 percent more hours. Similarly, the average American worked (100 − 75)/75 = 33 percent more hours than the average German. The average Japanese, on the other hand, worked (104 − 100)/100 = 4 percent more hours than the average American. Why?

Edward Prescott found that most of these differences can be explained by the variation in marginal tax rates on labor income among these countries.[10] The Japanese,

TABLE 15.4
Hours Worked per Person and Marginal Tax Rates, 1993–1996

Country	Hours worked per person per year relative to the U.S. (U.S. = 100)	Marginal tax rate
Japan	104	37%
United States	100	40
United Kingdom	88	44
Canada	88	52
Germany	75	59
France	68	59
Italy	64	64

SOURCE: Edward C. Prescott, "Why Do Americans Work So Much More Than Europeans?" Federal Reserve Bank of Minneapolis *Quarterly Review*, July 2004, pp. 2–13.

[9]Students who have taken introductory microeconomics may recognize this as an example of substitution and income effects.
[10]Prescott's marginal tax rates include taxes on consumption as well as income.

for example, worked the most and had the lowest marginal tax rate of 37 percent, while the Italians worked the least and had the highest marginal tax rate of 64 percent. Moreover, during the period 1970–1974, when the marginal tax rates in Europe were much closer to those in the United States, the average European worked as much as the average American. Prescott concludes that reductions in marginal tax rates in Europe would considerably increase both labor supply and potential output.

Most economists agree that higher tax rates help to explain why continental Europeans work fewer hours than Americans, but many note that there are other explanations as well. These explanations include Europe's higher unionization rates and government regulations that limit workweeks and the number of hours that stores may remain open. The differences in workhours also may be related to more generous social security systems supporting the unemployed, the sick and disabled, and those who retire early in many European countries.[11]

Some observers also have suggested that Europeans simply have a greater taste for leisure and the "good life" than Americans do. However, as Prescott points out, people in most European countries worked much longer hours in the past (when, among other things, tax rates were lower) than they do today, which suggests that the underlying preferences of Europeans and Americans may not be all that different. Yet, the decrease in hours worked over time among a larger sample of European countries is only weakly related to the increase in tax rates.[12] Clearly, this remains a controversial issue.

If lower tax rates tend to increase potential output, why not reduce taxes to zero? The answer is that, ultimately, government expenditures can be paid for only through taxes. Of course, the government can run a deficit for a while, borrowing to cover the difference between what it spends and what it collects in taxes. But deficits can be harmful (they may reduce national saving, as we saw in the chapter "Saving and Capital Formation"), and in any case the government's borrowing eventually must be repaid with future taxes. Thus, in the long run, taxes should be set at a level commensurate with the government's rate of spending.

The important message is that fiscal policy affects aggregate supply as well as aggregate demand. Thus, in making fiscal policy, government officials should take into account not only the need to stabilize aggregate demand but also the likely effects of government spending, taxes, and transfers on the economy's productive capacity.

RECAP	FISCAL POLICY AND THE SUPPLY SIDE

- A supply-side policy is a policy that affects potential output. Fiscal policies affect aggregate demand, but they also may be supply-side policies.
- Government expenditures on public capital—such as roads, airports, and schools—increase aggregate expenditure but also may increase potential output.
- Government tax and transfer programs affect the incentives, and thus the economic behavior, of households and firms.
- People may respond to reductions in their marginal tax rates by working more hours, investing more in education, and taking more entrepreneurial risks, all of which contribute to greater potential output. The size of the effect of tax changes on labor supply remains somewhat controversial.
- Fiscal policymakers should take into account the effects of spending and tax decisions on aggregate supply as well as on aggregate demand.

[11]Stephen Nickell, "Employment and Taxes," London School of Economics Centre for Economic Performance Discussion Paper No. 634, May 2004 and Alberto Alesina, Edward Glaeser, and Bruce Sacerdote, "Work and Leisure in the U.S. and Europe: Why So Different?" National Bureau of Economic Research Working Paper No. 11278, April, 2005.

[12]Olivier Blanchard, "The Economic Future of Europe," *Journal of Economic Perspectives* 18(1): 3–26, 2004.

■ SUMMARY ■

- This chapter extended the basic Keynesian model to include inflation. First, we showed how planned spending and short-run equilibrium output are related to inflation, a relationship that is summarized by the aggregate demand curve. Second, we discussed how inflation itself is determined. In the short run, inflation is determined by past expectations and pricing decisions, but in the longer run inflation adjusts as needed to eliminate output gaps.

- The *aggregate demand (AD) curve* shows the relationship between short-run equilibrium output and inflation. Because short-run equilibrium output is equal to planned spending, the aggregate demand curve also relates spending to inflation. Increases in inflation reduce planned spending and short-run equilibrium output, so the aggregate demand curve is downward-sloping.

- The inverse relationship of inflation and short-run equilibrium output is the result, in large part, of the behavior of the Federal Reserve. To keep inflation low and stable, the Fed reacts to rising inflation by increasing the real interest rate. A higher real interest rate reduces consumption and planned investment, lowering planned aggregate expenditure and hence short-run equilibrium output. Other reasons that the aggregate demand curve slopes downward include the effects of inflation on the real value of money, distributional effects (inflation redistributes wealth from the poor, who save relatively little, to the more affluent, who save more), uncertainty created by inflation, and the impact of inflation on foreign sales of domestic goods.

- For any given value of inflation, an exogenous increase in spending (that is, an increase in spending at given levels of output and the real interest rate) raises short-run equilibrium output, shifting the aggregate demand (AD) curve to the right. Likewise, an exogenous decline in spending shifts the AD curve to the left. The AD curve also can be shifted by a change in the Fed's monetary policy reaction function. If the Fed gets "tougher," shifting up its reaction function and thus choosing a higher real interest rate at each level of inflation, the aggregate demand curve will shift to the left. If the Fed gets "easier," shifting down its reaction function and thus setting a lower real interest rate at each level of inflation, the AD curve will shift to the right.

- In low-inflation industrial economies like the United States today, inflation tends to be inertial, or slow to adjust to changes in the economy. This inertial behavior reflects the fact that inflation depends in part on people's expectations of future inflation, which in turn depend on their recent experience with inflation. Long-term wage and price contracts tend to "build in" the effects of people's expectations for multiyear periods. In the aggregate demand–aggregate supply diagram, the *short-run aggregate supply (SRAS) line* is a horizontal line that shows the current rate of inflation, as determined by past expectations and pricing decisions.

- Although inflation is inertial, it does change over time in response to output gaps. An expansionary gap tends to raise the inflation rate, because firms raise their prices more quickly when they are facing demand that exceeds their normal productive capacity. A recessionary gap tends to reduce the inflation rate, as firms become more reluctant to raise their prices.

- The economy is in *short-run equilibrium* when the inflation rate equals the value determined by past expectations and pricing decisions, and output equals the level of short-run equilibrium output that is consistent with that inflation rate. Graphically, short-run equilibrium occurs at the intersection of the AD curve and the SRAS line. If an output gap exists, however, the inflation rate will adjust to eliminate the gap. Graphically, the SRAS line moves upward or downward as needed to restore output to its full-employment level. When the inflation rate is stable and actual output equals potential output, the economy is in *long-run equilibrium*. Graphically, long-run equilibrium corresponds to the common intersection point of the AD curve, the SRAS line, and the long-run aggregate supply (LRAS) line, a vertical line that marks the economy's potential output.

- Because the economy tends to move toward long-run equilibrium on its own through the adjustment of the inflation rate, it is said to be self-correcting. The more rapid the self-correction process, the smaller the need for active stabilization policies to eliminate output gaps. In practice, the larger the output gap, the more useful such policies are.

- Excessive spending, which increases aggregate demand, may lead to expansionary output gaps and result in higher inflation. The increase in spending can result from increases in private spending (consumption or private investment) or increases in government spending.

- Aggregate supply shocks also may cause inflation. *Aggregate supply shocks* include both *inflation shocks*—sudden changes in the normal behavior of inflation, created, for example, by a rise in the price of imported oil—and shocks to potential output. Adverse supply shocks both lower output and increase inflation, creating a difficult dilemma for policymakers.

- Reductions in marginal tax rates on income will increase aggregate demand by increasing consumption, and reductions in taxes on business income may increase investment. Reductions in marginal tax rates also may increase aggregate supply by increasing work effort and the willingness to save and invest.

▪ KEY TERMS ▪

aggregate demand (*AD*) curve (420)
aggregate supply shock (442)
average tax rate (445)
inflation shock (439)

long-run aggregate supply (*LRAS*)
line (432)
long-run equilibrium (434)
marginal tax rate (445)

short-run aggregate supply (*SRAS*)
line (432)
short-run equilibrium (433)
supply-side policy (444)

▪ REVIEW QUESTIONS ▪

1. What two variables are related by the aggregate demand (*AD*) curve? Explain how the behavior of the Fed helps to determine the slope of this curve. List and discuss two other factors that lead the curve to have the slope that it does.

2. State how each of the following affects the *AD* curve and explain:
   a. An increase in government purchases.
   b. A cut in taxes.
   c. A decline in planned investment spending by firms.
   d. A decision by the Fed to increase its target rate of inflation.

3. Why does the overall rate of inflation tend to adjust more slowly than prices of commodities, such as oil or grain?

4. Discuss the relationship between output gaps and inflation. How is this relationship captured in the aggregate demand–aggregate supply diagram?

5. Sketch an aggregate demand–aggregate supply diagram depicting an economy away from long-run equilibrium. Indicate the economy's short-run equilibrium point. Discuss how the economy reaches long-run equilibrium over a period of time. Illustrate the process in your diagram.

6. True or false: The economy's self-correcting tendency makes active use of stabilization policy unnecessary. Explain.

7. What factors led to increased inflation in the United States in the 1960s and 1970s?

8. Why does an adverse inflation shock pose a particularly difficult dilemma for policymakers?

9. How does a reduction in the marginal tax rate affect both aggregate demand and aggregate supply?

▪ PROBLEMS ▪

1. We saw in the last chapter that short-run equilibrium output falls when the Fed raises the real interest rate. Suppose the relationship between short-run equilibrium output Y and the real interest rate r set by the Fed is given by

$$Y = 1,000 - 1,000r.$$

   Suppose also that the Fed's reaction function is the one shown in Table 14.1. For whole-number inflation rates between 0 and 4 percent, find the real interest rate by the Fed and the resulting short-run equilibrium output. Graph the aggregate demand curve numerically.

2. For the economy in problem 1, suppose that potential output $Y^* = 960$. From the monetary policy reaction function in Table 14.1, what can you infer about the Fed's objective for the inflation rate in the long term?

3. An economy's aggregate demand curve (the relationship between short-run equilibrium output and inflation) is described by the equation

$$Y = 13,000 - 20,000\pi.$$

   Initially, the inflation rate is 4 percent, or $\pi = 0.04$. Potential output Y^* equals 12,000.
   a. Find inflation and output in short-run equilibrium.
   b. Find inflation and output in long-run equilibrium.

   Show your work.

4. This problem asks you to trace out the adjustment of inflation when the economy starts with an output gap. Suppose that the economy's aggregate demand curve is

$$Y = 1,000 - 1,000\pi,$$

where Y is short-run equilibrium output and π is the inflation rate, measured as a decimal. Potential output Y^* equals 950, and the initial inflation rate is 10 percent ($\pi = 0.10$).
   a. Find output and inflation for this economy in short-run equilibrium and in long-run equilibrium.
   b. Suppose that, each quarter, inflation adjusts according to the following rule:

   This quarter's inflation = Last quarter's inflation − 0.0004($Y^* - Y$).

   Starting from the initial value of 10 percent for inflation, find the value of inflation for each of the next five quarters. Does inflation come close to its long-run value?

5. For each of the following, use an *AD-AS* diagram to show the short-run and long-run effects on output and inflation. Assume the economy starts in long-run equilibrium.
   a. An increase in consumer confidence that leads to higher consumption spending.
   b. A reduction in taxes.
   c. An easing of monetary policy by the Fed (a downward shift in the monetary policy reaction function).
   d. A sharp drop in oil prices.
   e. A war that raises government purchases.

6. Suppose that the government cuts taxes in response to a recessionary gap, but because of legislative delays the tax cut is not put in place for 18 months. Using an *AD-AS* diagram and assuming that the government's objective is to stabilize output and inflation, show how this policy action might actually prove to be counterproductive.

7. Suppose that a permanent increase in oil prices both creates an inflationary shock and reduces potential output. Use an *AD-AS* diagram to show the effects of the oil price increase on output and inflation in the short run and the long run, assuming that there is no policy response. What happens if the Fed responds to the oil price increase by adopting a tighter monetary policy?

8. An economy is initially in recession. Using the *AD-AS* diagram, show the process of adjustment
   a. If the Fed responds by adopting a looser monetary policy (moving its monetary policy reaction function down).
   b. If the Fed does not change its monetary policy reaction function.

   What are the costs and benefits of each approach, in terms of output loss and inflation?

■ ANSWERS TO IN-CHAPTER EXERCISES ■

15.1 a. At the current level of inflation, output, and real interest rate, an exogenous reduction in business spending on new capital will reduce planned investment, causing a decline in planned aggregate expenditures (*PAE*) and a reduction in short-run equilibrium output. Because output has fallen for a given level of inflation, the decrease in business spending leads to a leftward shift in the *AD* curve.
   b. At the current level of inflation, output, and real interest rate, a reduction in federal income taxes increases consumers' disposable income ($Y - T$), which leads to an exogenous increase in consumption at all income levels, as illustrated in the chapter "Spending and Output in the Short Run." The upward shift in the consumption function increases overall planned aggregate expenditures (*PAE*) and leads to an increase in short-run equilibrium output. Because output has increased for a given level of inflation, the reduction in income taxes leads to a rightward shift in the *AD* curve.

15.2 An increase in the Fed's target inflation rate would shift the monetary policy function down, or to the right. The Fed would then set the real interest rate at a lower level than usual for each given rate of inflation. This change in monetary policy shifts the *AD* curve to the right.

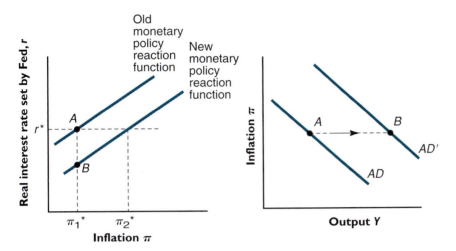

15.3 a. An upward shift in the Fed's monetary policy reaction function means that the Federal Reserve is raising the real interest rate associated with a given level of inflation. An increase in the real interest rate causes both consumption and planned investment spending to fall, reducing overall aggregate expenditures and short-run equilibrium output. Thus, a shift in the Fed's monetary policy reaction function causes the output level to fall for a given level of inflation, resulting in a leftward shift in the *AD* curve.

   b. The Federal Reserve's monetary policy reaction function illustrates that the Federal Reserve responds to rising inflation rates by raising the real interest rate (a move *along* the monetary policy reaction function), which causes a reduction in overall aggregate expenditures and short-run equilibrium output. However, in this case, the Fed's response to higher inflation causes a *move along* a given *AD* curve.

   Note that while the two actions appear to be similar, there is a key difference. In the first case, the Fed is changing its policy rule for a *given inflation rate,* while in the second case, the Fed is responding to a *changing inflation rate.* Changes in aggregate spending for a given inflation rate shift the *AD* curve, while changes in aggregate spending resulting from Fed policy responses to a rise or fall in inflation lead to moves along a given *AD* curve. Alternatively, in the first case the Fed is changing its (long-run) target rate of inflation, causing the monetary policy reaction function and the *AD* curve to shift. In the second case, the Fed's (long-run) target rate of inflation does not change.

15.4 a. If inflation is expected to be 2 percent next year and workers are expecting a 2 percent increase in their real wages, then they will expect, and ask for, a 4 percent increase in their nominal wages.

   b. If inflation is expected to be 4 percent next year, rather than 2 percent, workers will expect, and ask for, a 6 percent increase in their nominal wages.

   c. If wage costs rise, firms will need to increase the prices of their goods and services to cover their increased costs, leading to an increase in inflation. In part b, when expected inflation was 4 percent, firms will be faced with larger increases in nominal wages than in part a, when expected inflation was only 2 percent. Thus, we can expect firms to raise prices by more when expected inflation is 4 percent than when expected inflation is 2 percent. From this example, we can conclude that increased inflationary expectations lead to higher inflation.

15.5 If the inflation rate is high, the economy will tend to stay in this high-inflation state due to expectations of high inflation and the existence of long-term wage and price contracts, while if the inflation rate is low, the economy will likewise tend to stay in this low-inflation state for similar reasons. However, since high inflation rates impose economic costs on society, as pointed out in the chapter "Measuring the Price Level and Inflation," the Federal Reserve has an incentive to avoid the high-inflation state by keeping inflation low, which helps to maintain people's expectations of low inflation and leads to lower future inflation rates—perpetuating the "virtuous circle" illustrated in Figure 15.5.

15.6 An increase in spending on new capital by firms for a given level of inflation, output, and real interest rate increases aggregate expenditures and short-run equilibrium output. Since the economy was originally operating at potential output, the increase in investment spending will lead to an expansionary gap; actual output, Y, will now be greater than potential output, Y^*. When $Y > Y^*$, the rate of inflation will tend to rise.

15.7 The effects will be the opposite of those illustrated in Figure 15.9. Beginning in a long-run equilibrium with output equal to potential output and stable inflation (that is, where the aggregate demand (AD) curve intersects both the short-run and long-run aggregate supply lines ($SRAS$ and $LRAS$, respectively)), the fall in consumption spending will initially lead to a leftward shift in the AD curve and the economy moves to a new, lower, short-run equilibrium output level at the same inflation rate. The shift in AD creates a recessionary gap, since Y is now less than Y^*. The immediate effect of the decrease in consumption spending is only to reduce output. However, over time inflation will fall because of the recessionary gap. As inflation falls, the $SRAS$ line will shift downward. The Federal Reserve responds to the fall in inflation by reducing real interest rates, leading to an increase in aggregate expenditure and output, a move down along the new AD curve. When inflation has fallen enough (and real interest rates have fallen enough) to eliminate the output gap, the economy will be back in long-run equilibrium where output equals potential output but the inflation rate will be lower than before the fall in consumption spending.

15.8 A decrease in oil prices is an example of a "beneficial" inflation shock and the economic effects of such a shock are the reverse of those illustrated in Figure 15.10. In this case, starting from a long-run equilibrium where output equals potential output, a beneficial inflation shock reduces current inflation, causing the $SRAS$ line to shift downward. The downward shift in the $SRAS$ curve leads to a short-run equilibrium with lower inflation and higher output, creating an expansionary gap. If the Fed does nothing, eventually the $SRAS$ will begin to shift upward and the economy will return to its original inflation and output levels. However, the Fed may instead choose to tighten its monetary policy by shifting up its monetary policy reaction function, raising the current real interest rate, shifting the AD curve to the left, and restoring equilibrium at potential GDP, but at the new, lower inflation rate.

15.9 If productivity growth hadn't increased in the last half of the 1990s, the $LRAS$ would not have shifted as far to the right as it actually did. As a consequence, the average inflation rate would not have fallen as much as illustrated in Table 15.1 and average real GDP growth would have been smaller. Similarly, if productivity growth slows in the future from its actual 1995–2000 rate, we can expect higher inflation and lower GDP growth than we otherwise would have experienced.

15.10 If Tom earned $5,000, he would pay no taxes, so his average tax rate would be 0 percent. If he earned $5,001, he would still pay no taxes, so his marginal tax rate also would be 0 percent.

If Tom earned $11,000, he would pay $0.20(\$11,000 - \$10,000) = \$200$ in taxes, so his average tax rate would be $\$200/\$11,000 = 0.018$, or 1.8 percent. If his income rose by $1 so that he earned $11,001, his taxes would be $0.20(\$11,001 - \$10,000) = \$200.20$. Thus, he would pay an additional $.20 in taxes and his marginal tax rate would be 20 percent.

If Tom earned $15,000, he would pay $0.20(\$15,000 - \$10,000) = \$1,000$ in taxes, and his average tax rate would be $\$1,000/\$15,000 = 0.067$, or 6.7 percent. If his income rose by $1 to $15,001, he would pay an additional $.20 in taxes, so his marginal tax rate would still be 20 percent.

15.11 Your answer depends on your particular circumstances.

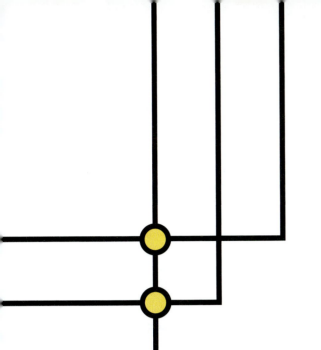

THE PRACTICE AND PITFALLS OF MACROECONOMIC POLICY

O n October 6, 1979, the Federal Open Market Committee, the policy-making committee of the Federal Reserve (see the chapter "Money, Prices, and the Federal Reserve"), held a highly unusual—and unusually secretive—Saturday meeting. Fed Chairman Paul Volcker may have called the Saturday meeting because he knew the financial markets would be closed and thus would not be able to respond to any "leaks" to the press about the discussions. Or perhaps he hoped that the visit of Pope John Paul II to Washington on the same day would distract the news media from goings-on at the Fed. However unnoticed this meeting may have been at the time, in retrospect it marked a turning point in postwar U.S. economic history.

When Volcker called the October 6 meeting, he had been chairman of the Fed for only six weeks. Six feet eight inches tall with a booming bass voice, and a chain-smoker of cheap cigars, Volcker had a reputation for financial conservatism and personal toughness. Partly for those qualities, President Carter had appointed Volcker to head the Federal Reserve in August 1979. Carter needed a tough Fed chairman to restore confidence in both the economy and the government's economic policies. The U.S. economy faced many problems, including a doubling of oil prices following the overthrow of the Shah of Iran and a worrisome slowdown in productivity growth. But in the minds of the public, the biggest economic worry was an inflation rate that seemed to be out of control. In the second half of 1979, the annual rate of increase in consumer prices had reached 13 percent; by the spring of 1980 the inflation rate had risen to nearly 16 percent. Volcker's assignment: to bring inflation under control and stabilize the U.S. economy.

Paul Volcker faced a tough assignment.

Volcker knew that getting rid of inflation would not be easy, and he warned his colleagues that a "shock treatment" might be necessary. His plan was couched in technical details, but in essence he proposed to reduce the rate of growth of the money supply sharply. Everyone in the room knew that slowing the growth of the money supply would cause interest rates to rise and aggregate spending to fall. Inflation might be brought down, but at what cost in terms of recession, lost output, and lost jobs? And how would the financial markets, which were already shaky, react to the new approach?

Officials in the room stirred nervously as Volcker spoke about the necessity of the move. Finally, a vote was called. Every hand went up.

What happened next? We will discuss the policies of the Volcker Fed and their effects later in this chapter. First, however, we must develop more background on the links between monetary policy and inflation.

We begin this chapter by extending the model used in preceding chapters to illustrate the short-run and long-run effects of tightening monetary policy in order to reduce inflation. We then use the model to discuss how the Fed can maintain low inflation when the economy is hit by shocks to aggregate demand or aggregate supply, and we also describe the ways in which monetary policy might be made more effective. Finally, we examine several practical difficulties in devising and implementing monetary and fiscal policy.

REDUCING HIGH INFLATION

High or even moderate rates of inflation are economically costly. What, then, should policymakers do if the inflation rate is too high? As Example 16.1 shows, inflation can be slowed by policies that shift the aggregate demand curve leftward. Although they produce the long-term gains in productivity and economic growth associated with low inflation, such policies are likely to impose significant short-run costs in the form of lost output and increased unemployment.

EXAMPLE 16.1

The effects of anti-inflationary monetary policy

Figure 16.1 illustrates both the short-run and long-run effects of an anti-inflationary monetary policy. In Figure 16.1(a), we depict the Fed's monetary policy reaction function we introduced in the chapter "Stabilizing the Economy." Recall that the Fed's monetary policy reaction function is described in Equation 14.2 as

$$r = r^* + g(\pi - \pi^*)$$

In Figure 16.1(a), the line labeled *MPRF* represents the monetary policy reaction function corresponding to an initial target inflation rate of 10 percent. When inflation is at its target, Equation 14.2 indicates that the actual real interest rate r will be equal to the Fed's target for the real interest rate r^*. Thus, at point A in Figure 16.1(a), $\pi = \pi_1^* = 10$ percent, and $r = r^*$.

In Figure 16.1(b), we connect the monetary policy reaction function to the aggregate demand–aggregate supply curves we introduced in the last chapter. The initial equilibrium at point A is depicted as a short-run equilibrium because it occurs at the intersection of the initial aggregate demand curve AD and the initial short-run aggregate supply line *SRAS*. Point A is also a long-run equilibrium because it is located at the intersection of AD and the long-run aggregate supply line *LRAS*. Consequently, at point A, actual output is equal to potential output $(Y = Y^*)$. Note that inflation, which is measured on the horizontal axis in Figure 16.1(a), is measured on the vertical axis in Figure 16.1(b).

Suppose the Fed decides that the high inflation is impeding economic performance and long-run economic growth. Consequently, it decides to adopt a tighter monetary policy, under which the long-run target inflation rate is 3 percent, rather than 10 percent. As we will show, the economic effects of adopting a tighter monetary policy are very different in the short run and in the long run. The Fed begins to

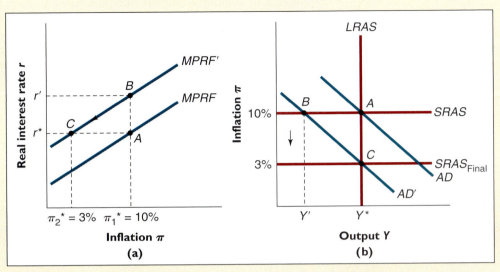

FIGURE 16.1

Short-Run and Long-Run Effects of an Anti-inflationary Monetary Policy.

(a) The economy is initially in long-run equilibrium at point A. Actual inflation is equal to the Fed's target rate of inflation of 10 percent, the real interest rate is equal to the target real interest rate r^*, and actual output is equal to potential. If the Fed reduces its target inflation rate to 3 percent, the monetary policy reaction function MPRF shifts left (upwards) to MPRF'. At the initial inflation rate of 10 percent, this will require an increase in the real interest rate to r'.

(b) The shift in the monetary policy reaction function shifts the aggregate demand curve to the left, from AD to AD', and the economy reaches a new short-run equilibrium at point B. Output falls to Y', but inflation doesn't change.

The recessionary gap that exists at point B eventually causes inflation to decline, shifting the short-run aggregate supply line downward. Long-run equilibrium is restored at point C, at which point real output returns to potential, inflation falls to the new lower target inflation rate of 3 percent, and the real interest rate returns to its target, r^*.

reduce inflation by decreasing its target rate of inflation. In Figure 16.1(a), we assume that the Fed reduces its target inflation rate to 3 percent. As we saw in the last chapter, the monetary policy reaction function will then shift to the left (or upwards) in Figure 16.1(a) so that $r = r^*$ when $\pi = \pi^* = 3$ percent, at point C. The economy, however, does not move directly from point A to point C. At the initial rate of inflation of 10 percent, the Fed must first increase the real interest rate to r' at point B.

An increase in the real interest rate will reduce consumption and investment spending, lowering aggregate demand at every inflation rate and shifting the aggregate demand curve to the left in Figure 16.1(b) from AD to AD'. After the Fed's action, the AD' curve and the SRAS line intersect at point B, the new short-run equilibrium. Actual output has fallen to Y', which is less than potential output Y^*. In other words, the Fed's action has allowed a recessionary gap to develop, so that unemployment will exceed the natural rate. At point B, however, the inflation rate is still 10 percent. Thus, in the short run, a monetary tightening pushes the economy into recession but has little or no effect on the inflation rate because of inflation inertia.

The short-run effects of the anti-inflationary shift in monetary policy—lower output, higher unemployment, and little or no reduction of inflation—are not encouraging, and they explain why such policy shifts are often unpopular in their early stages. Fortunately, the economy will not remain at point B indefinitely. The existence of a recessionary gap at point B eventually causes inflation to decline, as firms become more reluctant to raise their prices in the face of weak demand.

The eventual decline in inflation that results from a recessionary gap is illustrated by the gradual downward shift of the short-run aggregate supply line, from SRAS to

$SRAS_{Final}$ in Figure 16.1(b) and the movement along the new monetary policy reaction function $MPRF'$ in Figure 16.1(a). As the economy moves from point B to point C in Figure 16.1(a), inflation falls. This allows the Fed to lower the real interest rate from r' to r^* while staying on its new monetary policy reaction function (with its lower target inflation rate). The reduction in the real interest rate spurs investment from its depressed level and moves output back to potential, reflected by the move from point B to point C along the AD' curve in Figure 16.1(b). Inflation will continue to fall until the economy returns to long-run equilibrium at point C in both graphs. At that point, actual output has returned to potential, the inflation rate has stabilized at the new target inflation rate of 3 percent, and the real interest rate is once again equal to its target, r^*.

The adoption of a tighter monetary policy (reflected by a reduction in the Fed's target rate of inflation) therefore inflicts short-term pain (a decline in output, high unemployment, and a temporarily high real interest rate) to achieve a long-term gain (a permanent reduction in inflation). In the long run, however, the adoption of a tighter monetary policy will result in lower inflation but will affect neither real output nor the real interest rate. Recall that any change in the Fed's target for inflation will shift its monetary policy reaction function. Any shift in the Fed's monetary policy reaction function will then shift the aggregate demand curve. The adoption of a tighter monetary policy (a shift in $MRPF$ up or to the left) will shift the AD curve left; the adoption of a looser monetary policy (a shift in $MPRF$ down or to the right) will shift the AD curve right.

EXERCISE 16.1

Show the typical time paths of output, inflation, and the real interest rate when the Fed adopts a tighter (more anti-inflationary) monetary policy. Draw a separate graph for each variable, showing time on the horizontal axis. Be sure to distinguish the short run from the long run. Specific numerical values are not necessary.

"I don't like 6 per-cent unemployment, either. But I can live with it."

Now that we have seen how the adoption of a tighter monetary policy affects the economy, Economic Naturalist 16.1 discusses the situation faced by the Fed and Paul Volcker that we introduced at the beginning of this chapter.

How was inflation conquered in the 1980s?

After reaching double-digit levels in the late 1970s and 13.5 percent in 1980, inflation in the United States fell all the way to 3.2 percent in 1983, and it remained in the 2–5 percent range for the rest of the decade. In the 1990s, inflation fell even lower, in the 2–3 percent range in most years. How was inflation conquered in the 1980s?

ECONOMIC NATURALIST 16.1

The person who was most directly responsible for the conquest of inflation in the 1980s was the Federal Reserve's chairman, Paul Volcker. Following the secret Saturday meeting he called on October 6, 1979 (described in the introduction to this chapter), the Federal Open Market Committee agreed to adopt a strongly anti-inflationary monetary policy. The results of this policy change on the U.S. economy are shown in Table 16.1, which includes selected macroeconomic data for the period 1978–1985.

The data in Table 16.1 fit our analysis of anti-inflationary monetary policy quite well. First, as our model predicts, in the short run the Fed's adoption of a tighter monetary policy led to a recession. In fact, two recessions followed the Fed's action in 1979, a short one in 1980 and a deeper one in 1981–1982. Note that growth in real GDP was negative in 1980 and 1982, and the unemployment rate rose significantly, peaking at 9.7 percent in 1982. Nominal and real interest rates also rose, a direct effect of the shift in monetary policy. Inflation, however, did not respond much during the period 1979–1981. All these results are consistent with the short-run analysis in Figure 16.1.

By 1983, however, the situation had changed markedly. The economy had recovered, with strong growth in real GDP in 1983–1985 (see Table 16.1). In 1984 the unemployment rate, which tends to lag the recovery, began to decline. Interest rates remained relatively high, perhaps reflecting other factors besides monetary policy. Most significantly, inflation fell in 1982–1983 and stabilized at a much lower level. Inflation has remained low in the United States ever since.

TABLE 16.1
U.S. Macroeconomic Data, 1978–1985

Year	Growth in real GDP (%)	Unemployment rate (%)	Inflation rate (%)	Nominal interest rate (%)	Real interest rate (%)
1978	5.5	6.1	7.6	8.3	0.7
1979	3.2	5.8	11.4	9.7	−1.7
1980	−0.2	7.1	13.5	11.6	−1.9
1981	2.5	7.6	10.3	14.4	4.1
1982	−2.0	9.7	6.2	12.9	6.7
1983	4.3	9.6	3.2	10.5	7.3
1984	7.3	7.5	4.3	11.9	7.6
1985	3.8	7.2	3.6	9.6	6.0

SOURCE: *Economic Report of the President* (http://www.gpoaccess.gov/eop) and calculations by the author.

disinflation a substantial
reduction in the rate of inflation

A substantial reduction in the rate of inflation, like the one the Fed engineered in the 1980s, is called a **disinflation**. But again, disinflation may come at the cost of a large recessionary gap and high unemployment like that experienced by the United States in the early 1980s. Is this cost worth bearing? This question is not an easy one to answer because the costs of inflation are difficult to measure. Policymakers around the world appear to agree on the necessity of containing inflation, however, as many countries fought to bring their own inflation rates down to 2 percent or less in the 1980s and 1990s. Canada and Great Britain are among the many industrial countries that have borne the costs of sharp reductions in inflation.

Can the costs of disinflation be reduced? Unfortunately, no one has found a pain-free method of lowering the inflation rate. Accordingly, in recent years central banks around the world have striven to keep inflation at manageable levels, to avoid the costs of disinflation. In the next section, we discuss how the Fed can maintain a low rate of inflation when the economy is buffeted by shocks to aggregate demand or aggregate supply.

RECAP	**REDUCING HIGH INFLATION**

Inflation can be reduced by policies that shift the aggregate demand curve leftward, such as the adoption of a "tighter" monetary policy (an upward or leftward shift in the monetary policy reaction function). In the short run, the effects of a change to a tighter, more anti-inflationary monetary policy are felt largely on output, so that a disinflation (a substantial reduction in inflation) may create a significant recessionary gap. In the long run, output should return to potential and inflation should decline. These predictions were borne out during the Volcker disinflation of the early 1980s.

KEEPING INFLATION LOW

In the two decades since the Volcker disinflation, the United States has had relatively low inflation. Although inflation briefly rose above 5 percent in 1990, it has stayed below the 3.6 percent achieved in 1986 in all but three years. During this same period, real GDP growth has averaged 3.2 percent per year and the two economic recessions the United States has experienced have been short and relatively mild. Most economists believe that low inflation is an important reason for increased economic growth and greater economic stability. Moreover, a low inflation rate makes costly disinflations unnecessary. Thus, keeping inflation low is one of the best things that the Federal Reserve can do for the U.S. economy.

In this section, we examine the Fed's policy choices in a low-inflation environment. We illustrate how policy responses and the consequences of anti-inflationary policies may differ according to whether the disturbances in the economy are caused by shocks in spending or shocks to aggregate supply.

EXAMPLE 16.2

Responding to shocks in spending

As we learned in the last chapter, changes in monetary policy are not the only factors that shift the aggregate demand curve. The aggregate demand curve also will shift in response to changes in fiscal policy and other exogenous changes in spending. As we will see, if these changes in spending are permanent, the Fed will be able to maintain inflation at its original target inflation rate in the long run only if it changes its target real interest rate.

To understand this important point, let's re-examine the analysis of the effects of a change in fiscal policy that we began in the last chapter. In Figure 16.2(b), we depict the situation in Figure 15.8, where we examined the effects of an increase in military spending. As before, we begin at point A, at which output is equal to potential output Y^* and inflation is steady. In Figure 16.2(a), note that this corresponds to a point on the Fed's monetary policy reaction function at which actual inflation π is equal to the Fed's target rate of inflation π^* and the actual real interest rate r is equal to the Fed's target real interest rate r_1^*.

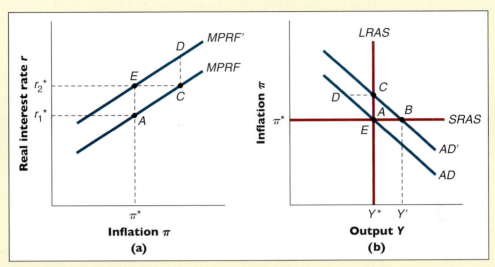

FIGURE 16.2

Maintaining Low Inflation After a Change in Spending.

Initially the economy is in long-run equilibrium at point A. Actual inflation is equal to the Fed's target rate of π^*, and actual output is equal to potential output Y^*. An increase in spending shifts the AD curve to the right, to AD'. In the short run, real GDP rises to Y', but inflation does not change. The expansionary gap leads to rising inflation, causing the SRAS line to shift up. If the Fed accommodates this increase in inflation, the economy moves to point C in the long run. Actual output returns to its potential level with a higher inflation rate.

If, however, the Fed does not want inflation to exceed its target, it can raise the target real interest rate to r_2^*. This will shift the monetary policy reaction function up to MPRF', and the aggregate demand curve will shift back to AD. Actual output will again be equal to its potential level in the long run, but inflation will return to the target level of π^*.

Now let us suppose an increase in military spending shifts the aggregate demand curve to the right. The shift in aggregate demand also could come from a cut in taxes or a sudden increase in consumption or investment spending. If the Fed does not shift its monetary policy reaction function, the economy moves from point A to point B in Figure 16.2(b) in the short run. Real GDP rises, creating an expansionary gap, but initially inflation does not change. Over time, however, the short-run aggregate supply line shifts up in response to the expansionary gap. As a result, inflation will begin to rise.

At this point, the Fed has a choice. If it allows inflation to rise above its target, the economy will gradually move to point C in Figure 16.2(a) and (b). Inflation will continue to rise, and the economy will gradually move back to potential output in the long run at a permanently higher rate of inflation. At point C, however, both inflation and the real interest rate will exceed the Fed's targets (π^* and r_1^*).

The Fed, however, can prevent inflation from rising by raising its target for the real interest rate to r_2^*. Recall that the monetary policy reaction function is drawn so that when actual inflation is equal to the Fed's target for inflation, the real interest rate is equal to the Fed's target real interest rate. Consequently, an increase in the Fed's target real interest rate will shift the Fed's monetary policy reaction function up (to the left) from MPRF to MPRF'. This shift in the Fed's monetary policy reaction function will shift the aggregate demand curve back to AD. Output will return to potential and inflation will eventually return to π^* at point E in Figures 16.2(a) and 16.2(b). While output returns to potential regardless of what the Fed does, the Fed can prevent inflation from permanently rising by increasing its target real interest rate and acting accordingly.

If the Fed waits to raise r^* until the economy moves from point B to point C, it will temporarily have to raise the real interest rate to point D in Figure 16.2(a). The economy will then experience a period of rapid growth followed by a period of contraction until it returns to potential output at point E in Figure 16.2(b). The Fed, however, may decide to act earlier and avoid both the elevated inflation and the boom-bust cycle in output. It can act *preemptively* by raising its target real interest rate immediately to r_2^*.[1] This increase in r^* would shift the monetary policy reaction function up immediately. Although the initial increase in spending may shift the aggregate demand curve from AD to AD', the Fed's action would shift it relatively quickly back to AD. As a result, the economy would remain at full employment and inflation would never change from its initial level. Output can be stabilized at potential and inflation can be kept low.

As we saw in the last chapter, changes in fiscal policy and other changes in spending do not change real output in the long run. Now, however, we see that inflation will change only if the Fed allows it to change. Sometimes economists use the word *accommodating* to describe a policy that allows the effects of a shock to occur. In this example, the Fed's **accommodating policy** would allow the spending shock to increase output in the short run and inflation in the long run. Rather than accommodate the spending shock, however, the Fed could block its effects on both output and inflation by raising its target real interest rate.

Why does the Fed have to increase its target for the real interest rate in order to maintain stable output and inflation? Recall from the chapter "Saving and Capital Formation" that the real interest rate is determined by saving and investment in the long run. An increase in military spending, or any other increase in government spending (or reduction in net taxes) will increase the government budget deficit. As we saw in Figure 9.9, an increase in the federal budget deficit reduces national saving and increases the real interest rate in the long run. In order to avoid long-run inflationary consequences, the Fed must raise its target real interest rate to a level that is compatible with long-run equilibrium in the market for saving and investment.

This model also can be used to analyze a sudden reduction in spending. Starting again at potential output, a reduction in spending will shift the aggregate demand curve to the left. The Fed can eliminate the recessionary gap resulting from this shift by reducing its real interest rate target. Once again, real GDP returns to potential and inflation returns to the Fed's target rate of inflation.

accommodating policy a policy that allows the effects of a shock to occur

EXERCISE 16.2

Suppose the economy is initially in long-run equilibrium and there is a sudden decrease in spending. Use the monetary policy reaction function graph and aggregate supply–aggregate demand graphs to illustrate and explain what happens to output and inflation in the short run and the long run. Assume that after the economy moves back to potential output, the Fed lowers its target real interest rate to the new real interest rate at which saving equals investment in the long run. Then explain what the differences would be if the Fed lowers its target real interest rate immediately after the decrease in spending.

[1]Note that r_2^* is also the actual real interest rate that is consistent with full employment after the shift in aggregate demand.

Why did the Fed lower interest rates again in 2003?

ECONOMIC NATURALIST 16.2

As we discussed in the last chapter, the Fed reduced the federal funds rate from 6.50 percent in January 2001 to 1.75 percent in December 2001 in order to fight the 2001 recession. After the economy began to recover in 2002 and 2003, however, the Fed again reduced the federal funds rate to 1.25 percent in November 2002 and 1.0 percent in June 2003. Why did the Fed continue to reduce the federal funds rate even during the recovery?

There were several reasons for the Fed's policy choices. First, as we mentioned before, economic growth even during the recovery was slower than it had been in previous recoveries. Second, job growth did not keep up with the growth in output, due to the unusual increases in productivity. In addition, there was a major slow-down in investment spending as businesses became more cautious, especially following the decline in the stock market. As a result, the Fed was concerned that aggregate demand might fall and create a recessionary gap. The reduction in investment spending also implied that there might have been a reduction in the long-run real interest rate at which saving equaled investment. In response, the Fed reduced its target real interest rate, which shifted its monetary policy reaction function down (to the right).

The Fed's action prevented the aggregate demand curve from falling further and thereby avoided a recession. This is another illustration of how the Fed can stabilize both inflation and output when there is a shock to aggregate demand.

Example 16.2 and Economic Naturalist 16.2 illustrated that shocks in aggregate demand do not require the Fed to make a difficult choice between inflation and the stability of output. The Fed can maintain stable inflation and output by adjusting its target real interest rate to the real interest rate at which saving equals investment in the long run. We examine the Fed's possible responses to an aggregate supply shock in the next example.

Responding to shocks in aggregate supply

EXAMPLE 16.3

Although shocks to aggregate demand do not require the Fed to choose between inflation and output stability, shocks to aggregate supply do create such a dilemma. If the Fed maintains its initial target inflation rate, the economy may experience a protracted recessionary or expansionary gap. If, on the other hand, it wants to hasten the return to potential GDP, it may have to change its inflation target.

We illustrate this situation in Figure 16.3. Once again, the economy starts at point A in both diagrams, with $Y = Y^*$, $\pi = \pi_1^*$, and $r = r^*$. Now suppose an adverse inflation shock shifts the short-run aggregate supply line up in Figure 16.3(b), just as in Figure 15.9. In the short run, the economy moves to point B, with higher inflation and a recessionary gap.

At this point, the Fed faces the dilemma we introduced in the last chapter. If it wants to avoid a recession, it can increase its target inflation rate to π_2^*. This will shift the monetary policy reaction function down (to the right) to $MPRF'$ and the aggregate demand curve to the right, to AD'. Output will return quickly to potential at point C, but inflation will be permanently higher. The initial bulge in inflation following the supply shock will be followed by a second round of inflation. In the second round, the initial increase in inflation leads to a change in inflationary expectations. Workers and firms will then expect prices to continue to rise, so they push for continued increases in wages and prices. Consequently, the higher inflation rate will be sustained.

Alternatively, when the economy is buffeted by an adverse inflation shock, the Fed can prevent inflation from becoming permanently higher by maintaining its original target inflation rate. By doing so, the Fed can preempt the second round of inflation and prevent the bulge in inflation from becoming permanent. If the Fed

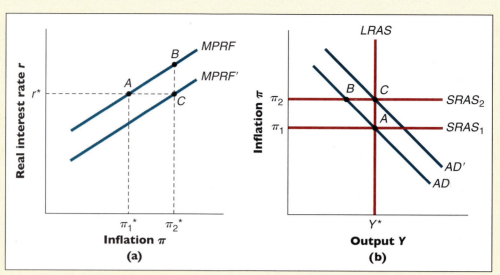

FIGURE 16.3

Maintaining Low Inflation after an Adverse Inflation Shock.

Initially the economy is in long-run equilibrium at point *A* with actual inflation equal to the Fed's initial target rate of π_1^* and actual output equal to potential output Y^*. An oil price increase or another adverse inflation shock shifts the *SRAS* line up to $SRAS_2$. If the Fed accommodates the supply shock, it increases its target inflation rate to π_2^*. This shifts the monetary policy reaction function downwards (to the right) to *MPRF'*, and the *AD* curve also shifts right to *AD'*. The economy moves quickly to point *C* and any recession is short-lived.

If, however, the Fed does not change its target inflation rate, neither the monetary policy reaction function nor the aggregate demand curve will shift. In the short run, we move to point *B* and real GDP falls. The recessionary gap at point *B* will gradually shift the short-run aggregate supply line down until real output again returns to potential and inflation falls back to its unchanged target at point *A*.

does not change its monetary policy (in which case the monetary policy reaction function does not shift), the recessionary gap that exists at point *B* will gradually shift the short-run aggregate supply line back down to $SRAS_1$, and the economy will move back to point *A* in the long run. Inflation will return to its initial rate and real GDP will return to potential. In the interim, however, the economy may experience a recession.

In deciding which of these two policy alternatives to follow, the Fed might like to know how long it would take for the economy to return to potential (at point *A*) if it did not change monetary policy. The answer depends on the speed with which the short-run aggregate supply line shifts down when an adverse inflation shock creates a recessionary gap. If the *SRAS* line shifts down quickly, the Fed is more likely to keep its target inflation rate unchanged at π_1^* because any recession will probably be short. If, on the other hand, the *SRAS* line shifts down very slowly, the Fed may be more inclined to increase its target inflation rate to avoid a lengthy recession.

Ironically, the speed with which the short-run aggregate supply line shifts back down following an adverse inflation shock depends partly on the public's expectation of how the Fed will act. If people are confident that the Fed will maintain its original target inflation rate, their expectations of future inflation will not change even if inflation rises temporarily. If this is the case, we describe people's expectations of inflation as being **anchored**. When an adverse supply shock increases inflation, people with anchored expectations believe that the Fed

anchored inflationary expectations when people's expectations of future inflation do not change even if inflation rises temporarily will act to ensure that inflation quickly falls back to its initial level. Workers will then be less likely to ask for inflationary wage increases and firms will be less likely to raise prices. The second round of inflation will be eliminated, the short-run aggregate supply line will shift back to $SRAS_1$ more rapidly, and output will return to potential more quickly. Because any recession will be shorter if inflationary expectations are anchored, the Fed also will be comfortable keeping its target inflation rate unchanged.

If, on the other hand, the Fed has frequently accommodated higher inflation rates in the past, expectations of inflation may not be anchored. If the public believes the Fed will raise its target inflation rate, expectations of future inflation will be higher. Workers will then demand larger wage increases and firms will raise prices more rapidly. In that event, the short-run aggregate supply line will shift down more slowly, and the return to full employment will be prolonged. Thus, the Fed has a stake in convincing the public that it will maintain its original target inflation rate. In Economic Naturalists 16.3 and 16.4, we suggest two periods during which anchored inflationary expectations may have contributed to improved macroeconomic performance.

Why has macroeconomic volatility in the United States declined so much since 1985?

Since about 1985, both real GDP growth and inflation have become much less volatile than they were prior to 1985. As shown in Figure 16.4, the variability in the growth rate of real GDP has been about half of what it was prior to 1985. In addition, the rate of inflation has declined by two-thirds.[2]

Reduced macroeconomic volatility has numerous benefits for the economy. It improves market functioning, makes economic and business planning easier, and reduces the resources devoted to managing inflation risks. More stable output and employment reduce the economic uncertainty confronting households and

ECONOMIC NATURALIST 16.3

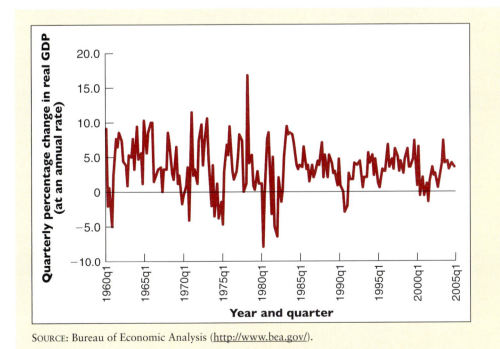

FIGURE 16.4
The Changing Volatility of Real GDP.
Since 1985 there has been a dramatic reduction in the volatility of real GDP.

SOURCE: Bureau of Economic Analysis (http://www.bea.gov/).

[2]Olivier J. Blanchard and John A. Simon, "The Long and Large Decline in U.S. Output Volatility," *Brookings Papers on Economic Activity*, 1: 135–164, 2001. Students who have taken statistics know that scientists generally use the variance of a variable (or its square root, called the standard deviation) to measure its variability.

firms. But why has macroeconomic volatility in the United States declined so markedly?

Many economists believe that better macroeconomic policy, especially monetary policy, is responsible for the reduced variability in both output and inflation. Prior to 1981, the Federal Reserve often allowed inflation to rise in response to shocks to aggregate demand and aggregate supply. This was followed by periodic attempts to rein in the inflation that followed. These swings in monetary policy from ease to tightness contributed to volatility in both output and inflation. Since the early 1980s, however, the Fed has been more consistent in its efforts to keep inflation from rising. These efforts have paid off by anchoring inflationary expectations, which, as we have just discussed, can stabilize not only inflation, but output, too.[3]

While most economists attribute the reduced variability in inflation to actions of the Fed, others believe that structural changes in the economy, and not the Fed, are largely responsible for the reduced variability in output. These structural changes include changes in technology, business practices, and other structural features that have improved the ability of the economy to absorb shocks. Some examples of these changes include better management of inventories, deregulation, the shift away from manufacturing and toward services, and an increased openness to trade and international capital flows.

ECONOMIC
NATURALIST
16.4

Why didn't the oil price increases of 2003–2005 lead to a recession or a substantial increase in inflation?

Economic Naturalist 15.2 discussed the experience of the U.S. economy following the substantial oil price increases of 1973–1974 and 1979. The world price of crude oil was about $3 per barrel in 1972; by the end of 1974, that price had quadrupled to $12. After remaining relatively constant for the next four years, the price nearly tripled again between 1978 and 1981, reaching $35 per barrel in 1981. In both cases, the price increases caused inflation shocks and were followed by stagflation— a period of recession and high inflation. With the exception of several periods of very low prices and an upward spike in 1999–2000, the price of oil fell gradually after 1981, reaching about $23 per barrel in 2002.

Starting in 2002, oil prices again rose dramatically, and the increase accelerated in 2003, 2004, and 2005.[4] By late 2004, average oil prices had exceeded $40 per barrel and prices rose above $65 per barrel in August 2005. At the time this edition is being written, however, the oil price increase has led to neither a recession nor a substantial increase in inflation. Real GDP grew at an annual rate of 2.7 percent in 2003, 4.2 percent in 2004, and 3.5 percent during the first half of 2005. Although the consumer price index rose by 1.9 percent in 2003, 3.4 percent in 2004, and 3.5 percent (at an annual rate) during the first seven months of 2005, this increase was much less dramatic than in earlier periods. Why did the economy respond so differently after the most recent oil price increase? Several explanations have been offered.

The first thing to note is that the real price of oil, which is the price of oil relative to the CPI, reached its (annual average) peak in 1981, when its price was $35 per barrel and the CPI was 0.91. By July 2005, the CPI had risen to 1.95. Consequently, a price of $35 per barrel in 1981 was equivalent to a price of $35(1.95/0.91) = $75 per barrel in July 2005. In real terms, the actual price of $65 in August 2005 was still below its peak in 1981.

Prior to the first inflation shock of 1973, the technology used in U.S. factories was based on cheap oil. When the real price rose sharply during the next decade, some energy-intensive factories became obsolete and were shut down.

---

[3]Ben Bernanke, "The Great Moderation," February 20, 2004, http://www.federalreserve.gov/boarddocs/speeches/2004/20040220/default.htm.
[4]U.S. Department of Energy, *Monthly Energy Review*, (www.eia.doe.gov/emeu/mer/prices.html).

Over time, new energy-saving technologies were also developed and adopted. Consequently, by the time real oil prices increased again in 2003–2004, U.S. factories already employed technologies that were profitable even with high energy prices.

Furthermore, the U.S. economy as a whole is now less reliant on energy. Manufacturing, which is still energy-intensive, comprises a smaller share of GDP as the United States has become a more service-oriented economy. New homes are better insulated and appliances and cars (even some SUVs) have become more energy efficient. As a result, the ratio of energy use per dollar of output fell from 14,427 Btus[5] per dollar of real GDP (in 2000 dollars) in 1981 to 9,462 Btus per dollar of real GDP in 2003.

A third reason for the (to-date) relatively benign response of the American economy to the latest oil price increase is related to inflationary expectations and the inflation-fighting reputation of the Fed. When the first two oil price increases shifted the short-run aggregate supply line up, the initial bulges in inflation were followed by second rounds of inflation. The oil price increases led to increases in inflationary expectations because the public thought the Fed might accommodate the higher inflation, and higher inflationary expectations in turn led to further increases in wages and prices. In this manner, the higher inflation was sustained.

In contrast, today most economists believe that inflationary expectations are more firmly anchored than they were in the 1970s. Much of the credit for this development belongs to Paul Volcker and Alan Greenspan. During their terms as chair of the Federal Reserve, the Fed acquired a reputation as an inflation fighter. Similar to the earlier oil price shocks, the 2003–2005 oil price increase also pushed the short-run aggregate supply line up. In this later period, however, people believed the Fed would quickly act to keep inflation low and preempt the second round of inflation. Consequently, expectations of inflation did not rise, and the short-run aggregate supply line shifted down much more quickly.

THE CORE RATE OF INFLATION

A bulge in inflation is not inevitable when there is an adverse aggregate supply shock, such as a sharp increase in energy prices. In principle, the Fed could prevent inflation from rising by adopting such a tight monetary policy that the initial bulge coming from higher energy prices would be offset by declines in nonenergy prices. Yet experience suggests that such a policy is likely to be too costly in terms of lost output as well as unnecessary for keeping inflation under control in the longer term. Instead, some economists suggest that the Fed accept the immediate inflationary effect of an oil price increase but act to minimize any second-round effect that occurs if the shock changes inflationary expectations and thereby affects wages and nonoil prices. If the Fed can prevent energy price increases from changing inflationary expectations, it can prevent inflation from becoming permanently higher.

To allow a temporary bulge but keep long-term inflationary expectations from rising, the Fed can focus on the **core rate of inflation,** defined as the rate of increase of all prices *except energy and food,* the two items most frequently responsible for inflation shocks.[6] Because core inflation excludes the sources of the most volatile price changes, it is considered to be a useful short-term measure of the underlying inflation trend. If the core rate of inflation does not change, the initial supply shock probably has not led to any second-round effects. Thus, the Fed may decide to adopt a tighter monetary policy only if the core rate of inflation exceeds its target inflation rate. Note that the Fed's focus on core inflation does not mean that it does not care about overall inflation, which includes oil and food prices. Rather, by

core rate of inflation the rate of increase of all prices except energy and food

---

[5]A British thermal unit (Btu) is a measure of energy consumption.
[6]Since energy and food are used as inputs in many other industries, some of the indirect effects of an increase in the prices of energy and food will be included even in the core rate of inflation.

focusing on the core rate of inflation, the Fed can prevent the bulge in inflation following an inflation shock from becoming permanent.

Table 16.2 presents the general and core rates of inflation from July 2002, through July 2005. During this period the general rate of inflation rose significantly, reflecting the sharp increase in oil prices. The core rate of inflation, however, was both lower and increased by less, implying that the Fed had so far successfully mitigated the second-round effects.

TABLE 16.2
U.S. Annualized Inflation Rates, July 2002–July 2005

Period	Annualized CPI inflation (%)	Annualized core inflation (CPI inflation excluding food and energy) (%)
July 2002–July 2003	2.1	1.5
July 2003–July 2004	3.0	1.8
July 2004–July 2005	3.2	2.1

SOURCE: U.S. Bureau of Labor Statistics (http://www.bls.gov/data/).

RECAP	KEEPING INFLATION LOW

In response to changes in spending that create shocks in aggregate demand, the Fed can maintain stable inflation and output by adjusting its target real interest rate to the real interest rate at which saving equals investment in the long run. Shocks to aggregate supply (such as inflation shocks), however, force the Fed to choose between maintaining inflation and stabilizing output. If inflationary expectations are anchored, however, the return to potential output following an inflation shock will occur more rapidly. By monitoring the core rate of inflation, the Fed can determine whether an inflation shock has led to any second-round effects on inflation and can act accordingly.

INFLATIONARY EXPECTATIONS AND CREDIBILITY

As we saw in the previous section, macroeconomic performance may be improved if inflationary expectations are anchored. But what determines whether expectations are anchored? Most economists believe that it depends on the **credibility of monetary policy,** which is the degree to which the public believes the central bank's promises to keep inflation low, even if doing so may impose short-run economic costs.

The importance of credibility was illustrated in Example 16.3 following an adverse inflation shock. In that case, the Fed's credibility as an inflation-fighter preempted the second-round effects of inflation and hastened the return to full employment at the original rate of inflation. Economists have identified several institutional characteristics that may affect the credibility of the central bank's pronouncements to keep inflation low and thus its ability to do so. These include the degree of central bank independence, the announcement of explicit inflation targets, and the establishment of a reputation for fighting inflation.

CENTRAL BANK INDEPENDENCE

The credibility of monetary policy may be enhanced if central bankers are insulated from short-term political considerations, a condition that is sometimes referred to

credibility of monetary policy the degree to which the public believes the central bank's promises to keep inflation low, even if doing so may impose short-run economic costs

as **central bank independence.** Independent central banks will be better able to take a long-term view of the economy. In particular, they can pursue anti-inflation policy when it is necessary, even if it leads to a temporary recession. Elected politicians, on the other hand, face frequent reelections, and they may be swayed by short-term political considerations to allow the economy to overexpand at the cost of higher inflation in the long run. Because of its enhanced credibility, an independent central bank may find it easier to anchor the public's expectations of inflation, reducing the duration of any inflationary or recessionary gap and promoting overall economic stability.

Various factors contribute to a central bank's independence. Among the many possible factors, we list four:

- The length of appointments to the central bank. Central banks are considered to be more independent if their central bankers are appointed for long terms, especially if the terms are staggered so that a single president or group of legislators cannot replace them all at once.

- Whether the central bank's actions are subject to frequent interference, review, or veto by the legislative branch. Central banks are considered to be more independent if their actions are not subject to frequent interference or review.

- Whether the central bank has the obligation, as it does in some countries, to finance the national deficit by buying newly issued government bonds. The obligation to do so reduces a central bank's independence.

- The degree to which the central bank's budget is controlled by the legislative or executive branch of government. Central banks are considered to be more independent if they are allowed to set and control their own budgets.

The U.S. Federal Reserve is generally considered to be a relatively independent central bank. The seven members of the Federal Reserve are appointed to staggered terms of 14 years, in contrast to the members of the U.S. House of Representatives, the president, and members of the Senate, who must face reelection every two, four, and six years, respectively. Although appointments to the Fed's Board of Governors must be approved by the Senate, and the Federal Reserve is subject to general oversight by the Congress, the daily policy actions of the Fed are not subject to review, approval, or veto by either the executive, legislative, or judicial branches of government. Finally, the Fed is under no obligation to finance the national deficit, and it controls its own budget. On the other hand, the law that created the Fed (the Federal Reserve Act) does not explicitly prohibit interference in monetary policy decisions by the legislative and executive branches of government. This prohibition is explicit in the central banking laws of many other countries.

Empirical evidence supports the proposition that countries should foster the independence of their central banks. Countries whose central banks are more independent have lower rates of inflation. More importantly, the lower inflation does not appear to come at the cost of lower output or higher unemployment, according to most studies. By enhancing a central bank's credibility, greater central bank independence leads to better overall economic outcomes.

ANNOUNCING A NUMERICAL INFLATION TARGET

Some economists believe that expectations are more firmly anchored and the central bank is perceived as more credible in those countries in which the central bank announces an explicit, numerical target for inflation. We have already introduced the idea of a target rate of inflation, or π^*, in our discussion of the monetary policy reaction function. Generally speaking, central banks must have an idea of the inflation rate they would like to achieve in order to make sensible policy. The more controversial question is whether central banks should announce their target inflation

central bank independence
when central bankers are insulated from short-term political considerations and are allowed to take a long-term view of the economy

rate to the public. Proponents argue that announcing a numerical target for long-run inflation, and then sticking to it, will increase credibility and better anchor inflation expectations.

Many central banks publicly announce their inflation target. The Bank of Canada, for example, began announcing its inflation target in 1991. Since 1995, that target has been 2 percent. In April 2005, the Bank of England's inflation target was 2 percent, and the Central Bank of Brazil's target was 4.5 percent. Other central banks provide a range for their target rather than, or in addition to, a single number. The Bank of Israel and the Reserve Bank of New Zealand, for example, both had a 1–3 percent target range as of April 2005; in Chile the range was 2–4 percent. Of course, the inflation targets must be consistently met if they are to be effective. The Reserve Bank of Zimbabwe's target range of 20–35 percent as of March 2005, for example, was generally believed to be implausibly low since prices more than doubled in 2004. It subsequently raised the target to 75–80 percent in April.

Central banks that announce their targets typically provide additional information to the public. This information may include their forecasts of inflation, real GDP, and other variables, as well as some discussion of the specific policies that will be needed to meet their targets. Advocates believe that announcing inflation targets and accompanying them with supporting information enhances the credibility of the central bank and reduces uncertainty among households and firms. This helps to anchor inflationary expectations, keep inflation low, and maintain full employment. Note that it makes sense for a central bank to announce a long-run inflation target, in that the central bank is able to control the rate of inflation in the long run. It would *not* make sense for a central bank to announce a long-run target for real GDP or employment, because these variables are determined by a host of factors (such as productivity and the supply of labor) that are not under the control of the central bank.

Once an inflation target is announced, the central bank may choose to adhere to it strictly, or it may be more flexible. A central bank that sets a strict target tries to meet the target all the time without regard for the consequences for output. As we have seen, this policy keeps output at potential when the economy is beset by spending shocks, but it may result in a recession if the central bank acts to eliminate even the initial bulge in inflation following a shock to aggregate supply, such as an inflation shock. In practice, virtually all central banks that announce an inflation target are flexible inflation targeters—they try to hit their inflation target in the long run or on average over a long period while responding to short-term shocks to aggregate supply in a way that takes account of both output gaps and inflation. In these cases, the announced inflation targets correspond to the target inflation rate in the monetary policy reaction function π^*.

Advocates of announcing explicit numerical targets believe that this practice reduces uncertainty in financial markets and among the public. Reduced uncertainty allows people to plan more effectively, save the resources used to protect themselves from unexpected inflation, and improve market functioning. By putting the prestige of the central bank behind its commitment to meet the target, the advocates also believe that explicit inflation targets enhance the central bank's credibility and anchor inflation expectations.

Supporters of inflation targets emphasize that it has been successful in both developing and industrialized countries. They believe that explicit targets in Brazil, Chile, Mexico, and Peru are one important reason why the central banks in nine of the most populous Latin American countries were able to reduce their inflation rates from 160 percent per year in the 1980s and 235 percent during the first half of the 1990s to only 13 percent per year in 1995–1999 and less than 8 percent in the period 2000–2004.[7]

---

[7]Ben Bernanke, "Inflation in Latin America: A New Era?" February 11, 2005, http://www.federalreserve.gov/boarddocs/speeches/2005/20050211/default.htm.

Those central banks, such as the Federal Reserve, that do not announce an explicit target to the public still may have a target or range in mind when making policy. Instead of announcing a specific number to the public, however, these banks typically state that they are interested in keeping inflation low, without defining exactly what that means. Proponents of this approach believe that a system of publicly announced targets is too rigid and may reduce the flexibility of the central bank to deal with unexpected circumstances. They worry that having an explicit inflation target may lead the central bank to pay too much attention to inflation and not enough attention to stabilizing output and maintaining full employment. Finally, opponents of explicit inflation targeting for the United States emphasize that the Fed has achieved good results without having a publicly announced target. They suggest following the adage, "if it ain't broke, don't fix it."

Why shouldn't the inflation target be zero?

ECONOMIC NATURALIST 16.5

Because central banks often state that they are in favor of stable prices, it would seem that the logical long-run target for inflation is 0 percent. However, most economists believe that an inflation target of zero is too low, and central banks that announce an explicit inflation target usually choose values that are low but above zero. Why shouldn't the inflation target be zero?

Several reasons have been offered. First, because hitting the target at all times is impossible in practice, an inflation target of 0 percent increases the risk that the economy will experience periods of deflation (negative inflation). The deflationary experiences of the United States in the 1930s and, more recently, in Japan illustrate that deflation can be difficult to stop once it starts, and it can lead to painful and persistent declines in real GDP, especially if people expect it to continue. Many policymakers prefer to reduce the risk of deflation by choosing an inflation target above 0 percent.

Second, there are times when the Fed may wish to counteract negative shocks to the economy with a negative real interest rate, but this requires that inflation be greater than zero. Recall that the real interest rate is equal to the nominal interest rate minus the rate of inflation. Thus, a negative real interest rate requires setting a nominal interest rate less than inflation. If inflation is zero (or less than zero), however, a negative real interest rate would require a negative nominal interest rate. But the federal funds rate cannot fall below zero because banks would rather keep their reserves than lend them out at a negative nominal interest rate. Consequently, a negative real interest rate must be accompanied by inflation greater than zero.

Third, as we saw in the chapter "Measuring the Price Level and Inflation," some evidence suggests that the conventional measures of inflation tend to overstate the "true" rate of inflation by about one percentage point. Consequently, if the Fed wanted to maintain "true" price stability (that is, "true" inflation of 0 percent), this would require conventionally measured rates of inflation of at least 1 percent.

Finally, some economists believe that a small amount of inflation is necessary to "grease" our economic engine. The analysis in the chapter "Workers, Wages, and Unemployment in the Modern Economy" indicated that technological change and shifts in product demand may require real wages in some industries or occupations to fall in an efficiently operating economy, even when real wages in other industries and occupations are rising. If inflation is positive, a worker's real wage will fall whenever her nominal wage rises by less than the rate of inflation. If, for example, her nominal wage rises by 4 percent but prices rise by 5 percent, her real wage (that is, the amount of goods and services she can buy with her earnings) will fall. If, however, inflation is 0 percent and prices are not changing, the only way in which a worker's real wage can fall is if her nominal wage itself falls. Some evidence suggests that workers will strenuously resist cuts in their nominal wages.[8] They seem to be less resistant to having their nominal wages rise by a smaller percent than inflation even though this, too, reduces their real wage. Consequently, inflation can provide the "grease" required to reduce real wages in some industries and achieve economic efficiency.[9] Critics of the "grease" theory, however, argue that workers will become less resistant to nominal wage cuts at very low or zero rates of inflation. In a low inflation environment, nominal wage cuts would, of necessity, be more common and workers would get used to the idea.

ECONOMIC NATURALIST 16.6

Was inflation almost too low in 2002–2003?

By late 2002, some Fed policymakers began to worry that inflation might actually be too low. Minutes of the Federal Reserve's September 24, 2002, Federal Open Market Committee meeting indicate that committee members were concerned that continuing weakness in the U.S. economy was likely to lead to "quite low and perhaps declining inflation" well into 2003.[10] With prices of consumer goods rising only about 1.5 percent from September 2001 to September 2002, members noted that "further sizable disinflation . . . could create problems for the implementation of monetary policy through conventional means in the event of an adverse shock to the economy."

During 2001 and 2002 the Federal Reserve had reduced the federal funds rate to 1.75 percent, the lowest level in four decades, in an attempt to provide economic stimulus to an economy slowly emerging from recession. Why did low inflation and a low federal funds rate create a potential problem for the Fed?

As pointed out in the chapter "Stabilizing the Economy," business and consumer spending respond to real interest rates, not nominal interest rates. With a federal funds rate of 1.75 percent and an inflation rate of 1.5 percent, the resulting real rate of interest—the difference between the nominal interest rate and the inflation rate—was already down to 0.25 percent. If the Fed was forced in the future to stimulate aggregate spending further in response to a negative economywide spending shock, it might need to reduce the real rate of interest below 0 percent, which, as we have learned in Economic Naturalist 16.5, requires a positive rate of inflation. Thus, if the inflation rate fell to 0 percent, the Fed's ability to conduct expansionary monetary policy to offset a recessionary gap would be limited. Indeed, partly as a preemptive measure to prevent further economic weakening and declines in inflation, the Fed acted at its next meeting, in November 2002, to cut the federal funds rate to 1.25 percent, and it was reduced even further, to 1.0 percent, in June 2003.

Even if the federal funds rate were reduced all the way to 0 percent, however, Fed officials at the time also noted that the Fed would still have options available to stimulate aggregate spending. Although the federal funds rate is a very short-term interest rate, large portions of investment and especially mortgage lending are influenced more by long-term interest rates. Long-term rates are typically higher than and may not move in concert with the federal funds rate. If the Fed wanted to spur investment and the federal funds rate was pushed to zero, it could offer to buy large quantities of long-term U.S. Treasury bonds. Recall from the chapter "Financial Markets and International Capital Flows" that bond prices and interest rates move in opposite directions. Consequently, if the Fed bought long-term bonds, bond prices would rise and long-term interest rates would fall. Alternatively, a central bank could buy other financial assets. For example, some central banks,

---

[8]This does not mean that nominal wages never fall. Many workers in the airline industry, for example, have had to accept lower nominal wages as their employers compete with newer low-cost airlines, such as Southwest and Jet Blue.

[9]George A. Akerlof, William T. Dickens, and George L. Perry, "The Macroeconomics of Low Inflation," *Brookings Papers on Economic Activity,* 1:1–76, 1996.

[10]Minutes from the Federal Reserve's September 2002 FOMC meeting are available online at http://www.federalreserve.gov/fomc/minutes/20020924.htm.

although not the Fed, are allowed to buy stocks. Central bank purchases of stocks would increase stock prices and household wealth and might stimulate consumption. When short-term interest rates fell to zero in Japan, for example, the Bank of Japan bought a limited amount of stocks from Japanese banks that were in financial trouble.

Another option might be for the Fed to commit itself to keeping both the current and future federal funds rate very low. This policy, which was actually implemented by the Bank of Japan in its "zero interest rate policy" (called ZIRP), might give some firms the confidence to invest today, which would increase spending and raise output. By using these "nontraditional" monetary policy tools, the Fed could, if necessary, stimulate the economy even if the federal funds rate fell to 0 percent. However, these alternative tools are largely untested and would be difficult to apply with precision. Hence, the Fed and most other central banks try to keep inflation from falling so low that achieving a negative real interest rate is impossible.

CENTRAL BANK REPUTATION

Ultimately, credibility can be won and maintained only by performance, and a central bank's performance will depend partly on its reputation as being an "inflation hawk" or an "inflation dove." An **inflation hawk** is someone who is committed to achieving and maintaining low inflation, even at some short-run cost in reduced output and employment. An **inflation dove** is someone who is not strongly committed to achieving and maintaining low inflation.

Inflation hawks believe that low and stable inflation allows the economy to grow more rapidly in the long run and therefore will be worth the possible short-run cost. Somewhat paradoxically, inflation hawks also may achieve more stable output and employment, even in the short run. Central banks that have acquired reputations as an inflation hawk will find it easier to anchor inflationary expectations. As we have learned, anchored expectations reduce the inflationary impact of an inflation shock by minimizing the second-round effects of that shock. Recall that anchored expectations also increase the speed with which the short-run aggregate supply line shifts down following an adverse inflation shock or an aggregate demand shock. Consequently, by anchoring expectations, a central bank that is viewed as an inflation hawk may be better able to stabilize output at potential GDP, even in the short run.

But how does a central bank acquire a reputation as an inflation hawk? Some central bankers acquire this reputation only after conducting monetary policy like an inflation hawk. Sometimes, however, the president can select people to serve on the Fed who already have acquired reputations as inflation hawks, based on their professional or academic backgrounds. Jimmy Carter's appointment of Paul Volcker as chair of the Fed is a famous example of a chair coming to the Fed with a well-established reputation as an inflation hawk.

inflation hawk someone who is committed to achieving and maintaining low inflation, even at some short-run cost in reduced output and employment

inflation dove someone who is not strongly committed to achieving and maintaining low inflation

RECAP	INFLATIONARY EXPECTATIONS AND CREDIBILITY

Macroeconomic performance may be improved if expectations of inflation are anchored. Anchored expectations, in turn, depend on the extent to which a central bank's anti-inflation pronouncements are viewed as credible. Several institutional characteristics may help to enhance a central bank's credibility: the extent to which the central bank is independent from the executive and legislative branches of the government, the announcement of a numerical inflation target, and the reputation of the central bank as an "inflation hawk."

POLICYMAKING: ART OR SCIENCE?

In the last four chapters, we have analyzed the basic economics underlying fiscal and monetary policy. We worked through some examples showing how much fiscal policymakers would have to increase government spending or cut taxes in order to eliminate a specific recessionary gap and restore output to its full employment level in the short run. We also calculated the real interest rate the Fed would have to set in order to eliminate other output gaps. While those examples are useful in understanding how fiscal and monetary policy works, they overstate the precision of policymaking.

In analyzing macroeconomic policy, one might be tempted to think of the economy as an automobile and the policymaker as its driver. By judiciously steering, braking, or accelerating at the appropriate times, the driver of a car can safely control it. He can steer it around obstacles. He can accelerate when the car is sluggish going up hills or if it needs an extra boost to pass another car. And he can step on the brake if the car is going too fast down a hill or if a hazard lies ahead.

Unfortunately, conducting macroeconomic policy is much more difficult than driving a car. The driver of a car typically knows exactly where he is at all times. He also knows his destination and can clearly see the road ahead. He has precise control over the accelerator, brake, and steering wheel. Finally, in most instances, he knows from experience how and when the car will respond to his actions. The real-world economy, on the other hand, is more complex because the economic policymaker has less information and control than the driver of a car.

Perfect macroeconomic policy would require each of the following: (1) accurate knowledge of the current state of the economy, (2) knowledge of the future path of the economy if no policy changes are implemented, (3) the precise value of potential output to determine the existence and size of any output gap, (4) complete and immediate control over the tools of fiscal and monetary policy, and (5) knowledge of how and when the economy will respond to changes in policy.

Unfortunately, macroeconomic policy in reality is far from this ideal. The current levels of many macroeconomic indicators such as real GDP often are not known until several months later, and even after that they are subject to multiple revisions. Because policymakers do not have very precise knowledge of the current state of the economy, they may not be able to act decisively.

Second, policymakers are often unsure about the future path of the economy if no policy changes are implemented. If the economy will move to its potential level in the near future in the absence of any policy changes, it will be unnecessary and often unwise for policymakers to act now to eliminate an output gap. Instead of hastening the move back to full employment, policy changes may lead the economy to overshoot, necessitating a policy reversal in the future and potentially destabilizing the economy.

Economists are also unsure about the exact levels of potential output and the natural rate of unemployment. For example, most economists now believe that macroeconomic policy was often too expansionary (and, hence, too inflationary) during the 1970s because policymakers overestimated the potential level of output and hence underestimated the natural rate of unemployment.

inside lag (of macroeconomic policy) the delay between the date a policy change is needed and the date it is implemented

Even when policy changes are needed, it can take a long time for policymakers to implement the appropriate policy changes. The **inside lag** of macroeconomic policy refers to the delay between the date a policy change is needed and the date that policy change is implemented. During this period, the policymakers' economic advisers must recognize that a persistent output gap exists and determine the correct policy change. The policymakers must then accept the desirability of that policy change and implement it.

The inside lag for monetary policy is substantially shorter than the inside lag for fiscal policy. Once monetary policymakers accept the desirability of a change in the federal funds rate, they only have to wait until the next meeting of the Federal Open Market Committee. Since this committee meets eight times per year, the maximum delay is about seven weeks. In urgent situations, the Committee has been known to act during conference calls in between meetings. And once the Committee decides to change the federal funds rate, the Federal Reserve Bank of New York almost immediately conducts the open-market operations sufficient to move the rate to its desired level.

The inside lag for fiscal policy, on the other hand, is considerably longer. After the president proposes a change in tax rates or government spending, both houses of Congress must approve it. This process can take a long time, especially when one or both of the houses of Congress are controlled by the opposing political party. One of the reasons for these delays is that the exact form of a change in taxes or government spending can vary considerably. Should personal income taxes or business taxes be cut? Should defense spending or spending on education be increased? Even after Congress has approved the policy change and the president has signed the bill, it sometimes takes a long time to implement the tax changes or make the additional expenditures.

Finally, economists have only an approximate idea of the exact output effect of a change in policy. The marginal propensity to consume is not known with certainty and need not be the same for all changes in income. Similarly, Fed policymakers have only an approximate idea of the effect of a given change in the real interest rate on planned spending. Economists have constructed statistical models of the economy that track the historical performance of the economy reasonably well. Yet these same statistical models have often yielded disappointing and unreliable forecasts of the future path of the economy. Part of the problem is that it is difficult to predict the values of the exogenous variables in the economy, such as government spending or tax rates. In addition, the economic structure of the economy itself occasionally changes over time. The extent to which investment responds to changing real interest rates, for example, has varied over time.

Furthermore, both fiscal and monetary policymakers are never sure about the length of time before the effects on planned spending will occur. The **outside lag** of macroeconomic policy refers to the delay between the date a policy change is implemented and the date by which most of its effects on the economy have occurred. Although fiscal policy has a longer inside lag than monetary policy, its outside lag may be shorter. Changes in government spending have an immediate effect on real GDP and the economy, although the multiplier effects continue into the future. Similarly, households often respond to tax cuts by increasing their consumption expenditures immediately. On the other hand, investment responds more slowly when the Fed changes the real interest rate since the interest rate is one among many factors that businesses look at before building a new factory or buying an expensive new machine.

outside lag (of macroeconomic policy) the delay between the date a policy change is implemented and the date by which most of its effects on the economy have occurred

Because our knowledge of the economy is imperfect, policymaking at its best also will be imperfect. In terms of our aggregate supply–aggregate demand model, policymakers don't know exactly how much or how fast the aggregate demand curve will shift in response to policy changes. They also don't know how fast the short-run aggregate supply line shifts up when output exceeds its potential level or how fast it shifts down if output is less than potential.

During the 1960s, economists were more confident about their ability to maintain output at its potential level using the appropriate monetary and fiscal policies. They believed they could compute the size of any output gaps, and devise policies to eliminate these gaps. Many also believed they could easily predict the future path of the economy under alternate policy scenarios, and they were comfortable implementing frequent policy changes in order to "fine-tune" the economy. Finally, many economists mistakenly thought policymakers could deliver a permanently higher level of output with just a bit more inflation and did not believe the now generally accepted view that the long-run aggregate supply line is vertical.

The experience of the past few decades has made economists more humble, even about identifying an output gap. Some economists believe that we are at potential output when the unemployment rate is 4.5 percent, while others believe the natural rate of unemployment is as high as 5.5 or even 6.0 percent. Consequently, whenever the actual unemployment rate lies between 4.5 and 6 percent, some economists think they see a recessionary gap while others see an expansionary gap.

Because of these uncertainties, macroeconomic policymakers tend to proceed cautiously. The Fed, for example, avoids large changes in interest rates and rarely raises or lowers the federal funds rate more than one-half of a percentage point (from 5 percent to 5.5 percent, for example) at any one time. Indeed, the typical change in the interest rate is one-quarter of a percentage point. Similarly, policymakers are now less likely to try to "fine-tune" the economy.

Is macroeconomic policymaking an art or a science, then? In practice it appears to be both. Scientific analyses, such as the development of detailed statistical models of the economy, have proved useful in making policy. But human judgment based on long experience—what has been called the "art" of macroeconomic policy—plays a crucial role in successful policymaking and is likely to continue to do so.

RECAP	POLICYMAKING: ART OR SCIENCE?

Macroeconomic policymaking is a difficult and inexact science. Policymakers do not know the precise state of the economy, the future path of the economy if no policy changes are implemented, or the precise level of potential output. They also have imperfect control over policy instruments and imprecise knowledge of the effects of any policy changes. The existence of inside and outside lags make policymaking even more difficult. Consequently, macroeconomic policymaking is an art as well as a science.

■ SUMMARY ■

- To reduce inflation, monetary policymakers must shift the aggregate demand curve and the monetary policy reaction function to the left, usually by decreasing the target rate of inflation and adopting a "tighter" monetary policy. In the short run, the main effects of an anti-inflationary policy may be reduced output and higher unemployment, as the economy experiences a recessionary gap. These short-run costs of disinflation must be balanced against the long-run benefits of a lower rate of inflation. Over time, output and employment will return to their maximum sustainable levels and inflation declines. The disinflation engineered by the Fed under Chairman Paul Volcker in the early 1980s followed this pattern.

- Changes in exogenous spending shift the aggregate demand curve. In response, the Fed can maintain stable inflation and output by adjusting its target real interest rate to the real interest rate at which saving equals investment in the long run.

- Supply shocks, such as inflation shocks, however, force the Fed to choose between maintaining inflation and stabilizing output. If inflationary expectations are anchored, the return to potential output following a supply shock will occur more rapidly.

- Changes in the core rate of inflation allow the Fed to determine whether an inflation shock has changed inflationary expectations and led to further changes in wages and nonoil and nonfood prices, which are sometimes called the second-round effects of the inflation shocks. If the core rate of inflation does not change, the effects of the supply shock on inflation are more likely to be temporary.

- Anchored inflationary expectations will improve economic performance in the long run and also may reduce the volatility of output and inflation in the short run. Inflationary expectations are more likely to be anchored if the central bank's policies are viewed as credible and the public believes the central bank's promises to keep inflation low.

- A central bank's credibility may be enhanced if it is insulated from short-term political considerations and is allowed to take a long-term view of the economy. Credibility also may be enhanced if the central bank publicly announces a numerical inflation target and if it has a reputation as an "inflation hawk."

- Economists now recognize that the analogy between driving a car and managing the economy is a poor one. Unlike driving a car, macroeconomic policymaking is an inexact science. Policymakers do not know the precise state of the economy, the future path of the economy if no policy changes are implemented, or the precise level of potential output. In addition, they have imperfect control over policy instruments and imprecise knowledge of the effects of any policy changes. During the past few decades, economic policymakers have become more humble about their ability to "fine-tune" the economy.

■ KEY TERMS ■

accommodating policy (462)

anchored inflationary
   expectations (464)

central bank independence (469)

core rate of inflation (467)

credibility of monetary policy (468)

disinflation (460)

inflation dove (473)

inflation hawk (473)

inside lag (474)

outside lag (475)

■ REVIEW QUESTIONS ■

1. How does the adoption of a tighter monetary policy, like that conducted by the Volcker Fed in the early 1980s, affect output, inflation, and the real interest rate in the short run? In the long run?

2. Most central banks place great value on keeping inflation low and stable. Why do they view this objective as so important?

3. Suppose there is an increase in taxes. What is the short-run effect on output, inflation, and the real interest rate, assuming any supply-side effects are minimal? What will be the effect in the long run if the Fed chooses to adjust its target real interest rate to the new long-run real interest rate at which saving equals investment?

4. Suppose there is a sudden increase in oil prices. What will be the effect on output and inflation in the short run? What is the "dilemma" faced by the Fed as a result of the adverse inflation shock?

5. What are anchored inflationary expectations and how do they reduce the cost of an adverse inflation shock?

6. What are the concerns about having an inflation rate that is "too low?"

7. What is the core rate of inflation and what is its relevance for macroeconomic policymaking?

8. Name two reasons why the 2003–2004 increase in oil policies had not led to a recession or a substantial increase in the core rate of inflation as of June 2005.

9. What factors determine a central bank's independence? What are the benefits of having an independent central bank?

10. In what ways is the Federal Reserve independent? In what ways is it not?

11. What are inside and outside lags? What is their relevance for macroeconomic policymaking?

12. Why are economists now more humble about their ability to fine-tune the economy?

■ PROBLEMS ■

1. The Bank of Lotusland, the central bank, has announced that it will set the real interest rate according to the following monetary policy reaction function: $r = .03 + 1.0 (\pi - .01)$. Thus, the target real interest rate is 3 percent and the target inflation rate is 1 percent. (The value of the parameter g also is equal to 1.)
   a. Construct a table indicating the level of the real interest rate at each of the following rates of inflation: 0, 1, 2, 3, and 4 percent.
   b. From either your table or the equation, draw the Bank of Lotusland's monetary policy reaction function.

2. Suppose the economy is initially in long-run equilibrium, and the Fed adopts a looser monetary policy by raising its target inflation rate.
   a. Illustrate what this switch to a looser monetary policy would do to the Fed's monetary policy reaction function and the aggregate demand curve.
   b. Use your results from part a and aggregate supply–aggregate demand graphs to illustrate and explain what will happen to real GDP and inflation in both the short run and the long run.

3. Suppose the economy is initially in long-run equilibrium and the Fed reduces its target real interest rate. Illustrate what this would do to the monetary policy reaction function and the aggregate demand curve.

4. Using the theory presented in this chapter, explain why the adoption of a tighter, more anti-inflationary monetary policy might be politically unpopular.

5. Suppose there is a large increase in oil or food prices.
   a. If the core rate of inflation remains unchanged, what might the Fed infer about inflationary expectations and the second-round effects of the inflation shock? How might it respond?
   b. If the core rate of inflation rises substantially, what might the Fed infer about inflationary expectations and the second-round effects of the inflation shock? How might it respond?

6. What is the advantage of having an independent central bank and what institutional features make a central bank independent?

7. Explain how the recognition that macroeconomic policymaking is an inexact science affects your recommended policy response to the following situations:
   a. Your estimate of the natural rate of unemployment is 5 percent, and the actual unemployment rate is 5.5 percent.
   b. Your estimate of the natural rate of unemployment is 5 percent, and the actual unemployment rate is 8 percent.

8.*Suppose an economy is described by the following equations:

$$C = 1,600 + 0.6(Y - T) - 2,000r,$$
$$I^P = 2,500 - 1,000r,$$
$$G = \overline{G} = 2,000,$$
$$NX = \overline{NX} = 50,$$
$$T = \overline{T} = 2,000.$$

   a. Find an equation relating planned spending to output and the real interest rate.
   b. Suppose the central bank's monetary policy reaction function is the same as in problem 1 above. Compute the short-run equilibrium output at each rate of inflation between 0 and 4 percent and graph the AD curve for this economy.

9.*For the economy described in problem 8a, suppose that the central bank adopts a tighter monetary policy by reducing its target inflation rate to 0.5 percent, while maintaining its target real interest rate of 3 percent. Consequently, it changes its monetary policy reaction function to $r = .03 + 1.0(\pi - .005)$.

   a. Construct a table indicating the level of the real interest rate at each of the following rates of inflation: 0, 1, 2, 3, and 4 percent. Draw the new monetary policy reaction function and compare it to the monetary policy reaction function you derived in problem 1.
   b. Use the planned expenditure equations in problem 8 to construct a table showing the new relationship between short-run equilibrium output and the inflation rate for values of inflation between 0 and 4 percent. Graph the new aggregate demand curve of the economy and compare it to the aggregate demand curve you derived in problem 8b.

10.*For the economy described in problem 8a and the monetary policy reaction function described in problem 1, suppose government purchases increase by 100 to 2,100.

   a. Find the new equation relating planned spending to output and the real interest rate.
   b. Compute the short-run equilibrium output at each rate of inflation between 0 and 4 percent.
   c. Graph the AD curve for this economy and compare it to the AD curve in problem 8b.

*Problems marked with an asterisk (*) are more difficult.

■ ANSWERS TO IN-CHAPTER EXERCISES ■

16.1

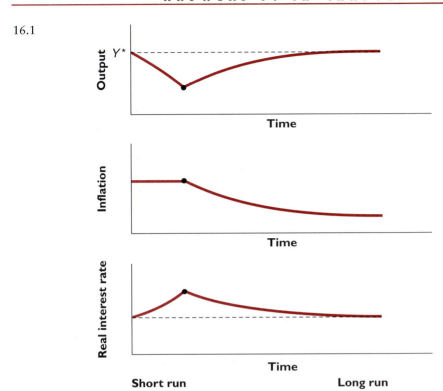

16.2 A sudden decrease in spending will shift the aggregate demand curve to the left, to *AD'* in the graph below. In the short run, output will fall to point *B*, but inflation will be unaffected. Over time, output will return to potential at point *C*. If the Fed then lowers its target real interest rate, the monetary policy reaction function will shift right (down) and the aggregate demand curve will shift back to *AD*. In the long run, output will remain at potential and inflation will return to its initial level at point *E* if the new target real interest rate is equal to the real interest rate that equates saving and investment in the long run.

If the Fed changes r^* immediately after the reduction in spending, the leftward shift in the aggregate demand curve caused by the decrease in spending will be offset by the rightward shift caused by the reduction in r^* (and shift in the *MPRF*). Output and inflation will remain unchanged at Y^* (points *A* and *E*) even in the short run.

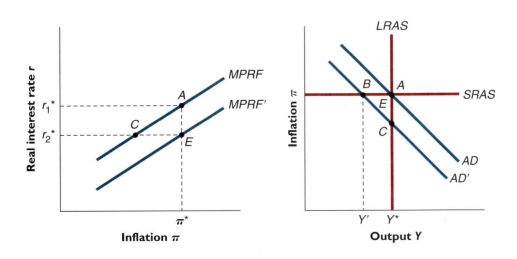

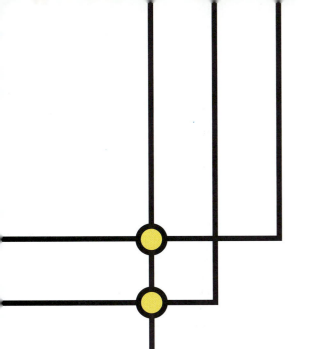

THE ALGEBRA OF AGGREGATE DEMAND AND AGGREGATE SUPPLY

In this appendix, we derive the aggregate demand curve algebraically. Then we show how together aggregate demand and aggregate supply determine the short-run and long-run equilibrium points of the economy.

THE AGGREGATE DEMAND CURVE

In the appendix to the chapter "Stabilizing the Economy," Equation 14A.1 showed that short-run equilibrium output depends on both exogenous components of expenditure and the real interest rate:

$$Y = \left(\frac{1}{1 - mpc}\right)\left[\overline{C} - mpc\overline{T} + \overline{I} + \overline{G} + \overline{NX} - (a + b)r\right], \quad (14A.1)$$

where $1/(1 - mpc)$ is the multiplier, $\overline{C} - mpc\overline{T} + \overline{I} + \overline{G} + \overline{NX}$ is the exogenous component of planned spending, the term in brackets is autonomous expenditure, and a and b are positive numbers that measure the effect of changes in the real interest rate on consumption and planned investment, respectively.

The aggregate demand curve incorporates the behavior of the Fed, as described by its monetary policy reaction function. According to its policy reaction function, when inflation rises, the Fed raises the real interest rate. Thus, the

Fed's monetary policy reaction function can be written as an equation relating the real interest rate r to inflation π and the target levels of the real interest rate r^* and inflation π^*:

$$r = r^* + g(\pi - \pi^*), \tag{16A.1}$$

where r^*, π^*, and the parameter g are positive constants chosen by Fed officials. This equation states that when inflation π rises by one percentage point—say from 2 to 3 percent per year—the Fed responds by raising the real interest rate by g percentage points. So, for example, if $g = 0.5$, an increase in inflation from 2 to 3 percent would lead the Fed to raise the real interest rate by 0.5 percent. If actual inflation is equal to the Fed's target π^*, the term in parentheses is equal to 0 and the Fed sets the real interest rate equal to its target real interest rate r^*.

Equations 14A.1 and 16A.1 together allow us to derive the aggregate demand curve. We can think of the curve as being derived in two steps: First, for any given value of inflation π (and the fixed values of the three constants r^*, π^*, and g), use the monetary policy reaction function, Equation 16A.1, to find the real interest rate set by the Fed. Second, for that real interest rate, use Equation 14A.1 to find short-run equilibrium output Y. The relationship between inflation and short-run equilibrium output derived in these two steps is the aggregate demand curve.

Alternatively, we can combine the equation for short-run equilibrium output with the equation for the monetary policy reaction function by substituting the right-hand side of Equation 16A.1 for the real interest rate r in Equation 14A.1:

$$Y = \left(\frac{1}{1 - mpc}\right)\left[\overline{C} - mpc\overline{T} + \overline{I} + \overline{G} + \overline{NX} - (a + b)(r^* + g(\pi - \pi^*))\right],$$

or

$$Y = \left(\frac{1}{1 - mpc}\right)\left[\overline{C} - mpc\overline{T} + \overline{I} + \overline{G} + \overline{NX}\right.$$
$$\left. - (a + b)(r^* - g(\pi^*)) - (a + b)g(\pi)\right] \tag{16A.2}$$

This equation, which is the general algebraic expression for the AD curve, summarizes the link between inflation and short-run equilibrium output, as shown graphically in Figure 15.1. Note that Equation 16A.2 implies that an increase in inflation π reduces short-run equilibrium output Y, so that the AD curve is downward-sloping.

For a numerical illustration, we can use the parameter values from Example 14.3. For the economy studied in Example 14.3, we assumed that $\overline{C} = 640$, $\overline{T} = 250$, $\overline{I} = 250$, $\overline{G} = 300$, $\overline{NX} = 20$, $mpc = 0.8$, $a = 400$, and $b = 600$. To derive the aggregate demand curve, we also need values for the Fed's monetary policy reaction function; for illustration, we use the policy reaction function presented in Table 14.1. $r = 0.04 + 1.0(\pi - 0.02)$. This implies that the Fed's targets for the real interest rate and inflation are 4 percent and 2 percent, respectively. Furthermore, the value of g, the slope of the monetary policy reaction function, is 1.0. Several specific values of r and π (shown in Table 14.1) are reproduced here for convenience.

Substituting these numerical values into Equation 16A.2 and simplifying, we get the following numerical equation for the AD curve:

$$Y = 5\left[640 - 0.8(250) + 250 + 300 + 20\right.$$
$$\left. - (400 + 600)(0.04 - 0.02) - (400 + 600)\pi\right] \tag{16A.3}$$

$$Y = 4{,}950 - 5{,}000\pi \tag{16A.4}$$

TABLE 14A.1
A Policy Reaction Function for the Fed

Rate of inflation, π	Real interest rate set by Fed, r
0.00 (= 0%)	0.02 (= 2%)
0.01	0.03
0.02	0.04
0.03	0.05
0.04	0.06

Note that in this equation, higher values of inflation imply lower values of short-run equilibrium output, so the aggregate demand curve is downward-sloping. To check this equation, suppose that inflation is 3 percent, so that the Fed sets the real interest rate at 5 percent (see Table 14A.1, which is reproduced above). Setting $\pi = 0.03$ in Equation 16A.4 yields $Y = 4,800$. This is consistent with the answer we found in Example 14.4, where we showed for the same economy that when $r = 0.05$ (the value of the real interest rate set by the Fed when $\pi = 0.03$), then short-run equilibrium output $Y = 4,800$.

SHIFTS OF THE AGGREGATE DEMAND CURVE

Recall that exogenous changes in spending or in the Fed's monetary policy reaction function will shift the AD curve. These results follow from Equation 16A.2. First, the equation shows that for a given rate of inflation π, an increase in exogenous spending, $\overline{C} - mpc\overline{T} + \overline{I} + \overline{G} + \overline{NX}$, will raise short-run equilibrium output Y. Thus, an increase in exogenous spending shifts the AD curve to the right; conversely, a decrease in exogenous spending shifts the AD curve to the left. A shift in the Fed's monetary policy reaction function can be captured by a change in the target rates of interest r^* or inflation π^* in Equation 16A.1. For example, suppose the Fed tightens monetary policy by reducing its target rate of inflation by one percentage point to 1 percent. If $g = 1$, it would then set the real interest rate 1 percentage point higher than before at every level of inflation. If you look at Equations 16A.2 and 16A.3, you will see that with the level of inflation held constant, a reduction in π^* reduces short-run equilibrium output. Thus, a tightening of monetary policy (an upward movement in the monetary policy reaction function) shifts the AD curve to the left. Conversely, an easing of monetary policy (represented by a decline in π^* or a downward shift in the monetary policy reaction function) shifts the AD curve to the right.

EXERCISE 16A.1

a. For the economy described above, find an algebraic equation for the AD curve after an exogenous increase in spending (say, in planned investment) of 10 units.

b. For the economy described above, find an algebraic equation for the AD curve after a tightening of monetary policy that involves setting the real interest rate one percentage point higher at each level of inflation.

SHORT-RUN EQUILIBRIUM

Recall that in short-run equilibrium, inflation is equal to its previously determined value, and the $SRAS$ line is horizontal at that value. At that level of inflation, the level of output in short-run equilibrium is given by the aggregate demand curve,

Equation 16A.2. For instance, in the economy described, suppose the current value of inflation is 5 percent. The value of short-run equilibrium output is therefore

$$Y = 4{,}950 - 5{,}000\pi = 4{,}950 - 5{,}000(0.05)$$
$$= 4{,}700.$$

LONG-RUN EQUILIBRIUM

In long-run equilibrium, actual output Y equals potential output Y^*. Thus, in long-run equilibrium, the inflation rate can be obtained from the equation for the AD curve by substituting Y^* for Y. To illustrate, let's write the equation for the AD curve in this sample economy, Equation 16A.4, once again:

$$Y = 4{,}950 - 5{,}000\pi.$$

Suppose, in addition, that potential output $Y^* = 4{,}850$. Substituting this value for Y in the aggregate demand equation yields

$$4{,}850 = 4{,}950 - 5{,}000\pi.$$

Solving for the inflation rate π we get

$$\pi = 0.02 = 2\%.$$

When this economy is in long-run equilibrium, then, the inflation rate will be 2 percent. If we start from the value of inflation in short-run equilibrium, 5 percent, we can see that the short-run aggregate supply line must shift downward until inflation reaches 2 percent before long-run equilibrium can be achieved.

■ ANSWERS TO IN-APPENDIX EXERCISE ■

16A.1 The algebraic solutions for the AD curve in each case, obtained by substituting the numerical values into the formula, are given below.
    a. $Y = 5{,}000 - 5{,}000\pi.$
    b. $Y = 4{,}900 - 5{,}000\pi.$

PART

5

THE INTERNATIONAL ECONOMY

One of the defining economic trends of recent decades is the "globalization" of national economies. Since the mid-1980s, the value of international trade has increased at nearly twice the rate of world GDP, and the volume of international financial transactions has expanded at many times that rate. From a long-run perspective, the rapidly increasing integration of national economies we see today is not unprecedented: Before World War I, Great Britain was the center of an international economic system that was in many ways nearly as "globalized" as our own, with extensive international trade and lending. But even the most far-seeing nineteenth-century merchant or banker would be astonished by the sense of *immediacy* that recent revolutionary changes in communications and transportation have imparted to international economic relations. For example, teleconferencing and the Internet now permit people on opposite sides of the globe to conduct "face-to-face" business negotiations and transactions.

We introduced international dimensions of the economy at several points in this book already (for example, in our discussion of comparative advantage and trade in Chapter 2 and our analysis of the labor market effects of globalization in the chapter "Workers, Wages, and Unemployment in the Modern Economy"). Chapter 17 continues our analysis of international trade, considering both the broad benefits of trade and the reasons why we sometimes see attempts to block or reduce trade. Chapter 18 focuses on a particularly important variable in international economics, the *exchange rate*. The exchange rate plays a key role in determining patterns of trade. Furthermore, as we will see, the type of exchange rate system a country adopts has important implications for the effectiveness of its macroeconomic policies.

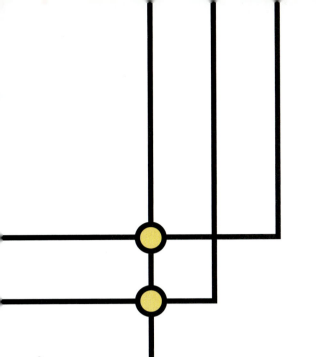

INTERNATIONAL TRADE

On April 13, 1861, Southern troops fired on Fort Sumter in Charleston harbor, initiating the American Civil War. Less than a week later, on April 19, President Lincoln proclaimed a naval blockade of the South. Code-named the Anaconda Plan (after the snake that squeezes its prey to death), the blockade required the Union navy to patrol the Southern coastline, stopping and boarding ships that were attempting to land or depart. The object of the blockade was to prevent the Confederacy from shipping cotton to Europe, where it could be traded for military equipment, clothing, foodstuffs, and other supplies.

In the early years of the war, the North had too few ships to cover the 3,600-mile Southern coastline, so "running" the blockade was not difficult. But in the latter part of the war, the number of Union ships enforcing the blockade increased from about 90 to over 600, and sailing ships were replaced with faster, more lethal ironclad vessels. Still, private blockade-runners—like the fictitious Rhett Butler in Margaret Mitchell's novel *Gone with the Wind*—attempted to elude the Union navy in small, fast ships. Because the price of raw cotton in Great Britain was between 10 and 20 times what it was in the Confederacy (a differential that indicated disruption in the normal flow of trade), blockade-runners enjoyed huge profits when they were successful. But despite their efforts, by 1864 the Southern war effort was seriously hampered by a lack of military equipment and supplies, at least in part as a result of the blockade.

The use of a naval blockade as a weapon of war highlights a paradox in contemporary attitudes toward trade between nations. Presumably, an attempt by a foreign power to blockade U.S. ports would today be considered a hostile act that would elicit a strong response from the U.S. government. Yet one often hears politicians and others arguing that trade with other nations is harmful to the United States and should be restricted—in effect, that the United States should blockade its own ports! Despite support from President Clinton and virtually all professional economists, for example, many politicians opposed the 1993 signing

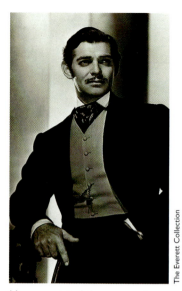

He appreciated the economic benefits of trade.

of the North American Free Trade Agreement (NAFTA), which was intended to increase U.S. trade with Mexico and Canada, on the grounds that it might cost American jobs. In December 1999, opponents of increased trade demonstrated in Seattle, disrupting meetings of the World Trade Organization, an international body set up to promote trade and enforce trade agreements. And in the years since, organized opposition to trade has grown further. So is trade a good thing or not? And if it is, why does it sometimes face determined and even violent opposition?

This chapter addresses international trade and its effects on the broader economy. We will begin by reviewing the idea of *comparative advantage,* which was introduced in Chapter 2. We will show that everyone can enjoy more goods and services if nations specialize in those products in which they have a comparative advantage, and then trade freely among themselves. Furthermore, if trade is unrestricted, market forces will ensure that countries produce those goods in which they have a comparative advantage.

Having shown the potential benefits of trade, we will turn next to the reasons for opposition to trade. Although opening the economy to trade increases economic welfare overall, some groups—such as workers used intensively in industries that face competition from foreign producers—may be made worse off. The fact that open trade may hurt some groups creates political pressure to enact measures restricting trade, such as taxes on imported goods (called *tariffs*) and limits on imports (called *quotas*). We will analyze the effects of these trade restrictions, along with other ways of responding to concerns about affected industries and workers. From an economic point of view, providing direct assistance to those who are hurt by increased trade is preferable to blocking or restricting trade.

COMPARATIVE ADVANTAGE AS A BASIS FOR TRADE

Climate, soil, and long experience give France a comparative advantage in producing fine wines.

Chapter 2 began with the story of the Nepalese cook Birkhaman, a remarkable jack-of-all-trades who could do everything, from butchering a goat to fixing an alarm clock. Yet despite his range of skills, Birkhaman, like most Nepalese, was quite poor. The reason for Birkhaman's poverty, as we saw in Chapter 2, was precisely his versatility. Because he did so many different things, he could not hope to become as productive in each separate activity as someone who specialized entirely in that activity.

The alternative to a nation of Birkhamans is a country in which each person specializes in the activity at which he is relatively best, or has a *comparative advantage.* This specialization, combined with trade between producers of different goods and services, allows a society to achieve a higher level of productivity and standard of living than one in which each person is essentially self-sufficient.

This insight, that specialization and trade among individuals can yield impressive gains in productivity, applies equally well to nations. Factors such as climate, natural resources, technology, workers' skills and education, and culture provide countries with comparative advantages in the production of different goods and services. For example, as we saw in Chapter 2, the large number of leading research universities in the United States gives that nation a comparative advantage in the design of technologically sophisticated computer hardware and software. Likewise, the wide international use of the English language endows the United States with a comparative advantage in producing popular films and TV shows. Similarly, France's climate and topography, together with the accumulated knowledge of generations of vintners, provide that country a comparative advantage in producing fine wines, while Australia's huge expanses of arable land give that country a comparative advantage in producing grain.

The *principle of comparative advantage* tells us that we can all enjoy more goods and services when each country produces according to its comparative advantage, and then trades with other countries. In the next section we explore this fundamental idea in greater detail.

PRODUCTION AND CONSUMPTION POSSIBILITIES AND THE BENEFITS OF TRADE

In this section we will consider how international trade benefits an individual country. To do so, we will contrast the production and consumption opportunities in a **closed economy**—one that does not trade with the rest of the world—with the opportunities in an **open economy**—one that does trade with other economies.

Recall from Chapter 2 that the production possibilities curve (PPC) for a two-good economy is a graph that shows the maximum amount of one good that can be produced for every possible level of production of the other good. For purposes of illustration, we consider an economy that produces only two goods, coffee and computers. In such an economy, the point C on the PPC shown in Figure 17.1 tells us that the maximum production of coffee is 100,000 pounds per year when the economy is producing 1,000 computers per year.

Recall also from Chapter 2 that the smoothly bowed shape of the PPC in Figure 17.1 is typical for an economy that employs a large number of workers. The slope of the PPC at each point reflects the opportunity cost of producing an additional computer. For instance, the opportunity cost, in terms of coffee, of producing an extra computer at point C is given by the slope of the line tangent to the PPC at that point. Because computers will be produced first by workers with the greatest comparative advantage (the lowest opportunity cost), the slope of the PPC becomes more and more sharply negative as we move from left to right along the curve. Thus, at Point D, where the economy is producing 40,000 pounds per year of coffee and 2,000 computers per year, the slope of the PPC is steeper than at C. This means that the opportunity cost of an additional computer (the number of pounds of coffee that must be forgone to produce an additional computer) is greater at D than at C.

closed economy an economy that does not trade with the rest of the world

open economy an economy that trades with other countries

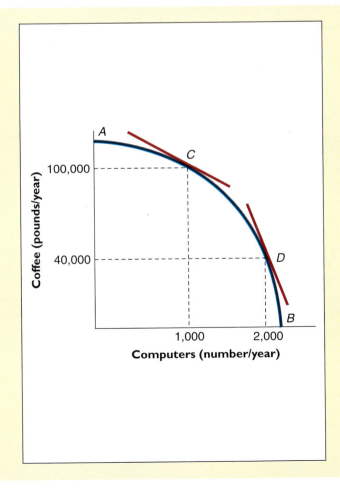

FIGURE 17.1

Production Possibilities Curve for a Many-Worker Economy.

The PPC for a many-worker economy has a smooth, outwardly bowed shape. At each point on the PPC, the slope of the curve reflects the opportunity cost, in terms of coffee forgone, of producing an additional computer. For example, the opportunity cost of a computer at point C equals the slope of the line tangent to the PPC at that point, and the opportunity cost of a computer at point D equals the slope of the line tangent to the PPC there. Because the opportunity cost of producing another computer increases as more computers are produced, the slope of the PPC becomes more and more negative as we read from left to right on the graph.

RECAP	PRODUCTION POSSIBILITIES CURVES (PPCs)

- The *production possibilities curve* (PPC) for a two-good economy is a graph that shows the maximum amount of one good that can be produced at each possible level of production of the other good.

- The slope of a PPC at any point indicates the opportunity cost, in terms of forgone production of the good on the vertical axis, of increasing production of the good on the horizontal axis by one unit.

- The more of a good that is already being produced, the greater the opportunity cost of increasing production still further. Thus the slope of the PPC becomes more and more negative as we move from left to right, imparting the characteristic outwardly bowed shape of the curve.

CONSUMPTION POSSIBILITIES WITH AND WITHOUT INTERNATIONAL TRADE

A country's production possibilities curve shows the quantities of different goods that its economy can produce. However, economic welfare depends most directly not on what a country can *produce*, but on what its citizens can *consume*. The combinations of goods and services that a country's citizens might feasibly consume are called the country's **consumption possibilities.**

consumption possibilities
the combinations of goods and services that a country's citizens might feasibly consume

The relationship between a country's consumption possibilities and its production possibilities depends on whether or not the country is open to international trade. In a closed economy with no trade, people can consume only the goods and services produced within their own country. *In a closed economy, then, society's consumption possibilities are identical to its production possibilities.* A situation in which a country does not trade with other nations, producing everything its citizens consume, is called **autarky.**

autarky a situation in which a country does not trade with other nations

The case of an open economy, which trades with the rest of the world, is quite different. In an open economy, people are not restricted to consuming what is produced in their own country, because part of what they produce can be sent abroad in exchange for other goods and services. Indeed, we will see in this section that opening an economy up to trade may allow citizens to consume more of everything. Thus, *in an open economy, a society's consumption possibilities are typically greater than (and will never be less than) its production possibilities.*

In the examples that follow, our focus will be on Costa Rica, which for simplicity is assumed to produce and consume only two goods, coffee and computers. Consider the PPC shown as curve *ACDB* in Figure 17.2. Point *A*, where the PPC intercepts the vertical axis, indicates the maximum amount of coffee that Costa Rica can produce, and point *B*, the horizontal intercept of the PPC, shows the maximum number of computers it can produce. As before, the intermediate points on the PPC represent alternative combinations of coffee and computers that can be produced.

Now suppose that the Costa Rican economy, which was operating at point *D* as a closed economy (meaning that it both produced and consumed 2,000 computers per year and 50,000 pounds per year of coffee), gains the opportunity to buy or sell either good in the world market at prices of $10 per pound for coffee and $500 per computer. Without changing its production at all, we see that it immediately enjoys a new range of consumption possibilities. For example, if it sold its entire production of 2,000 computers in the world market at $500 apiece, the $1,000,000 it would earn would enable it to purchase an additional 100,000 pounds of coffee each year. Thus, the point *E* in Figure 17.2, which was not available to Costa Ricans in the absence of international trade, is now attainable.

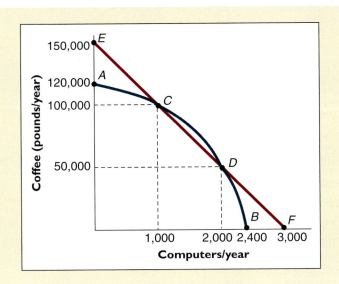

FIGURE 17.2

Buying and Selling in World Markets.

If Costa Rica produces at point *D* and can buy or sell computers and coffee in world markets at prices of $500 per computer and $10 per pound, respectively, it can consume any point along the line *EF*.

Alternatively, suppose that Costa Ricans again start at *D* and now sell their annual production of 50,000 pounds of coffee in the world market. The $500,000 they receive from this sale will enable them to buy an additional 1,000 computers each year. Thus, the point *F* in Figure 17.2, which was also not a consumption option in the absence of international trade, now becomes available. And as you can easily verify, any other point along the line *EF* also becomes available to Costa Ricans if they produce at *D* and can exchange their goods in world markets at the stated prices.

EXERCISE 17.1

Suppose prices in world markets are again $500 per computer and $10 per pound for coffee. Show that if Costa Rica starts by producing at point *C* in Figure 17.2, it can consume 500 computers per year and 125,000 pounds per year of coffee. To do so, how many units of each good will it buy or sell in world markets?

EXERCISE 17.2

If prices remain as before and if Costa Rica again starts by producing at point *C* in Figure 17.2 and can trade in world markets, it can consume 2,500 computers per year and 25,000 pounds per year of coffee. To do so, how many units of each good will it buy or sell in world markets?

If Costa Rica could buy or sell in world markets at $500 per computer and $10 per pound for coffee, would its best option be to produce at point *C* in Figure 17.2? No, because it could do better by producing at point *G* in Figure 17.3.

If Costa Rica produces at point *G* in Figure 17.3 and can buy or sell computers and coffee in world markets at prices of $500 per computer and $10 per pound, the country's consumption possibilities will now lie along the line *LM*. This line has two key features. First, it is drawn so that it is tangent to the PPC at point *G* in Figure 17.3. Second, the slope of line *LM* is determined by the relative prices of coffee and computers on the world market. Specifically, the slope of line *LM*, which is

(160,000 pounds of coffee/year)/(3,200 computers/year)
$$= 50 \text{ pounds of coffee per computer}$$

FIGURE 17.3

Production Possibilities, Consumption Possibilities, and the Optimal Production Mix for an Open Economy.

If Costa Rica can buy or sell computers and coffee in world markets at prices of $500 per computer and $10 per pound, the line *LM* maximizes the country's consumption possibilities. The slope of this line is the rate at which coffee can be traded for computers at the stated world prices—namely, 50 pounds of coffee per computer. The line *LM* is tangent to the production possibilities curve at *G*. Costa Rica's best option is to produce at point *G* and then trade in world markets (either sell computers and buy coffee or vice versa) so as to reach its most desired point on the line *LM*.

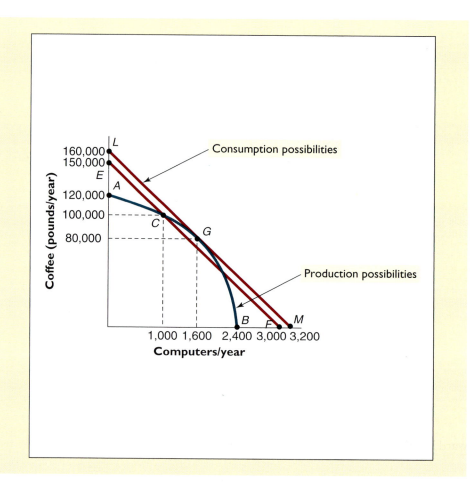

tells us how much coffee must be exchanged on world markets to obtain an additional computer.

With access to international trade, Costa Rica can consume the greatest amount of both coffee and computers by producing at point *G* on the PPC and

"The repairs will take awhile. We need a part from Mexico, a part from Brazil and one from Taiwan."

trading on the international market to obtain the desired combination of coffee and computers on line *LM*. (The exact combination of coffee and computers Costa Ricans will choose depends on the preferences of its population.)

Why should the Costa Ricans produce at point *G*? At point *G*, and only at that point, the slope of the PPC equals the slope of the consumption possibilities line, *LM*. Hence, only at point *G* is the opportunity cost of increasing domestic computer production equal to the opportunity cost of purchasing an extra computer on the world market. If the opportunity cost of producing a computer domestically exceeded the opportunity cost of purchasing a computer on the world market, Costa Rica would gain by reducing its computer production and importing more computers. Likewise, if the opportunity cost of producing a computer domestically were less than the opportunity cost of purchasing a computer abroad, Costa Rica would gain by increasing computer production and reducing computer imports. Costa Rica's best production combination, therefore, is at point *G*, where the domestic and international opportunity costs of acquiring an extra computer, measured in terms of coffee forgone, are equal. The combination of goods at point *G* is also the one whose sale at world prices produces the largest possible total revenue.

We have already stated the general conclusion that can be drawn from this analysis. Once again, by opening itself up to trade, a country can consume more of *every* good than if it relied solely on its own production (a situation of *autarky*). Graphically, the consumption possibilities line in Figure 17.3 lies above the production possibilities curve, showing that through trade, Costa Rica can consume combinations of computers and coffee that would not be attainable if its economy were closed to trade.[1]

As we saw in Chapter 2, production possibilities curves do not always bow outward like the ones shown in Figures 17.1 through 17.3. In the following example, we consider the case of a two-good economy in which the opportunity cost of producing each good is independent of the amount of it produced.

How do world prices affect what a country produces?

EXAMPLE 17.1

The 100 workers in Islandia, a small island open economy, are equally productive in producing coffee and tea. In a day's work, each can produce either eight pounds of coffee or eight pounds of tea. Workers who divide their time between the two activities will produce each good in proportion to the amount of time spent producing it. Describe Islandia's consumption possibilities curve if the world price of coffee is twice that of tea. What if the world price of coffee is half that of tea? What will Islandia produce if the world price of coffee happens to equal the world price of tea?

Islandia's production possibilities curve is shown in Figure 17.4. At one extreme, if everyone works full time producing coffee, it can produce 800 pounds of coffee per day and no tea (point *A*). At the other extreme, if everyone works full time producing tea, it can produce 800 pounds of tea per day and no coffee (point *D*). Any other point on the straight line joining *A* and *D* is also feasible. For example, Islandians could produce 600 pounds of coffee per day and 200 pounds of tea (point *B*), or 200 pounds of coffee per day and 600 pounds of tea (point *C*).

Given that Islandia can trade with other nations, the country's goal should be to produce the combination of tea and coffee that will sell for the largest possible amount at world prices. If the world price of coffee is twice that of tea, Islandia's best bet would thus be to produce only coffee—that is, to produce at point *A* in Figure 17.4. Its consumption possibilities curve would then be the curve labeled *AD'* in

---

[1]The single point at which consumption possibilities do *not* lie above production possibilities in Figure 17.3 is at point *G*, where production possibilities and consumption possibilities are the same. If Costa Rican residents happen to prefer the combination of computers and coffee at point *G* to any other point on *LM*, then they realize no benefit from trade.

FIGURE 17.4

A Straight-Line Production Possibilities Curve.

When this economy devotes all of its labor to coffee production, it can produce 800 pounds per day of coffee (point A). When it devotes all of its labor to tea production, it also can produce 800 pounds per day of tea (point D). When it divides its labor between the two activities (e.g., as at points B and C), the output of each good is proportional to the amount of labor devoted to its production.

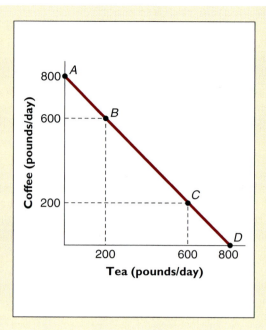

Figure 17.5(a). Since the price of coffee is twice the price of tea, the money earned by selling 800 pounds of coffee would be enough to buy as much as 1,600 pounds of tea (point D'). With the money earned by selling the coffee it produces at point A in world markets, the country could then consume any combination of coffee and tea along the line AD'.

Conversely, if the world price of tea is twice the world price of coffee, Islandians do best by specializing completely in tea production, as at point D in Figure 17.5(b). By selling the 800 pounds of tea produced at point D, they could buy as many

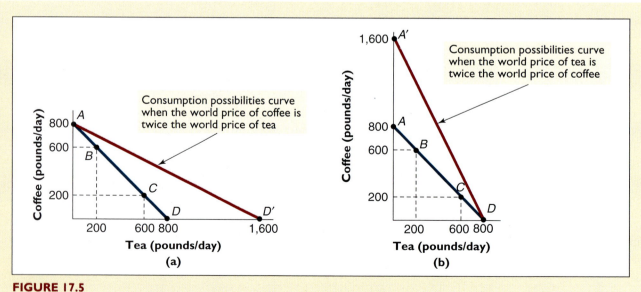

FIGURE 17.5

Two Consumption Possibilities Curves.

When the world price of coffee is twice the world price of tea, the country should specialize in coffee production at point A in panel (a). When the world price of coffee is half the world price of tea, the country should specialize in tea production (b).

as 1,600 pounds of coffee, or point A' in Figure 17.5(b). With the money earned by selling the tea it produces at point D in world markets, the country could then consume any combination of coffee and tea along the line $A'D$.

Finally, if the world price of coffee were the same as the world price of tea, it would not matter which point Islandians chose on their production possibilities curve, because every bundle along the PPC would sell for the same amount. In this case, Islandia's PPC would be identical to its consumption possibilities curve. It would gain nothing from being able to participate in world markets.

EXERCISE 17.3

How would your answer to the questions posed in Example 17.1 differ if a new variety of coffee plant made each Islandian worker able to produce three times as much coffee as before?

As Example 17.1 and Exercise 17.3 illustrate, the case of a straight-line production possibilities curve is different from the case of a bow-shaped production possibilities curve. In the latter case, a country typically maximizes its consumption possibilities by producing at the point where the consumption possibilities line is tangent to the PPC, and then trading so as to reach its most preferred point on the consumption possibilities line. In contrast, completely specialized production is the standard outcome in the case of a straight-line production possibilities curve. In that case, a country typically maximizes its consumption possibilities by devoting all its resources to production of the good for which the output per unit of resource input sells for the highest price.

RECAP	CONSUMPTION POSSIBILITIES AND PRODUCTION POSSIBILITIES

- A country's *consumption possibilities* are the combinations of goods and services that its citizens might feasibly consume.

- In an economy that is closed to trade, residents can consume only what is produced domestically (a situation of *autarky*). Hence, in a closed economy, consumption possibilities equal production possibilities.

- The residents of an open economy can trade part of what they produce on international markets. According to the principle of comparative advantage, trade allows everyone to do better than they could otherwise. Thus, in an open economy, consumption possibilities are typically greater than, and will never be less than, production possibilities.

- Graphically, consumption possibilities in an open economy are described by a downward-sloping straight line whose slope equals the amount of the good on the vertical axis that must be traded on the international market to obtain one unit of the good on the horizontal axis. In the case of a bow-shaped production possibilities curve, a country maximizes its consumption possibilities by producing at the point where the consumption possibilities line is tangent to the PPC, and then trading so as to reach its most preferred point on the consumption possibilities line. In the case of a straight-line PPC, a country typically maximizes its consumption possibilities by specializing in the good for which an hour's production sells for the largest dollar amount in world markets.

ECONOMIC
NATURALIST
17.1

Does "cheap" foreign labor pose a danger to high-wage economies?

Some people argue that high-wage industrialized countries lose by trading with low-wage developing nations. The concern is that the lower average wage that prevails in developing nations will allow those countries to produce most or all goods and services at lower cost. Unable to compete, the industrialized countries will suffer declining wages and rising unemployment. Does "cheap" foreign labor pose a danger to high-wage economies?

The "cheap foreign labor" argument is fallacious because it ignores the principle of comparative advantage and the advantages of specialization. To illustrate the key issues, suppose the United States produces both software and beef. Trade negotiators have proposed to open trade between the United States and a developing nation, Fredonia, which produces the same two products. Real wages are much lower in Fredonia than in the United States. Does this fact imply that Fredonia will undersell the United States in both the software and the beef markets, threatening American workers with the loss of their jobs?

To answer this question, let's first ask *why* wages are lower in Fredonia. As suggested in Chapter 2 as well as the chapter on perfectly competitive supply, wages are determined by the productivity of labor. Hence, if wages in Fredonia are radically lower than in the United States, Fredonian workers must be much less productive than U.S. workers. This observation is enough to show why Fredonian producers will not be able to undersell American producers in both industries. Even though Fredonian firms pay lower wages, because of differences in factors such as technology, physical capital, and human capital, a Fredonian worker produces much less output per hour than an American worker. Thus, lower Fredonian wages do not necessarily translate into lower production costs.

Indeed, Fredonia's production costs will tend to be lower than U.S. production costs only in those industries in which Fredonia is *relatively* more productive. Recall the principle of comparative advantage. Suppose that Fredonia is half as productive as the United States in producing beef, but only one-tenth as productive in producing software. In that case, the United States has an absolute advantage in producing both goods, but Fredonia has a comparative advantage in producing beef and the United States has a comparative advantage in producing software. The United States can gain by producing more software and trading the extra software to Fredonians for beef. Fredonia can gain too by trading its beef for software. Far from being hurt by trading with Fredonia, U.S. consumers can have more of both goods through trade.

Does cheap foreign labor pose a danger to high-wage economies?

While the U.S. economy as a whole gains from trade with Fredonia, the United States will have a larger software sector and a smaller beef-producing sector than it would in the absence of trade. That is, some U.S. software will be exported to Fredonia, but some U.S.-produced beef will be replaced by imported Fredonian beef. Hence, although opportunities for workers in the software sector will increase as a result of trade, employment and wages in the beef sector will fall. We will discuss the sectoral impacts of trade in the next section.

A SUPPLY-AND-DEMAND PERSPECTIVE ON TRADE

To this point we have shown that a country can improve its overall consumption possibilities by trading with other countries. In this section we will look more carefully at how international trade affects supply and demand in the markets for

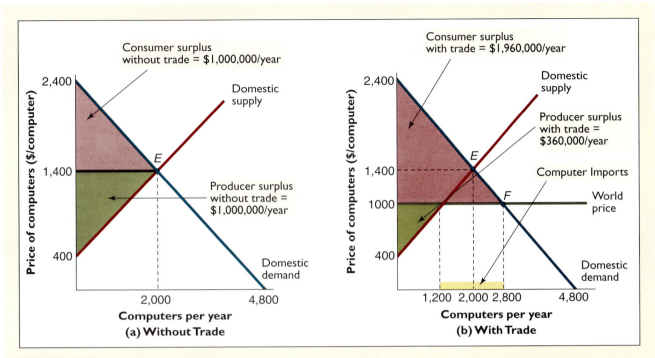

FIGURE 17.6

The Market for Computers in Costa Rica.

If Costa Rica is closed to international trade (a), the equilibrium price and quantity of computers are determined by the intersection of the domestic supply and demand curves at E. But if Costa Rica is open to trade (b), the domestic price of computers must equal the world price of $1,000. At that price, Costa Ricans will demand 2,800 computers each year, but domestic producers will supply only 1,200. Thus, 2,800 − 1,200 = 1,600 computers must be imported each year from abroad. Compared to the closed-economy outcome, computer buyers gain $960,000 per year of additional consumer surplus with trade, and domestic computer sellers lose $640,000 per year of producer surplus. For Costa Rican computer buyers and sellers as a whole, total economic surplus is thus $320,000 per year larger with trade.

specific goods. We will see that when it is costly for workers and firms to change industries, opening up trade with other countries may create groups of winners and losers among producers, even as it helps consumers.

Let's see how trade affects the markets for computers and coffee in Costa Rica. Figure 17.6 shows the supply and demand for computers in that country. As usual, the price is shown on the vertical axis and the quantity on the horizontal axis. We assume that computers sell in the world market for a price of $1,000 each. The upward-sloping curve in Figure 17.6 is the supply curve of computers, in this case for computers produced in Costa Rica; and the downward-sloping curve is the demand curve for computers by Costa Rican residents.

If the Costa Rican economy is closed to international trade, then market equilibrium occurs where the domestic supply and demand curves intersect, at point *E* in Figure 17.6(a). The equilibrium price will be $1,400 per computer and the equilibrium quantity, 2,000 computers per year. Domestic computer buyers enjoy a consumer surplus of $1 million per year, and domestic computer producers enjoy a producer surplus of $1 million per year.

If Costa Rica opens its market to trade, however, the relevant price for computers becomes the **world price** of computers, the price at which computers are traded internationally. The world price for computers is determined by the worldwide supply and demand for computers. If we assume that Costa Rica's computer market is too small to affect the world price for computers very much, the world price can be treated as fixed, and represented by a horizontal line in the figure.

world price the price at which a good or service is traded on international markets

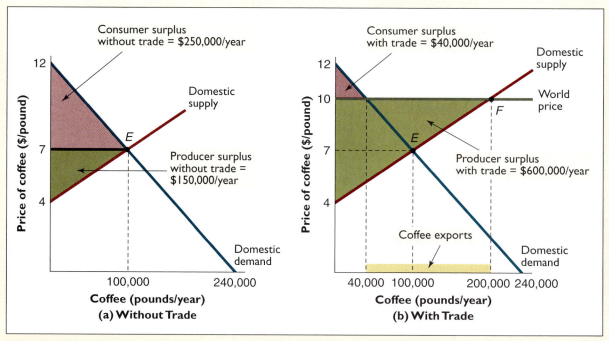

FIGURE 17.7

The Market for Coffee in Costa Rica.

With no international trade (a), the equilibrium price and quantity of coffee in Costa Rica are determined by the intersection of the domestic supply and demand curves (point *E*). But if the country opens to trade (b), the domestic price of coffee must equal the world price. At the higher world price, Costa Ricans will demand only 40,000 pounds of coffee each year, which is less than the 200,000 pounds Costa Rican producers supply at that price. The difference, 160,000 pounds of coffee, is exported from Costa Rica each year. Compared to the closed-economy outcome, domestic coffee buyers suffer a loss of $210,000 per year of consumer surplus from trade, and domestic coffee sellers gain $450,000 per year of producer surplus from trade. For Costa Rican coffee buyers and sellers as a whole, total economic surplus is thus $240,000 per year larger with trade.

Figure 17.6(b) shows the world price of $1,000 per computer as being lower than Costa Rica's closed-economy price of $1,400.

If Costa Ricans are free to buy and sell computers on the international market, then the price of computers in Costa Rica must be the same as the world price. (No one in Costa Rica will buy a computer at a price above the world price, and no one will sell one at a price below the world price.) Figure 17.6(b) shows that at the world price, Costa Rican consumers and firms demand 2,800 computers each year, but Costa Rican computer producers will supply only 1,200. The difference between the two quantities, 1,600, is the number of computers that Costa Rica must import from abroad each year. Figure 17.6(b) illustrates a general conclusion: *If the price of a good or service in a closed economy is greater than the world price, and that economy opens itself to trade, the economy will tend to become a net importer of that good or service.*

Note in Figure 17.6(b) that domestic computer buyers now enjoy $1,960,000 per year of consumer surplus, or $960,000 per year more than before trade. Domestic computer producers, for their part, now receive only $360,000 per year of producer surplus, or $640,000 less than before trade. On balance, then, domestic participants in the Costa Rican computer market experience a net increase of $320,000 per year in total economic surplus.

A different outcome occurs in Costa Rica's coffee market, shown in Figure 17.7. The price of coffee is shown on the vertical axis and the quantity of coffee on the horizontal axis. The downward-sloping demand curve in the figure shows how much coffee Costa Rican consumers want to buy at each price, and the upward-sloping supply curve, how much coffee Costa Rican producers are willing to supply at each price. If Costa Rica's economy is closed to trade with the rest of the world, then equilibrium in the market for coffee will occur at point E, where the domestic demand and supply curves intersect. The quantity produced will be 100,000 pounds of coffee each year and the price will be $7 per pound of coffee, as shown in Figure 17.7(a). Domestic coffee buyers enjoy a consumer surplus of $250,000 per year and domestic coffee producers enjoy a producer surplus of $150,000 per year.

Now imagine that Costa Rica opens its coffee market to international trade. As in the case of computers, if free trade in coffee is permitted, then the prevailing price for coffee in Costa Rica must be the same as the world price. Unlike the case of computers, however, the world price of coffee as shown in Figure 17.7(b) is *higher* than the domestic equilibrium price. We know that the world price of coffee will be higher than the domestic price because, in an example with only two goods, if non–Costa Rican producers have a comparative advantage in computers, as reflected in the fact that computers exchange for coffee at a lower price in the world market than in the domestic Costa Rican market, then Costa Rican producers must have a comparative advantage in coffee. And that means that the domestic price of coffee in Costa Rica without trade will be lower than the world price.

Figure 17.7(b) shows that at the world price for coffee, Costa Rican producers are willing to supply 200,000 pounds of coffee each year, while Costa Rican consumers want to purchase a much smaller amount, only 40,000 pounds. The difference between domestic production and domestic consumption, 200,000 − 40,000 = 160,000 pounds per year, is exported to the world market each year. Note in Figure 17.7(b) that domestic coffee buyers now enjoy a consumer surplus of $40,000 per year, a reduction of $210,000 per year in comparison with the surplus they enjoyed without trade. But domestic coffee producers now receive $600,000 per year of producer surplus, or $450,000 per year more than before trade. As in the case of the domestic computer market, domestic participants in the Costa Rican coffee market come out ahead on balance. Their total economic surplus is $240,000 per year higher as a result of opening the coffee market to trade. Note, finally, that the proceeds from the export of coffee ($1,600,000 per year) is just enough to enable the Costa Ricans to pay for the 1,600 computers per year they import (see Figure 17.6(b)).

The general conclusion of Figure 17.7 is this: *If the price of a good or service in a closed economy is lower than the world price, and that economy opens itself to trade, the economy will tend to become a net exporter of that good or service.* And again the result will be a net increase in the total economic surplus experienced by domestic buyers and sellers.

These examples illustrate how the market translates comparative advantage into mutually beneficial gains from trade. If trade is unrestricted, then countries with a comparative advantage in a particular good will profit by supplying that good to the world market and using the revenue earned to import goods in which they do not have a comparative advantage. Thus, the workings of the free market automatically ensure that goods will be produced where the opportunity cost is lowest, leading to the highest possible consumption possibilities for the world as a whole.

EXERCISE 17.4

If the domestic supply and demand curves for computers in Costa Rica are as shown in the diagram and the world price of computers is $1,200, how will opening the country to the possibility of buying computers in the world market affect consumer and producer surpluses in its domestic computer market?

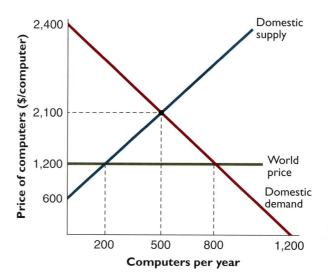

WINNERS AND LOSERS FROM TRADE

If trade is so wonderful, why do politicians so often resist free trade and "globalization"? The reason, as we have already seen, is that although free trade benefits the economy as a whole, specific groups may not benefit. If groups who are hurt by trade have sufficient political influence, they may be able to persuade politicians to enact policies that restrict the free flow of goods and services across borders.

The supply-and-demand analyses shown in Figures 17.6 and 17.7 are useful in understanding who gains and who loses when an economy opens up to trade. Look first at Figure 17.6, which shows the market for computers in Costa Rica. When Costa Rica opens its computer market to international competition, Costa Rican consumers enjoy a larger quantity of computers at a lower price. Clearly, Costa Rican computer users benefit from the free trade in computers. In general, *domestic consumers of imported goods benefit from free trade.* However, Costa Rican computer producers will not be so happy about opening their market to international competition. The fall in computer prices to the international level implies that less efficient domestic producers will go out of business, and that those who remain will earn lower profits. Unemployment in the Costa Rican computer industry will rise and may persist over time, particularly if displaced computer workers cannot easily move to a new industry.[2] We see that, in general, *domestic producers of imported goods are hurt by free trade.*

Consumers are helped, and producers hurt, when imports increase. The opposite conclusions apply for an increase in exports (see Figure 17.7). In the example of Costa Rica, an opening of the coffee market raises the domestic price of coffee to the world price and creates the opportunity for Costa Rica to export coffee. Domestic producers of coffee benefit from the increased market (they can now sell coffee abroad as well as at home) and from the higher price of their product. In short, *domestic producers of exported goods benefit from free trade.* Costa Rican coffee drinkers will be less enthusiastic, however, since they must now have to pay the higher world price of coffee, and will therefore consume less. *Thus, domestic consumers of exported goods are hurt by free trade.*

Free trade is *efficient,* in the sense that it increases the total economic surplus available to the economy. Indeed, the efficiency of free trade is an application of the

---

[2]The wages paid to Costa Rican computer workers also will fall, reflecting the lower relative price of computers. The other side of this coin, however, is that the wages paid to Costa Rican coffee growers will rise.

RECAP	**TRADE WINNERS AND LOSERS**

Winners

- Consumers of imported goods

- Producers of exported goods

Losers

- Consumers of exported goods

- Producers of imported goods

equilibrium principle, that markets in equilibrium leave no unexploited opportunities for individuals. Despite the efficiency of free trade, however, some groups lose from trade, which generates political pressures to block or restrict trade. In the next section we will discuss the major types of policies used to restrict trade.

PROTECTIONIST POLICIES: TARIFFS AND QUOTAS

The view that free trade is injurious and should be restricted is known as **protectionism.** Supporters of this view believe the government should attempt to "protect" domestic markets by raising legal barriers to imports. (It is interesting that protectionists rarely attempt to restrict exports, even though they hurt consumers of the exported good.) Two of the most common types of such barriers are *tariffs* and *quotas*. A **tariff** is a tax imposed on an imported good. A **quota** is a legal limit on the quantity of a good that may be imported.

protectionism the view that free trade is injurious and should be restricted

tariff a tax imposed on an imported good

quota a legal limit on the quantity of a good that may be imported

Tariffs

The effects of tariffs and quotas can be explained using supply-and-demand diagrams. Suppose that Costa Rican computer makers, dismayed by the penetration of "their" market by imported computers, persuade their government to impose a tariff—that is, a tax—on every computer imported into the country. Computers produced in Costa Rica will be exempt from the tax. Figure 17.8 shows the likely effects of this tariff on the domestic Costa Rican computer market. The lower of the two horizontal lines in Figure 17.8(a) indicates the world price of computers, not including the tariff—shown in the diagram as $1,000 per computer. The higher of the two lines indicates the price Costa Rican consumers will actually pay for imported computers, including the tariff, shown in the diagram as $1,200 per computer. The vertical distance between the two lines equals the amount of the tariff that is imposed on each imported computer—here, $200 per computer.

From the point of view of domestic Costa Rican producers and consumers, the imposition of the tariff has the same effects as an equivalent increase in the world price of computers. Because the price (including the tariff) of imported computers has risen, Costa Rican computer producers will be able to raise the price they charge for their computers to the world price plus tariff, or $1,200 per computer. Thus, the price Costa Rican consumers must pay—whether their computers are imported or not—equals $1,200 per computer, represented by the upper horizontal line in Figure 17.8.

The rise in the price of computers created by the tariff affects the quantities of computers supplied and the quantities demanded by Costa Ricans. Domestic computer producers, facing a higher price for computers, increase their production from 1,200 to 1,600 computers per year (see Figure 17.8(b)). Costa Rican consumers, also reacting to the higher price, reduce their computer purchases from 2,800 to 2,400 per year. As a result, the number of imported computers—the

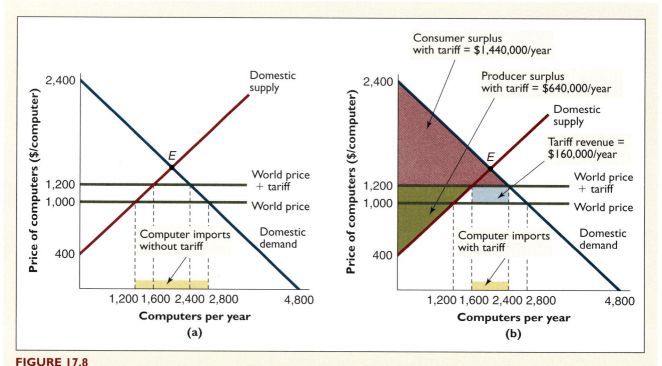

FIGURE 17.8

The Market for Computers after the Imposition of an Import Tariff.
The imposition of a tariff of $200 per imported computer raises the price of computers in Costa Rica from the world price ($1,000) to the world price plus the tariff ($1,200), represented by the upper horizontal line. Domestic production of computers rises from 1,200 to 1,600 per year. Domestic purchases of computers fall from 2,800 to 2,400 per year, and computer imports fall from 1,600 to 800 per year. Compared to the alternative of free trade (Figure 17.6(b)), Costa Rican computer buyers lose $520,000 per year of consumer surplus, and Costa Rican producers of computers gain $280,000 per year of producer surplus. The Costa Rican government collects revenue from the tariff equal to $160,000 per year, the area of the blue rectangle. The net effect of the tariff in the computer market is thus a reduction in total economic surplus of $80,000 per year.

difference between domestic purchases and domestic production—falls from 1,600 to 800 per year.

Who are the winners and the losers from the tariff, then? Relative to an environment with free trade and no tariff, the winners are the domestic computer producers and the losers are Costa Rican consumers, who must now pay more for their computers. Another winner is the government, which collects revenue from the tariff. The blue area in Figure 17.8(b) shows the amount of revenue the government collects, equal to the quantity of computer imports after the imposition of the tariff, 800 per year, times the amount of the tariff, $200 per computer, for a total of $160,000 per year.

How does the tariff affect total economic surplus? From Figure 17.6(b), recall that computer buyers reaped a consumer surplus of $1,960,000 per year under free trade. In Figure 17.8(b), we see that imposition of the $200 tariff on computers results in a consumer surplus of only $1,440,000 per year, a decline of $520,000 per year. Similarly, we saw in Figure 17.6(b) that domestic computer sellers reaped a producer surplus of $360,000 per year in the absence of tariffs. In Figure 17.8(b), note that the producer surplus rises to $640,000 per year with the imposition of the $200 tariff, a gain for producers of $280,000 per year. And note finally in Figure 17.8(b) that the government collects $160,000 per year in tariff revenue. Taking all these changes into account, the net effect of the imposition of the tariff is to cause a reduction in total economic surplus of $80,000 per year:

$$-\$520,000/\text{year} + \$280,000/\text{year} + \$160,000/\text{year} = -\$80,000/\text{year}$$

EXERCISE 17.5

If Costa Rica's supply and demand curves in its domestic computer market are as shown and buyers are currently able to import computers at the world price of $1,200, how will the imposition of a tariff of $300 per computer affect total economic surplus?

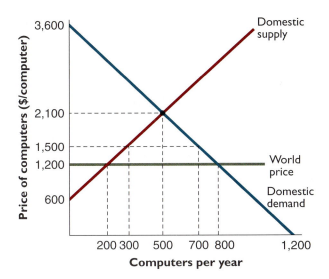

Why do consumers in the United States pay more than double the world price for sugar?

In 2005, Americans paid an average of 22 cents per pound of raw sugar as compared with an average world price of only 10 cents. What explains this huge price gap?

ECONOMIC
NATURALIST
17.2

The short answer is that the United States imposes a tariff of more than 100 percent on imported sugar. But that begs the following question: Why would legislators in Congress approve a tariff that costs their constituents about $2 billion each year? The most plausible answer is that in the political arena the incentive principle plays out in very different ways for domestic consumers of sugar than for domestic producers.

Because the typical family spends only a small fraction of one percent of its income each week on sugar, few people would ever take the trouble to write their representatives to complain about the price of sugar. Indeed, most people probably don't even realize that the sugar tariff exists. (Did you?)

For producers, the incentives are very different. For example, the sugar tariff was estimated to increase the profits of one large producer in Florida by some $65 million per year. With that much at stake, producers not only write letters, they also hire skilled lobbyists to promote their case. And more importantly, they make substantial political campaign contributions to legislators who support the tariff.

The gain to producers from the tariff is less than half the cost it imposes on consumers. The country would thus enjoy an additional $1 billion in economic surplus if the tariff was eliminated. Yet the fact remains that the costs of the tariff are diffuse while its benefits are highly concentrated. Because of that asymmetry, political support for tariff repeal promises to remain elusive.

Quotas

An alternative to a tariff is a quota, or legal limit, on the number or value of foreign goods that can be imported. One means of enforcing a quota is to require importers to obtain a license or permit for each good they bring into the country. The

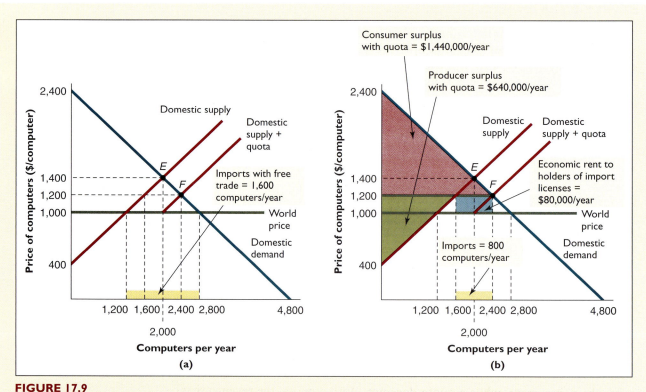

FIGURE 17.9

The Market for Computers after the Imposition of an Import Quota.

The figure shows the effects of the imposition of an import quota of 800 computers per year. The total supply of computers to the domestic economy is the domestic supply curve shifted to the right by 800 units (the amount of imports allowed under the quota). Market equilibrium occurs at point F. The effects of the quota on the domestic market are identical to those of the tariff analyzed in Figure 17.8. The domestic price rises from $1,000 to $1,200 per computer, domestic production of computers rises from 1,200 to 1,600 computers per year, domestic purchases of computers fall from 2,800 to 2,400 computers per year, and computer imports fall from 1,600 to 800 computers per year. Consumer and producer surpluses are the same under quotas as under tariffs. The tax revenue the government collected under the tariff goes instead as an economic rent to the holders of import licenses.

government then distributes exactly the same number of permits as the number of goods that may be imported under the quota.

How does the imposition of a quota on, say, computers affect the domestic market for computers? The effect is shown in Figure 17.9, which is similar to Figure 17.8. As before, assume that at first there are no restrictions on trade. Consumers pay the world price for computers, and 1,600 computers are imported each year (Figure 17.9(a)). Now suppose once more that domestic computer producers complain to the government about competition from foreign computer makers, and the government agrees to act. However, this time, instead of a tariff, the government imposes a quota on the number of computers that can be imported. For comparability with the tariff analyzed in Figure 17.8, let's assume that the quota permits the same level of imports as entered the country under the tariff: specifically, 800 computers per year. What effect does this ruling have on the domestic market for computers?

After the imposition of the quota, the quantity of computers supplied to the Costa Rican market is the production of domestic firms plus the 800 imported computers allowed under the quota. Figure 17.9(a) shows the quantity of computers supplied inclusive of the quota. The total supply curve, labeled "Domestic supply plus quota," is the same as the domestic supply curve except for one change: For all prices above the world price of $1,000 per computer, it is shifted 800 units to the right. (Even though the quota would allow foreign producers to sell 800 units at prices below $1,000, none would do so, because they could get $800 for them in the world market.) The domestic demand curve is the same as in Figure 17.8. Equilibrium in the domestic market for computers occurs at point F in Figure 17.9(a), at the intersection of the supply curve including the quota and the domestic demand curve.

The figure shows that, relative to the initial situation with free trade, the quota (1) raises the domestic price of computers by $200 per computer above the world price; (2) reduces domestic purchases of computers from 2,800 to 2,400 computers per year; (3) increases domestic production of computers from 1,200 to 1,600 computers per year; and (4) reduces imports from 1,600 to 800 computers per year, the full amount permitted under the quota. Similarly, note in Figure 17.9(b) that both consumer surplus and producer surplus are the same in the domestic computer market under a quota as they were in that market under a tariff (Figure 17.8(b)). So, like a tariff, the quota helps domestic producers by increasing their sales and the price they receive for their output, while hurting domestic consumers by forcing them to pay a higher price.

Under our assumption that the quota is set so as to permit the same level of imports as the tariff, the effects on the domestic market of the tariff (Figure 17.8) and the quota (Figure 17.9) are not only similar, they are *identical*. Comparing Figures 17.8 and 17.9, you can see that the two policies have precisely the same effects on the domestic price, domestic purchases, domestic production, and imports.

Although the market effects of a tariff and a quota are the same, there is one important difference between the two policies, which is that a tariff generates revenue for the government, while a quota does not. With a quota, the revenue that would have gone to the government goes instead as an economic rent to those firms who hold the import licenses. A holder of an import license can purchase a computer at the world price of $1,000 and resell it in the domestic market at price of $1,200, pocketing the difference. This difference is an economic rent, much like the economic rent received by the owner of a taxi medallion. As long as the number of licenses is fixed, it cannot be competed away. Thus, with a tariff, the government collects the difference between the world price and the domestic market price of the good; with a quota, private firms or individuals collect that difference, in both cases $80,000 per year.

Why then would the government ever impose a quota rather than a tariff? One possibility is that the distribution of import licenses is a means of rewarding the government's political supporters. Sometimes, international political concerns also may play a role (see Economic Naturalist 17.3 for a possible example).

Who benefited from, and who was hurt by, voluntary export restraints on Japanese automobiles in the 1980s?

ECONOMIC NATURALIST 17.3

After the oil price increases of the 1970s, American consumers began to buy small, fuel-efficient Japanese automobiles in large numbers. Reeling from the new foreign competition, U.S. automobile producers petitioned the U.S. government for assistance. In response, in May 1981 the U.S. government negotiated a system of so-called *voluntary export restraints*, or VERs, with Japan. Under the VER system, each Japanese auto producer would "voluntarily" restrict exports to the United States to an agreed-upon level. VER quotas were changed several times before the system was formally eliminated in 1994. Who benefited from, and who was hurt by, VERs on Japanese automobiles?

Several groups benefited from the VER system. As should be expected, U.S. auto producers saw increased sales and profits when their Japanese competition was reduced. But Japanese automobile producers also profited from the policy, despite the reduction in their U.S. sales. The restrictions on the supply of their automobiles to the U.S. market allowed them to raise their prices in the U.S market significantly—by several thousand dollars per car by the latter part of the 1980s, according to some estimates. From an economic point of view, the VERs functioned like a tariff on Japanese cars, except that the Japanese automobile producers, rather than the U.S. government, got to keep the tariff revenue. A third group that benefited from the VERs was European automobile producers, who saw U.S. demand for their cars rise when Japanese imports declined.

The biggest losers from the VER system were clearly American car buyers, who faced higher prices (particularly for Japanese imports) and reduced selection. During this period, dealer discounts on new Japanese cars largely disappeared, and customers often found themselves paying a premium over the list price. Because the economic losses faced by American car buyers exceeded the extra profits received by U.S. automobile producers, the VERs produced a net loss for the U.S. economy that at its greatest was estimated at more than $3 billion per year.

The U.S. government's choice of a VER system, rather than a tariff or a quota, was somewhat puzzling. If a tariff on Japanese cars had been imposed instead of a VER system, the U.S. government would have collected much of the revenue that went instead to Japanese auto producers. Alternatively, a quota system with import licenses given to U.S. car dealers would have captured some revenue for domestic car dealers rather than Japanese firms. The best explanation for why the U.S. government chose VERs is probably political. U.S. policymakers may have been concerned that the Japanese government would retaliate against U.S. trade restrictions by imposing its own restrictions on U.S. exports. By instituting a system that did minimal financial harm to—or even helped—Japanese auto producers, they may have hoped to avoid retaliation from the Japanese.[3]

Tariffs and quotas are not the only barriers to trade that governments erect. Importers may be subject to unnecessarily complex bureaucratic rules (so-called red-tape barriers), and regulations of goods that are nominally intended to promote health and safety sometimes have the side effect, whether intentionally or unintentionally, of restricting trade. One example is European restrictions on imports of genetically modified foods. Although these regulations were motivated in part by concerns about the safety of such foods, they also help to protect Europe's politically powerful farmers from foreign competition.

Who benefited from "voluntary" export restraints on Japanese cars?

THE INEFFICIENCY OF PROTECTIONISM

Free trade is efficient because it allows countries to specialize in the production of goods and services in which they have the greatest comparative advantage. Conversely, protectionist policies that limit trade are inefficient—they reduce total economic surplus. (Recall Chapter 3's *efficiency principle*, that efficiency is an important social goal.) Why, then, do governments adopt such policies? The reason is similar to why some city governments impose rent controls (see Chapter 3). Although rent controls reduce economic welfare overall, some people benefit from them—namely, the tenants whose rents are held artificially below market level. Similarly, as we have seen in this section, tariffs and quotas benefit certain groups. Because those who benefit from these restrictions (such as firms facing import competition) are often better organized politically than those who lose from trade barriers (such as consumers in general), lawmakers are sometimes persuaded to enact the restrictions.

The fact that free trade is efficient suggests an alternative to trade restrictions, however. Because eliminating restrictions on trade increases total economic surplus, in

---

[3]President Reagan's autobiography confirms that policymakers were concerned that an alternative method of limiting Japanese imports would provoke the Japanese into taking measures to limit U.S. exports to Japan. See Ronald Reagan, *An American Life* (New York: Simon and Schuster, 1990), p. 274.

general the winners from free trade will be able to compensate the losers in such a way that everyone becomes better off. Government programs that assist and retrain workers displaced by import competition are an example of such compensation. As the incentive principle reminds us, people are likely to resist policy changes that threaten their incomes. Spreading the benefits of free trade—or at least reducing its adverse effects on certain groups—reduces the incentives of those groups to inhibit free trade.

Although we have focused on the winners and losers from trade, not all opposition to free trade is motivated by economic interest. For example, many opponents of trade have focused on environmental concerns. Protecting the environment is an important and laudable goal, but once again the *efficiency principle* suggests that restricting trade is not the most effective means of achieving that goal. Restricting trade lowers world income, reducing the resources available to deal with environmental problems. (High levels of economic development are in fact associated with lower, not higher, amounts of pollution.) Furthermore, much of the income loss arising from barriers to trade is absorbed by poor nations trying to develop their economies. For this reason, leaders of developing countries are among the strongest advocates of free trade.

RECAP	A SUPPLY-AND-DEMAND PERSPECTIVE ON TRADE

- For a closed economy, the domestic supply and demand for a good or service determine the equilibrium price and quantity of that good or service.

- In an open economy, the price of a good or service traded on international markets equals the *world price*. If the domestic quantity supplied at the world price exceeds the domestic quantity demanded, the difference will be exported to the world market. If the domestic quantity demanded at the world price exceeds the domestic quantity supplied, the difference will be imported.

- Generally, if the price of a good or service in a closed economy is lower than the world price, and the economy opens to trade, the country will become a net exporter of that good or service. If the closed-economy price is higher than the world price, and the economy opens to trade, the country will tend to become a net importer of the good or service.

- Consumers of imported goods and producers of exported goods benefit from trade, while consumers of exported goods and producers of imported goods are hurt by trade. If those groups that are hurt have sufficient political influence, they may persuade the government to enact barriers to trade. The view that free trade is injurious and should be restricted is called *protectionism*.

- The two most common types of trade barriers are *tariffs*, or taxes on imported goods, and *quotas*, legal limits on the quantity that can be imported. A tariff raises the domestic price to the world price plus the tariff. The result is increased domestic production, reduced domestic consumption, and fewer imports. A quota has effects on the domestic market that are similar to those of a quota. The main difference is that, under a quota, the government does not collect tariff revenue.

- Trade barriers are inefficient; they reduce the overall size of the economic pie. Thus, in general, the winners from free trade should be able to compensate the losers in such a way that everyone becomes better off. Government programs to help workers displaced by import competition are an example of such compensation.

OUTSOURCING

outsourcing a term increasingly used to connote having services performed by low-wage workers overseas

An issue very much in the news in recent years has been the **outsourcing** of U.S. service jobs. Although the term once primarily meant having services performed by subcontractors anywhere outside the confines of the firm, increasingly it connotes the act of replacing relatively expensive American service workers with much cheaper service workers in overseas locations.

A case in point is the transcription of medical records. In an effort to maintain accurate records, many physicians dictate their case notes for later transcription after examining their patients. In the past, transcription was often by the physician's secretary in spare moments. But secretaries also must attend to a variety of other tasks that disrupt concentration. They must answer phones, serve as receptionists, prepare correspondence, and so on. As insurance disputes and malpractice litigation became more frequent during the 1980s and 1990s, errors in medical records became much more costly to physicians. In response, many turned to independent companies that offered transcription services by full-time, dedicated specialists.

These companies typically served physicians whose practices were located in the same community. But while many of the companies that manage transcription services are still located in the United States, an increasing fraction of the actual work itself is now performed outside the United States. For example, Eight Crossings, a company headquartered in Northern California, enables physicians to upload voice dictation files securely to the Internet, whereupon they are transmitted to transcribers who perform the work in India. The finished documents are then transmitted back, in electronic form, to physicians, who may edit and even sign them online. The advantage for physicians, of course, is that the fee for this service is much lower than for the same service performed domestically, because wage rates in India are much lower than in the United States.

In China, Korea, Indonesia, India, and elsewhere, even highly skilled professionals still earn just a small fraction of what their counterparts in the United States are paid. Accordingly, companies face powerful competitive pressure to import not just low-cost goods from overseas suppliers, but also a growing array of professional services.

As Microsoft chairman Bill Gates put it in a 1999 interview,

> As a business manager, you need to take a hard look at your core competencies. Revisit the areas of your company that aren't directly involved in those competencies, and consider whether Web technologies can enable you to spin off those tasks. Let another company take over the management responsibilities for that work, and use modern communication technology to work closely with the people—now partners instead of employees are doing the work. In the Web work style, employees can push the freedom the Web provides to its limits.

In economic terms, the outsourcing of services to low-wage foreign workers is exactly analogous to the importation of goods manufactured by low-wage foreign workers. In both cases, the resulting cost savings benefit consumers in the United States. And in both cases, jobs in the United States may be put in jeopardy, at least temporarily. An American manufacturing worker's job is at risk if it is possible to import the good he produces from another country at lower cost. By the same token, an American service worker's job is at risk if a lower-paid worker can perform that same service somewhere else.

Is PBS economics reporter Paul Solman's job a likely candidate for outsourcing?

Paul Solman and his associate Lee Koromvokis produce video segments that provide in-depth analysis of current economic issues for the PBS evening news program *The NewsHour with Jim Lehrer*. Is it likely that his job will someday be outsourced to a low-wage reporter from Hyderabad?

ECONOMIC
NATURALIST
17.4

In a recent book, the economists Frank Levy and Richard Murnane attempt to identify the characteristics of a job that make it a likely candidate for outsourcing.[4] In their view, any job that is amenable to computerization is also vulnerable to outsourcing. To computerize a task means to break it down into units that can be managed with simple rules. ATM machines, for example, were able to replace many of the tasks that bank tellers once performed, because it was straightforward to reduce these tasks to a simple series of questions that a machine could answer. By the same token, the workers in offshore call centers who increasingly book our airline and hotel reservations are basically following simple scripts much like computer programs.

So the less rules-based a job is, the less vulnerable it is to outsourcing. Safest of all are those that Levy and Murnane describe as "face-to-face" jobs. Unlike most rules-based jobs, these jobs tend to involve complex face-to-face communication with other people, precisely the kind of communication that dominates Mr. Solman's economics reporting.

In an interview for the *NewsHour*, Mr. Solman asked Mr. Levy what he meant, exactly, by "complex communication."

Is a low-wage foreign economics reporter likely to replace Paul Solman?

> "Suppose I say the word *bill*," Levy responded, "and you hear that. And the question is what does that mean? . . . Am I talking about a piece of currency? Am I talking about a piece of legislation, the front end of a duck? The only way you're going to answer that is to think about the whole context of the conversation. But that's very complicated work to break down into some kind of software."[5]

Levy and Murnane describe a second category of tasks that are less vulnerable to outsourcing—namely, those that for one reason or another require the worker to be physically present. For example, it is difficult to see how someone in China or India could build an addition to someone's house in a Chicago suburb, or repair a blown head gasket on someone's Chevrolet Corvette in Atlanta, or fill a cavity in someone's tooth in Los Angeles.

So on both counts, Paul Solman's job appears safe for the time being. Because it involves face-to-face, complex communication, and because many of his interviews can be conducted only in the United States, it is difficult to see how a reporter from Hyderabad could displace him.

Of course, the fact that a job is relatively safe does not mean that it is completely sheltered. For example, although most dentists continue to think themselves immune from outsourcing, it is now possible for someone requiring extensive dental work to have the work done in New Delhi and still save enough to cover his airfare and a two-week vacation in India.

There are more than 135 million Americans in the labor force. Every three months or so, approximately 7 million of them lose their jobs and 7 million find new ones. At various points in your life, you are likely to be among this group in transition. In the long run, the greatest security available to you or any other worker is the ability to adapt quickly to new circumstances. Having a good education provides no guarantee against losing your job, but it should enable you to develop a comparative advantage at the kinds of tasks that require more than just executing a simple set of rules.

---

[4]Frank Levy and Richard Murnane, *The New Division of Labor: How Computers Are Creating the Next Job Market* (Princeton, NJ: Princeton University Press, 2004).
[5]http://www.pbs.org/newshour/bb/economy/july-dec04/jobs_8-16.html.

■ SUMMARY ■

- According to the principle of comparative advantage, the best economic outcomes occur when each nation specializes in the goods and services at which it is relatively most productive, and then trades with other nations to obtain the goods and services its citizens desire.

- The production possibilities curve (PPC) of a country is a graph that describes the maximum amount of one good that can be produced at every possible level of production of the other good. At any point the slope of a PPC indicates the opportunity cost, in terms of forgone production of the good on the vertical axis, of increasing production of the good on the horizontal axis by one unit. The more of a good that is already being produced, the greater the opportunity cost of increasing production still further. Thus, the slope of a PPC becomes more and more negative as we read from left to right. When an economy has many workers, the PPC has a smooth, outwardly bowed shape.

- A country's *consumption possibilities* are the combinations of goods and services that might feasibly be consumed by its citizens. In a *closed economy*—one that does not trade with other countries—the citizens' consumption possibilities are identical to their production possibilities. But in an *open economy* that does trade with other countries, consumption possibilities are typically greater than, and never less than, the economy's production possibilities. Graphically, an open economy's consumption possibilities are described by a downward-sloping line that just touches the PPC, whose slope equals the amount of the good on the vertical axis that must be traded to obtain one unit of the good on the horizontal axis. A country achieves its highest consumption possibilities by producing at the point where the consumption possibilities line touches the PPC and then trading to obtain the most preferred point on the consumption possibilities line.

- In a closed economy, the relative price of a good or service is determined at the intersection of the supply curve of domestic producers and the demand curve of domestic consumers. In an open economy, the relative price of a good or service equals the world price—the price determined by supply and demand in the world economy. If the price of a good or service in a closed economy is greater than the world price, and the country opens its market to trade, it will become a net importer of that good or service. But if the closed-economy price is below the world price, and the country opens itself to trade, it will become a net exporter of that good or service.

- Although free trade is beneficial to the economy as a whole, some groups—such as domestic producers of imported goods—are hurt by free trade. Groups that are hurt by trade may be able to induce the government to impose *protectionist* measures, such as tariffs or quotas. A *tariff* is a tax on an imported good that has the effect of raising the domestic price of the good. A higher domestic price increases domestic supply, reduces domestic demand, and reduces imports of the good. A *quota*, which is a legal limit on the amount of a good that may be imported, has the same effects as a tariff, except that the government collects no tax revenue. (The equivalent amount of revenue goes instead to those firms with the legal authority to import goods.) Because free trade is efficient, the winners from free trade should be able to compensate the losers so that everyone becomes better off. Thus, policies to assist those who are harmed by trade, such as assistance and retraining for workers idled by imports, are usually preferable to trade restrictions.

■ KEY TERMS ■

autarky (490)	open economy (489)	quota (501)
closed economy (489)	outsourcing (508)	tariff (501)
consumption possibilities (490)	protectionism (501)	world price (497)

■ REVIEW QUESTIONS ■

1. Why are production possibilities curves often bowed outward from the origin?

2. What is meant by the *consumption possibilities* of a country? How are consumption possibilities related to production possibilities in a closed economy? In an open economy?

3. True or false and explain: If a country is more productive in every sector than a neighboring country, then there is no benefit in trading with the neighboring country.

4. Show graphically the effects of a tariff on imported automobiles on the domestic market for automobiles. Who is hurt by the tariff, and why? Who benefits, and why?

5. Show graphically the effects of a quota on imported automobiles on the domestic market for automobiles. Whom does the quota hurt, and who benefits? Explain.

▪ PROBLEMS ▪

Problems 1–5 refer to a small open economy whose production possibilities curve is as shown by the curve *ACGDB* in the diagram.

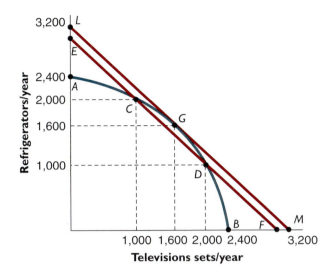

1. What is the maximum number of television sets this country can produce each year? What is the maximum number of refrigerators?

2. If refrigerators and television sets can each be bought or sold for $500 in the world market, what is the maximum number of refrigerators this country can consume each year? The maximum number of television sets? How would your answers change if refrigerators and television sets both sold for $1,000?

3. If refrigerators and television sets both sell for $1,000 in the world market, is it possible for this country to consume 1,000 television sets per year and 2,200 refrigerators? Could the country consume 1,000 refrigerators each year and 2,500 television sets?

4. If refrigerators and television sets both sell for $1,000 in the world market, how many units of each good should this country produce?

5. If the world price of refrigerators rose to $1,200 and the price of television sets remained $1,000, how will this country alter the mix of the two goods it produces? How will it alter the mix of the two goods it consumes?

6. A small open economy is equally productive in producing coffee and tea—that is, for each additional pound of coffee it produces, it must sacrifice the production of exactly one pound of tea. What will this economy produce if the world price of coffee is 20 percent higher than that of tea?

7. A developing economy requires 1,000 hours of work to produce a television set and 10 hours of work to produce a bushel of corn. This economy has available a total of 1,000,000 hours of work per day.
   a. Draw the PPC for daily output of the developing economy. Give numerical values for the PPC's vertical intercept, horizontal intercept, and slope. Relate the slope to the developing country's opportunity cost of producing each good. If this economy does not trade, what are its consumption possibilities?
   b. The developing economy is considering opening trade with a much larger, industrialized economy. The industrialized economy requires 10 hours of work to produce a television set and one hour of work to produce a bushel of corn. Show graphically how trading with the industrialized economy affects the developing economy's consumption possibilities. Is opening trade desirable for the developing economy?

8. Suppose that a U.S. worker can produce 1,000 pairs of shoes or 10 industrial robots per year. For simplicity, assume there are no costs other than labor costs and firms earn zero profits. Initially, the U.S. economy is closed. The domestic price of shoes is $30 per pair,

so a U.S. worker can earn $30,000 annually by working in the shoe industry. The domestic price of a robot is $3,000, so a U.S. worker also can earn $30,000 annually working in the robot industry. Now suppose that the United States opens trade with the rest of the world. Foreign workers can produce 500 pairs of shoes or one robot per year. The world price of shoes after the United States opens its markets is $10 per pair, and the world price of robots is $5,000.

a. Describe the new consumption possibilities curve for the United States.

b. What do foreign workers earn annually, in dollars?

c. When it opens to trade, which good will the United States import and which will it export?

d. Find the real income of U.S. workers after the opening to trade, measured in (1) the number of pairs of shoes annual worker income will buy and (2) the number of robots annual worker income will buy. Compare this real income to the situation before the opening of trade.

e. Does trading in goods produced by "cheap foreign labor" hurt U.S. workers?

f. How might your conclusion in part *c* be modified in the short term if it is costly for workers to change industries? What policy response might help with this problem?

9. If the domestic supply and demand curves for toasters in Islandia are as shown in the diagram and the world price of toasters is $18, how will opening the country to the possibility of buying toasters in the world market affect consumer and producer surpluses in its domestic computer market?

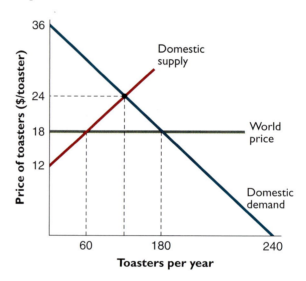

10. If Islandia's supply and demand curves in its domestic market for toasters are as shown and buyers are currently able to import toasters at the world price of $18, how will the imposition of a tariff of $3 per toaster affect total economic surplus?

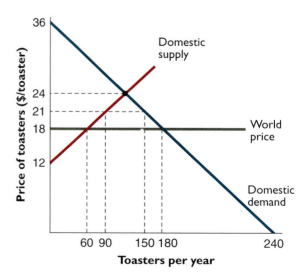

■ ANSWERS TO IN-CHAPTER EXERCISES ■

17.1 If Costa Rica produces at point C and can trade in the world market at the rate of 500 pounds of coffee per computer, it can sell 500 computers for 25,000 pounds of coffee. By so doing, Costa Rica can consume 125,000 pounds of coffee and 500 computers per year (point X in the diagram).

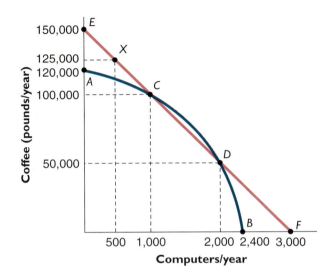

17.2 At the point Y in the diagram, Costa Rica consumes 2,500 computers per year and 25,000 pounds of coffee. Costa Rica can go from C to Y by selling 75,000 pounds of coffee in the world market at the world price of 0.02 computer per pound of coffee. At that price, its revenue from the sale of 75,000 pounds of coffee will enable it to purchase 2,000 computers.

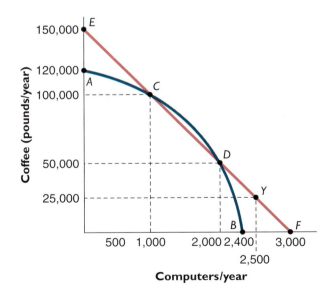

17.3 Now each Islandian worker can produce either 24 pounds of coffee per day or 8 pounds of tea. Workers who divide their time between the two activities will again produce each good in proportion to the amount of time spent producing it. Islandia's production possibilities curve will now be the line AD in the left panel of the diagram. If the world price of coffee is twice the world price of tea, Islandia should again specialize completely in coffee production. Its consumption possibilities curve is the line AD' in the left panel.

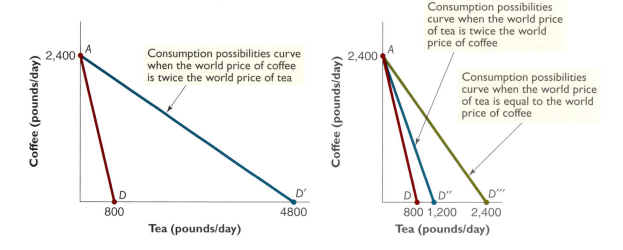

If the world price of tea is twice the world price of coffee, Islandians will still maximize their revenue from sales in world markets by specializing completely in coffee production. After all, an hour devoted to coffee production yields 24 pounds of coffee, which is enough to buy 12 pounds of tea at world prices, whereas an hour devoted to tea production would only yield 8 pounds of tea. In this case Islandia's consumption possibilities curve would be line AD'' in the right panel of the diagram. Finally, if the world price of coffee is equal to the world price of tea, Islandia's consumption possibilities curve would be line AD''' in the right panel.

17.4 Domestic consumers and producers in the computer market each reaps a surplus of $375,000 per year in the absence of trade (left panel), for a total economic surplus of $750,000. With trade, the country imports 300 computers per year at the world price of $1,200 per computer. Computer buyers reap a consumer surplus of $960,000 per year, or $585,000 per year more than before trade. Computer sellers receive a producer surplus of $60,000 per year, or $315,000 less than before trade. The net gain in total economic surplus from trade is $270,000 per year.

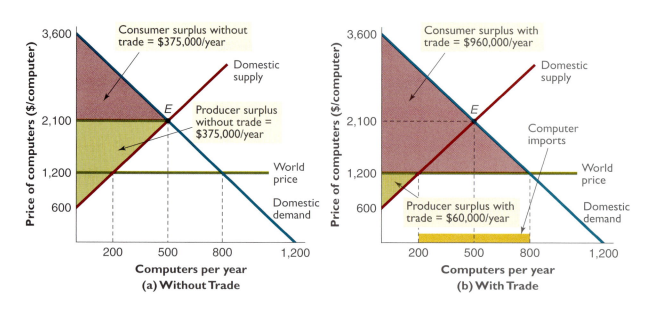

17.5 Total economic surplus without the tariff is $1,020,000 per year (left panel). With the tariff, consumer surplus falls by $225,000 per year, producer surplus rises by $75,000 per year, and government revenue rises by $120,000 per year. The net decrease in total economic surplus caused by the tariff is $30,000 per year.

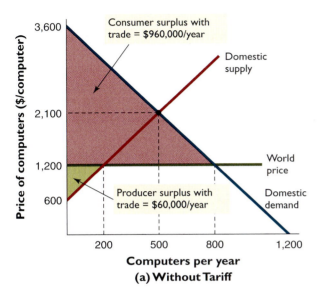

(a) Without Tariff

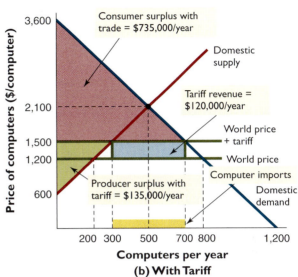

(b) With Tariff

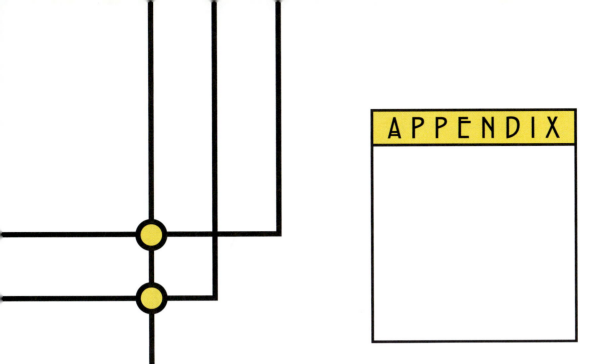

AN ALGEBRAIC APPROACH
TO TRADE ANALYSIS

In the text of this chapter, we used a graphical approach to show how international trade and various restrictions on trade affect economic welfare. In this appendix, we illustrate how the same issues can be approached in an algebraic framework.

EXAMPLE 17A.1

A Tariff on Imported Computers

Suppose the demand for computers by Costa Rican consumers is given by

$$P_C = 6,000 - 2Q^D,$$

where Q^D is the annual quantity of computers demanded and P_C is the price per computer in dollars.

The supply of computers by domestic Costa Rican producers is

$$P_C = 2Q^S,$$

where Q^S is the annual quantity of computers supplied.

a. Assuming that the Costa Rican economy is closed to trade, find the equilibrium price and quantity in the Costa Rican computer market.

b. Assume the economy opens to trade. If the world price of computers is $1,500, find annual Costa Rican consumption, production, and imports of computers.

c. At the request of domestic producers, the Costa Rican government imposes a tariff of $500 per imported computer. Find Costa Rican consumption, production, and imports of computers after the imposition of the tariff. How much revenue does the tariff raise for the government?

a. To find the equilibrium quantity Q^* for the closed economy, we note that the right-hand sides of the supply and demand equations will yield the same value for price at Q^*. So equating the right-hand sides of the supply and demand equations, we have

$$6,000 - 2Q^* = 2Q^*,$$

which solves for $Q^* = 1,500$ computers per year. Substituting this equilibrium quantity into either the supply equation or the demand equation, we find the equilibrium price of computers in the Costa Rican market, equal to $3,000 per computer. This equilibrium price and quantity correspond to point E in Figure 17A.1.

FIGURE 17A.1

The Effect of a Tariff.

The imposition of a tariff of $500 per computer increases the quantity of computers supplied domestically from 750 to 1,000 per year and reduces the quantity of computers demanded domestically from 2,250 to 2,000 per year. The tariff causes imports to fall from 1,500 to 1,000 computers per year. Government collects $500,000 in tariff revenue.

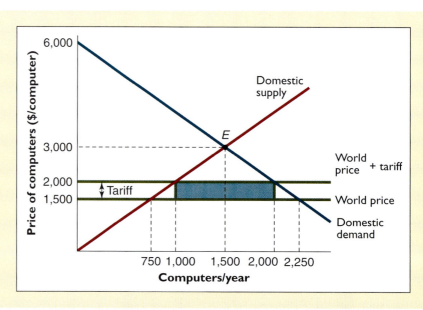

b. If the economy opens to trade, the domestic price of computers must equal the world price, which is $1,500. To find the domestic quantity demanded at this price, we can either consult Figure 17A.1 or else plug the world price into the domestic demand equation and solve for $Q^D = 2,250$ computers per year; in similar fashion, we see that the domestic quantity supplied is 750 computers per year. Imports equal the difference between domestic quantities demanded and supplied, or $2,250 - 750 = 1,500$ computers per year.

c. The imposition of a tariff of $500 per computer raises the price from $1,500 (the world price without the tariff) to $2,000. To find Costa Rican consumption and production at this price, we set the price equal to $2,000 in the demand and supply equations and solve for the relevant quantities. (Alternatively, we can locate these quantities in Figure 17A.1.) Thus, the domestic quantity demanded is 2,000 computers per year, and the domestic quantity supplied is 1,000 computers per year. Imports, the difference between the quantity demanded by Costa Ricans and the quantity supplied by domestic firms, equal 1,000 computers per year. Thus, the tariff has raised the price of computers by $500 and reduced imports by 500 computers per year. The tariff revenues collected by the government equal $500 per imported computer times 1,000 computers per year, or $500,000 per year.

EXERCISE 17A.1

Repeat parts *b* and *c* of Example 17A.1 under the assumption that the world price of computers is $1,000. What happens if the world price is $2,000 and the tariff is $1,500?

Effects of an Import Quota

EXAMPLE 17A.2

Suppose the supply of and demand for computers in Costa Rica is as given in Example 17A.1, and the government imposes an import quota of 1,000 computers. Find the equilibrium price in the domestic computer market, as well as the quantities produced by domestic firms and purchased by domestic consumers.

The supply curve of domestic Costa Rican producers of computers was stated in Example 17A.1 to be $P_C = 2Q^S$. The quota allows 1,000 computers per year to be imported. Let $Q^{S'}$ denote the new total quantity of computers supplied, including both domestic production and imports: $Q^{S'} = 1,000 + Q^S$. The new supply curve is thus the original supply curve shifted to the right by 1,000 units at every price above the world price. To find the equation for the new supply curve, we solve the original supply curve for $Q^S = P/2$, then add 1,000 to both sides to obtain

$$Q^S + 1,000 = P/2 + 1000 = Q^{S'}.$$

Solving back for P yields

$$P = -2,000 + 2QS'.$$

At the market equilibrium quantity Q^*, the price on this new supply curve will be equal to price on the demand curve:

$$-2,000 + 2Q^* = 6,000 - 2Q^*,$$

which solves for $Q^* = 2,000$ computers per year. Plugging $Q^* = 2,000$ into the demand curve, we solve for the new equilibrium price of computers, $P_C = 6,000 - 2Q^* = \$2,000$. Of the 2,000 computers sold each year domestically, 1,000 are produced in Costa Rica and another 1,000 are imported. These results are summarized in Figure 17A.2.

FIGURE 17A.2

The Effect of a Quota.
The imposition of a quota of 1,000 imported computers per year increases the quantity of computers supplied domestically from 750 to 1,000 per year and reduces the quantity of computers demanded domestically from 2,250 to 2,000 per year. The quota causes imports to fall from 1,500 to 1,000 computers per year. Government collects no tariff revenue.

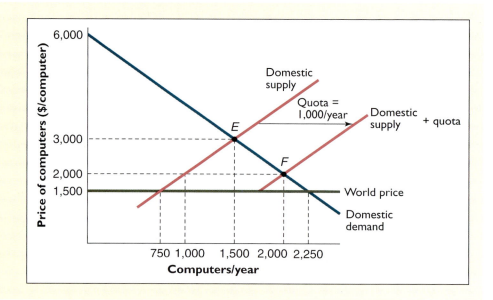

Note that the effects of the quota on domestic price, domestic production, and domestic demand are the same as the corresponding effects of a tariff identified in Example 17A.1. Thus, the tariff and the quota have the same effects on the domestic market for computers. The only difference between the two policies is that with a quota, the government does not get the tariff revenue it got in Example 17A.1. That revenue goes instead to the holders of import licenses, who can buy computers on the world market at $1,500 and sell them in the domestic market at $2,000.

▪ PROBLEMS ▪

1. The demand for automobiles in a certain country is given by

$$P = 60 - (Q^D/200),$$

   where P is the price of a car and Q^D is the quantity demanded. Supply by domestic automobile producers is

$$P = -140 + (Q^S/50),$$

   where Q^S is the quantity supplied.
   a. Assuming that the economy is closed, find the equilibrium price and production of automobiles.
   b. The economy opens to trade. The world price of automobiles is 18. Find the domestic quantities demanded and supplied and the quantity of imports or exports.
   c. Who will favor the opening of the automobile market to trade, and who will oppose it?
   d. The government imposes a tariff of 1 unit per car. Find the effects on domestic quantities demanded and supplied and on the quantity of imports or exports. Also find the revenue raised by the tariff. Who will favor the imposition of the tariff, and who will oppose it?
   e. Can the government obtain the same results as you found in part c by imposing a quota on automobile imports? Explain.

2. Suppose the domestic demand and supply for automobiles are as given by problem 1. The world price of automobiles is 16. Foreign car firms have a production cost of 15 per automobile, so they earn a profit of 1 per car.
   a. How many cars will be imported, assuming this country trades freely?
   b. Now suppose foreign car producers are asked "voluntarily" to limit their exports to the home country to half of free-trade levels. What will be the equilibrium price of

cars in the domestic market if foreign producers comply? Find domestic quantities of cars supplied and demanded.

c. How will the "voluntary" export restriction affect the profits of foreign car producers?

ANSWER TO IN-APPENDIX EXERCISE

17A.1 If the world price of computers is $1,000, the domestic quantity of computers demanded is 2,500 per year. The domestic quantity supplied is 500 computers per year. The difference between the quantity demanded and the quantity supplied, 2,000 computers per year, is imported.

A tariff of $500 raises the domestic price of computers to $1,500. Now the domestic quantity demanded is 2,250 per year, and domestic quantity supplied is 750. The difference, 1,500 computers per year, equals imports. Revenue for the government is $500 per computer times 1,500 imported computers, or $750,000 per year.

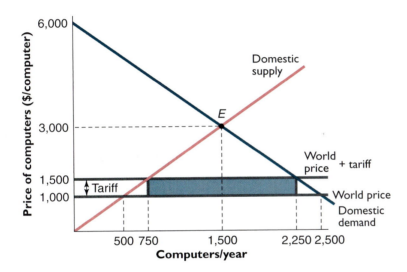

If the world price of computers is $2,000 and there is no tariff, the domestic quantity demanded is 2,000 computers per year and the domestic quantity supplied is 1,000 computers per year. The difference, 1,000 computers per year, is imported. A tariff of $1,500 per computer raises the world price plus tariff to $3,500, which is greater than the domestic price when there is no trade ($3,000). No computers are imported in this case and no tariff revenue is raised. 1,500 computers are produced and sold domestically each year at a price of $3,000.

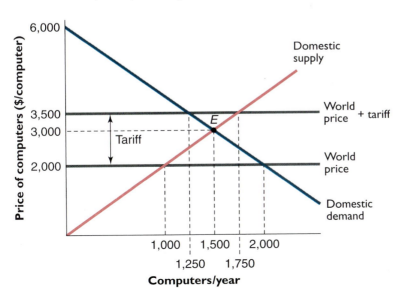

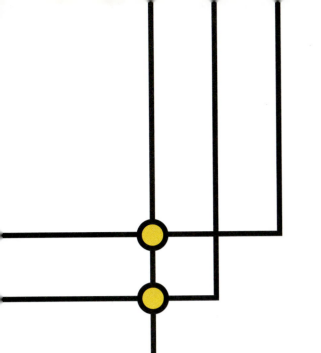

EXCHANGE RATES AND THE OPEN ECONOMY

Two Americans visiting London were commiserating over their problems understanding English currency. "Pounds, shillings, tuppence, thruppence, bob, and quid, it's driving me crazy," said the first American. "This morning it took me 20 minutes to figure out how much to pay the taxi driver."

The second American was more upbeat. "Actually," he said, "since I adopted my new system, I haven't had any problems at all."

The first American looked interested. "What's your new system?"

"Well," replied the second, "now, whenever I take a taxi, I just give the driver all the English money I have. And would you believe it, I have got the fare exactly right every time!"

Dealing with unfamiliar currencies—and translating the value of foreign money into dollars—is a problem every international traveler faces.[1] The traveler's problem is complicated by the fact that *exchange rates*—the rates at which one country's money trades for another—may change unpredictably. Thus, the number of British pounds, Russian rubles, Japanese yen, or Australian dollars that a U.S. dollar can buy may vary over time, sometimes quite a lot.

The economic consequences of variable exchange rates are much broader than their impact on travel and tourism, however. For example, the competitiveness of U.S. exports depends in part on the prices of U.S. goods in terms of foreign currencies, which in turn depend on the exchange rate between the U.S. dollar and

---

[1]However, British money today is less complicated to understand than suggested by the introductory story. In 1971 the British switched to a decimal monetary system, under which each pound is worth 100 pence. At that time, the traditional British system, under which a pound equaled 20 shillings and each shilling equaled 12 pence, was abandoned.

Foreign currency conundrums.

those currencies. Likewise, the prices Americans pay for imported goods depend in part on the value of the dollar relative to the currencies of the countries that produce those goods. Exchange rates also affect the value of financial investments made across national borders. For countries that are heavily dependent on trade and international capital flows—the majority of the world's nations—fluctuations in the exchange rate may have a significant economic impact.

This chapter discusses exchange rates and the role they play in open economies. We will start by introducing the *nominal exchange rate*—the rate at which one national currency trades for another. We will then show how exchange rates affect the prices of exports and imports, and thus the pattern of trade.

Next we will turn to the question of how exchange rates are determined in the short run. Exchange rates may be divided into two broad categories: flexible and fixed. The value of a *flexible* exchange rate is determined freely in the market for national currencies, known as the *foreign exchange market*. Flexible exchange rates vary continually with changes in the supply of and demand for national currencies. In contrast, the value of a *fixed* exchange rate is set by the government at a constant level. Because most large industrial countries, including the United States, have a flexible exchange rate, we will focus on that case first. We will see that a country's monetary policy plays a particularly important role in determining the exchange rate. Furthermore, in an open economy with a flexible exchange rate, the exchange rate becomes a tool of monetary policy, in much the same way as the real interest rate.

Although most large industrial countries have a flexible exchange rate, many small and developing economies fix their exchange rates, so we will consider the case of fixed exchange rates as well. We will explain first how a country's government (usually, its central bank) maintains a fixed exchange rate at the officially determined level. Though fixing the exchange rate generally reduces day-to-day fluctuations in the value of a nation's currency, we will see that, at times, a fixed exchange rate can become severely unstable, with potentially serious economic consequences. We will then discuss the relative merits of fixed and flexible exchange rates. We will close the chapter by introducing the *real exchange rate*—the rate at which one country's goods trade for another's—and discussing how exchange rates are determined in the long run.

EXCHANGE RATES

The economic benefits of trade between nations in goods, services, and assets are similar to the benefits of trade within a nation. In both cases, trade in goods and services permits greater specialization and efficiency, whereas trade in assets allows financial investors to earn higher returns while providing funds for worthwhile capital projects. However, there is a difference between the two cases. Trade in goods, services, and assets *within* a nation normally involves a single currency—dollars, yen, pesos, or whatever the country's official form of money happens to be—whereas trade *between* nations usually involves dealing in different currencies. So, for example, if an American resident wants to purchase an automobile manufactured in South Korea, she (or more likely, the automobile dealer) must first trade dollars for the Korean currency, called the won. The Korean car manufacturer is then paid in won. Similarly, an Argentine who wants to purchase shares in a U.S. company (a U.S. financial asset) must first trade his Argentine pesos for dollars and then use the dollars to purchase the shares.

NOMINAL EXCHANGE RATES

Because international transactions generally require that one currency be traded for another, the relative values of different currencies are an important factor in international economic relations. The rate at which two currencies can be traded for each other is called the **nominal exchange rate,** or more simply the *exchange rate*, between the two currencies. For example, if one U.S. dollar can be exchanged for 110 Japanese yen, the nominal exchange rate between the U.S. and Japanese currencies is 110 yen per dollar. Each country has many nominal exchange rates, one corresponding to each currency against which its own currency is traded. Thus the dollar's value can be quoted in terms of English pounds, Swedish kroner, Israeli shekels, Russian rubles, or dozens of other currencies.

Table 18.1 gives exchange rates between the dollar and six other important currencies as of the close of business in New York City on May 16, 2005. As Table 18.1 shows, exchange rates can be expressed either as the amount of foreign currency needed to purchase one U.S. dollar (left column) or as the number of U.S. dollars needed to purchase one unit of the foreign currency (right column). These two ways of expressing the exchange rate are equivalent: each is the reciprocal of the other. For example, on May 16, 2005, the U.S.–Canadian exchange rate could have been expressed either as 1.2697 Canadian dollars per U.S. dollar or as 0.7876 U.S. dollars per Canadian dollar, where 0.7876 = 1/1.2697.

nominal exchange rate the rate at which two currencies can be traded for each other

TABLE 18.1
Nominal Exchange Rates for the U.S. Dollar

Country	Foreign currency/U.S. dollar	U.S. Dollars/foreign currency
United Kingdom (pound)	0.5442	1.8376
Canada (Canadian dollar)	1.2697	0.7876
Mexico (peso)	11.0096	0.0908
Japan (yen)	106.85	0.009359
Switzerland (Swiss franc)	1.2222	0.8182
South Korea (won)	1,007.46	0.0009926

SOURCE: *The Wall Street Journal*, May 17, 2005.

EXAMPLE 18.1

Nominal exchange rates

Based on Table 18.1, find the exchange rate between the British and Canadian currencies. Express the exchange rate in both Canadian dollars per pound and pounds per Canadian dollar.

From Table 18.1, we see that 0.5442 British pounds will buy a U.S. dollar, and that 1.2697 Canadian dollars will buy a U.S. dollar. Therefore, 0.5442 British pounds and 1.2697 Canadian dollars are equal in value:

0.5442 pounds = 1.2697 Canadian dollars.

Dividing both sides of this equation by 1.2697, we get

0.4286 pounds = 1 Canadian dollar.

In other words, the British–Canadian exchange rate can be expressed as 0.4286 pounds per Canadian dollar. Alternatively, the exchange rate can be expressed as 1/0.4286 = 2.33 Canadian dollars per pound.

EXERCISE 18.1

From the business section of the newspaper or an online source (try the Federal Reserve Bank of St. Louis FRED database, http://research.stlouisfed. org/fred2/), find recent quotations of the value of the U.S. dollar against the British pound, the Canadian dollar, and the Japanese yen. Based on these data, find the exchange rate (a) between the pound and the Canadian dollar and (b) between the Canadian dollar and the yen. Express the exchange rates you derive in two ways (e.g., both as pounds per Canadian dollar and as Canadian dollars per pound).

Figure 18.1 shows the nominal exchange rate for the U.S. dollar from 1973 to 2004. Rather than showing the value of the dollar relative to that of an individual foreign currency, such as the Japanese yen or the British pound, the figure expresses the value of the dollar as an average of its values against other major currencies. This average value of the dollar is measured relative to a base value of 100 in 1973. So, for example, a value of 120 for the dollar in a particular year implies that the dollar was 20 percent more valuable in that year, relative to other major currencies, than it was in 1973.

FIGURE 18.1

The U.S. Nominal Exchange Rate, 1973–2004.

This figure expresses the value of the dollar from 1973 to 2004 as an average of its values against other major currencies, relative to a base value of 100 in 1973.

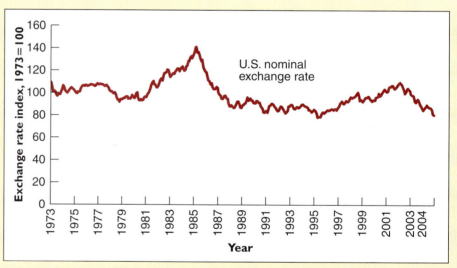

SOURCE: Federal Reserve Bank of St. Louis, FRED database (http://research.stlouisfed.org/fred2/).

You can see from Figure 18.1 that the dollar's value has fluctuated over time, sometimes increasing (as in the period 1980–1985) and sometimes decreasing (as in 1985–1987 and 2003–2004). An increase in the value of a currency relative to other currencies is known as an **appreciation;** a decline in the value of a currency relative to other currencies is called a **depreciation.** So we can say that the dollar appreciated in 1980–1985 and depreciated in 1985–1987 and 2003–2004. We will discuss the reasons a currency may appreciate or depreciate later in this chapter.

In this chapter, we will use the symbol e to stand for a country's nominal exchange rate. Although the exchange rate can be expressed either as foreign currency units per unit of domestic currency, or vice versa, as we saw in Table 18.1, let's agree to define e as *the number of units of the foreign currency that each unit of the domestic currency will buy.* For example, if we treat the United States as the "home" or "domestic" country and Japan as the "foreign" country, e will be defined as the number of Japanese yen that one U.S. dollar will buy. Defining the nominal exchange rate this way implies that an *increase* in e corresponds

appreciation an increase in the value of a currency relative to other currencies

depreciation a decrease in the value of a currency relative to other currencies

to an *appreciation*, or a strengthening, of the home currency, since each unit of the domestic currency will then buy more units of the foreign currency. Similarly, a *decrease* in *e* implies a *depreciation*, or weakening, of the home currency.

"On the foreign-exchange markets today, the dollar fell against all major currencies and the doughnut."

FLEXIBLE VERSUS FIXED EXCHANGE RATES

As we suggested in Figure 18.1, the exchange rate between the U.S. dollar and other currencies isn't constant but varies continually. Indeed, changes in the value of the dollar occur daily, hourly, even minute by minute. Such fluctuations in the value of a currency are normal for countries like the United States, which have a *flexible* or *floating exchange rate*. The value of a **flexible exchange rate** is not officially fixed but varies according to the supply and demand for the currency in the **foreign exchange market**—the market on which currencies of various nations are traded for one another. We will discuss the factors that determine the supply and demand for currencies shortly.

Some countries do not allow their currency values to vary with market conditions but instead maintain a *fixed exchange rate*. The value of a **fixed exchange rate** is set by official government policy. (A government that establishes a fixed exchange rate typically determines the exchange rate's value independently, but sometimes exchange rates are set according to an agreement among a number of governments.) Some countries fix their exchange rates in terms of the U.S. dollar (Hong Kong, for example), but there are other possibilities. Many African countries fix the value of their currencies in terms of the euro, the currency of the European Economic Community. Under the gold standard, which many countries used until its collapse during the Great Depression, currency values were fixed in terms of ounces of gold.

flexible exchange rate an exchange rate whose value is not officially fixed but varies according to the supply and demand for the currency in the foreign exchange market

foreign exchange market the market on which currencies of various nations are traded for one another

fixed exchange rate an exchange rate whose value is set by official government policy

RECAP	NOMINAL EXCHANGE RATES

- The nominal exchange rate between two currencies is the rate at which the currencies can be traded for each other. More precisely, the nominal exchange rate *e* for any given country is the number of units of foreign currency that can be bought for one unit of the domestic currency.

- An appreciation is an increase in the value of a currency relative to other currencies (a rise in e); a depreciation is a decline in a currency's value (a fall in e).

- An exchange rate can be either flexible—meaning that it varies freely according to supply and demand for the currency in the foreign exchange market—or fixed, meaning that its value is established by official government policy.

THE DETERMINATION OF THE EXCHANGE RATE IN THE SHORT RUN

Countries that have flexible exchange rates, such as the United States, see the international values of their currencies change continually. What determines the value of the nominal exchange rate at any point in time? In this section, we use supply and demand analysis to answer this question for the short run. Our focus for the moment is on flexible exchange rates, whose values are determined by the foreign exchange market. Later in the chapter we discuss the case of fixed exchange rates, the costs and benefits of each type of exchange rate, and the determination of exchange rates in the long run.

A SUPPLY AND DEMAND ANALYSIS

As we will see, dollars are demanded in the foreign exchange market by foreigners who seek to purchase U.S. goods, services, and assets and are supplied by U.S. residents who need foreign currencies to buy foreign goods, services, and assets. The market equilibrium exchange rate is the value of the dollar that equates the number of dollars supplied and demanded in the foreign exchange market. In this section, we will discuss the factors that affect the supply and demand for dollars, and thus the U.S. exchange rate.

One note before we proceed: In the chapter "Stabilizing the Economy," we described how the supply of money by the Fed and the demand for money by the public help to determine the nominal interest rate. However, the supply and demand for money in the domestic economy, as presented in that chapter, are *not* equivalent to the supply and demand for dollars in the foreign exchange market. As mentioned, the foreign exchange market is the market in which the currencies of various nations are traded for one another. The supply of dollars to the foreign exchange market is *not* the same as the money supply set by the Fed; rather, it is the number of dollars U.S. households and firms offer to trade for other currencies. Likewise, the demand for dollars in the foreign exchange market is *not* the same as the domestic demand for money, but the number of dollars holders of foreign currencies seek to buy. To understand the distinction, it may help to keep in mind that while the Fed determines the total supply of dollars in the U.S. economy, a dollar does not "count" as having been supplied to the foreign exchange market until some holder of dollars, such as a household or firm, tries to trade it for a foreign currency.

The Supply of Dollars

Anyone who holds dollars, from an international bank to a Russian citizen whose dollars are buried in the backyard, is a potential supplier of dollars to the foreign exchange market. In practice, however, the principal suppliers of dollars to the foreign exchange market are U.S. households and firms. Why would a U.S. household or firm want to supply dollars in exchange for foreign currency? There are two major reasons. First, a U.S. household or firm may need foreign currency *to purchase foreign goods or services*. For example, a U.S. automobile importer may need yen to purchase Japanese cars, or an American tourist may need yen to make purchases in Tokyo. Second, a U.S. household or firm may need foreign currency *to purchase foreign assets*. For example, an American mutual fund may wish to acquire stocks issued by Japanese companies, or an individual U.S. saver may want to purchase Japanese government bonds. Because Japanese assets are priced in yen, the U.S. household or firm will need to trade dollars for yen to acquire these assets.

The supply of dollars to the foreign exchange market is illustrated by the upward-sloping curve in Figure 18.2. We will focus on the market in which dollars are traded for Japanese yen, but bear in mind that similar markets exist for every other pair of traded currencies. The vertical axis of the figure shows the U.S.–Japanese exchange rate as measured by the number of yen that can be purchased with each dollar. The horizontal axis shows the number of dollars being traded in the yen–dollar market.

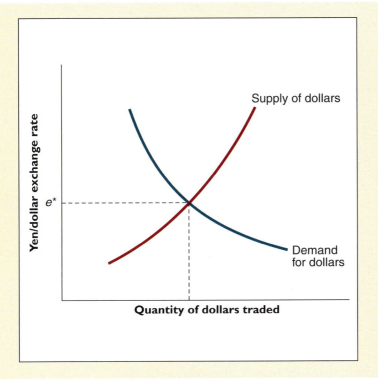

FIGURE 18.2
The Supply and Demand for Dollars in the Yen–Dollar Market.
The supply of dollars to the foreign exchange market is upward-sloping, because an increase in the number of yen offered for each dollar makes Japanese goods, services, and assets more attractive to U.S. buyers. Similarly, the demand for dollars is downward-sloping, because holders of yen will be less willing to buy dollars the more expensive they are in terms of yen. The *market equilibrium exchange rate e** equates the quantities of dollars supplied and demanded.

The supply curve for dollars is upward-sloping indicating that the more yen each dollar can buy, the more dollars people are willing to supply to the foreign exchange market. Why? At given prices for Japanese goods, services, and assets, the more yen a dollar can buy, the cheaper those goods, services, and assets will be in dollar terms.

For example, suppose a video game costs 5,000 yen in Japan, and a dollar can buy 100 yen, the dollar price of the video game will be

$$5{,}000 \text{ yen} \times \$1/100 \text{ yen} = \$50.^2$$

If, however, the yen price of a dollar rises to 200 yen, the dollar price of the same video game that costs 5,000 yen in Japan will then be

$$5{,}000 \text{ yen} \times \$1/200 \text{ yen} = \$25.$$

---

[2]Recall that an exchange rate of one dollar per 100 yen is the same as 100 yen per dollar. We are writing it the first way in this example so that the yen will cancel when we perform the multiplication and we are left with the dollar price.

If lower dollar prices will induce Americans to increase their total dollar expenditures on Japanese goods, services, and assets, a higher yen–dollar exchange rate will increase the supply of dollars to the foreign exchange market. Thus, the supply curve for dollars is upward-sloping.

The Demand for Dollars

In the yen–dollar foreign exchange market, demanders of dollars are those who wish to acquire dollars in exchange for yen. Most demanders of dollars in the yen–dollar market are Japanese households and firms, although anyone who happens to hold yen is free to trade them for dollars. Why demand dollars? The reasons for acquiring dollars are analogous to those for acquiring yen. First, households and firms that hold yen will demand dollars *so that they can purchase U.S. goods and services*. For example, a Japanese firm that wants to license U.S.-produced software needs dollars to pay the required fees, and a Japanese student studying in an American university must pay tuition in dollars. The firm or the student can acquire the necessary dollars only by offering yen in exchange. Second, households and firms demand dollars *in order to purchase U.S. assets*. The purchase of Hawaiian real estate by a Japanese company or the acquisition of Microsoft stock by a Japanese pension fund are two examples.

The demand curve for dollars will be downward-sloping, as illustrated in Figure 18.2. The demand for dollars will be low when dollars are expensive in terms of yen and high when dollars are cheap in terms of yen.

Suppose the licensing fee for a piece of U.S.-produced software is $30. If it costs a Japanese business 200 yen to buy $1, the software will cost the Japanese

$$\$30 \times 200 \text{ yen}/\$1 = 6{,}000 \text{ yen.}^3$$

If, however, the price of a dollar falls to 100 yen, the yen price of the same software that costs $30 in the United States will then be

$$\$30 \times 100 \text{ yen}/\$1 = 3{,}000 \text{ yen.}$$

As the yen price per dollar falls, U.S. goods, services, and assets become cheaper and more attractive to the Japanese. They respond by buying more U.S. goods, services, and assets and thereby demanding more dollars.

The Market Equilibrium Value of the Dollar

As mentioned earlier, the United States maintains a flexible, or floating, exchange rate, which means that the value of the dollar is determined by the forces of supply and demand in the foreign exchange market. In Figure 18.2, the equilibrium value of the dollar is e^*, the yen–dollar exchange rate at which the quantity of dollars supplied equals the quantity of dollars demanded. In general, the **market equilibrium value of the exchange rate** is not constant but changes with shifts in the supply of and demand for dollars in the foreign exchange market.

market equilibrium value of the exchange rate the exchange rate that equates the quantities of the currency supplied and demanded in the foreign exchange market

The U.S. trade deficit and the value of the dollar

ECONOMIC NATURALIST 18.1

The United States maintains a flexible exchange rate, allowing the value of the dollar to be determined by market forces. As we discussed in the chapter "Financial Markets and International Capital Flows," the United States also runs a large trade deficit, with imports greatly exceeding exports. Since the supply of dollars by Americans who want to buy foreign goods and services is so much greater than the foreign demand for dollars to buy U.S. goods and services, why doesn't the market equilibrium value of the dollar fall until the trade deficit is eliminated?

---

[3]In this calculation, we use the yen per dollar exchange rate so that the dollars cancel when we perform the multiplication and we are left with the price in yen.

In Economic Naturalist 11.4, we showed how a country's trade deficit equals the excess of its domestic investment over its national saving. Here we have another way to make the same point. Recall that the supply of dollars depends on the U.S. demand for foreign assets as well as on Americans' desire to purchase foreign goods and services. Likewise, the demand for dollars depends on foreigners' desire to hold U.S. assets as well as on their demand for U.S. goods and services. In the markets for goods and services, the supply of dollars exceeds the demand for dollars, reflecting the fact that the U.S. imports more goods and services than it exports. Thus, if there were no trade in assets, the dollar's value would decline sufficiently to eliminate the imbalance of imports and exports. However, in fact, international trade in assets is quite active, and the quantity of U.S. assets purchased by foreigners exceeds the quantity of foreign assets purchased by U.S. residents. Foreign demand for U.S. assets reflects the expectation of foreign investors that investments in the United States will pay a healthy return. Foreign central banks also purchase U.S. assets (see Economic Naturalist 18.5 for a discussion of the case of China).

Because foreigners are net purchasers of U.S. assets, in asset markets the demand for dollars exceeds the supply of dollars, which makes up for the fact that, in the markets for goods and services, the demand for dollars is less than the supply. The existence of a trade deficit thus does not necessarily imply a decline in the value of the dollar, at least so long as foreigners have a strong demand for U.S. assets. Note that the net demand by foreigners for U.S. assets corresponds to the amount of foreign capital flowing into the United States. As we saw in the chapter "Financial Markets and International Capital Flows," the net capital inflow to the United States from abroad equals the excess of domestic investment over national saving, which in turn equals the U.S. trade deficit.

CHANGES IN THE SUPPLY OF DOLLARS

Recall that people supply dollars to the yen–dollar foreign exchange market in order to purchase Japanese goods, services, and assets. Factors that affect the desire of U.S. households and firms to acquire Japanese goods, services, and assets therefore will affect the supply of dollars to the foreign exchange market. Some factors that will *increase* the supply of dollars, shifting the supply curve for dollars to the right, include

- An increased preference for Japanese goods. For example, suppose that Japanese firms produce some popular new consumer electronics. To acquire the yen needed to buy these goods, American importers will increase their supply of dollars to the foreign exchange market.

- An increase in U.S. real GDP. An increase in U.S. real GDP will raise the incomes of Americans, allowing them to consume more goods and services (recall the consumption function, introduced in the chapter "Spending and Output in the Short Run"). Some part of this increase in consumption will take the form of goods imported from Japan. To buy more Japanese goods, Americans will supply more dollars to acquire the necessary yen.

- An increase in the real interest rate on Japanese assets or a decrease in the real interest rate on U.S. assets. Recall that U.S. households and firms acquire yen in order to purchase Japanese assets as well as goods and services. Other factors, such as risk, held constant, the higher the real interest rate paid on Japanese assets (or the lower the real interest rate paid on U.S. assets), the more Japanese assets Americans will choose to hold. To purchase additional Japanese assets, U.S. households and firms will supply more dollars to the foreign exchange market.

Supplying dollars, demanding yen.

Conversely, reduced demand for Japanese goods, a lower U.S. GDP, a lower real interest rate on Japanese assets, or a higher real interest rate on U.S. assets will *reduce* the number of yen Americans need, in turn reducing their supply of dollars to the foreign exchange market and shifting the supply curve for dollars to the left. Of course, any shift in the supply curve for dollars will affect the equilibrium exchange rate, as Example 18.2 shows.

EXAMPLE 18.2

Video games, the yen, and the dollar

Suppose Japanese firms come to dominate the video game market, with games that are more exciting and realistic than those produced in the United States. All else being equal, how will this change affect the relative value of the yen and the dollar?

The increased quality of Japanese video games will increase the demand for the games in the United States. To acquire the yen necessary to buy more Japanese video games, U.S. importers will supply more dollars to the foreign exchange market. As Figure 18.3 shows, the increased supply of dollars will reduce the value of the dollar. In other words, a dollar will buy fewer yen than it did before. At the same time, the yen will increase in value: A given number of yen will buy more dollars than it did before.

FIGURE 18.3

An Increase in the Supply of Dollars Lowers the Value of the Dollar.

Increased U.S. demand for Japanese video games forces Americans to supply more dollars to the foreign exchange market to acquire the yen they need to buy the games. The supply curve for dollars shifts from S to S′, lowering the value of the dollar in terms of yen. The market equilibrium value of the exchange rate falls from e* to e*′.

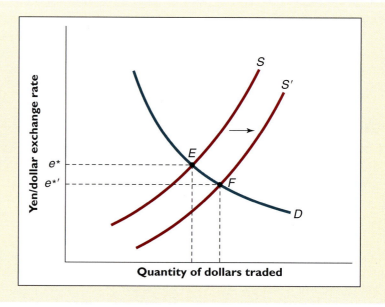

EXERCISE 18.2

The U.S. goes into a recession, and real GDP falls. All else equal, how is this economic weakness likely to affect the value of the dollar?

CHANGES IN THE DEMAND FOR DOLLARS

The factors that can cause a change in the demand for dollars in the foreign exchange market, and thus a shift of the dollar demand curve, are analogous to the factors that affect the supply of dollars. Factors that will *increase* the demand for dollars include

- An increased preference for U.S. goods. For example, Japanese airlines might find that U.S.-built aircraft are superior to others, and decide to expand the number of American-made planes in their fleets. To buy the American planes, Japanese airlines would demand more dollars on the foreign exchange market.

■ An increase in real GDP abroad, which implies higher incomes abroad, and thus more demand for imports from the United States.

■ An increase in the real interest rate on U.S. assets or a reduction in the real interest rate on Japanese assets would make U.S. assets more attractive to foreign savers. To acquire U.S. assets, Japanese savers would demand more dollars.

Does a strong currency imply a strong economy?

Politicians and the public sometimes take pride in the fact that their national currency is "strong," meaning that its value in terms of other currencies is high or rising. Likewise, policymakers sometimes view a depreciating ("weak") currency as a sign of economic failure. Does a strong currency necessarily imply a strong economy?

ECONOMIC NATURALIST 18.2

Contrary to popular impression, there is no simple connection between the strength of a country's currency and the strength of its economy. For example, Figure 18.1 shows that the value of the U.S. dollar relative to other major currencies was greater in the year 1973 than in the year 2004, though U.S. economic performance was considerably better in 2004 than in 1973, a period of deep recession and rising inflation. Indeed, the one period shown in Figure 18.1 during which the dollar rose markedly in value, 1980–1985, was a time of recession and high unemployment in the United States.

One reason a strong currency does not necessarily imply a strong economy is that an appreciating currency (an increase in e) tends to hurt a country's net exports. For example, if the dollar strengthens against the yen (that is, if a dollar buys more yen than before), Japanese goods will become cheaper in terms of dollars. The result may be that Americans prefer to buy Japanese goods rather than goods produced at home. Likewise, a stronger dollar implies that each yen buys fewer dollars, so exported U.S. goods become more expensive to Japanese consumers. As U.S. goods become more expensive in terms of yen, the willingness of Japanese consumers to buy U.S. exports declines. A strong dollar therefore may imply lower sales and profits for U.S. industries that export, as well as for U.S. industries (like automobile manufacturers) that compete with foreign firms for the domestic U.S. market.

MONETARY POLICY AND THE EXCHANGE RATE

Of the many factors that could influence a country's exchange rate, among the most important is the monetary policy of the country's central bank. Monetary policy affects the exchange rate primarily through its effect on the real interest rate.

Suppose the Fed is concerned about inflation and tightens U.S. monetary policy in response. The effects of this policy change on the value of the dollar are shown in Figure 18.4. Before the policy change, the equilibrium value of the exchange rate is e^*, at the intersection of supply curve S and the demand curve D (point E in the figure). The tightening of monetary policy raises the domestic U.S. real interest rate r, making U.S. assets, such as bonds, more attractive to both foreign and American financial investors. The increased willingness of foreign investors to buy U.S. assets increases the demand for dollars, shifting the demand curve rightward from D to D'. The willingness of American investors to buy more U.S. assets (and presumably fewer foreign assets) decreases the supply of dollars and shifts the supply curve leftward from S to S'. The equilibrium moves from point E to point F, and the market equilibrium value of the dollar rises from e^* to $e^{*'}$.

In short, a tightening of monetary policy by the Fed raises the demand for dollars and reduces the supply of dollars, causing the dollar to appreciate. By similar logic,

FIGURE 18.4
A Tightening of Monetary Policy Strengthens the Dollar.
Tighter monetary policy in the United States raises the domestic real interest rate, increasing the demand for U.S. assets by foreign and American savers. An increased demand for U.S. assets by foreigners increases the demand for dollars, shifting the demand curve rightward from D to D'. An increased demand for U.S. assets by American savers decreases the supply of dollars, shifting the supply curve to the left. The exchange rate appreciates from e^* to $e^{*'}$.

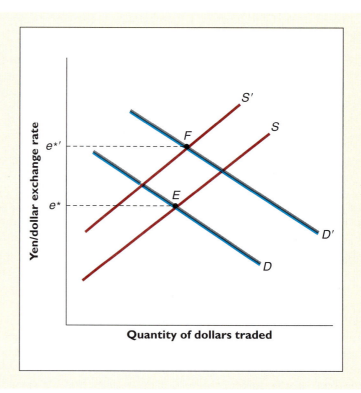

an easing of monetary policy, which reduces the real interest rate, would make U.S. assets, such as bonds, less attractive to both Americans and foreigners. This would weaken the demand for dollars but increase the supply of dollars (as Americans buy more foreign assets), causing the dollar to depreciate.

Why did the dollar appreciate nearly 50 percent in the first half of the 1980s?

Figure 18.1 showed the strong appreciation of the U.S. dollar in 1980–1985, followed by a sharp depreciation in 1986–1987. Why did this happen?

ECONOMIC NATURALIST 18.3

Tight monetary policy and the associated high real interest rate were important causes of the dollar's remarkable appreciation during 1980–1985. As we saw in Economic Naturalist 16.1, U.S. inflation peaked at 13.5 percent in 1980. Under the leadership of Chairman Paul Volcker, the Fed responded to the surge in inflation by raising the real interest rate sharply in hopes of reducing aggregate demand and inflationary pressures. As a result, the real interest rate in the United States rose from negative values in 1979 and 1980 to more than 7 percent in 1983 and 1984 (see Table 16.1). Attracted by these high real returns, U.S. and foreign savers rushed to buy U.S. assets, driving the value of the dollar up significantly.

The Fed's attempt to bring down inflation was successful. By the middle of the 1980s, the Fed was able to ease U.S. monetary policy. The resulting decline in the real interest rate reduced the demand for U.S. assets, and thus for dollars, at which point the dollar fell back almost to its 1980 level.

Why did the dollar depreciate more than 25 percent in 2002–2004?

Figure 18.1 also showed that the dollar depreciated substantially starting in early 2002. There are several reasons for this depreciation, but we will focus on two. First, the U.S. economy grew faster during this period than that of most of the countries to which we export (Canada, Mexico, and Japan). Consequently, the supply of dollars (to pay for imports) increased. Second, as we saw in Economic Naturalist 14.3, the Fed reduced the federal funds rate from 6 percent in early 2001 to

ECONOMIC NATURALIST 18.4

1 percent in June 2003 and kept it at 1 percent until June 2004. Although the steep decline in the federal funds rate was not accompanied by equal declines in long-term nominal and real interest rates, they, too, fell. The decline in U.S. real interest rates reduced the attractiveness of U.S. bonds to both Americans and foreigners. Consequently, the supply of dollars rose and the demand for dollars fell, contributing to the depreciation of the dollar.

THE EXCHANGE RATE AS A TOOL OF MONETARY POLICY

In a closed economy, monetary policy affects aggregate demand solely through the real interest rate. For example, by raising the real interest rate, a tight monetary policy reduces consumption and investment spending. We will see next that in an open economy with a flexible exchange rate, the exchange rate serves as another channel for monetary policy, one that reinforces the effects of the real interest rate.

To illustrate, suppose that policymakers are concerned about inflation and decide to restrain aggregate demand. To do so, they increase the real interest rate, reducing consumption and investment spending. But, as Figure 18.4 shows, the higher real interest rate also increases the demand for dollars and reduces the supply of dollars, causing the dollar to appreciate. The stronger dollar, in turn, further reduces aggregate demand. Why? As we saw in discussing the exchange rate, a stronger dollar reduces the cost of imported goods, thereby increasing imports. It also makes U.S. exports more costly to foreign buyers, which tends to reduce exports. Recall that net exports—or exports minus imports—is one of the four components of aggregate demand. Thus, by reducing exports and increasing imports, a stronger dollar (more precisely, a higher exchange rate) reduces aggregate demand.[4]

In sum, when the exchange rate is flexible, a tighter monetary policy reduces net exports (through a stronger dollar) as well as consumption and investment spending (through a higher real interest rate). Conversely, an easier monetary policy weakens the dollar and stimulates net exports, reinforcing the effect of the lower real interest rate on consumption and investment spending. Thus, relative to the case of a closed economy we studied earlier, *monetary policy is more effective in an open economy with a flexible exchange rate.*

The tightening of monetary policy under Fed Chairman Volcker in the early 1980s illustrates the effect of monetary policy on net exports (the trade balance). As we saw in Economic Naturalist 18.2, Volcker's tight-money policies were a major reason for the 50 percent appreciation of the dollar during 1980–1985. In 1980 and 1981, the United States enjoyed a trade surplus, with exports that modestly exceeded imports. Largely in response to a stronger dollar, the U.S. trade balance fell into deficit after 1981. By the end of 1985, the U.S. trade deficit was about 3 percent of GDP, a substantial shift in less than half a decade.

RECAP	DETERMINING THE EXCHANGE RATE IN THE SHORT RUN

- Supply and demand analysis is a useful tool for studying the short-run determination of the exchange rate. U.S. households and firms supply dollars to the foreign exchange market to acquire foreign currencies, which they need to purchase foreign goods, services, and assets. Foreigners demand dollars in the foreign exchange market to purchase U.S. goods, services, and assets. The market equilibrium exchange rate equates the quantities of dollars supplied and demanded in the foreign exchange market.

[4]We are temporarily assuming that the prices of U.S. goods in dollars and the prices of foreign goods in foreign currencies are not changing.

■ An increased preference for foreign goods, an increase in U.S. real GDP, an increase in the real interest rate on foreign assets, or a decrease in the real interest rate on U.S. assets will increase the supply of dollars on the foreign exchange market, lowering the value of the dollar. An increased preference for U.S. goods by foreigners, an increase in real GDP abroad, an increase in the real interest rate on U.S. assets, or a decrease in the real interest rate on foreign assets will increase the demand for dollars, raising the value of the dollar.

■ A tight monetary policy raises the real interest rate, increasing the demand for dollars, reducing the supply of dollars, and strengthening the dollar. A stronger dollar reinforces the effects of tight monetary policy on aggregate spending by reducing net exports, a component of aggregate demand. Conversely, an easy monetary policy lowers the real interest rate, weakening the dollar.

FIXED EXCHANGE RATES

So far we have focused on the case of flexible exchange rates, the relevant case for most large industrial countries like the United States. However, the alternative approach, fixing the exchange rate, has been quite important historically and is still used in many countries, especially small or developing nations. In this section, we will see how our conclusions change when the nominal exchange rate is fixed rather than flexible. One important difference is that when a country maintains a fixed exchange rate, its ability to use monetary policy as a stabilization tool is greatly reduced.

HOW TO FIX AN EXCHANGE RATE

In contrast to a flexible exchange rate, whose value is determined solely by supply and demand in the foreign exchange market, the value of a fixed exchange rate is determined by the government (in practice, usually the finance ministry or treasury department, with the cooperation of the central bank). Today, the value of a fixed exchange rate is usually set in terms of a major currency (for instance, at the time this book went to press, China pegged its currency at 8.11 yuan per U.S. dollar), or relative to a "basket" of currencies, typically those of the country's trading partners. Historically, currency values were often fixed in terms of gold or other precious metals, but in recent years precious metals have rarely if ever been used for that purpose.

Once an exchange rate has been fixed, the government usually attempts to keep it unchanged for some time.[5] However, sometimes economic circumstances force the government to change the value of the exchange rate. A reduction in the official value of a currency is called a **devaluation;** an increase in the official value is called a **revaluation.** The devaluation of a fixed exchange rate is analogous to the depreciation of a flexible exchange rate; both involve a reduction in the currency's value. Conversely, a revaluation is analogous to an appreciation.

The supply and demand diagram we used to study flexible exchange rates can be adapted to analyze fixed exchange rates. Let's consider the case of a country called Latinia, whose currency is called the peso. Figure 18.5 shows the supply and demand for the Latinian peso in the foreign exchange market. Pesos are *supplied* to

devaluation a reduction in the official value of a currency (in a fixed-exchange-rate system)

revaluation an increase in the official value of a currency (in a fixed-exchange-rate system)

---

[5]There are exceptions to this statement. Some countries employ a *crawling peg* system, under which the exchange rate is fixed at a value that changes in a preannounced way over time. For example, the government may announce that the value of the fixed exchange rate will fall 2 percent each year. Other countries use a *target zone* system, in which the exchange rate is allowed to deviate by a small amount from its fixed value. To focus on the key issues, we will assume that the exchange rate is fixed at a single value for a protracted period.

the foreign exchange market by Latinian households and firms who want to acquire foreign currencies to purchase foreign goods, services, and assets. Pesos are *demanded* by holders of foreign currencies who need pesos to purchase Latinian goods, services, and assets. The exchange rate on the vertical axis of Figure 18.5 will now be the number of dollars (foreign currency) per peso (domestic currency). Figure 18.5 shows that the quantities of pesos supplied and demanded in the foreign exchange market are equal when a peso equals 0.1 dollar (10 pesos to the dollar). Hence 0.1 dollars per peso is the *market equilibrium value* of the peso. If Latinia had a flexible-exchange-rate system, the market supply and demand for pesos would determine the exchange rate, and the peso would trade at 10 pesos to the dollar in the foreign exchange market.

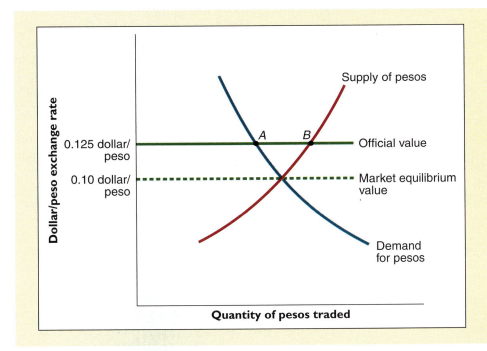

FIGURE 18.5

An Overvalued Exchange Rate.

The peso's official value (0.125 dollar) is shown as greater than its market equilibrium value (0.10 dollar), as determined by supply and demand in the foreign exchange market. Thus, the peso is overvalued. To maintain the fixed value, the government must purchase pesos in the quantity *AB* each period.

But let's suppose that Latinia has a fixed exchange rate and that the government has decreed the value of the Latinian peso to be 8 pesos to the dollar, or 0.125 dollars per peso. This official value of the peso, 0.125 dollars, is indicated by the solid horizontal line in Figure 18.5. Notice that it is greater than the market equilibrium value, corresponding to the intersection of the supply and demand curves. When the officially fixed value of an exchange rate is greater than its market equilibrium value, the exchange rate is **overvalued**. The official value of an exchange rate also can be lower than its market equilibrium value, in which case the exchange rate is **undervalued**.

In this example, Latinia's commitment to hold the peso at 8 to the dollar is inconsistent with the market equilibrium value of 10 to the dollar, as determined by supply and demand in the foreign exchange market (the Latinian peso is overvalued). How could the Latinian government deal with this inconsistency? There are several possibilities. First, Latinia could simply devalue its currency, from 0.125 dollars per peso to 0.10 dollars per peso, which would bring the peso's official value into line with its market equilibrium value. As we will see, devaluation is often the ultimate result of an overvaluation of a currency. However, a country with a fixed exchange rate will be reluctant to change the official value of its exchange rate every time the market equilibrium value changes. If a country must continuously adjust its exchange rate to market conditions, it might as well switch to a flexible exchange rate.

As a second alternative, Latinia could try to maintain its overvalued exchange rate by restricting international transactions. Imposing quotas on imports and prohibiting domestic households and firms from acquiring foreign assets would effectively reduce the supply of pesos to the foreign exchange market, raising the market

overvalued exchange rate an exchange rate that has an officially fixed value greater than its market equilibrium value

undervalued exchange rate an exchange rate that has an officially fixed value less than its market equilibrium value

equilibrium value of the currency. An even more extreme action would be to prohibit Latinians from exchanging the peso for other currencies without government approval, a policy that would effectively allow the government to determine directly the supply of pesos to the foreign exchange market. Such measures might help to maintain the official value of the peso. However, restrictions on trade and capital flows are extremely costly to the economy, because they reduce the gains from specialization and trade and deny domestic households and firms access to foreign capital markets. Thus, a policy of restricting international transactions to maintain a fixed exchange rate is likely to do more harm than good.

The third and most widely used approach to maintaining an overvalued exchange rate is for the government to become a demander of its own currency in the foreign exchange market. Figure 18.5 shows that at the official exchange rate of 0.125 dollars per peso, the private sector supply of pesos (point *B*) exceeds the private sector demand for pesos (point *A*). To keep the peso from falling below its official value, in each period the Latinian government could purchase a quantity of pesos in the foreign exchange market equal to the length of the line segment *AB* in Figure 18.5. If the government followed this strategy, then at the official exchange rate of 0.125 dollars per peso, the total demand for pesos (private demand at point *A* plus government demand *AB*) would equal the private supply of pesos (point *B*). This situation is analogous to government attempts to keep the price of a commodity, like grain or milk, above its market level. To maintain an official price of grain that is above the market-clearing price, the government must stand ready to purchase the excess supply of grain forthcoming at the official price. In the same way, to keep the "price" of its currency above the market-clearing level, the government must buy the excess pesos supplied at the official price.

To be able to purchase its own currency and maintain an overvalued exchange rate, the government (usually the central bank) must hold foreign currency assets, called **international reserves,** or simply *reserves.* For example, the Latinian central bank may hold dollar deposits in U.S. banks or U.S. government debt, which it can trade for pesos in the foreign exchange market as needed. In the situation shown in Figure 18.5, to keep the peso at its official value, in each period the Latinian central bank will have to spend an amount of international reserves equal to the length of the line segment *AB.*

Because a country with an overvalued exchange rate must use part of its reserves to support the value of its currency in each period, over time its available reserves will decline. The net decline in a country's stock of international reserves over a year is called its **balance-of-payments deficit.** Conversely, if a country experiences a net increase in its international reserves over the year, the increase is called its **balance-of-payments surplus.**

international reserves foreign currency assets held by a government for the purpose of purchasing the domestic currency in the foreign exchange market

balance-of-payments deficit the net decline in a country's stock of international reserves over a year

balance-of-payments surplus the net increase in a country's stock of international reserves over a year

EXAMPLE 18.3

Latinia's balance-of-payments deficit

The demand for and supply of Latinian pesos in the foreign exchange market are

$$\text{Demand} = 25{,}000 - 50{,}000e,$$

$$\text{Supply} = 17{,}600 + 24{,}000e,$$

where the Latinian exchange rate e is measured in dollars per peso. Officially, the value of the peso is 0.125 dollars. Find the market equilibrium value of the peso and the Latinian balance-of-payments deficit, measured in both pesos and dollars.

To find the market equilibrium value of the peso, equate the demand and supply of pesos:

$$25{,}000 - 50{,}000e = 17{,}600 + 24{,}000e.$$

Solving for *e*, we get

$$7,400 = 74,000e$$

$$e = 0.10.$$

So the market equilibrium value of the exchange rate is 0.10 dollars per peso, as in Figure 18.5.

At the official exchange rate, 0.125 dollars per peso, the demand for pesos is $25,000 - 50,000(0.125) = 18,750$, and the supply of pesos is $17,600 + 24,000(0.125) = 20,600$. Thus, the quantity of pesos supplied to the foreign exchange market exceeds the quantity of pesos demanded by $20,600 - 18,750 = 1,850$ pesos. To maintain the fixed rate, the Latinian government must purchase 1,850 pesos per period, which is the Latinian balance-of-payments deficit. Since pesos are purchased at the official rate of 8 pesos to the dollar, the balance-of-payments deficit in dollars is $(1,850 \text{ pesos}) \times (0.125 \text{ dollars/peso}) = \$(1,850/8) = \$231.25$.

EXERCISE 18.3

Repeat Example 18.3 under the assumption that the fixed value of the peso is 0.15 dollars per peso. What do you conclude about the relationship between the degree of currency overvaluation and the resulting balance-of-payments deficit?

Although a government can maintain an overvalued exchange rate for a time by offering to buy back its own currency at the official price, there is a limit to this strategy, since no government's stock of international reserves is infinite. Eventually the government will run out of reserves, and the fixed exchange rate will collapse. As we will see next, the collapse of a fixed exchange rate can be quite sudden and dramatic.

EXERCISE 18.4

Diagram a case in which a fixed exchange rate is *undervalued* rather than overvalued. Show that, to maintain the fixed exchange rate, the central bank must use domestic currency to purchase foreign currency in the foreign exchange market. With an undervalued exchange rate, is the country's central bank in danger of running out of international reserves? (*Hint:* Keep in mind that a central bank is always free to print more of its own currency.)

Should China change the way it manages its exchange rate?

ECONOMIC NATURALIST 18.5

At the time this book was going to press, the United States and other industrialized countries were putting pressure on China to change the way it manages its currency, the yuan.[6] Between 1995 and July 2005, the Chinese fixed the value of the yuan at 8.28 yuan per dollar. During this same period, U.S. imports from China soared, while U.S. exports to China rose much more slowly. In 2004, U.S. imports from China exceeded U.S. exports to China by more than $150 billion, representing almost one-quarter of the entire U.S. trade deficit. Moreover, with the elimination of tariffs on Chinese textiles in early 2005, a further increase in Chinese exports to the United States seemed likely. Critics argued that, at 8.28 yuan per dollar, the value of

---

[6]See, for example, U.S. Treasury, *Report to Congress on International Economic and Exchange Rate Policies*, May 2005, (http://www.treas.gov/press/releases/reports/js2448_report.pdf).

the yuan was set below its market equilibrium value, making Chinese exports artificially cheap (in dollar terms) and giving Chinese goods an unfair advantage in the international marketplace.

Under pressure from the United States and other nations, China revalued the yuan in July 2005 to 8.11 yuan per dollar. They also took some steps that raised the possibility that the yuan might be more flexible in the future. Many economists, however, believe that a larger revaluation is necessary.

Is the yuan still undervalued? Most experts say that it is, with many estimating that, at 8.11 yuan per dollar, the Chinese currency is still about 15–30 percent below its market equilibrium value. The claim that the yuan is undervalued is supported by the fact that the Chinese central bank has had to buy hundreds of billions of dollars of U.S. assets (mostly Treasury bonds) in order to keep the yuan at its current value. Although the yuan appears to be undervalued, estimating the precise extent of undervaluation is not easy. One reason that the market equilibrium value for the yuan is hard to determine is that China has severely restricted the ability of its citizens to buy foreign assets, and it also closely regulates foreign investment in China. If these restrictions were lifted, both the Chinese demand for foreign assets and the foreign demand for Chinese assets might change significantly. Changes in the demands for assets would affect the supply of and demand for yuan, with effects on its market equilibrium value that are difficult to predict.

Should China change the way it manages its exchange rate? As a developing country, China may have benefited from having a fixed exchange rate in the past. However, as the Chinese economy grows and becomes more sophisticated, this system may begin to create some problems for the country. One concern is that, in order to keep the value of the yuan fixed, China must purchase large quantities of U.S. assets, as mentioned above. However, the Chinese savings used to buy these U.S. assets might be put to better use financing domestic investment in China. An undervalued exchange rate also has the effect of making imports from other countries to China expensive, which makes Chinese households and firms worse off and may contribute to inflation.

If China decided to change its current system, it would have several options. For example, it could simply revalue the yuan again, to a level closer to its market equilibrium value, and then keep the currency fixed at that level. Or it could allow the yuan's value to be determined by the market, perhaps within some limits. An advantage of adopting a more market-oriented system is that the value of the yuan would automatically adjust to its market equilibrium value, making the purchases of U.S. assets by the Chinese central bank unnecessary.

A higher value for the yuan, by making Chinese goods more expensive in dollar terms, would probably reduce U.S. imports from China. By itself, however, this change would probably not reduce the overall U.S. trade deficit dramatically, in part because U.S. consumers might react to increased dollar prices for Chinese goods by shifting their demand to other foreign producers. Greater improvement in the U.S. trade deficit might occur if the Chinese leadership allowed (or even encouraged) Chinese households and firms to import more from abroad.

SPECULATIVE ATTACKS

speculative attack a massive selling of domestic currency assets by financial investors

A government's attempt to maintain an overvalued exchange rate can be ended quickly and unexpectedly by the onset of a *speculative attack*. A **speculative attack** involves massive selling of domestic currency assets by both domestic and foreign financial investors. For example, in a speculative attack on the Latinian peso, financial investors would attempt to get rid of any financial assets—stocks, bonds, deposits in banks—denominated in pesos. A speculative attack is most likely to occur when financial investors fear that an overvalued currency will soon be devalued, since in a devaluation, financial assets denominated in the domestic currency suddenly become worth much less in terms of other currencies. Ironically, speculative attacks, which are usually prompted by *fear* of devaluation, may turn out to be the *cause* of devaluation. Thus, a speculative attack actually may be a self-fulfilling prophecy.

The effects of a speculative attack on the market for pesos are shown in Figure 18.6. At first, the situation is the same as in Figure 18.5: The supply and demand for Latinian pesos are indicated by the curves marked *S* and *D,* implying a market equilibrium value of the peso of 0.10 dollars per peso. As before, the official value of the peso is 0.125 dollars per peso—greater than the market equilibrium value—so the peso is overvalued. To maintain the fixed value of the peso, each period the Latinian central bank must use its international reserves to buy back pesos, in the amount corresponding to the line segment *AB* in the figure.

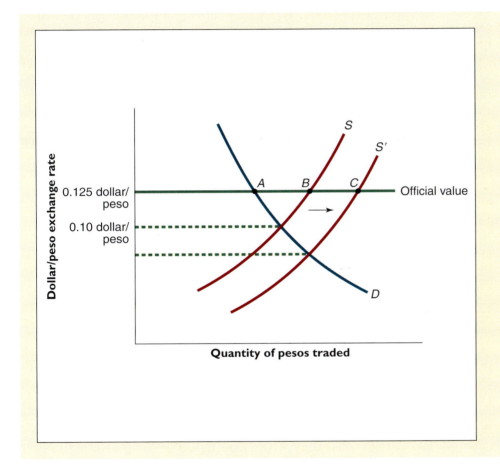

FIGURE 18.6

A Speculative Attack on the Peso.

Initially, the peso is overvalued at 0.125 dollars per peso. To maintain the official rate, the central bank must buy pesos in the amount *AB* each period. Fearful of possible devaluation, financial investors launch a speculative attack, selling peso-denominated assets and supplying pesos to the foreign exchange market. As a result, the supply of pesos shifts from *S* to *S'*, lowering the market equilibrium value of the currency still further and forcing the central bank to buy pesos in the amount *AC* to maintain the official exchange rate. This more rapid loss of reserves may lead the central bank to devalue the peso, confirming financial investors' fears.

Suppose, though, that financial investors fear that Latinia may soon devalue its currency, perhaps because the central bank's reserves are getting low. If the peso were to be devalued from its official value of 0.125 dollars per peso to its market equilibrium value of 0.10 dollars per peso, then a 1 million peso investment, worth $125,000 at the fixed exchange rate, would suddenly be worth only $100,000. To try to avoid these losses, financial investors will sell their peso-denominated assets and offer pesos on the foreign exchange market. The resulting flood of pesos onto the market will shift the supply curve of pesos to the right, from *S* to *S'* in Figure 18.6.

This speculative attack creates a serious problem for the Latinian central bank. Prior to the attack, maintaining the value of the peso required the central bank to spend each period an amount of international reserves corresponding to the line segment *AB*. Now, suddenly, the central bank must spend a larger quantity of reserves, equal to the distance *AC* in Figure 18.6, to maintain the fixed exchange rate. These extra reserves are needed to purchase the pesos being sold by panicky financial investors. In practice, such speculative attacks often force a devaluation by reducing the central bank's reserves to the point where further defense of the fixed exchange rate is considered hopeless. Thus, a speculative attack ignited by fears of devaluation may actually end up producing the very devaluation that was feared.

ECONOMIC NATURALIST 18.6

Can a speculative attack occur under flexible exchange rates?

The last section described the self-fulfilling nature of speculative attacks in a fixed-exchange rate system: fears of a currency devaluation often lead to actual currency devaluation. Can a speculative attack occur in a flexible-exchange-rate system?

As noted earlier, a speculative attack on a currency involves large-scale selling of a country's domestic currency assets by both domestic and foreign financial investors based on fears of a future decline in the value of the country's currency. The economic effects of a speculative attack are illustrated in Figure 18.6. The resulting increase in the supply of the domestic currency lowers the market equilibrium value of the currency, often dramatically. Brazil experienced this sort of deterioration in the value of its currency, the real (pronounced *ray-al*), during 2002, in anticipation of a presidential victory by Brazilian Worker's Party candidate, Luis Inacio da Silva, who goes by the nickname "Lula." Investors were concerned that da Silva would break from the economic policies of outgoing president Fernando Henrique Cardoso, who helped to stabilize Brazil's economy, South America's largest, since his first presidential election in 1994.

In the early 1990s, just prior to Mr. Cardoso's election, high inflation stunted Brazil's economic performance and reduced foreign investment, weakening future economic growth prospects. Inflation averaged over 20 percent per month since the late 1980s and reached a monthly rate of nearly 50 percent (over 10,000 percent per year!) by June 1994, when newly elected president Cardoso instituted a bold economic plan that included the creation of a new currency—the real—that was directly linked to the value of the U.S. dollar. Immediately the inflation rate dropped to less than 10 percent per month, and by 1997 the *annual* inflation rate was in the single digits. However, by 1998, increasing Brazilian budget and current-account deficits led to a speculative attack that led to a dramatic devaluation of the real in January 1999 and an uncoupling of the real from the U.S. dollar. Since 1999, the Brazilian currency has been allowed to fluctuate freely but has remained relatively stable, along with the Brazilian economy: Except for a period in 2002–2003, inflation has remained in the single digits, poverty has been reduced, and a variety of social indicators have improved. Progress has come with a cost, however: rising government debt to pay for Cardoso's social programs.

Concerns about the growing government debt and the increasing popularity of opposition party candidate da Silva led to another round of downward pressure on the real during 2002 as investors began to sell off financial assets denominated in reals. Investors were concerned that da Silva, if elected president, would be unwilling to make the tough government spending and taxing decisions that would be necessary to stabilize the government's debt, raising concerns of a government default, higher inflation, and even further downward pressure on the real. As a result, by the end of September, the real had reached record lows and inflation was on the rise.

However, following da Silva's landslide election victory in early October, pledges that he would continue Cardoso's fight against inflation and promote fiscal policy discipline, along with a new international loan package from the International Monetary Fund, helped to calm currency and financial markets, sparking hopes for continued economic growth with low inflation, rising currency values, and falling interest rates. Since da Silva's election, both the exchange rate and inflation have remained relatively steady.

MONETARY POLICY AND THE FIXED EXCHANGE RATE

We have seen that there is no really satisfactory way of maintaining a fixed exchange rate above its market equilibrium value for an extended period. A central bank can maintain an overvalued exchange rate for a time by using international reserves to buy up the excess supply of its currency in the foreign exchange market. But a country's international reserves are limited and may eventually be exhausted by the attempt to keep the exchange rate artificially high. Moreover, speculative attacks often hasten the collapse of an overvalued exchange rate.

An alternative to trying to maintain an overvalued exchange rate is to take actions that increase the market equilibrium value of the exchange rate. If the exchange rate's market equilibrium value can be raised enough to equal its official value, then the overvaluation problem will be eliminated. The most effective way to change the exchange rate's market equilibrium value is through monetary policy. As we saw earlier in the chapter, a tight monetary policy that raises the real interest rate will increase the demand for the domestic currency, as domestic assets become more attractive to foreign financial investors. Higher real interest rates also will decrease the supply of domestic currency as domestic assets become more attractive to domestic citizens, too. Increased demand and decreased supply of the currency will, in turn, raise its market equilibrium value.

The use of monetary policy to support a fixed exchange rate is shown in Figure 18.7. At first, the demand and supply of the Latinian peso in the foreign

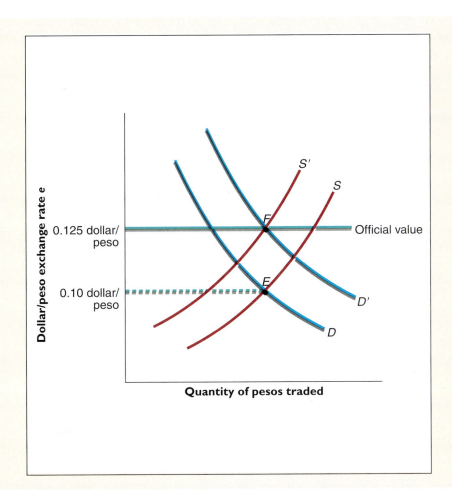

FIGURE 18.7

A Tightening of Monetary Policy Eliminates an Overvaluation.

With the demand for the peso given by D and the supply given by S, equilibrium occurs at point E and the market equilibrium value of the peso equals 0.10 dollars per peso—below the official value of 0.125 dollars per peso. The overvaluation of the peso can be eliminated by tighter monetary policy, which raises the domestic real interest rate, making domestic assets more attractive to both foreign and domestic financial investors. The demand for pesos will increase from D to D′, and the supply of pesos will fall from S to S′. These changes in supply and demand raise the peso's market equilibrium value to 0.125 dollars per peso, the official value. The peso is no longer overvalued.

exchange market are given by the curves D and S, so the market equilibrium value of the peso equals 0.10 dollars per peso—less than the official value of 0.125 dollars per peso. Just as before, the peso is overvalued. This time, however, the Latinian central bank uses monetary policy to eliminate the overvaluation problem. To do so, the central bank increases the domestic real interest rate, making Latinian assets more attractive to both foreign and domestic financial investors. This increase in the real interest rate thus will raise the demand for pesos from D to D' and reduce the supply of pesos from S to S'. After the changes in supply and demand, the market equilibrium value of the peso equals the officially fixed value, as can be seen in Figure 18.7. Because the peso is no longer overvalued, it can be maintained at its fixed value without loss of international reserves or fear of speculative attack. Conversely, an easing of monetary policy (a lower real interest rate) could be used to remedy an undervaluation, in which the official exchange rate is below the market equilibrium value.

Although monetary policy can be used to keep the market equilibrium value of the exchange rate equal to the official value, using monetary policy in this way has some drawbacks. In particular, *if monetary policy is used to set the market equilibrium value of the exchange rate equal to the official value, it is no longer available for stabilizing the domestic economy.* Suppose, for example, that the Latinian economy were suffering a recession due to insufficient aggregate demand at the same time that its exchange rate is overvalued. The Latinian central bank could lower the real interest rate to increase spending and output, or it could raise the real interest rate to eliminate overvaluation of the exchange rate, *but it cannot do both.* Hence, if Latinian officials decide to maintain the fixed exchange rate, they must give up any hope of fighting the recession using monetary policy. The fact that a fixed exchange rate limits or eliminates the use of monetary policy for the purpose of stabilizing aggregate demand is one of the most important features of a fixed-exchange-rate system.

"It's just a flesh wound. I got it defending the dollar."

The conflict monetary policymakers face, between stabilizing the exchange rate and stabilizing the domestic economy, is most severe when the exchange rate is under a speculative attack. A speculative attack lowers the market equilibrium value of the exchange rate still further, by increasing the supply of the currency in the foreign exchange market (see Figure 18.6). To stop a speculative attack, the central bank must raise the market equilibrium value of the currency a great deal, which requires a large increase in the real interest rate. (In a famous episode in 1992, the Swedish central bank responded to an attack on its currency by raising the short-term interest rate to 500 percent!) However, because the increase in the real interest rate that is necessary to stop a speculative attack reduces aggregate demand, it can cause a severe economic slowdown. Economic Naturalist 18.7 describes a real-world example of this phenomenon.

What were the causes and consequences of the East Asian crisis of 1997–1998?

During the past three decades, the countries of East Asia have enjoyed impressive economic growth and stability. But the "East Asian miracle" seemed to end in 1997, when a wave of speculative attacks hit the region's currencies. Thailand, which had kept a constant value for its currency in terms of the U.S. dollar for more than a decade, was the first to come under attack, but the crisis spread to other countries, including South Korea, Indonesia, and Malaysia. Each of these countries was ultimately forced to devalue its currency. What caused this crisis, and what were its consequences?

ECONOMIC NATURALIST 18.7

Because of the impressive economic record of the East Asian countries, the speculative attacks on their currencies were unexpected by most policymakers, economists, and financial investors. With the benefit of hindsight, however, we can identify some problems in the East Asian economies that contributed to the crisis. Perhaps the most serious problems concerned their banking systems. In the decade prior to the crisis, East Asian banks received large inflows of capital from foreign financial investors hoping to profit from the East Asian miracle. Those inflows would have been a boon if they had been well invested, but unfortunately, many bankers used the funds to make loans to family members, friends, or the politically well-connected—a phenomenon that became known as *crony capitalism*. The results were poor returns on investment and defaults by many borrowers. Ultimately, foreign investors realized that the returns to investing in East Asia would be much lower than expected. When they began to sell off their assets, the process snowballed into a full-fledged speculative attack on the East Asian currencies.

Despite assistance by international lenders such as the International Monetary Fund (see Box 18.1), the effects of the speculative attacks on the East Asian economies were severe. The prices of assets such as stocks and land plummeted, and there were banking panics in several nations. (See the chapter "Money, Prices, and the Federal Reserve" for a discussion of banking panics.) In an attempt to raise the market equilibrium values of their exchange rates and stave off additional devaluation, several of the countries increased their real interest rates sharply. However, the rise in real interest rates depressed aggregate demand, contributing to sharp declines in output and rising unemployment.

Fortunately, by 1999 most East Asian economies had begun to recover. Still, the crisis impressed the potential dangers of fixed exchange rates quite sharply in the minds of policymakers in developing countries. Another lesson from the crisis is that banking regulations need to be structured so as to promote economically sound lending rather than crony capitalism.

> ## BOX 18.1: THE INTERNATIONAL MONETARY FUND
>
> The International Monetary Fund (IMF) was established after World War II. An international agency, the IMF is controlled by a 24-member executive board. Eight executive board members represent individual countries (China, France, Germany, Japan, Russia, Saudi Arabia, the United Kingdom, and the United States); the other 16 members each represents a group of countries. A managing director oversees the IMF's operations and its approximately 2,700 employees.
>
> The original purpose of the IMF was to help manage the system of fixed exchange rates, called the *Bretton Woods system,* put in place after World War II. Under Bretton Woods, the IMF's principal role was to lend international reserves to member countries who needed them so that those countries could maintain their exchange rates at the official values. However, by 1973 the United States, the United Kingdom, Germany, and most other industrial nations had abandoned fixed exchange rates for flexible rates, leaving the IMF to find a new mission. Since 1973 the IMF has been involved primarily in lending to developing countries. It lent heavily to Mexico when that country experienced speculative attacks in 1994, and it made loans to East Asian countries during the 1997–1998 crisis. Other countries that received large IMF loans in recent years include Russia, Turkey, and Brazil.
>
> The IMF's performance in recent crises has been controversial. Many observers credit the IMF with helping Mexico, the East Asian nations, and others to recover quickly from the effects of speculative attacks and contend that the IMF plays a vital role in maintaining international economic stability. However, some critics have charged that the IMF has required recipients of its loans to follow economic policies—such as tight monetary policies and fiscal cutbacks—that have turned out to be ill-advised. Others have claimed that the IMF's loans help foreign financial investors and the richest people in the countries receiving loans, rather than the average person. (The IMF has been severely embarrassed by reports that much of the nearly $5 billion it lent to Russia in 1998 has disappeared into the bank accounts of unscrupulous citizens, including gangsters.)
>
> The IMF also has come into conflict with the World Bank, a separate international institution that was set up at about the same time as the IMF. The World Bank, whose mission is to provide long-term loans to help poor nations develop their economies, has complained that IMF interventions in poor countries interfered with World Bank programs and objectives. In 2000, a report commissioned by the U.S. Congress recommended reducing the IMF's powers (as well as, incidentally, those of the World Bank). The debate over the IMF's proper role will no doubt continue.

ECONOMIC NATURALIST 18.8

How did policy mistakes contribute to the Great Depression?

The chapter "Macroeconomics" introduced the study of macroeconomics with the claim that policy mistakes played a major role in causing the Great Depression. Now that we are close to completing our study of macroeconomics, we can be more specific about that claim. How did policy mistakes contribute to the Great Depression?

Many policy mistakes (as well as a great deal of bad luck) contributed to the severity of the Depression. For example, U.S. policymakers, in an attempt to protect domestic industries, imposed the infamous Hawley-Smoot tariff in 1930. Other countries quickly retaliated with their own tariffs, leading to the virtual collapse of international trade.

However, the most serious mistakes by far were made in the realm of monetary policy.[7] As we saw in the chapter "Money, Prices, and the Federal Reserve," the U.S. money supply contracted by one-third between 1929 and 1933 (Table 10.7). Associated with this unprecedented decline in the money supply were sharply falling output and prices and surging unemployment.

At least three separate policy errors were responsible for the collapse of the U.S. money supply between 1929 and 1933. First, the Federal Reserve tightened monetary policy significantly in 1928 and 1929, despite the absence of inflation. Fed officials took this action primarily in an attempt to "rein in" the booming stock market, which they feared was rising too quickly. Their "success" in dampening stock market speculation was more than they bargained for, however, as rising interest rates and a slowing economy contributed to a crash in stock prices that began in October 1929.

The second critical policy error was allowing thousands of U.S. banks to fail during the banking panics of 1930 to 1933. Apparently, officials believed that the failures would eliminate only the weakest banks, strengthening the banking system overall. However, the banking panics sharply reduced bank deposits and the overall money supply, for reasons discussed in Economic Naturalist 10.2.

The third policy error, related to the subject of this chapter, arose from the U.S. government's exchange rate policies. When the Depression began, the United States, like most other major countries, was on the gold standard, with the value of the dollar officially set in terms of gold.[8] By establishing a fixed value for the dollar, the United States effectively created a fixed exchange rate between the dollar and other currencies whose values were set in terms of gold. As the Depression worsened, Fed officials were urged by Congress to ease monetary policy to stop the fall in output and prices. However, as we saw earlier, under a fixed exchange rate, monetary policy cannot be used to stabilize the domestic economy. Specifically, policymakers of the early 1930s feared that if they eased monetary policy, foreign financial investors might perceive the dollar to be overvalued and launch a speculative attack, forcing a devaluation of the dollar or even the abandonment of the gold standard altogether. The Fed therefore made no serious attempt to arrest the collapse of the money supply.

In hindsight, we can see that the Fed's decision to place a higher priority on remaining on the gold standard than on stimulating the economy was a major error. Indeed, countries that abandoned the gold standard in favor of a floating exchange rate, such as Great Britain and Sweden, or those that had never been on the gold standard (Spain and China) were able to increase their money supplies and to recover much more quickly from the Depression than the United States. The Fed evidently believed, erroneously as it turned out, that stability of the exchange rate would somehow translate into overall economic stability.

Upon taking office in March 1933, Franklin D. Roosevelt reversed several of these policy errors. He took active measures to restore the health of the banking system, and he suspended the gold standard. The money supply stopped falling and began to grow rapidly. Output, prices, and stock prices recovered rapidly from 1933 to 1937, although unemployment remained high. Ultimate recovery from the Depression was interrupted by another recession in 1937–1938.

RECAP	**FIXED EXCHANGE RATES**

- The value of a fixed exchange rate is set by the government. The official value of a fixed exchange rate may differ from its market equilibrium value, as determined by supply and demand in the foreign exchange market.

[7]A classic 1963 book by Milton Friedman and Anna Schwartz, *A Monetary History of the United States: 1867–1960* (Princeton University Press), was the first to provide detailed support for the view that poor monetary policy helped to cause the Depression.
[8]The value of the dollar in 1929 was such that the price of one ounce of gold was fixed at $20.67.

An exchange rate whose officially fixed value exceeds its market equilibrium value is overvalued; an exchange rate whose officially fixed value is below its market equilibrium value is undervalued.

■ For an overvalued exchange rate, the quantity of the currency supplied to the foreign exchange market at the official exchange rate exceeds the quantity demanded. The government can maintain an overvalued exchange rate for a time by using its international reserves (foreign currency assets) to purchase the excess supply of its currency. The net decline in a country's stock of international reserves during the year is its balance-of-payments deficit.

■ Because a country's international reserves are limited, it cannot maintain an overvalued exchange rate indefinitely. Moreover, if financial investors fear an impending devaluation of the exchange rate, they may launch a speculative attack, selling domestic currency assets and supplying large amounts of the country's currency to the foreign exchange market—an action that exhausts the country's reserves even more quickly. Because rapid loss of reserves may force a devaluation, financial investors' fear of devaluation may prove a self-fulfilling prophecy.

■ A tight monetary policy, which increases the real interest rate, raises the demand for the currency and hence its market equilibrium value. By raising a currency's market equilibrium value to its official value, tight monetary policies can eliminate the problem of overvaluation and stabilize the exchange rate. However, if monetary policy is used to set the market equilibrium value of the exchange rate, it is no longer available for stabilizing the domestic economy.

SHOULD EXCHANGE RATES BE FIXED OR FLEXIBLE?

Should countries adopt fixed or flexible exchange rates? In briefly comparing the two systems, we will focus on two major issues: (1) the effects of the exchange rate system on monetary policy and (2) the effects of the exchange rate system on trade and economic integration.

On the issue of monetary policy, we have seen that the type of exchange rate a country has strongly affects the central bank's ability to use monetary policy to stabilize the economy. A flexible exchange rate actually strengthens the impact of monetary policy on aggregate demand. However, a fixed exchange rate prevents policymakers from using monetary policy to stabilize the economy because they must instead use it to keep the exchange rate's market equilibrium value at its official value (or else risk speculative attacks).

In large economies like that of the United States, giving up the power to stabilize the domestic economy via monetary policy makes little sense. Thus large economies should nearly always employ a flexible exchange rate. However, in small economies, giving up this power may have some benefits. An interesting case is that of Argentina, which for the period 1991–2001 maintained a one-to-one exchange rate between its peso and the U.S. dollar. Although prior to 1991 Argentina had suffered periods of hyperinflation, while the peso was pegged to the dollar, Argentina's inflation rate essentially equaled that of the United States (as we will see in Figure 18.8). By tying its currency to the dollar and giving up the freedom to set its monetary policy, Argentina attempted to commit itself to avoiding the inflationary policies of the past, and instead placed itself under the "umbrella" of the Federal Reserve. Unfortunately, early in 2002, investors' fears that Argentina would not be able to repay its international debts led to a speculative attack on the Argentine peso. The fixed exchange rate collapsed, the peso depreciated, and Argentina experienced an economic crisis from which it has not yet fully recovered. The lesson is that a fixed exchange rate alone cannot stop inflation in a small economy if other policies are not sound as well. Large fiscal deficits, which were financed by foreign borrowing, ultimately pushed Argentina into crisis.

The second important issue is the effect of the exchange rate on trade and economic integration. Proponents of fixed exchange rates argue that fixed rates promote international trade and cross-border economic cooperation by reducing uncertainty about future exchange rates. For example, a firm that is considering building up its export business knows that its potential profits will depend on the future value of its own country's currency relative to the currencies of the countries to which it exports. Under a flexible-exchange-rate regime, the value of the home currency fluctuates with changes in supply and demand and is therefore difficult to predict far in advance. Such uncertainty may make the firm reluctant to expand its export business. Supporters of fixed exchange rates argue that if the exchange rate is officially fixed, uncertainty about the future exchange rate is reduced or eliminated.

One problem with this argument, which has been underscored by episodes like the East Asian crisis and the Argentine crisis, is that fixed exchange rates are not guaranteed to remain fixed forever. Although they do not fluctuate from day to day as flexible rates do, a speculative attack on a fixed exchange rate may lead suddenly and unpredictably to a large devaluation. Thus, a firm that is trying to forecast the exchange rate 10 years into the future may face as much uncertainty if the exchange rate is fixed as if it is flexible.

The potential instability of fixed exchange rates caused by speculative attacks has led some countries to try a more radical solution to the problem of uncertainty about exchange rates: the adoption of a common currency. Economic Naturalist 18.9 describes an important instance of this strategy.

Why have 11 European countries adopted a common currency?

ECONOMIC NATURALIST 18.9

Effective January 1, 1999, 11 western European nations, including France, Germany, and Italy, adopted a common currency, called the *euro*. In several stages, the euro replaced the French franc, the German mark, the Italian lira, and other national currencies. The process was completed in early 2002, when the old currencies were completely eliminated and replaced by euros. Why have these nations adopted a common currency?

For some decades the nations of western Europe have worked to increase economic cooperation and trade among themselves. European leaders recognized that a unified and integrated European economy would be more productive and perhaps more competitive with the U.S. economy than a fragmented one. As part of this effort, these countries established fixed exchange rates under the auspices of a system called the European Monetary System (EMS). Unfortunately, the EMS did not prove stable. Numerous devaluations of the various currencies occurred, and in 1992 severe speculative attacks forced several nations, including Great Britain, to abandon the fixed-exchange-rate system.

In December 1991, in Maastricht in the Netherlands, the member countries of the European Community (EC) adopted a treaty popularly known as the Maastricht Treaty. One of the major provisions of the treaty, which took effect in November 1993, was that member countries would strive to adopt a common currency. This common currency, known as the euro, was formally adopted on January 1, 1999. The advent of the euro means that Europeans will no longer have to change currencies when trading with other European countries, much as Americans from different states can trade with each other without worrying that a "New York dollar" will change in value relative to a "California dollar." The euro should help to promote European trade and cooperation while eliminating the problem of speculative attacks on the currencies of individual countries.

Because western Europe now has a single currency, it also must have a common monetary policy. The EC members agreed that European monetary policy would be put under the control of a new European Central Bank (ECB), a multinational institution located in Frankfurt, Germany. The ECB, in effect, has become "Europe's Fed." One potential problem with having a single monetary policy for 11 different countries is that different countries may face different economic conditions, so a single monetary policy cannot respond to all of them. For example, in recent years, some countries in Europe (such as Germany) have grown slowly, suggesting the need for an easier monetary policy, while other countries (such as Ireland) have seen increases in inflation, which implies a need for adopting a tighter monetary policy. Because the ECB can choose only a single monetary policy for all the countries using the euro, conflicts of interest may arise among the member nations of the European Community.

DETERMINATION OF THE EXCHANGE RATE IN THE LONG RUN

In this section, we discuss how exchange rates are determined in the long run. In our short-run analysis, we assumed that both the dollar price of U.S. goods and the foreign currency price of foreign goods (for example, the price of Sony Playstations in yen) did not change. In discussing the long run, we must relax this assumption. The theory we shall use to discuss the long-run determination of the exchange rate is called the theory of *purchasing power parity*. In order to explain this theory, we must first introduce the *real exchange rate*.

THE REAL EXCHANGE RATE

The nominal exchange rate tells us the price of the domestic currency in terms of a foreign currency. As we will see in this section, the *real exchange rate* is the price of the average domestic *good or service* in terms of the average foreign *good or service*.

To provide background for discussing the real exchange rate, imagine you are in charge of purchasing for a U.S. corporation that is planning to acquire a large number of new computers. The company's computer specialist has identified two models, one Japanese-made and one U.S.-made, that meet the necessary specifications. Since the two models are essentially equivalent, the company will buy the one with the lower price. However, since the computers are priced in the currencies of the countries of manufacture, the price comparison is not so straightforward. Your mission—should you decide to accept it—is to determine which of the two models is cheaper.

To complete your assignment, you will need two pieces of information: the nominal exchange rate between the dollar and the yen and the prices of the two models in terms of the currencies of their countries of manufacture. Example 18.4 shows how you can use this information to determine which model is cheaper.

EXAMPLE 18.4   **Comparing prices expressed in different currencies**

A U.S.-made computer costs $2,400, and a similar Japanese-made computer costs 242,000 yen. If the nominal exchange rate is 110 yen per dollar, which computer is the better buy?

To make this price comparison, we must measure the prices of both computers in terms of the same currency. To make the comparison in dollars, we first convert the Japanese computer's price into dollars. The price in terms of Japanese yen is ¥242,000 (the symbol ¥ means "yen"), and we are told that ¥110 = $1. As we did earlier, we find the dollar price of the Japanese computer by observing that for any good or service,

$$\text{Price in yen} = \text{Price in dollars} \times \text{Value of dollar in terms of yen.}$$

Note that the value of a dollar in terms of yen is just the yen–dollar exchange rate. Making this substitution and solving, we get

$$\text{Price in dollars} = \frac{\text{Price in yen}}{\text{Yen–dollar exchange rate}}$$

$$= \frac{¥242,000}{¥110/\$1} = \$2,200.$$

Notice that the yen symbol appears in both the numerator and the denominator of the ratio, so it cancels out. Our conclusion is that the Japanese computer is cheaper than the U.S. computer at $2,200, or $200 less than the price of the U.S. computer, $2,400. The Japanese computer is the better deal.

EXERCISE 18.5

Continuing Example 18.4, compare the prices of the Japanese and American computers by expressing both prices in terms of yen.

In Example 18.4, the fact that the Japanese computer was cheaper implied that your firm would choose it over the U.S.-made computer. In general, a country's ability to compete in international markets depends in part on the prices of its goods and services *relative* to the prices of foreign goods and services, when the prices are measured in a common currency. In the hypothetical example of the Japanese and U.S. computers, the price of the domestic (U.S.) good relative to the price of the foreign (Japanese) good is $2,400/$2,200, or 1.09. So the U.S. computer is 9 percent more expensive than the Japanese computer, putting the U.S. product at a competitive disadvantage.

More generally, economists ask whether *on average* the goods and services produced by a particular country are expensive relative to the goods and services produced by other countries. This question can be answered by the country's *real exchange rate*. Specifically, a country's **real exchange rate** is the price of the average domestic good or service *relative* to the price of the average foreign good or service, when prices are expressed in terms of a common currency.

To obtain a formula for the real exchange rate, recall that e equals the nominal exchange rate (the number of units of foreign currency per dollar) and that P equals the domestic price level, as measured, for example, by the consumer price index. We will use P as a measure of the price of the "average" domestic good or service. Similarly, let P^f equal the foreign price level. We will use P^f as the measure of the price of the "average" foreign good or service.

The real exchange rate equals the price of the average domestic good or service relative to the price of the average foreign good or service. It would not be correct, however, to define the real exchange rate as the ratio P/P^f, because the two price levels are expressed in different currencies. As we saw in Example 18.4, to convert foreign prices into dollars, we must divide the foreign price by the exchange rate. By this rule, the price in dollars of the average foreign good or service equals P^f/e. Now we can write the real exchange rate as

$$\text{Real exchange rate} = \frac{\text{Price of domestic good}}{\text{Price of foreign good, in dollars}}$$

$$= \frac{P}{P^f/e}$$

real exchange rate the price of the average domestic good or service *relative* to the price of the average foreign good or service, when prices are expressed in terms of a common currency

To simplify this expression, multiply the numerator and denominator by *e* to get

$$\text{Real exchange rate} = \frac{eP}{P^f} \tag{18.1}$$

which is the formula for the real exchange rate.

To check this formula, let's use it to re-solve the computer example, Example 18.4. (For this exercise, we imagine that computers are the only good produced by the United States and Japan, so the real exchange rate becomes just the price of U.S. computers relative to Japanese computers.) In that example, the nominal exchange rate *e* was ¥110/$1, the domestic price *P* (of a computer) was $2,400, and the foreign price *P^f* was ¥242,000. Applying Equation 18.1, we get

$$\text{Real exchange rate (for computers)} = \frac{(\text{¥}110/\$1) \times \$2,400}{\text{¥}242,000}$$

$$= \frac{\text{¥}264,000}{\text{¥}242,000}$$

$$= 1.09,$$

which is the same answer we got earlier.

The real exchange rate, an overall measure of the cost of domestic goods relative to foreign goods, is an important economic variable. It incorporates both the nominal exchange rate and the relative prices of goods and services across countries. As Example 18.4 suggests, when the real exchange rate is high, domestic goods are on average more expensive than foreign goods (when priced in the same currency). A high real exchange rate implies that domestic producers will have difficulty exporting to other countries (domestic goods will be "overpriced"), while foreign goods will sell well in the home country (because imported goods are cheap relative to goods produced at home). Since a high real exchange rate tends to reduce exports and increase imports, we conclude that *net exports will tend to be low when the real exchange rate is high.* Conversely, if the real exchange rate is low, then the home country will find it easier to export (because its goods are priced below those of foreign competitors), while domestic residents will buy fewer imports (because imports are expensive relative to domestic goods). *Thus, net exports will tend to be high when the real exchange rate is low.*

In our earlier analysis, we showed how an increase in the nominal exchange rate *e* will reduce net exports by making exports more expensive to foreigners and by making imports cheaper for Americans. Equation 18.1 shows that an increase in *e* also will increase the real exchange rate, all other things equal, most notably, the ratio *P/P^f*. And an increase in the real exchange rate will again reduce net exports.

A SIMPLE THEORY OF EXCHANGE RATES: PURCHASING POWER PARITY (PPP)

The most basic theory of how nominal exchange rates are determined in the long run is called *purchasing power parity,* or PPP. To understand this theory, we must first discuss a market equilibrium economic concept, called *the law of one price.* The **law of one price** states that if transportation costs are relatively small, the price of an internationally traded commodity must be the same in all locations. For example, if transportation costs are not too large, the price of a bushel of wheat ought to be the same in Bombay, India, and Sydney, Australia. Note that this condition implies that the real exchange rate must equal one in the long run. Suppose that were not the case—that the price of wheat in Sydney were only half the price

law of one price if transportation costs are relatively small, the price of an internationally traded commodity must be the same in all locations

in Bombay. In that case, grain merchants would have a strong incentive to buy wheat in Sydney and ship it to Bombay, where it could be sold at double the price of purchase. As wheat left Sydney, reducing the local supply, the price of wheat in Sydney would rise, while the inflow of wheat into Bombay would reduce the price in Bombay. According to the *equilibrium principle* (Chapter 3), the international market for wheat would return to equilibrium only when unexploited opportunities to profit had been eliminated—specifically, only when the prices of wheat in Sydney and in Bombay became equal or nearly equal (with the difference being less than the cost of transporting wheat from Australia to India).

If the law of one price were to hold for all goods and services, and the real exchange rate were equal to one (which is not a realistic assumption, as we will see shortly), then the value of the nominal exchange rate would be determined as Example 18.5 illustrates.

How many Indian rupees equal one Australian dollar? (1)

EXAMPLE 18.5

Suppose that a bushel of grain costs 5 Australian dollars in Sydney and 150 rupees in Bombay. If the law of one price holds for grain, what is the nominal exchange rate between Australia and India?

Because the market value of a bushel of grain must be the same in both locations, we know that the Australian price of wheat must equal the Indian price of wheat, so that

$$5 \text{ Australian dollars} = 150 \text{ rupees.}$$

Dividing by 5, we get

$$1 \text{ Australian dollar} = 30 \text{ Indian rupees.}$$

Thus, the nominal exchange rate between Australia and India should be 30 rupees per Australian dollar.

Alternatively, if we use Equation 18.1 and the PPP assumption that the real exchange rate will equal one,

$$1 = \frac{eP}{P^f}$$

and

$$e = P^f/P = 150 \text{ Indian rupees}/5 \text{ Australian dollars}$$
$$= 30 \text{ Indian rupees per 1 Australian dollar.}$$

EXERCISE 18.6

The price of gold is $180 per ounce in New York and 2,500 kronor per ounce in Stockholm, Sweden. If the law of one price holds for gold, what is the nominal exchange rate between the U.S. dollar and the Swedish krona?

Example 18.5 and Exercise 18.6 illustrate the application of the purchasing power parity theory. According to the **purchasing power parity (PPP) theory**, nominal exchange rates are determined as necessary for the law of one price to hold.

A particularly useful prediction of the PPP theory is that in the long run, the *currencies of countries that experience significant inflation will tend to depreciate.* To see why, we will extend the analysis in Example 18.5.

purchasing power parity (PPP) the theory that nominal exchange rates are determined as necessary for the law of one price to hold

EXAMPLE 18.6   **How many Indian rupees equal one Australian dollar? (2)**

Suppose India experiences significant inflation so that the price of a bushel of grain in Bombay rises from 150 to 300 rupees. Australia has no inflation, so the price of grain in Sydney remains unchanged at 5 Australian dollars. If the law of one price holds for grain, what will happen to the nominal exchange rate between Australia and India?

As in Example 18.5, we know that the market value of a bushel of grain must be the same in both locations. Therefore,

$$5 \text{ Australian dollars} = 300 \text{ rupees.}$$

Equivalently,

$$1 \text{ Australian dollar} = 60 \text{ rupees.}$$

The nominal exchange rate is now 60 rupees per Australian dollar. Before India's inflation, the nominal exchange rate was 30 rupees per Australian dollar (Example 18.5). So, in this example, inflation has caused the rupee to depreciate against the Australian dollar. Conversely, Australia, with no inflation, has seen its currency appreciate against the rupee.

This link between inflation and depreciation makes economic sense. Inflation implies that a nation's currency is losing purchasing power in the domestic market. Analogously, exchange rate depreciation implies that the nation's currency is losing purchasing power in international markets.

Figure 18.8 shows annual rates of inflation and nominal exchange rate depreciation for the 10 largest South American countries from 1995 to 2004.[9] Inflation is measured as the annual rate of change in the country's consumer price index;

FIGURE 18.8
Inflation and Currency Depreciation in South America, 1995–2004.
The annual rates of inflation and nominal exchange-rate depreciation (relative to the U.S. dollar) in the ten largest South American countries varied considerably during 1995–2004. High inflation was associated with rapid depreciation of the nominal exchange rate. (Data for Ecuador refer to the period 1995–2000.)

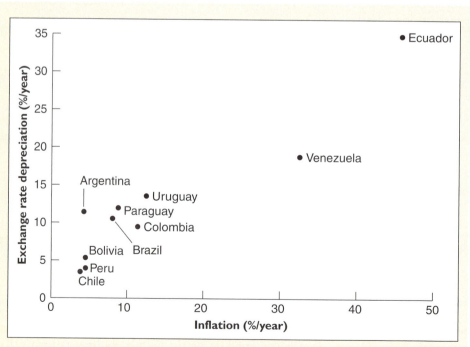

SOURCE: International Monetary Fund, *International Financial Statistics*, and authors' calculations.

[9]Since Ecuador, the 10th country, adopted the U.S. dollar as its currency in 2000, the data for Ecuador refer to the period 1995–2000.

depreciation is measured relative to the U.S. dollar. As you can see, inflation varied greatly among South American countries during the period. For example, Chile's inflation rate was within two percentage points of the inflation rate of the United States, while Venezuela's inflation was 33 percent per year.

Figure 18.8 shows that, as the PPP theory implies, countries with higher inflation during the 1995–2004 period tended to experience the most rapid depreciation of their currencies.

SHORTCOMINGS OF THE PPP THEORY

Empirical studies have found that the PPP theory is useful for predicting changes in nominal exchange rates over the relatively long run. In particular, this theory helps to explain the tendency of countries with high inflation to experience depreciation of their exchange rates, as shown in Figure 18.8. However, the theory is less successful in predicting short-run movements in exchange rates.

A particularly dramatic failure of the PPP theory occurred in the United States in the early 1980s. As Figure 18.1 indicates, between 1980 and 1985, the value of the U.S. dollar rose nearly 50 percent relative to the currencies of U.S. trading partners. This strong appreciation was followed by an even more rapid depreciation during 1986 and 1987. PPP theory could explain this roller-coaster behavior only if inflation were far lower in the United States than in U.S. trading partners from 1980 to 1985, and far higher from 1986 to 1987. In fact, inflation was similar in the United States and its trading partners throughout both periods.

Why does the PPP theory work less well in the short run than the long run? Recall that this theory relies on the law of one price, which says that the price of an internationally traded commodity must be the same in all locations. The law of one price works well for goods such as grain or gold, which are standardized commodities that are traded widely. However, *not all goods and services are traded internationally,* and *not all goods are standardized commodities.*

Many goods and services are not traded internationally because the assumption underlying the law of one price—that transportation costs are relatively small—does not hold. For example, for Indians to export haircuts to Australia, they would need to transport an Indian barber to Australia every time a Sydney resident desired a trim. Because transportation costs prevent haircuts from being traded internationally, the law of one price does not apply to them. Thus, even if the price of haircuts in Australia were double the price of haircuts in India, market forces would not necessarily force prices toward equality in the short run. (Over the long run, some Indian barbers might emigrate to Australia.) Other examples of nontraded goods and services are agricultural land, buildings, heavy construction materials (whose value is low relative to their transportation costs), and highly perishable foods. In addition, some products use nontraded goods and services as inputs: A McDonald's hamburger served in Moscow has both a tradable component (frozen hamburger patties) and a nontradable component (the labor of counter workers). In general, the greater the share of nontraded goods and services in a nation's output, the less precisely the PPP theory will apply to the country's exchange rate.[10]

The second reason the law of one price and the PPP theory sometimes fail to apply is that not all internationally traded goods and services are perfectly standardized commodities, like grain or gold. For example, U.S.-made automobiles and Japanese-made automobiles are not identical; they differ in styling, horsepower, reliability, and other features. As a result, some people strongly prefer one nation's cars to the other's. Thus, if Japanese cars cost 10 percent more than American cars, U.S. automobile exports will not necessarily flood the Japanese market, since many

[10]Trade barriers, such as tariffs and quotas, also increase the costs associated with shipping goods from one country to another. Thus, trade barriers reduce the applicability of the law of one price in much the same way that physical transportation costs do.

Japanese will still prefer Japanese-made cars even at a 10 percent premium. Of course, there are limits to how far prices can diverge before people will switch to the cheaper product. But the law of one price, and hence the PPP theory, will not apply exactly to nonstandardized goods.

RECAP	**THE REAL EXCHANGE RATE AND THE DETERMINATION OF THE NOMINAL EXCHANGE RATE IN THE LONG RUN**

- The real exchange rate is the price of the average domestic good or service relative to the price of the average foreign good or service, when prices are expressed in terms of a common currency. A useful formula for the real exchange rate is eP/P^f, where e is the nominal exchange rate, P is the domestic price level, and P^f is the foreign price level.

- An increase in the real exchange rate implies that domestic goods are becoming more expensive relative to foreign goods, which tends to reduce exports and stimulate imports. Conversely, a decline in the real exchange rate tends to increase net exports.

- The most basic theory of nominal exchange rate determination in the long run, purchasing power parity (PPP), is based on the law of one price. The law of one price states that if transportation costs are relatively small, the price of an internationally traded commodity must be the same in all locations. According to the PPP theory, the nominal exchange rate between two currencies can be found by setting the price of a traded commodity in one currency equal to the price of the same commodity expressed in the second currency.

- A useful prediction of the PPP theory is that the currencies of countries that experience significant inflation will tend to depreciate over the long run. However, the PPP theory does not work well in the short run. The fact that many goods and services are nontraded, and that not all traded goods are standardized, reduces the applicability of the law of one price, and hence of the PPP theory.

▪ SUMMARY ▪

- The *nominal exchange rate* between two currencies is the rate at which the currencies can be traded for each other. A rise in the value of a currency relative to other currencies is called an *appreciation*; a decline in the value of a currency is called a *depreciation*.

- Exchange rates can be flexible or fixed. The value of a *flexible exchange rate* is determined by the supply and demand for the currency in the *foreign exchange market*, the market on which currencies of various nations are traded for one another. The government sets the value of a *fixed exchange rate*.

- Supply and demand analysis is a useful tool for studying the determination of exchange rates in the short run. The equi-

librium exchange rate, also called the *market equilibrium value of the exchange rate*, equates the quantities of the currency supplied and demanded in the foreign exchange market. A currency is supplied by domestic residents who wish to acquire foreign currencies to purchase foreign goods, services, and assets. An increased preference for foreign goods, an increase in the domestic GDP, an increase in the real interest rate on foreign assets, or a decrease in the real interest rate on domestic assets all will increase the supply of a currency on the foreign exchange market and thus lower its value. A currency is demanded by foreigners who wish to purchase domestic goods, services, and assets. An increased preference for domestic goods by foreigners, an increase in real GDP abroad, an increase in the domestic real interest rate, or a decrease in the foreign real interest rate all will increase the demand for the currency on the foreign exchange market and thus increase its value.

- If the exchange rate is flexible, a tight monetary policy (by raising the real interest rate) increases the demand for the currency, reduces the supply of currency, and causes it to appreciate. The stronger currency reinforces the effects of the tight monetary policy on aggregate demand by reducing net exports. Conversely, easy monetary policy lowers the real interest rate and weakens the currency, which in turn stimulates net exports.

- The value of a fixed exchange rate is officially established by the government. A fixed exchange rate whose official value exceeds its market equilibrium value in the foreign exchange market is said to be *overvalued*. An exchange rate whose official value is below its market equilibrium value is *undervalued*. A reduction in the official value of a fixed exchange rate is called a *devaluation*; an increase in its official value is called a *revaluation*.

- For an overvalued exchange rate, the quantity of the currency supplied at the official exchange rate exceeds the quantity demanded. To maintain the official rate, the country's central bank must use its *international reserves* (foreign currency assets) to purchase the excess supply of its currency in the foreign exchange market. Because a country's international reserves are limited, it cannot maintain an overvalued exchange rate indefinitely. Moreover, if financial investors fear an impending devaluation of the exchange rate, they may launch a *speculative attack*, selling their domestic currency assets and supplying large quantities of the currency to the foreign exchange market. Because speculative attacks cause a country's central bank to spend its international reserves even more quickly, they often force a devaluation.

- A tight monetary policy, by raising the market equilibrium value of the exchange rate, can eliminate the problem of overvaluation. However, if monetary policy is used to set the market equilibrium value of the exchange rate equal to the official value, it is no longer available for stabilizing the

domestic economy. Thus, under fixed exchange rates, monetary policy has little or no power to affect domestic output and employment.

- Because a fixed exchange rate implies that monetary policy can no longer be used for domestic stabilization, most large countries employ a flexible exchange rate. A fixed exchange rate may benefit a small country by forcing its central bank to follow the monetary policies of the country to which it has tied its rate. Advocates of fixed exchange rates argue that they increase trade and economic integration by making the exchange rate more predictable. However, the threat of speculative attacks greatly reduces the long-term predictability of a fixed exchange rate.

- The *real exchange rate* is the price of the average domestic good or service *relative* to the price of the average foreign good or service, when prices are expressed in terms of a common currency. The real exchange rate incorporates both the nominal exchange rate and the relative levels of prices among countries. An increase in the real exchange rate implies that domestic goods and services are becoming more expensive relative to foreign goods and services, which tends to reduce exports and increase imports. Conversely, a decline in the real exchange rate tends to increase net exports.

- A basic theory of nominal exchange rate determination in the long run, the *purchasing power parity* (PPP) theory, is based on the law of one price. The *law of one price* states that if transportation costs are relatively small, the price of an internationally traded commodity must be the same in all locations. According to the PPP theory, we can find the nominal exchange rate between two currencies by setting the price of a commodity in one of the currencies equal to the price of the commodity in the second currency. The PPP theory correctly predicts that the currencies of countries that experience significant inflation will tend to depreciate in the long run. However, the fact that many goods and services are not traded internationally, and that not all traded goods are standardized, makes the PPP theory less useful for explaining short-run changes in exchange rates.

■ KEY TERMS ■

appreciation (526)
balance-of-payments deficit (538)
balance-of-payments surplus (538)
depreciation (526)
devaluation (536)
fixed exchange rate (527)
flexible exchange rate (527)

foreign exchange market (527)
international reserves (538)
law of one price (552)
market equilibrium value of the exchange rate (530)
nominal exchange rate (525)
overvalued exchange rate (537)

purchasing power parity (PPP) (553)
real exchange rate (551)
revaluation (536)
speculative attack (540)
undervalued exchange rate (537)

■ REVIEW QUESTIONS ■

1. Japanese yen trade at 110 yen per dollar and Mexican pesos trade at 10 pesos per dollar. What is the nominal exchange rate between the yen and the peso? Express in two ways.

2. Why do U.S. households and firms supply dollars to the foreign exchange market? Why do foreigners demand dollars in the foreign exchange market?

3. Under a flexible exchange rate, how does an easing of monetary policy (a lower real interest rate) affect the value of the exchange rate? Does this change in the exchange rate tend to weaken or strengthen the effect of the monetary ease on output and employment? Explain.

4. Define *overvalued exchange rate*. Discuss four ways in which government policymakers can respond to an overvaluation. What are the drawbacks of each approach?

5. Use a supply and demand diagram to illustrate the effects of a speculative attack on an overvalued exchange rate. Why do speculative attacks often result in a devaluation?

6. Contrast fixed and flexible exchange rates in terms of how they affect (a) the ability of monetary policy to stabilize domestic output and (b) the predictability of future exchange rates.

7. Define *nominal exchange rate* and *real exchange rate*. How are the two concepts related?

8. Would you expect the law of one price to apply to crude oil? To fresh milk? To taxi rides? To compact discs produced in different countries by local recording artists? Explain your answer in each case.

▪ PROBLEMS ▪

1. Using the data in Table 18.1, find the nominal exchange rate between the Mexican peso and the Japanese yen. Express in two ways. How do your answers change if the peso appreciates by 10 percent against the dollar while the value of the yen against the dollar remains unchanged?

2. Suppose a French bottle of champagne costs 20 euros.
   a. If the euro–dollar exchange rate is 0.8 euro per dollar, so that a dollar can buy 0.8 euro, how much will the champagne cost in the United States?
   b. If the euro–dollar exchange rate rises to 1 euro per dollar, how much will the champagne cost in the United States?
   c. If an increase in the euro–dollar exchange rate leads to an increase in Americans' dollar expenditures on French champagne, what will happen to the amount of dollars supplied to the foreign exchange market as the euro–dollar exchange rate rises?

3. Consider an Apple iPod model that costs $240.
   a. If the euro–dollar exchange rate is 1 euro per dollar, so that it costs a European 1 euro to buy a dollar, how much will the iPod cost in France?
   b. If the euro–dollar exchange rate falls to 0.8 euro per dollar, how much will the iPod cost in France?
   c. Consequently, what will happen to French purchases of iPods and the amount of dollars demanded in the foreign exchange market as the euro–dollar exchange rate falls?

4. How would each of the following be likely to affect the value of the dollar, all else being equal? Explain.
   a. U.S. stocks are perceived as having become much riskier financial investments.
   b. European computer firms switch from U.S.-produced software to software produced in India, Israel, and other nations.
   c. As East Asian economies recover, international financial investors become aware of many new, high-return investment opportunities in the region.
   d. The U.S. government imposes a large tariff on imported automobiles.
   e. The Federal Reserve reports that it is less concerned about inflation and more concerned about an impending recession in the United States.
   f. The European Central Bank becomes less concerned about European inflation and more concerned about an impending recession in Europe.

5. The demand for and supply of shekels in the foreign exchange market are

$$\text{Demand} = 30{,}000 - 8{,}000e,$$

$$\text{Supply} = 25{,}000 + 12{,}000e,$$

where the nominal exchange rate is expressed as U.S. dollars per shekel.
   a. What is the market equilibrium value of the shekel?

b. The shekel is fixed at 0.30 U.S. dollar. Is the shekel overvalued, undervalued, or neither? Find the balance-of-payments deficit or surplus in both shekels and dollars. What happens to the country's international reserves over time?

c. Repeat part b for the case in which the shekel is fixed at 0.20 U.S. dollars.

6. The annual demand for and supply of shekels in the foreign exchange market is as given in problem 5. The shekel is fixed at 0.30 dollars per shekel. The country's international reserves are $600. Foreign financial investors hold checking accounts in the country in the amount of 5,000 shekels.

a. Suppose that foreign financial investors do not fear a devaluation of the shekel, and thus do not convert their shekel checking accounts into dollars. Can the shekel be maintained at its fixed value of 0.30 U.S. dollars for the next year?

b. Now suppose that foreign financial investors come to expect a possible devaluation of the shekel to 0.25 U.S. dollars. Why should this possibility worry them?

c. In response to their concern about devaluation, foreign financial investors withdraw all funds from their checking accounts and attempt to convert those shekels into dollars. What happens?

d. Discuss why the foreign investors' forecast of devaluation can be considered a "self-fulfilling prophecy."

7. Eastland's currency is called the eastmark, and Westland's currency is called the westmark. In the market in which eastmarks and westmarks are traded for each other, the supply of and demand for eastmarks are given by

$$\text{Demand} = 25{,}000 - 5{,}000e - 50{,}000(r_E - r_W),$$

$$\text{Supply} = 18{,}500 + 8{,}000e - 50{,}000(r_E - r_W).$$

The nominal exchange rate e is measured as westmarks per eastmark, and r_E and r_W are the real interest rates prevailing in Eastland and Westland, respectively.

a. Explain why it makes economic sense for the two real interest rates to appear in the demand and supply equations in the way they do.

b. Initially, $r_E = r_W = 0.10$, or 10 percent. Find the market equilibrium value of the eastmark.

c. The Westlandian central bank grows concerned about inflation and raises Westland's real interest rate to 12 percent. What happens to the market equilibrium value of the eastmark?

d. Assume that the exchange rate is flexible and that Eastland does not change its real interest rate following the increase in Westland's real interest rate. Is the action of the Westlandian central bank likely to increase or reduce aggregate demand in Eastland? Discuss.

e. Now suppose that the exchange rate is fixed at the value you found in part b. After the action by the Westlandian central bank, what will the Eastlandian central bank have to do to keep its exchange rate from being overvalued? What effect will this action have on the Eastlandian economy?

f. In the context of this example, discuss the effect of fixed exchange rates on the ability of a country to run an independent monetary policy.

8. A British-made automobile is priced at £20,000 (20,000 British pounds). A comparable U.S.-made car costs $26,000. One pound trades for $1.50 in the foreign exchange market. Find the real exchange rate for automobiles from the perspective of the United States and from the perspective of Great Britain. Which country's cars are more competitively priced?

9. Between last year and this year, the CPI in Blueland rose from 100 to 110 and the CPI in Redland rose from 100 to 105. Blueland's currency unit, the blue, was worth $1 (U.S.) last year and is worth 90 cents (U.S.) this year. Redland's currency unit, the red, was worth 50 cents (U.S.) last year and is worth 45 cents (U.S.) this year.

Find the percentage change from last year to this year in Blueland's *nominal* exchange rate with Redland and in Blueland's *real* exchange rate with Redland. (Treat Blueland as the home country.) Relative to Redland, do you expect Blueland's exports to be helped or hurt by these changes in exchange rates?

10. The demand for U.S.-made cars in Japan is given by

$$\text{Japanese demand} = 10,000 - 0.001(\text{Price of U.S. cars in yen}).$$

Similarly, the demand for Japanese-made cars in the United States is

$$\text{U.S. demand} = 30,000 - 0.2(\text{Price of Japanese cars in dollars}).$$

The domestic price of a U.S.-made car is $20,000, and the domestic price of a Japanese-made car is ¥2,500,000. From the perspective of the United States, find the real exchange rate in terms of cars and net exports of cars to Japan if
a. The nominal exchange rate is 100 yen per dollar.
b. The nominal exchange rate is 125 yen per dollar.

How does an appreciation of the dollar affect U.S. net exports of automobiles (considering only the Japanese market)?

11. a. Gold is $350 per ounce in the United States and 2,800 pesos per ounce in Mexico. What nominal exchange rate between U.S. dollars and Mexican pesos is implied by the PPP theory?
   b. Mexico experiences inflation so that the price of gold rises to 4,200 pesos per ounce. Gold remains $350 per ounce in the United States. According to the PPP theory, what happens to the exchange rate? What general principle does this example illustrate?
   c. Gold is $350 per ounce in the United States and 4,200 pesos per ounce in Mexico. Crude oil (excluding taxes and transportation costs) is $30 per barrel in the United States. According to the PPP theory, what should a barrel of crude oil cost in Mexico?
   d. Gold is $350 per ounce in the United States. The exchange rate between the United States and Canada is 0.70 U.S. dollars per Canadian dollar. How much does an ounce of gold cost in Canada?

■ ANSWERS TO IN-CHAPTER EXERCISES ■

18.1   Answers will vary, depending on when the data are obtained.

18.2   A decline in U.S. GDP reduces consumer incomes and hence imports. As Americans are purchasing fewer imports, they supply fewer dollars to the foreign exchange market, so the supply curve for dollars shifts to the left. Reduced supply raises the market equilibrium value of the dollar.

18.3   At a fixed value for the peso of 0.15 dollars, the demand for the peso equals $25,000 - 50,000(0.15) = 17,500$. The supply of the peso equals $17,600 + 24,000(0.15) = 21,200$. The quantity supplied at the official rate exceeds the quantity demanded by 3,700. Latinia will have to purchase 3,700 pesos each period, so its balance-of-payments deficit will equal 3,700 pesos, or $3,700 \times 0.15 = 555$ dollars. This balance-of-payments deficit is larger than we found in Example 18.3. We conclude that the greater the degree of overvaluation, the larger the country's balance-of-payments deficit is likely to be.

18.4   The figure shows a situation in which the official value of the currency is *below* the market equilibrium value, as determined by the supply of and demand for the currency in the foreign exchange market, so the currency is undervalued. At the official value of the exchange rate, the quantity demanded of the domestic currency (point *B*) exceeds the quantity supplied (point *A*). To maintain the official value, the central bank must supply domestic currency to the foreign exchange market each period in the amount *AB*. In contrast to the case of an overvalued exchange rate, here the central bank is providing its own currency to the foreign exchange market and receiving foreign currencies in return.

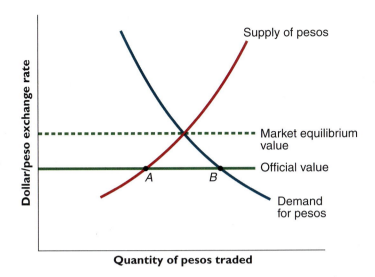

Quantity of pesos traded

The central bank can print as much of its own currency as it likes, and so with an undervalued currency, there is no danger of running out of international reserves. Indeed, the central bank's stock of international reserves increases in the amount *AB* each period, as it receives foreign currencies in exchange for the domestic currency it supplies.

18.5   The dollar price of the U.S. computer is $2,400, and each dollar is equal to 110 yen. Therefore, the yen price of the U.S. computer is (110 yen/dollar) × ($2,400), or 264,000 yen. The price of the Japanese computer is 242,000 yen. Thus, the conclusion that the Japanese model is cheaper does not depend on the currency in which the comparison is made.

18.6   Since the law of one price holds for gold, its price per ounce must be the same in New York and Stockholm:

$$\$300 = 2{,}500 \text{ kronor.}$$

Dividing both sides by 300, we get

$$\$1 = 8.33 \text{ kronor.}$$

So the exchange rate is 8.33 kronor per dollar.

GLOSSARY

A

Absolute advantage. One person has an absolute advantage over another if he or she takes fewer hours to perform a task than the other person.

Accommodating policy. A policy that allows the effects of a shock to occur.

Aggregate demand (*AD*). Total planned spending on final goods and services.

Aggregate demand (*AD*) curve. Shows the relationship between aggregate demand and inflation; because short-run equilibrium output equals aggregate demand, the aggregate demand curve also shows the relationship between short-run equilibrium output and inflation; increases in inflation reduce aggregate demand and short-run equilibrium output, so the aggregate demand curve is downward-sloping.

Aggregate supply shock. Either an inflation shock or a shock to potential output; adverse aggregate supply shocks of both types reduce output and increase inflation.

Aggregation. The adding up of individual economic variables to obtain economywide totals.

Anchored expectations. When people's expectations of future inflation do not change even if inflation rises temporarily.

Appreciation. An increase in the value of a currency relative to other currencies.

Assets. Anything of value that one owns.

Attainable point. Any combination of goods that can be produced using currently available resources.

Autarky. A situation in which a country is economically self-sufficient; that is, it does not trade with other nations.

Automatic stabilizers. Provisions in the law that imply automatic increases in government spending or decreases in taxes when real output declines.

Autonomous expenditure. The portion of planned aggregate expenditure that is independent of output.

Average benefit. Total benefit of undertaking *n* units of an activity divided by *n*.

Average cost. Total cost of undertaking *n* units of an activity divided by *n*.

Average labor productivity. Output per employed worker.

Average tax rate. Total taxes divided by total before-tax income.

B

Balance-of-payments deficit. The net decline in a country's stock of international reserves over a year.

Balance-of-payments surplus. The net increase in a country's stock of international reserves over a year.

Balance sheet. A list of an economic unit's assets and liabilities on a specific date.

Bank reserves. Cash or similar assets held by commercial banks for the purpose of meeting depositor withdrawals and payments.

Banking panic. An episode in which depositors, spurred by news or rumors of the imminent bankruptcy of one or more banks, rush to withdraw their deposits from the banking system.

Barter. The direct trade of goods or services for other goods or services.

Bequest saving. Saving done for the purpose of leaving an inheritance.

Board of Governors. The leadership of the Fed, consisting of seven governors appointed by the president to staggered 14-year terms.

Bond. A legal promise to repay a debt, usually including both the principal amount and regular interest, or coupon, payments.

Boom. A particularly strong and protracted expansion.

Buyer's reservation price. The largest dollar amount the buyer would be willing to pay for a good.

Buyer's surplus. The difference between the buyer's reservation price and the price he or she actually pays.

C

Capital gains. Increases in the value of existing assets.

Capital good. A long-lived good that is used in the production of other goods and services.

Capital inflows. Purchases of domestic assets by foreign households and firms.

Capital losses. Decreases in the value of existing assets.

Capital outflows. Purchases of foreign assets by domestic households and firms.

Cash on the table. Economic metaphor for unexploited gain from exchange.

Central bank independence. When central bankers are insulated from short-term political considerations and are allowed to take a long-term view of the economy.

Change in demand. A shift of the entire demand curve.

Change in supply. A shift of the entire supply curve.

Change in the quantity demanded. A movement along the demand curve that occurs in response to a change in price.

Change in the quantity supplied. A movement along the supply curve that occurs in response to a change in price.

Closed economy. An economy that does not trade with the rest of the world.

Comparative advantage. One person has a comparative advantage over another if his or her opportunity cost of performing a task is lower than the other person's opportunity cost.

Complements. Two goods are complements in consumption if an increase in the price of one causes a leftward shift in the demand curve for the other (or if a decrease causes a rightward shift).

Compound interest. The payment of interest not only on the original deposit but on all previously accumulated interest.

Constant. A quantity that is fixed in value.

Consumer price index (CPI). For any period, measures the cost in that period of a standard basket of goods and services relative to the cost of the same basket of goods and services in a fixed year, called the *base year*.

Consumption expenditure. Spending by households on goods and services such as food, clothing, and entertainment.

Consumption function. The relationship between consumption spending and its determinants, in particular, disposable (after-tax) income.

Consumption possibilities. The combination of goods and services that a country's citizens might feasibly consume.

Contraction. *See* **Recession.**

Contractionary monetary policy. An increase in interest rates by the Fed, made with the intention of reducing an expansionary gap.

Contractionary policies. Government policy actions designed to reduce planned spending and output.

Core rate of inflation. The rate of increase of all prices except energy and food.

Coupon payments. Regular interest payments made to the bondholder.

Coupon rate. The interest rate promised when a bond is issued; the annual coupon payments are equal to the coupon rate times the principal amount of the bond.

Credibility of monetary policy. The degree to which the public believes the central bank's promises to keep inflation low, even if doing so may impose short-run economic costs.

Crowding out. The tendency of increased government deficits to reduce investment spending.

Cyclical unemployment. The extra unemployment that occurs during periods of recession.

D

Deflating (a nominal quantity). The process of dividing a nominal quantity by a price index (such as the CPI) to express the quantity in real terms.

Deflation. A situation in which the prices of most goods and services are falling over time so that inflation is negative.

Demand curve. A schedule or graph showing the quantity of a good that buyers wish to buy at each price.

Demand for money. The amount of wealth an individual or firm chooses to hold in the form of money.

Dependent variable. A variable in an equation whose value is determined by the value taken by another variable in the equation.

Deposit insurance. A system under which the government guarantees that depositors will not lose any money even if their bank goes bankrupt.

Depreciation. A decrease in the value of a currency relative to other currencies.

Depression. A particularly severe or protracted recession.

Devaluation. A reduction in the official value of a currency (in a fixed-exchange-rate system).

Diminishing returns to capital. If the amount of labor and other inputs employed is held constant, then the greater the amount of capital already in use, the less an additional unit of capital adds to production.

Diminishing returns to labor. If the amount of capital and other inputs in use is held constant, then the greater the quantity of labor already employed, the less each additional worker adds to production.

Discount rate. The interest rate that the Fed charges commercial banks to borrow reserves.

Discount window lending. The lending of reserves by the Federal Reserve to commercial banks.

Discouraged workers. People who say they would like to have a job but have not made an effort to find one in the past four weeks.

Disinflation. A substantial reduction in the rate of inflation.

Diversification. The practice of spreading one's wealth over a variety of different financial investments to reduce overall risk.

Dividend. A regular payment received by stockholders for each share that they own.

Duration. The length of an unemployment spell.

E

Economic surplus. The economic surplus from taking any action is the benefit of taking the action minus its cost.

Economics. The study of how people make choices under conditions of scarcity and of the results of those choices for society.

Efficiency (or economic efficiency). Condition that occurs when all goods and services are produced and consumed at their respective socially optimal levels.

Efficient point. Any combination of goods for which currently available resources do not allow an increase in the production of one good without a reduction in the production of the other.

Entrepreneurs. People who create new economic enterprises.

Equation. A mathematical expression that describes the relationship between two or more variables.

Equilibrium. A balanced or unchanging situation in which all forces at work within a system are canceled by others.

Equilibrium price and equilibrium quantity. The price and quantity of a good at the intersection of the supply and demand curves for the good.

Excess demand (or shortage). The difference between the quantity supplied and the quantity demanded when the price of a good lies below the equilibrium price; buyers are dissatisfied when there is excess demand.

Excess supply (or surplus). The difference between the quantity supplied and the quantity demanded when the price of a good exceeds the equilibrium price; sellers are dissatisfied when there is excess supply.

Expansion. A period in which the economy is growing at a rate significantly above normal.

Expansionary gap. A negative output gap, which occurs when actual output is higher than potential output ($Y > Y^*$).

Expansionary monetary policy. A reduction in interest rates by the Fed, made with the intention of reducing a recessionary gap.

Expansionary policies. Government policy actions intended to increase planned spending and output.

F

Federal funds rate. The interest rate that commercial banks charge each other for very short-term (usually overnight) loans; because the Fed frequently sets its policy in terms of the federal funds rate, this rate is closely watched in financial markets.

Federal Open Market Committee (or FOMC). The committee that makes decisions concerning monetary policy.

Federal Reserve System (or Fed). The central bank of the United States; also called the *Fed*.

Final goods or services. Goods or services consumed by the ultimate user; because they are the end products of the production process, they are counted as part of GDP.

Financial intermediaries. Firms that extend credit to borrowers using funds raised from savers.

Fiscal policy. Decisions that determine the government's budget, including the amount and composition of government expenditures and government revenues.

Fisher effect. The tendency for nominal interest rates to be high when inflation is high and low when inflation is low.

Fixed cost. A cost that does not vary with the level of an activity.

Fixed exchange rate. An exchange rate whose value is set by official government policy.

Flexible exchange rate. An exchange rate whose value is not officially fixed but varies according to the supply and demand for the currency in the foreign exchange market.

Flow. A measure that is defined per unit of time.

Foreign exchange market. The market on which currencies of various nations are traded for one another.

Fractional-reserve banking system. A banking system in which bank reserves are less than deposits so that the reserve-deposit ratio is less than 100 percent.

Frictional unemployment. The short-term unemployment associated with the process of matching workers with jobs.

G

Government budget deficit. The excess of government spending over tax collections $(G - T)$.

Government budget surplus. The excess of government tax collections over government spending $(T - G)$; the government budget surplus equals public saving.

Government purchases. Purchases by federal, state, and local governments of final goods and services; government purchases do *not* include *transfer payments,* which are payments made by the government in return for which no current goods or services are received, nor do they include interest paid on the government debt.

Gross domestic product (GDP). The market value of the final goods and services produced in a country during a given period.

H

Hyperinflation. A situation in which the inflation rate is extremely high.

I

Income effect. The change in the quantity demanded of a good that results because a change in the price of a good changes the buyer's purchasing power.

Income-expenditure multiplier. The effect of a one-unit increase in autonomous expenditure on short-run equilibrium output.

Independent variable. A variable in an equation whose value determines the value taken by another variable in the equation.

Indexing. The practice of increasing a nominal quantity each period by an amount equal to the percentage increase in a specified price index. Indexing prevents the purchasing power of the nominal quantity from being eroded by inflation.

Induced aggregate demand. The portion of aggregate demand that is determined within the model.

Induced expenditure. The portion of planned aggregate expenditure that depends on output Y.

Inefficient point. Any combination of goods for which currently available resources enable an increase in the production of one good without a reduction in the production of the other.

Inferior good. A good whose demand curve shifts leftward when the incomes of buyers increase.

Inflation dove. Someone who is not strongly committed to achieving and maintaining low inflation.

Inflation hawk. Someone who is committed to achieving and maintaining low inflation, even at some short-run cost in reduced output and employment.

Inflation-protected bonds. Bonds whose holders receive a nominal interest rate each year equal to the fixed real rate plus the actual rate of inflation during that year.

Inflation shock. A sudden change in the normal behavior of inflation, unrelated to the nation's output gap.

Inside lag (of macroeconomic policy). The delay between the date a policy change is needed and the date it is implemented.

Intermediate goods or services. Goods or services used up in the production of final goods and services and therefore not counted as part of GDP.

International capital flows. Purchases or sales of real and financial assets across international borders.

International reserves. Foreign currency assets held by a government for the purpose of purchasing the domestic currency in the foreign exchange market.

Investment. Spending by firms on final goods and services, primarily capital goods.

L

Labor force. The total number of employed and unemployed people in the economy.

Law of one price. If transportation costs are relatively small, the price of an internationally traded commodity must be the same in all locations.

Liabilities. The debts one owes.

Life-cycle saving. Saving to meet long-term objectives, such as retirement, college attendance, or the purchase of a home.

Long-run aggregate supply (*LRAS*) line. A vertical line showing the economy's potential output Y^*.

Long-run equilibrium. A situation in which actual output equals potential output and the inflation rate is stable; graphically, long-run equilibrium occurs when the AD curve, the $SRAS$ line, and the $LRAS$ line all intersect at a single point.

M

M1. Sum of currency outstanding and balances held in checking accounts.

M2. All the assets in M1 plus some additional assets that are usable in making payments but at greater cost or inconvenience than currency or checks.

Macroeconomic policies. Government actions designed to affect the performance of the economy as a whole.

Macroeconomics. The study of the performance of national economies and the policies that governments use to try to improve that performance.

Marginal benefit. The marginal benefit of an activity is the increase in total benefit that results from carrying out one additional unit of the activity.

Marginal cost. The marginal cost of an activity is the increase in total cost that results from carrying out one additional unit of the activity.

Marginal propensity to consume (*mpc*). The amount by which consumption rises when disposable income rises by \$1; we assume that $0 < mpc < 1$.

Marginal tax rate. The amount by which taxes rise when before-tax income rises by one dollar.

Market. The market for any good consists of all buyers or sellers of that good.

Market equilibrium. Occurs when all buyers and sellers are satisfied with their respective quantities at the market price.

Market equilibrium value of the exchange rate. The exchange rate that equates the quantities of the currency supplied and demanded in the foreign exchange market.

Maturation date. The date at which the principal of a bond will be paid.

Medium of exchange. An asset used in purchasing goods and services.

Menu costs. The costs of changing prices.

Microeconomics. The study of individual choice under scarcity and its implications for the behavior of prices and quantities in individual markets.

Monetary policy. Determination of the nation's money supply.

Money. Any asset that can be used in making purchases.

Money demand curve. Shows the relationship between the aggregate quantity of money demanded M and the nominal interest rate i; because an increase in the nominal interest rate increases the opportunity cost of holding money, which reduces the quantity of money demanded, the money demand curve slopes down.

Multiplier. *See* **Income-expenditure multiplier.**

Mutual fund. A financial intermediary that sells shares in itself to the public, then uses the funds raised to buy a wide variety of financial assets.

N

National saving. The saving of the entire economy, equal to GDP less consumption expenditures and government purchases of goods and services, or $Y - C - G$.

Natural rate of unemployment, *u**. The part of the total unemployment rate that is attributable to frictional and structural unemployment; equivalently, the unemployment rate that prevails when cyclical unemployment is zero, so the economy has neither a recessionary nor an expansionary output gap.

Net capital inflows. Capital flows that are equal to foreign purchases of domestic assets (which bring funds into the country) minus domestic purchases of foreign assets (which send funds out of the country); that is, capital inflows minus capital outflows.

Net exports. Exports minus imports.

Nominal exchange rate. The rate at which two currencies can be traded for each other.

Nominal GDP. A measure of GDP in which the quantities produced are valued at current-year prices; nominal GDP measures the *current dollar value* of production.

Nominal interest rate. The annual percentage increase in the nominal value of a financial asset; also known as the *market interest rate.*

Nominal quantity. A quantity that is measured in terms of its current dollar value.

Normal good. A good whose demand curve shifts rightward when the incomes of buyers increase.

Normative analysis. Addresses the question of whether a policy *should* be used; normative analysis inevitably involves the values of the person doing the analysis.

Normative economic principle. One that says how people should behave.

O

Okun's law. States that each extra percentage point of cyclical unemployment is associated with about a 2 percentage point increase in the output gap, measured in relation to potential output.

100 percent reserve banking. A situation in which banks' reserves equal 100 percent of their deposits.

Open economy. An economy that trades with other countries.

Open-market operations. Open-market purchases and open-market sales.

Open-market purchase. The purchase of government bonds from the public by the Fed for the purpose of increasing the supply of bank reserves and the money supply.

Open-market sale. The sale by the Fed of government bonds to the public for the purpose of reducing bank reserves and the money supply.

Opportunity cost. The opportunity cost of an activity is the value of the next-best alternative that must be forgone to undertake the activity.

Output gap, $Y^* - Y$. The difference between the economy's potential output and its actual output at a point in time.

Outside lag (of macroeconomic policy). The delay between the date a policy change is implemented and the date by which most of its effects on the economy have occurred.

Outsourcing. A term increasingly used to connote having services performed by low-wage workers overseas.

Overvalued exchange rate. An exchange rate that has an officially fixed value greater than its fundamental value.

P

Parameter. *See* Constant.

Participation rate. The percentage of the working-age population in the labor force (that is, the percentage that is either employed or looking for work).

Peak. The beginning of a recession, the high point of economic activity prior to a downturn.

Planned aggregate expenditure (*PAE*). Total planned spending on final goods and services.

Policy reaction function. Describes how the action a policymaker takes depends on the state of the economy.

Portfolio allocation decision. The decision about the forms in which to hold one's wealth.

Positive analysis. Addresses the economic consequences of a particular event or policy, not whether those consequences are desirable.

Positive economic principle. One that predicts how people will behave.

Potential output, *Y**. The maximum sustainable amount of output (real GDP) that an economy can produce; also known as *potential GDP* or *full-employment output*.

Precautionary saving. Saving for protection against unexpected setbacks, such as the loss of a job or a medical emergency.

Price ceiling. A maximum allowable price, specified by law.

Price index. A measure of the average price of a given class of goods or services relative to the price of the same goods and services in a base year.

Price level. A measure of the overall level of prices at a particular point in time as measured by a price index such as the CPI.

Principal amount. The amount originally lent.

Private saving. The saving of the private sector of the economy is equal to the after-tax income of the private sector minus consumption expenditures ($Y - T - C$); private saving can be further broken down into household saving and business saving.

Production possibilities curve. A graph that describes the maximum amount of one good that can be produced for every possible level of production of the other good.

Protectionism. The view that free trade is injurious and should be restricted.

Public saving. The saving of the government sector is equal to net tax payments minus government purchases ($T - G$).

Purchasing power parity (PPP). The theory that nominal exchange rates are determined as necessary for the law of one price to hold.

Q

Quantity equation. Money times velocity equals nominal GDP: $M \times V = P \times Y$.

Quota. A legal limit on the quantity of a good that may be imported.

R

Rate of inflation. The annual percentage rate of change in the price level, as measured, for example, by the CPI.

Rational person. Someone with well-defined goals who tries to fulfill those goals as best he or she can.

Real exchange rate. The price of the average domestic good or service *relative* to the price of the average foreign good or service, when prices are expressed in terms of a common currency.

Real GDP. A measure of GDP in which the quantities produced are valued at the prices in a base year rather than at current prices; real GDP measures the actual *physical volume* of production.

Real interest rate. The annual percentage increase in the purchasing power of a financial asset; the real interest rate on any asset equals the nominal interest rate on that asset minus the inflation rate.

Real quantity. A quantity that is measured in physical terms—for example, in terms of quantities of goods and services.

Real wage. The wage paid to workers measured in terms of purchasing power; the real wage for any given period is calculated by dividing the nominal (dollar) wage by the CPI for that period.

Recession (or contraction). A period in which the economy is growing at a rate significantly below normal.

Recessionary gap. A positive output gap, which occurs when potential output exceeds actual output ($Y^* > Y$).

Relative price. The price of a specific good or service *in comparison* to the prices of other goods and services.

Reservation price. The highest price someone is willing to pay to obtain any good or service, or the lowest payment someone would accept for giving up a good or performing a service.

Reserve requirements. Set by the Fed, the minimum values of the ratio of bank reserves to bank deposits that commercial banks are allowed to maintain.

Reserve-deposit ratio. Bank reserves divided by deposits.

Revaluation. An increase in the official value of a currency (in a fixed-exchange-rate system).

Rise. *See* Slope.

Risk premium. The rate of return that financial investors require to hold risky assets minus the rate of return on safe assets.

Run. *See* Slope.

S

Saving. Current income minus spending on current needs.

Saving rate. Saving divided by income.

Seller's reservation price. The smallest dollar amount for which a seller would be willing to sell an additional unit, generally equal to marginal cost.

Seller's surplus. The difference between the price received by the seller and his or her reservation price.

Short-run aggregate supply (SRAS) line. A horizontal line showing the current rate of inflation, as determined by past expectations and pricing decisions.

Short-run equilibrium. A situation in which inflation equals the value determined by past expectations and pricing decisions, and output equals the level of short-run equilibrium output that is consistent with that inflation rate;

graphically, short-run equilibrium occurs at the intersection of the *AD* curve and the *SRAS* line.

Short-run equilibrium output. The level of output at which output *Y* equals planned aggregate expenditure *PAE*; the level of output that prevails during the period in which prices are predetermined.

Shortage. *See* **Excess demand.**

Skill-biased technological change. Technological change that affects the marginal products of higher-skilled workers differently from those of lower-skilled workers.

Slope. In a straight line, the ratio of the vertical distance the straight line travels between any two points (*rise*) to the corresponding horizontal distance (*run*).

Socially optimal quantity. The quantity of a good that results in the maximum possible economic surplus from producing and consuming the good.

Speculative attack. A massive selling of domestic currency assets by financial investors.

Stabilization policies. Government policies that are used to affect planned aggregate expenditure, with the objective of eliminating output gaps.

Stock. A measure that is defined at a point in time.

Stock (or equity). A claim to partial ownership of a firm.

Store of value. An asset that serves as a means of holding wealth.

Structural policy. Government policies aimed at changing the underlying structure, or institutions, of the nation's economy.

Structural unemployment. The long-term and chronic unemployment that exists even when the economy is producing at a normal rate.

Substitutes. Two goods are substitutes in consumption if an increase in the price of one causes a rightward shift in the demand curve for the other (or if a decrease causes a leftward shift).

Substitution effect. The change in the quantity demanded of a good that results because buyers switch to substitutes when the price of the good changes.

Sunk cost. A cost that is beyond recovery at the moment a decision must be made.

Supply curve. A graph or schedule showing the quantity of a good that sellers wish to sell at each price.

Supply-side policy. A policy that affects potential output.

Surplus. *See* **Excess supply.**

T

Target inflation rate. The Fed's long-run goal for inflation.

Target real interest rate. The Fed's long-run goal for the real interest rate.

Tariff. A tax imposed on an imported good.

Total surplus. The difference between the buyer's reservation price and the seller's reservation price.

Trade balance (or net exports). The value of a country's exports less the value of its imports in a particular period (quarter or year).

Trade deficit. When imports exceed exports, the difference between the value of a country's imports and the value of its exports in a given period.

Trade surplus. When exports exceed imports, the difference between the value of a country's exports and the value of its imports in a given period.

Transfer payments. Payments the government makes to the public for which it receives no current goods or services in return.

Trough. The end of a recession; the low point of economic activity prior to a recovery.

U

Unattainable point. Any combination of goods that cannot be produced using currently available resources.

Undervalued exchange rate. An exchange rate that has an officially fixed value less than its fundamental value.

Unemployment rate. The number of unemployed people divided by the labor force.

Unemployment spell. A period during which an individual is continuously unemployed.

Unit of account. A basic measure of economic value.

V

Value added. For any firm, the market value of its product or service minus the cost of inputs purchased from other firms.

Variable. A quantity that is free to take a range of different values.

Velocity. A measure of the speed with which money circulates in transactions involving final goods and services. Numerically, $V = (P \times Y)/M$, where V is velocity, $P \times Y$ is nominal GDP, and M is the money supply whose velocity is being measured.

Vertical intercept. The value taken by the dependent variable when the independent variable equals zero.

W

Wealth. The value of assets minus liabilities.

Wealth effect. The tendency of changes in asset prices to affect households' wealth and thus their spending on consumer goods.

Worker mobility. The movement of workers between jobs, firms, and industries.

World price. The price at which a good or service is traded on international markets.

INDEX

T